ROUTLEDGE HANDBOOK OF HIGHER EDUCATION FOR SUSTAINABLE DEVELOPMENT

The *Routledge Handbook of Higher Education for Sustainable Development* gives a systematic and comprehensive overview of existing and upcoming research approaches for higher education for sustainable development. It provides a unique resource for researchers engaged in the field of higher education for sustainable development by connecting theoretical aspects of the range of relevant methodologies, showing the interdisciplinary aspects of the research field and illustrating the breadth of research directions.

With a team of international authors from leading universities in research and teaching in higher education for sustainable development, this Handbook brings together a broad range of research approaches and shows how these approaches are reflected in the research practice in higher education for sustainable development. Key topics include:

- Research paradigms and methodologies
- Ongoing and future directions of research
- Meta-analysis and reviews
- Policy and politics
- Challenges for implementation
- Action research and transdisciplinary perspectives
- Gender, diversity and post-colonial perspectives
- Operationalising competencies
- Outcome-oriented research
- Curriculum change
- Organisational change and organisational learning
- Community and partnerships
- University appraisal systems and indicators
- Evaluation approaches
- Engaging academic teachers
- Good practice learning and teaching
- Transformative leadership and change strategies.

This Handbook is an invaluable research and teaching tool for all those working in higher education for sustainable development.

Matthias Barth is Professor of Education for Sustainable Development at Leuphana University of Lüneburg, Germany.

Gerd Michelsen is Senior Professor of Sustainability Science and UNESCO Chair of Higher Education for Sustainable Development at Leuphana University of Lüneburg, Germany.

Marco Rieckmann is Assistant Professor of Higher Education Development at the University of Vechta, Germany.

Ian Thomas is Honorary Associate Professor with the School of Global, Urban and Social Studies, RMIT University, Australia.

Thirty years on, the promise that higher education would serve as a fulcrum to leverage the larger culture toward the dream of a sustainable future seems greatly diminished. Yet this volume demonstrates that the important research goes on. With its breadth of theoretical perspective and research design, and its depth of inquiry and critique of research practice, this edited collection substantially advances our critically important field. The editors have assembled a who's who and what's what of higher education for sustainable development; the book gives me hope.

Peter Blaze Corcoran, Professor of Environmental Studies and Environmental Education, Director of the Center for Environmental and Sustainability Education, Florida Gulf Coast University, USA

Higher education has a crucial role to play in ensuring that students as future decision-makers are equipped to manage the complex and uncertain problems that confront our planet. As such it is essential that we research the policies and processes of higher education as they interlink with sustainability. This book includes chapters from some of the leading experts in sustainability in higher education, and provides an important contribution to this growing research area. It is a much-needed update on a fast-changing field, and will be of interest both to early career researchers and experienced academics.

Debby Cotton, Professor of Higher Education and Head of Educational Development, Plymouth University, UK

Regarding higher education as a potential transformative social practice and the University as a social institution which plays a key role in the construction of a more sustainable future, this Handbook brings together reflections and concrete experiences from different countries and diverse higher education contexts, offering generative perspectives for the construction of a sustainable world, in which social and environmental justice is taken as a common goal.

Luiz Marcelo de Carvalho, São Paulo State University, Brazil

The UN reaffirmed sustainability reform must be based on sound research. All realms of higher education must be engaged as society itself must change dramatically. Today's graduates will lead this change as leaders in government, the private sector, and civil society. This book is a crucial guide assisting effective institutional change.

Charles Hopkins, UNESCO Chair in Reorienting Teacher Education, Canada

The Handbook of Higher Education for Sustainable Development structures this emerging field of research and practice. By offering this structure, it is a foundational contribution to HESD. It thereby contributes to engage new generations to work on the great challenges of our times.

Karel Mulder, Initiator of the Engineering for Sustainable Development network, The Netherlands

Moving from the UN decade on education for sustainable development into the more action-oriented Global Action Programme, this Handbook is a timely and much needed contribution to the field of higher education for sustainable development. The Handbook presents a highly useful collection of reviews, descriptions and discussions of research efforts, and has contributions by many of the big names in the field.

Magdalena Svanström, Professor of Chemical Environmental Science, Chalmers University of Technology, Gothenburg, Sweden

ROUTLEDGE HANDBOOK OF HIGHER EDUCATION FOR SUSTAINABLE DEVELOPMENT

Edited by Matthias Barth, Gerd Michelsen, Marco Rieckmann and Ian Thomas

Routledge
Taylor & Francis Group
LONDON AND NEW YORK

earthscan
from Routledge

First published 2016
by Routledge
2 Park Square, Milton Park, Abingdon, Oxon OX14 4RN

and by Routledge
711 Third Avenue, New York, NY 10017

First issued in paperback 2018

Routledge is an imprint of the Taylor & Francis Group, an informa business

British Library Cataloguing-in-Publication Data
A catalogue record for this book is available from the British Library.

Library of Congress Cataloging-in-Publication Data
Routledge handbook of higher education for sustainable development /
edited by Matthias Barth, Gerd Michelsen, Marco Rieckmann, and Ian Thomas.
pages cm. — (Routledge international handbooks)
Includes bibliographical references and index.
1. Education, Higher—Economic aspects—Handbooks, manuals, etc.
2. Sustainable development—Study and teaching (Higher)—Handbooks, manuals, etc.
3. Economic development—Effect of education on—Handbooks, manuals, etc. I. Barth, Matthias, 1974- editor of compilation.
LC67.6.R68 2015
338.4'3378—dc23
2015016776

ISBN 13: 978-1-138-59754-9 (pbk)
ISBN 13: 978-0-415-72730-3 (hbk)

Typeset in Bembo
by FiSH Books Ltd, Enfield

CONTENTS

FIGURES

TABLES

BOXES

CONTRIBUTORS

Vanessa de Oliveira Andreotti holds a Research Chair in Race, Inequalities and Global Change, at the Department of Educational Studies, University of British Columbia, Canada. She has extensive experience across sectors in the areas of international development and global citizenship education. Her research focuses on analyses of historical and systemic patterns of reproduction of inequalities and how these mobilise global imaginaries that limit or enable different possibilities for existence.

Pilar Aznar is Professor of Theory of Education and a member of the Theory of Education Department at the Faculty of Philosophy and Education Sciences of the University of Valencia, Spain. She has more than 35 years of teaching experience. She has been the head of the Sustainability and Higher Education Research Team of the University of Valencia since 2003.

Matthias Barth is Professor of Education for Sustainable Development at Leuphana University of Lüneburg, Germany. He has worked on various projects in Germany and Australia, researching higher education for sustainable development on the micro-level of teaching and learning settings and the macro-learning of curriculum change.

Michael J. Bernstein is a Doctoral Candidate in the School of Sustainability, a member of the Sustainability Transition and Intervention Research Lab, and a Research Associate at the Center for Nanotechnology in Society at Arizona State University, USA. He researches interventions in science and technology policy and practice for sustainability.

Belinda Christie is a Sessional Academic in the School of Life and Environmental Sciences at Deakin University in Melbourne, Australia. Her research and teaching focus on environmental sustainability and management, and education for sustainability.

Matthew Cohen is Assistant Professor of Sustainability Science at Furman University, USA. He holds a PhD from the School of Sustainability at Arizona State University, USA. His research and teaching focus on sustainability competencies, transformational sustainability learning, and urban planning for sustainability.

Barbara de la Harpe is the Executive Dean of the Faculty of Education, Law and Arts at the University of Southern Queensland in Australia. She is a Professor of Higher Education and an established scholar in the areas of student learning, pedagogy, leadership and change, and academic staff professional development. A distinguishing feature of her work is its focus on the nexus of theory and real world practice.

Neus (Snowy) Evans is an Education Lecturer in the College of Arts, Society and Education at James Cook University in Cairns, Australia. Her main research and teaching interests focus on the embedding of education for sustainability in the school and higher education sectors and, more specifically, teacher education.

Antonio Fernández-Crispín is Professor of Management and Conservation of Natural Resources at the Biology Faculty of the Meritorious Authonomous University of Puebla, Mexico. His major research and teaching interests are environmental education and social representation of environmental problems.

Rider W. Foley is an Assistant Professor in the Department of Engineering and Society at the University of Virginia, USA, and a team leader at the Center for Nanotechnology in Society at Arizona State University, USA. He holds a PhD from the School of Sustainability at Arizona State University. His research and teaching focuses on socio-technical innovation processes and solutions to complex sustainability problems.

Nigel Forrest is a Doctoral Candidate in the School of Sustainability and a member of the Sustainability Transition and Intervention Research Lab at Arizona State University, USA. His research interests include urban sustainability transitions, municipal sustainability programs, and small-scale community transitions. He has taught transformational-oriented sustainability at high school, community college and university levels.

Angela Franz-Balsen is an independent expert in sustainability communication and education for sustainable development. Her research interests are professional development and gender and diversity competence in sustainability communication/education, with a focus on higher education for sustainable development.

Edgar J. González-Gaudiano is Senior Research Fellow at the Institute of Researches in Education, at the Universidad Veracruzana, Mexico, where he leads the research line of environmental education for sustainability. His current research focus is on social representations of climate change, vulnerability, risk and social resilience.

Steve Gough is Professor of Environment and Society and Associate Dean at the University of Bath, UK. He has researched and published widely on higher education and education for sustainable development.

Gary P. Hampson is an independent scholar and creative life artist. He has published on such topics as global worldview regeneration, ecological education, complex integrative approaches, and transformative human identity. His PhD on transformative higher education was nominated for the Australian National Doctoral Award in Education.

Kathryn Hegarty is a Lecturer in Environment and Sustainability at RMIT University in

Melbourne, Australia. Her research interests include educational design for professional education, interdisciplinary responses to climate change imperatives, and academics' subjectivities.

Krista Hiser is Professor of English at Kapi'olani Community College in Honolulu, Hawaii. She teaches composition in the context of sustainability and coordinates faculty work in developing sustainability curriculum and service-learning pedagogy. Her research focuses on student perspectives towards sustainability and global environmental issues.

Sarah Holdsworth is a Lecturer within the School of Global Property Construction and Project Management at RMIT University, Melbourne, Australia. Her professional roles have involved change projects in relation to tertiary learning and teaching, and academic development in higher education. Her main research focus is the identification of key mechanisms required to turn sustainability innovations into embedded practice in a university context; specifically, the development of curriculum, learning and teaching methodologies and pedagogic change related to sustainability for higher education.

Margarita Juárez-Nájera is Professor at the Universidad Autónoma Metropolitana, CBI-Azcapotzalco, Mexico. She has worked in pollution prevention projects in the industry sector. Her major research interest is on sustainable behaviour among members of higher educational institutions.

Braden Kay is a Sustainability Project Manager for the City of Orlando, Florida, USA. He obtained his doctoral degree at the School of Sustainability at Arizona State University, USA. He teaches solution-oriented sustainability courses at high school and university levels. He managed community engagement and sustainability strategy building for the City of Phoenix's Reinvent Phoenix grant, funded by the US Department of Housing and Urban Development.

Christopher Kuzdas is an Associate Researcher and Consultant for the Tropical Agricultural Research and Higher Education Center, USA. He holds a PhD in Sustainability and a Masters of Public Administration from Arizona State University. He has collaborated with researchers, policy makers and community members on sustainable water governance, water conflict mitigation, and drought planning in Costa Rica since 2009.

Regula Kyburz-Graber is Professor of Education for secondary school teachers at University of Zurich, Switzerland. She was leader of various cooperative research projects with teachers in national and international contexts. Her research interests are environmental education, education for sustainable development, science education, science at the interface of nature and society, cross-curricular teaching and learning, reflective teaching, and self-regulated learning.

David Lara-González is Professor at the Science Institute of the Meritorious Authonomous University of Puebla, Mexico. His major research and teaching interests are evaluation, use, management and conservation of natural resources with emphasis on soil and water.

Heila Lotz-Sisitka is Professor and Murray & Roberts Chair of Environmental Education at Rhodes University, South Africa. She has been actively engaged in various national and international research and policy initiatives in education for sustainable development, and is founding member of the Mainstreaming Environment and Sustainability in African Universities network. Her research interests include critical research approaches, and the relationship between learning, agency and social change in various educational settings, including higher education.

Clemens Mader is Senior Researcher at the UNESCO Chair in Higher Education for Sustainable Development at Leuphana University of Lüneburg, Germany, and at the Sustainability Team of University of Zurich, Switzerland. He is President of the COPERNICUS Alliance – the European Network on Higher Education for Sustainable Development. He has teaching and research experience from universities in Austria, Germany, Switzerland, Serbia and Japan and has published in the fields of sustainability assessment and transformations at the interface of education, research, policy and practice.

M. Pilar Martínez-Agut is a Doctor in Pedagogy, Professor of Secondary Education and part-time Associate Professor at the Theory of Education Department of University of Valencia, Spain, specialising in social education and sustainability education.

Cynthia N. Martínez-Fernández is a Senior Doctorate in Educational Research at the Universidad Veracruzana, Mexico. The title of her doctoral research is 'Sustainability Policies in Institutions of Higher Education. Analysis in Three Mexican Public Universities'.

Jorge Megid Neto is a Professor at University of Campinas (UNICAMP), Brazil, since 1996. He has worked in both undergraduate and postgraduate courses and his major research interests are in science education and environmental education, with a particular focus on state of the art research, methods in education research, initial and continuing teacher education, and evaluation of teaching materials.

Pablo Á. Meira-Cartea is Professor of Environmental Education at the University of Santiago de Compostela, Spain. His research interests are social and educational dimensions of climate change, the theoretical foundations of environmental education, and development of public environmental education policies to generate a culture of sustainability.

Gerd Michelsen was Professor of Sustainability and Environmental Communication at Leuphana University Lüneburg, Germany, from 1995 to October 2013. Since then he is Senior Professor of Sustainability Science. Research and publications are in the areas of (higher) education for sustainable development, sustainability and environmental communication, and sustainable consumption.

Kelly Miller is a Senior Lecturer in the School of Life and Environmental Sciences at Deakin University in Melbourne, Australia, and Course Director for the Bachelor of Environmental Science (Environmental Management and Sustainability). Her teaching and research focus on the human dimensions of wildlife management, environmental planning, and education for sustainability.

Yoko Mochizuki is Head of Curriculum Team at UNESCO Mahatma Gandhi Institute of Education for Peace and Sustainable Development (MGIEP) in New Delhi, India. She has been engaged in the global implementation of Education for Sustainable Development (ESD) since the beginning of the Decade of ESD, as an ESD specialist at the United Nations University-Institute of Advanced Studies, and as a Programme Specialist at the Section of ESD at UNESCO Paris.

Meyrav Mor is a PhD student at Bath University, UK. Her research focus is on traditional cultural knowledge and its possible contributions to sustainable education. She is currently undertaking her fieldwork in the Nepal Himalayas with the Rai Bahing ethnic group. Her professional background includes establishing schools in Nepal with an emphasis on integrating Himalayan culture into the school curriculum.

Susanne Müller-Lindeque works as a Research Fellow at the Institute of Primary School Education of the Pädagogische Hochschule FHNW Liestal, Switzerland. Her research interests focus on discourses and policies of education for sustainable development and sustainable higher education especially in relation to the formation of academic subjects and subjectivities.

Rob O'Donoghue is an Associate Professor in the Environmental Education and Sustainability Centre at Rhodes University, South Africa. Much of his work has been centred on situated (indigenous) knowledge and learning-led change in curriculum and community contexts where environment and sustainability education is approached as a process of co-engaged evaluation and reflexive learning.

Albert Piñero is a Doctor in Sociology and Associated Professor at the Department of Sociology and Social Anthropology of University of Valencia, Spain, currently retired from teaching.

Christian Rammel is Assistant Professor at the Institute of Ecological Economics at the Vienna University of Economics and Business, Austria. He is also the Head of the Regional Centre of Expertise on Education for Sustainable Development Vienna (RCE Vienna) and works mainly in the area of sustainable development and transformative education.

Jonathan Reams is an Associate Professor at the University of Science and Technology, Norway, teaching and doing research in the field of leadership development. He serves as Editor-in-Chief of the open access online journal *Integral Review*, and is a co-founder of the Center for Transformative Leadership as well as the European Center for Leadership Practice. He brings awareness-based leadership development technology to his work, focusing on how the inner workings of human nature can develop leadership capacities for today's complex challenges.

Alan Reid is a member of the Education, Environment and Sustainability research group at Monash University, Australia. His research interests focus on teachers' thinking and practice in environmental and sustainability education, and traditions, capacities and issues in environmental and sustainability education theory, research and practice. He edits the international journal *Environmental Education Research*.

Mark Rickinson is an Associate Professor and Associate Dean (Engagement) in the Faculty of Education at Monash University, Australia. His research focuses on the role of evidence in educational policy and practice, and the role of learning in environmental and sustainability education.

Marco Rieckmann is Assistant Professor of Higher Education Development at the University of Vechta, Germany. His major research and teaching interests are in higher education development, competence development and assessment, (higher) education for sustainable development, and global education.

Juliana Rink is Assistant Professor of Environmental Education and Environmental Management at the Paula Souza Technology Educational Center (FATEC JD), Brazil. Her major teaching and research interests are science education, environmental education and higher education for sustainable development, especially related to the curricular greening of undergraduate courses.

Debra Rowe is Professor of Renewable Energies, Energy Efficiency, Sustainable Development and Psychology at Oakland Community College, Michigan, USA. She also teaches sustainable development at the University of Vermont. As President of the US Partnership for Education for Sustainable Development, she has created higher education for sustainable development networks for over 50 national higher education associations with a focus on both faculty and administrators. She helps higher education integrate sustainable development into curricula, research, operations, and campus life, with a focus on engagement in regional to national community-based projects for systemic change.

Kerry Shephard is Professor of Higher Education Development at the University of Otago, New Zealand. He researches what learners choose to do with the knowledge and skills that they learn in higher education, such as opting to think critically and making sustainable and integrious academic and life choices; and if and how university teachers encourage such things.

Mandy Singer-Brodowski studied educational science at the University of Erfurt, Germany, and has recently submitted her PhD project on 'Self-organised and Probem-based Learning for Sustainability' at the Leuphana University of Lüneburg, Germany. She is employed by the Wuppertal Institute for Climate, Energy and Environment.

Anna Sowter is a PhD student at the University of Bath, UK. Her research focuses on water, learning and sustainability. Recent fieldwork in the Occupied Palestinian Territories explores the meanings around water in order to examine water interventions and the processes of engagement at the local level. She has worked on various projects in Uganda, researching environmental education in formal and non-formal contexts, and therapeutic horticulture in the UK.

Stephen Sterling is Professor of Sustainability Education at Plymouth University, UK, and has worked as a consultant in environmental and sustainability education in the academic and NGO fields nationally and internationally for over three decades. His research interest is in ecological thinking, systemic change, and learning at individual and institutional scales, and the challenge of accelerating the educational response to the sustainability agenda.

Paul Sylvestre is a PhD candidate in the Department of Geography at Queen's University, Canada. His major research focus centres drawing on lessons of anti-colonial and critical pedagogy to inform the development of higher education for sustainable development and how to deploy such radical approaches within conventional institutional contexts.

Valentina C. Tassone is Lecturer at Wageningen University, Education and Competence Studies group, Netherlands. She has conducted scientific research and educational activities in Europe (Italy, the Netherlands, Malta, Estonia, Poland) and South Africa, especially focusing on participatory processes, community development, empowerment, transformative learning and competence development supporting transition towards sustainability.

Ian Thomas is Honorary Associate Professor at RMIT University, Australia. His research has covered environmental management and most recently has focused on implementation of education for sustainable development in universities, particularly in relation to relevant pedagogy and competencies.

Daniella Tilbury is Professor of Education for Sustainable Development and Vice-Chancellor of the University of Gibraltar. She is recognised for her expertise in leadership, learning and institutional change for sustainable development in higher education. She is the recipient of several research awards including the Macquarie Innovation Award for Research (Australia 2007); a Marie Curie International Research Fellowship (European Commission 2009) and Green Gown Awards (2008; 2010). She directs the University Educators for Sustainable Development initiative (2014–16) and served as Chair of the UNESCO Global Monitoring and Evaluation Expert Group on ESD (2005–14).

Jana Timm is a PhD student at the UNESCO Chair 'Higher Education for Sustainable Development' at Leuphana University of Lüneburg, Germany. Her major research interests are in higher education for sustainable development, social and sustainability entrepreneurship as well as sustainability entrepreneurship teaching methods.

M. Angeles Ull is Professor of Biochemistry and Molecular Biology at the Faculty of Biological Sciences of University of Valencia, Spain. She has more than 30 years of teaching experience and in recent years she has focused her research on sustainability in higher education.

Paul Vare is Course Leader for the Masters in Education programme at the University of Gloucestershire, UK, and is a founding director of the South West Learning for Sustainability Coalition, a non-governmental cross-sector network. In the past he has developed education and community development projects in settings as diverse as western Ghana and northern Alaska. A key area of interest in relation to ESD is exploring the boundary between individual and social learning. Between 2002 and 2012 he represented the NGO coalition, European ECO Forum, at the United Nations Economic Commission for Europe (UNECE) where he contributed to drafting the UNECE Strategy for ESD, a set of ESD indicators and competences for ESD educators.

Luis Velázquez has 25 years of experience as Industrial Engineer and since 1994 he has served as Director of Sustainable Development Group in the Engineering College at the University of Sonora, Mexico. He is Senior Researcher in the Sustainability, Cleaner Production and Pollution Prevention fields. He holds a doctoral degree in the major of Cleaner Production and Pollution Prevention from the University of Massachusetts Lowell, USA. Currently he is Professor and Researcher in the University of Sonora in Mexico and Adjunct Professor in the University of Massachusetts Lowell.

Fiona Wahr recently completed a PhD investigating academic engagement in sustainability related curriculum change at RMIT University, Melbourne, Australia. She currently works at Melbourne Polytechnic in the role of Senior Lecturer, Curriculum Transformations. She has extensive experience as an academic developer, working to support higher education curriculum change and enhanced student learning. Her research reinforces her professional work by exploring the theory and practice of facilitating transformative professional learning for academics.

Arjen E.J. Wals is Professor of Transformative Learning and Socio-Ecological Sustainability at Wageningen University in The Netherlands and a UNESCO Chair. He is also a guest professor in Sustainability Education at Gothenburg University in Sweden and an Adjunct Faculty member of the Department of Natural Resources of Cornell University in the USA.

Paul Warwick is a Research Fellow at the Centre for Sustainable Futures, Plymouth University, UK. His major research and teaching interests are innovation and reform in education, education for sustainable development and citizenship education.

Arnim Wiek is an Associate Professor in the School of Sustainability at Arizona State University, USA, and the Head of the Sustainability Transition and Intervention Research Lab. His research group develops evidence-supported solutions to sustainability challenges in close collaboration with government, businesses and community groups. He holds a PhD in Environmental Sciences from the Swiss Federal Institute of Technology, Zurich. He had research and teaching engagements at the Swiss Federal Institute of Technology, Zurich, the University of British Columbia, Canada, the University of Tokyo, Japan, and Leuphana University of Lüneburg, Germany.

Lauren Withycombe Keeler is a Postdoctoral Researcher in the Faculty of Sustainability at Leuphana University Lüneburg, Germany. She holds a PhD from the School of Sustainability at Arizona State University, USA. She conducted research on key competencies in sustainability and has taught sustainability courses in the US and Germany. Currently she applies methods of anticipation and future studies to inform urban sustainability transformations and build anticipatory competence in future change agents.

Tarah Wright is Director of the Education for Sustainability Research Group and Professor in the Faculty of Science at Dalhousie University, Canada. Her research interests include sustainability in higher education, and the role of performance art in creating positive change toward a sustainable future.

Lynne Wyness is Senior Research Administrator at the Centre for Sustainable Futures and an Educational Developer at Plymouth University, UK. Her research interests include the intersection of sustainability and entrepreneurship education through creativity, critical thinking, and values-based learning, teaching and learning as an embodied, emotional process, wellbeing and sustainability education, and the geographies of education.

Masaru Yarime is Project Associate Professor of Science, Technology, and Innovation Governance (STIG) at the Graduate School of Public Policy of the University of Tokyo, Japan, and Honorary Reader in the Department of Science, Technology, Engineering & Public Policy (STEaPP) of University College London, United Kingdom. His research interest centres around public policy, corporate strategy, and institute design for innovation for sustainability.

ACKNOWLEDGEMENTS

Bringing together so many different voices views and ideas can only happen through interacting deeply with friends and colleagues. The editors would therefore like to take the opportunity to thank first of all the authors who have contributed to this Handbook and have put their energy and work into producing high quality contributions. Special thanks also go to the members of the editorial board for their collaboration and support in particular during the elaboration of the concept for this Handbook: Aklilu Dalelo, Addis Ababa University, Ethiopia; Luiz Marcelo de Carvalho, Universitàe Estadual Paulista, Brazil; Edgar J. González-Gaudiano, University of Veracruz, Mexico; Heila Lotz-Sisitka, Rhodes University, South Africa; Yoko Mochizuki, UNESCO Mahatma Gandhi Institute of Education for Peace and Sustainable Development, India; Daniella Tilbury, University of Gibraltar; and Tarah Wright, Dalhousie University, Canada. We also acknowledge the financial support from the German Academic Exchange Service (DAAD) as the funding agency of the project 'Graduate capabilities to contribute to a more sustainable future – An emerging field of research in education for sustainability' between RMIT University, Melbourne, Australia, and Leuphana University of Lüneburg, Germany. This project made possible several meetings in Australia and Germany during 2012 and 2013, in which the idea for this Handbook was born and the Handbook concept was elaborated. Finally, the editors thank our colleagues from all over the world who reviewed the chapters of this Handbook for their enormous and very important support.

INTRODUCTION

In 2012, twenty years after the 1992 World Summit on Environment and Development in Rio de Janeiro, the normative idea of sustainable development was celebrated with a follow-up conference – again in Rio de Janeiro (Rio+20). In this time, a growing awareness of the increasing scale of human impacts on the natural environment not only contributed to the emergence of the *concept of sustainable development* but also fostered a scientific response to the fundamental social, cultural, economic and ecological changes that humankind is confronted with. This search for ways for a transition towards sustainability is a process of social learning in its broadest sense. Accordingly, it is not only learning that is at issue but education and educational science, which is about exploring the preconditions of and opportunities for learning and education – whether individual or social, whether in formal or informal settings.

The emerging area of *education for sustainable development* (ESD) emphasises aspects of learning that enhance the transition towards sustainability, 'translates' research outcomes of sustainability science into educational practices and is an integrative approach to teaching and learning. Thus, it represents a changed educational paradigm, rather than yet another 'adjectival' education. ESD supports individuals in reflecting on their own actions by taking into account their current and future social and environmental effects – from a global perspective – and to intervene productively in shaping them in a sustainable manner. Individuals should be empowered to act in complex situations which may require the individual to strike out in new directions. Therefore, ESD aims to develop competencies that enable individuals to participate in socio-political processes and hence to move their society towards sustainable development.

How ESD matured in an academic area in its own right can be reconstructed on the three different but related levels of policy, pedagogies and research. The latter is witnessed by a fast growing number of articles and books on the topic, the establishment of specific journals as well as special issues on ESD in existing journals and finally a growing number of international conferences.

Among the educational sectors *universities* as research and teaching institutions are playing an important role since they not only generate and transfer relevant knowledge, but they also can educate future decision makers to enable them to contribute to a (more) sustainable future. Dealing with the concept of sustainable development, offers the opportunity for universities to understand and face up to complexity as well as to cope with uncertainty and diverging norms and values. Furthermore it facilitates systemic institutional and organisational change of universities and provides them with spaces for future-oriented and transformative thinking and learning.

Accordingly, *research on higher education for sustainable development* (HESD) features prominently in the ESD discourse – with distinctive topics and research approaches. Over the last decade, a number of research initiatives and postgraduate programmes worldwide gained momentum and engaged with research in this area. However, what is still missing is a systematic overview of existing approaches as well as an introduction in this emerging field of research. This *Handbook of Higher Education for Sustainable Development* aims at filling that gap and providing an orientation of existing and upcoming research approaches for HESD. Thus, it surveys where research on HESD is at the present time and where it may be going in the future. Its approach is twofold: while a more theoretical overview of existing approaches helps to understand the various foci and perspectives and to structure the emerging research area, these approaches are exemplified in tangible applications which offer insights in hands-on experiences and critically discusses content and methods of latest research projects.

The Handbook – with its international authors from leading universities in research and teaching in HESD – brings together a broad range of different research approaches and shows how these approaches are reflected in the research practice in HESD. Thus, the Handbook pioneers in its attempt to structure an emerging field while at the same time it complements existing resources for researchers in HESD, such as general introductions in educational research, and draws upon the tradition of environmental education and research in that field.

The Handbook targets those academics who conduct research on HESD or plan to do so. This means at least three distinctive groups of researchers are addressed: Early career researchers up from postgraduate level, who start to establish a research career and are already trained in courses or programmes explicitly dedicated to higher education for sustainable development; early and mid-career researchers coming from a variety of different disciplines such as educational science in general, educational psychology or environmental or sustainability (social) sciences who specialise in HESD as an area of research; and finally academics who engage with research on HESD as part of their sustainability related teaching and learning scholarship.

Organising any field of study, especially one as diverse as HESD, is no easy matter; whatever scheme we could have employed would have captured only part of the complexity of scholarship in HESD. We have decided to *structure the Handbook in four parts*: Part 1 – Education for sustainable development in higher education; Part 2 – Paradigms and methodologies of research on higher education for sustainable development; Part 3 – Issues and themes of research on higher education for sustainable development; and Part 4 – Examples of research on higher education for sustainable development.

Part 1: Education for sustainable development in higher education

This section deals with the evolution of (higher) education for sustainable development as well as the underlying paradigms, concepts and principles. It also discusses critical aspects of ESD in higher education institutions.

The first chapter by *Yoko Mochizuki and Masaru Yarime* starts with exploring relations between ESD and sustainability science in the context of re-purposing higher education and research. It discusses potential synergies between ESD and sustainability science and explores how ESD and sustainability science can reinforce each other.

In the second chapter *Arjen E.J. Wals and colleagues* look back at two evolutions: the evolution from nature conservation education to sustainability education, on the one hand, and the evolution within science and higher education from environmental science to sustainability science, on the other. They connect them using eco-socio innovation as a bridge resulting in, what they call, praxis-oriented sustainability, which is inevitably emergent, critically reflexive, potentially disruptive and ultimately transformative.

HESD has moved up the international political agenda. This agenda involves three elements: content and goals (policy), the activities of different actors (politics) engaged in HESD as well as its institutional and organisational infrastructure (polity). In order to better understand the path HESD has taken over the last years and decades, *Gerd Michelsen* examines in Chapter 3 the three political dimensions – policy, politics and polity – as they apply to the area of HESD.

Given the efforts over two decades that have been made to introduce ESD into the curricular of higher education institutions, it might be expected that its implementation would be more advanced than the data suggest. Against this background, Chapter 4 by *Ian Thomas* considers the literature associated with change in higher education institutions and specifically with curriculum change. From this discussion factors affecting the implementation of ESD in higher education institutions are identified and guidance is provided for how such changes may be facilitated in future.

In some concluding remarks for Part 1, *Edgar J. González-Gaudiano and colleagues* provide the reader in Chapter 5 with a perspective from Ibero-America. They critically reflect on the idea of sustainable development, the difficulties to put it into practice within universities and structural barriers – such as the disciplinary and overtly compartmentalised structure of knowledge and neoliberal capitalism – that hinder progress towards sustainability and HESD. The authors ask for rethinking and reformulating strategic frameworks for action that have been followed so far in order to facilitate a transition into a deep environmental sustainability in universities.

Part 2: Paradigms and methodologies of research on higher education for sustainable development

The second section takes a threefold approach. It gives an overview of existing research paradigms and methodologies and the state of the art in research on HESD, discusses some of the ongoing and future directions of research and its prominent representatives, and critically investigates key challenges of HESD.

The opening Chapter 6 by *Stephen Sterling and colleagues* provides an introductory overview of approaches to research on ESD and environmental education (EE) in the context of higher education. ESD research is viewed broadly as an approach to investigating policy, practice and pedagogy as they relate to the sustainability agenda across higher education, rather than being focused solely on the ESD community and its practitioners. Three questions inform the chapter: why ESD in higher education research is done, what distinguishes ESD in higher education research methodology, and what are the main foci and issues of ESD in higher education research.

Matthias Barth and Marco Rieckmann complement that view in Chapter 7. They present the results of a systematic literature review on current research trends in HESD since 1992 – concerning research foci, methods, research topics, key journals and authors' origins as well as general trends over time. By doing so, they hope to provide a basis for an international dialogue about needs for future research on HESD, especially in terms of critical aspects as a prevalent Western dominance, quality standards and research foci.

Chapter 8 by *Steve Gough and colleagues* reviews the historical origins of contemporary thinking on higher education and sustainable development, and also notes that much work in universities that is clearly education, and equally clearly related to or focused on sustainable development, takes place with no reference to the body of work known as HESD. The chapter suggests that there is a need for interdisciplinary engagement by educationalists and for a more developed meta-theory of how ESD knowledge develops, and how it relates to other knowledge.

In Chapter 9, *Regula Kyburz-Graber* looks into a first specific research approach that features prominently in HESD. She elaborates the special role and challenges of case study research on HESD and outlines the theoretical foundations and quality challenges of such a methodology. Based on the appreciation of existing case studies as well as the critique on deficiently documented research procedures, the chapter critically reflects on opportunities and drawbacks and introduces quality aspects of case study research. The procedure of a case study research is illustrated by cases of a reflective teaching approach, and claims for generalising findings and the role of cross-case-comparison are discussed.

Research synthesis has become increasingly prominent within education and social research over the last 10–15 years. Within the field of HESD however, to date there has been little or no strategic investment in research synthesis. *Mark Rickinson and Alan Reid* argue in Chapter 10 how and why the future development of HESD needs to involve strategic commissioning of synthesis projects, varied types of synthesis projects and methodologies, fuller involvement of research users in synthesis projects, and targeted uses of synthesis to inform policy, practice and research.

Chapter 11 by *Fiona Wahr and Barbara de la Harpe* takes a look at using a well-established action-oriented research approach to bring about change in universities in support of sustainability curriculum change. It explores the use of Action Research as a vehicle for supporting transformation in higher education contexts, bringing about meaningful and lasting change, and contributing to theory.

Angela Franz-Balsen states in Chapter 12 that a historical-epistemological overview of the changes that gender studies have undergone over the last decades, accompanied by a whole body of new terminology, is essential for understanding the current state of art, as characterised by the call for sex-gender-diversity-competence for researchers. The chapter explores the manifold relations between gender issues and (un)sustainability and, based on recently published research, it illustrates what it means to make HESD research gender-sensitive.

Chapter 13 by *Vanessa Andreotti* stresses the importance of questions emerging in postcolonial studies for research on sustainable development in higher education. It outlines key concepts and critiques of modern forms of knowledge production and their effects on social and political relations drawing on postcolonial and decolonial studies. Finally, it introduces an example of an approach to research in higher education that attempts to address the problematic issues identified in the first part of the chapter.

Heila Lotz-Sisitka suggests in Chapter 14 that critical HESD research needs to be based on a review of the emergence and development of three generations of critical theory. Through reference to examples of HESD research conducted in southern Africa, she considers how different generations of critical theory influence HESD research. She specifically considers the critique of an inadequate politics of emancipation within critical theory in the context of the dire need for emancipatory research in the context of sustainability concerns in southern Africa and elsewhere.

Chapter 15 by *Rob O'Donoghue* brings features of evaluation as a realm of professionally mediated measurement into question. ESD is approached as an evaluative process in its own right, and a start-up tool kit for situated evaluation processes is developed drawing on core aspects of appreciative inquiry, developmental evaluation and value creation assessment. A case study of a collaborative evaluation process is reported to begin to re-inscribe and integrate evaluation practices in Regional Centres of Expertise (RCEs) as situated critical processes of transformative social learning for the common good.

Part 3: Issues and themes of research on higher education for sustainable development

This section provides an overview of the field of research of ESD in higher education institutions. It identifies the 'needles' – the issues and elements of theory that provide the basis for researching, and the 'threads' – the ideas and experiences that join the issues, elements and experiences of researching together. Through this, it provides questions and directions for future research. The chapters of Part 3 deal with the different views on HESD from a micro, meso and macro level. The micro view of the individual learning process is asking about what is happening with the learner. The meso level is looking at what is happening in the classroom; and finally, on the macro level, the focus is more on curriculum change, organisational change and more general change that is happening in the educational system.

In Chapter 16, *Arnim Wiek and colleagues* look into the concept of competencies that has lately received increasing attention as critical reference point for the development of curricula and courses. As the operationalisation of competencies into specific learning objectives still lags – in particular, when it comes to specifications for different educational levels – the authors offer an initial system of operationalised competencies in sustainability, differentiated into novice, intermediate and advanced levels. The competencies can be applied to undergraduate and/or graduate education programmes, and even to prepare high school students for sustainability programmes in higher education institutions. The chapter concludes with a critical discussion of the proposed operationalisation and further research needs.

Chapter 17 by *Kerry Shephard* suggests that if higher education is to educate for sustainable development, it should be interested in how its efforts impact on its students' educational outcomes. The chapter explores the nature of some of these outcomes, and the challenges involved in addressing them via research. It asserts that outcomes that are affective in nature, or are underpinned by affective dispositions, are best researched at the level of individual, anonymous students.

According to *Daniella Tilbury*, student engagement in higher education is becoming the focus of academic conversations, policy documents and recent studies. This backdrop provides an important context to understanding current research into higher education studies in sustainability, and is explored in detail in Chapter 18. The student engagement narrative resonates deeply with proponents of sustainable development who seek transformative outcomes. Consequently a need for research to improve participation or empowerment levels is elaborated and a call for research that can truly support student leadership for sustainability is made.

Curriculum change in higher education is a fundamental plank of the diffusion of ESD in universities, and therefore, in the professions and the world. Chapter 19 by *Kathryn Hegarty and Sarah Holdsworth* reflects on a range of current curriculum change practices in higher education through a review of key ESD journals throughout the UN DESD. It explores some 'epistemological tensions' which impede curriculum change, and researches into it. It identifies the 'cascaded' layers of imperatives which drive curriculum change in universities and considers the scholarly and collegial processes through which the ESD project might move towards a framework for a rigorous and defensible curriculum for ESD.

Chapter 20 by *Paul Sylvestre and Tarah Wright* looks into the macro level of learning and provides a brief overview of several dominant trajectories of thought within the scholarship of organisational learning, as well as a discussion of several approaches to organisational learning that could help promote sustained change in higher education. The purpose is to act as an entry point for researchers in the field of HESD seeking to ground their research in a more robust understanding of the nature of learning and change at universities.

Chapter 21 by *Debra Rowe and Krista Hiser* highlights the importance of student learning in the context of community-based projects and partnerships, with an emphasis on real world project-based research, learning, and sustainability competence acquisition. Action research, community engaged research, and indigenous research methodologies as they are currently used in education and public health fields are suggested as frameworks to be integrated with engaged pedagogies for HESD. By learning through authentic, reciprocal community partnerships, it is argued, students attain the interpersonal skills and proactive problem solving that twenty-first-century employers are requesting, and that the development of sustainable systems and improved quality of life requires.

In Chapter 22 *Christian Rammel and colleagues* provide a general conceptual framework for sustainability assessment in higher education and highlight essential cornerstones of an assessment approach that is aiming at internal learning processes, participation and transformation. Assessing sustainability is seen as significant support for incorporating sustainability into the institutional setting of universities that drives the process of mainstreaming sustainable development in higher education. Nevertheless, the authors argue, in many cases sustainability assessment at universities is missing an integrative and holistic approach and shows conceptual gaps and shortcomings when it comes to tackle the demands of a 'sustainable university'.

Part 4: Examples of research on higher education for sustainable development

The final part provides a noticeably different experience for the reader on three levels. Whereas the preceding parts provide an overview of the range of issues associated with HESD research, the chapters in this part are always based on one research project, and an emphasis in these chapters is the authors' reflection on the research process. Further, unlike the preceding chapters, contributions for this part were specifically sought from emerging researchers, people who have recently gained research experience and credentials and who do not have extensive research profiles. In this respect many of the chapters represent the work of the emerging researchers themselves, while for some there has been collaboration with more experienced researchers. Finally, the editors made a specific effort to have contributions from a range of cultures and countries. Initial responses to the 'call for chapters' demonstrated interest from all continents and a wide range of cultures. However, the pressures of producing draft chapters led to the withdrawal of some authors, and a smaller range being represented in the final selection.

As a result the chapters encompass a wide range of topics associated with HESD, a range of styles, and a range of research methodologies and related methods. The variation exhibited means that there is little that links the chapters, as in previous parts; rather the reader has the opportunity to experience the diversity that HESD is built on. Nevertheless, there are clear relationships between the chapters in Part 4 and those of Parts 1, 2 and 3 in regard to the topics covered, theories used and research approaches; and some are examples of particular approaches that are presented in overview in the previous parts.

In Part 2, in chapters by *Matthias Barth and Marco Rieckmann* and *Regula Kyburz-Graber* the prevalence of case study approaches of HESD research is noted, and several chapters of this Part 4 provide examples of the case study approach. The chapters by *Antonio Fernández-Crispín and David Lara-González*, *Mandy Singer-Brodowski* and *Pilar Aznar and colleagues* are clearly in this category, while the chapter by *Susanne Müller-Lindeque* embodies a comparative case study design. Otherwise, we see the spectrum of research approaches discussed. The chapter by *Juliana Rink and Jorge Megid Neto* is effectively a desk study reviewing the data from a sample of research theses, while in the chapter by *Pilar Aznar and colleagues* the sources of data are the teacher (subject) guides for university subjects. Distinctly different is the approach of the research presented in the chapters by *Margarita Juárez-Nájera* and *Belinda Christie and Kelly Miller*, which has been based on large samples and where the analyses of the data have used statistical techniques to identify similarities and differences. In addition, the chapter by *Jana Timm* shows leanings towards an ethnographic approach, specifically basing the research on an action-theoretical understanding to explore the experiences of practitioners of sustainable development. The action-research base of the research discussed in the chapter by *Neus (Snowy) Evans* illustrates an even closer focus on the role of reflection and learning by the researcher.

As well as the variety of research approaches, the chapters also illustrate a wide range of data collection methods. Questionnaires, paper-based and electronic (online), have been implemented for data collection for the research discussed in the chapters by *Margarita Juárez-Nájera, Antonio Fernández-Crispín and David Lara-González, Belinda Christie and Kelly Miller* and *Neus (Snowy) Evans*. The other main survey tool of interviews provided data discussed in the chapters by *Jana Timm, Mandy Singer-Brodowski*, and *Susanne Müller-Lindeque*. For some of the research presented multiple methods were used, for example the combination of questionnaires and interviews (as discussed in the chapters by *Belinda Christie and Kelly Miller* and *Neus (Snowy) Evans*), however, other methods have also contributed data, such as group discussions and observations in parallel with interviews. As already indicated, the research discussed in the chapters by *Juliana Rink and Jorge Megid Neto* and *Pilar Aznar and colleagues* relied on secondary data collection and analysis. A clearly different method was that of a weekly planning and reflection journal, in combination with a student questionnaire and selective interviews, discussed in the chapter by *Neus (Snowy) Evans*.

For the authors of all the chapters, their research experiences have provided rich material for them to reflect on their research results, but more especially to reflect on the methodology and methods they used. Again the chapters demonstrate a range of insights, and some proposals for future research. In this regard the chapter by *Jana Timm* provides an extensive discussion of the research process and experiences, with considerable learning that will be of value to others seeking deep understanding of their topic. Likewise, the action-research approach of the chapter by *Neus (Snowy) Evans* lends itself to reflection on the overall experience. More broadly the chapter by *Susanne Müller-Lindeque*, based on the experiences of interviewing practitioners of sustainable higher education, raises questions about the role of 'post-qualitative inquiry'. In addition, reflections about the efficacy of particular research methods are provided by the authors, and will be important guides for future research.

Pulling together a handbook like this with a great variety of voices, approaches and topics is a huge undertaking and the selection and structure of this variety will always leave some blind spots and underrepresented areas. While we are fully aware that there will be numerous other possible structures and conceptualisations of this area of research – some we might have considered, some we did not even think of – we also hope that the structure we have chosen is useful and transparent for the readers to engage with the text. In an intense process of selecting topics and authors and at the same time ensuring a high quality throughout the book with a full peer review process, we tried to provide a resource that might serve as a catalyst for an intense engagement with the heterogeneity and richness of approaches in higher education for sustainable development. In other words, we invite and encourage readers to engage, critique and challenge this synthesis of knowledge and ideas to shape their own understanding of what research in higher education is, will be and could be.

Matthias Barth, Gerd Michelsen, Marco Rieckmann and Ian Thomas
August 2015

PART 1

Education for sustainable development in higher education

1

EDUCATION FOR SUSTAINABLE DEVELOPMENT AND SUSTAINABILITY SCIENCE

Re-purposing higher education and research

Yoko Mochizuki and Masaru Yarime

Introduction

Normative discussions surrounding the role of higher education in contributing to sustainable development abound, from the perspectives of Education for Sustainable Development (ESD), Sustainability Education, or more specifically Higher Education for Sustainable Development (HESD). Despite familiar calls for interdisciplinarity and more research to advance higher education to facilitate a global transition to sustainability, however, such discussions rarely involve natural scientists, engineers or technologists striving to establish 'Sustainability Science' as an academic field and are often silent on crucial relations between ESD and Sustainability Science in the context of re-purposing higher education and research. This can be partly explained by different 'epistemic communities' formed by ESD experts on the one hand, and scientists who promote Sustainability Science on the other. This chapter discusses potential synergies between ESD and Sustainability Science by 1) contextualising them in global 'policyscapes' (Carney 2009), and 2) exploring how ESD and Sustainability Science can reinforce each other.

Literature investigating links between ecological science and environmental education has long pointed out the importance for knowledge producers and knowledge users to identify problems and develop solutions to them together (see, for example, Beal *et al.* 1986; Maarleveld and Dabgbégnon 1999). In recent years, literature on 'social learning' for natural resources management has inspired practitioners and scholars of ESD to highlight the importance of stakeholder communication and interaction in change-oriented learning processes (Lotz-Sisitka 2012). The added value of this chapter is not so much underscoring the importance of developing learning partnerships as drawing attention to the fact that calls for integration of knowledge are gaining prominence in an emerging policy common sense or global 'policyscapes'. Whereas context embedded research and education, starting from real-life problems, are important aspects of Sustainability Science and ESD, the purpose of this chapter is not to show how they manifest themselves in different settings. Rather, this chapter intends to enhance HESD stakeholders' understanding of global frameworks that would affect directly and indirectly the implementation of HESD on the ground in the coming decade. The chapter aims at enriching the field of HESD by identifying common challenges and opportunities faced by ESD and Sustainability Science in the international policy community's ongoing efforts to set post-2015 education and development agendas as well as the scientific community's efforts to set a new knowledge agenda.

ESD and sustainability science in global 'policyscapes'

In 1999, UNESCO and the International Council for Science (ICSU) organised the World Conference on Science in Budapest and declared the importance of 'science in society, and science for society'. The concept of 'Sustainability Science' was originally introduced at the World Congress 'Challenges of a Changing Earth 2001' in Amsterdam organised by the ICSU and other international organisations. Although the linkages between ESD and Sustainability Science have been recognised since the beginning of the United Nations (UN) Decade of ESD (DESD 2005–2014) by ESD researchers as well as advocates of Sustainability Science in Japan, where the government has supported these two initiatives through various funding schemes, it was not until recently that UNESCO explicitly came to endorse the idea of Sustainability Science.

In 2011, the Japanese National Commission for UNESCO submitted to the UNESCO Secretariat a proposal to request that UNESCO introduce the concept of 'Sustainability Science' in formulating its programmes (MEXT 2011). Consequently, 'Sustainability Science' came to be recognised in UNESCO's medium-term strategy covering the period between 2014 and 2021 as 'integrated, "problem-solving" approaches' to science and engineering for sustainable development which 'draw on the full range of scientific, traditional and indigenous knowledge in a trans-disciplinary way to identify, understand and address economic, environmental, ethical and societal challenges' (UNESCO 2014a: 22, paragraph 52). This section contextualises ESD and Sustainability Science in relation to the 'real world' of global politics, international organisations, and international agenda setting – in other words, in global 'policyscapes' (Carney 2009), created around notions of sustainable development and composed of a particular constellation of visions, values, policies and practices. It pays special attention to the changing role of the UN as 1) a diagnostician of the global illness, and 2) a tool for global governance and governance of global commons.

Diagnosing and curing the global illness

An analogy often invoked in discussing the need for efforts like ESD and Sustainability Science is that of physicians. Just as a physician has a vision of a healthy human-being, most ESD and sustainability researchers have a vision of a healthy society and healthy relations between human and earth systems. It is especially telling that the International Commission for Education for Sustainable Development Practice (ICESDP) – launched in 2007 with the support of the John D. and Catherine T. MacArthur Foundation and tasked to identify practical initiatives to reorient education and training of development professionals – was inspired by the 1910 Flexner Report, which transformed medical education in the United States.[1] Based on the recommendations of the ICESDP (2008), the Global Master's in Development Practice (MDP) was created to offer a two-year degree providing graduate-level students with the skills and knowledge required to better identify and address the global challenges of sustainable development. What motivated John MacArthur to support the ICESPD and the ensuing creation of MDP programmes across the globe was the perceived need to reorient training of development professionals who make decisions about the well-being of millions of people in developing countries.

Physicians seek out knowledge on what needs to be done to allow their patients to attain a vision of a healthy human being. In the same way, sustainability education and sustainability science researchers attempt to produce knowledge that would facilitate attainment of a vision of a sustainable world. The analogy of physicians, however, is in no way new. In ancient Greece, for example, many philosophers saw themselves as analogous to physicians. If physicians treat and heal the body, the role of the philosopher was to provide comparable therapy for the soul to realise human flourishing. What is new today in the early years of the twenty-first century is the diagnosis and proposed remedy of the world we live in. The UN system has long served as the 'main diagnostician of the global illness of poverty, ecological destruction, human rights violation, and violent conflicts' (Osseiran and Reardon 1998: 386). The idea for the MDP comes from the US economist Jeffrey Sachs, an architect of the Millennium Development Goals (MDGs), which form a blueprint agreed to by all the world's countries and all the world's leading development institutions.

With the target date of MDGs approaching in 2015, the UN Conference on Sustainable Development in 2012 (Rio+20) and the ongoing discussion on the post-MDGs have provided ample opportunities for the UN agencies and other entities such as international NGOs and think tanks to point out the interconnected nature of the global illness and make propositions about how to realise a preferred future – to borrow the title of the Rio+20 outcome document, 'The Future We Want'. There are diverse visions of preferred futures found in the broad sustainable development community, leading to varied and sometimes irreconcilable views on the nature of interventions required in attaining sustainability (see Table 1.1). Whereas there seems to be an increasing consensus on the need for 'transformative shifts' required for realising sustainable development, a proposed cure for the global illness can range from interventions for accelerating economic globalisation to anti-capitalist and anti-globalisation movements. This poses, for example, a question to those who design educational and research programmes in HESD on how to embed equity in the curriculum.

What is rather unique about ESD is that it seems to embrace a whole range of competing worldviews. This is both a strength and weakness of ESD. On the one hand, ESD is open to a diverse array of disciplines and theoretical traditions. On the other hand, ESD lacks a clear definition and there is no consensus on competencies to be fostered through ESD or education for sustainability. For example, Wolbring and Burke (2013), examining the practice and purpose of sustainability-focused education through the lens of ability studies, have concluded that no consensus has been reached within ESD discourses on the process of how to identify essential abilities and a list of such abilities. Whereas there seems to be some shared understanding about sustainability competencies (Mochizuki and Fadeeva 2010; Wiek *et al.* 2011; Wiek *et al.* in this Handbook), what is meant by integration of sustainability into the curriculum or the whole institution may be different from one higher education institution to another (for various types of tools for assessing integration of sustainability in higher education institutions, see Yarime and Tanaka 2012).

The MDP degree aspires to integrate the four 'core areas' of 1) health sciences, 2) the natural sciences and engineering, 3) the social sciences, and 4) management for sustainable development. On the surface, MDP resonates with ESD and Sustainability Science in that it seeks to foster future leaders who can work flexibly across intellectual, professional and geographic boundaries to contribute to sustainable development. Exposure to a wide range of development problems and different disciplines, however, will not automatically foster the kind of critical and systemic thinking or collaborative skills needed for facilitating a transition to sustainability. While MDP achieves its purpose by solving problems, ESD ultimately 'achieves its purpose by transforming society' (UNESCO 2014b: 12). This difference between education

Table 1.1 Competing pathways to sustainable development

	Capitalism with a Green Face	*Sustainable Development as Defined by the UN*	*Social Economy*	*Limits to Growth*	*Sustainable Cities*
Worldview	Market liberals (grounded in neoclassical economics)	Institutionalists (grounded in political science and international relations)	Social greens (grounded in Marxist thought)	Bioenvironmentalists (grounded in natural sciences and ecological economics)	Urban greens City-based approach One system approach
Timeframe	Short-medium	Medium	Short and long	Long	Medium-long
Problems to be tackled	Lack of economic growth, market distortions, bad policies (e.g. subsidies)	Lack of global cooperation/ global regimes that manage the global environment; lack of state capacity	Capitalism as a primary driver of injustice	The assumption of infinite economic growth; rising population and consumption	Sustainability and design concerns for large cities (e.g. energy, transport, water/ sewage, green areas, brownfields, building)
Social	Green jobs Social protection for vulnerable groups Equality of opportunity Consultation Green consumerism	Global cooperation Redistribution (income) Stronger institutions Inter- & intra-generational equity Capacity building Social dialogue	Redistribution (power) Rights-based Social justice Equality of outcomes Empowerment Citizen action	Radical decrease in consumption and population growth Inclusivity Needs Rights	Social inclusion Platform for collaborative design and decision-making Consensus building
Environment	Eco-efficiency Technology transfer REDD[1]	Eco-regulation Strengthen global governance regimes REDD+[2]	Environmental justice Agroecology Grassroots action	Eco-centric valuing of nature for its own sake Enforced regulation of global commons	Cities as social-ecological systems Ecological cities as economic cities Urban metabolism
Economy	Green growth Voluntary CSR Carbon markets, PES[3] Production focused Private governance	Economic/trade reform Green finance Green taxes State governance CDM[4]	De-globalisation Localisation Institutional reform Regional solidarity Green economics	No-growth/de-growth Measures beyond GDP Ecological economics	Investment framework that values sustainability and resiliency Industrial ecology

Table 1.1 continued

	Capitalism with a Green Face	*Sustainable Development as Defined by the UN*	*Social Economy*	*Limits to Growth*	*Sustainable Cities*
Representative organisations, publications, publishers	WTO, IMF, WBCSD[5] World Economic Forum *The Economist*	World Bank, UNEP, UNFCCC,[6] GEF,[7] OECD	World Social Forum Third World Network *The Ecologist* New Society Publishers Chelsea Green	World Watch Institute WWF network IUCN Pachamama Earthscan, Island Press	ICLEI[8] C40 Eco^2 Cities
ESD agenda	Greening TVET[9], green skills Entrepreneurial Education Climate Change Education Education for Sustainable Consumption (soft version) DRR[10] Education (to build resilience of vulnerable groups)	Greening TVET[9], green skills Environmental Education Education for Sustainability Climate Change Education Biodiversity Education DRR[10] Education (Global) Citizenship Education Capacity building of policymakers	Human Rights Education Global (Citizenship) Education Development Education Climate Justice Education Community Learning Centres	Social-Critical Environmental Education Education for Sustainable Consumption and Production (radical version)	Regional Centres of Expertise on ESD (RCEs) coordinated by the United Nations University Multi-stakeholder approaches Social learning
Primary locus of action and attitude towards globalisation	Top-down globalist	Top-down globalist	Bottom-up anti-globalist	Top-down and bottom-up, anti-globalist	Bottom-up and top-down, often silent on issues of globalisation and justice

Source: The first five columns except for the last two rows have been adapted from UNRISD (2012), which is based on four worldviews put forward by Clapp and Dauvergne (2011). The Sustainable Cities column was added based on Marien (2011).

Notes: [1] REDD: Reducing Emissions from Deforestation and Forest Degradation; [2] REDD+: REDD with sustainable management of forests, conservation of forest carbon stocks and enhancement of forest carbon stocks; [3] PES: Payments for Ecological Services; [4] CDM: Clean Development Mechanism; [5] WBCSD: World Business Council for Sustainable Development; [6] UNFCCC: United Nations Framework Convention on Climate Change; [7] GEF: Global Environment Facility; [8] ICLEI: Local Governments for Sustainability; [9] TVET: Technical and Vocational Education and Training; [10] DRR: Disaster Risk Reduction for 'problem solving' and education for 'transforming society' is echoed by a tension between 'problem solving' research and 'world shaping' research observed by social scientists who aim to enhance the role of the social sciences in integrated research on global environmental change (Crowley 2012). These tensions are expected to continue as the world is not likely to forge a consensus on the diagnosis and cure for the global illness overnight.

Addressing the science-policy gap and transforming global governance

While a proposed cure for the global illness may range from mild to radical treatment, there is a growing international consensus on the need for taking a more integrated approach to address sustainable development and strengthening the role of the UN system as a diagnostician of the global illness of the twenty-first century. The UN Secretary-General Ban Ki-moon has convened multiple initiatives aimed at a global transition to sustainability in the lead up to Rio+20 and in the ongoing effort to forge an international consensus on the post-2015 agenda. Immediately following Rio+20, Ban Ki-moon established the Sustainable Development Solutions Network (SDSN), a global network of research centres, universities and businesses led by Jeffrey Sachs and tasked with informing the development of the Sustainable Development Goals (SDGs). He also established the UN Scientific Advisory Board, a board of 26 scientists, including not only natural scientists but also political scientists.[2] The Board, inaugurated in January 2014, marked the first time in the history of the UN system that its Secretary-General had a team of chief scientific advisers.

Another example of efforts to enhance an interface between the scientific community and policy makers is the Intergovernmental Science-Policy Platform on Biodiversity and Ecosystem Services (IPBES). IPBES aims at building capacity for and strengthening the use of science in policy making. It can also be considered as an updated science-policy interface compared to the Intergovernmental Panel on Climate Change (IPCC) in that it includes capacity building in its mandate. UNESCO works with the United Nations Environment Programme (UNEP), Food and Agriculture Organization (FAO), United Nations Development Programme (UNDP) and other relevant organisations to operationalise IPBES.

At the same time, international sustainable development research is itself undergoing a major transition. This transformation is being spearheaded by the ten-year research programme Future Earth, which was launched in 2013, integrating the existing four major international research programmes on global environmental change.[3] Future Earth aims to provide critical knowledge required for societies to face the challenges posed by global environmental change and to identify opportunities for transformation towards global sustainability (Future Earth 2013). In particular, the mandate of Future Earth includes *co-design* of research agendas, *co-production* of knowledge, and *co-dissemination* of findings and perspectives with key stakeholders, so that scientific knowledge makes an important contribution to decision-making.

While these are promising signs, the problems run deeper than the science-policy links. The inclusion of political scientists in the UN Scientific Advisory Board reflects a growing awareness that the governance arrangements of the twentieth century can no longer cope adequately with the challenges of today and tomorrow. The increasing interdependence among nation-states has not been accompanied by sufficient adjustments in the global governance regime, including global economic governance and global environmental governance (UN System Task Team on the Post-2015 UN Development Agenda 2013). While gaps in the international trade, finance and technology regimes are exacerbating global inequalities, climate change and increased activities in the global commons are making individual states more susceptible to policies adopted by others. There is therefore a need to improve international arrangements for collective decision making.

Whereas researchers in the field of sustainability education tend to see the UN mechanisms like the UN Decade as *the* major push for efforts for a better future, it is important to recognise the very limitation of the UN as state-centred governance arrangements, which can be a double-edged sword in efforts to transform existing systems. For example, the very limitation of the UN as peace educator was pointed out in the 1990s by prominent peace education researchers:

> [The United Nations has not been] able to persuade [the member states] to educate their publics toward the construction of alternatives to a system that perpetuates and is perpetuated by war. ... the United Nations cannot acknowledge that peace-building requires peace-learning on the part of the member states themselves as well as those whose education they design and deliver.
>
> *(Osseiran and Reardon 1998: 388)*

In addition, there is a need to enhance coordination and policy-making across the UN system (UN System Task Team on the Post-2015 UN Development Agenda 2013). Within the UN system, myriad organisations, secretariats of conventions, programmes, funds, commissions and panels work on what can be grouped under the heading of sustainable development, which makes it challenging to ensure policy coherence and coordination. This is partly evidenced by the experience of the UN DESD. Although the UN Inter-Agency Committee on the DESD consists of 22 UN entities, those who use the term ESD explicitly and consistently in their programming have been limited to a handful of active and committed members among them.

Furthermore, consideration should also be given to proposals for enabling participatory and accountable collective decision-making on sustainable development by way of enhancing the involvement of diverse stakeholders in governmental and inter-governmental processes. In this connection, the UN Secretary-General's Global Education First Initiative (GEFI) launched in 2012 deserves attention. The GEFI has three priorities: 1) put every child in school; 2) improve the quality of learning; and 3) foster global citizenship. While the first two pillars of the GEFI echo the education goal of the MDGs, the third pillar of preparing global citizens departs from the MDG discourses and is particularly relevant to mainstreaming ESD in the post-2015 agenda.

The concept and term of global citizenship are gaining traction in the education work of the UN as well as in higher education. With higher education's growing interest in internationalisation in recent years, the concept of civics and citizenship education has broadened to include a more global focus. Discussions on student learning about and for global citizenship, world citizenship (Nussbaum 1997), and global civics (Altinay 2011) deeply resonate with those on student learning about and for sustainability. Learning *about* and *for* global citizenship involves an individual's awareness of the interdependence of individuals and systems and the interconnected nature of the world – and a sense of responsibility that emanates from such awareness. As Altinay (2011: 1) suggests, 'a university education which does not provide effective tools and forums for students to think through their responsibilities and rights as one of the several billions on planet Earth, and along the way develop their moral compass, would be a failure'. This opens a door for HESD stakeholders to engage with the faculties of the Humanities who are under increasing pressure to safeguard liberal arts education in the neo-liberal era.

Exploring synergies between ESD and sustainability science

What is central to the ongoing reconfiguration of both the global development agenda and the international research on global environmental change is improving collective decision making about existing and future challenges facing humanity. There is growing consensus that we need new educational approaches as well as new approaches to knowledge production to address the complexity, uncertainty and socio-political controversy that characterise sustainability challenges. ESD can contribute to improvement in collective decision making by enabling individuals to make more informed decisions as citizens, workers and consumers. In the context of HESD in particular, this includes building capacities of educators and decision makers as well as producing knowledge which helps improve collective decision making. The latter is particularly relevant in discussing synergies between ESD and Sustainability Science.

Sustainability science aims to understand complex and dynamic interactions between natural and human systems for transforming and developing these sustainably (Clark and Dickson 2003; Jerneck *et al.* 2011; Kates *et al.* 2001; Komiyama and Takeuchi 2006). It is considered by many as an academic field defined by the problems it addresses, rather than by the disciplines it employs, similar to agricultural science or health science (Clark 2007). In other words, sustainability science is understood as a field characterised by what is called the 'use-inspired basic research' in Pasteur's Quadrant of the modern science and technology (Stokes 1997). Increasingly reaching out to encompass relevant work in the curiosity-driven theorising of Bohr's Quadrant and pragmatic problem solving of Edison's Quadrant, sustainability science intends to advance useful knowledge as well as informed action by creating a dynamic bridge between the two quadrants (Clark 2007).

Three stages of ESD and multi-, inter-, trans-disciplinarity

ESD can be considered in three stages which involve progressive levels of learning: first-order, second-order and third-order learning. They correspond to education *about*, education *for* and education *as* sustainability (Lucas 1979; Sterling 2009). The first form is an essential first step which aims at deepening awareness, knowledge and understanding of the concerns of sustainability. The second form is vital to individual and social change, as it involves questioning of the usual frame of reference to respond to the challenges of sustainability. The third form involves epistemic change and leads to cultivating a culture of sustainability. Corresponding to the distinction of the three stages for ESD, sustainability science is also considered to have three dimensions in terms of the degree of integration of knowledge aimed for: *multi*-disciplinarity, *inter*-disciplinarity, and *trans*-disciplinarity (see Table 1.2).

It is important to note that these three stages are neither mutually exclusive nor meant to indicate the relative usefulness of particular approaches and associated scholarship. If the first form transmits to learners what is already known about problems at stake, for example climate change, the second form encourages them to examine existing climate change mitigation and adaptation measures critically and to take concrete actions themselves. At the third stage, ESD and sustainability science aim at developing interventions and solutions to context-specific climate change challenges, by engaging what is already known in a process of explorative and reflexive deliberation. In the context of HESD, the third stage requires a carefully designed process where multiple actors can share knowledge and perspectives and develop an understanding of one another's interests and concerns, which in turn open opportunities for them to reach a shared diagnosis of a specific sustainability challenge as a foundation of deciding on particular interventions or solutions. Many programmes in HESD combine courses focusing

Table 1.2 Three stages of ESD and Sustainability Science

ESD	*Sustainability Science*
'education about sustainability' ➔ *content based sustainability literacy*	**'Multi-disciplinarity'** identifies and assembles relevant knowledge and expertise in traditional academic disciplines for addressing sustainability problems
'education for sustainability' ➔ *a critical questioning of assumptions; contribution to problem-solving*	**'Inter-disciplinarity'** connects and integrates disciplinary knowledge and expertise to advance basic understanding of the complex, dynamic interactions of human-environment systems.
'education as sustainability' ➔ *a shift of worldview*	**'Trans-disciplinarity'** promotes active collaboration with various stakeholders throughout society, organising processes of mutual learning among science and society.

on the first two forms and practice-oriented courses focusing on the third. All three forms of learning can take place in a single undergraduate or graduate course as well.

Barth and Michelsen (2013) have identified three types of ESD scholarship as particularly relevant to sustainability science: 1) scholarship that examines educational contribution to fostering competencies of individuals; 2) scholarship that addresses organisational change and social learning; and 3) scholarship on situated learning and 'communities of practice' in the context of inter- and trans-disciplinary collaboration. At the first stage of education *about* sustainability, the first type of ESD scholarship can advance discussions on sustainability literacy and improve teaching and learning to foster these competencies. Sustainability science in turn can inform the content of what is taught as a multidisciplinary field that consists of related research fields, including agriculture, fishery, forestry, water, energy, economics, sociology, and other relevant sciences (Kajikawa *et al.* 2007). Accordingly, the function of sustainability science is defined to identify and assemble relevant knowledge and expertise in traditional academic disciplines for addressing sustainability problems. To tackle the challenge of climate change, for example, learners first need to understand the mechanisms of greenhouse effect and heat circulation in complex interactions between the atmosphere and the ocean. This requires natural science knowledge. Engineering knowledge is vital in designing and developing technologies for utilising renewable energy sources efficiently and effectively. Also economics is critically important in examining the behaviour of relevant actors in response to economic incentives provided through carbon taxes and emission permits. Multidisciplinary knowledge covering natural sciences, engineering and social sciences is indispensable in learning about many issues related to sustainability.

At the second stage of education *for* sustainability, sustainability science can contribute to overcoming the fragmentation of knowledge through inter-disciplinary approaches. They allow us to 1) better address symptoms of unsustainable development, and 2) tackle the root causes of the fundamental 'unsustainability' of the current model of progress. Here sustainability science is expected to connect and integrate the knowledge and expertise accumulated in traditional academic disciplines, as sustainability problems cut across diverse academic disciplines, ranging from natural sciences to social sciences and humanities (Yarime *et al.* 2012). Interdisciplinarity helps advance basic understanding of the complex, dynamic interactions of human-environment systems, which constitute an essential aspect of sustainability. In the case of climate change, the behaviour of the relevant actors influences their emissions of carbon dioxide, which will have impacts on the climate. That, in turn, will affect how the actors behave with regard to reducing energy consumptions and consequently CO_2 emissions or making investments in developing new technological measures. Natural, social and technological phenomena are intermingled with each other in complex ways, which requires interdisciplinary knowledge for tackling sustainability issues. Although there are attempts to enhance the role and relevance of ESD-related scholarship in sustainability science (see, for example, Barth and Michelsen 2013), the contribution of educational sciences in sustainability science is yet to be fully recognised. In the context of HESD, educational sciences should inform and support the design and delivery of interdisciplinary as well as transdisciplinary education and research programmes to purposely drive reflexive learning and change.

At the third stage of education *as* sustainability, sustainability science can contribute to bringing about epistemic change by systematically involving knowledge users in the research process. For addressing complex, real-world sustainability problems, interdisciplinarity *per se* would not suffice. Active collaboration with various stakeholders throughout society, that is, transdisciplinarity, must form another critical component of sustainability science (Yarime *et al.* 2012). Whereas Barth and Michelsen (2013) do not highlight distinctions between interdisciplinary and transdisciplinary research, we note the particular significance of 'transdisciplinarity' as a stage where ESD and sustainability science are approached as reflexive learning and change processes for re-purposing education and research.

While interdisciplinarity fuses methods and concepts from different scientific disciplines, transdisciplinarity goes beyond sciences, organises processes of mutual learning between science and society, and innovates conventional patterns of knowledge exchange. Transdisciplinarity integrates experiential knowledge and values about real-world problems (provided by practitioners and stakeholders) with scientific knowledge about systems (provided by researchers). The issue of global climate change demands actions to be implemented throughout the world by a large number of people having considerably different backgrounds and interests. As they comprise a highly heterogeneous group, the contexts in which technologies are designed and utilised are diverse. Also the long time span of climate change implies that there is a significant degree of uncertainty in the process of climate evolution and technological improvement. The existence of diversity and uncertainty inevitably leads to a situation in which scientific knowledge produced by academia would not be sufficient in dealing with climate change. This requires effective integration of various types of knowledge involving science and practice as transdisciplinarity.

Challenges and opportunities

Like ESD, Sustainability Science has been proposed and discussed mainly in industrialised countries. In Japan, the Fukushima nuclear disaster in 2011 highlighted the need for timely decision making about urgent problems where both stakes and uncertainty are paramount, providing a renewed impetus for achieving 'science for society' in Japan (Mori 2014). The dramatic event of the Fukushima disaster is just one important example of an abysmal failure on the part of policy makers and more broadly knowledge users to benefit from science.

Recently, countries in the developing world have also started establishing research and educational programmes to integrate sustainability in policy making. Stakeholders involved in society's attempts to move towards sustainability are diverse in terms of their perceptions, beliefs, incentives and behaviour, which have been shaped by particular economic, social and cultural contexts. This will have significant implications for public policies, corporate strategies and institutional design for promoting cooperation and collaboration in making a transition towards a more sustainable society. Context-specific views on the field of sustainability science as well as practices of implementing it deserve careful consideration and proper respect, especially in developing and emerging economies. From the perspective of HESD, it would be important to discuss which dimensions of sustainability science would be relevant and how they could be incorporated into HESD for effective synergies.

To address global sustainability problems, often ill-defined and intermingled, we need to integrate knowledge from various academic disciplines in the natural sciences, social sciences and humanities. This is essential to better understand complex and dynamic interactions between natural and human systems and enablers and barriers for societal actions for sustainable transformation. Furthermore, with the necessary expertise and experience involving a significant degree of diversity and uncertainty, a major challenge in sustainability science is how to design and implement serious engagement and fruitful collaboration between academia and stakeholders, including industry, government and civil society. With often diverging understanding of problems by researchers from different disciplines, as well as by different stakeholders, it is crucial to create and manage stakeholder platforms that can encourage dialogue and lead to a shared understanding of the problem to be addressed. The creation and management of equitable learning partnerships between different disciplines, sectors and stakeholders would be the key for *co-creating* knowledge, *co-designing* targets, and *co-implementing* processes (for recent examples of university-led initiatives on collaboration with stakeholders, see, for example, Trencher *et al.* 2013, 2014a, 2014b). What is needed, although hard to realise, is precisely such platforms that can facilitate sharing knowledge and expertise through mutual understanding and trust and contribute to establishing socially robust strategies for sustainability.

Sustainability science is relevant not only in gathering data for understanding dynamic interactions between natural and human systems, or synthesising and analysing information for decision making, but also in enhancing the involvement of scientists in decision making and the use of scientific knowledge in social contexts. A novel kind of interaction is encouraged between sustainability scientists and those who shape learning processes to facilitate the use of scientific and other forms of knowledge.

Ways forward

There is an increased demand for higher education and research on sustainable development and a growing consensus on the need to increase higher education's contributions to developing more effective and equitable responses to a diverse array of sustainability challenges. Although important efforts have been made by a number of academic groups, networks, alliances and scientific institutions, bringing the different sciences together in integrated research on sustainable development remains a daunting task. Sustainability science can be understood as one of such efforts.

Much work remains to be done to build a shared understanding of what integration entails in practice and to adjust institutional practices to enable it. A new set of internationally agreed sustainable development goals (expected to be formulated as SDGs) and global programmes and platforms like Future Earth and IPBES have a potential to become a driving force in adjusting institutional practices, for better or worse. At best, they can serve to adjust institutional practices for realising meaningful and effective interdisciplinarity and transdisciplinarity; often, they invite opportunistic repackaging of existing programmes without necessary adjustments to institutional structures; at worst, they can privilege certain agendas, disciplines and stakeholders at the expense of others that are critical for achieving sustainable development.

To advance HESD and sustainability science, and to realise 'education as sustainability' and transdisciplinarity, more research is needed to understand what types of joint initiatives and networking contribute to identifying desirable goals and targets and developing complementary skills and capacities, what mechanisms and stakeholder relations have been developed to drive existing practices and initiatives, and what factors promote or obstruct their successful implementation. As institutional structures, reward systems, and evaluation criteria play a crucial role in providing incentives and legitimacy to new and cross-cutting efforts like ESD and sustainability science, the structure and processes of their institutionalisation in the academia also need to be addressed seriously.

Notes

1 When the Carnegie Foundation commissioned Abraham Flexner to write his report, many American medical schools were small trade schools unaffiliated with a college or university, with a degree often awarded after only two years of study. Flexner's recommendations led to requirements for collegiate study in basic sciences prior to medical school, and to a four-year medical degree at medical schools that were incorporated into universities.

2 To formulate a new blueprint for sustainable development, the UN Secretary-General's High-Level Panel on Global Sustainability produced a report titled *Resilient People, Resilient Planet*, which included a recommendation that 'the Secretary-General should consider naming a chief scientific adviser or establishing a scientific advisory board with diverse knowledge' (UN Secretary-General's High-Level Panel on Global Sustainability 2012: 75, Recommendation 51). Building on *Resilient People, Resilient Planet* and also on *21 Issues for the 21st Century*, UNEP's report prepared for Rio+20 which highlighted what it called 'broken bridges' between science and policy (UNEP 2012), Ban Ki-moon set up the UN Scientific Advisory Board, a board of 26 scientists.

3 *Future Earth* integrates four major international research networks on global environmental change: the International Geosphere-Biosphere Programme (IGBP); International Human Dimensions Programme on Global Environmental Change (IHDP); the DIVERSITAS International Programme on Biodiversity Science; and the World Climate Research Programme (WCRP).

References

Altinay, H. (ed.), 2011. *Global Civics.* Washington, DC: Brookings.

Barth, M. and Michelsen, G., 2013. 'Learning for Change: An Educational Contribution to Sustainability Science', *Sustainability Science*, 8(1), 103–19.

Beal, G.M., Dissanayake, W., and Konoshima, S., 1986. *Knowledge Generation, Exchange and Utilization.* Boulder, CO: Westview Press.

Carney, S., 2009. 'Negotiating Policy in an Age of Globalization: Exploring Educational 'Policyscapes' in Denmark, Nepal and China', *Comparative Education Review*, 53(1), 63–88.

Clapp, J. and Dauvergne, P., 2011. *Paths to a Green World: The Political Economy of the Global Environment* (Second Edition). Cambridge, MA: The MIT Press.

Clark, W.C., 2007. 'Sustainability Science: A Room of its Own', *Proceedings of the National Academy of Sciences*, 104(6), 1737–8.

Clark, W.C. and Dickson, N.M., 2003. 'Sustainability Science: The Emerging Research Program', *Proceedings of the National Academy of Sciences,* 100(14), 8059–61.

Crowley, J., 2012. *Making Knowledge Work: From Social Science Research to Socially Reflexive Sustainability.* Report of UNESCO and the International Social Science Council (ISSC). Paris: ISSC and UNESCO.

Future Earth, 2013. *Future Earth Initial Design: Report of the Transition Team.* Paris: International Council for Science (ICSU).

ICESDP, 2008. *International Commission for Education for Sustainable Development Practice Final Report.* New York: The Earth Institute of Columbia University.

Jerneck, A., Olsson, L., Ness, B., Anderberg, S., Baier, M., Clark, E., Hickler, T., Hornborg, A., Kronsell, A., Lövbrand, E., and Persson, J., 2011. 'Structuring Sustainability Science', *Sustainability Science*, 6(1), 69–82.

Kajikawa, Y., Ohno, J., Takeda, Y., Matsushima, K., and Komiyama, H., 2007. 'Creating an Academic Landscape of Sustainability Science: An Analysis of the Citation Network', *Sustainability Science*, 2(2), 221–31.

Kates, R.W., Clark, W.C., Corell, R., Hall, J.M., Jaeger, C.C., Lowe, I., McCarthy, J.J., Schellnhuber, H.J., Bolin, B., Dickson, N.M., Faucheux, S., Gallopin, G.C., Grubler, A., Huntley, B., Jager, J., Jodha, N.S., Kasperson, R.E., Mabogunje, A., Matson, P., Mooney, H., Moore, B., O'Riordan, T., and Svedin, U., 2001. 'Sustainability Science', *Science*, 292(5517), 641–2.

Komiyama, H. and Takeuchi, K., 2006. 'Sustainability Science: Building a New Discipline', *Sustainability Science*, 1(1), 1–6.

Lotz-Sisitka, H.B. (ed.), 2012. *(Re) Views on Social Learning Literature: A Monograph for Social Learning Researchers in Natural Resources Management and Environmental Education*. Grahamstown/Howick: Environmental Learning Research Centre, Rhodes University/EEASA/SADC REEP.

Lucas, A.M., 1979. *Environment and Environmental Education: Conceptual Issues and Curriculum Implications.* Melbourne: Australian International Press and Publications.

Marien, M., 2011. *Clapp and Dauvergne, Paths to a Green World* (book review). www.globalforesightbooks.org/Book-of-the-Month/jennifer-clapp-paths-to-a-green-world.html [accessed 11 February 2015].

Marleveld, M. and Dabgbégnon, C., 1999. 'Managing Natural Resources: A Social Learning Perspective', *Agriculture and Human Values*, 16(3), 267–80.

MEXT (Ministry of Education, Culture, Sports, Science and Technology, Office of the Director-General for International Affairs), 2011. *Proposal to UNESCO on 'Sustainability Science'.* www.mext.go.jp/english/unesco/1323150.htm [accessed 11 February 2015].

Mochizuki, Y. and Fadeeva, Z., 2010. 'Competences for Sustainable Development and Sustainability: Significance and Challenges for ESD', *International Journal of Sustainability in Higher Education*, 1(4), 391–403.

Mori, S., 2014. *Discussion Paper on the Relationship between the Science Community and Stakeholders.* Tokyo: National Institute of Science and Technology Policy (NISTEP), Japan. www.nistep.go.jp/archives/15799 [accessed 11 February 2015].

Nussbaum, M.C., 1997. *Cultivating Humanity: A Classical Defence of Reform in Liberal Education.* Cambridge, MA and London: Harvard University Press.

Osseiran, S. and Reardon, B., 1998. 'The United Nation's Role in Peace Education', in Alger, C.F. (ed.), *The Future of the United Nations System: Potential for the Twenty-First Century.* New York: United Nations University Press, 385–408.

Sterling, S., 2009. 'Sustainable Education', in Gray, D., Colucci-Gray, L. and Camino, E. (eds), *Science, Society and Sustainability: Education and Empowerment for an Uncertain World.* New York and London: Routledge, 105–18.

Stokes, D.E., 1997. *Pasteur's Quadrant: Basic Science and Technological Innovation.* Washington, DC: Brookings Institution.

Trencher, G., Yarime, M., and Kharrazi, A., 2013. 'Co-creating Sustainability: Cross-sector University Collaborations for Driving Sustainable Urban Transformations', *Journal of Cleaner Production*, 50, 40–55.

Trencher, G., Yarime, M., McCormick, K., Doll, C. and Kraines, S., 2014a. 'Beyond the Third Mission: Exploring the Emerging University Function of Co-creation for Sustainability', *Science and Public Policy*, 41(2), 151–79.

Trencher, G., Bai, X., Evans, J., McCormick, K.B., and Yarime, M., 2014b. 'University Partnerships for Co-designing and Co-producing Urban Sustainability', *Global Environmental Change*, 28, 153–65.

UN Secretary-General's High-Level Panel on Global Sustainability, 2012. *Resilient People, Resilient Planet: A Future Worth Choosing.* New York: United Nations.

UN System Task Team on the Post-2015 UN Development Agenda, 2013. *Global Governance and Governance of the Global Commons in the Global Partnership for Development beyond 2015.* Thematic Think Piece by OHCHR, OHRLLS, UNDESA, UNEP, UNFPA. New York: United Nations.

UNEP, 2012. *21 Issues for the 21st Century: Result of the UNEP Foresight Process on Emerging Environmental Issues.* Nairobi, Kenya: United Nations Environment Programme (UNEP).

UNESCO, 2014a. *37 C/4: 2014–2021 Medium-term Strategy* (as approved by the General Conference at its 37th session [General Conference resolution 37 C/Res.1] and validated by the Executive Board at its 194th session [194 EX/Decision 18]), Paris: UNESCO. http://unesdoc.unesco.org/images/0022/002278/227860e.pdf [accessed 11 February 2015].

UNESCO, 2014b. *Roadmap for Implementing the Global Action Programme on Education for Sustainable Development*. Paris: UNESCO.

UNRISD (United Nations Research Institute for Social Development), 2012. *From Green Economy to Green Society: Bringing the Social to Rio+20*. Geneva: UNRISD.

Wiek, A., Withycombe, L., and Redman, C.L., 2011. 'Key Competencies in Sustainability: A Reference Framework for Academic Program Development', *Sustainability Science*, 6(2), 203–18.

Wolbring, G. and Burke, B., 2013. 'Reflecting on Education for Sustainable Development Through Two Lenses: Ability Studies and Disability Studies'. *Sustainability*, 5(6), 2327–42.

Yarime, M. and Tanaka, Y., 2012. 'The Issues and Methodologies in Sustainability Assessment Tools for Higher Education Institutions: A Review of Recent Trends and Future Challenges', *Journal of Education for Sustainable Development*, 6(1), 63–77.

Yarime, M., Trencher, G., Mino, T., Scholz, R.W., Olsson, L., Ness, B., Frantzeskaki, N., and Rotmans, J., 2012. 'Establishing Sustainability Science in Higher Education Institutions: Towards an Integration of Academic Development, Institutionalization, and Collaborations with Stakeholders', *Sustainability Science*, 7(Supplement 1), 101–13.

2

LEARNING FOR WALKING THE CHANGE

Eco-social innovation through sustainability-oriented higher education

Arjen E.J. Wals, Valentina C. Tassone, Gary P. Hampson and Jonathan Reams

Introduction

As we seek to re-orient education to enable humanity to find some kind of dynamic balance with the planet that hosts us and all life in the universe as far as we know, it is good to look ahead and explore emerging forms of learning and innovation, but also to have a sense of history by looking back. First we will look back at two somewhat parallel 'evolutions' that share some common characteristics: the evolution from nature conservation education to sustainability education on the one hand, and the evolution within science and higher education from environmental science to sustainability science on the other. We realise that the interpretation of history is somewhat biased as we do so from our own, mostly Western, vantage points which blind us from seeing history from a different socio-cultural perspective that might be just as or perhaps even more informative. Nonetheless we hope that readers who come to this Handbook from a different perspective will still find merit in our attempt to make sense of the past and the way we use it to inform possible future orientations of higher education.

Let us begin by re-capping in a nutshell the movement from nature conservation education to sustainability education with environmental education (EE) as a linking pinch between them (Wals 2012). First of all we do not mean to suggest that nature conservation education and what might be considered its younger cousin, biodiversity education, and environmental education are now passé and no longer relevant; on the contrary they are still very much alive but in some cases have been drowned out by the sustainability education movement of the last decade or so. Nature conservation education can be seen as foundational for teaching and learning that seeks to develop a better understanding of the natural world, to develop a better relationship with and appreciation of the natural world, with the ultimate goal of protecting the carrying capacity of the Earth and, indeed, a more respectful and ethically justifiable and morally defensible relationship with the natural world in all its diversity. Nature conservation education was born out of a concern, among scientists, mainly biologists and an urban elite of concerned citizens with a deep appreciation for nature, that natural areas were rapidly disappearing due to urbanisation and industrialisation. Since its early beginnings, well over a century ago, the learning associated with nature conservation education can be characterised by experiential, affective/emotive, place-based, but also analytical especially when emphasis was placed on the cognitive understanding of the web of life and how nature works. Arguably some strands of nature conservation education were rather anthropocentric with a focus on the importance of nature for the well-being and future prospects of us humans, while others were more eco- and/or biocentric emphasising the intrinsic 'value' of nature and all species.

Roughly half a century later, in the 1950s, concerns about pollution of water, air and soil, and the accumulation of toxins in food chains, perhaps best articulated by Rachel Carson's *Silent Spring* (Carson 1962), led to the rise of the environmental movement with environmental education as one of its spin-offs (Stapp 1969). Unlike nature conservation education, early EE focused not so much on understanding, appreciating and connecting nature, but rather on educating citizens in becoming environmentally responsible in their behaviour. The environmental crises at the time seemed too urgent for establishing a time-consuming deep connection with the natural world as a foundational stepping stone for such behaviour. Furthermore, most people by now were living in cities far removed from nature which limited the possibilities for such connections. With environmental science as the new science that could somewhat authoritatively inform policy-makers what the most desirable behaviour looked like, there was little doubt about both the urgency and the desired behavioural outcome. It is no surprise that environmental education back then paid much attention to social and behavioural psychology as these fields worked hard on dissecting and modelling human behaviour and understanding the way we might influence or shape behaviour (Hungerford and Volk 1990). Not until the relationship between environmental awareness, attitudes, locus of control, values and behaviour was critiqued and questioned – there did not seem to be a direct causal relation between them as was initially thought or assumed – did environmental educators begin to look at their field from an education and human development perspective rather than from an instrumental environmental behaviour perspective (Kollmuss and Agyeman 2002). At the international policy-level this seemed to be acknowledged much earlier than within environmental education research as the landmark Tbilisi declaration from 1977 (UNESCO-UNEP 1978) reflects this shift quite well as it explicitly and sometimes more implicitly refers to critical thinking, capacity building and human development.

The IUCN's World Conservation Strategy and shortly thereafter the Brundtland report (WCED 1987), leading up to the UNCED or Earth Summit in Rio in 1992, enters notions of sustainable development which typically call for taking into account the socio-economic, environmental and ecological implications of all that we do bearing in mind future generations (granted with a bias towards future *human* generations) and people living not just near where we live but elsewhere as well. Agenda 21 and Local Agenda 21 (United Nations 1992) emphasise the role of education and communication in engaging people in finding ways to balance people-planet-profit/prosperity without compromising the lives of others here and elsewhere, now and in the future. There has been an assumption, at least in the beginning of the sustainable development era, that these different dimensions and interspatial and inter-temporal interests can somehow be balanced in good harmony and that there is some kind of optimum that allows everyone, everywhere to prosper and develop forever. More recently we are seeing discourses emerge that argue that such an assumption is inherently flawed at best and at worst represents a distraction from a more fundamental transition towards a new world order based on radically different principles and values than the one represented by hegemonic growth-oriented models.

It can be argued that early Education for Sustainable Development (ESD) worked from the same premise as early EE in that there was an assumption that there is some consensus about the desired behavioural outcomes. In other words, there was a general idea of what sustainable development requires and what it meant to live sustainably and that we need to educate, communicate and train people so that they can become sustainable citizens. Just like in the development of EE the second phase of ESD – sometimes referred to as 'Mode 2 ESD' (Scott and Gough 2003) – more or less abandoned this deterministic and instrumental position (Mode 1 ESD) to make room for a more emancipatory and human development perspective. The latter perspective addresses early criticism of ESD by emancipatory environmental educators who argued that the concept of sustainable development was flawed and ESD was too prescriptive and lacked grounding in local contexts (Jickling 1992; Jickling and Wals 2008). Mode 2 ESD on the other hand centres around the notion that sustainability above all requires reflexivity and the ability to continuously experiment, test, recalibrate and question one's actions, individually and collaboratively and that there will always uncertainty, confusion and controversy around what sustainability is. This recalibrating should be done against criteria for sustainability that are not frozen in time and place but established with the knowledge of today with the full understanding that this knowledge will change and that the context in which these actions are tested and recalibrated affects what knowledge is relevant.

Now let us turn to higher education. The evolution to date of sustainability and sustainable development – two related but not identical concepts (Hampson 2012) – in higher education has been described (Wals and Blewitt 2010) as a three-staged process consisting of: 1) the rise of environmentalism in the 1970s and 1980s which led to environmental engineering, environmental studies, environmental law, etc. as a part of university education and research; 2) the greening of the ivory tower with a focus on universities' own environmental impact and management in the 1990s and 2000s; and 3) the emergence of sustainability science representing holistic, systemic, integrative and 'post-normal' approaches and methodologies linking education, research and outreach. The latter perspective questions deeply ingrained methodological, organisational and educational routines which lead to the commodification of education and research for serving economic interests rather than people and the planet. Instead it promotes ontological and epistemological pluralism and transformative forms of interconnected research and education that improve our knowing, doing, being and our ability to make change. Sometimes the concept of a 'whole-institution approach to sustainability' is used to refer to such a perspective although this concept does not always include a rethinking of ontological and epistemological assumptions.

In a recent review of three edited volumes focusing on sustainability in higher education rooted in highly Western-contexts (USA, UK and Australia) Bill Scott makes a helpful distinction between loose and tight conceptual framings of sustainability within universities (Scott 2014). The former refers to an institution that takes sustainability seriously in what it does, 'without having in place values, dispositions and orientations, and an appropriate conceptually grounded vision'. Whereas the latter refers to an institution that 'embodies a vision, values and values-informed practices that have been shifted to fit a particular conceptualization of sustainability which gives meaning, not just to what that institution does, but also to what it is trying to become' (ibid.: 1). He argues:

> (i) that the essential distinction here is between that of doing sustainability, and a shift to being sustainable as a whole institution; (ii) that any developmental journey to a tight framing would need to be a deliberate one; (iii) that changes to curriculum, management, leadership and governance would need to be in place before this can start; and (iv) that an important step on the journey will involve institution-wide deliberations on the conceptual framing(s) to adopt.
>
> *(ibid.: 1)*

To achieve all four in some coordinated way will require unconventional ways of looking at management, leadership, knowledge creation and the interface between science and society.

Some of these 'unconventional ways' are captured by sustainability science (Lang *et al.* 2012) and so-called 'post-normal science' perspectives (Funtowicz and Ravetz 1993). Sustainability science, in particular, is born out of the realisation, within a small but critical mass within the science community, that global challenges – such as climate change, food and nutrition security for all, rising inequity and the continued loss of (bio)diversity – are urgent and require that we explore new ontologies (way of being in the world) and epistemologies (ways of knowing). These challenges are further compounded by the 'disconnect' between people and places by hyper-consumption-driven information and communication technologies. Ad-hoc, piecemeal solutions that are comfortably described and even the optimisation of the 'clever' systems that we have created during the last centuries, do not do the trick anymore, if they ever did. This realisation might lead to a wider recognition that addressing sustainability issues requires alternative modes of interaction, ones that allow for more systemic responses as well as the exploration of alternative values and ways of being in and relating to the world which acknowledge the inevitable uncertainty and continuous change (Peters and Wals 2013). Parallel to this there is the emergence of movements in the international policy arena that point to the need for 'responsive and responsible research' (Stilgoe *et al.* 2013). Although these developments appear to coincide and show a high family resemblance, they lack synergy, despite optimists' beliefs that a 'perfect storm is brewing' – one which will lead to a values and learning-based transition.

It is no surprise that in light of this there is a rise of: community engaged science (e.g. citizen science), new forms of learning (e.g. social learning, transformative learning), thinking (e.g. anticipatory thinking, systems thinking), competence (e.g. sustainability competence, innovation competence), new methodologies such as practical theory building (Peters and Wals 2013), new networks in higher education such as the living knowledge network (www.livingknowledge.org) and, finally, new forms of education and learning around 'real' locally grounded sustainability issues (GUNI 2011). The notion of sustainability competence in particular seems to have gained a lot of traction among sustainability education scholars during the last few years (see Wiek *et al.* in this Handbook). In line with the post-normal sustainability perspective we take in this chapter we do not consider 'competence' as an analytical term that cuts up human behaviour into smaller pieces that can somehow be measured or captured in a rubric. Rather we view sustainability competence as a relational, contextual and emergent property. As such sustainability competence refers to a way of knowing, doing, being and transforming in action that leads to a temporary outcome that is considered the most sustainable given what we know, value and strive for at that moment in time while working on sustainability challenges in a concrete setting.

The nature conservation education – environmental education – sustainability education evolution on the one hand and the environmental science – environmental engineering and management – sustainability science evolution on the other, have occurred in relative isolation from each other but there are clear connections. We suggest that both sustainability education and sustainability science can benefit from making those connections more visible and establishing linkages (see Mochizuki and Yarime in this Handbook). A key question is: How can higher education become the broker of this perfect storm and lead the way in values and learning-based transitions towards socio-ecological sustainability? We intentionally preface 'sustainability' with 'socio-ecological' to indicate that the social and ecological appears to be lost or marginalised within current sustainability discourse which seems to be hijacked by economic interests and values (Parr 2009). In the so-called triple bottom line of people-planet-profit which is increasingly becoming the new mantra in business and industry the 'p' for profit seems uncontested and in a way legitimised as an inevitable part of sustainability. Arguably the 'p' for profit has done much better that the 'p' for people and planet during the last century. There is a concern that with the emphasis on sustainability, the emergence of the green economy and a focus on green jobs, issues having to do with biodiversity loss, equity, values and ethics are overshadowed. In the next section we will introduce the idea of eco-social innovation as a bridging concept between sustainability education and sustainability science.

The emergence of social innovation

Higher education is increasingly seen as a catalyst for innovation and social change with the goal of creating sustainable societies (Sterling *et al.* 2013). A growing number of universities appear to be engaging in the task of reorienting teaching and learning in a way that will lead to new mental models, new capabilities and innovations that can contribute to sustainability (Wals 2012). At the same time, within academia and in society, we see the emergence of Social Innovation (SI) concepts and practices attempting to bring about changes in our society, in our way of thinking, being and operating. Let us have a closer look at SI.

Godin provides the following useful historical context for SI (Godin 2012). The term 'Social Innovation' was originally used in Europe (c. fifteenth century) in a pejorative way to signify religious heresy. By the nineteenth century, the pejorative sense was transferred to the context of socialism – mostly taken to mean a violent threat to the established order. However, the supporters of social change gradually began to acquire more influence, and so SI also began to be used positively by the supporters of radical social thinkers such as Charles Fourier (Molz and Hampson 2010). A positive meaning was also given by Auguste Comte, the founder of sociology. The term was then applied positively to the rise of social reform initiatives such as cooperatives. The twentieth century saw the development of theorising in relation to SI, particularly as a complement to technological innovation (Ward 1903; Ogburn 1922; Bernard 1923; Noss 1944; Drucker 1957; Fairweather 1967; Lapierre 1968; Gabor 1970; Pike 1973). However, it wasn't until the beginning of the twenty-first century that interest in SI grew suddenly and rapidly, such that it became a term variously used in a myriad of discourses – a 'super category' (Harris 2005). The contemporary literature identifies SI in relation to its critical global context including interrelated current ecological (often referred to as environmental) and societal challenges. Ecological (or environmental) challenges are, for example, climate change, resource depletion and biodiversity loss. Societal challenges are, for example, social inequalities, an ageing population, unemployment. Together, we argue that these can be aptly identified as pertaining to *eco-social innovation*. Such identification thwarts attempts at maintaining the inadequate modernistic conception of society which ignores or marginalises the ecological context within which global society is situated and the complex interrelation between ecological and social aspects. Additionally it aims to highlight the capability and potential of social innovation to include and tackle socio-ecological concerns.

Key features of eco-social innovation

Fuzziness (multiple perspectives, open-endedness and complexity)

Firstly eco-social innovation (ESI) can be typified as *fuzzy* for, at least, two reasons: 1) different people in different contexts approach, conceptualise and implement ESI in different manners and there are different ways to address socio-ecological issues; 2) ESI emerges without set boundaries and it evolves in an open-ended fashion. We do not know yet how ESI will evolve in the future and we cannot prescribe in advance what the best ESI is, but we can think that there can be endless forms of innovation capable of tackling our critical socio-ecological condition. This fuzziness also holds true for sustainability. In fact, the term sustainability is characterised too by a proliferation of definitions and applications (Connelly 2007; Johnston *et al.* 2007; White 2013). It is influenced within society by a variety of perspectives, value orientations and beliefs (van Egmond and de Vries 2011; de Vries and Petersen 2009). It is characterised by indeterminacy, the impossibility of knowing in advance what the best approach or the best course of action is, and thus it evolves in an open-ended fashion. Additionally, the social and ecological challenges that ESI attempts to address are highly complex. Many of those challenges are wicked issues (Jordan *et al.* 2014). They are explored from a multitude of perspectives, they involve interconnections among environmental, social, economic, cultural, ethical etc. factors, and there is no agreement on standards for successful outcomes. All this calls for new capacities to handle complexity and to deal with fuzziness.

Social change (newness and well-doing)

Secondly, in spite of the diversity of approaches and applications, the literature indicates that ESI is essentially about *social change* (to innovate – stemming from the latin *innovatus* and from *in* 'into' and *novus* 'new' – implies going into the new; it means 'to renew', 'to change'). Rueede and Lurtz, based on an extensive literature review, have identified two main interpretations of SI, namely a normative one – SI as an effort to do something good for society, and a sociological one – SI as an effort to change social practices and/or structures (Rueede and Lurtz 2012). By adopting an integrative approach we suggest to position ESI at their crossing point. Additionally, if one takes into account the contemporary significance of the critical state of the biosphere (Hampson 2010), then 'something good for society' would implicitly prioritise addressing our uniquely challenging ecological situation, such that an authentically-centred SI implicates the pertinence of the term 'Eco-Social Innovation' (ibid.). In our view, a process of innovation in the quest towards sustainability can benefit from people that hold values not purely based on the material side of the existence, but also on care for others and for our natural environment, and that develop new capacities to address socio-ecological concerns, individually and collectively, now and in the future. We infer, then, that an ESI is about social change, i.e. doing good for society by changing social practices and/or structures. Viewed as such ESI implies a process of transformation and, indeed, a profound transformation of the way people think and operate, in the use of assets and resources, in production and consumption patterns, in social structures, etc. We suggest that such social transformation, fuelled by current challenges, can be a vehicle towards a values-driven socio-ecological oriented sustainability. In the context of this transition towards sustainability we envision ESI could play a leading role.

Following our line of argumentation, facilitating ESI in higher education with the goal of creating socio-ecologically sustainable societies implies, at least, two things: dealing with fuzziness and fostering a process of social change for the good of people and planet.

Facilitating eco-social innovation through higher education

In order to foster ESI, deal with its inherent fuzziness and stimulate a process of socio-ecological change we propose a praxis-oriented learning process that supports learners to 'walk the change' towards a socio-ecological oriented sustainability. Central to our approach is the idea of transformation through praxis which constitutes a cyclical iterative journey of reflection and action which engages learners in understanding why things are the way they are (current state), what keeps them from changing (maladaptive resilience), how things should be (more desirable state), what needs to be done to bring about change, trying out new ways of doing things, learning from the experience and re-entering the cycle until a more desirable state has been reached. Such learning is: context dependent (time, space, culture, politics, hierarchies, etc.); future-oriented but taking into account the history of the present; holistic in that the issues are looked at from a bigger picture perspective and addressed in all known dimensions from multiple vantage points; inevitably open-ended and transformative as it leads to a change in the learners, the issue and in the context in which the learning takes place. There are at least two kinds of normativity in play: 1) its emphasis on multi-stakeholder interaction, participation, agency and praxis which might be described as a 'learning-based perspective', and 2) its focus on sustainability and eco-social innovation and the improvement of the well-being of people and planet. Both normative underpinnings require evolving criteria which can be used to assess whether the learning taking place is actually contributing to the realisation of the norms that have been privileged. Figure 2.1 represents an attempt to graphically represent this approach.

Given that ESI involves substantive shifts of understandings, capabilities and behaviours in people, we argue that this calls for a type of learning that not only addresses surface ideas and accumulation of knowledge, but also works with more deep-seated structures requiring an understanding of both *what* is learned and *how* it is learned (Millard 2012). This type of deep learning can be categorised as transformative learning which brings us to the work of Mezirow (Mezirow 1978; Mezirow and Taylor 2009). Mezirow urged the recognition of a crucial dimension of learning in adulthood that enables us to recognise and modify the structures of assumptions and beliefs that frame our tacit points of view and influence our understandings, our values and interpretation about the world, others and ourselves and that determine our line of action (Mezirow 1978). Transformative learning can support a shift in the lenses of meaning

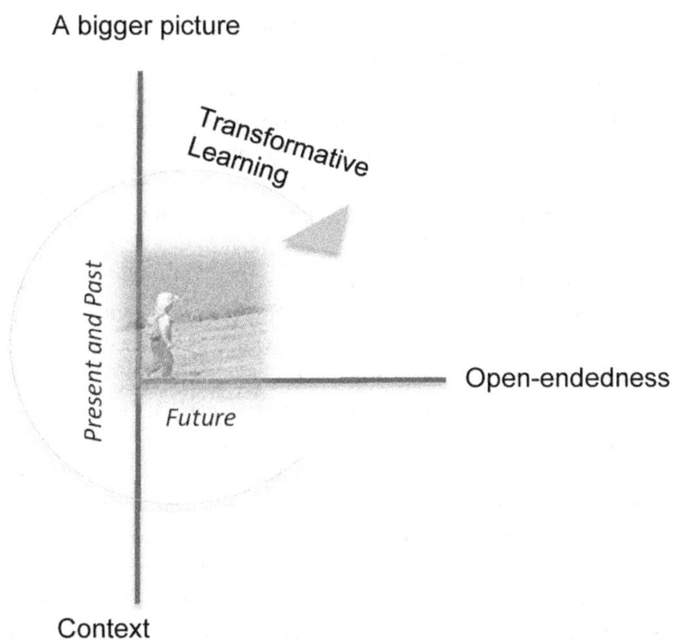

Figure 2.1 Learning for walking the change

making and lead to more inclusive, discriminating and integrative perspectives. It opens up new lenses of perception and it can allow the development of capacities for understanding and navigating complex challenges, like the ones of addressing socio-ecological challenges and advancing ESI with the goal of creating sustainable societies.

For those reasons, we suggest placing transformative learning at the heart of sustainability educational efforts. Below we elaborate briefly on those reasons. We introduce the notion of cognitive or epistemic structures in order to understand fuzziness and the process of transformation of meaning perspectives. Then, especially by drawing on the notion of adaptive leadership, we reflect on the process of social change and the implications for learning.

The notion of *cognitive or epistemic structures* was first developed by James Mark Baldwin (Baldwin 1906) and more famously extended by Jean Piaget (Piaget 1932, 1954, 1970). Loevinger researched stages of ego development, while Kohlberg examined stages of moral development (Loevinger 1976; Kohlberg 1984). Numerous other researchers have also contributed to the growth of understanding of how cognitive and epistemic understanding evolves (Reams 2014). Fischer developed a model of dynamic skill theory which also described patterns of development focused on the complexity of cognitive skills in a dynamic relation to the immediate environment (Fischer 1980; Fischer and Bidell 2006; Mascolo and Fischer 2010). In this model, Fischer describes tiers ranging from reflexes, through sensory motor skills, representations and abstractions to the tier of principles. Within each of these tiers are levels of single sets, mappings between single sets, systems of mappings, and systems of systems, which become chunked into a single set at the next tier. What is relevant about this, when it comes to facilitating ESI through sustainability education, is that we can use this lens of cognitive complexity to understand and navigate fuzziness, as well as to be more specific about the transformation we are after.

Fischer uses the concept of developmental change which refers to 'structural transformation in patterns of thinking, feeling, and action within particular domains and context' (Mascolo and Fischer 2010: 168). The nature of the transformational processes themselves can be seen as a set of rules. While the levels of development themselves describe the macro developmental process, transformation rules can provide micro, or within level predictions. Those transformation rules (including inter-coordination, compounding, focusing, substitution and differentiation) 'specify how a skill is transformed into a new, more advanced skill' (Fischer 1980: 497). Through those micro development transformations, skills of gradually increasing complexity can be constructed. In turn, developing those skills can transform the capability of the individual to learn, to interpret things and to face complex challenges. All of these processes go on in the context and immediate environment within which one is situated. Those insights can be useful for educators aspiring to facilitate ESI in the quest for sustainability. By supporting a process of cognitive development and transformation in learners, educators are providing tools that can enable learners to expand and develop their capabilities to make sense of complex and messy issues, like socio-ecological ones, and to navigate them.

Another important aspect to be addressed in this discussion is the one of *social change*. We find Heifetz's view of *adaptive leadership* to be a useful approach to explore the challenge of moving individuals and groups of people through processes aimed at social change, i.e. at doing good for society and contribute to socio-ecological oriented sustainability by changing social practices and/or structures (Heifetz 1994; Heifetz *et al.* 2009). An important distinction we like to make is the one between technical problems and adaptive challenges. Technical problems may be very complex and critically important for communities, organisations and society but they have clearly defined boundaries and known solutions that can be implemented with current know-how. Their resolution comes through the application of authoritative expertise and draws on current contextual structures, procedures and ways of doing things. Adaptive challenges, on the other hand, are more like ill-structured problems (Brown *et al.* 2010) in that they are not able to be defined and understood in terms of existing knowledge. They do not have clear boundaries and there are not ready-made solutions to address them. Rather than relying on current know-how, adaptive challenges require a process of experimentation, sensitivity to the context and an attitude of curiosity and discovery. Additionally, they involve issues that lie 'below the neck' like beliefs, assumptions and loyalties. Knowing this distinction, we suggest approaching social change as an *adaptive change*, rather than as a technical endeavour. The capacity to do good for society and contribute to socio-ecological oriented sustainability by changing social practices and/or structures, requires a profound transformation of individuals and of the system. It requires a move from a dominant materialistic mentality to a socio-ecological inclusive one. This is not a technical endeavour with ready-made solutions. It is an adaptive challenge that requires changes in people's hearts and minds.

Additionally, social change is related to people's sense of *agency*. Any fundamental change in society requires the motivation and the abilities of people to act in order to change lifestyles and the basic structures of the system and to further empower others to act. Underlying all this is the assumption that participation can foster innovation and transformation of the societal and political system.

Heifetz notes that, in relation to adaptive challenges, most people look to leaders to take responsibility for fixing the problem (Heifetz 1994). In this way, they avoid any personal responsibility for action, and if the solutions are not to their liking, they can then scapegoat the leader as being the source of this failure rather than having any broader accountability for their own actions or lack of actions. On the other hand adaptive challenges require adaptive leadership. This is about going beyond the use of expertise and authority to enable people to do the learning, or 'work' of examining assumptions, beliefs, habits and loyalties. This leads to another aspect of adaptive leadership we find relevant; that leadership functions by utilising the existing tensions, diversity and complexity of socio-ecological sustainability issues to create a holding environment where this kind of work can be done. A holding environment is a kind of container, a space where sufficient challenge and support (Kegan 1994) is present to enable learning and growth. This holding environment allows people to deal with pressing global challenges, to question own values, habits and beliefs that run us as reflexes, to learn from each other by mirroring one's perspective with that of others, and go beyond those reflexes by experimenting new ways of doing and being.

Those insights can be useful for educators in their efforts to foster social change and advance ESI and socio-ecological sustainability. Educators can approach social change as an adaptive change, they can foster agency and provide space for experimentation. This would mean that next to transferring knowledge educators could adopt an emancipatory approach to education (Wals and Jickling 2002) that can support a transformative learning process. This includes encouraging learners to go through a process of questioning and revision of their perspectives, value orientations and deeply held assumptions around issues, supporting them to critically and creatively reflect on current global socio-ecological challenges, and empowering and equipping them to experiment and act on addressing those challenges at the interface between the classroom and society (Tassone and Wals 2014).

Walking the talk

In an attempt to walk the talk ourselves in this chapter we will provide two brief examples that we are personally familiar with as they come from our own higher education institution,

Wageningen University.[1] The examples consist of: 1) a single course called *Empowerment for Sustainability* (six study points) that can be freely elected by Masters students, and 2) the Science Shop which represents a hybrid learning and research arrangement between the university and societal actors who could benefit from research but lack the resources to commission paid research.

Empowerment for sustainability

Empowerment for Sustainability engages students intensively for a total of 168 hours spread over four weeks (six study points or ECTS).[2] It offers a holistic approach to sustainability through which the student gains knowledge and reflects, in an integrative fashion, on a variety of sustainability-related worldviews, discourses, facts and applications which revolve around socio-ecological concerns. Students are asked to create and implement a real-life personal sustainability action project of their own choice. Through this action project, students are meant to contribute to sustainability in a manner that fits their own vision, capabilities and inspiration, by addressing a particular sustainability concern or by enhancing a state of play within their own sphere of influence (e.g. their own community, university, family, lifestyle, etc.).

Examples of action projects implemented by students are: creation and execution of plans to stimulate recycling and the reduction of plastic waste in universities, supermarkets, shops and students houses; execution of social entrepreneurial innovation plans; workshop design and delivery to foster ecological awareness in schools and boy-scout groups; and the organisation of meetings to foster social cohesion in neighbourhoods and among various cultural and religious groups. The learning process is supported by a process of reflection on the impacts of the actions undertaken, but also on the underlying personal beliefs, values, knowledge, context-awareness and capabilities when it comes to being an agent of change for sustainability.

One main assumption, within the context of this course, is that a praxis-oriented approach to education – which involves an iterative journey of reflection and action – leads to process of transformation and empowerment of the students within the context of sustainability. This assumption has been researched recently in a thesis (van Lingen 2014).

Results of van Lingen's research indicate that engaging students in real life actions appears to be crucial when it comes to empowering and equipping students for sustainability. The educational activity that students appreciated the most, when it comes to their empowerment, is the development and execution of a personal sustainability action project. According to the students, it is especially through the action project that they were able to contextualise, personalise and operationalise their understanding about sustainability and to get to know themselves as agents of change within their own sphere of influence. The research also suggests that engaging into an action project increases students' perception of own self-efficacy (the belief that one can reach goals and persevere in the face of challenges) but also that engaging into an action project increases students' conviction that they have the power to impact their own surroundings through their actions.

The results also appear to indicate that at the end of the course, on average, students have shifted and/or enlarged the way they frame the concept of sustainability and moved towards a more integrative understanding of sustainability. On this matter, students indicate they especially appreciated to be exposed to a variety of worldviews, concepts and applications that characterise the quest for sustainability. At the end of the course students perceive an increased capability to position themselves within the sustainability debate, and that connecting to own values, qualities and things they particularly care about in their surroundings positively influenced their learning process.

The three most important elements supporting their learning process in the classroom are (in order of importance): 1) engaging in an open dialogue with peers and lecturers and learning from each other; 2) being exposed to different lecturers having different backgrounds and expertise, who provided them with different views and approaches to sustainability; 3) having a safe and trustworthy climate in the classroom, supporting an open process of inquiry and sharing (which links to the first element).

The science shop[3]

Science shops are not 'shops' in the traditional sense of the word. They are small entities that carry out scientific research in a wide range of (inter)disciplines – usually free of charge – on behalf of citizens and local civil society. The fact that science shops respond to civil society's needs for expertise and knowledge is a key element that distinguish them from conventional knowledge transfer mechanisms. Science shops are often linked to universities, where students conduct the research as part of their curriculum.

Science shops define themselves as 'a unit that provides independent, participatory research support in response to concerns experienced by civil society' (www.livingknowledge.org). Science shops use the term 'science' in its broadest sense, incorporating social and human sciences, as well as natural, physical, engineering and technological sciences. The word 'provide' in the definition means that science shops make their services available on an affordable basis, free of financial barriers. Furthermore, science shops seek to create equitable and supportive partnerships with civil society organisations, hence the word 'participatory'. The provision of 'research support' can include educational projects, but also stresses that there is a difference with regular social/welfare based support to society. The phrase 'in response to', is meant to indicate that the research is not driven by a science or technology push but rather by societal 'concerns'. This also means that science shops are not there to answer curiosity-driven questions.

For the most part, these units belong to universities, though some are organised as separate NGOs or not-for-profit companies. Science shops combine research (and teaching where applicable) with service to society. Civil society organisations can simply approach a science shop with a problem in which they feel some research would be helpful for them to solve their problem. The science shop staff will then transfer these requests into research projects and find students and/or staff to work on these projects, in close contact with the 'client'. The results are handed over to the client and the science shop staff will support the use of these scientific results by the client and will help to formulate follow-up proposals, both those relevant to the client and those relevant to further research. This process means that new knowledge is generated, or at least existing knowledge is combined and adapted to context. Box 2.1 lists some of the main goals of a typical science shop.

A variety of other tasks are sometimes performed by science shops, such as regular university teaching and research, contract research, education and training for civil society, etc.

In a critical review of three exemplary science shop projects supported by the Wageningen University, Beunen *et al.* conclude that projects of this kind can challenge and even change stuck power structures that maintain unhelpful binaries (e.g. truth and un-truth) (Beunen *et al.* 2012). The projects reviewed also helped question and debate scientific knowledge produced which led to increased political involvement of citizens and the inclusion of informal local knowledge. They further conclude that such projects can inspire innovations in decision-making, in knowledge and in self-efficacy. As such they become a laboratory for experimenting with democratic traditions that strive for the inclusion of marginalised voices and perspectives

Box 2.1 Mission statement of science shops

Science shops seek to:

- provide civil society with knowledge and skills through research and education;
- provide their services on an affordable basis;
- promote and support public access to, and public influence on, science and technology;
- create equitable and supportive partnerships with civil society organizations;
- enhance understanding among policymakers and education and research institutions of the research and education needs of civil society;
- strengthen the transferable skills and knowledge of students, community representatives and researchers.

Source: www.livingknowledge.org

and create space for citizens' own initiatives. But there are cautionary notes as well as the analysis shows that there is a tension between, what they call, 'performative' and reflexive science, where the former requires a kind of partisanship with those seeking change in a particular direction, while the latter requires more distance between the academic researcher and those seeking change.

The two examples we described briefly all have in common that they are praxis-oriented, work on a real issue that is meaningful to all involved, that there is attention for the quality of the process of interaction between multiple-stakeholders and that it is not known ahead of time what the result will be (open-ended). If we look back at Figure 2.1 we can say the science shop example does not show the transformative aspect very well, neither does it become clear how engaging in the described activities leads participants to see, what we called, 'the big picture'. In part this is a result of inadequate or a lack of monitoring and evaluation – we have not integrated more reflexive forms of monitoring and evaluation that could capture transformations taking place at the various levels – and in part this is the result of the focus on local and/or more personal issues which can be a barrier for seeing the big picture. The latter requires the ability to see local and personal issues as manifestations of wider global issues and to mirror one's own situation with those of others to see how they are related.

Conclusion

Higher education is at the crossroads having to choose between the path of commodification of knowledge creation and learning focusing on optimisation and efficiency with the well-being of the economy as a key driver or the path of socio-ecological transitions requiring new forms of research and learning as well as alternative capabilities and values that contribute to the well-being of planet and people. The latter path currently represents the road less travelled and is disruptive in that it leads to a questioning of prevailing routines and values that are increasingly seen as manifestations and causes of unsustainability. The convergence of sustainability education and sustainability science represents an opportunity for higher education to take the lead in praxis-oriented transformative experiments where research, education, learning and capacity-building blend. These experiments must take place at the interface between science and society in what some refer to as hybrid coalitions of multiple stakeholders representing the world of science, work, governance, civic society and education. The social innovation perspective – which indeed can be critiqued as yet another attempt by growth driven interests serving the economy first and foremost to coopt sustainability-oriented transition movements – can, when coupled to socio-ecological and participatory perspectives, become a bridging concept that is generative for the renewal of higher education.

Obviously universities will need to be bold and create space for praxis-oriented transformative learning in which students and staff become co-learners seeking to resolve a sustainability issue that they have jointly identified with those affected by the issue at stake. Not only does this renewal imply a different outlook on knowledge and knowledge creation with notions of knowledge-in-action of living knowledge, the recognition of multiple 'knowledges' alongside of scientific knowledge and of different ways of knowing associated with different ways of being, it also implies new forms of teaching, learning and doing research as well as new ways of assessing their value and impact.

Around the world we are seeing some niches in higher education in which these spaces are opening up and much 'boundary work' is being done which could inform the renewal of higher education in the (un)sustainability era. It is crucial to learn from these experiences and to understand what triggers their emergence, how they develop, what keeps them from developing further, what conditions are conducive or limiting, what capabilities are needed both to support new forms of teaching, learning and research, and how to assess their merits, but also to be able to contribute to reflexively and critically 'walking the talk'. This Handbook highlights and explores some of these niches, conditions, levers, capabilities and processes which is a good start and represents some kind of progress, especially considering that a handbook like this would be unimaginable at, say, the turn of the millennium. We are still in the pioneering stage which – indeed more good news – according to ecologists is the stage in which species learn the most.

Notes

1 Note 'our own' refers to the first two authors of this chapter: Arjen Wals and Valentina Tassone.
2 ECTS represents a European standard for expressing the course load for students.
3 This text comes from www.livingknowledge.org which represents a network of European science shops of which the Wageningen University Science Shop is one.

References

Baldwin, M., 1906. *Social and Ethical Interpretations in Mental Development*. New York: Macmillan.

Bernard, L., 1923. 'Invention and Social Progress', *American Journal of Sociology*, 29(1), 1–33.

Beunen, R., Duineveld, M., During, R., Straver, G.H.M.B. and Aalvanger, A., 2012. 'Reflexivity in Performative Science Shop Projects', *Gateways: International Journal of Community Research and Engagement,* 5(1), 135–51.

Brown, V.A., Harris, J.A. and Russell, J.Y., 2010. *Tackling Wicked Problems through the Transdisciplinary Imagination*. London: Earthscan.

Carson, R., 1962. *Silent Spring*. New York: Fawcett Crest.

Connelly, S., 2007. 'Mapping Sustainable Development as a Contested Concept', *Local Environment*, 12(3), 259–78.

de Vries, B.J.M. and Petersen, A.C., 2009. 'Conceptualizing Sustainable Development: An Assessment Methodology Connecting Values, Knowledge, Worldviews and Scenarios', *Ecological Economics*, 68(4), 1006–19.

Drucker, P.F., 1957. *Landmarks of Tomorrow*. New York: Harper and Brothers.

Fairweather, G.W., 1967. *Methods for Experimental Social Innovation*. New York: John Wiley.

Fischer, K,. 1980. 'A Theory of Cognitive Development: The Control and Construction of Hierarchies of

Skills', *Psychological Review*, 87(6), 477–531.

Fischer, K. and Bidell, T., 2006. 'Dynamic Development of Action, Thought, and Emotion', in Damon, W. and Lerner, R. (eds), *Handbook of Child Psychology: Theoretical Models of Human Development*. New York: Wiley, 313–99.

Funtowicz, S.O. and Ravetz, J.R., 1993. 'Science for the Post-normal Age', *Futures*, 25(7), 739–55.

Gabor, D., (1970). *Innovations: Scientific, Technological, and Social*. Oxford: Oxford University Press.

Godin, B., 2012. *Social Innovation: Utopias of Innovation from c.1830 to the Present*. Project on the Intellectual History of Innovation (11). www.csiic.ca/ [accessed 11 February 2015].

GUNI (eds), 2011. *Higher Education's Commitment to Sustainability: from Understanding to Action Global University Network for Innovation* (GUNI). Series on the Social Commitment of Universities, Higher Education in the World Part 4. Basingstoke, UK: Palgrave/Macmillan.

Hampson, G.P., 2010. 'Facilitating Eco-logical Futures through Postformal Poetic Ecosophy', *Futures*, 42(10), 1064–72.

Hampson, G.P., 2012. 'Eco-logical Education for the Long Emergency', *Futures*, 44(1), 71–80.

Harris, R., 2005. *The Semantics of Science*. London: Continuum.

Heifetz, R.A., 1994. *Leadership Without Easy Answers*. Cambridge, MA: Belknap Press of Harvard University Press.

Heifetz, R., Linsky, M. and Grashow, A., 2009. *The Practice of Adaptive Leadership. Tools and Tactics for Changing your Organization and the World*. Cambridge, MA: Harvard Business School Press.

Hungerford, H. and Volk, T., 1990. 'Changing Learner Behavior through Environmental Education', *Journal of Environmental Education*, 21(3), 8–21.

Jickling, Bob, 1992. 'Why I don't want my Children to be Educated for Sustainable Development', *Journal of Environmental Education*, 23(4), 5–8.

Jickling, B. and Wals, A.E.J., 2008. 'Globalization and Environmental Education: Looking beyond Sustainable Development', *Journal of Curriculum Studies*, 40(1), 1–21.

Johnston, P., Everard, M., Santillo, D. and Robèrt K.H., 2007. 'Reclaiming the Definition of Sustainability', *Environmental Science and Pollution Research*, 1(60), 60–6.

Jordan, M.E., Kleinsasser, R.C. and Roe, M.F., 2014. 'Wicked Problems: Inescapable Wickedity', *Journal of Education for Teaching: International Research and Pedagogy*, 40(3), 415–30.

Kegan, R., 1994. *In over our Heads: The Mental Demands of Modern Life*. Cambridge, MA: Harvard University Press.

Kohlberg, L., 1984. *The Psychology of Moral Development: The Nature and Validity of Moral Stages*. San Francisco, CA: Harper & Row.

Kollmuss, A. and Agyeman, J., 2002. 'Mind the Gap: Why do People Act Environmentally and What are the Barriers to Pro-environmental Behavior?', *Environmental Education Research*, 8(3), 239–60.

Lang, D.J., Wiek, A., Bergmann, M., Stauffacher, M., Martens, P., Moll, P., Swilling, M. and Thomas, C., 2012. 'Transdisciplinary Research in Sustainability Science: Practice, Principles, and Challenges', *Sustainability Science*, 7(1), 25–43.

Lapierre, J.W., 1968. *Essai sur le fondement du pouvoir politique*. Aix-en-Provence: Ophrys.

Loevinger, J., 1976. *Ego Development: Concepts and Theories*. San Francisco, CA: Jossey-Bass.

Mascolo, M.F. and Fischer, K.W., 2010. 'The Dynamic Development of Thinking, Feeling, and Acting over the Life Span', in Overton, W.F. (ed.), *Biology, Cognition, and Methods across the Lifespan*. Hoboken, NJ: Wiley, 1, 149–94.

Mezirow, J., 1978. 'Perspective Transformation'. *Adult Education Quarterly Journal*, 28(2), 100–10.

Mezirow, J., Taylor E. (and Associates) (eds), 2009. *Transformative Learning in Practice: Insights from Community, Workplace and Higher Education*. San Francisco, CA: Jossey-Bass.

Millard, J., 2012. *Social Innovation in the Age of the Sharing Economy: Local Challenges that Meet the Network Effect*. TEPSIE (in association with MESHLABS), European Commission, 7th Framework Programme, Brussels: European Commission, DG Research.

Molz, M. and Hampson, G.P., 2010. 'Elements of the Under-acknowledged History of Integral Education', in Esbjorn-Hargens, S., Reams, J. and Gunnlaugson, O., (eds). *Integral Education: New Directions for Higher Learning*. Albany, NY: SUNY, 35–46.

Noss, T.K., 1944. *Resistance to Social Innovation in the Literature Regarding Innovations Which Have Proved Successful*. Chicago, IL: University of Chicago.

Ogburn, W.F., 1922. *Social Change with Respect to Culture and Original Nature*. New York: B.W. Huebsch.

Parr, A,. 2009. *Hijacking Sustainability*. Cambridge, MA: The MIT Press.

Peters, S. and Wals, A.E.J., 2013. 'Learning and Knowing in Pursuit of Sustainability: Concepts and Tools for Trans-Disciplinary Environmental Research', in Krasny, M., and Dillon, J. (eds), *Trading Zones in Environmental Education: Creating Transdisciplinary Dialogue.* New York: Peter Lang, 79–104.

Piaget, J., 1932. *Moral Judgment of the Child.* New York: Free Press.

Piaget, J., 1954. *The Construction of Reality in the Child.* New York: Basic Books.

Piaget, J., 1970. *Structuralism* (C. Maschler, trans.). New York: Harper&Row.

Pike, F.B., 1973. *Spanish America, 1900–1970: Tradition and Social Innovation.* New York: Norton.

Reams, J., 2014. 'A Brief Overview of Developmental Theory, or what I Learned in the FOLA Course', *Integral Review,* 10(1), 122–52.

Rueede, D. and Lurtz, K., 2012. *Mapping the Various Meanings of Social Innovation: Towards a Differentiated Understanding of an Emerging Concept.* EBS Business School Research Paper No. 12-03. Available from SSRN: http://ssrn.com/abstract=2091039 or http://dx.doi.org/10.2139/ssrn.2091039 [accessed 12 February 2015].

Scott, W.B., 2014. 'Exploring a Transformative Orientation to Sustainability in Universities: A Question of Loose and Tight Framings', *Environmental Education Research,* DOI: 10.1080/13504622.2014.954238.

Scott, W. and Gough, S. (eds), 2003. *Key Issues in Sustainable Development and Learning: A Critical Review.* London: Routledge Falmer.

Stapp, W.B., 1969. 'The Concept of Environmental Education', *Journal of Environmental Education,* 1(1), 30–2.

Sterling, S., Maxey, L., and Luna, H. (eds), 2013. *The Sustainable University: Progress and Prospects.* Abingdon: Routledge, Earthscan.

Stilgoe, J., Owen, R. and Macnaghten, P., 2013. 'Developing a Framework for Responsible Innovation', *Research Policy,* 42(9), 1568–80.

Tassone, V.C. and Wals, A.E.J., 2014. 'EYE for Sustainability: A Learning Tool for Change Agents', in Corcoran, P.B., Hollingshead, B.P., Lotz-Sisitka, H., Wals, A.E.J. and Weakland, J.P. (eds). *Intergenerational Learning and Transformative Leadership for Sustainable Futures.* United Nation Decade of Education for Sustainable Development, Wageningen: Wageningen Academic Publishers.

UNESCO-UNEP, 1978. *Intergovernmental Conference on Environmental Education.* 78 pp. Tbilisi (USSR). 14–26 October 1977, Final Report. Paris: UNESCO.

United Nations, 1992. *Agenda 21: The United Nations Programme of Action from Rio.* 38. New York: United Nations Publications.

van Egmond, N.D. and de Vries, H.J.M., 2011. 'Sustainability: The Search for the Integral Worldview', *Futures,* 43(8), 853–67.

van Lingen, T., 2014. 'Empowerment for Sustainability through Higher Education: Exploring the Effects of the EYE for Sustainability Learning Tool applied in the Classroom at Wageningen University'. BSc thesis, Wageningen University, Education and Competences Studies chair group.

Wals, A.E.J., 2012. 'Learning our Way out of Un-sustainability: The Role of Environmental Education', in Clayton, S. (ed.), *Oxford Handbook on Environmental and Conservation Psychology,* London: Oxford University Press, 628–44.

Wals, A.E.J. and Blewitt, J., 2010. 'Third Wave Sustainability in Higher Education: Some (Inter)national Trends and Developments', in Jones, P., Selby, D. and Sterling, S. (eds). *Green Infusions: Embedding Sustainability across the Higher Education Curriculum.* London: Earthscan, 55–74.

Wals, A.J. and Jickling, B., 2002. 'Sustainability in Higher Education: From Doublethink and Newspeak to Critical Thinking and Meaningful Learning', *International Journal of Sustainability in Higher Education,* 3(3), 221–32.

Ward, L.F., 1903. *Pure Sociology: A Treatise on the Origin and Spontaneous Development of Society.* New York: Macmillan.

WCED, 1987. *Our Common Future – The Brundtland Report.* Oxford: Oxford University Press.

White, M.A., 2013. 'Sustainability: I know it when I see it'. *Ecological Economics,* 86(February), 213–17.

3

POLICY, POLITICS AND POLITY IN HIGHER EDUCATION FOR SUSTAINABLE DEVELOPMENT

Gerd Michelsen

Introduction

Higher education for sustainable development has moved up the international political agenda, at the latest since the Johannesburg World Summit on Sustainable Development (WSSD) in 2002. This agenda involves three elements: content and goals (policy), the activities of different actors (politics) engaged in higher education for sustainable development, as well as its institutional and organizational infrastructure (polity). Since the Johannesburg summit meeting the United Nations Educational, Scientific and Cultural Organization (UNESCO) has taken up the challenge of promoting the integration of education for sustainable development in the different educational sectors, from elementary schooling to higher education and informal education, in every region in the world. A key political activity was the United Nation's World Decade on Education for Sustainable Development (2005-2014), which will be continued in 2015 as a Global Action Programme (GAP) in order to maintain support for the activities, together with their actors, that started during the Decade (Michelsen 2011, Leal Filho 2011, Barth 2015). Higher education for sustainable development played an important role in the World Decade and it should be continued in the Global Action Plan.

Policy, politics and polity

In order to better understand the path higher education for sustainable development has taken over the last years and decades, I will examine more closely three political dimensions – namely, *policy, politics* and *polity* – as they apply to this area (Fischer and Miller 2006):

- *Policy* describes the content of politics – its goals, activities and objects. The particular shape of politics and its realisation depend on societal interests that can vary greatly depending on individual substantive and ideological agendas and may be contradictory or potentially conflictual.
- *Politics* is concerned with this procedural dimension of mediating these interests through conflict and consensus. However, the continuous process of policy-making and the mediation of societal interests cannot be understood solely by examining the contents of policy and its actors.

- *Polity* as the third political dimension requires an analysis of institutions that are based on the constitution and legal order as well as on tradition.

All three dimensions will be the basis of the further analysis in this chapter.

The analysis of the *policy* dimension involves examining declarations, programmes and other documents (see Table 3.1) containing policy statements on higher education in the context of the environment and sustainability, as well as important conferences that have played a role in setting the strategic agenda. Topics include concepts of education for sustainable development (in particular higher education), inter- and transdisciplinarity in teaching as well as the whole-institution approach for transforming the university towards sustainability.

In the *politics* dimension the focus is on political processes in connection with the interests that higher education for sustainable development is advancing and their respective achievement. In order to characterise these processes, it is important to take account of not only key declarations and policy statements, but also the networks that have emerged over the last years and decades. Here the main topics are: activities of the network, orientation (environment, sustainability or both), and range (global, regional, national or local).

If we look at the *polity* dimension of higher education for sustainable development, then we see that it is about not only norms and institutions but also about the organisation and regulations that support the process and goal-setting as well as content development. The World Decade can be seen as an example for the institutional framework provided by the United Nations and UNESCO, which in turn is then implemented on the national level with the necessary organisation and procedural regulations.

The *development phases* in higher education for sustainable development are identified by compiling a list of declarations, charters and programmes together with their year of publication (Table 3.1), networks together with their foundation year (Tables 3.2 and 3.3) as well as depicting in Figure 3.1 the development of the total quantity of declarations and networks over time.

The policy dimension of higher education for sustainable development

The starting point of an analysis of the role of education in sustainable development is provided by the first UN Conference on Human Environment (UNCHE) in Stockholm in 1972. The declaration adopted by the members of the conference refers to the role that education has to play and calls on UNESCO to address this challenge and hold a conference on environmental education. The resulting Tbilisi Conference (1977) endorsed the Tbilisi Declaration, which had as a consequence that UNESCO would put on its educational agenda environmental issues in all formal as well as informal and non-formal educational contexts. In this declaration the goals of environmental education are formulated as creating an awareness and knowledge of the importance of the environment, promoting attitudes, values and responsibility for the environment, developing practical skills to identify and solve environmental problems, and promoting the participation of groups and individuals in processes to overcome environmental problems. From a programmatic perspective, education is located in the context of environmental challenges, with a focus on the analysis and identification of ways to solve environmental problems.

The UN Conference on Environment and Development in Rio de Janeiro in 1992 extended the scope of the environment to the concept of sustainability. Almost 180 countries adopted Agenda 21, which in Chapter 36 deals in detail with education, including higher education. This chapter emphasises the importance of educational processes in the context of

Table 3.1 Declarations, charters und programmes in higher education (1972–2014)

Declaration/ Charter/ Programme	*Initiator/Partner*	*Year*	*Idea/Keywords*	*Challenge*	*Approach*
Declaration of the UN Conference on the Human Environment	United Nations	1972	Environmental education in general	Environment	
Tbilisi Declaration	UNESCO/ UNEP	1977	Environmental Education	Environment	Interdisciplinarity
Talloires Declaration	University Leaders for a Sustainable Future (ULSF)	1990	Higher education Leadership for sustainability	Environment Sustainability	Interdisciplinarity Transdisciplinarity
Halifax Declaration	Canadian institutions, IAU, UNU	1991	Ethical obligation Participation Leadership	Environment Sustainability	Whole-institution approach
Agenda 21	United Nations	1992	Chapter 36 Environmental education	Environment Sustainability	
Kyoto Declaration	IAU	1993	Sustainability action plan Environmental education	Environment Sustainability	Whole-institution approach
Swansea Declaration	Association of Commonwealth Universities	1993	Ethical obligation Environmental literacy and curriculum	Environment Sustainability	Whole-institution approach
COPERNICUS Charter	COPERNICUS and European Universities	1994	Embedding the environment and sustainability across higher education	Environment Sustainability	Interdisciplinarity
World Declaration for Higher Education	UNESCO	1998	Responsibility Societal problems	Environmental Sustainability	Inter- and transdisciplinarity Whole-institution approach
Lüneburg Declaration	GHESP	2001	Key role of universities Social change Curriculum reorientation	Sustainability	Whole-institution approach
Ubuntu Declaration	UNU, UNESCO, COPERNICUS GHESP, ULSF *et al.*	2002	Learning for sustainability Review of programs and curriculum MDGs	Sustainability	Whole-institution approach

Table 3.1 continued

Declaration/ Charter/ Programme	*Initiator/Partner*	*Year*	*Idea/Keywords*	*Challenge*	*Approach*
Johannesburg Declaration/ Johannesburg Plan	United Nations	2002	Education for sustainable development UN Decade ESD	Sustainability	
UNECE Strategy on ESD	UNECE	2005	ESD in general and in higher education	Sustainability	Interdisciplinarity Whole-institution approach
Graz Declaration	COPERNICUS, Oikos, UNESCO	2005	Embedding sustainability across higher education	Sustainability	Interdisciplinarity Whole-institution approach
Bologna Declaration/Bergen Communiqué	Ministers of Education in Europe	1998/ 2005	Sustainability Curriculum reform process	Sustainability	
Sapporo Sustainability Declaration	G8 University Network	2008	Need for global sustainability Reorientation of education and curriculum	Sustainability	
Bonn Declaration	UNESCO	2009	ESD Higher education institutions	Sustainability	Multidisciplinarity Whole-institution approach
The Future We Want – Rio+20 Declaration	United Nations	2012	ESD Quality education	Sustainability	Interdisciplinarity
Rio+20 Treaty on Higher Education	COPERNICUS, MESA, GUNI, GUPES, IAU, ISCN, UNU RCE *et al.*	2012	Responsibility of universities ESD in higher education Transformation research	Sustainability	
Aichi-Nagoya Declaration on Education for Sustainable Development	UNESCO	2014	ESD in general Responsibility Transformative knowledge	Sustainability	Whole-institution approach

sustainable development. Ten years later, at the World Summit on Sustainable Development in Johannesburg in 2002, the United Nations was called on to proclaim a World Decade on Education for Sustainable Development. And at the General Assembly Meeting of the UN in December 2002 the Decade was adopted, creating an institutional framework for the promotion of education for sustainable development with UNESCO acting as a lead agency in its implementation. The World Decade has resulted in concrete policy proposals and practical activities in many countries around the world and has given impulses in politics, administration as well as educational practice for the implementation of education for sustainable development in the different educational sectors.

Among the most important recent international conferences focusing on education for sustainable development, the following should be mentioned: the Bonn Conference on Moving into the Second Half of the World Decade in 2009, with its Bonn Declaration, the 36th General Assembly Meeting of the UN in 2011, where 68 countries referred in their statements to the importance of education for sustainable development, and the Rio+20 Conference in 2012, with its final document once again emphasising the importance of education for sustainable development.

A closer look at the process of reaching an understanding of education for sustainable development reveals the crucial importance of a number of policy statements. Sustainable development, as formulated in the Brundtland Report, cannot be achieved without comprehensive and far-reaching social change processes and fundamental shifts in perspective (e.g. in the human-nature relationship) along with other policy actions as found, for example, in Agenda 21. Such fundamental reorientations and changes require bringing about a new consciousness in individuals, which will undoubtedly only be possible through learning. Such a change in mentality must be systematically initiated as an integral goal of the educational system. Education is thus an essential element in the sustainability process, with its role explicitly defined in Agenda 21:

> Education is critical for promoting sustainable development and improving the capacity of the people to address environment and development issues.
>
> *(United Nations Division for Sustainable Development 1992: Chapter 36.3)*

In order for education to adequately address these demands, sustainable development must be understood as a cross-cutting issue. Since the 1990s there have been numerous efforts worldwide to introduce elements of education for sustainable development in formal, non-formal and informal educational sectors. The United Nations Economic Commission for Europe (UNECE) has thus reformulated and further elaborated its understanding of education for sustainable development in its strategy:

> Education for sustainable development develops and strengthens the capacity of individuals, groups, communities, organizations and countries to make judgments and choices in favour of sustainable development. It can promote a shift in people's mindsets and in so doing enable them to make our world safer, healthier and more prosperous, thereby improving the quality of life. Education for sustainable development can provide critical reflection and greater awareness and empowerment so that new visions and concepts can be explored and new methods and tools developed.
>
> *(UNECE 2005: 1)*

To this end, education for sustainable development should contribute to developing critical thinking competence in individuals so they will be better able to help shape the process of sustainable development as well as question their own attitudes and actions. A key goal in education for sustainable development is to foster the development of such individual competences. In addition, it is important to debate what knowledge and values are especially relevant to a vision of sustainable development – in particular as they are related to the preservation of the natural basis of life, human dignity and justice. This fundamental understanding of education for sustainable development is relevant for all educational sectors, and thus also for higher education for sustainable development.

For the higher education sector, alongside initiatives originating in the United Nations and the UNESCO, it is above all non-governmental organisations, networks and interest groups that have contributed with their declarations and programmatic proposals to the intensive discussions about sustainability in higher education that have taken place since the 1990s. If sustainability was at first seen as closely related to the environment, then this view has changed considerably since the beginning of the new millennium. Both the 2001 Lüneburg Declaration and the 2002 Ubuntu Declaration explicitly refer to the key role of universities and call for essential changes in teaching towards inter- and transdisciplinary approaches. They also take a holistic view of universities and call for a whole-institution approach to their transformation.

In Europe the COPERNICUS Charter and the Bologna Declaration together with the Bergen Communiqué have also played an important role. As a consequence of the Earth Summit in 1992, the European Rectors' Conference adopted the COPERNICUS University Charter in 1994, which then served as a mission statement for many European universities. By signing the Charter, universities voluntarily commit themselves to ten principles of action, encompassing environmental ethics, the education of university employees, programmes in environmental education, interdisciplinarity, the dissemination of knowledge, networking, partnerships, continuing education programmes and technology transfer. The Charter defines the voluntary commitment of universities to act in accordance with the principles of sustainable development and to integrate the idea of sustainability into the university system across teaching and learning, research and operational practice.

On the policy level, the so-called Bergen Communiqué of the Conference of European Ministers Responsible for Higher Education in 2005 marked a major step toward acknowledging sustainability as a guiding principle for building the European higher education area and the Bologna Process. The UNECE places the Strategy for Education for Sustainable Development (ESD), also established in 2005 in Vilnius (Lithuania), high on the political agenda and serves as a driving force for creating structures and provisions for ESD in the region. The strategy serves as a flexible framework for European countries and outlines a range of objectives underlying the regional implementation, e.g. ensuring that policies support ESD, promoting sustainable development through all forms of learning, equipping the education sector with the competences to engage in ESD, developing special tools and materials, promoting research and development of ESD, fostering the use of indigenous knowledge and strengthening cooperation on ESD in the UNECE region. Detailed descriptions of the goals and measures necessary for the introduction of ESD can be found in this strategy.

The politics dimension of higher education for sustainable development

Higher education for sustainable development relies on strong networks not only for its members to share experiences and learn from each other, but also to achieve its interests with as much consensus as possible. Over the last two decades, a number of national as well as international networks have been formed to facilitate such exchange activities and to pursue their interests and conduct the lobbying work necessary to that end. Table 3.2 lists some of the most influential networks around the world. Not surprisingly, the number of networks has increased considerably since the beginning of the UN World Decade on Education for Sustainable Development. There are now possibilities for universities in every region of the world to actively engage in networks on global, regional, national and local scales. The growing interest

Table 3.2 Networks on higher education for sustainable development – an overview

Networks	*Activities*	*Year established*	*Orientation*	*Global/ regional/ national*	*Internet address*
IAU – International Association of Universities	Promoting and facilitating universities' responsibility with regard to sustainability	Since 1993 (Kyoto Declaration)	Environment Sustainability	Global	www.iau-aiu.net/sd/sd_dkyoto.html
ISCN – International Sustainable Campus Network	Sharing best practices on building design, transportation and teaching (world-wide)	2007	Sustainability	Global	www.international-sustainable-campus-network.org
GUNI – Global Universities Network for Innovation	Strengthening the role of higher education in society contributing to the renewal of the visions, missions and policies of higher education	1998	Innovation Social responsibility	Global	www.guninetwork.org
GUPES – Global University Network for Environment and Sustainability	Mainstreaming of environment and sustainability practices and curricula into universities around the world	2010	Environment Sustainability	Global	www.gupes.org
UN-PRME – United Nations Principles for Responsible Leadership Education	Responsible management education, research and leadership	2007	Environment Sustainability	Global	www.unprme.org
COPERNICUS Alliance	Improving higher education and research for sustainable development in partnership with the society	1993/2007	Sustainability	Europe	www.copernicus-alliance.org
NSCN – Nordic Sustainable Campus Network	Strengthening sustainability in research and teaching; supporting green campus activities	2012	Sustainability	Europe	https://nordicsustainablecampusnetwork.wordpress.com
EAUC – Environmental Association for Universities and Colleges	Embedding the principles and values of environmental, economic and social sustainability in higher education	1996	Environment Sustainability	National	www.eauc.org.uk/home

Table 3.2 continued

Networks	*Activities*	*Year established*	*Orientation*	*Global/ regional/ national*	*Internet address*
AUT – Allianz Nachhaltige Universitäten in Österreich	Establishing sustainability in universities	2012	Sustainability	National	http://nachhaltige universitaeten.at/
AASHE – Association for the Advancement of Sustainability in Higher Education	Inspiring and catalysing higher education to lead the the global sustainability transformation	2005	Sustainability	North America	www.aashe.org
NWF – Campus Ecology	Campus Ecology program to protect wildlife and habitat, and improve campuses overall green educational programming and onsite sustainability	1989	Environment Sustainability	North America	www.nwf.org/ Campus-Ecology.aspx
ARIUSA – Alianza de Redes Ibero-americanas de Universidades por la Sustentabilidad y el Ambiente	Improving higher education for environment and sustainability; greening the campus	2007	Environment Sustainability	South America	http://ariusa.net
MESA Universities Partnership	Mainstreaming/ integrating of environment and sustainability concerns into teaching, research and community engagement and management of African universities		Environment Sustainability	Africa	www.unep.org/ training/ programmes/ mesa.asp
ProSPER.Net	Promoting sustainability in postgraduate education and research; young scientist award; leadership programme	2007	Sustainability	Asia	www.prospernet.ias. unu.edu
KAGCI	Sustainability in higher education; green campus declaration of university presidents	2008	Sustainability	Asia	www.kagci.org

Table 3.2 continued

Networks	*Activities*	*Year established*	*Orientation*	*Global/ regional/ national*	*Internet address*
ACTS – Australian Campuses Towards Sustainability	Inspiring, promoting and supporting change towards best practice sustainability within the operations, curriculum and research of universities	2006	Environment Sustainability	Australia	www.acts.asn.au

in network-building underscores two developments: firstly, the interest in changing universities towards more sustainability, and secondly, the role that networks play as instruments in further strengthening the political process establishing sustainability in universities.

The potential of such networks is exemplified on the regional level by the European network COPERNICUS Alliance, which was re-established in 2007 (Mader 2011). Founded by ten core member institutions, the network's vision is to promote the role of sustainable development in European higher education in partnership with societal actors. Its main goals are to exchange knowledge on ESD between European higher education institutions and student organisations that work for sustainability, to promote ESD in European policy-making, to disseminate tools for sustainability integration in higher education and to represent European higher education in international committees on ESD. The network takes up earlier networking activities from the former Copernicus Campus network and is strongly connected to the COPERNICUS Charter. On a national level we can see in the example of Austria how different actors in the higher education sector network exert influence on political processes on a global level (e.g. through ISCN or GUPES), but also on a regional level (e.g. through the COPERNICUS Alliance) and on a national level (e.g. through AUT).

Student networks engaged in issues concerning the integration of sustainability in higher education also play a special role (Table 3.3). Even though the number of global student networks is not very high, it is clear that there is substantial interest on the part of students in the environment and sustainability.

If we look at the development process of higher education and sustainability, then we see that at the latest with the start of the new millennium there has been a considerable increase in engagement. On an international level the United Nations and the UNESCO have taken up the cause of education for sustainable development by proclaiming the UN World Decade of Education for Sustainable Development, giving an important impulse to countries in different regions of the world. Even if education for sustainable development has been taken up by individual countries around the world with varying degrees of enthusiasm in the different sectors of their educational systems, the Decade has provided an important stimulus for higher education. The establishment of new networks for 'higher education and sustainability' span every continent and show not only that many actors are interested in initiating change processes in their own institutions but also that these actors are influencing political decision-making so as to promote a transformation of higher education towards sustainability. In the Bologna Process, which was established to create a unified European higher education area,

Table 3.3 Student networks worldwide

Networks	*Activities*	*Year established*	*Orientation*	*Global/ regional/ national*	*Internet address*
Oikos International – Students for Sustainable Economics and Management	Empowering future leaders to drive change towards sustainability worldwide	1987	Sustainability	Global	www.oikos-international.org
WSEN – World Student Environmental Network	Supporting creative student initiatives for the incorporation of sustainability into higher education systems, policies and institutions	2008	Environment Sustainability	Global	http://wsen.org
NetImpact	Community of students and professionals committed to solving the world's toughest social and environmental problems	1993	Environment	Global	https://netimpact.org

policy-makers called on institutions of higher education to integrate elements of sustainability into all new programmes of study. The cooperation of governmental, non-governmental and societal institutions and organisations has, both before and during the UN Decade, led to processes exploring how changes can be made in higher education that would lead to greater sustainability.

The polity dimension of higher education for sustainable development: the example of the UN world decade education for sustainable development

Following the recommendation of the World Summit for Sustainable Development in Johannesburg 2002, the General Assembly of the United Nations proclaimed the World Decade on Education for Sustainable Development for the period 2005–2014 to be coordinated by UNESCO. Its goal was to develop educational measures to contribute to the implementation of Agenda 21, which was adopted at the 1992 Rio Summit and then reaffirmed at the 2002 Johannesburg Summit, anchoring the principles of sustainable development in national educational systems around the world. All member nations of the United Nations were called on to develop national and international educational activities that would show pathways to preserving and enhancing the living conditions and chances of survival for both existing and future generations.

In a number of countries, institutional frameworks were created for the implementation of Decade activities and for promoting the process of establishing education for sustainable development in all sectors of education. An example of which structures were created for the activities during the UN World Decade for National Development can be found for the German-speaking countries of Austria, Switzerland and Germany (Michelsen 2014; see Table 3.4).

We can now look more closely at the institutional and organisational implementation of the Decade, using Germany as an example with the structures and procedures created there. Organisationally, a Decade Office was established at the German UNESCO Commission for the implementation of the Decade, receiving financial support for its operation from the German Federal Ministry for Education and Research (BMBF). A National Committee Education for Sustainable Development was appointed and met twice a year to deal with important issues related to the monitoring and implementation of the Decade. The results and recommendations they reported were then addressed to the respective decision-makers in politics, administration and educational practice and negotiated with them. The National Committee was composed of members from the relevant ministries at federal and state levels as well as from politics, associations, non-governmental organisations and institutions such as universities, broadcasting companies, from the media and from relevant foundations. Representatives of educational practice met annually at the Round Table and agreed on concrete practical educational activities.

From the very beginning of the decade, the working group 'Higher Education' played a crucial role with more than 100 academics from universities and universities of applied science participating. Work of the group covered teaching and learning in higher education, whole-institution approaches and finally the development of a sustainability codex. An important milestone was the memorandum 'Higher Education and Sustainability' which was approved by the German UNESCO commission as well as the Germans Rectors' conference in 2009 (Deutsche UNESCO-Kommission 2014).

Table 3.4 Structures for implementing the UN World Decade Education for Sustainable Development

Country	*Structures and activities*
Germany	• National Committee with Decade Office • Round table with stakeholders • Recognition of Decade projects • Research programme in education for sustainable development • Activities specific to each federal state • Establishing Regional Centres of Expertise
Switzerland	• Swiss Coordination Conference Education for Sustainable Development • Action Plan 2007–2014 Education for Sustainable Development • Recognition of Decade projects • Programme Sustainable Development in Universities (2013–2017)
Austria	• Austrian Strategy for Education for Sustainable Development • Decade Office • Recognition of Decade projects • Sustainability Award for Austrian universities • Establishing Regional Centres of Expertise

An important tool for encouraging initiatives and projects on education for sustainable development was a recognition process for so-called Decade projects. Over the Decade, nearly 2,000 projects were awarded recognition. At the federal level, a research program was also launched to study education for sustainable development, and at the federal state level specific initiatives were put in place in individual states, for example, modifying framework guidelines for schools, while in a number of universities programmes of study containing elements of sustainability were introduced. On the federal state level contractual arrangements in the form of target agreements between individual universities and the relevant ministry were made, which explicitly included the integration of sustainability into the strategy of higher education development.

Higher education for sustainable development: from the environmental perspective to sustainability

A closer look at the role of education in the context of the environment and sustainability shows what changes there have been in discussions revolving around these topics. The declarations published over the past 40 years along with the networks and the institutional frameworks that have been established (see Figure 3.1) can be divided into three different phases:

1. Orientation and experimental phase (1970 to 1990)
2. Transition and development phase (1990 to 2000)
3. Expansionary phase (to 2014)

In the *orientation and experimental phase* the background is characterised by the environmental destruction, together with the growing realisation that raw materials are a finite resource, that was experienced in many countries around the world and was documented in numerous publications including *Silent Spring, Limits to Growth, Global 2000, Seveso ist überall* (Seveso is Everywhere). In reaction to these developments, the UN Conference on Human Environment (1972) called for involving education as an instrument for preventing or solving environmental problems, which led to the UNESCO holding, as mentioned above, the first conference on environmental education in Tbilisi (Georgia). The Tbilisi Declaration that was adopted at the end of the conference had as a consequence that many countries undertook both policy initiatives and practical actions in education that aimed at establishing environmental education in the different educational sectors. At the same time a scientific discussion on environmental education began. With the Brundtland Report (1987) it became clear that human development on earth in a traditional sense (for example, continued growth on a planet with finite resources, environmental destruction, unequal distribution of resources) was no longer possible. The report shaped the 'modern' idea of sustainability and produced the concept of sustainable development that has since become an important element in global political and societal discourse. The discussion on education has also been strongly influenced by this thinking.

An important landmark in the *transition and development phase* was Agenda 21, which was adopted at the Rio Conference in 1992. This document describes the action that must be taken in order to achieve the goal of sustainable development. Although almost all chapters in Agenda 21 contain references to the importance of education, it is Chapter 36 that exclusively deals with education, public awareness and training. It is a catalogue of proposals showing pathways to implementing the actions listed in this chapter. This document gave the discussion about the role of education in the context of sustainable development a central reference point, one that

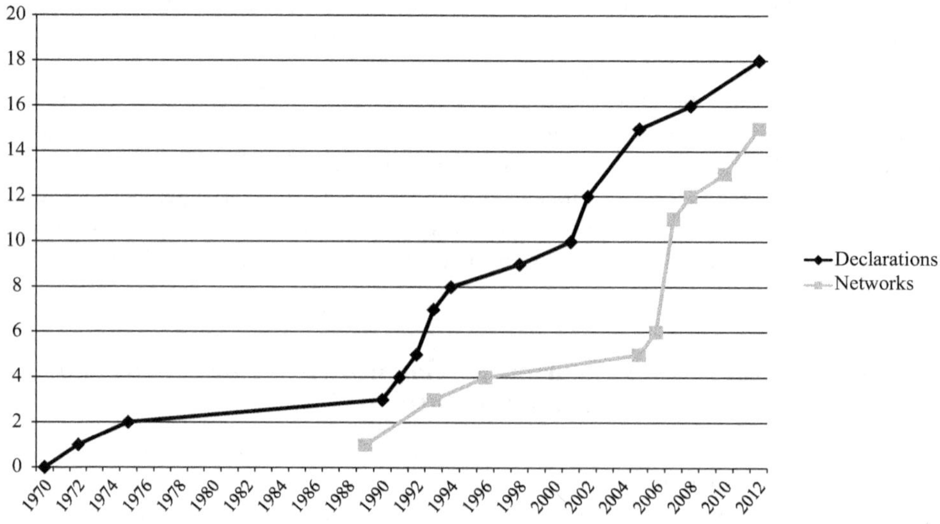

Figure 3.1 Number of declarations and networks: development since 1970

has since repeatedly appeared in educational policy initiatives and activities in national context. The activities that were initiated world-wide had however consequences that need to be critically evaluated. The first efforts to implement Agenda 21 focused on schools (that is, on only one area of the formal educational system), were mostly limited to environmental education and concentrated on the ecological dimension of sustainability. The first initiatives (political declarations, establishing networks) in higher education recognised the role of universities in meeting the challenge of sustainability.

In the *expansionary phase* an important role was played by the World Summit for Sustainable Development in Johannesburg in 2002. The Johannesburg Declaration on Sustainable Development and the Johannesburg Plan of Implementation both stressed the special importance of education and lifelong learning for promoting sustainable development. The role of education as an integral component in sustainable development was strengthened:

> we will work together to assist one another to have access to financial resources, … ensure capacity building, … and make sure that there is technology transfer, human resource development, education and training to banish forever underdevelopment.
>
> *(United Nations 2002)*

A number of chapters emphasise the key role of education for specific fields of action such as gender equality, rural development, healthcare and patterns of consumption and formulated the goal to:

> Integrate sustainable development into education systems at all levels of education in order to promote education as a key agent for change.
>
> *(United Nations 2002)*

Furthermore the Plan of Implementation argues for the creation and implementation of local, sub-national and national educational guidelines that include education for sustainable development. It also proposes as an important measure the implementation of a World Decade of Education for Sustainable Development to start in 2005. This position statement and the UN Decade of Education for Sustainable Development both call for all educational sectors, including that of informal education, to devote greater efforts to integrating the concept of sustainability. In this phase we can also see increased activities in higher education. It will be a challenge in the next phase to create the necessary structures for the implementation of sustainability in higher education.

The Decade was undoubtedly successful overall (Wals 2012). As a result of the UN World Decade there have been many initiatives and activities all over the world that have shown what education for sustainable development is about. This includes major conferences and publications as well as specific initiatives. For example, in China education for sustainable development was integrated in the medium and long term planning for national educational reform (2010–20) and over 1,000 experimental schools for education for sustainable development were established. In India the campaign CO_2 Pick Right was started in over 70,000 schools. In Japan education for sustainable development was codified in the national curriculum guidelines. Sweden is supporting the training and education of teachers in education for sustainable development in Asia and Africa. The MESA programme by UNEP has introduced education for sustainable development and sustainable development in over 80 universities in 40 African countries. Alongside numerous European initiatives (see Stoltenberg and Holz 2012), Sweden has passed legislation requiring all universities to take up education for sustainable development and sustainable development. In Germany close to 2,000 so-called Decade Projects were recognised, a good 4,000 teachers in day-care centres were certified in education for sustainable development, and in general schools sustainable development has gained importance. The United Nations University has been able to establish over 100 Regional Centres for Expertise (RCE) around the world that focus on education for sustainable development on a local or regional level. Research programs on education for sustainable development (for example in Germany) are beginning to take shape.

Outlook

Education for sustainable development has become an established concept that fundamentally reinterprets the goals, methods and content of education, enhancing its quality, as well as creating opportunities for change processes in individual educational sectors. However despite the countless political initiatives and activities as well as practical projects described, education for sustainable development is not yet 'mainstream'. And it is for this reason that at the final Decade conference in Nagoya (2014) the UNESCO announced it will continue the UN World Decade as a Global Action Programme. The Aichi-Nagoya Declaration states:

> that the Global Action Programme (GAP) on ESD, endorsed by the 37th session of the General Conference of UNESCO as a follow up to the Decade of ESD and a concrete contribution to the post-2015 agenda, aims at generating and scaling up ESD actions in all levels and areas of education, training and learning.
>
> *(UNESCO 2014: 1)*

Moreover the member countries of UNESCO are called on to continue to work for further progress in education for sustainable development; in particular that they should:

> Review the purposes and values that underpin education, assess the extent to which education policy and curricula are achieving the goals of ESD; reinforce the integration of ESD into education, training, and sustainable development policies, with a special attention paid to system-wide and holistic approaches and multi-stakeholder cooperation and partnerships between actors of the education sector, private sector, civil society and those working in the various areas of sustainable development; and ensure the education, training and professional development of teachers and other educators to successfully integrate ESD into teaching and learning.
>
> *(UNESCO 2014: 2)*

The Global Action Programme is expected to give further impulses for the implementation of education for sustainable development. The programme is concentrated on five priority action areas:

1. Processes for the political integration of education for sustainable development at national and international levels must be strengthened, and the success factors for its establishment identified.
2. Support is needed for holistic approaches for schools and higher education (whole-institution approaches) to sustainability, not viewing it merely as a topic for lessons and teaching but as a comprehensive mission that will impact the shape of educational institutions.
3. The Global Action Programme should aim at strengthening activities integrating education for sustainability development in the areas of pre-service and in-service teacher education and training.
4. Young people should not only be seen as target groups of education but should instead be more closely involved in educational processes and provided opportunities to serve as change agents, especially in the informal and non-formal educational sectors.
5. Finally, efforts should be increased to promote education for sustainable development on a local level and to support network local actors.

We can expect that the five strategic action areas identified in the Global Action Program, in particular the greater efforts to empower young people, will play a more prominent role in further developing practice and research in the area of sustainable development over the coming years. Consequently, with the years coming, the following activities come into play and will be crucial for HESD:

- The 'whole-institution approach' needs to be embedded more systematically in institutions. This way, universities have the opportunity to take over organisational responsibility and serve as a role model in society.
- Higher Education Institutions need to develop and implement new study programmes, especially but not limited to teacher education, in which sustainability is a key issue. This will help to educate future change agents that will contribute to a sustainability transformation.
- The role of professional development of academics in higher education as well as of key actors in economy, administration, education and academia must be supported with respect to key challenges in sustainability.
- In research on HESD an output- and outcome-oriented perspective that provides evidence-based recommendations is needed, especially focusing on the development of key competencies in sustainability.

In the course of these activities the UNESCO Chairs that are engaged in issues related to sustainable development should also take on a greater role internationally. The UNESCO Chairs belong to the UNITWIN/UNESCO Chairs Programme, which promotes interuniversity cooperation and networking to enhance institutional capacities through knowledge sharing and collaboration. In many instances, the UNESCO Chairs serve as think tanks and as bridge builders between academia, civil society, local communities, research institutions and policy makers. In the context of UNESCO initiatives they have so far been an underutilised resource, but in their intermediary function in their own countries they have been able to make a considerable contribution to focusing the attention of universities and colleges on education for sustainable development. For teaching but also for research, all of the strategic action areas are of interest for the UNESCO Chairs as well as for other actors in higher education.

References

Barth, M., 2015. *Implementing Sustainability in Higher Education. Learning in an Age of Transformation.* London: Routledge.

Deutsche UNESCO-Kommission (DUK), ed., 2014. *Hochschulen für eine nachhaltige Entwicklung. Netzwerke fördern, Bewusstsein verbreiten.* Bonn: DUK.

Fischer, F. and Miller, G.J., eds., 2006. *Handbook of Public Policy Analysis: Theory, Politics, and Methods.* Boca Raton, CA: crc Press.

Leal Filho, W., 2011. 'Applied Sustainable Development. A Way Forward in Promoting Sustainable Development in Higher Education Institutions', in Leal Filho, W. (ed.), *World Trends in Education for Sustainable Development.* Frankfurt a.M.: Peter Lang, 11–30.

Mader, C., 2011. 'Launching the COPERNICUS Alliance. European Network on Higher Education for Sustainable Development', *Journal of Education for Sustainable Development,* 5(1), 7–8.

Michelsen, G., 2011. 'Future Challenges in the Context of Sustainable Development from a European Point of View', in Barth, M., Rieckmann, M. and Sanusi, Z.A. (eds), *Higher Education for Sustainable Development. Looking Back and Moving Forward.* Bad Homburg: VAS-Verlag für akademische Schriften, 59–77.

Michelsen, G., 2014. 'Education for Sustainable Development. Status Quo and Perspectives', in O'Farrell, L., Schonman, S. and Wagner, E. (eds), *Yearbook of Research in Arts Education.* Münster: Waxmann, 121–9.

Stoltenberg, U. and Holz, V., 2012. *Education for Sustainable Development – European Approaches.* Bad Homburg: VAS-Verlag für akademische Schriften.

UNECE, 2005. *UNECE Strategy for Education for Sustainable Development.* CEP/AC.13/2005/3/Rev.1 (adopted at the High Level Meeting in Vilnius, 17–18 March 2005).

UNESCO, 2014. *Aichi-Nagoya Declaration on Education for Sustainable Development.* www.unesco.org/new/fileadmin/MULTIMEDIA/HQ/ERI/pdf/Aichi-Nagoya_Declaration_EN.pdf [accessed 10 March 2015].

United Nations, 2002. *Johannesburg Declaration on Sustainable Development.* A/CONF.199/20. www.un-documents.net/jburgdec.htm [accessed 10 March 2015].

United Nations Division for Sustainable Development, 1992. *Agenda 21. Rio Declaration on Environment and Development.* www.un.org/esa/sustdev/documents/agenda21/english/agenda21toc.htm [accessed 10 March 2015].

Wals, A.E.J., 2012. *Shaping the Education of Tomorrow: 2012 Full-length Report on the UN Decade for Education for Sustainable Development.* Wageningen: Wageningen Universiteit.

4

CHALLENGES FOR IMPLEMENTATION OF EDUCATION FOR SUSTAINABLE DEVELOPMENT IN HIGHER EDUCATION INSTITUTIONS

Ian Thomas

Context

As Wals *et al.* (Chapter 2 in this Handbook) and Michelsen (Chapter 3 in this Handbook) indicate, Education for Sustainable Development (ESD) has been a maturing field of practice, research and theory over almost three decades. After this time we could expect to see evidence of Higher Education Institutions (HEI) embracing ESD, and their curricular developing relevant competencies in graduates. Yet in HEIs we see few examples of where ESD has been integrated.

A sober reflection on the complexity of HEIs indicates that this slow rate of change is not surprising. This chapter is designed to explore the range of issues that make change in any HEI complicated, and consequently relatively slow. Once we have an appreciation of these factors we can, perhaps, appreciate and understand the achievements so far in implementing ESD.

Implementing ESD in higher education: focusing on curriculum change

Broadly we see ESD as having three components: operations within the institution (e.g. waste management, energy management); curriculum that guides the education of students; and interactions with the broader community (where students, academics and sections of the community exchange experiences). Community interactions largely occur after students and academics have developed experiences through the curriculum and operations; however, both internal HEI and community components can develop in parallel, without there being any necessarily close connection between them. Yet the centre of ESD at any institution is the curriculum experienced by students, supported by the practical examples provided by the institution's operations and by interested sections of the community.

As in any field of curriculum, implementation of ESD represents a curriculum change, a process that is complicated, and frequently difficult. This point is emphasised by Lattuca and Stark (2009: 301) who comment that, regarding curriculum:

> Broad changes … require leadership, coordination, and, often, professional development for faculty and administrators. Successful leadership for such changes must recognize and build upon the college or university culture, including its institutional traditions, norms, and values; politics and power; individual and collective beliefs and attitudes related to proposed changes; and existing social relations and practices.

Broad redirections amount to an exercise in organisational change for an institution, as discussed by de la Harpe and Thomas (2009). Such changes may be thought to be a simple exercise in planning. However, Eckel and Kezar (2002) emphasise that changing the curriculum at an HEI requires transformational organisational change in order to change all courses, programmes, disciplines and institutional experiences. As a consequence, there is broad agreement that curriculum change in a HEI is a challenging task, and the attempt often fails to meet the expectations of the change agents (for example Arnold 2004; Blackmore and Kandiko 2012; Eckel and Kezar 2002).

However, this is not a failure of knowing what to change, but rather how to institutionalise a change (Merton *et al.* 2009). Generally change projects assume that academics and the institutions' behaviours are rational, but Arnold (2004) argues that in reality political agendas are to be expected in HEIs so that actors and stakeholders will have their own agendas that will inevitably influence decision making about any change. As an example, Arthur (2007) argues that market and institutional reasons are rarely the cause for curriculum change, but can be used as supporting rationales for change agents, who are usually academics and students.

There is no shortage of literature regarding organisational change, especially in the context of business organisations, however, HEIs, in particular universities, are unique and complex organisations. They have a history going back over several centuries (Ford 2002), but with considerable growth in recent times. The twenty-first century has seen a significant growth in the number of students undertaking Higher Education (Higher Education Statistics Agency, no date; Larkins 2012; National Center for Education Statistics, no date). To cater for these increases there has been a growth in the number of universities and their size; Larkins (2012) reports on there being 'nine Australian Universities with more than 40,000 students enrolled in 2010'. Management of such large organisations now requires formal structures, systems, policies and procedures. Further, the increasing size of universities brings with it an increased management task, an aspect of which, as Marginson and Considine (2000: 4) report, leads to:

> forms of organisation and methods of work [that] are undergoing crucial changes. University purpose is now defined by forms of strong executive control. University missions and governing bodies start to take on a distinctly corporate character … marketing mediates much of the relationship with the world outside, and performance targets are superimposed on scholarly honorifics.

This evolution suggests a move from a 'collegial' to a 'managerial' culture, as described by Berquist (1992) (cited in Eckel and Kezar 2002). In addition, 'developmental' and 'negotiating' cultures had been identified by Berquist at some institutions.

These conclusions encompass trends in HEI internationally, and they suggest a growing complexity of management and governance; a complexity that any curriculum change has to emerge from. Advice about change in these situations draws on business and public sector experiences, for example Kotter (1996). However, work by researchers like de la Harpe and Radloff (2003) have related factors critical for successful curriculum change more closely to the situations encountered in HEIs (for example see Box 4.1). From the other perspective,

Box 4.1 Factors critical for successful curriculum transformation

- engaging in an intellectual effort to develop an agreed vision and shared understanding;
- gaining active involvement and ownership by senior leadership;
- providing opportunities to debate and discuss issues and to recognise and resolve concerns;
- providing professional development for staff to reflect on their conceptions of themselves, their profession and their work, and their approaches to the curriculum;
- communicating widely and regularly the endorsement of the project, its goals, progress and outcomes;
- ensuring that tasks are completed by those assigned responsibility for them;
- demonstrating that change is worth the effort and results in superior outcomes;
- ensuring that systems and processes are developed or modified to support and monitor the change agenda.

Source: de la Harpe and Radloff (2003)

barriers to curriculum change have been identified as: lack of consultation with staff; an unhelpful organisational culture; insufficient funding; political challenges; academics and/or their departments considering a change to be irrelevant to their discipline; and an individualistic culture that inhibits collaboration (Blackmore and Kandiko 2012; Eckel and Kezar 2002; Leask 2001; Uchiyama and Radin 2009).

At this point is it useful to be clear about the degree of curriculum change that ESD will require. The scope of a proposed change, or how it will alter institutional practices, can be considered in terms of depth (e.g. requiring instructors and students to think differently) and pervasiveness of the change (i.e. whether it affects many units and programs) (Lattuca and Stark 2009). Combinations of these two dimensions have been discussed by Lattuca and Stark (2009) in relation to the four possibilities outlined in Table 4.1. At one end of the spectrum, 'adjustment' (quadrant 1), change is localised (e.g. to a specific subject/unit/course, and one taken by only a small number of students). At the other end is 'transformational' change (quadrant 4) where curricular across an institution are changed and the majority of students and academics are affected. Clearly transformational change is the sort of broad change relevant to ESD.

Lattuca and Stark (2009) also suggest that there are several models that can provide guidance for curricular change, i.e. diffusion theories (addressing external influences); planned

Table 4.1 Spectrum of curriculum change possibilities

		Depth	
		Low	*High*
Pervasiveness	Low	Adjustment (Quadrant 1)	Isolated change (Q2)
	High	Far-reaching change (Q3)	Transformational change (Q4)

Source: after Lattuca and Stark, 2009

change models (problem solving and research and development, continuous improvement); political models; and social-cognition models. Each has its individual attributes, while drawing on commonalities discussed above. Even with these models, Lattuca and Stark (2009: 319) emphasise the complexity of trying to achieve effective change:

> Those who wish to achieve active curricular change must use several models simultaneously and consider many factors: institutional and program histories, traditions and norms; individual and collective understanding of local values and practices; power and interest groups; and the limitations of rational plans.

These points have much in common with implementation of policies, i.e. processes for change, where there is frequently talk of adopting either a 'top-down' or 'bottom-up' approach (Hogwood and Gunn 1989). With the first, the senior management-staff of the organisation direct the other levels of staff to follow the policy. With the second, junior, lower level, staff introduce changes that are subsequently valued by management and incorporated into a formal policy that 'legitimises' the change. Of the factors listed in Box 4.1, most epitomise a top-down approach; yet, 'providing opportunities to debate and discuss issues' gives a small opening for bottom-up actions. However, the range of actors/stakeholders, structures and values that interact around HEI curriculum means that the reality of a change process has to recognise, and actively encourage, the interactions of many contributors. For instance, Hegarty (2008) points the role of 'communities of practice' in bringing stakeholders together for change process in HEIs.

As with general policy situations, a curriculum change is a process rather than a single outcome (Holley 2009; Walkington, cited in Roger 2011). As such the process will need both the 'top' to provide coordination, structures and resources, as well as the 'bottom' to provide the knowledge and energy to interpret the concepts and put them into action. A critical path for this sort of interactivity is via academic development. Several researchers have noted that staff engagement and professional development are key, and this requires allocating time in their work plans (Hannan *et al.* 1999; Blackmore and Kandiko 2012). Importantly the interconnections between stakeholders are illustrated by Barth and Rieckmann (2012) in their discussion of the effects of academic development programmes for ESD, for social learning across the HEI, and for supporting moves to embed ESD.

Another consequence of the process of curriculum change is that it requires time before a change will be seen to be operating. Periods of five to ten years may be needed according to the experiences of Blackmore and Kandiko (2012), and Simsek and Louis (1994). This all leads to the consideration of what the main actors may need to recognise, and the critical interactions that would have to be managed.

Complexities in curriculum change: reality or myth

In a broad sense Thomas *et al.* (2012) have identified the 'tip of the iceberg' of factors that may play a role in curriculum change. These factors focus on aspects of the roles of: the university/HEI; its operational activities; its academics; and particular groups outside the HEI. In summary, the stakeholders, or actors, and the related factors include:

- HEI, to guide and resource –
    - organisational change for the development and implementation of curriculum
    - structures and institutional culture

    - establish graduate attributes, or competencies, that are consistent with ESD
    - academic development to assist academics to develop the material for the curriculum, and plan the pedagogy for the delivery of the material
    - operational activities in line with sustainable development principles to establish the campus as a 'learning laboratory'
- academics, to develop the ESD curriculum relevant to their discipline and profession, including the curriculum content, the learning and teaching practice and pedagogy
- professional associations, other accrediting bodies, and industry advisors to provide guidance to the academics, and HEIs, about the competencies (core and specific) sought in graduates seeking employment
- communities, external to the HEI, to provide broad guidance and support for sustainable development to be practiced in HEI and provide a base for education of students.

To gain a deeper insight into the components of the change process it is worth reminding ourselves about the aim of ESD, and consider the factors that are likely to influence the achievement of that aim. It is acknowledged that there are different explanations of ESD, but taking the definition adopted by UNESCO:

> Education for Sustainable Development (ESD) is a learning process (or approach to teaching) based on the ideals and principles that underlie sustainability and is concerned with all levels and types of learning to provide quality education and foster sustainable human development – learning to know, learning to be, learning to live together, learning to do and learning to transform oneself and society.
>
> *(Education for Sustainable Development Unit, no date)*

So we see that, in addition to providing quality education, the aim is to foster sustainable development through learning processes. This learning will be achieved by the intervention of teachers, and in the context of HEIs, it will be the academics employed to assist students to learn. The teacher, or academic, is then the direct link to the students. Yet, the content that the academic presents to the learners, and how it is presented, will be influenced by a range of factors associated with the academic her/himself, and from both within and external to the HEI; as outlined above.

An academic may wish to introduce curriculum changes themselves, without being asked to do so. In these situations, and through their surveys of academics, Hannan *et al.* (1999) determined that the most important reasons for change were to improve the learning experience for students and to respond to changes in student intake. In this context, the factors were the numbers of students, and their expectations; as Lattuca and Stark (2009) note students have goals, attitudes, personal traits and increasingly seek freedom and relevance from their studies. While these influences occur regularly, and academics are responding with modified pedagogy, implementation of ESD requires transformational change, involving many academics, and is likely to be initiated by others. However, not all will see change to be in their interest; Hannan *et al.* (1999) point out that curriculum innovation by an individual staff can be both a career opportunity (higher status as a teacher) as well as a threat (the time taken may impact on research output).

Considering the broader influences on academics we see a strong similarity with the concept of 'nested' policies (Bregha *et al.* 1990), or there being a 'hierarchy' of policies (Dovers 1999). In this situation broad-scale policies ('meta-policy' such as those developed by the United Nations) provide direction for the policies of nations ('macro-policy' of Mozambique for example), which in turn guides regional policies ('meso-policy' of Niassa), which directs activities at the regional and local HEIs (and their 'micro-policy').

The academics become a fifth stage in this hierarchy. Guided by policies such as UNESCO's Decade of ESD (UNESCO 2005), nations and then regions have developed their responses, which have in turn shaped the plans of HEIs; for example, by the mid-2000s a sizable proportion of Australian universities had policies related to sustainable development (Lang *et al.* 2006). Academics, guided by the broad 'learning and teaching' strategies or more specific ESD strategies, have then been in the position of responding with their own individual 'nano-policies' (i.e. curriculum designs) to achieve the aim of ESD, as noted above.

With these policy stages we can identify the types of curricular changes that Lattuca and Stark (2009: 306) have categorised in relation to deep and persuasive curricular changes i.e.:

> (a) those that result from institutional response to external societal pressures; (b) those that result from diffusion of educational ideas developed outside the institution; and (c) those that emerge from planning efforts of faculty and administrators within a program, college, or university.

While type (a) changes are likely to be associated with meta and macro policies, and (b) with macro or meso policies, type (c) will be most closely linked to the micro policy level.

Irrespective of how we prefer to label the curriculum change for ESD, it will be at the deepest and most pervasive level. That there are few reports of ESD being integrated into HEIs suggests that only a few HEIs have approached transformational change, even if a range of academics have responded with a 'strategy' of 'nano' curriculum change. Looking at the complexity of the curriculum change process, in the following sections, it is not surprising that this is the case.

Factors affecting the implementation of ESD in HEIs

Associated with the development of policies for ESD, by the international community through to the regional governments (meta-policy to meso-policy), there will be many influences that will shape the policies; both the content and how they will be implemented (Thomas 2007). However, it is at the micro-policy and nano-policy levels that influences can have a profound effect on the pace of the implementation, and the details of what is changed. Policies at these levels equate to the curriculum designs that academics, or the 'street level bureaucrats' of Hill (2005), implement. As a result it is the academics who have substantial influence in the policy-process; for development of their specific curriculum.

Those of us involved with ESD in HEIs have limited opportunities to affect the higher level policies (meta to meso), but there is opportunity with the other levels of policy. Hence it is important to appreciate the issues involved with the delivery of ESD in an HEI, and specifically the role of the academic, if we wish to identify ways to improve the speed at which ESD is implemented. Eckel *et al.* (1999) note that curriculum change processes rely on understanding the change process, understanding why change is needed, and implementing change. These elements are closely related to a variety of factors that are variously: structural (related to the physical and governance arrangements of the HEI); cultural (the values and ways of working within the HEI); and personal (values and traits of the individuals).

With a framework guided by these categories (structural, cultural and personal), the research discussed above, together with some experience in working in a HEI, it is possible to identify a range of factors that may influence a curriculum change process, and specifically the ways that individual academics will respond. Table 4.2 is an outcome of such consideration, where the range of factors takes account of matters external to the HEI, but focuses on internal issues. Development of this table draws on Thomas *et al.* (2012), and de la Harpe and Thomas (2009), where a range of factors related to the implementation of ESD have been discussed. Recent reviews of the progress of ESD contribute to the depth of the range, such as the review of the role of government by Martin *et al.* (2013); a workshop that identified 'limiting factors' associated with ESD curriculum adoption noted by Sterling (2012); and the role of institutional factors (Moore 2005), academics, and students in curriculum implementation discussed by van der Leeuw *et al.* (2012). Further, consideration of the literature and a study of a sample of German HEIs helped Barth (2013) to highlight some specific factors that affected the implementation of ESD, specifically institutional size, opportunities for participation in ESD, change processes, and supportive internal structures. While his study examined a range of HEI situations, across his range of cases clear commonalities could be seen. Likewise, case studies from four southern African universities highlighted to Lotz-Sisitka and Lupele (2006) the range of structural factors (such as power relations and hierarchies) and socio-cultural factors (e.g. regional networking) influencing curriculum change, all of which must work in with pressures less experienced in developed countries.

External influences will be those that individual HEIs, or even the sector as a whole, have little or no power over, for example the increased accountability by governments noticeable at the beginning of the twenty-first century (Lattuca and Stark 2009). Additional influences may come from specific regional situations, such as the environment and sustainability risks associated with economic development and production, plus vulnerabilities and risks and associated with poverty, reported by Lotz-Sisitka and Lupele (2006). In some cases the institutions may be engaged in the issue, but not have control over the outcomes such as changes in technology and thinking about instructional processes (Lattuca and Stark 2009).

Internal influences are many and varied. Appreciation of these influences is critical for Lattuca and Stark (2009: 106) who note: 'suggestions for integrating curricula that require dramatic changes on college and university organizational structure and relationships are unlikely to be accepted and, experience suggests, often fail'. One influence that connects across external and internal levels, and particularly across internal elements (Table 4.2) of academic staff, is the role of disciplines. I have used the term disciplines in a broad sense, however, Lattuca and Stark (2009) draw a distinction that may be important in some institutions. They draw a difference between the concepts of academic fields (an inclusive term encompassing disciplines, interdisciplinary, and undergraduate professional study and occupational study), and disciplines (academic subjects traditionally taught in the arts and science colleges). Within each field the authors suggest there will be considerations of: organisational structure within the field and its connections to other fields; discourse and symbolic structures within the field; values and value structures; and the academic community of the field (being internally insular or connected). The importance of recognising the role of academic fields is emphasised by the observation that: 'Effective course and program planning does not require overhauling departments or units; instead, it acknowledges the essential role of academic fields in curriculum planning and seeks to balance the impact of academic fields with the educational needs of students' (Lattuca and Stark 2009: 106).

However, the 15-year experience of Turpin-Marion *et al.* indicated that 'the engineering community is not aware enough and ready to have a change of this magnitude' (Turpin-Marion *et al.* 2006: 97) to introduce environmental perspectives into engineering programs. While this was the experience in Mexico, Mulder and Jansen (2006) noted similar disciplinary culture issues in the Netherlands, as has Shi (2006) in the cultures associated with physical and social sciences in China.

The 'elements' and 'issues' that are presented in Table 4.2 are derived from the expansion of the many factors noted previously. In particular they draw on the observation of Barth (2013) that the focus of related research is on the roles of students, academic staff, HEI administration and external factors. Yet, the limited research in the area means that Table 4.2 is not intended to represent the full listing of influences. The reason being that depending on the experiences of the researcher additional issues may be identifiable, while some currently included may be considered to be of less importance. Rather, Table 4.2 is intended as a starting point for thinking about the complexity of change in HEIs.

A specific focus in Table 4.2 is the emphasis on academics. This emphasis derives from observations such as that of Barth (2013: 172) who notes that academics are '"transmitters" of implementation processes ... to bridge any gap between students and management, as well as between learning and campus operation.'

In other contexts, Holdsworth *et al.* (2008) and Barth and Rieckmann (2012) have made similar observations, while the research of Martin *et al.* (2006) highlights the issue of providing the staff with the contexts to become involved in ESD implementation. Importantly, as outlined by these researchers the personal situations and characteristics of the academics involved in ESD projects are critical, and become much of the focus in Table 4.2. We can be more specific and re-figure the material to focus on the range of aspects related to academics, which is the function of Figure 4.1 where the central role that academics play is highlighted (closely related elements of Table 4.2 have been amalgamated in Figure 4.1 to simplify the diagrammatic representation). This emphasis is consistent with the point discussed earlier where academics are in the position of being the most direct connection to students/learners for their exposure to ESD. The academics' connections have been assisted by the guides, toolkits and frameworks, such as that compiled for The Higher Education Academy (Sterling 2012). These resources provide assistance for academics who are looking to engage with ESD. Importantly these resources have evolved from a focus on content (examples of material to be included in a curriculum), to the discussion of the outcomes expected from ESD curriculum (competencies of graduates) and the relevant pedagogy.

When it comes to an individual academic, s/he will have to choose which content to include in their classes, which learning outcomes they will expect from the students (and the assessment tasks to evaluate the students' outcomes), and what pedagogy s/he will guide their teaching. All these choices and decisions will be strongly influenced by the individual's values. In Figure 4.1 we see that values are associated with all segments (directly with personal values, sense of self, reflective, self-learner, and less directly with pedagogy, information sources, and professional culture), and so will play an important role in the way that an academic will respond to proposals to introduce ESD. These values, and the academic's background, will shape the academic's thinking about the content that would be included (someone from an artistic background is unlikely to immediately consider the inclusion of organic chemistry), and about the pedagogy that would be appropriate to convey the material. Values shape the way we think and are at the base of how disciplines have developed. The role of disciplines is explicitly recognised by Sterling (2012) where he identifies curriculum activities relevant to specific disciplines. This discussion recognises the values and background of the academics; however, a deep understanding of the external and internal elements (of Table 4.2), such as the relevance of sustainability, would be required if the academics using this framework were opposed to ESD concepts, or even uninterested in teaching ESD.

It is not within the scope of this chapter to consider all the aspects noted in Table 4.2, to provide a plan for how each aspect can be used to facilitate ESD. Even examining the more focused relationships illustrated in Figure 4.1 would require the discussion of a range of issues

Table 4.2 Factors that may affect the implementation of education for sustainable development in higher education institutions

Relative to HEI	*Aspect of HEI or group*	*Element*	*Issue*
External to HEI	Government (international, national, regional, local)	Policies	To either direct the uptake of sustainability in HEIs, or to encourage it – for both physical activities/projects, and for educational activities
		Resources	Construction of sustainability initiatives
			Maintenance of sustainability activities
			Projects and research
		Structures	Sections of government have sustainability as their focus
			Adequate numbers of staff are appointed to promote and maintain initiatives
		By example	By their actions show how sustainability can be implemented
		Engagement with HEIs	Opportunities for engagement and willingness to engage
	Community groups, NGOs	Engagement with sustainability	Whether the focus of their activities is on sustainability
		Engagement with HEIs	Opportunities for engagement and willingness to engage
	Professional associations and/or Accrediting bodies	Policies	Mission-statement (broad vision) to encourage and support sustainability activities
			Clarity of the capabilities expected in the profession
		Role in accrediting graduates	Whether they have direct control, or are invited to advise HEIs
		By example	By their actions show how sustainability can be implemented
		Engagement with HEIs	Opportunities for engagement and willingness to engage
	Private enterprise	Policies	Mission-statement (broad vision) to encourage and support sustainability activities
		Resources	Construction of sustainability initiatives
			Maintenance of sustainability activities
			Projects and research related to sustainability
		Structures	Sections of government have sustainability as their focus
			Adequate numbers of staff are appointed to promote and maintain initiatives
		By example	By their actions show how sustainability can be implemented
		Engagement with HEIs	Opportunities for engagement and willingness to engage

Table 4.2 continued

Relative to HEI	*Aspect of HEI or group*	*Element*	*Issue*
Internal to HEI	Physical characteristics	Location	Proximity to communities for collaboration
		Size	Space for physical structures as examples of environmental management and sustainability initiatives
		Climate	Solar access; growing seasons; possibilities of biological processes
	Organisational	Resources	Construction of sustainability initiatives
			Maintenance of sustainability activities
			Projects and research
			Support staff
			Capturing savings to fund initiatives
			Staff development funds available
		Policies	Mission-statement (broad vision) to encourage and support sustainability activities
			Avoid perverse-incentives that discourage (or actively counter) sustainability
			For management of resources, pollution control
			For governance that supports respectful, ethical and equitable interactions
			Ethical engagement with the community
			Curriculum that is sustainability focused
		Staffing (in general)	Recruitment encourages equity and sustainability opportunities
			Recognition given to promotion and support of sustainability
			Staff development focuses on sustainability
			Sufficient staff numbers for a Community of Practice to operate
		Structures	Sustainability staff employed
			Sustainability staff in decision-making positions
			Sustainability staff report to top levels of the HEI
			Sustainability staff are supported by a broad-ranging committee, which reports to and engages with the top levels of the HEI
		Culture	Historical connection with sustainability
			Tacit knowledge of sustainability is communicated
			Norms of sustainability are supported by the majority

Table 4.2 continued

Relative to HEI	*Aspect of HEI or group*	*Element*	*Issue*
	Executive staff	Decision-making	Follow the sustainability policies
		Leadership	Actively seek opportunities to promote sustainability in the HEI
		By example	By their actions show how sustainability can be implemented
	General/support staff	Employment conditions	Encourage and enable staff to participate in sustainability thinking and activities
		Reward structures	Positively acknowledge the contributions of individuals and groups
		Communication	Systems encourage sharing of ideas and resources within the HEI and with external colleagues
		Values	Willingness to engage positively with sustainability actions at home and at their HEI
	Students	Background	Experience and enthusiasm for sustainability
		Values	Willingness to engage positively with sustainability actions at home and at their HEI
		Motivation	Willingness to take up opportunities presented in their curriculum to learn and engage with sustainability activity
	Academic staff	Personal and professional values	Whether inclined to support sustainability principles and actions
		By example	By their actions show how sustainability can be implemented
		Disciplinary culture	Extent to which their discipline engages with sustainability
		Personal background	Cultural background and personal experience and enthusiasm for sustainability
		Professional background	Whether through employment or research experience their understanding and enthusiasm for sustainability is facilitated
		Institutional confidence	Having a sense of purpose in the HEI and education generally
		Sense of self	Whether confident to take risks with their teaching and research to incorporate, or actively promote, sustainability
		Pedagogical approach	Either originally appropriate to ESD or sufficiently adaptable to change that way
		Professional development	Openness to undertake PD generally, and to engage in PD for ESD
		Sources of information	Whether they know where to find sustainability information (own and others' research, professional networks, HEI networks)
		Networks	Whether their communities of practice and networks of peers, colleagues and general contacts focus on, or at least include, sustainability
		Reflective capability	Ability to analyse their own values, plans and actions and consider if change is needed.
		Awareness of graduate capabilities	Understanding of the expectations of the employers of their graduates, and the centrality of generic capabilities (closely associated with ESD)

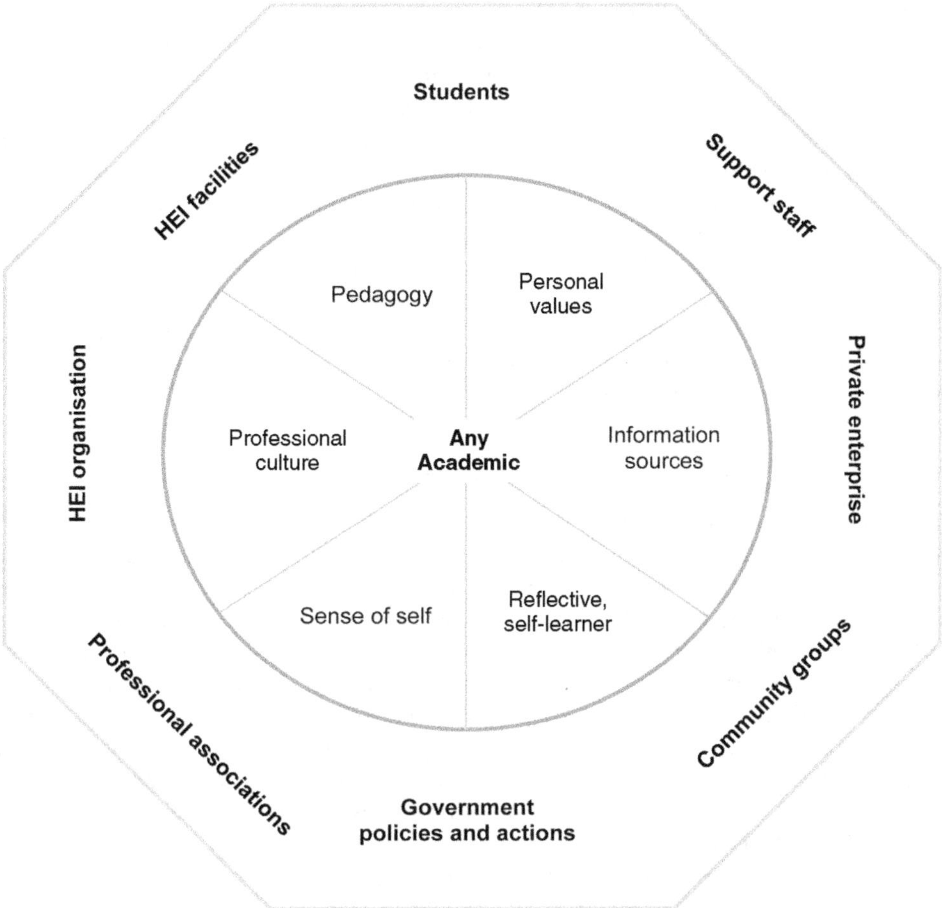

Figure 4.1 Influences on the implementation of education for sustainable development in higher education institutions; emphasising the key role of academics

that require more than this chapter could allow. Rather, this level of investigation must be left to the future work by a variety of researchers.

The facilitating role of academic development

Yet how might we use these ideas? Even though we do not have anything like a precise path for curricular change, nor do we currently have the research that could lead to such a plan, the elements of Table 4.2 and Figure 4.1 provide a starting point for individual academics, or teams, to introduce ESD. Specifically, academic professional development is a direction that links several elements and their related aspects. Introduction of such programmes will require the academics' HEI to have recognised the need for the programme, as part of a policy to introduce ESD, possibly encouraged by government or the actions of other HEIs. There is the possibility too that the professional associations to which academics belong will also have decided to promote sustainability, with related policies and guidance.

The importance of academic development programmes is highlighted by Barth and Rieckmann (2012). In their discussion of the effects of these programmes for ESD they identified that the programmes: 'facilitated the personal competence development of the participating academic staff and changed their teaching practice' (28); offered the opportunity to introduce new and innovative learning and teaching approaches; and 'influenced the general organisational development of the university' (28). They concluded: 'deep-rooted implementation of higher education for sustainable development, can be more effectively facilitated by an approach which links staff development and organisational change' (34).

Here we see, from Table 4.2, a number of elements, associated with the 'internal HEI' aspect of 'organisational', being important; in particular resources, policies, staffing and culture. In addition the majority of elements of the aspect 'academic staff' will become relevant, starting with 'professional development' and 'awareness of graduate capabilities' (to match their teaching with the students' ultimate needs).

Researching for the ESD future

The discussion to date may appear very logical and straightforward. The implication is that if we have diagrams like Table 4.2 and Figure 4.1 then we can develop a checklist to lead our ESD implication. Yet use of the material in this Table and Figure in such a deterministic fashion would be 'courageous' (i.e. risky). While we have some understanding of the ways in which HEIs bring in significant changes, such as that for ESD, we have little evidence of what is the process to follow for curriculum change in an HEI. We have case studies, such as that of Rowe (2002), which describe a change process at particular institutions, but we have little insight to show that the described process would work equally well at another institution. As chapters in this book illustrate, case studies are a most frequent way in which ESD researchers to date have explored the field. Case study results provide us with ideas, but not always the knowledge that is applicable in all, or most, situations.

Some chapters in Part D of this Handbook contribute further case studies that add to the information about implementing ESD, but more research in this topic is needed. I trust that the insights and ideas presented in this Handbook will generate future research to improve our ability to introduce ESD to the curriculum of more HEIs. In the meantime, what can be gained from the likes of Table 4.2 and Figure 4.1?

First, the information presented builds on the results of past research to provide starting points for future researchers to: examine the role of academics; see how the aspects internal to the HEI can facilitate ESD; determine how the aspects external to HEIs can be developed to support ESD; and, considering the interactions of these aspects, and elements, to assess their relative influence in the range of situations that HEIs encounter.

Second, as I have pointed out, the current information should not be taken as the base of a checklist approach for ESD. Rather, the information acts as a caution to those wanting to implement ESD. It shows how many factors interact, and how complicated the curricular change process can be; and made more complicated by no one person or group having control over the change process or its stages. At each stage there will be a range of individuals who have a role, which they may or may not understand, and may or may not choose to support.

Third, cautions are negative and tend to discourage people trying anything. Anyone would be discouraged by the warning notice of a mine-field, however, they would be empowered once they had a map of the field and were able to navigate their way through. Similarly, Table 4.2 and Figure 4.1 provide a map of the features that lead to ESD. They provide a 'road-map' to show what may be encountered and some of the interconnections. Like any map they do not provide all the details, but outline the main features. At this stage in our understanding of curriculum change it is not appropriate to be talking about, or hoping for, the equivalent of a Global Positioning System that would talk us through the path to ESD. Rather, in the journey to ESD our current map will have to be interpreted by the individuals making the journey: each will decide how important the aspects of Table 4.2 will be for their specific HEI.

Many and varied steps to the future

Progress since the 1992 Rio Conference and the beginning of the Decade for Education for Sustainable Development may seem slow. The number of articles, such as the review by Martin *et al.* (2013), indicate that ESD is by no means mainstream in HEIs. Given the complexity of curriculum change and the range of influences that can be identified (see Table 4.2) it is impressive that so much has been achieved; chapters in Part 4 of the Handbook in particular will attest to some of this achievement.

When discussing curricular change generally, Lattuca and Stark (2009) suggest that those promoting a change can ask targeted questions that 'encourage instructors to use rational planning and problem solving modes while also acknowledging the social and political dimensions of change' (325). These questions ask: is there a need for curricular change?; who and what will be affected by the change?; is the proposed change appropriate for the local context?; and what will the change process look like? Such questions can provide the starting point for discussion of the critical elements of ESD, and especially the engagement of the academics who are the key players in the curriculum development and its implementation. Inevitably they will also identify issues to be researched.

As I have argued, any curriculum change, and especially that for ESD which is a relatively new concept for most disciplines, will be slow, probably piecemeal, and will certainly require conscious strategies. The critical players in this change will be the academics, and I have outlined a number of influences that will have to be considered to support academics during this process, or to help convince some that the changes are worthwhile. These influences are presented in Figure 4.1, and given more depth through the elements associated with change presented in Table 4.2.

The influences and elements do not in themselves represent any sort of plan for implementing ESD. Every HEI will have its own unique set of circumstances coming from the aspects listed in Table 4.2. However, within these individual HEIs the influences and elements identified provide a basis for thinking through a strategy for the introduction of ESD. It is unlikely that each influence could be taken into account in the development of a strategy, but being able to recognise how they may affect a plan for curriculum change provides us with a better chance of a successful change, and achievement of ESD.

References

Arnold, G.B., 2004. 'Symbolic Politics and Institutional Boundaries in Curriculum Reform: The case of National Sectarian University', *Journal of Higher Education*, 75(5), 572–93.

Arthur, M.M.L., 2007. 'Getting Away from the Basics: Competing Explanations for Curricular Change'. http://search.proquest.com/docview/304829822/fulltextPDF/CC55066984844708PQ/1?accountid=13552 [accessed 12 February 2015].

Barth, M., 2013. 'Many Roads Lead to Sustainability: a Process Orientated Analysis of Change in Higher Education', *International Journal of Sustainability in Higher Education*, 14(2), 160–75.

Barth, M. and Rieckmann, M., 2012. 'Academic Staff Development as a Catalyst for Curriculum Change towards Education for Sustainable Development: An Output Perspective', *Journal of Cleaner Production*, 26(1), 28–36.

Blackmore, P. and Kandiko, C.B., 2012. 'Change: Processes and Resources', in Blackmore, P. and Kandiko, C.B. (eds), *Strategic Curriculum Change: Global Trends in Universitie.* London: Routledge, 111–27.

Bregha, F., Benidickson, J., Gamble, D., Shillington, T. and Weick, E., 1990. *The Integration of Environmental Considerations into Government Policy*, report for the Canadian Environmental Assessment Research Council, Hull. Quebec: Canadian Environmental Assessment Research Council.

de la Harpe, B. and Radloff, A., 2003. 'The Challenges of Integrating Generic Skills at Two Australian Universities' [Special Edition], *Staff and Education Development International*, 7(3), 235–44.

de la Harpe, B. and Thomas, I., 2009. 'Curriculum Change in Universities: Why Education for Sustainable Development is so Tough', *Journal of Education for Sustainable Development,* 3(1), 75–85.

Dovers, S., 1999. 'Institutionalising Ecologically Sustainable Development: Promises, Problems and Prospects', in Walker, K. and Crowley, K. (eds), *Australian Environmental Policy 2: Studies in Decline + Devolution*. Sydney: UNSW Press, 204–23.

Eckel, P.D. and Kezar, A.J., 2002. 'The Effect of Institutional Culture on Change Strategies in Higher Education: Universal Principles or Culturally Responsive Concepts?' *Journal of Higher Education*, 73(4), 435–60.

Eckel, P., Green, M., Hill, B., and Mallon, W., 1999. *Taking Charge of Change: A Primer for Colleges and Universities.* Washington DC: American Council on Education.

Education for Sustainable Development Unit (no date). *Definition of ESD.* www.unescobkk.org/education/esd-unit/definition-of-esd/ [accessed 12 February 2015].

Ford, M., 2002. *Beyond the Modern University: Towards a Constructive Post-Modern University*. Westport, CT: Praeger.

Hannan, A., English, S. and Silver, H., 1999. 'Why Innovate? Some Preliminary Findings from a Research Project on "Innovations in Teaching and Learning in Higher Education"', *Studies in Higher Education*, 24(3), 279–89

Hegarty, K., 2008. 'Sustaining Knowledges: Using Communities of Practice to Foster Sustainability Literacy in Disciplines and Curriculum', *Ed.- The RMIT Learning and Teaching Journal*, 3(2), [online]. http://emedia.rmit.edu.au/edjournal/node/365 [accessed 12 February 2015].

Higher Education Statistics Agency, no date. *Students and Qualifiers Data Tables.* www.hesa.ac.uk/index.php/content/view/1973/239/ [accessed 12 February 2015].

Hill, M., 2005. *The Public Policy Process*, 4th edn. Harlow: Pearson-Longman.

Hogwood, B. and Gunn, L., 1989. *Policy Analysis for the Real World.* Oxford: Oxford University Press.

Holdsworth, S., Wyborn, C., Bekessy, S. and Thomas, I., 2008. 'Professional Development for Education for Sustainability: How Advanced are Australian Universities?', *International Journal of Sustainability in Higher Education*, 9(2), 131–46.

Holley, K.A., 2009. 'Interdisciplinary Strategies as Transformative Change in Higher Education', *Innovative Higher Education*, 34(5), 331–44.

Kotter, J.P., 1996. *Leading Change.* Cambridge, MA: Harvard Business School Press.

Lang, J., Thomas, I. and Wilson, A., 2006. 'Education for Sustainability in Australian Universities: Where is the Action?' *Australian Journal for Environmental Education*, 22(2), 45–58.

Larkins, F., 2012. *Student and Teaching Staff Trends in Selected Australian Universities*, LH Martin Institute. [online]. www.lhmartininstitute.edu.au/insights-blog/2012/03/81-student-and-teaching-staff-trends-in-selected-australian-universities [accessed 12 February 2015].

Lattuca, L.R. and Stark, J.S., 2009. *Shaping the College Curriculum – Academic Plans in Context*, 2nd edn. San Francisco, CA: Jossey-Bass.

Leask, B., 2001. 'Internationalisation: Changing Contexts and their Implications for Teaching, Learning and Assessment', in Richardson, L. and Lidstone, J. (eds), *Flexible Learning for a Flexible Society*, Proceedings of ASET-HERDSA 2000 Conference, Toowoomba, Qld, 2–5 July 2000. ASET and HERDSA, 389–401.

Lotz-Sisitka, H. and Lupele, J., 2006. 'Curriculum Transformation in Higher Education Institutions: Some Perspectives from Africa', in Holmberg, J. and Samuelsson, B.E. (eds), *Drivers and Barriers for Implementing Sustainable Development in Higher Education*, Göteborg Workshop, 7–9 December, UNESCO Education for Sustainable Development in Action, Technical Paper No.3. Paris: UNESCO, 49–54.

Marginson, S. and Considine, M., 2000. *The Enterprise University: Power, Governance and Reinvention in Australia.* Cambridge: Cambridge University Press.

Martin, S. Dawe, G. and Jucker, R., 2006. 'Embedding Education for Sustainable Development in Higher Education in the UK', in Holmberg, J. and Samuelsson, B.E. (eds), *Drivers and Barriers for Implementing*

Sustainable Development in Higher Education, Göteborg Workshop, 7–9 December, UNESCO Education for Sustainable Development in Action, Technical Paper No.3. Paris: UNESCO, 59–67.

Martin, S., Dillon, J., Higgins, P., Peters, C. and Scott, W., 2013. 'Divergent Evolution in Education for Sustainable Development Policy in the United Kingdom: Current Status, Best Practice, and Opportunities for the Future', *Sustainability*, 5(4), 1522–44.

Merton, P., Froyd, J.E., Clark, M.C. and Richarson, J., 2009. 'A Case Study of Relationships between Organizational Culture and Curricular Change in Engineering Education', *Innovation in Higher Education*, 34(4), 219–33.

Moore, J., 2005. 'Seven Recommendations for Creating Sustainability Education at the University Level: A Guide for Change Agents', *International Journal of Sustainability in Higher Education*, 6(4), 326–39.

Mulder, K.F. and Jansen, J.L.A., 2006. 'Integrating Sustainable Development in Engineering Education Reshaping University Education by Organizational Learning', in Holmberg, J. and Samuelsson, B.E. (eds), *Drivers and Barriers for Implementing Sustainable Development in Higher Education*, Göteborg Workshop, 7–9 December, UNESCO Education for Sustainable Development in Action, Technical Paper No.3. Paris: UNESCO, 69–73.

National Center for Education Statistics, no date. *Fast Facts*. http://nces.ed.gov/fastfacts/display.asp?id=98 [accessed 12 February 2015].

Roger, S., 2011. 'Good Practice Guide 3: Principles of Curriculum Renewal and Change', in *Building Capacity among Emerging Occupational Therapy Academic Leaders in curriculum Renewal and Evaluation at UQ and Nationally*. Canberra: Office for Learning and Teaching, Australian Government. www.olt.gov.au/resource-building-capacity-among-emerging-occupational-therapy-academic-leaders-curriculum-renewal-a [accessed 12 February 2015].

Rowe, D., 2002. 'Environmental Literacy and Sustainability as Core Requirements: Success Stories and Models', in Filho, W.L. (ed.), *Teaching Sustainability at Universities: Towards Curriculum Greening*. Frankfurt: Peter Lang, 79–104.

Shi, C., 2006. 'Exploring Effective Approaches For "Education for Sustainable Development" in Universities of China', in Holmberg, J. and Samuelsson, B.E. (eds), *Drivers and Barriers for Implementing Sustainable Development in Higher Education*, Göteborg Workshop, 7–9 December, UNESCO Education for Sustainable Development in Action, Technical Paper No.3. Paris: UNESCO, 83–7.

Simsek, H. and Louis. K.S., 1994. 'Organizational Change as Paradigm Shift: Analysis of the Change Process in a Large, Public University', *Journal of Higher Education*, 65(6), 670–95.

Sterling, S., 2012. *The Future Fit Framework: An Introductory Guide to Teaching and Learning for Sustainability in HE*. London: The Higher Education Academy. https://www.heacademy.ac.uk/sites/default/files/Future_Fit_270412_1435.pdf [accessed 28 April 2013].

Thomas, I., 2007. *Environmental Policy: Australian Practice in the Context of Theory*. Sydney: Federation Press.

Thomas, I., Hegarty, K. and Holdsworth, S., 2012. 'The Education for Sustainability Jig-Saw Puzzle: Implementation in Universities', *Creative Education*, 3, Special Issue, 840–6.

Turpin-Marion, S., Espinosa-Valdemar, R.M., Juárez-Nájera, M. and Cisneros-Ramos, A., 2006. 'Barriers for Incorporating the Environmental Perspective into Engineering Programs in a Mexican University', in Holmberg, J. and Samuelsson, B.E. (eds), *Drivers and Barriers for Implementing Sustainable Development in Higher Education*, Göteborg Workshop, 7–9 December, UNESCO Education for Sustainable Development in Action, Technical Paper No.3. Paris: UNESCO, 97–102.

UNESCO, 2005. *UN Decade of Education for Sustainable Development, 2005–2014*; The DESD at a glance. http://unesdoc.unesco.org/images/0014/001416/141629e.pdf [accessed 12 February 2015].

Uchiyama, K.P. and Radin, J.L., 2009. 'Curriculum Mapping in Higher Education: A Vehicle for Collaboration', *Innovation in Higher Education*, 33(4), 271–80.

van der Leeuw, S., Wiek, A., Harlow, J. and Buize, A., 2012. 'How Much Time do we Have? Urgency and Rhetoric in Sustainability Science', *Sustainability Science*, 7 (Supplement 1), 115–20.

5

LITURGY AND GLASS CEILING IN THE PROCESS OF STRENGTHENING THE SUSTAINABILITY IN INSTITUTIONS OF HIGHER EDUCATION

A perspective from Ibero-America

Edgar J. González-Gaudiano, Pablo Á. Meira-Cartea and Cynthia N. Martínez-Fernández

Some basic background

The incorporation of sustainability in higher education institutions in the region of Ibero-America (Latin America, Spain and Portugal) is a relatively recent process. Among its most remote antecedents stand out the creation of the International Training Centre of Environmental Science (CIFCA, for its acronym in Spanish) in 1975 and, of particular interest for the purposes of this essay, the Seminar on University and Environment in Latin America and the Caribbean, held in Bogotá, Colombia, in 1985.[1]

CIFCA started its activities with an intensive programme that included a series of publications and seminars, such as the Seminar on Science, Research and Environment, also convened by United Nations Environmental Programme (UNEP) in January 1982 (Bogotá). Its main intention was to analyse the situation of basic and applied environmental research in the region, with emphasis on conceptual and methodological aspects of different disciplines, to observe and analyse the way they have been affected by the emergence of environmental problems (Leff 1986). A few years earlier it had released the first inventory of curricula related to the environment and natural resources offered by the universities in the region. It was called Panorama of Environmental Higher Education in Latin America (1977).

Subsequently, the Seminar on University and Environment continued this undertaking, emphasising the important role of universities in developmental processes in the region and, therefore, the imperative to link higher education with environmental issues. The seminar discussed two important documents (Ruscheinsky *et al.* 2014). The first one was 'Ten Theses on Environment in Latin America' by Fernando Tudela (1991) which states that the current international economic order is the one that has determined, in Latin American countries, a development style that causes the degradation of ecosystems as well as an impoverishment of a vast part of the population. Diverse forms of exploitation of natural resources produce a deterioration that greatly exceeds the regenerative capacity of natural systems. The report also states that the region is endowed with sufficient natural resources to meet the basic needs of its population and also with an ecological and human potential to induce a sustained development process. Nevertheless an unfortunate mismanagement of resources has led either to the elimination or drastic alteration of natural ecosystems.

In that document environment is conceived as a productive potential for an alternative, equitable and sustainable development based on the integrated management of their ecological, technological and cultural resources so that solutions to specific environmental problems ultimately depend on a new organisational capacity of society as a whole based on community cultural values, people's creativity and innovative potential. Such solutions cannot be located out of an adequate framework of political will that strives to break with the economic, ideological and technological dependence, and leads forward the conditions conducive to a participatory and democratic management of resources.

The other document discussed at the seminar was 'The Charter of Bogotá on University and Environment in Latin America' (González-Gaudiano 1989). It stated that the introduction of the environmental dimension into higher education requires rethinking the role of the university as a primordial institution in society, and in the context of the new world order, in which Latin American and Caribbean realities are configured. Therefore, it is necessary to insist on the deep significance and role of the university as a laboratory of contemporary reality considering the concrete conditions of the region in the global context. Hence the incorporation of environmental issues in university functions and the internalisation of the environmental dimension in the production of knowledge, restate the problem of interdisciplinary research and teaching, and in that context, the responsibility of universities in the process of development of our countries.

The Charter of Bogota also emphasises that the environmental issues have generated new interdisciplinary themes which require outstripping previous multidisciplinary efforts and methods. These issues are, among others, the need for the decentralisation of power and economic processes based on environmental criteria, and the generation of a more balanced development style in the region – ecologically sustainable, which allows a more democratic management of productive resources.

It is in such a framework where complex and global problems such as the rationality of production processes, food requirements of our peoples, the integrated management of our resources, meeting the basic necessities of the population and improving their quality life can be analysed.

Sustainability as a liturgical event

The previous background, and some other antecedents, allows us to emphasise that the notion of environment that has prevailed in our region has been characterised by strong economic and political constituents. It has been understood therefore as a complex concept with deep historical and cultural roots. This conception prevents us from understanding the environment just as the mere physical medium from which ecosystem services are derived. Furthermore, it restrains us from perceiving it as a natural capital that provides goods and services, seen in the economist jargon as positive externalities that contribute to increase the wellbeing of people and communities (Barzev 2002). By contrast, the environment has been assumed as a complex intersection among human and natural systems in specific sociocultural frames.

Thus when the Brundtland Report was published (1987), it became clear that the concept of sustainable development is a political and not a scientific notion, whose expectations are deposited mainly in the technological potential and not in the social. On the other hand, the necessary articulation of ecological, social and economic components was implicit in the very concept of environment in the region. The fact of being a political notion caused the definitions of sustainable development to enter below a halo of ambiguity that was the breeding ground which led to their success (Naredo 1997), enabling it to be used as an empty signifier in the discursive constellation of varied political, economic and environmental affiliations (González-Gaudiano 2009). However that same ambiguity has been one of the main difficulties in implementing public policies related to the environment.

The conceptual debate on sustainable development was positioned around two nodal points: 1) its vision focused on the intergenerational rather than on the intragenerational aspect, and 2) the association with the discredited notion of development, which some authors assume as an oxymoron (Meira Cartea 2005). The discussion soon gave birth to a distinct proposal that revalued critical thinking, which had been metabolised by the system. Hence sustainability emerged as something different to sustainable development and in that debate a distinction between strong and weak sustainability was established; such categories have been questioned (Martínez-Alier 1995; Beckerman 1994). The conceptual debate perseveres but the clear operational dimensions of the two proposals has still not been clarified, even if the definition of indicators has progressed (United Nations 2007; Gutiérrez Garza and González-Gaudiano 2010; Benayas del Álamo 2014b; Complexus 2013).

Nevertheless more than 1,000 higher education institutions have signed declarations on the implementation of sustainability, often adopting the definition of 'Our Common Future' (WCED 1987). Numerous universities have eluded the discussion about it and used interchangeably sustainability and sustainable development (Tilbury 2007). In other words, without exception, in the university arena a conceptual confusion prevails eschewing the political implications of using one or another concept. They are used to apply conventionally accepted definitions, although the vast majority tends to defend a bias view of it as environmental sustainability. Moreover, a large number of such declarations and policies of the higher education sector encourages the naive belief that we can solve the great crisis from within academia. The full inscription of institutional sustainability policies boisterously announced in documents and speeches by authorities has become a kind of liturgical act.

In the region in question, the public university faces a very precarious and uncertain situation. In the Americas the development experienced by the economies of emerging countries such as Mexico, Brazil and Chile is forcing us to rethink – very often in a traumatic way – the role of training systems and advanced research, mainly of public university systems, caught between market requirements, its own inertia and the needs of their societies of reference. In the Iberian countries, Spain and Portugal, academic institutions, mainly public, have been heavily impacted by an economic crisis that has drastically lessen its funding and, as if it could not get any worse, they have suffered a reduction of their academic autonomy for the sake of the deficit control in order to meet the debt transferred from the banking system to the states.

On both sides of the Atlantic Ocean it is easy to realise that underlying the particularities of the crisis of each national university system is the crisis of the public university. One can clearly perceive the project to predispose every social device to the service of the market interests, be they global, dominated by a neoliberal, developmental and competitive logic that is at odds with the purpose of enlightened, modern and humanistic *universitas*. In this scenario, on the one hand, society as a whole urges it increasingly to meet their needs as well as to encourage innovation processes of very different types and scopes; secondly, the state increasingly restricts their required funding and seeks to limit their autonomy. Threefold challenged by society, the state and the global market, universities do not seem able to face many challenges (Santos 1998), especially the so complex defiance of injecting sustainability in their structure, operation and substantive functions.

Shriberg and Tallent (2003) point out that from Taillores, the field of sustainability in higher education institutions (HEIs) has been nurtured with many theoretical recommendations and lessons as well as with learned narratives. However, nor enough data, deep rigorous empirical evidence or theoretical developments are being offered. Thus, universities and educators lack a coordinated evaluation of initiatives on campuses to provide a well-founded approach for success.

Those who encourage sustainability in HEIs still insist on finding a guiding and unifying strategy for all universities, despite their marked differences. The results of a survey of 59 American universities and colleges conducted by the University Leaders for a Sustainable Future (ULSF) in 2001 reveal that the usual operational measures of campus waste separation predominate, but resistance to more ambitious activities such as promoting alternative transport measures or the use of renewable energy is strongly shown. Members of these universities – signatories of the Declaration of Taillores – answered in this survey that the implementation of sustainable proposals have as a main motivation the contribution to institutional reputation and cost savings (Shriberg 2002).

On the other hand, the integration of sustainability in research and the curriculum is manifested in various patterns and its approval depends on academic committees and authorities which are not usually favourable to transform traditions and customs. Besides, policies for sustainability are neither part of the main institutional agenda nor are generally applicable to the entire campus; faculties and centres are added slowly to the actions under uncoordinated efforts; bureaucratic and hierarchical structures discourage any advance – even if precarious – in sustainability and recurrently allege financial issues as the main constraint, although the true underlying problem is a deep lack of understanding and commitment from senior management in relation to sustainability.

Such an intricate web of situations that resist change to promote nodal steps and to move towards sustainability does not necessarily involve finding a one and only inclusive model. Definitively this should not be seen as the search for a holy grail. As a matter of fact, like any other institution, universities function accordingly to their own identities, dressed in specific socio-historical contexts, and adopt a new ethos through slow processes. A more appropriate question would be to discover: What is expected from universities in relation to the transition towards sustainability? If the answer to the crisis of civilisation relies on the field of sustainability then: Why are so few universities working on it? This is a question that Leal Filho had already raised in 2000.

Leal Filho (2000) performed a study similar to USLF but following more qualitative strategies. His intention was to build an approximate profile of the reasons why universities are reluctant to actively pursue goals towards sustainability. The research was conducted with 40 European universities through interviews and informal discussions, whose investigation focused on two axes: 1) What is your personal opinion about sustainability? and 2) What is perceived as an obstacle to achieve sustainability in the context of your institutions? Leal Filho sought to identify whether the issue of sustainability was considered to be important. As for obstacles, he explored those areas where action is needed. Going back to the discussion about the polysemy of sustainability and sustainable development in higher education institutions, in Leal Filho results show that this issue is a much more complex one because various confusions and misunderstandings, which the author describes as 'false thoughts', were detected (Leal Filho 2000):

- Sustainability is too abstract. The representatives of universities address the issue as abstract and remote from reality.
- Sustainability is very wide. So wide that it can be applied to any area of the university and some activities can be considered as sustainable even when they are not.
- Sustainability is an issue only for specialists. There is the belief that highly qualified staff are needed to implement sustainability.
- Sustainability does not have any scientific basis. Although referred to a lesser extent, this is still an argument for inaction.
- Sustainability is expensive. The financial resources for its implementation are not justified.

While USLF questions the fulfilment of international commitments, Leal Filho ponders in different investigations: Why is it so difficult to understand sustainability on an operational level? Making an addition to the above list of ideas about obstacles, Waas *et al.* (2012) argue that absence of vision on the part of the leaders, lack of motivation, lack of coordination and financial resources, as well as a rigid structure of the organisation around the faculties of universities, make it very difficult to achieve an integrative thinking, cooperation and interdisciplinary learning. Sustainability is assumed as a patch and not as an integrated dimension. Academics perceive that scientific basis for a proper operation is missing. Some others even consider it a radical issue that interferes with academic freedom since it tends to blur the academic boundaries (Waas *et al.* 2012).

From the point of view of institutional policies it is observed that there is no consistency with the alleged purpose of transcending towards a sustainable university. Thus, HEIs have conducted their planning processes for sustainability independently of other academic plans, without the proper linkage through a transverse plan. A masterfully crafted plan is of little help if its effects are reduced to a limited scope of action, due to the fact that it is opposed to hierarchically more important policies or policies that maintain an institutional inertia.

In sum, a problem that frames such a situation is the lack of a full understanding of the significance of sustainability in our times, and the difficulties of putting it into practice within universities. The underlying conflict is the resistance shown by HEIs —but not only by them – to substantial changes in their academic and management structure, the main effect of which is that sustainability proposals crash against a glass ceiling in higher education institutions.

The glass ceiling

When migrating the glass ceiling concept of the feminist field towards the analysis of university environmentalisation processes in Ibero-America we want to draw attention to a contradictory reality. After two decades, the majority of HEIs that endorse more or less ambitious environmentalisation plans or programmes, in many cases reinforced with administrative structures (vice-rectories, offices, services) specifically focused on its application. The universities in the region that have failed to incorporate sustainability into their strategic social responsibility objectives are very few, thus formally recognising the need for changes in management and in focusing their main functions (training, research and extension) towards that horizon. However, this formal progress does not translate itself into deep structural transformations of the university community. Nor has it led to the transformation of these institutions in environmental coherence models for the societies they serve. Just as it occurs in gender politics, a rhetoric definition of a doctrine that strategically focuses on the environmentalisation of universities ends in a crash against strongly established social and economic barriers as well as an academic inertia that prevents real and significant progress. That is to say, there is a considerable distance between the devised environmentalisation goals and the final achievements.

What are the barriers and obstacles implied in the glass ceiling metaphor made of? To begin with, in the same way that gender equality policies collide with patriarchal and sexist structures that constitute a very subtle and difficult barrier to traverse to the extent that it can permeate the culture at all levels and dimensions of social life, it is possible that policies designed to establish universities in the wave of sustainability also collide with other structural barriers linked to developmental and mercantilist conceptions of society. Undeniably, the latter permeate and determine increasingly intense HEIs policies and socio-cultural patterns; the members of the university community – from the faculty to the students themselves – are guided by them. Both the generation of knowledge and the provision of higher education, even in public universities are subjected to growing commercialisation; this is a clear indicator of the process of submission of HEIs to the interests and imperatives of the market.

The trivialisation of environmental sustainability in HEIs (increasingly diluted in a concept of 'social responsibility' that has been transferred from the world of the private enterprise) is part of the growing mismatch between a formal pro-environmental strategic discourse and political, economic and academic practices in which the market and criteria interests prevail. In this sense, think about the growing importance of competition between universities and academic bodies: how incoherent rankings can be from the point of view of a socially and environmentally responsible discourse. This also affects environmental sustainability policies. As a whole, it is not at all different to what is happening globally, where the spheres of social life tend to be increasingly colonised by the dogmas of growth and free-market in its most radical phase of neoliberal capitalism.

To this structural barrier related to the glass ceiling – undoubtedly the most powerful and insidious – that hinders progress towards sustainability, one must add some others related to the difficulty of HEIs to break the inertia inherited from the nineteenth century and compartmentalised view of knowledge, both in the field of research and in the organisation of disciplinary curriculum. In fact, most of the evaluative studies on university environmentalisation policies in Ibero-America acknowledge that this progress has been barely achieved in the field of curriculum environmentalisation as well as in the incorporation of the complexity of environmental problems (and not only of scientific knowledge associated with these problems) to the training curriculum and research programmes. Available experiences, even if they are innovative and exemplary of transdisciplinary academic models to make some progress in this line, are still very few and specific, limited to small groups of innovative teachers in a career or a faculty, but with poor incidence in the development of more general training plans (Geli *et al.* 2003; Aznar *et al.* 2011).

Nor do we think that these barriers in the university area are particularly distinctive in our region if compared to some other areas of the planet. For example, the global report prepared in 2012 by the Global University Network for Innovation (GUNI-UNESCO) on the challenges and commitments of universities with sustainability, points out that one of the major difficulties that they face is to introduce changes in a fundamentally unsustainable social context. A limitation identified precisely in this study is the disciplinary and overtly compartmentalised structure that persists in most universities, which inhibits an inclusive and global approach to the environmental crisis. In the report it is also observed that there is a significant commitment based on technological innovation without discussing the limitations involved in applying solutions. Another observation resides in the teacher programmes that often contain a hidden agenda based on unsustainable actions that are not conducive to reflection on the ethical dilemmas associated with human interaction with environment practices. In regard to research, the report claims that it seems to be more focused on the impact factor of publications than in promoting the social and environmental relevance of advances and solutions produced by researchers.

As Benayas del Álamo (2014a: 9) points out, one can identify some other limitations and barriers that Ibero-American universities are facing today, but their main deficiency 'is that they are not involving their teachers and teaching their students and future leaders of society on the principles of sustainability', since 'they have not made significant progress for students of various careers … to receive basic training to build an economic and social system based on the principles of sustainability'. In other words, sustainability has permeated only superficially and in a very limited way into the culture of the university community. All of this takes place even despite the supposedly optimal conditions for institutions to which a specific social responsibility inherent to its mission is attributed: to create scientific and humanistic knowledge useful in the training of the professional and intellectual elites of their reference societies. It is hard to think that universities can serve as models to generate profound social changes in the medium or long term relationship with the biosphere if their training of students continues to reproduce fundamental knowledge, cultural practices and production models that are environmentally unsustainable and socially unjust since they have placed us on the threshold of a socio-environmental collapse.

Do those Ibero-American university communities that are more involved in environmentalisation perceive the existence of this 'glass ceiling'? There are not many studies in this respect, but there are some contributions that may help to answer this question. For example, UNIVERSIA virtual platform has made a survey of the university community as part of the preparatory activities of the III Latin American Meeting of Rectors, held between 28 and 29 July 2014 in Rio de Janeiro, under the slogan 'The University of XXI Century: A Reflection from Latin America'.[2] In that consultation the following question was asked: 'Do Ibero American universities fulfil their role as leaders of socio-environmental sustainability?'

The university experts that participated in the survey could choose between two possible answers. The first one stated that universities have made in recent years significant efforts to make commitments and implement specific measures related to sustainability, with activities in the field of managing their campus, expanding and diversifying green areas, improving waste management and hazardous waste collection, reducing energy consumption and promoting alternative forms of transportation. Those who chose this option assumed that higher education institutions are clearly moving towards sustainability. In contrast, the alternative answer considered that the HEIs are not meeting the challenge of sustainability; that is, although they have made some first steps, there is still a long way to go since in most universities sustainability policies 'are emerging, rare and isolated, lacking a global plan of action that changes profoundly the way in which the university functions'.[3] The main shortcoming was the already mentioned disconnection between university community and the main principles of sustainability.

Of the 156 Latin American experts who responded to the survey – a large representation of the university area – 70 per cent opted for the second option, i.e. the existence of little progress in the response of universities to the challenge of sustainability; while only 30 per cent acknowledged that there have been significant advances in this way. Even more relevant than the quantitative data are some of the arguments used by experts to justify their choices since they point out precisely the existence of multiple barriers and inertia in the universities that either block or slow progress towards sustainability, even when contemplated as a target in the strategic horizon of its universities.

It should be noted that many experts who opted for the pessimistic view nevertheless recognise that there have been some advances, even if clearly valued as partial and insufficient. The

Spanish case exemplifies this situation. Recent reports have been made about Spanish universities that have incorporated the principles and objectives of environmental sustainability since the mid-1990s up to the middle of the first decade of this century, are in agreement with the idea that some progress has been made in areas such as urban and architectural campus management, treatment of waste and reduction of energy consumption (Alba *et al.* 2011; Comisión Técnica de la Estrategia Universidad-2015 2011; Larrán 2014). Many of these advances were unavoidable for universities, such as the application of normative-legal EU and national frameworks for the proper control and management of toxic and hazardous waste generated in the university activity. Others are more inclined to obey economic reasons than pro-environmental ones, such as savings in energy consumption. Faced with relatively important advances in the field of management, however, these reports indicate limited progress in the impregnation of the culture of sustainability in university communities, in the curriculum environmentalisation, in the necessary research work and in the role of universities as models of environmental coherence for society as a whole. A very important fact is that virtually no Spanish university monitors systematically the evolution of its ecological footprint, although some of them have made significant efforts in this regard.[4] Another observed deficiency is the lack of visibility of environmentalisation plans for the same university communities. These reports agree in the remark that this stalemate worsened with the outbreak of the economic crisis in 2007, causing significant cuts in funding for public universities that have limited further development of still incipient policies for environmentalisation.

Beyond the glass ceiling

The ability to break the glass ceiling that limits the transition into a deep environmental sustainability in the work of Ibero-American universities possibly requires rethinking and reformulating strategic frameworks for action that have been followed so far. There have been significant advances, and they must be consolidated, particularly in the field of management. But the initiatives developed in order that HEIs internalise the culture of sustainability and are able to disseminate it to the whole of society have scarcely achieved the permeation of the values and practices of the university community.

In fact, Ibero-American universities are at a crossroads. On the one hand, the pressures of the market strongly act to put HEIs training resources and researchers into its own service; but, on the other hand, there are very strong social demands for the university to put this potential into service of the welfare, social equality and proper management and distribution of common goods within their social contexts. The deterioration of public university systems in Spain and Portugal as a result of unbridled financial, social and economic crisis since 2007 in southern Europe, is highlighting the conflict between a type of higher education subordinated to the interests of the market – identified by the neoliberal discourse with the interests of society – and a type of higher education that serves the interests and requirements of society. At least in the Iberian scenario, the impact of the crisis in their university systems goes far beyond the financial constraints and affects the very conception and utilities that need to put their skills into the service of society. The sustainability plans painstakingly designed in the last decade of the last century and the first half of this, are either frozen or backward, due to scarce funding and organisational structures that barely remain or languish waiting for their disappearance. And what is worse, without the university communities have realised kick for recognition and assessment strategies, policies and programs of sustainability had before within the same university communities.

The commodification of higher education, with a growing private supply and an increasing pressure to reduce both funding and autonomy of public universities, is being reinforced by the imposition of criteria and evaluation indicators pondering the quality and academic excellence in terms of its profitability and its ability to respond to the demands of the market. Any other social or environmental purpose is considered secondary or, at most, subject to the neoliberal vision that pervades and determines everything.

It is possible to state that we cannot see the forest (the crisis of sustainability in universities) for the trees (indicators). Many of the HEIs networks constituted within states in Ibero-America and even transnationally have devised certain systems of indicators to assess progress in the process of university environmental sustainability. No doubt they are necessary initiatives, but the underlying competitive logic of the rankings can be also perceived; this logic is very important in university policies because they are focused on competition and efficiency, seeking to transfer into university policies the same criteria and standards of success used in the business world. These assessment processes are based on generalised batteries and indicators, which are applied with varying degrees of critical capacity, but often ignore the anthropological, ideological and social model to which university policy should respond.

In countries like Spain this fundamental conflict is increasingly evident and is revealed through the different approaches to assessing university sustainability. Face to face with systemic reports designed to consolidate progress and identify alternatives and best practices to overcome the glass ceiling in those areas in which these advances have been limited (CADEP 2011; Comisión Técnica de la Estrategia Universidad-2015 2011), some other studies transfer into academic practices, a language and a philosophy of evaluation of social responsibility good and proper for the business world (Larrán 2014), making a characterisation of the sectors that integrate the university community as 'employees', 'clients' or 'providers'.

Furthermore, whichever the approach, indicators are susceptible to turning a process that is cooperative and supportive necessarily – core values in a culture of deep sustainability – into a competitive process followed to enter the rankings that universities use in their marketing strategies forced upon them by the struggle to attract increasingly scarce public and private resources. What the protocols used to develop the rankings of existing environmental sustainability fail to demonstrate – and probably cannot be demonstrated at all – is whether those universities at the top have developed in their university community and social environment a truly alternative culture with respect to the causes of the socio-environmental crisis or if they have simply introduced some more or less superficial changes in areas that may be important (waste management, energy conservation, awareness-raising on mobility, etc.), but that do not really involve a transformation of the university in regard to the key elements of sustainability culture.

From this perspective, the challenge of universities with reference to sustainability does not lie only in the field of environmentalisation of the management, knowledge creation or curriculum. Neither in its relationship with their communities of reference and society as a whole, although in this dimension it is obviously a requirement to rethink and reformulate its role with respect to the socio-environmental crisis and its governance. The central question must be now, at least in Ibero-American universities on both sides of the Atlantic, how to challenge an institutional status conditioned by the market hegemony and its insidious strategy to destroy management mechanisms and democratic deliberation in universities, which are the basis of their academic, political and economic autonomy. Fiscal crisis is the small scale dynamite that is being used for a demolition without explosives. But this demolition is accompanied by a series of strategies inspired by neoliberal competitiveness (such as producing knowledge, training, seeking 'clients', generating 'profitable' patents, etc.) that are valued as supreme goals. The commodification of knowledge through those companies that manage publishers, academic journals and databases, the treatment of patents and their transfer to the private sector, the increasing commodification of training subject to the laws of supply and demand but not to social interest or criteria of equity and equality of opportunity, etc., are some of the manifestations that this neoliberal inspiration derives from. The knowledge society augured by UNESCO in the 1980s and 1990s has turned into a society of knowledge understood as a commodity, accordingly to which universities are asked to define their role and identity: submission or critical spirit.

Are there any alternative approaches that allow HEIs to question this stage and respond more realistically to the challenges of socio-environmental crisis? Like any attempt to develop a praxis against the hegemony of the market, this does not have an easy solution, and even more, it is hard to imagine possible practical alternatives. The Ibero-American university conjuncture, as has been characterised here, tends to prevail and become naturalised as the only one possible, presenting low margins for innovation and change. Here we seek to open, even if hypothetically, some other strategies to try to build universities in which the culture of sustainability and social contexts can be permeated.

It is common to refer to the university as a 'community'. In fact, this term is frequently used in the documentation governing their administrative, teaching and research activities, as well as its social outreach activity. We emphasise the idea that these institutions are notable for being composed of a body of people who have common interests, in reference to knowledge, management or professional development. Being a 'body' means that it consists of unique and individual elements; however, sharing the same identity and sense of belonging to a common institutional framework.

The 'university community' is an institutional aggregate that performs functions of public interest (mainly teaching and research) and is a type of key organisation in the education system of any modern state. It also has well-structured and differentiated organs, normally equipped with a high degree of autonomy and a democratic character to a certain extent, because we should not forget that it preserves a strong stratified component. Since they are close to the sources of scientific, technical and humanistic knowledge, it is also true that university communities have varying degrees of social prestige in society

As an institution, the University (capitalised) is assumed to possess the ability to exert a great influence on its members, balancing between safeguarding the status quo and the constant renewal of its structures and models of academic, scientific and administrative organisation. Nevertheless, the expectations generated in the societies they serve are often contradictory: it is expected that HEIs are at the pinnacle of social innovation – since they are in a privileged position in terms of production and access to knowledge; in contrast, they are also expected to be conservative, since neither sudden nor radical changes are well tolerated. Hence the frequent accusation that university communities live outside of reality, while they are expected to offer innovative and effective solutions to the challenges and uncertainties posed by that same reality in the Ibero-American social space.

Related to sustainability, the university can be understood as 'a human activity, embedded in a territory, influential on a certain area, that produces a series of impacts over the environment' (Alba *et al.* 2011: 147). We can derive from this notion that the measures taken by the university in regard to how to regulate its activity in relation to environmental issues have an impact on the community of persons who manages and, in a parallel manner, on other communities related to it, be it directly or indirectly; thus it becomes an inspiring 'model' of change for other institutional and social contexts.

The formulas to enter from a different view of the inertia of the established (the current economic and social model that demonstrates unsustainable) require engagement strategies and the involvement of community members. It is useless to manage space, waste, energy, and so on from greener approaches if the conscious participation of the different sectors within it is absent. That is why Alba *et al.* (2011: 148) state that 'management and environmental education are closely related; a sustainable environmental management at the University will hardly operate if only executed by technical groups: an active participation from the part of the entire university community must be encouraged'. A culture of sustainability requires, in short, a shift that permeates all levels of the university community; in relation to its members, it is urgent to modify substantially the way of being and living in that community; this transformation must extend, from their academic and professional fields (linked to their roles as teachers, researchers, students or management staff), to their personal and social sphere (linked to their roles as citizens committed to the sustainability of their communities and society as a whole).

This strategic intent is encouraging us to transfer the model 'communities in transition' into the university arena (Iglesias 2013; Pardellas *et al.* 2013). 'Communities in transition' – also known as 'transition initiatives' or 'transition towns' – are a social movement led by environmentalist Rob Hopkins that began in Kinsale (Ireland), and then spread to Totnes (England), back in early 2005 (Hopkins 2008, 2011). Its aim is to build, through a participatory methodology, processes driven by civil society to tackle seriously both the climate change and Peak Oil (Suriñach 2008). Concerned by the social changes that will result from these environmental problems, the purpose of 'initiatives in transition' is to build a social model that strengthens local communities (neighbourhoods, towns, cities), developing their sense of community and reducing their energy dependence. This results in achieving a larger goal: an increasing resilience of people and communities.[5]

The HEIs or academic groups from a university that have opted for this framework have a renewed interest in developing transformative learning experiences that permeate the culture of sustainability in all university bodies, by adopting an eminently educational approach. The implementation of initiatives in transition in university has brought a revitalised impetus towards already existing projects and programmes. However, these initiatives have not had sufficient continuity and are not easily supported by social institutions, so that they are hindered from causing tangible changes in structural aspects of the university organisation or in the exercise of their basic roles in education and research, that which will allow them to reach a more important projection in their work of social extension (Iglesias 2013).

With all this in mind, courses, conferences, workshops, seminars, discussion groups and social innovation initiatives, consumer cooperatives, etc. have been launched. Their aim is the search of new ways to socialise, engage and mobilise the university community in a sharing and cooperative transformation, with a focus on integral development.

If what is characteristic of hegemonic ideas and practices is to be displayed as natural and inevitable (neoliberalism as unique thought, capitalism without viable alternatives, patriarchy without equal options, etc.), it could be that those university communities in transition will be able to toughly display its singularity and autonomy, to resist the cultural and economic homogenisation (which is one of the pillars of unsustainability), to become laboratories for testing practices and cultural patterns, models of social relations of production and consumption, in sum, to walk in the opposite direction. A university that assumes the model of communities in transition will also be subject to market pressures, this is unavoidable. But it is possible to generate alternative public spheres for mobilising its scientific, technological and organisational assets in order to contribute to the construction of alternative models of society. In that way, it would free itself to some extent from the pharisaic, efficient-like and economist barriers that configure the glass ceiling that prevents more ambitious steps towards sustainability.

In contrast to other communities in transition, universities build collectively the sustainability of their community. Through internal mobilisation, they can – and should – generate far-reaching diffuser effects because one of their main missions is to prepare people for being professionals and citizens with great capacity to influence other communities, be they near to or distant from the HEIs where they received education. It is a requirement of the community as a whole, where knowledge, ethics and behaviour must be referenced consistently and coherently. In addition, changes can and should be proposed and implemented at different scales, from those small changes that involve only objective or subjective costs for those who assume them (as replacing incandescent light bulbs by low power ones), to the abandonment of high-impact practices, whose adoption involves radical changes in normalised life styles (a refusal to fly, a renouncement of private transport and practices of conspicuous consumption). In the middle we could find those changes that translate into more expensive options (to moderate the average temperature of the air conditioning and heating or renounce eating red meat). This kind of practices would be positioned within the framework of degrowth philosophy.[6]

With a more critical perspective, a part of the university community participant in the Transition Network poses the following question:

> If the future for which we are educating the youth is not the future that lies ahead, how can we set the course of our monolithic educational system? What are the skills and abilities required for a world of economic contraction, of rising energy costs, environmental degradation and climate change? Have we traced our route guided by a false North Star?
>
> *(Hopkins 2013)*

With more or less success, some university communities – some of them Ibero-American – have launched transition initiatives that explore, even if in an incipient form, innovative alternatives to meet the challenge of establishing a university community composed of citizens (male and female) aware of environmental threats and engaged in the arduous task of overcoming or minimising their consequences at local, regional and global levels.

Notes

1 CIFCA was founded at the initiative of the Spanish government and UNEP, as a result of the UN Conference on the Human Environment (Stockholm, 1972) and in response to the need to strengthen cooperation between Spain and Latin America and Caribbean. Its activity was oriented towards environmental training at the highest level, understanding that the countries of this region should encourage their development processes to meet growing social demands, but without degrading ecosystems and reducing the quality of their environment.

2 The approach and the results of this survey can be found online at: http://universiario2014.com/es/debates/debate26.html.

3 This idea is in survey results in the cited webpage – Option B: www.universiario2014.com/es/debates/debate26.html.

4 The University of Santiago de Compostela has followed up its ecological footprint between 2010 and 2013 as part of the assessment of its policy of social responsibility towards environmental sustainability. The results are available at www.usc.es/export/sites/default/gl/goberno/vrcalidade/descargas/MRS2013galego/Ecoloxxa_interna.pdf. Others, such as the universities of Málaga, Granada and León, have made precise calculations or pilot studies on the ecological footprint of some of its campuses and faculties.

5 Transition Network suggests a 12-step model for the launch of an initiative in transition in a city/town/neighborhood: 1) Set up a steering group and design its demise/transformation from the outset; 2) Start raising awareness; 3) Lay the foundations; 4) Organise a Great Unleashing; 5) Form

theme (or special interest) groups; 6) Use Open Space; 7) Develop visible practical manifestations of the project; 8) Facilitate the 'Great Reskilling'; 9) Build a bridge to Local Government; 10) Honour the elders; 11) Let it go where it wants to go…; and 12) Create an Energy Descent Action Plan (https://www.transitionnetwork.org/support/12-ingredients; Brangwyn and Hopkins 2009). The adaptation of this model to the peculiarities of the university community and greening strategies is an unmet challenge.

6 The 'degrowth' is a current of thought and action that puts into question the need to grow that the capitalist economy has been established as a system of production and consumption. Its approaches denounce the inability of modern life model to produce welfare and therefore advocate a rational and respectful production with the resources of nature and the planet. Benchmark authors may be Serge Latouche (2008) and Carlos Taibo (2011), in Ibero-America. As a socio-economic approach clearly counter-hegemonic academic presence in the university environment is marginal.

References

Alba, D., Alonso, I. and Benayas, J., 2011. 'La Agenda 21 Educativa en la Universidad',in Melendro, M., Murga, M.A. and Cano, A. (eds), *IDEAS. Iniciativas de Educación Ambiental para la Sostenibilidad.* Madrid: UNED, 119–39.

Aznar, P., Martínez-Agut, M., Palacios, B., Piñero, A. and Ull, M.A., 2011. 'Introducing Sustainability into University Curricula: An Indicator and Baseline Survey of the Views of University Teachers at the University of Valencia', *Environmental Education Research*, 17(2), 145–66.

Barzev, R., 2002 *Valoración Económica Integral de los Bienes y Servicios ambientales de la Reserva del Hombre y la Biosfera de Río Plátano.* Proyecto Manejo Reserva del Hombre y la Biosfera de Río Plátano Corredor Biológico Mesoamericano (CBM).

Beckerman, Wilfred, 1994. 'Sustainable Development: Is it a Useful Concept?', *Environmental Values*, 3(3), 191–209.

Benayas del Álamo, J., 2014a. *Universidad y sostenibilidad. Reflexiones para un debate. ¿la universidad está liderando los cambios necesarios para que la sociedad se comprometa con un futuro más sostenible?.* Carpeta Informativa del CENEAM, 7–10.

Benayas del Álamo, J., 2014b. *RISUPROJECT. Development of Indicators to Assess the Implementation of Sustainability Policies in Latin American Universities. Executive Summary.* Madrid: UAM.

Brangwyn, B. and Hopkins, R., 2009. *Compendio de iniciativas de transición.* Totnes: Transition Network.

CADEP, 2011. *Evaluación de las políticas universitarias de sostenibilidad como facilitadoras para el desarrollo de los campus de excelencia internacional. Madrid, Conferencia de Rectores de Universidades Españolas.* www.crue.org/Sostenibilidad/CADEP/Documents/Documentos/21.CADEP2011finalbaja.pdf [accessed 27 January 2015).

Comisión Técnica de la Estrategia Universidad-2015, 2011. *La Responsabilidad Social de la Universidad y el Desarrollo Sostenible.* Madrid, Ministerio de Educación-Secretaría General de Universidades. www.crue.org/Sostenibilidad/CADEP/Documents/Documentos/24.La_RSU_y_el_desarrollo_sostenible_2011.pdf [accessed 27 January 2015).

Complexus, 2013. *Indicadores para medir la contribución de las instituciones de educación superior a la sustentabilidad.* Guanajuato: Universidad de Guanajuato.

Geli, A.M., Junyent, M. and Sánchez, S., 2003. *Ambientalización curricular de los Estudios Superiores.* Girona: Universidad de Girona – Red Aces.

Global University Network for Innovation, 2012. *Higher Education in the World.* Suffolk: Palgrave Macmillan.

González Gaudiano, E., 1989. 'La Carta de Bogotá sobre Universidad y Medio Ambiente', *Revista de la Educación*, Superior, México, 18(71), 1–4.

González Gaudiano, E.J., 2009. 'Environmental Education: A Field in Tension or in Transition?', in Reid, A. and Scott, W. (eds), 2009, *Researching Education and the Environment. Retrospect and Prospect.* New York: Routledge, 45–54.

Gutiérrez Garza, E. and González-Gaudiano, E.J., 2010. *De las teorías del desarrollo al desarrollo sustentable.* México: Siglo XXI eds.

Hopkins, R., 2008. *The Transition Handbook. From Oil Dependency to Local Resilience.* Totnes: Green Books.

Hopkins, R., 2011. *The Transition Companion.* Totnes: Green Books.

Hopkins, R., 2013. *One Year in Transition and the Power of Alternatives to University.* https://www.transitionnetwork.org/blogs/rob-hopkins/2013-07/one-year-transition-and-power-alternatives-university [accessed 27 January 2015].

Iglesias, L., ed., 2013. *Comunidades en Transición y Educación Ambiental. Análisis de tres Universidades pioneras: Santiago De Compostela, Minho y Edimburgo.* Santiago de Compostela, Grupo de Investigación en Pedagogía Social y Educación Ambiental. Informe de investigación inédito.

Larrán, M., ed., 2014. *Análisis del nivel de implantación de políticas de responsabilidad social en las universidades españolas. Madrid, Fundación Carolina-Conferencia de Consejos Sociales de las Universidades Públicas Españolas.* http://ccsu.es/sites/default/files/analisis_del_nivel_de_implantacion_de_politicas_de_responsabilidad_social_en_las_universidades_espanolas.pdf [accessed 27 January 2015).

Latouche, S., 2008. *La apuesta por el decrecimiento. ¿Cómo salir del imaginario dominante?* Barcelona: Icaria.

Leal Filho, W., 2000. 'Dealing with Misconceptions on the Concept of Sustainability', *International Journal of Sustainability in Higher Education*, 1(1), 9–19.

Leff, E., ed., 1986. *Los problemas del conocimiento y la perspectiva ambiental del desarrollo.* México: Siglo XXI eds.

Martinez-Alier, J., 1995. 'The Environment as a Luxury or 'Too Poor to be Green'?', *Ecological Economics*, 13(1), 1–10.

Meira Cartea, P.A., 2005. 'In Praise of Environmental Education', *Educational Philosophy and Theory*, 3(3), 284–95.

Naredo, J.M., 1997. 'Sobre el "pensamiento único", Archipiélago', *Cuadernos de Crítica de la Cultura*, 29, 11–24.

Pardellas, M., Iglesias, L. and Meira, P.Á., 2013. 'Iniciativas en transición: nuevos escenarios para una educación ambiental comunitaria', *Cuadernos de pedagogía*, 439, 53–5.

Ruscheinsky, A. Guerra, A.F.S., Figueiredo, M.L., Silva Leme, P.C., Lima Ranieri, V.E. and Carvalho Delitti, W.B., 2014. *Ambientalização nas instituições de educação superior no Brasil.* São Carlos: EESC/USP.

Shriberg, M., 2002. *Research: Talloires in Action: Creating Leaders and Laggards in the U.S.* www.ulsf.org/pub_declaration_resvol61.htm [accessed 8 January 2015].

Shriberg, M. and Tallent, H., 2003. *Beyond Principles: Implementing the Talloires Declaration.* www.ulsf.org/pdf/ShribergTallentFinal.pdf [accessed 8 January 2015].

Sousa Santos, B. de (2011), 'A Encruzilhada da Universidade Europeia', *Revista do SNESup*, 41, 1–8.

Suriñach, R., 2008. 'Volviendo a lo local', *Opcions*, 28, 27–9.

Taibo, C., 2011. *El decrecimiento explicado con sencillez.* Madrid: La Catarata.

Tilbury, D., 2007. 'Learning Based Change for Sustainability: Perspectives and Pathways', in Wals, A. (ed.), *Social Learning toward a more Sustainable World: Principles, Perspectives, and Praxis.* Wageningen, The Netherlands: Wageningen Academic Publishers, 117–31.

Tudela, Fernando, 1991. 'Diez tesis sobre desarrollo y medio ambiente en América Latina y el Caribe', *Ecológicas. Boletín bimestral de Instituto Autónomo de Investigaciones Ecológicas*, 2(2), 14–16.

United Nations, 2007. *Indicators of Sustainable Development: Guidelines and Methodologies.* New York: United Nations Publication.

Waas, T., Hugé, J., Ceulemans, K., Lambrechts, W., Vandenabeele, J., Lozano, R. and Wright, T., 2012. *Sustainable Higher Education: Understanding and Moving Forward.* www.lne.be/doelgroepen/onderwijs/ecocampus/over-ecocampus/sustainable-higher-education-understanding-and-moving-forward-waas-et-al-.pdf [accessed 10 January 2015].

WCED, 1987. *Our Common Future. Brundtland Report.* www.un-documents.net/wced-ocf.htm [accessed 23 March 2015].

PART 2

Paradigms and methodologies of research on higher education for sustainable development

6

UNDERSTANDING APPROACHES TO ESD RESEARCH ON TEACHING AND LEARNING IN HIGHER EDUCATION

Stephen Sterling, Paul Warwick and Lynne Wyness

Introduction

To begin a review of the purpose(s) of ESD research, we must first ask the basic question of the purpose of research generally. Definitions of research normally centre on it comprising systematic investigation which contributes to knowledge or understanding of phenomena or a problem. A distinction is commonly drawn between pure or basic research which focuses on understanding phenomena and issues, and applied research where the primary emphasis is on research which contributes to the solution of problems or some systemic improvement rather than knowledge for its own sake. Some commentators see action research as a third category as it is predicated on the researcher being part of the research process which itself is committed to personal or social change. ESD research as an area of interest is perhaps unusual because it accommodates and crosses these categories. It also engages in philosophic research regarding cultural, worldview and ethical dimensions of sustainability education – critically important dimensions of ESD research, but not within the scope of this chapter.

Research on – say – the relative effect of different pedagogies, or how a learning environment affects learning, may be thought of as basic research, but at another level, ESD research is often purposeful beyond the accumulation of understanding about educational processes. At a prosaic level, the motivation for research could be little more than funding opportunities or academic profile and advancement: these factors play an influential role in ESD research as in any other area of education research. However, for many ESD researchers, their primary purpose and motivation often operates at a deeper level and relates to the grand challenge of securing a more sustainable societal and planetary future, through the agency and processes of education and learning which are perceived as having a critical role. For example, commenting on action research, Reason and Bradbury (2001: 2) suggest that its 'wider purpose' is to contribute 'to the increased well-being – economic, political, psychological, spiritual – of human persons and communities, and to a more equitable and sustainable relationship with the wider ecology of the planet of which we are an intrinsic part'.

This kind of argument – what Wals *et al.* (2013: 542) call 'engaged scholarship with a planetary conscience' – relates to a broad discussion on the purposes not just of research in higher education, but to the purposes of HE generally (Sterling 2013: 17–50). For example Chase and Bartlett (2013: 15) suggest: 'Sustainability in higher education calls us to new sets of relationships – with our students, with each other, with what we learn, and with ourselves'.

Put alternatively, policy, practice and research in ESD is commonly motivated and shaped by the desire for change – in staff and student understanding and engagement, in organisational orientation, and in social processes towards conditions perceived as consistent with a safer, more sustainable world (Reunamo and Pipere 2011). Importantly, this agentive approach to ESD and by extension, to HE as a whole, is endorsed and promoted by UNESCO (2012a) and UNECE (2013). ESD work therefore can be marked out as often having an implicit or explicit ethical or teleological dimension which is much less evident in most mainstream discourse on higher education. Arguably, this latter discourse has been influenced by a narrow instrumentalism in recent years through the dominance of neo-liberal policies advocating marketisation and commodification of the sector (Blewitt 2013).

However, the overall picture is not simple, and this complexity derives from two main factors. First, the fact that 'education for sustainable development' draws on and attempts a synthesis of two (often otherwise separate) areas of work and discourse: *education*, and *sustainable development*. Whereas the above point about teleology is generally valid, the history of ESD research reveals a distinction between those researchers who are *primarily* interested in learning and educational processes and who therefore are likely to stress intrinsic values in education, and those researchers who are *primarily* interested in the role of education and learning ultimately in advancing sustainable development, and who hold more instrumental values. For the former, intellectual curiosity and a desire to understand learning may precede their interest in its contribution to sustainable development. The emphasis is on the quality of learning, and often, on building the individual's capacity (for example, to think critically, systemically and reflexively), rather than encouraging particular social or environmental outcomes. For the latter the reverse tends to hold. The former are more likely to put emphasis on research *about* change, the latter on research *for* change, or – in the case of action research – research *as* change, stressing the transformative role of education. This is a tension in ESD research which relates to the matter of research paradigms and methodology, and also – more generally – educational paradigms which influence thinking and practice, and this is returned to below.

The second complicating factor is that whereas movement towards sustainability requires the sufficient development of learning and capacity *through* the effect of educational systems, this is reliant on the achievement of adequate learning and capacity *within* educational systems (Richmond 2010). We can therefore make a useful distinction between two interrelated *arenas* of learning in HE, being *designed learning* and *institutional learning*. Both are of interest to the ESD research community. As Sterling and Maxey (2013: 7) have outlined previously:

> Designed learning is the concern of all educational programmes: it is planned, resourced and provided for all the different student groups that experience higher education. Institutional learning refers to the social and organisational learning that the policy-makers and providers may themselves undergo or experience: senior managers, academic staff, support staff, and policy-makers and stakeholders. In the movement to align HE towards sustainability over recent years, it has become clear that substantive progress in *designed learning* is dependent on sufficient depth and extent of *institutional learning* and capacity building.

This analysis yields a simple table (Table 6.1) which allows a rough categorisation of ESD research interests.

Table 6.1 Broad categorisation of ESD research interests

	ESD: primary interest in process of HE education and learning	*ESD: primary interest in contribution of HE to SD*
Designed learning (courses, programmes)	-A- *Focus on curriculum change and the learning process*	-C- *Focus on sustainability competence, action and engagement*
Institutional learning (social and organisational learning)	-B- *Focus on systemic change and learning in the institution*	-D- *Focus on the impact of the institution on the community and in effecting change towards sustainability*

Theoretical bases

As noted above, when considering the nature of ESD research in HE it is important to consider the paradigm(s) upon or within which the research is based. The concept of paradigm can be defined variously, but Capra's view, derived from Kuhn's work, is representative. He defines paradigm as: 'a constellation of concepts, values, perceptions and practices shared by a community, which forms a particular vision of reality that is the basis of the way the community organises itself' (Capra 1996: 5).

Therefore 'paradigm' and 'worldview' is often held to mean the same thing, except that 'paradigm' is held by a group, while a worldview can be held by an individual as well as by a group. The shared group paradigm legitimates and gives rise to methodology and practice. Hence, Marglin and Marglin (1990: 24) describe 'knowledge systems' which are defined in terms of four characteristics: epistemology, transmission, innovation and power:

> Each system has its own theory of knowledge (or epistemology), its own rules for sharing knowledge, its own distinctive ways for changing the content of what counts as knowledge, and finally, its own political rules for governing relationships both among insiders … and between insiders and outsiders'.

Alternatively, a paradigm or knowledge system can be seen to comprise of epistemology, ontology and methodology, and this is evident both in research paradigms and broader cultural paradigms. A long standing feature of research discourse has been the subject of how far distinct paradigms are commensurable (not least the basic distinction between quantitative and qualitative methodologies).

Reviewing educational and research paradigms, various writers present models setting out three or four educational paradigm positions which apply across HE (not just ESD). For example, Robottom and Hart (1993) wrote an influential book setting out three key positions in environmental education (positivist, interpretivist and critical). In the same year, drawing on Kemmis's work, Fien (1993) suggested a model of educational positions (vocational/neo-classical, liberal/progressive, socially critical), which corresponded with Robottom and Hart's three positions. Similarly, Sauvé (1996) suggests 'rational, humanistic, and inventive' stances. These models still have currency, and can be used to interpret positions within educational debate. In more recent years, a wider spectrum tends to be acknowledged. Hence a range of methodological positions (such as positivist, postpositivist, interpretivist, transformative, postmodern, poststructuralist) are distinguished (Gough and Reid 2000; Denzin and Lincoln 2000).

Fien (2002) distinguishes four distinct research paradigms to frame research into institutional and programme change in relation to sustainability:

1. The *positivist,* or empirical-analytical paradigm. Used to describe, control and predict.
2. The *interpretive* or hermeneutic paradigm. Used to empathise, interpret and understand.
3. The *critical* or reconstructionist paradigm. Used to critique power and structures and assist change processes especially as regards social justice.
4. The *poststructural* paradigm. Used to deconstruct and analyse discourse.

He suggests that these approaches also apply to the philosophical position through which sustainability is understood. Whilst many in the ESD research community would think Fien's four-part typology sufficient, we would argue that it omits a fifth paradigm, which Heron (1996) and Reason and Bradbury (2001) call the 'participative paradigm' – a holistic, systemic, relational position based upon an emergent postmodern ecological (i.e. relational) worldview – a fifth paradigm which is postmodern, postpositivist, and ecological. This emergent paradigm emphasises our role in co-creating our reality, recognising that we are deeply enmeshed in a reality which is both existent and created, and that these are inextricably linked: how we see the world shapes the world, and this in turn shapes us. This co-evolutionary state of inseparability gives rise to a drive to research meaning, purpose and action in the interests of human and ecological flourishing through participative research.

Clearly, these five research positions give rise to methodological stances and issues. As Fien notes (in relation to his four positions):

> Each of these paradigms has an appropriate part to play in educational research, depending on the type of problem being investigated. For example, all four are used in environmental education research although the empirical-analytic paradigm has been most dominant until recent years.
>
> *(Fien 2002: 247)*

The primary tension in research methodology, which stems directly from paradigmatic bases, is reflected in this quote by Breiting (2009: 203):

> are we as researchers seeing ourselves as contributors to a quest for supporting education that solves current problems through whatever educational processes necessary, or are we striving to support the creation of future educated citizens that are capable of making their own decisions?

Breiting argues that more prescriptive environmental or ESD research focused on the implementation of interventions and techniques to change behaviour, is counterintuitive to the deeper purpose of ESD, which is to bring about educational contexts that nurture critical, creative, and compassionate citizens through the opening up, rather than diminishment, of teaching approaches.

This echoes the distinction made earlier between those primarily interested in the 'sustainable development' part of ESD (the C and D positions in Table 6.1), and those primarily interested in the 'education' component of ESD (positions A and B). Clearly, these positions are not exclusive, and many researchers have interests beyond one position or in the relationship between these foci. Indeed, we would argue that they are not exclusive, but need to be seen as components of the urgent challenge to realign higher education to address the critical issues facing global society (Wals and UNESCO 2012).

Research paradigms and methodologies

Reunamo and Pipere (2011) believe a 'typology' of ESD/environmental education (EE) researchers can be conceived, where researchers find themselves drawn towards particular research paradigms that they believe sit more comfortably with the notion of sustainability and environmentalism. They suggest this results in four distinct methodological approaches to ESD and attempt to provide a framework of 'agentive perception' for understanding the agency and accommodation of ESD researchers and their chosen research paradigms – theoretic, participatory, quantitative and qualitative. In a later paper, Reunamo and Pipere (2012: 314) ask if there is 'room for objectivity in the politically and morally loaded topic of ESD?' and demonstrate how, when researchers describe their research orientations, they reveal the personal motivations behind their research. The participatory paradigm, whereby ESD is seen as a cultural product that affords societal change towards sustainability, appears to be most prevalent (Reunamo and Pipere 2011). As chapter authors, this is the position that we would endorse but also believe that, properly understood, it can subsume – rather than negate – other research paradigms reflecting an historic shift from positivism to constructivism, and from constructivism to an emergent participativism (relationalism). Thus methodologies associated with previous paradigms are employed according to appropriateness to context, rather than rejected, affording an integrative framework incorporating multiple paradigms (Taylor *et al.* 2012).

The participatory paradigm stems from a relational or ecological view of the world, which concomitantly gives rise to a collaborative methodology of participative inquiry and practice (Reason and Bradbury 2001), epitomised by forms of action research, including cooperative inquiry (Heron 1996), and participatory action research (PAR) (Kemmis and McTaggart 2005), and interest in systemic change and transformative learning (Blackmore and Ison 2012).

Action research is described by McNiff *et al.* (2003) as a process for systematically leading a change in practice that is driven by a concern for justice, and values of compassion and respect that need to be both explored and defended by educators' reflexive engagement throughout the change process. An interesting example of PAR in ESD, underpinned by a strong empowerment ethic, is provided by the work of Wierenga and Guevara (2013).

Whilst as authors, we believe the participatory paradigm offers an integrative direction for ESD research, we recognise that this view is not necessarily widely shared or appreciated. Meanwhile, some commentators critique the lack of clear theoretical underpinning of research where a pluralist mix of approaches obscures the theoretical bases of research. Hence, Dillon and Wals (2006) highlight the tendency towards 'blurring' of research methods/methodologies within environmental education research, and remind researchers of the need to root their chosen methods and methodologies in appropriate contexts. They call for more attention to the ontological, epistemological and axiological considerations of research, and advocate that research should always be driven by research questions, rather than by preferred or tried-and-tested research methods. 'In order to move forward we need to start seeing ourselves as members of a community of reflective scholars, and not just as aggregates of individuals, or as competing camps, or as a pluralistic field of multiple unconnected research paradigms without common interests' (Dillon and Wals 2006: 557).

Cutting and Cook (2009) also note the lack of cohesive discourse from EE and ESD and conclude there is a lack of rigour and critical analysis. Similarly, Fien (2002: 245) notes the preponderance of non-theoretical research into sustainability in HE and charts the tendency towards more descriptive, narrative and evaluative accounts of institutional change, and audit reports of beneficial interventions, arguing that 'few studies have sought to go beyond description to include a critical and theoretical analysis or to ground explanations in social or organisational theory' (Fien 2002: 244). He warns researchers not to bypass the grounding of their research in a philosophical paradigm in favour of the 'real business' of making improvements and finding interventions that effect change.

Further, a number of commentators have drawn attention to what is perceived by many in the critical educational research field to be a worrying (neoliberal) drift towards researching efficacy in education and building an evidence base for policy (Heimlich 2007). Heimlich (2007) believes the trend in USA towards accountability in educational outcomes, measured through test scores and behavioural change, carries the consequence of research operating in a manner contrary to the social and environmental moral compass of EE. Rather, he presents other research areas in which different paradigms, methodologies and principles are at work – for example, action research, place-based education, experiential learning and cultural relevance.

In sum, whilst at first glance the field of ESD research in HE might appear a unified field, the discussion above indicates that, on examination, it is revealed as a complex field of inquiry. This results from differences in:

- researchers' individual and collective starting points and motivations;
- preferred research paradigms and methodologies;
- the degree to which such paradigms and methodologies are explicit and recognised;
- a primary emphasis on education and learning processes, or on sustainable development actions and behavioural outcomes;
- interest in different levels of individual and collective learning, from first order change to transformative and epistemic learning; and
- focus – from the *micro* level of individual learning and change, and *meso* level of teaching and learning ('designed learning'), to the *macro* level of organisational change ('institutional learning') and beyond this, wider systemic change in educational systems.

Taking the last distinction regarding 'focus', we now review very briefly some selected examples of research under the micro/meso/macro headings which together give some indication of ESD interests and directions in recent years (although the reader is directed to the key journals for a fuller picture). However, it is important to note that these three levels are systemically interrelated and need to be considered integratively.

Researching learning and change

Micro level

At this level of ESD research, the focus tends to be on the experience of the individual learner. The diversity of research paradigms and methodologies as well as of range of interests is evident.

Key questions arising include: What is the current state of awareness, attitudinal stance, knowledge and understanding amongst students? How is it possible to measure and evaluate the affective realm of the individual learner? What is the process of transformative learning?

What constitutes sustainability literacy in learners whereby sustainability competencies and dispositions are developed? How are students' attitudes and values affected and how does this change their behaviours? Are changes in student views, understanding and action sustained over time?

These are all very pertinent – and often complex – research areas. Some examples follow.

- The sustainability literacy or sustainability competencies of individual learners/graduate attributes (Mann *et al.* 2013; Wiek *et al.* in this Handbook). Emphasis on enhancing students' capacity to act as change agents in transforming the world towards a more sustainable direction (Elliot 2010).
- The link between understanding, values and change in behaviours. Buissink-Smith *et al.* (2011) argue that ESD addresses 'affective attributes' – values, dispositions, attitudes, behaviours and sense of responsibility that are hard to measure in terms of change (except for behavioural change in pro-environmental behaviours) (cf. Chapter 17 in this Handbook).
- The attitudes of students towards sustainable development (Drayson *et al.* 2013).
- Development of graduate attributes and the use of metrics and quantitative analysis to measure worldviews and progression towards more sustainability-orientated perspectives; use of the revised New Environmental Paradigm (NEP) to understand students' worldviews (Harraway *et al.* 2012).
- The pursuit of individual transformative learning (Elliot 2010) and effect on the learner (Haigh 2013).
- The role of subjective knowledge: dreams (Gough and Gough 2004), embodiment and race (Grange 2004), and spirituality (Beringer 2007).
- Longitudinal research that charts students' acquisition of sustainability literacy or transformation of attitudes and behaviours from start to finish of Higher Education experience (Winter *et al.* 2012; Cotton and Alcock 2013).

Meso level

At this level, the focus is on teaching and learning practices in HE, teacher-learner interaction, and the learning environment. Key questions include: What constitutes ESD pedagogy? How can innovative pedagogies be introduced? How can new ESD programmes be evaluated? How do staff conceptions and understanding of ESD affect practice? What is the effect of Continuous Professional Development in promoting good ESD practice? How can teachers/researchers experience transformative learning, as well as students? How can student engagement and initiatives enrich ESD experiences? What are the effects of different learning spaces? How are sustainable development competencies taught and learnt? How does interdisciplinarity affect student learning? What is the role of the campus in formal and non-formal ESD? How does the hidden curriculum affect student learning?

Some examples follow:

- ESD pedagogy. Eilam and Trop (2010) argue that curriculum content has changed over 30 years of EE and latterly ESD, but pedagogical approaches have not – they propose a framework of four principles of ESD pedagogy (academic/cognitive, multi-disciplinary, multi-dimensional [time/space] and emotional learning), each of which is necessary to bring about ESD. Cotton and Winter (2010) review the use of sustainability pedagogies in HE; Ryan and Cotton (2013) examine the role of sustainability pedagogies in HE.
- Training the trainers. The difficulties of introducing participatory action research with

trainee teachers in Jamaica (Down 2006), and a global learning module to trainee teachers in England (Scoffham 2013) – due to prior values and beliefs.
- Learning spaces and transformational learning environments (Blake *et al.* 2013).
- Attitudes and knowledge of lecturers in HE relating to ESD, and implications for other HEIs (Cotton *et al.* 2007).
- Developing sustainability competencies in HE (Barth *et al.* 2013).
- Use of campus and extra-curricular learning (Lipscombe 2008).

Macro level

At this level, the focus is on curriculum change, organisational learning and change in educational systems. Key questions include: In what ways can policy help or hinder change towards a sustainability curriculum? How do university communities change towards sustainability through organisational learning? How does ESD relate to other university agendas and priorities? What is the process of whole institutional change? What is the role of leadership? How can ESD research engage with other sectors and policy arenas effectively?

Examples of research themes at this level include:

- Whole institutional change. Connection between university strategy, curriculum development, research agendas and cultural change within departments (Qian 2013; Hopkinson *et al.* 2008; Dyer *et al.* 2006)
- Developing a holistic curriculum across the university (Ryan 2012).
- Progress towards the sustainable university (Sterling *et al.* 2013, Chase and Bartlett 2013).
- University leadership and sustainability (Scott *et al.* 2012; Shiel 2013).
- International trends on ESD teaching and learning (UNESCO 2012b).
- Engaging with the public sphere and policy arenas (Fear *et al.* 2006; McKenzie 2009).

Conclusion

ESD research is a remarkably rich field of inquiry, not least considering that it is relatively young: one of the first and leading journals *Environmental Education Research* has only been existence since 1995. While the common commitment and enthusiasm of its researchers characterise this field, a critical aspect is the sheer breadth of themes and foci that come under the broad umbrella of ESD research related to teaching and learning. Given also the cultural shift in research paradigms that is underway in research generally, this makes ESD in HE research peculiarly difficult to capture and understand synoptically, and therefore the comparison of research findings, and the identification of gaps and priorities, is not a simple matter.

However, there are number of areas which arguably need further focus:

- More research on longitudinal effects of ESD. The use of graduate surveys, use of leavers' employment statistics; emphasis on story and narratives of change, rooted in particular changes in attitudes and values (Barth and Thomas 2012), would be helpful here.
- Research which is better theoretically underpinned and having coherent methodological direction.
- More large scale comparative research, particularly internationally. On the whole, ESD research has tended to be small-scale and localised.
- Better communication with researchers in non-English speaking countries, given that ESD literature is dominated by research from USA, UK and Northern Europe, Canada,

Australia and South Africa, plus strengths for example in German-speaking countries of Germany, Austria and Switzerland (Nikel and Reid 2006) as well as further afield (South Africa).

- Stronger engagement with communities beyond the university.
- More interaction between ESD researchers and sustainable development researchers and activists.
- Stronger engagement with other sectors and disciplines beyond the usual players, including NGOs, business, media, local and national government.

We believe the nature of the current eco-cultural crises affecting the global world requires a change in cultural consciousness towards a more systemic, holistic and integrative sensibility, understanding and ability to engage. The role of research in facilitating transformative change has never been more important or urgent. Given that learning for sustainable change takes time, the overall argument is for a rapid and widespread scaling up of research 'about', 'for' and 'as' change in the years to come. This will necessitate environmental education and ESD research intentionally blurring any niche boundaries, forming partnerships with myriad interest groups, and determinedly influencing and engaging educational researchers, communities and policy-makers way beyond those already committed.

References

Barth, M. and Thomas, I., 2012., 'Synthesising Case-study Research – Ready for the Next Step?', *Environmental Education Research*, 18(6), 751–64.

Barth, M., Thomas, I. and Day, T., 2013. 'Education for Sustainability, Graduate Capabilities, Professional Employment: How they all Connect', *Australian Journal of Education*, 29, 2–15.

Beringer, A., 2007. 'The "Spiritual Handshake": Toward a Metaphysical Sustainability Metrics', *Canadian Journal of Environmental Education* 12(1), 143–59.

Blackmore, C. and Ison, R., 2012. 'Designing and Developing Learning Systems for Managing Systemic Change in a Climate Change World', in Wals, A. and Corcoran, P. (eds), *Learning for Sustainability in Times of Accelerating Change*. Waginengen: Waginengen Academic Publishers, 347–63.

Blake, J., Sterling, S. and Goodson, I., 2013. 'Transformative Learning for a Sustainable Future: An Exploration of Pedagogies for Change at an Alternative College', *Sustainability*, 5(12), 5347–72 [online]. www.mdpi.com/2071-1050/5/12/5347 [accessed 17 February 2015].

Blewitt, J., 2013. 'EfS: Contesting the Market Model of Higher Education', in Sterling, S., Maxey, L. and Luna, H. (eds), *The Sustainable University – Progress and Prospects*. Abingdon: Routledge/Earthscan, 71–86.

Breiting, S., 2009. 'Issues for Environmental Education and ESD Research Development: Looking Ahead from WEEC 2007 in Durban', *Environmental Education Research*, 15(2), 199–207.

Buissink-Smith, N., Mann, S. and Shephard, K., 2011. 'How Do We Measure Affective Learning in Higher Education?', *Journal of Education for Sustainable Development*, 5(1), 101–14.

Capra, F., 1996. *The Web of Life – A New Synthesis of Mind and Matter*. London: Harper Collins.

Chase, G. and Bartlett, P., 2013. *Sustainability in Higher Education: Stories and Strategies for Transformation*. Cambridge, MA: The MIT Press.

Cotton, D.R.E and Alcock, I., 2013. 'Commitment to Environmental Sustainability in the UK Student Population', *Studies in Higher Education*, 38(10), 1457–71.

Cotton, D. and Winter, J., 2010. 'It's Not Just Bits of Paper and Light Bulbs: A Review of Sustainability Pedagogies and their Potential for Use in Higher Education', in Jones, P., Selby, D. and Sterling, S. (eds), *Sustainability Education: Perspectives and Practice Across Higher Education*. London: Earthscan, 39–54.

Cotton, D., Warren, M.F., Maiboroda, O. and Bailey, I., 2007. 'Sustainable Development, Higher Education and Pedagogy: A Study of Lecturers' Beliefs and Attitudes', *Environmental Education Research*, 13(5), 579–97.

Cutting, R. and Cook, R., 2009. 'The World Environmental Education Congress 2007: A Critical Appraisal', *Environmental Education Research*, 15(2),177–87.

Denzin, N. and Lincoln, Y., 2000. *Handbook of Qualitative Research*, 2nd edn. Thousand Oaks, CA: Sage Publications.

Dillon, J. and Wals, A., 2006. 'On the Danger of Blurring Methods, Methodologies and Ideologies in Environmental Education Research', *Environmental Education Research*, 12(3–4), 549–58.

Down, L., 2006. 'Addressing the Challenges of Mainstreaming Education for Sustainable Development in Higher Education', *International Journal of Sustainability in Higher Education*, 7(4), 390–9.

Drayson, R., Bone, L., Agombar, J. and Kemp, S., 2013. '2013: Student Attitudes Towards and Skills for Sustainable Development'. York: NUS/Higher Education Academy. www.heacademy.ac.uk/resources/detail/sustainability/2013_student_skills_final_report&nation=scotland [accessed 10 December 2014].

Dyer, A., Selby, D. and Chalkley, B., 2006. 'A Centre for Excellence in Education for Sustainable Development', *Journal of Geography in Higher Education*, 30(2), 307–12.

Eilam, E. and Trop, T., 2010. 'ESD Pedagogy: A Guide for the Perplexed', *Journal of Environmental Education*, 42(1), 43–64.

Elliot, J., 2010, 'Insights to Transformative Learning through Education for Sustainable Development', *Learning and Teaching in Higher Education*, 5, 96–113.

Fear, F., Rosaen, C., Bawden, R. and Foster-Fishman, P., 2006. *Coming to Critical Engagement*. Lanham, MD: University Press of America.

Fien, J., ed., 1993. *Education for the Environment*. Geelong: Deakin University.

Fien, J., 2002. 'Advancing Sustainability in Higher Education – Issues and Opportunities for Research', *International Journal of Sustainability in Higher Education*, 3(3), 243–53.

Gough, A. and Gough, N., 2004. 'Environmental Education Research in Southern Africa: Dilemmas of Interpretation', *Environmental Education Research*, 10(3), 409–24.

Gough, S. and Reid, A., 2000. 'Environmental Education Research as Profession, as Science, as Art and as Craft: Implications for Guidelines in Qualitative Research', *Environmental Education Research,* Special Issue: Qualitative Methods of Inquiry, 6(1), 47–59.

Grange, L.L., 2004. 'Embodiment, Social Praxis and Environmental Education: Some Thoughts', *Environmental Education Research*, 10(3), 387–99.

Haigh, M., 2013. 'Gaia: "Thinking like a Planet" as Transformative Learning', *Journal of Geography in Higher Education*, 38(1), 49–68.

Harraway, J., Broughton-Ansin, F., Deaker, L., Jowett, T. and Shephard, K., 2012. 'Exploring the Use of the Revised New Ecological Paradigm Scale (NEP) to Monitor the Development of Students' Ecological Worldviews', *Journal of Environmental Education*, 43(3), 177–91.

Heimlich, J.E., 2007. 'Research Trends in the United States: EE to ESD', *Journal of Education for Sustainable Development*, 1(2), 219–27.

Heron, J., 1996. *Cooperative Inquiry – Research into the Human Condition*. London: Sage.

Hopkinson, P., Hughes, P. and Layer, G., 2008. 'Sustainable Graduates: Linking Formal, Informal and Campus Curricula to Embed Education for Sustainable Development in the Student Learning Experience', *Environmental Education Research*, 14(4), 435–54.

Kemmis, S. and McTaggart, R., 2005. 'Participatory Action Research. Communicative Action and the Public Sphere', in Denzin, N. and Lincoln, Y. (eds), *Handbook of Qualitative Research,* 3. Thousand Oaks, CA: Sage, 559–603.

Lipscombe, B.P., 2008. 'Exploring the Role of the Extra curricular Sphere in Higher Education for Sustainable Development in the United Kingdom', *Environmental Education Research*, 14(4), 455–68.

McKenzie, M., 2009. 'Scholarship as Intervention: Critique, Collaboration and the Research Imagination', *Environmental Education Research*, 15(2), 217–26.

McNiff, J., Lomax, P. and Whitehead, J., 2003. *You and Your Action Research Project*. London: Routledge Falmer.

Mann, S., Harraway, J., Broughton-Ansin, F., Deaker, L. and Shephard, K., 2013. 'Seeking Richer Descriptions of Learners' Sustainability Attributes and Learning Needs', *International Journal of Sustainability in Higher Education*, 14(1), 90–100.

Marglin, F.A. and Marglin S.A., 1990. *Dominating Knowledge – Development, Culture and Resistance*. Oxford: Clarendon Press.

Nikel, J. and Reid, A., 2006. 'Environmental Education in three German speaking Countries: Tensions and Challenges for Research and Development', *Environmental Education Research*, 12(1), 129–48.

Qian, W., 2013. 'Embracing the Paradox in Educational Change for Sustainable Development: A Case of Accounting', *Journal of Education for Sustainable Development*, 7(1), 75–93.

Reason, P. and Bradbury, H., 2001. 'Introduction: Inquiry and Participation in a Search of a World Worthy of Human Aspiration', in Reason, P. and Bradbury, H. (eds), *Handbook of Action Research – Participative Practice and Enquiry*. London: Sage Publications, 1–14.

Reunamo, J. and Pipere, A., 2011. 'Doing Research on Education for Sustainable Development', *International Journal of Sustainability in Higher Education,* 12(2), 110–24.

Reunamo, J. and Pipere, A., 2012. 'Education for Sustainable Development Research from the Researchers' Point of View', *Journal of Education for Sustainable Development*, 6(2), 313–26.

Richmond, R., 2010. 'Envisioning, Coordinating and Implementing the UN Decade of Education for Sustainable Development', in Witthaus, M., McCandless, K. and Lambert, R. (eds), *Tomorrow Today*. Leicester: Tudor Rose on behalf of UNESCO, 19–22.

Robottom, I. and Hart, P., 1993. *Research in Environmental Education*. Geelong: Deakin University.

Ryan, A., 2012. *Education for Sustainable Development and Holistic Curriculum Change*. York: Higher Education Academy.

Ryan, A. and Cotton, D., 2013. 'Times of Change – Shifting Pedagogy and Curricula for Future Sustainability', in Sterling, S., Maxey, L. and Luna, H. (eds), *The Sustainable University – Progress and Prospects*. Abingdon: Routledge/Earthscan, 151–67.

Sauvé, L., 1996. 'Environmental Education and Sustainable Development: Further Appraisal', *Canadian Journal of Environmental Education*, 1, 7–34.

Scoffham, S., 2013. 'Do We Really Need to Know This? The Challenge of Developing a Global Learning Module for Trainee Teachers', *International Journal of Development Education and Global Learning*, 5(3), 28–47.

Scott, G., Tilbury, D., Deane, L. and Sharp, L., 2012. *Turnaround Leadership for Sustainability in Higher Education Australian Government*. Australia: Office for Learning and Teaching Canberra, 89.

Shiel, C., 2013. 'Leadership', in Sterling, S., Maxey, L. and Luna, H. (eds), *The Sustainable University – Progress and Prospects*. Abingdon: Routledge/Earthscan, 110–31.

Sterling, S., 2013. 'Introduction', in Sterling, S., Maxey, L. and Luna, H. (eds), *The Sustainable University – Progress and Prospects*. Abingdon: Routledge/Earthscan, 17–50.

Taylor, P.C., Taylor, E. and Luitel, B.C., 2012. 'Multi-paradigmatic Transformative Research as/for Teacher Education: An Integral Perspective', in Tobin, K., Fraser, B. and McRobbie, C. (eds), *Second International Handbook of Science Education*. Dordrecht, The Netherlands: Springer, 373–87.

UNECE Expert Group, 2013. *Empowering Educators for a Sustainable Future*, Geneva: UNECE/UN. http://anea.org.mx/docs/DRAFT_PUBLICATION_26-02-%202013.pdf [accessed 17 February 2015].

UNESCO, 2012a. *Shaping the Education of Tomorrow: 2012 Report on the UN Decade of Education for Sustainable Development*. Paris: UNESCO.

UNESCO, 2012b. ESD Sourcebook, *Learning & Training Tools,* 4. Paris: UNESCO. http://unesdoc.unesco.org/images/0021/002163/216383e.pdf [accessed 17 February 2015].

Wals, A. and UNESCO, 2012. *Shaping the Education of Tomorrow: 2012 Full-length Report on the UN Decade of Education for Sustainable Development*. Paris: UNESCO, DESD Monitoring and Evaluation.

Wals, A.E.J., Stephenson, B., Brody, M. and Dillon, J., 2013. 'Tentative Directions for Environmental Education Research in Uncertain Times', in Stephenson, B., Brody, M., Dillon, J. and Wals, A.E.J. (eds), *International Handbook of Environmental Education Research*. London: Routledge, 542–47.

Wierenga, A. and Guevara, R. (eds), 2013. *Educating for Global Citizenship – A Youth-led Approach to Learning Through Partnerships*. Melbourne: Melbourne University Press.

Winter, J., Cotton, D. and Grant, V., 2012. 'Experiencing Transformation: A Student Perspective', in Filho, W.L. (ed.), *Sustainable Development at Universities: New Horizons*. Frankfurt: Peter Lang, 85–97.

7

STATE OF THE ART IN RESEARCH ON HIGHER EDUCATION FOR SUSTAINABLE DEVELOPMENT

Matthias Barth and Marco Rieckmann

Introduction

The fundamental reorientations and transformations in terms of sustainable development require a far-reaching change of thinking and acting in individuals and society as a whole. This can only be brought about by learning; hence sustainable development has to be understood as a learning process (Vare and Scott 2007). Education for sustainable development (ESD) is expected both to make people more aware and better qualified to take part in shaping future developments responsibly, and to raise their awareness of the problems related to sustainable development and bring forth innovative contributions to all economic, social, environmental and cultural issues.

Universities play an important role for fostering ESD 'by addressing sustainability through their major functions of education, research and outreach' (Fadeeva and Mochizuki 2010: 250). By involving higher education in ESD, UNESCO (2009: 5) wants to 'encourage and enhance scientific excellence, research and new knowledge development for ESD'. Universities are key actors in the process of implementing sustainable development, 'because they form a link between knowledge generation and knowledge transfer to society both by educating future decision-makers and through societal outreach and service' (Adomßent and Michelsen 2006: 87–8). Dealing with the concept of sustainable development offers for universities the opportunity to understand and face up to complexity as well as to cope with uncertainty and diverging norms and values, and it facilitates systemic institutional and organisational change of universities and provides them with spaces for future-oriented and transformative thinking and learning (Adomßent *et al.* 2007).

Higher education for sustainable development (HESD) aims at enabling people to not only acquire and generate knowledge, but also to reflect on further effects and the complexity of behaviour and decisions in a future-oriented and global perspective of responsibility (Rieckmann 2012). Consequently, many universities from all over the world have already initiated activities to address sustainability in their teaching and learning at course level and in the curricula. Research complements these activities and features prominently in the ESD discourse – with distinctive topics and research approaches (Karatzoglou 2013). Over the last decade, a number of research initiatives and postgraduate programmes worldwide gained momentum and engaged with research in this area. However, what is still missing is a systematic overview of state of the art of research on HESD.

Literature reviews on (higher) education for sustainable development

With the maturation of every area of research and educational practice, at a certain point the question arises as to what actually constitutes this area. What is typical for research in the area, what specific approaches or common themes may we find? The moment in which such questions are considered explicitly is an important stepping point in the development of every discipline or research area and consequently also features prominently in the furthering of educational science.

Examples can be found for every educational sector from primary (McEwan 2014) to higher education (Teixeira 2013), in more specific areas like e.g. distance education (Lee *et al.* 2004), as well as for various sub-disciplines such as science education (Tsai and Lydia Wen 2005; Lee *et al.* 2009) or medical education (Regehr 2004). Such reviews differ significantly in terms of their methodology (from descriptive to qualitative to quantitative), their regional scope (local to global) and their coverage (period, number of journals). Together they form an important source for reflection on how a field develops, what the state of the art is and what the future might bring.

If we focus on ESD's 'older brother', environmental education, we can clearly see such an increasingly systematic tracing of the field's progress and an elaboration of the state of the art in research practices in environmental education. Andrew and Malone (1995) provide us with a typical example of one of the earlier approaches here, as they analyse a decade of articles published from 1984 to 1994 in the *Australian Journal of Environmental Education*, one of the lead journals of the field. Similar work has been done in a follow-up study by Stevenson and Evans (2011). In a widely debated review, Rickinson (2001) contributed a more detailed qualitative analysis about learner and learning in environmental education (see also Marcinkowski 2003, Sauvé and Berryman 2003, and Reid and Nikel 2003 for comments on the review).

Within the much younger field of ESD research very few such attempts to structure the existing body of knowledge have been undertaken until recently – a fact that is probably typical for this emerging and still somewhat fluid area of research. One of the first attempts to capture the development of the area was undertaken by Heimlich (2007) and his qualitative-descriptive approach to trace the development from a focus on environmental education towards the broader area of ESD in the US. Wright and Pullen (2007) were among the first to offer some quantitative insights as they prepared a bibliometric study of the existing body of literature. This has been recently complemented by Reunamo and Pipere (2011) with a slightly different but very telling approach, as they based their observations on a questionnaire that was sent out to ESD researchers.

A first and even more specific focus on higher education for sustainable development was taken by Karatzoglou (2013) with an analysis of articles in the two journals *International Journal of Sustainability in Higher Education* and *Journal of Cleaner Production*, covering the years from 2003 to 2011. Similar but slightly broader, Vaughter *et al.* (2013) analysed 272 articles in total published in eight journals between 2003 and 2012. While the latter two approaches provide us already with some interesting insights, two main flaws become obvious and are influenced by research strategies and a change over time.

First, in an emerging research area such as higher education for sustainable development there are two somehow contradictory strategies to get research published: new journals and special issues of existing journals offer new opportunities to present this sort of research and create a new community. Simultaneously researchers approach more traditional journals and link this new sort of research to existing discourses and traditions. With reviews considering only the first approach and focussing on 'leading' or 'main' journals, the numerous articles published in different established journals and often functioning as 'ice-breakers' in existing discourses are not acknowledged in their important role.

Second, the establishment of a research area such as higher education for sustainable development goes through a number of very different stages that can be expected to be seen in the way research is conducted and reported. A full understanding of the emergence of the field thus can only be brought about by a coverage of articles from the very beginning. In the case of higher education for sustainable development the United Nations Conference on Environment and Development (UNCED) in 1992 can be seen as a starting point with publications from 1992 onwards.

Research focus

To provide a better overview of the emerging area of research in higher education the following study explicitly addresses the two flaws described above. It examines current research trends in higher education for sustainable development and traces the development over time. The aim was to provide as robust data as possible on research paradigms and methodologies, topics and methods of journals, and an overview of key journals and authors in this emerging area of research. Therefore a systematic review has been carried out of all articles available that are published in English and peer reviewed and that can be described as having an explicit focus on higher education *and* education for sustainable development. It covers the period from 1992 to 2012, thus the first two decades from the first appearance of research in higher education for sustainable development.

Methodological design

Systematic reviews in educational science represent a typical way of mapping the field and tracing recent developments (Petticrew and Roberts 2009). From being a rather vague 'catch phrase' for a preparatory step prior to the actual research it developed into a systematic method of investigation in its own right (Light and Pillemer 1984; Hart 2002; Littell *et al.* 2008; see Foster and Hammersley 1998 for a meta-review). Examples encompass quantitative (e.g. Tsai and Lydia Wen 2005) as well as qualitative (e.g. Trede *et al.* 2011) approaches, content analysis (e.g. Lee *et al.* 2009) and the use of mixed methods (e.g. Thurlings *et al.* 2013).

In the present study we follow the systematic review approach outlined in Fink (2009). By following that approach we intended to provide a systematic and replicable search and analysis strategy which is fully documented and transparent. Going through the steps of 1) data collection, 2) data processing and coding, and 3) data analysis, we have produced a bibliometric overview that combines quantitative analysis with a qualitative analysis of content areas and research methodologies.

Data collection

To provide a sample universe as complete as possible, for subsequent steps we structured the process of data collection (see Figure 7.1). First, we conducted a search within four major databases. Besides Web of Science and Scopus as the two biggest databases covering the social sciences, we chose ERIC as the most important provider for data collections in educational science, and Sustainability Science Abstracts as its counterpart in sustainability science. The literature search was conducted using the following keywords: ('higher education' OR 'university' OR 'universities' OR 'tertiary education' OR 'college') AND ('education for

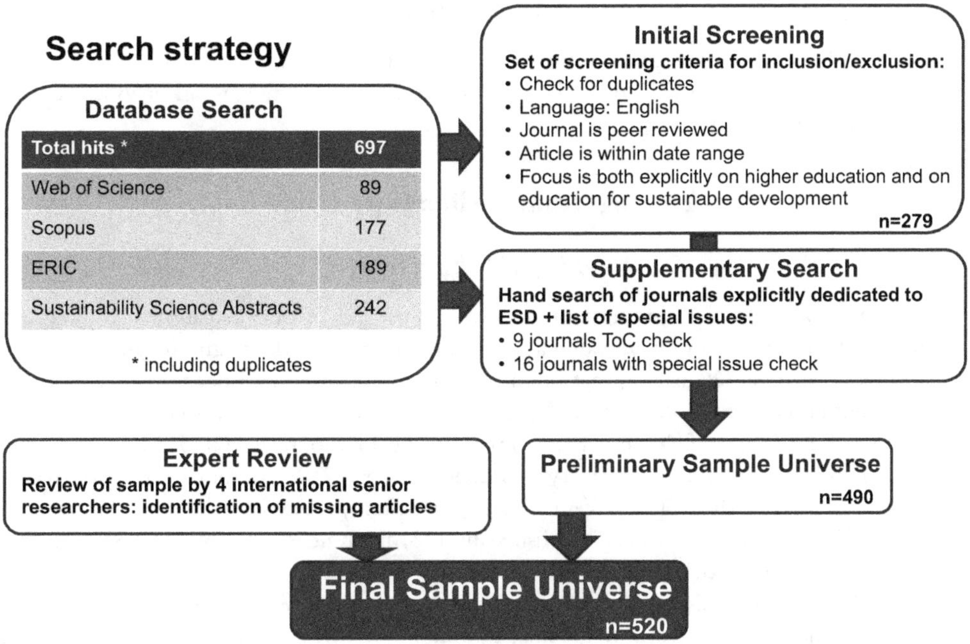

Figure 7.1 Search procedure

sustainability' OR 'education for sustainable development'). This produced a total of 697 hits, including numerous duplicates as the databases cover a significant overlap.

In the second step, the results went through an initial screening process with predefined criteria for inclusion and exclusion to remove duplicates and justify that the article is within the date range, peer reviewed and focusing explicitly on higher education for sustainable development. We completed this systematic search in the third step with an additional search of journals that are explicitly dedicated to ESD and/or produced one or more special issues on the subject, leading to a preliminary sample universe of 490 articles. Finally, we sent this sample out to four international experts in the field for review and comments on blind spots which again produced an additional 30 articles, adding up to a total of 520 articles.

Data processing and coding

Out of the sample universe a database was created including all available bibliographic data, the abstract and the full text. Two research assistants added missing data, with the results checked for sufficient inter-coder reliability. Additional variables were created for the research focus, methods and content. Based on the abstracts and, if needed, the full text, for each variable every article was coded following pre-defined coding instructions. This last step was done by the two authors with an inter-coder reliability of 0.85 and subsequent discussion of all differences.

Data analysis

Data was analysed in three steps. A statistical analysis of the bibliometric variables was followed by an analysis of each variable over time. This was complemented by an analysis of word frequency within the keywords.

Findings from the literature review

Who is publishing where?

An analysis of authors and their affiliation as well as the places of publication highlights two significant characteristics of this research area. Firstly, especially in the beginning, it is a strongly fragmented area. The 520 articles that build our sample universe have been written by nearly 800 different authors from 366 institutions around the globe. The institutions which are most present in the research field are: the University of Plymouth (UK), RMIT University (Australia) and the Technical University of Catalonia (Spain). While four leading journals of the field cover more than 50 per cent of all publications, articles on higher education for sustainable development have been published in 113 different journals with 105 journals in which fewer than ten articles appear (see Table 7.1).

Secondly, the global distribution of authorship represents an Anglo-American dominance that exists in the academic world in general, although here it is Europe that plays a major role. Accordingly, almost 50 per cent of all authors come from Europe (with an emphasis on the UK) and an additional quarter from North America. Africa contributes less than 3 per cent (see Table 7.2). This clearly shows that while the focus on HESD is said to be global and in policy statements action around the globe is called for, the academic discourse is mostly Western-dominated.

Regarding the geographical area of concern, the majority of the articles report on research which has been conducted in Europe, followed by articles with a global focus, North America, Australia/Oceania, Asia, Latin America and the Caribbean, and finally Africa. It is worth noting that only 15 articles present research from African countries. Studies from 57 different countries

Table 7.1 Key journals of HESD research

Journal	*n*	%
International Journal of Sustainability in Higher Education	171	32.9
Journal of Education for Sustainable Development	40	7.7
Journal of Cleaner Production	39	7.5
Environmental Education Research	33	6.3
Sustainability: The Journal of Record	16	3.1
Journal of Geography in Higher Education	15	2.9
Journal of Teacher Education for Sustainability	14	2.7
European Journal of Engineering Education	12	2.3
Higher Education Policy	9	1.7
Journal of Education for Teaching	8	1.5
Sustainability Science	8	1.5
The Journal of Sustainability Education	7	1.3
101 other journals	148	28.5

Table 7.2 Origin of the authors

Origin	*n*	%
Europe	491	46.9
North America	248	23.7
Australia/Oceania	153	14.6
Asia	89	8.5
Latin America and the Caribbean	43	4.1
Africa	23	2.2

are represented in the sample. However, more than one third of the articles focus on research from the USA (13.3 per cent), UK (12.3 per cent), and Australia (8.6 per cent).

What is published?

To gain a better understanding of the sort of research that is being published, we defined the research focus according to one of the four foci described in Box 7.1.

Box 7.1 Research foci

Exploratory Studies:
Open questions, curiosity at the beginning of the research process; to provide better understanding for general interest; to examine the feasibility of further study by indicating what might be relevant to study in more depth; to illuminate on a process or problem. Questions focus on the how, what, when and where. Studies tend to be small scale and often informal in structure, for example, illuminative evaluation.

Explanatory Studies:
To explain the cause or non-occurrence of a phenomenon; to show causal connections and relationships between variables of the types 'if A then B'; to suggest reasons for events and make recommendations for change. Questions focus on the why and aim to uncover laws and regularities of a universal nature. Studies can be large or small scale and are often based on hypothetico-deductivism and associated quantitative data.

Descriptive Studies:
To understand a common or uncommon social phenomenon by observing the detail of the elements that make it a phenomenon in order to provide an empirical basis for valid argument. Questions focus on the how and what. Studies tend to be small scale and qualitative, for example, ethnomethodological research.

Conceptual Papers:
Papers of a rather abstract, philosophical, normative nature, with the focus on understanding theoretical distinctions.

Against these four categories it becomes obvious that the vast majority of the articles are of descriptive or conceptual nature with explanatory research playing only a minor role (see Table 7.3).

A similar picture can be drawn if we look into the use of research methods. Here all articles have been coded against the educational research methods described in Cohen *et al.* (2009) (see Table 7.4). Case studies represent by far the most often indicated research method, followed by surveys, longitudinal, cross-sectional and trend studies, and naturalistic and ethnographic research.

Thus, the existent diversity of research methods is reflected only to a very limited degree in HESD research. Somehow alarming is the fact that many of the case studies do not meet minimum standards of case study research (see Kyburz-Graber in this Handbook); some do not even refer to a research question, but just describe the implementation of ESD in one higher education institution, for instance.

Details about the process of data collection are only given in 46 per cent of all articles. When we take into account that about 23 per cent of all articles are conceptual in nature and per se do not include data collection, there are however still 31 per cent of the articles which are not conceptual, but nevertheless do not refer to any sort of data collection. Among those that do refer to data collection, the most common method of data collection is the survey method, followed by document analysis, interviews and focus groups (see Table 7.5).

Table 7.3 Research focus

Research focus	*n*	%
Descriptive	232	44.6
Exploratory	118	22.7
Conceptual	118	22.7
Explanatory	52	10.0

Table 7.4 Research methods

Research method	*n*	%
Case studies	265	51.3
Conceptual papers	118	22.8
Surveys, longitudinal, cross-sectional and trend studies	58	11.2
Naturalistic and ethnographic research	31	6.0
Action research	19	3.7
Historical and documentary research	19	3.7
Experiments, quasi experiments, single case research and meta-analysis	5	1.0
Ex post facto research	2	0.4

Table 7.5 Methods of data collection

Data collection	*n*	%
Survey	124	35.7
Document analysis	85	24.5
Interview	48	13.8
Focus groups	35	10.1
Tests, Assignments	30	8.6
Observation	15	4.3
Other	10	2.9

What are the main research topics?

Among the research topics, curriculum development features prominently with about one third of all publications related to that content area. Together with approaches of teaching and learning, organisational change and research on students' as well as lecturers' views and opinions, this covers three out of four papers (see Table 7.6). Linking to the recent prominent discussion in educational science on accountability and assessment, it may surprise that less than 6 per cent of all articles deal with the assessment of learning outcomes. Thus, while HESD research tells us in particular a lot about how ESD can be integrated in university curricula and about what teaching and learning approaches might be especially adequate for HESD, still little evidence-based research is focusing on what students actually learn and which competencies they develop.

A word cloud of all the articles' key words as provided by the authors underlines the impression of the dominant discourse around curriculum (see Figure 7.2). It also provides insights into disciplinary priorities such as engineering and management.

Table 7.6 Content focus

Content	*n*	%
Curriculum development	176	33.8
Teaching and learning approaches	100	19.2
Organisational change/learning	64	12.3
Students'/lecturers' views and opinions	55	10.6
Development of ESD in higher education in a particular nation/region	31	6.0
Assessing student learning outcomes	30	5.8
Philosophical	23	4.4
Research in HESD	9	1.7
Others	32	6.2

Figure 7.2 Word cloud of key words

How has HESD research developed since its beginning?

The growth in the number of articles over the time period that has been analysed is presented in Figure 7.3. It shows that it took about ten years from the emergence of the first articles to see a notable growth in quantity, which becomes clearly visible around the beginning of the UN Decade on Education for Sustainable Development (2005–2015) with an increase that outnumbers the overall growth of published papers in that time. Since 2008 the number of published articles has settled to between 60 and 70 articles per year.

A cross-tabulation of the first authors' origins (continent) per year of publication is presented in Table 7.7. The figure reveals that European and North American researchers pioneered the field of HESD. While at the end of the twentieth century researchers from Latin America and the Caribbean started making a notable contribution, researchers from other continents joined in only more recently.

Although there is a slight variation from year to year, an overall trend in terms of the distribution between authors from different continents becomes obvious. Not unlike research in international peer reviewed journals as such, the field of HESD research is still dominated by researchers from Europe and North America. While for the period between 2008 and 2012 on average 44 per cent of the first authors came from Europe and 25 per cent from North America, only 15 per cent came from Australia/Oceania, 11 per cent from Asia, 3 per cent from Latin America and the Caribbean and only 1.6 per cent from Africa. There is no evidence that the European and North American dominance decreases.

A cross-tabulation of the research focus per year of publication reveals another notable development (see Table 7.8). It shows how the descriptive focus was predominant over more than a decade, a fact that might not be surprising for a newly emerging research area. While between 2004 and 2008 descriptive research was present in about 50 per cent (in 2005 even

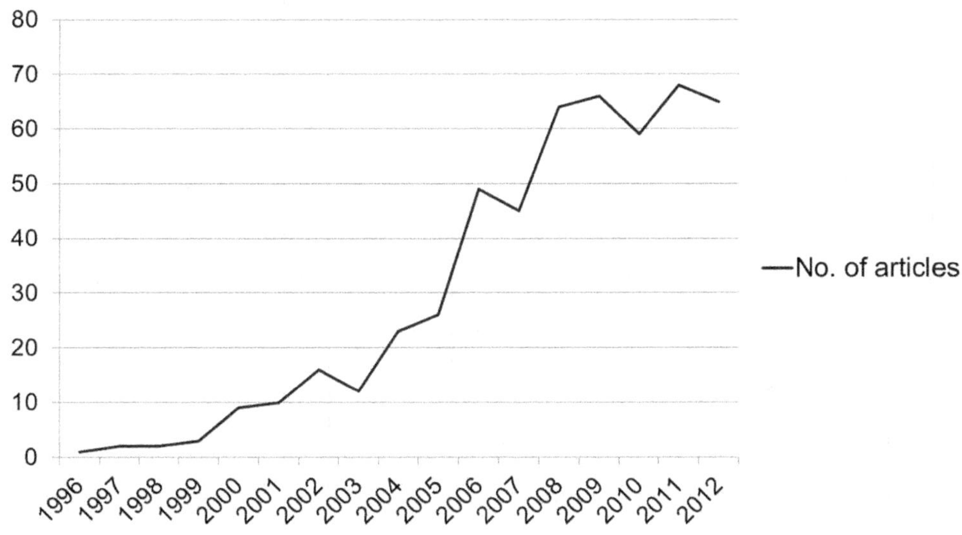

Figure 7.3 Published articles from 1992 to 2012

about 60 per cent) of all articles, there is a steady decrease over the last years. Between 2009 and 2011 this number has reached only about 40 per cent, in 2012 only about 30 per cent. The percentage of exploratory research has been constantly around 25 per cent since 2007, while the quantity of explanatory studies and conceptual papers has been slightly increasing during the last years.

Discussion of the findings

The systematic review provides us with an impression of HESD as a field of research that has emerged in the 1990s and has become fairly stable and significant in terms of its output. This confirms an existing general appraisal given the growing number of dedicated journals and conferences (Barth and Michelsen 2013) and contradicts partly the findings of the literature review by Karatzoglou (2013) who came up with a significantly lower number and relatively low publication numbers in 2010 and 2011.

Although a thorough and systematic search strategy has been applied, the process shed light on a number of limitations. As not all articles especially from the early 1990s have been digitalised and made available in databases there might be still articles missing in that sample. Similarly, the increase in the sample throughout the research steps shows another systemic problem of reviews in such a young and emerging field. As there has been no 'academic arena' with established journals for the field during the first years, articles have been published in a wide array of journals, not all of them easily accessible and indexed in databases. New journals that emerged in response to the growing need for places for this discourse are by now integrated into database indexes (e.g. *Environmental Education Research, International Journal of Sustainability in Higher Education*) but only from the time of acceptance. Thus, for as full a picture as possible, intensive additional search steps have been necessary.

In terms of the authorship and distribution of research, our results confirm Karatzoglou's (2013) findings of a strong predominance of European and North-American researchers in the

Table 7.7 First authors' origin from 1992 to 2012

Authors' origin		*1996*	*1997*	*1998*	*1999*	*2000*	*2001*	*2002*	*2003*	*2004*	*2005*	*2006*	*2007*	*2008*	*2009*	*2010*	*2011*	*2012*
Europe	n	0	2	1	2	5	5	5	6	10	14	29	21	38	27	24	23	28
	%	0.0	100.0	50.0	66.7	55.6	50.0	31.3	50.0	43.5	53.8	59.2	46.7	59.4	40.9	40.7	33.8	43.1
North-America	n	1	0	0	0	2	1	4	3	5	8	7	11	9	20	14	21	17
	%	100.0	0.0	0.0	0.0	22.2	10.0	25.0	25.0	21.7	30.8	14.3	24.4	14.1	30.3	23.7	30.9	26.2
Australia/Oceania	n	0	0	0	0	1	1	3	1	3	3	7	7	10	12	4	13	10
	%	0.0	0.0	0.0	0.0	11.1	10.0	18.8	8.3	13.0	11.5	14.3	15.6	15.6	18.2	6.8	19.1	15.4
Asia	n	0	0	0	0	0	3	2	2	2	0	2	1	5	5	11	7	8
	%	0.0	0.0	0.0	0.0	0.0	30.0	12.5	16.7	8.7	0.0	4.1	2.2	7.8	7.6	18.6	10.3	12.3
Africa	n	0	0	0	0	1	0	1	0	3	0	1	3	1	0	2	1	1
	%	0.0	0.0	0.0	0.0	11.1	0.0	6.3	0.0	13.0	0.0	2.0	6.7	1.6	0.0	3.4	1.5	1.5
Latin America and	n	0	0	1	1	0	0	1	0	0	1	3	2	1	2	4	3	1
the Caribbean	%	0.0	0.0	50.0	33.3	0.0	0.0	6.3	0.0	0.0	3.8	6.1	4.4	1.6	3.0	6.8	4.4	1.5

Table 7.8 Research focus from 1992 to 2012

Research focus		*1996*	*1997*	*1998*	*1999*	*2000*	*2001*	*2002*	*2003*	*2004*	*2005*	*2006*	*2007*	*2008*	*2009*	*2010*	*2011*	*2012*
Exploratory	n	0	0	1	1	1	2	4	0	6	3	8	12	14	22	12	17	15
	%	0.0	0.0	50.0	33.3	11.1	20.0	25.0	0.0	26.1	11.5	16.3	26.7	21.9	33.3	20.3	25.0	23.1
Explanatory	n	0	0	0	0	1	0	0	3	0	2	3	4	6	8	5	10	10
	%	0.0	0.0	0.0	0.0	11.1	0.0	0.0	25.0	0.0	7.7	6.1	8.9	9.4	12.1	8.5	14.7	15.4
Descriptive	n	1	1	1	1	5	7	7	5	12	16	26	21	32	26	24	27	20
	%	100.0	50.0	50.0	33.3	55.6	70.0	43.8	41.7	52.2	61.5	53.1	46.7	50.0	39.4	40.7	39.7	30.8
Conceptual Paper	n	0	1	0	1	2	1	5	4	5	5	12	8	12	10	18	14	20
	%	0.0	50.0	0.0	33.3	22.2	10.0	31.3	33.3	21.7	19.2	24.5	17.8	18.8	15.2	30.5	20.6	30.8

field who in their studies also focus mainly on Western countries, and there is still no indication of any change in this respect. Given the development of ESD in non-European and North American countries it appears we still have much to learn about HESD in African, Asian and Latin-American countries. Encouraging, supporting and conducting more research in these so far underrepresented regions will help us to better understand the relevance of different contexts as well as general drivers and barriers for implementing HESD and will contribute to cross colonial boundaries (see in this respect also Andreotti in this Handbook).

In this context, it is worth stressing that a clear limitation of our study is its focus only on articles published in English. Including articles published in French, German, Portuguese and Spanish, for instance, would probably make visible a much stronger contribution to HESD research of researchers from Africa and Latin America. Nevertheless, it has to be considered that the international scientific discourse is mainly dominated by the English language. Thus, although it would be important to include articles in further languages in future HESD literature reviews, still it remains true that a stronger participation of non-Western researchers in the leading HESD research journals (as indicated in Table 7.1) and collaborative and comparative research would be important for creating a real North-South dialogue on HESD.

It can be highlighted that the quantity of explanatory studies has been increasing during the last years, but there is still a strong predominance of descriptive research often being designed as a case study. Case studies can offer important, context-sensitive insights that might not be achieved with other approaches, but therefore they need to meet the necessary quality standards (see Kyburz-Graber in this Handbook). The problems around this sort of research especially in environmental education and ESD have been discussed from early on (Corcoran *et al.* 2004) and strong calls for more rigour and comparative research have been raised (Barth and Thomas 2012; Barth 2015). These drawbacks seem to be visible with numerous case studies presented in the literature analysed in this study. The fact that still about one third of the articles do not detail the process of data collection and analysis is something that needs to be improved, to say the least.

Conclusion

Over the last decades, a number of research initiatives and postgraduate programmes worldwide gained momentum and engaged with research on higher education for sustainable development. Higher education for sustainable development has become a diverse, significant and stable field of research. In the light of the literature review presented in this chapter we draw the following main conclusions, which we take as a starting point for an international dialogue about needs for future research on higher education for sustainable development:

- *HESD research is characterised by a Western dominance:* There is a clear need for more research on higher education for sustainable development from non-Western researchers as well as for more research in non-Western countries. Conducting more research in the – so far underrepresented – non-Western regions will help us to better understand the relevance of different contexts as well as general drivers and barriers for implementing HESD and will contribute to cross colonial boundaries.
- *HESD research is (still) dominated by descriptive studies and only partly meets standards of high quality research:* Although the strong predominance of descriptive research often being designed as a case study has been decreasing during the last years, there is still a particular need for more explanatory studies. This kind of research would help to gain more gener-

alisable evidence on drivers and barriers for implementing HESD and the impacts of HESD. Furthermore, we should strive for more quality in HESD research – not only in case study research as mentioned before but in all kind of studies; of course, the research question should be made explicit, and in the case of empirical studies the process of data collection and analysis should be detailed. It is surprising that this is not a standard yet in articles which all went through peer review.

- *HESD research focuses particularly on curriculum development and teaching and learning approaches:* While HESD research tells us in particular a lot about how ESD can be integrated in university curricula and about which teaching and learning approaches might be especially adequate for HESD, still little evidence-based research is focusing on what students actually learn and which competencies they develop. There is a broad debate about competence concepts and about which teaching and learning approaches help students develop competencies. However, there is still only very limited research on learning outcomes. There is still much research to be done to operationalise competencies and develop instruments for assessing and monitoring students' competence development (see Wiek *et al.* in this Handbook).

By presenting data concerning research foci, methods, research topics, key journals and authors' origins, as well as general trends over time in HESD research, the literature review contributes to better understand and systematise the academic discourse on HESD. It illustrates the breadth of research directions and provides both challenges and guidance for directions emerging researchers – and others – may wish to pursue.

We hope that this Handbook will contribute to the further development of HESD research in terms of the needs described here – in particular the need for more global and more empirical HESD research.

References

Adomßent, M. and Michelsen, G., 2006. 'German Academia Heading for Sustainability? Reflections on Policy and Practice in Teaching, Research and Institutional Innovations', *Environmental Education Research*, 12(1), 85–99.

Adomßent, M., Godemann, J., and Michelsen, G., 2007. 'Transferability of Approaches to Sustainable Development at Universities as a Challenge', *International Journal of Sustainability in Higher Education*, 8(4), 385–402.

Andrew, J. and Malone, K., 1995. 'The First Ten Years. A Review of the *Australian Journal of Environmental Education*', *Australian Journal of Environmental Education*, 11, 131–62.

Barth, M., 2015. *Implementing Sustainability in Higher Education. Learning in an Age of Transformation.* London: Routledge.

Barth, M. and Michelsen, G., 2013. 'Learning for Change: An Educational Contribution to Sustainability Science', *Sustainability Science*, 8(1), 103–19.

Barth, M. and Thomas, I., 2012. 'Synthesising case study research. Ready for the Next Step?', *Environmental Education Research*, 18(6), 751–64.

Cohen, L., Manion, L. and Morrison, K., 2009. *Research Methods in Education*, 6th edn. London: Routledge Falmer.

Corcoran, P.B., Walker, K.E. and Wals, A.E.J., 2004. 'Case Studies, Make-your-case Studies, and Case Stories. A Critique of Case-study Methodology in Sustainability in Higher Education', *Environmental Education Research*, 10(1), 7–21.

Fadeeva, Z. and Mochizuki, Y., 2010. 'Higher Education for Today and Tomorrow: University Appraisal for Diversity, Innovation and Change towards Sustainable Development', *Sustainability Science*, 5(2), 249–56.

Fink, A., 2009. *Conducting Research Literature Reviews: From the Internet to Paper.* Los Angeles, CA: Sage.

Foster, P. and Hammersley, M., 1998. 'A Review of Reviews: Structure and Function in Reviews of Educational Research', *British Educational Research Journal*, 24(5), 609–28.

Hart, C., 2002. *Doing a Literature Review. Releasing the Social Science Research Imagination.* London: Sage.
Heimlich, J.E., 2007. 'Research Trends in the United States. EE to ESD', *The Journal of Education for Sustainable Development*, 1(2), 219–27.
Karatzoglou, B., 2013. 'An In-depth Literature Review of the Evolving Roles and Contributions of Universities to Education for Sustainable Development', *Journal of Cleaner Production*, 49 (June 2013), 44–53.
Lee, Y., Driscoll, M.P. and Nelson, D.W., 2004. 'The Past, Present, and Future of Research in Distance Education: Results of a Content Analysis', *American Journal of Distance Education*, 18(4), 225–41.
Lee, M., Wu, Y. and Tsai, C., 2009. 'Research Trends in Science Education from 2003 to 2007: A Content Analysis of Publications in Selected Journals', *International Journal of Science Education*, 31(15), 1999–2020.
Light, R.J. and Pillemer, D.B., 1984. *Summing Up. The Science of Reviewing Research.* Cambridge, MA: Harvard University Press.
Littell, J.H., Corcoran, J. and Pillai, V.K., 2008. *Systematic Reviews and Meta-analysis.* Oxford: Oxford University Press.
McEwan, P.J., 2014. 'Improving Learning in Primary Schools of Developing Countries: A Meta-Analysis of Randomized Experiments', *Review of Educational Research*, doi: 10.3102/0034654314553127.
Marcinkowski, T., 2003. 'Commentary on Rickinson's "Learners and Learning in Environmental Education: A Critical Review of the Evidence" (EER 7(3))', *Environmental Education Research*, 9(2), 181–214.
Petticrew, M. and Roberts, H., 2009. *Systematic Reviews in the Social Sciences. A Practical Guide*, 8th edn. Malden, MA: Blackwell Publishers.
Regehr, G., 2004. 'Trends in Medical Education Research', *Academic Medicine*, 79(10), 939–47.
Reid, A. and Nikel, J., 2003. 'Reading a Critical Review of Evidence: Notes and Queries on Research Programmes in Environmental Education', *Environmental Education Research*, 9(2), 149–65.
Reunamo, J. and Pipere, A., 2011. 'Doing Research on Education for Sustainable Development', *International Journal of Sustainability in Higher Education*, 12(2), 110–24.
Rickinson, M., 2001. 'Learners and Learning in Environmental Education: A Critical Review of the Evidence', *Environmental Education Research*, 7(3), 207–320.
Rieckmann, M., 2012. 'Future-oriented Higher Education: Which Key Competencies should be Fostered through University Teaching and Learning?', *Futures*, 44(2), 127–35.
Sauvé, L. and Berryman, T., 2003. 'Researchers and Research in Environmental Education: A Critical Review Essay on Mark Rickinson's Report on Learners and Learning', *Environmental Education Research*, 9(2), 167–80.
Stevenson, R.B. and Evans, N., 2011. 'The Distinctive Characteristics of Environmental Education Research in Australia', *Australian Journal of Environmental Education*, 27(2), 274–87.
Teixeira, P., 2013. 'Reflecting about Current Trends in Higher Education Research', in Kehm, B. and Musselin, C. (eds), *The Development of Higher Education Research in Europe.* Rotterdam/Boston/Taipei: SensePublishers, 103–21.
Thurlings, M., Vermeulen, M., Bastiaens, T. and Stijnen, S., 2013. 'Understanding Feedback: A Learning Theory Perspective', *Educational Research Review*, 9, 1–15.
Trede, F., Macklin, R. and Bridges, D., 2011. 'Professional Identity Development: A Review of the Higher Education Literature', *Studies In Higher Education*, 37(3), 365–84.
Tsai, C., and Lydia Wen, M., 2005. 'Research and Trends in Science Education from 1998 to 2002: A Content Analysis of Publication in Selected Journals', *International Journal of Science Education*, 27(1), 3–14.
United Nations Educational, Scientific and Cultural Organization (UNESCO), 2009. *Bonn Declaration. UNESCO World Conference on Education for Sustainable Development, Bonn, Germany on 31 March to 2 April 2009.* www.esd-world-conference-2009.org/fileadmin/download/ESD2009_Bonn Declaration080409.pdf [accessed 20 October 2010].
Vare, P. and Scott, W.A.H., 2007. 'Learning for a Change: Exploring the Relationship Between Education and Sustainable Development', *Journal of Education for Sustainable Development*, 1(2), 191–8.
Vaughter, P., Wright, T., McKenzie, M. and Lidstone, L., 2013. 'Greening the Ivory Tower: A Review of Educational Research on Sustainability in Post-Secondary Education', *Sustainability*, 5(5), 2252–71.
Wright, T. and Pullen, S., 2007. 'Examining the Literature: A Bibliometric Study of ESD Journal Articles in the Education Resources Information Center Database', *Journal of Education for Sustainable Development*, 1(1), 77–90.

8

ONGOING AND FUTURE DIRECTIONS OF RESEARCH ON HIGHER EDUCATION FOR SUSTAINABLE DEVELOPMENT

Steve Gough, Meyrav Mor, Anna Sowter and Paul Vare

Introduction

To understand the way we think about the present, we need to examine the past. The ideas academics have today do not spring into their minds from nowhere, but are rooted in earlier terminologies, practices and debates of which they are likely to be only partly aware. To understand the prospects for higher education for sustainable development we therefore need to examine its principle historical influences. Space is limited, so this discussion restricts itself to two such influences. These are work in environmental education, and education for sustainable development. With this brief analysis in hand, the rest of the chapter considers the successes and challenges of the present and the prospects for the future. In particular, it notes that much sustainable development education in higher education takes place in partial or absolute ignorance of the existence of something called 'Education for Sustainable Development' (ESD), and asks whether this matters and why. In particular, this gives rise to a discussion of the differences between, on the one hand, identifying and assessing ESD and, on the other hand, practising and developing ESD in a purposive way.

A brief and selective history

The perception that human societies are damaging their environment, and that there is something potentially catastrophic about this situation from a moral, ecological, economic, spiritual and/or social point of view, has been with us for a long time. To take one example, John Muir's National Park Bill was passed by the US Congress in 1890. It is certainly possible to argue, however, that this is a poor example because, in fact, 1890 is not very long ago at all. It may be that guilt about human activities that increase economic and cultural wealth but also transform the environment has been with us since the events sometimes known as the 'Urban Revolution' which happened around 6,000 years ago (Kriwaczek 2010), or perhaps since the Flood (whatever that actually was) which occurred only a little more recently.

In any case, and notwithstanding the fact that people have been teaching each other things about and in relation to the environment for *as long as there have been* people, the origins of *environmental education* as a distinct curriculum project, pedagogic endeavour and object of study are much more recent. Annette Gough (Greenall Gough 1993) dates it to roughly 1970, when the United States' Environmental Education Act was passed. In the 1970s and 1980s much time and effort was expended trying to delineate exactly what environmental education was, and to embed it in national education documents through United Nations conferences and the like. Much of this work was very good indeed and continues to have an influence, albeit usually an unrecognised influence, on how we think about higher education for sustainable development in the present. The following quotation illustrates the approach most frequently taken at that time:

> We might define an environmentally responsible citizen as one who has (1) an awareness and sensitivity to the total environment and its allied problems … (2) a basic understanding of the environment and its allied problems … (3) feelings of concern for the environment and motivation for actively participating in environmental improvement and protection, (4) skills for identifying and solving environmental problems … (5) active involvement at all levels in working towards resolution of environmental problems.
>
> *(Hungerford and Volk 1993: 8–9)*

There are a number of points that we might note here. Firstly, everything that is being proposed is sensible enough in itself. Teaching these kinds of understandings, awareness and skills seems reasonable, and there are, without doubt, academic colleagues around the world today teaching sustainability topics in science and engineering who might see the above as a pretty decent working definition of what they were hoping to achieve. It is hard to see why anyone would be *against* such teaching. It is quite straightforward to identify more recent work that would appear to be in some respects a development of the Hungeford and Volk approach, even if this is not necessarily made explicit. So, for example, when Disterheft *et al.* (2013) write of 'sustainability science' we might say that they are developing a new idea in a long-standing, and sometimes marginalised tradition:

> Sustainability science has emerged over the last decade as a new interdisciplinary field that attempts to conduct problem-driven and action-oriented research on the challenges mentioned above, striving to link knowledge to social actions and creating new visions of natural and social well-being.
>
> *(Disterheft* et al. *2013: 10)*

Secondly, however, the Hungerford and Volk text normalises a number of assumptions that are, in fact questionable. These are:

- The appropriate lever for bringing about change is action by citizens. This assumes that citizens have real power, that people think of themselves as citizens (rather than as employees, employers, Christians, Muslims, parents or something else) when making important choices, and, in fact, that everyone *actually is* a citizen.
- The 'problems' that we are concerned with reside *in the environment*. So if they are to be solved it is the environment and its workings that we need to understand. An alternative formulation would be that the problems ultimately reside in society.
- The rather more arcane but, as it has turned out, very significant assumption that scientific understandings can be separated from 'feelings'.

From about 1989 onwards these assumptions were in fact challenged by an alternative body of work originating, for the most part, in Australia and the UK. Initially, academics in this area made use of a distinction between 'education *in* the environment', 'education *about* the environment', and their preferred 'education *for* the environment'. This new approach has been characterised as 'red-green'. This designation has some merit, but is also an oversimplification. It does capture the attempt to link environmental and social justice issues – something that had also been done in the Brundtland Report of 1987, which offered what is still the most widely cited definition of sustainable development as the meeting of present needs without compromising the ability of future generations to meet their own needs. However, of those marching under the 'red-green' banner some were more red (e.g. John Huckle, Ian Robottom), some more green (e.g. Stephen Sterling, Paul Hart) and some already making the turn towards feminism, postmodernism and poststructuralism (e.g. Annette Gough). The 'red' element also derived methodological impetus from the influence of Kemmis and his work on critical curriculum theorising at Deakin University. The point made by Dobson as early as 1990 – that it is not in the least obvious that the exploitation of the natural world and the exploitation of people are linked in any systematic or predictable way (Dobson 1990) – was largely ignored. This was however a period during which some outstanding scholarship was produced, together with some landmark pedagogy in higher education, most particularly the superb Deakin University/Griffith University Environmental Education Project. Through this body of work 'environmental education' gradually began to lose the interest of academics (although not necessarily of practitioners, who were sometimes confused by the ways things were going) and be replaced by a variety of competing terminologies that eventually became consolidated as 'Education for Sustainable Development'. In fact, 1993 saw the publication – all within the Deakin/Griffith project – of John Fien's *Education for the Environment: Critical Curriculum Theorising and Environmental Education*, Fien and Trainer's edited volume *Environmental Education: A Pathway to Sustainability*, and, within the latter, Fien and Trainer's chapter entitled 'Education for Sustainability'.

To continue this historical account beyond this point would require a book in itself, since the idea of Education for Sustainable Development proved a most suggestive one. It was taken up across Western Europe and Scandinavia, in Russia, Canada, Japan, Africa and elsewhere. In every case academics and practitioners took ownership of the term in their own contexts and shaped it to their particular purposes. Further, in all of these settings work specifically focused on higher education was developed. There are some, perhaps most notably Hopkins, who have been ever present throughout these developments from the earliest days of environmental education, and have worked in most of these countries and continents. Professor Hopkins currently holds the UNESCO Chair in Reorienting Teacher Education to Sustainable Development at York University in Toronto.

Of course, the 'paradigm wars' are now over. As is often the case with wars, the passage of time has caused matters that were once the source of vehement debate – and even sometimes, sadly, ill-feeling between colleagues – to seem rather humdrum and obvious. Most contemporary scholarship takes the need for active and rigorous social science informed by methodologically scrupulous natural science as given. Recent illustrative examples include the following:

- Fuchs' (2012) observation that upcoming environmental challenges for society require not only a strong supply of technically competent engineers, but also changes in the way engineers think about their profession and their role in society, and thus changes in engineering education.

- Work by Thomas and Day (2014) to explore the relationship between the capabilities required of graduates by employers and by sustainability respectively. They note that these sets of capabilities have a great deal in common, so reflecting the reality that while many problems do indeed require technical expertise for their solution, the definition of what counts as a problem, and what an acceptable solution, is a social matter.
- Insights from the field of corporate social responsibility that recognise the complexity of change processes in universities, and the need to understand the interplay of, *inter alia*, their disciplinary and social missions in promoting sustainable development (Godemann *et al.* 2014)
- Sterling's (2014) prospectus for education and sustainable development post-2015, which notes the importance of both specialist competencies and creativity and imagination, and concludes by asking: 'what are the main elements of possible sustainability scenarios over the next 10–20 years with regard to such areas as water and sanitation, energy, health, sustainable cities, climate change, etc.? What competencies will (*i*) policymakers, (*ii*) specialists and (*iii*) the public need to ensure that desirable scenarios are realized?' (Sterling 2014: 111).

However, before moving on we should note one further tension that runs throughout the period and into the present. This is, quite simply, what ultimately is the purpose of (higher) education in this context. If we want to judge the success or failure of an initiative, what should we look for? Should we look for learning by students? Should we look for substantive improvements in environmental variables such as carbon emissions, biodiversity loss or water quality over time? It is very clear that these two different kinds of goal *do not* necessarily, or even very often, go hand in hand. Students do not have control of environmental variables, now or in the future: there are many factors in play including the economic, legal, political, social, technological and ecological contexts in which learning takes place and is applied. Students may, of course, have an influence: but that is not the same thing. Further, teachers and lecturers have a primary professional duty to their students: and students, by-and-large, are looking for an education that will serve them in *this* world, and not a world that, however regrettably, exists in the present only as an aspiration in the minds of their teachers.

Nevertheless, when policy-makers support ESD initiatives they usually do so because they want to see environmental (or wider social sustainability) outcomes. Of course, progress can be made towards these, but it is often difficult to show that education produces a stronger impact than, say, changes in regulatory environments, technological processes or financial incentives. An alternative view, squarely in the Deweyian pragmatist tradition in education, is that (good) education *is an inalienable and central component* of any sustainable way of life, enabling continuous, intelligent adaptation to a world that is always subject to change. The earliest expression of this conception is probably Foster's (2001) paper. It underpins his later work (see, for example, Foster 2008). In this view, the purpose of education for sustainable development is not to transmit a set of prescriptions that will bring about a sustainable form of life, because no sufficiently detailed and enduring set of prescriptions *can ever possibly* be available. Rather, it is to enable learners to make better decisions throughout their lives. The test of success is not environmental, but educational.

Such a proposition is not unique to an English language tradition. It is, for example, broadly consistent with the action competence approach developed in Denmark and Sweden (see, for example, Mogensen and Schnack 2010). However, this perspective does not render evaluation of ESD any less complex and problematic, if anything quite the reverse (see Kopnina and Meijers 2014, for a recent discussion of some of the issues and possibilities).

At this point we might usefully return to the title of this chapter and ask what it entails. The title is: (Ongoing and future directions of) Research on Higher Education (for Sustainable Development). The brackets serve to emphasise that the present project is an instance of research within the higher education system *into* research within the higher education system. The addition of the contents of the brackets narrows down the focus within a wider field of higher education research. In that wider field, one issue dominates all others: the impact of neo-liberal globalisation upon higher education provision around the world, particularly in relation to performativity and instrumentalism.

To illustrate the importance of this, contrast the following two quotations, both significant in their way in the development of higher education in Britain. The first comes from the Executive Summary of the October 2013 Witty Report into universities and growth:

> Universities should assume an explicit responsibility for facilitating economic growth, and all universities should have stronger incentives to embrace this 'enhanced Third Mission' – from working together to develop and commercialise technologies which can win in international markets to partnering with innovative local Small and Medium Enterprises.
>
> *(Department for Business, Innovation and Skills 2013: 6)*

The second comes from the work of the philosopher Oakeshott:

> This, then, to the undergraduate, is the distinctive mark of a university; it is a place where he has the opportunity of education in conversation with his teachers, his fellows and himself, and where he is not encouraged to confuse education with training for a profession, with learning the tricks of a trade, with preparation for future particular service in society, or with the acquisition of a kind of moral or intellectual outfit to see him through life. Whenever an ulterior purpose of this sort makes its appearance, education (which is concerned with persons, not functions) steals out of the back door with noiseless steps.
>
> *(Fuller 1989: 101)*

As academics in the field of education, the tension between these two kinds of position is part of our intellectual heritage. It leads us perhaps, sometimes anyway, to get unnecessarily bogged down in questions of ontology, epistemology and methodology: and while we are engaged by these arcane and difficult matters we can easily forget that our academic colleagues in other disciplines do not share out concerns, but are simply getting on with developing and delivering to students programmes that are, by any defensible standard, practical examples of education for sustainable development. They should, therefore, be studied by research into education for sustainable development. This is to suggest that while part of the task of developing or implementing sustainable development through higher education is clearly to refine the ESD concept, another is to be able to identify useful elements in the professional practice of others that do not, necessarily, accord with our currently most refined conceptualisations. The following discussion of a research example illustrates this point.

An English example, and more recent developments

In 2007 the Higher Education Funding Council for England (HEFCE) commissioned research into sustainability in the country's (then) 132 universities. This research tender was won by a consortium comprising the Policy Studies Institute, PA Consulting Ltd and the Centre for Research in Education and the Environment of the University of Bath. The research was conducted under three main headings: research in sustainability; sustainability through the management of university estates; and, teaching (see Katayama and Gough 2008 for an account of the work on teaching and sustainable development, the full report of the research is at www.hefce.ac.uk/pubs/rdreports/2008/rd03_08/).

As a result of this work a database of teaching in all universities in England was produced for the funder. The database is searchable by three primary headings:

- Discipline (for example, mathematics; sociology; chemical engineering)
- Institution (for example, University of Bath, Loughborough University)
- Academic level (for example, Diploma, Bachelors with Honours, Masters)

Standard headings were used throughout to ensure comparability. For example, courses were allocated to a discipline based on which of a set of national, standardised disciplinary headings host universities used when reporting to the Higher Education Statistics Agency (HESA). The database contains in excess of 1,600 items, of which a little over 300 are modules within programmes that have no other sustainability content. The remainder are programmes. The largest amount of sustainability-focused teaching was found to be at masters level. In terms of disciplinary areas, there were only three in which no sustainability-related teaching was found at all. These were 'clinical dentistry', 'pharmacy and pharmacology' and 'anatomy and physiology'. The most sustainability-related teaching nationwide was found in the areas of 'earth, marine and environmental science', 'architecture, built environment and planning', 'social studies', 'business and management' and 'geography'. It is also noteworthy that there appears to be no reliable correlation between the inclusion of 'sustainable development' as a goal within an institution's mission statement and the presence of teaching that promotes sustainable development.

An interesting finding was that the use of the terms 'sustainability' or 'sustainable development' in the names of programmes was typically a matter of the institution's position in the academic marketplace. So, for example, the Dean of a School in one of the country's elite universities reported that, although sustainable development lay at the intellectual heart of *all* programmes, the words themselves were *never* used in programme or module titles. The reason given was that the institution sought to attract the very best student applicants, and its internal research showed that such applicants *did not want* a qualification with a title that might appear to be unusual to future potential employers. Hence, for the best applicants, and on the whole, 'Mechanical Engineering' was attractive but 'Mechanical Engineering for Sustainable Development' was not, even if the programme content was the same in both cases. In less prestigious institutions that were competing for candidates with lower entry scores this situation was reversed, perhaps because the applicants hoped to improve their subsequent position in the labour market by demonstrating a fashionable specialism. An important lesson here is that it may well be factors of this sort, operating at the margin, that determine the attractiveness and success of offerings in sustainable development, rather than high-level rhetoric (however convincing and justified) about environment threats, saving the planet and so on.

Overall, a four-part classification of sustainable development teaching suggested itself. *Problem-oriented* courses set out to equip students to help address particular, serious issues in the modern world. These include contaminated land remediation, climate change, mathematical modelling in relation to, *inter alia*, biodiversity loss and habitat fragmentation, waste management, poverty, emergency disaster response and so on. *Responsibility-oriented* courses focus on corporate social responsibility in relation to a range of matters that include tourism management, ethical fashion, global supply chain management, social enterprise and land management. *Creativity-oriented* courses seek to use sustainability to acquire creative impetus across a wide range of areas that include garden design, product engineering, town planning and rural regeneration. Finally, *skills-oriented* courses offer training in sustainability skills for the labour market, and may be further subdivided into those dealing with manufacturing skills (for example in relation to energy efficiency, sustainable technologies and sustainable design), environmental management skills (in, for example, groundwater engineering, marine resources management, aquatic chemistry and quantitative environmental analysis), and social skills (such as participatory design, regeneration management and knowledge transfer).

This review provides a snapshot of universities in a particular country at a particular time, using a particular organising framework. That framework includes, for example, a clear distinction between learning and teaching, research and estates management; and, a four-part classification of sustainable development teaching in higher education. No claims are made for the merit of these particular conceptual devices, but it might be helpful if academics in the field could agree some basics of classification so that sequential reviews and studies could compare like with like. Now, of course, we do have available the findings of other, subsequent reviews undertaken in other places. They have tended to use quite different (and, no doubt, quite possibly better) methodologies, so making it difficult to develop iterative measures of progress. So, for example, a study of ESD in HE in Scotland was conducted in 2008 and reported in 2009 (HEA, 2009). It used a questionnaire, interviews and case studies, and found, *inter alia*, that;

- 9 of the 16 responding HEIs (56.25 per cent) had specific learning and teaching commitments to nurture ESD
- 32 UG and 47 PG programmes were identified as explicitly targeted to sustainability issues
- Various pedagogic approaches to ESD were emerging.
- All 16 responding HEIs anticipated some intentional increase in their formal sustainability provision. (HEA 2009: 3)

These findings are similar to the English ones, but it is hard to make detailed comparisons. More recent reviews reinforce the point. Sterling *et al.* (2012), for example, set out precisely to share lessons from UK experience with others around the world. They offer a wealth of case study examples, and organise their material under three headings, 'context', 'aspects' and 'institutional change'. The inclusion of the last of these, at the very least, is a significant step forward, and one which goes some considerable way to provide a framework in which the issue identified earlier, of synthesising the identification of ESD in higher education with its development, might be addressed.

Moving forward would be facilitated if we could be sure to preserve and build on such classificatory improvements. Other recent examples of attempts to review ESD in higher education across different contexts include the UNESCO review of ESD in the UK (UNESCO 2013) and the UE4SD (2014) report covering 33 countries. There is also a great deal of excellent work that would be more impactful if it could be more readily subjected to critical comparison. This would include, for example, the work of Wright and her colleagues in Canada on the ways in which sustainable development is conceptualised within higher education (Sylvestre *et al.* 2013; Wright and Defields 2012; Wright and Wilton 2012) and the work of Thomas and his collaborators in Australia on the relationship between the perceptions of employers and sustainable development in higher education (Thomas 2014; Thomas *et al.* 2012).

None of the foregoing should be taken as providing cause for despair, but it does suggest that educationalists working in higher education should be asking how they might best contribute to a creative team effort. So, for example: 'what sustainability knowledge and pedagogy will contribute to producing the best engineers?' is a question that invites a collaborative and iteratively-developing process leading to a shared goal. By contrast, simply asserting what every engineer needs to know about sustainability will usually seem unwarrantably intrusive to academic colleagues and students alike.

Happily, there is much work taking place in the field of education that points in a very promising direction. One recent example (Krasny and Dillon 2013) identifies environmental problems as being 'wicked' – in the sense of having multiple problem definitions – and experiments with innovative educational techniques in order to address them. In setting out these techniques the authors state:

> Our experiment showed that pairing individuals with common interests yet different disciplinary perspectives can produce novel ideas and approaches; the general idea of providing a structure for working across disciplines may have application to other cross-disciplinary settings such as research projects and academic departments.
>
> *(Krasny and Dillon 2013: 275)*

Here we begin to see the possibility of education for sustainable development in higher education as a facilitating tool, or set of techniques for bringing together different approaches to create new knowledge in the face of new and/or intractable problems. The problems we face often are both new and intractable. Of course, it may be objected at this point that dealing with new and intractable problems does not sit particularly well with the idea of standardised systems for classification of ESD. A more refined view, consistent with Krasny and Dillion's insight and also, at a more philosophical level, with the pragmatist tradition in education, would be that a settled classificatory system is likely to elude us, but discussions held in good faith about what one might best look like are likely to be most productive.

Sustainability in context: three examples

Each of the following three cases draws on recent or ongoing doctoral study, and is itself, therefore, a contemporary example of higher education for sustainable development. In each case, ESD in higher education is at the centre of things: in the first two examples because ESD learning is taking place in an HE setting, and because the idea of sustainability is at the heart of the research project. In the third case ESD in HE is the focus of research as well.

1. Nepal

It is not possible to separate sustainability according to geographical boundaries, as whatever happens in one part of the world is inevitably linked to another. As an example, Nepal's massive export of unskilled labourers to the Middle East and other wealthy Asian countries has far reaching effects on the prospects for sustainable development. It brings about great unplanned changes in Nepal's rural communities.

As one of the most underdeveloped countries in the world, Nepal has been experiencing massive changes due to the Maoist insurgency which raged for ten years and consequently forced men to flee their villages. So began the massive exodus from rural areas into safe cities and abroad. Nepal's economy and way of life is mostly based on subsistence farming, and the men play a vital role in keeping it balanced. Fieldwork observations at a cluster of villages in Solu Khumbu, Eastern Nepal revealed that most of the men of working age were working abroad on three-to-five-year employment contracts. One village, for example, has 23 houses (which is equivalent to 23 families); here 30 men between the ages of 20–55 are working abroad. At the same time, 25–50 per cent of the cultivable land is not being used due to lack of manpower. Effects on sustainable development include: reduction of food production leading to the import of food; distortions of family structure and the traditional village welfare system; loss within families and the community of male role models who would otherwise transfer traditional knowledge of agriculture, craft and survival skills in their natural environment (for example, only the older people know how to make a wooden plough which is still the only way they plough their terraces); economic distortions from money repatriated by migrant workers; and, difficulties in reintegration of returning workers.

In this context traditional knowledge is very much alive. Communities are active in seeking to preserve their way of life. They feel proud of who they are and their heritage but also would like life to be more comfortable for them. Research is needed to understand how to develop educational approaches that not only inform children about environmental issues and better practices, but also addresses sustainability from a holistic perspective. If moving towards sustainable living in developing countries is to be achieved it is not only about the survival of the natural environment but of diversity of cultures.

2. Palestine

Non-Governmental Organisations (NGOs) are powerful stakeholders in sustainable development policy and programmes. Within them, learning is often perceived as a tool for social change. NGOs have developed broad programme areas focusing on awareness raising and capacity building. Water is clearly a crucial resource in relation to any conception of sustainable development, is politically contested in Palestine, and is debated in relation to technical understandings generated by a range of disciplines. We may ask what the rationale for learning should be for NGOs and participants, in relation to the sustainability of community water interventions.

Research into the role of learning in addressing water issues needs to be both context sensitive and responsive to the needs, lived experiences and symbolic representations of people at the local level. As an approach to understanding local experiences of water issues, the research suggests a need to explore the broader meanings that people give to water, in order for community interventions to bring about valued improvements in people's lives. The research observed how the sustainability of community water interventions is limited, primarily because communities lack decision making capability due to power asymmetries. Where participation in water interventions is limited to voluntary labour and the maintenance of new technology, the potential for learning is curtailed. During this process, local people struggle to assert and defend their lives in a context of great uncertainty. Further work is needed to explore how learning can be supported between organisations and communities, and how NGOs and other organisations can support local people's ideas – ideas that are meaningful to their lives and help to build capacity.

3. The UK

Though based in the UK, this recent research is informed by very extensive international educational experience, much of it in remote and/or politically troubled settings. For most UK universities today, higher education appears to be centrally concerned with engaging more fully in the economy and responding to pressure to ensure that students emerge with 'employability skills'. This might be seen as the neo-liberal agenda running its course, or simply the search for relevance in a shifting scene. But, while this seems to reflect a narrow conception of the economy, simultaneously economists, enlightened employers and others now understand the economy more broadly, and are, for example, pursuing alternative ideas such as 'shared value', 'cradle-to-cradle' or 'working with the grain of nature'. So, rather than research Education for Sustainable Development per se, researchers would do well to leave that particular furrow and investigate instead the extent to which HE does *not* support any definition of a sustainable economy. Are broader conceptions of the economy – and less reductive visions of what it is to be 'at work' – reflected, accommodated, embraced or ignored by higher education, and what might be done about it? Assuming need for a more sustainable mode of development is self-evident, researchers might explore current practice and emerging patterns within higher education and ask: 'to what extent are these practices (1) cognisant of, (2) contributing to, (3) contradicting, or (4) challenging our notions of sustainable development?' This would take academics working in the field of higher education for sustainable development away from the 'making them more like us' approach of some higher education ESD projects (which must irritate most academics) in favour of a more truly investigative approach.

Discussion

It has been a recurring theme of this chapter that refining and developing ESD is one thing, and identifying ESD in action quite another. The first two of the foregoing examples build our understanding by identifying opportunities for sustainable development focused learning both *in and from* unique and complex contexts. The third points towards a conceptualisation of ESD in higher education that would require ESD practitioners to learn from engagement with other people in other contexts who may stand to benefit from ESD but are unlikely to engage with it as an idea. Sterling has written that learning:

> is commonly seen simply as the 'acquisition of skills and knowledge through experience or study'. But it is important to go a little deeper than this definition. Learning is a response by the individual or group to external change or feedback. This has two aspects: first, *meaning making*, that is, making sense of the change and second, making some internal adjustment or (in systems terms) '*correction*' to take account of the change such as acquiring a new understanding or perspective or a modification or shift in assumptions or beliefs. The changes and challenges that sustainability entails present a profound learning challenge – including *unlearning* some established patterns of thinking and behaviour, *relearning* sustainable patterns where appropriate and *new learning* to be able to recognize, create and engage with necessary alternatives. Where this occurs at a deep level, it is called *transformative learning*. Learning occurs at all levels: individual, organizational and social. Note: There is no change without learning, and no learning without change.
>
> *(Sterling 2014: 93)*

This applies in equal measure to the learning of those we teach and research, and to how we, as ESD professionals, should learn from them. As researchers in ESD in higher education we are contributors to a human project to move ourselves forward, not the deliverers of 'correct' answers fashioned from our own superior wisdom.

Conclusion: future directions

These examples serve to illustrate the necessarily interdisciplinarity of research in education for sustainable development in higher education. Achieving sustainability cannot be *only* about getting the science right and applying technological solutions: but nor can it be *only* about social dynamics, power relations, competing narratives or something similar. We need to be clear about what interdisciplinarity is. Krasny and Dillon (2013) show the way here when they refer to competing problem *definitions*. It is not about bringing an educational piece to the jigsaw, because everyone has a different jigsaw. It's about making a distinctively educational contribution to how we collectively cope with that situation, all the while respecting the contributions of our colleagues from other disciplines, and our research subjects, and listening to what they have to say about education. At its simplest, this can save us embarrassment. The first two of the foregoing examples engage ancient cultures grappling with irreversible change to produce as yet unforeseeable outcomes. Together, all three engage not only educational thinking, but also economics, soil science, international relations, hydrology, sociology and so on. Each of these disciplines has a body of knowledge that is well established. Proposals made in ignorance of such knowledge may turn out to be plain daft. For example, any policy proposal made in ignorance of the basic economic concept of opportunity cost is unlikely to gain much traction on reality (see Gough 2009, for a discussion of this, and related, issues).

What, then, would a distinctively educational contribution look like? Perhaps it would not be about foreseeing the future better than other people and telling them what to do, nor about delivering the social projects of others, whether they be radical socialists, environmentalists, deep ecologists, practical ecologists, development NGOs or someone else. Perhaps it would simply be about education, about remembering the learner, about the student who, in 50 years from now will need to make good decisions in a world that, however things turn out, will be nothing like anything we can imagine today. In 2001 Foster wrote:

> Environmental education – or, as we should now perhaps say, just education – is, after all, radically non-instrumental: an end in itself. Education properly conceived embodies and deploys our heuristic intelligence as the fundamental contemporary form of responsible – and that is, ultimately sustainable – human living. Like all real life, it is instrumental to nothing (though it is relevant without limit) and subserves nothing but itself.
>
> *(Foster 2001: 164)*

Perhaps, looking to the future, it is this conception of our own worth that should best inform those of us who care about research into education for sustainable development in higher education.

References

Department for Business Innovation and Skills, 2013. *Encouraging a British Invention Revolution: Sir Andrew Witty's Review of Universities and Growth*. London: UK Government ref. BIS/13/1241.

Disterheft, A., Caeiro, S., Azeiteiro, U.M. and Leal Filho, W., 2013. 'Sustainability Science and Education for Sustainable Development in Universities: A Way for Transition', in Caeiro, S., Leal Filho, W., Jabbour, C. and Azeiteiro, U.M. (eds), *Sustainability Assessment Tools in Higher Education. Institutions Mapping Trends and Good Practices Around the World*. London: Springer, 3–27.

Dobson, A., 1990. *Green Political Thought*. London: Harper Collins.

Fien, J., 1993. *Education for the Environment: Critical Curriculum Theorising and Environmental Education*. Geelong: Deakin University Press.

Fien, J. and Trainer, T., eds., 1993a. *Environmental Education: A Pathway to Sustainability*. Geelong: Deakin University Press.

Fien, J. and Trainer, T., 1993b. 'Education for Sustainability', in Fien, J. and Trainer, T. (eds), *Environmental Education: A Pathway to Sustainability*. Geelong: Deakin University Press, 11–23.

Foster, J., 2001. 'Education *as* Sustainability', *Environmental Education Research*, 7(2), 153–65.

Foster, J., 2008. *The Sustainability Mirage: Illusion and Reality in the Coming War on Climate Change*. London: Earthscan.

Fuchs, W., 2012. 'The New Global Responsibilities of Engineers Create Challenges for Engineering Education', *Journal of Education for Sustainable Development*, 6(1), 111–13.

Fuller, T., ed., 1989. *The Voice of Liberal Learning: Michael Oakeshott on Education*. New Haven, CT: Yale University Press.

Godemann, J., Bebbington, J., Herzig, C. and Moon, J., 2014. 'Higher Education and Sustainable Development', *Accounting, Auditing & Accountability Journal*, 27(2), 218–33.

Gough, S., 2009. 'Philosophy of Education and Economics: A Case for Closer Engagement', *Journal of Philosophy of Education*, 43(2), 269–83.

Greenall Gough, A., 1993. *Founders in Environmental Education*. Geelong: Deakin University Press.

Higher Education Academy, 2009. *2008 Review of Education for Sustainable Development (ESD) in Higher Education in Scotland. Final report*. London: Higher Education Academy.

Hungerford, H. and Volk, T., 1993. 'Changing Learner Behaviour through Environmental Education', *Journal of Environmental Education*, 21(3), 8–17.

Katayama, J. and Gough, S., 2008. 'Developing Sustainable Development within the Higher Education Curriculum: Observations on the HEFCE Strategic Review', *Environmental Education Research*, 14(4), 413–22.

Kopnina, H. and Meijers, F., 2014. 'Education for Sustainable Development (ESD)', *International Journal of Sustainability in Higher Education*, 15(2), 188–207.

Krasny, M.E. and Dillon, J., 2013. *Trading Zones in Environmental Education: Creating Transdisciplinary Dialogue*. New York: Peter Lang.

Kriwaczek, P., 2010. *Babylon: Mesopotamia and the Birth of Civilization*. London: Atlantic Books.

Mogensen, F. and Schnack, K., 2010. 'The Action Competence Approach and the "new" Discourses of Education for Sustainable Development, Competence and Quality Criteria', *Environmental Education Research*, 16(1), 59–74.

Sterling, S., 2014. 'Separate Tracks or Real Synergy? Achieving a Closer Relationship between Education and SD, Post-2015', *Journal of Education for Sustainable Development*, 8(2), 89–112.

Sterling, S., Maxey, L. and Luna, H., eds., 2012. *The Sustainable University: Progress and Prospects*. Abingdon: Taylor and Francis.

Sylvestre, P., Wright, T. and Sherren, K., 2013. 'Exploring Faculty Conceptualizations of Sustainability in Higher Education: Cultural Barriers to Organizational Change and Potential Resolutions', *Journal of Education for Sustainable Development*, 7(2), 223–44.

Thomas, I., 2014. 'Student Interest for Environment/Sustainability Undergraduate Programmes: Recent Australian Experience', *Journal of Education for Sustainable Development*, 8(1), 5–27.

Thomas, I. and Day, T., 2014. 'Sustainability Capabilities, Graduate Capabilities, and Australian Universities', *International Journal of Sustainability in Higher Education*, 15(2), 208–27.

Thomas, I., Hegarty, K., Whitman, S. and Macgregor, V., 2012. 'Professional Associations. Their Role in Promoting Sustainable Development in Australia', *Journal of Education for Sustainable Development*, 6(1), 121–36.

UE4SD, 2014. *Mapping Opportunities for Professional Development of University Educators in Education for Sustainable Development: A State of the Art Report across 33 UE4SD Partner Countries*. Cheltenham: University of Gloucestershire.

UNESCO, 2013. *Education for Sustainable Development (ESD) in the UK – Current Status, Best Practice and Opportunities for the Future*. London: UK National Commission for UNESCO.

Wright, T. and Defields, D., 2012. 'Determining the "Essentials" for an Undergraduate Sustainability Degree Program: A Delphi Study at Dalhousie University', *Journal of Education for Sustainable Development*, 6(1), 101–10.

Wright, T. and Wilton, H., 2012. 'Facilities Management Directors' Conceptualizations of Sustainability in Higher Education', *Journal of Cleaner Production*, 31, 118–25.

9

CASE STUDY RESEARCH ON HIGHER EDUCATION FOR SUSTAINABLE DEVELOPMENT

Epistemological foundation and quality challenges

Regula Kyburz-Graber

Case, case study and case study research

Case study research offers a range of accounts for in-depth research in fields of higher education, in the sense of identifying relevant issues for promoting sustainable development and creating knowledge within and between different groups (Wals *et al.* 2013), in and outside higher education institutions. This chapter about case study *research* is aimed at contributing to increase the reliability and credibility of case study research and to establish it as a methodology with high potential for analysing social situations. In a first step we have to be distinctive about the terms 'case', 'case study' and 'case study research'. In literature on environmental education and education for sustainable development the terms 'case' and 'case study' are quite commonly used (e.g. Karim *et al.* 2013; Togo and Lotz-Sisitka 2013; Evans *et al.* 2012; Svanström *et al.* 2012; James and Card 2012; Chapman 2011; Sanusi and Khelghat-Doost 2008; Baumgartner and Zabin 2008; Van Petegem *et al.* 2007; Newman 2005; Fisher 2003; Castillo *et al.* 2002). Not all authors do clearly differentiate between 'case' and 'case study' and related intentions and procedures. 'Case' is often used as a synonym for 'example' without claiming any research intentions. According to O'Leary (2010) a case is 'a bounded system, or a particular instance or entity that can be defined by identifiable boundaries' (O'Leary 2010: 174). 'Case study' is prevalently used whenever a confined system, a specific situation or a process is analysed and the findings are presented in a comprehensive way. The intention of such a process is the description of the case as closely as possible to give readers a picture and an understanding of the situation in question. O'Leary defines case study as 'a method of studying elements of the social through comprehensive description and analysis of a single situation or case, e.g. a detailed study of an individual, setting, group, episode, or event' (O'Leary 2010: 174).

Yet another purpose of a case study is its use as an educational or training method (Posch and Scholz 2006; Scholz *et al.* 2006; Stauffacher *et al.* 2006; Posch and Steiner 2006; Muhar *et al.* 2006; Kreber 2001). Those case studies are arranged to stimulate students by authentic complexity to engage them in investigating a social situation from various perspectives and come to conclusions. Case studies in educational contexts can vary in their structure and method as either open ended inquiry or else offering students prepared information inviting them to work out thoroughly founded solutions.

A case study can refer to single or multiple cases. As a most important aspect O'Leary (2010) argues that case study 'allows for the building of holistic understandings through prolonged engagement and the development of rapport and trust within a clearly defined and highly relevant context' (O'Leary 2010: 174). In similar ways other authors stress that a case study explores the complexity of a situation in its real life context from multiple perspectives (Stake 1995; Simons 2009; Yin 2013; Thomas 2011). Most authors do not explicitly distinguish between case study and case study research, but point out the difference between illustrative, atheoretical, configurative-idiographic, story-telling, descriptive case studies on one hand, and theory-guided case studies like theory testing, theory seeking, heuristic, explanatory case studies on the other hand (see Thomas 2011;Yin 2013). Analysing the considerably diverse criteria in existing typologies Thomas (2011) suggests founding decisions throughout a case study research on three criteria: *purpose* (intrinsic, instrumental, evaluative or exploratory), *approach* (illustrative/descriptive, theory-testing or theory-building) and *process* (single studies or multiple studies). In order to avoid the 'looseness of the case study as a form of inquiry' he claims that a case study is not only about a *subject* (a practical, historical unity as a case) but also about an *object*, that is an analytical or theoretical frame which the case 'illuminates and explicates' (Thomas 2011: 513), linked with the question 'what is this a case *of*' (Thomas 2011: 515). Emphasising the importance of the theoretical part in the research process, we argue for a distinction between 'case study' as a more illustrative piece of work and 'case study *research*', as a study embedded in a theoretical reflection, distinctively advocating for a high quality in explicit research approaches (see also Corcoran *et al.* 2004). Hence, authors who do not associate distinct research principles with their case study may not be blamed for shortcomings in research aspects if they have never intended to follow a clear-cut research strategy.

It may be criticised that case study approach has developed in a somewhat arbitrary conglomerate of methodical procedures and qualities. The purpose of this chapter follows an alternative strategy: It points out distinct quality aspects which distinguish case study *research* from case studies. Researchers deciding for case study research as a methodology have to do it consciously and well founded on ontological, epistemological and methodical grounds (Dillon and Reid 2004). If case study research is to be recognised as quality research and if related research outcomes are to be acknowledged as reliable knowledge, case study research has to be documented as research process with high quality standards (Yin 2013; Arthur *et al.* 2012; Morrison *et al.* 2011; Gerring 2006; Hancock and Algozzine 2006; Tavers 2001). As with any other research it has to provide traceable research procedures like documenting framing discourses, transparent data collection, analysis and documentation, inter-subjective validation and interpretation.

Before turning to those epistemological and methodical aspects of case study research, we will examine possible purposes that researchers in the field of higher education for sustainable development may pursue with case study research (for discussion on a wider range of purposes of case studies see Thomas 2011).

Intended purposes of case study research in HESD

Case study research in higher education for sustainable development may serve as informative analysis of promising developments in the field, and beyond, in a broader context, as a means for supporting transformative processes in higher education.

Case study research for illustrating accounts to promising developments in higher education

Promoting sustainable development in higher education embraces strategic and technical strategies on one hand, like integrating principles of sustainable development in mission statements, university strategies, and organisational processes, and on the other hand embedding those principles in the key areas of higher education institutions: in research and education. As Gough and Scott (2008) state, a main goal of higher education institutions must be 'to develop curricula, pedagogy and extracurricular activities that enable students to develop values, skills and knowledge to contribute to sustainable development' (Gough and Scott 2008: 76).

Researchers, teachers and learners who are already active in these fields presumably seek in some way or another, openly or concealed, to persuade others of the need to promote and support teaching and learning towards sustainable development. Seemingly case studies are assigned to be useful as a means to prove positive effects of any efforts aimed at integrating sustainable development issues in education. Case studies seem to be easy to conduct and easily accessible for illustrating success stories. It is particularly such assumptions about easy going case study research that may compromise the potential of case study research as a high quality and reliable research approach.

Case study research for meeting the challenges of transformation processes in higher education

Not reduced to telling success stories, case study *research* may be aimed at better knowing and understanding how teaching and learning within the specific conditions and culture develops towards sustainable development, and how students develop 'new skills' (Gough and Scott 2008: 77). And beyond this purpose, research may seek to analyse and explain what happens in a specific context, including barriers and drivers, identifying key issues and drawing evidence from the findings, for instance in terms of policy responses or support and exchange strategies (Gough and Scott 2008: 77). Case study research can provide in-depth views and an understanding how and why things in terms of sustainability are developing in certain ways. The overall goal of using case study research thus can be seen as a means to 'build the new skills, knowledge and tools needed for sustainable development through research' (Gough and Scott 2008: 76). A couple of authors are talking about transformation processes that are needed to meet the challenges (see e.g. Jones *et al.* 2010; Barth *et al.* 2007; Thomas 2004). As Jones *et al.* (2010) state higher education institutions should be 'less centres of transmission and delivery and more centres of transformation and inquiry' (Jones *et al.* 2010: 330).

Looking at higher education for sustainable development in a wider context it is evident that attempts at institutionalisation challenge the system of higher education in its very fundament and ask for discourses on how transformation in teaching, learning and researching might be initiated and accompanied (Barth *et al.* 2007). After years of studying developments and constraints in sustainable developments in higher education Gough and Scott (2008) come to this conclusion: 'To attempt to summarise the issues at stake is daunting to say the least, but it does seem clear that the level of complexity is such that any progress according to any criteria will require a degree of clear-headedness about two absolutely fundamental questions: "What is a university for?" and "What is education for?"' (Gough and Scott 2008: 82).

Case study research can serve as a means for supporting and nourishing those discourses if it is not reduced to simply documenting and describing processes of teaching and learning for sustainable development as (success) stories. If it is to go beyond a foreground kind of study the researchers have to be clear about the theoretical and epistemological foundation of case study as a research approach. This foundation is outlined and discussed in the following section providing the basis for quality claims, the choice of adequate methods, data analysis and interpretation of outcomes.

The ontological and epistemological basis of case study research

Of which reality are we talking about in higher education for sustainable development? – the ontological dimension of case study research

What makes case study research particular in its attempts is that it aims at exploring how social situations are conceived and interpreted (Chadderton and Torrance 2011). Case study research is most meaningful as research methodology for investigating social situations which are highly contextual, complex, subjectively and socially constructed and constantly interpreted and re-interpreted by people involved. If researchers accept social situations in their complexity and are driven to give a description and furthermore a meaning to what is going on in those situations, why people might act as they do and what conditions influence their acting and the way they give meaning to their actions, in those situations case study research is an adequate research methodology.

The constructive and re-constructive nature of sustainable development issues

Higher education for sustainable development generally manifests features of complex social contexts and processes. The notion of sustainable development as a 'regulative idea' (Raudsepp and Tamm 2004; Raudsepp 2002) or as a guiding idea ('gesellschaftspolitisches Leitbild', explored in Hirsch Hadorn and Brun 2007) cannot be handled as a scientifically fixed term; it is constantly defined and re-defined by the people involved (Raudsepp and Heidmets 2005). 'Sustainable development' in higher education can be a whole course subject, a topic within a course, an implicit principle within a higher education program, an overall goal for the higher education institution as a whole or for specific programs, an instance to progress to sustainable institutional processes, etc. In any case, people involved, students, lecturers, researchers, leaders, managers, technicians, laboratory staff, facilitators and others, give meaning to the notion of sustainable development and try – or do not try – to make sense of it in their praxis.

To illustrate the meaning of socially constructed situations as ontological basis of case studies let us take a situation presumably in similar ways familiar to readers: The situation is a university course on the topic 'Environment, Health and Sustainable Development as an educational challenge in secondary education'. What could be a research interest related to such a course? A most obvious research impulse might be to test evidence-based learning effects in students. The question is if a strategy like that could ever illuminate the problems the students are struggling with regarding their future teaching practice on sustainable development issues in school. They come with multiple ideas and images of what environmental education and education for sustainable development is about, often with behavioural change missions in their mind (not so much for themselves but for their future students), frequently based on their own experiences in school. Most of the students in that course are driven by the idea to make a difference, to substantially change teaching and learning in their future school, but the same time they are frustrated by the rigid conditions in schools and the absent interest and will of teachers and school leaders in schools to introduce sustainable development as a main principle in education. And they judge their own learning at school and at university in terms of sustainable development as poor, occasional and patchy. The challenge for the university teachers of that course is to conceptualise a curriculum that is personally relevant for the students, theoretically challenging and practically useful, encouraging and engaging without excluding constraints, frustration and fears of failure and disappointment. What can a case study research in this situation offer as research process?

Case study research may throw light on the various kinds of preconditions and beliefs the students bring with them when they take part in the course. The research may illuminate the teaching-learning condition in the course itself and pose the question if and how teaching-learning is experienced in alternative ways and what that experience means for becoming teachers. In case study research it is consciously acknowledged that it is the subjective views of students and teachers involved which build the data basis. The reality constructed by the people involved is relevant, not primarily a seemingly objective reality. Case study research does not deny the existence of the multiple subjectively meaningful experiences of students as well as of teachers but, on the contrary, uses those experiences as a source for understanding and explaining what is going on in the course and how the case study outcomes could be used for further curriculum development. The question arises how knowledge of a complex social situation can be generated, followed by the question of what knowledge counts as knowledge. Thus it raises the epistemological dimension of case study research.

The epistemological dimension in case study research

The potential of case study research is to provide knowledge on how people experience higher education for sustainable development and construct their meanings and judgements on sustainable development, on relevant teaching-learning situations and institutional processes. The nature of knowledge generated in case study research is contextual, reflective, critical with respect to conditions, traditions, values and prevailing beliefs, rather than predictive and fixed.

What counts as knowledge on higher education for sustainable development? This is a prior question in all higher education settings. Researchers have to be aware that the predominant discourse might follow – at least in natural science and social sciences – a positivist empirical research epistemology. Case study research will not generate scientific knowledge in that paradigm. Its objective is to understand and explain social situations rather than to statistically describe them (not excluding though that descriptive statistics may provide additional background information on the case). Case study research asks the questions what and why, not how many (Kyburz-Graber 2004). In well documented and traceable outcomes researchers have to show how they generate data and how they conduct the interpretation process and come to conclusions. It must be their aim to demonstrate reliability and validity of their research epistemology in a way that case study research will be seen as a research approach with high quality standards and accountable scientific knowledge (see quality claims below).

The methodological positioning of case study research within the established methodologies

Case study research 'is not easily summarized as a single, coherent form of research' (Stark and Torrance 2005: 33). It emphasises an approach as 'study-in-depth', privileging understanding of the situation over generalising, 'in-depth inquiry over coverage' (Stark and Torrance 2005: 33). According to Stark and Torrance (2005), a case study must seek to 'illuminate the readers' understanding of an issue'. Striving for depth may be seen as a key issue for case study research (Stark and Torrance 2005).

Has case study research to be positioned as a methodology on its own, or has it rather to be located within the established methodologies like ethnography, narrative inquiry, phenomenology, critical inquiry (Somekh and Lewin 2011)? Case study research is not an approach with distinct methodological strategies but integrates a range of various methodological accounts, depending on the research interests. In either way, case study research with its fundamental research attempts to provide in-depth views of social situations has to be positioned as a methodology, though using research strategies from established methodologies. Case study research is thus more than a research method; as a methodology it integrates epistemological reflections on ways of reliable knowledge generation. Choosing adequate research methods is then a follow-up step.

Genres and methods of case study research

Reflecting on various genres or typologies of case study research may help to clarify emerging questions throughout the research process (see Thomas 2011). Emphasising the case study *research* as theory-led inquiry we have found that the genres of case study research described by Yin (2013) offer a clear and most useful basis for decisions on the research conduct of a case study, following from one genre to the next an increasingly elaborated theory-based research approach. Researchers may start with a descriptive process and finally turn into an explanatory-causal inquiry.

Genres of case study research

Yin (2013) distinguishes case study genres relating to the degree of in-depth analysis and objectives: descriptive, explorative, explanatory-causal. The distinction offers a characterisation of what can be seen as the potentials conducting case study research (see also Kyburz-Graber 2004).

Descriptive case study

A descriptive case study gives a more or less close picture of a social situation without exploring it in depth. The aim in this case is to provide a characteristic picture of what is going on in the situation concerned, which people under what conditions are concerned. For case study descriptions, available documents may be used, such as mission statements, study programs, protocols, course readings, evaluation outcomes, examination results. In literature many cases are documented in such ways without claiming to present outcomes of a sound research process. An example for this genre is the case study of Leite *et al.* (2005). This case study shows a possible starting point in the way of description and giving recommendations for further research while not analysing in depth reasons for lacking knowledge, or else, resources for teachers to include the local environment in their teaching. Another example for a descriptive case study is Biedenweg *et al.* (2013).

Explorative case study

An explorative case study is aimed at understanding a case against the background of its context. For such a process data are collected from various perspectives including, for example, document analysis, various forms of interviews and observation. Lamnek (2010) sees in this genre an often used basis for hypothesis construction used for a quantitative survey research.

But an explorative case study as a research study in itself can (and should) also serve as an empirically based analysis of a situation offering assumptions and interpretations, and drawing evidence from analysed data. Examples of such explorative case studies can be seen in Lundholm (2005, 2004); Tormey *et al.* (2008); Kopnina (2013).

Explanatory-causal case study

An explanatory-causal case study as a research approach goes beyond interpreting the case as a phenomenon trying to answering questions of 'why' on a theoretical basis. Theoretical reasoning is done in an elaborated way by interpreting and re-interpreting emerging outcomes against theoretical reflections. Theorising in such research processes is an important procedure which has to be traceable in well documented research steps (see e.g. Stake 2005). Most famous is the case study research of Whyte, *Street Corner Society* (1993), which is based on accurate documentation of research procedures and data including the author's reflections on his own role as a sociologist and participating observer.

An example for the explanatory-causal genre of case study research in the context of education for sustainable development is given in Kyburz-Graber (2013: 28 et seq.): The researchers' interest was to identify potentials of critical reflection on socio-ecological issues in classrooms. They explored five cases of video recorded classroom discussions on topics at the interface between natural science and society (for example, 'potential benefits and risks of biotechnologies'), each class guided by a tandem-team formed of a biology teacher and a humanities teacher. In a first (explorative-analytical) step the researchers explored which issues were raised in the discussions and how they were discussed. In a second (explanatory-causal) step through iterative interpretative reconstruction and cross-case analysis it was searched for reasons why classroom discussions were mainly shaped by raising facts and less by critical reflections like discussing values, norms, feelings and uncertainties of knowledge. Drawing a chain of evidence the researchers found that the students attested natural science researchers a predominating unquestionable role in solving problems in the world by producing objective value-free knowledge while social science was attributed less importance due to subjective, value and culture based knowledge. The teachers representing 'their' science seemed to strongly influence students' images of natural and social science (Wolfensberger 2008).

Methods of case study research

Depending on the objectives researchers are aiming at and depending on the level of elaboration they want to conduct their case study research, the methods to collect and analyse data will vary. Given the ontological assumption that social situations are permanently constructed and re-constructed by people involved giving their own meaning to what they experience, document analysis alone will not be sufficient to conduct a sound case study research, at least if the researchers seek to go beyond a descriptive case study. They will try to come as close to the meanings students, teachers/researchers, managers or leaders are giving to their acting, intentions and experiences, and to learn from the people's beliefs and values they bring into the situation.

If researchers decide to follow an *ethnological* methodology for their case study research, focussing on the culture of a case and how people involved experience that culture, they will use methods which allow them to explore this culture, like participant observation or shadow studies, field notes (research diaries), ethnographic (guided) interviews to get information on how people experience and judge the culture of a setting or an institution (for an informative overview of research methods see Somekh and Lewin 2011; Merriam 1998). Additionally, discourses in the documents may be analysed to allow a critical stance on the way that various stakeholders conceptualise key issues like sustainability or sustainable development.

If researchers prefer a *narrative* methodology seeking to explore the narratives people involved tell about their experiences, the methods to choose will be at first narrative interviews. They may be conducted as open, unguided talks, or as more or less guided interviews (see e.g. Somekh and Lewin 2011; Bohnsack 2010; Nohl 2012; Mayring 2002, 2003). The art of collecting data lies in the way that the researchers can build an atmosphere inviting the interview partners to talk openly about their experiences and to thoroughly reflect on what they are talking about.

Another focus for doing case study research is *phenomenological*. If researchers decide to frame their case study with the focus to highlight a phenomenon, the essence of a situation, they will choose interview methods to find out from people what it is like for them to be involved in the case in question. The phenomenological methodology is not easy to follow; it needs thorough studies of the founding theories (see e.g. Somekh and Lewin 2011) in order to deeply understand how to unfold the procedure. But even, if the researchers do not decide to conduct case study research close to the phenomenological methodology, it can offer a better understanding of what is needed in the hermeneutic interpretation process which is a part anyway of an elaborative case study research project. For such procedures see e.g. Bohnsack (2010) who describes a way for an interpretation process in several steps by the approach of 'reconstructive social science research'.

Researchers aiming at a *critical reflection* on a case of higher education for sustainable development will ask questions about dominating discourses in documents like study programs and/or teaching/learning settings: How is teaching and learning organised and why? Who decides on what is important to learn about sustainable development? Is 'sustainable development' taken as a predefined, not questionable concept? What role is assigned to the students within the transformation process of sustainable development? Methodologies used in such critical research approaches are for instance discourse analysis, action research, researching policy, feminist methodologies (see e.g. Somekh and Lewin 2011). In case study research, critical approaches may be combined with other methodologies like ethnography or narrative inquiry in order to get a broad and critically reflected picture of the case.

Quality claims for case study research

General aspects of quality claims in qualitative research

In case study research quality claims are similar to those in other qualitative or mixed methods approaches. Quality criteria are thus not new but specifically described here in the light of conducting case study research (see e.g. Yin 2013; Hancock and Algozzine 2006; Kyburz-Graber 2004; Tavers 2001; Darke *et al.* 1998; Merriam 1998). For general quality discourse in qualitative research see e.g. Lamnek 2010; Somekh and Lewin 2011.

Quality criteria

A case study research project can be of high scientific quality if it is founded on a traceable procedure which provides the basis for scientific discussion on what is acknowledged as reliable knowledge. Quality criteria outlined below are: a theoretical basis, triangulation of data collection and interpretation ensured by multiple sources of evidence, a traceable chain of evidence, full documentation of the research process, inter-subjective communicative validation, iterative review and rewriting process (see e.g. Yin 2013; Kyburz-Graber 2004).

Theoretical basis

When researchers decide to conduct a case study research they usually do not start from scratch. They have in mind assumptions, beliefs, previous experiences, observations they have made in comparable situations, and they are driven by the aim to give evidence for what they expect. Reflection about the researchers' own starting point and interests and the reasons why they are interested in special cases: that is meant by founding case study research on theoretical basis. Subjective knowledge on higher education for sustainable development may be added by knowledge given in literature, be it from previous case studies, information on sustainable development discourses, or other knowledge sources. The researchers have to be clear where they are starting and why. Additional theoretical aspects often emerge during the evolving study. The theorising process is part of the research process and has to be documented as part of the case study, ending in research questions guiding case study research. The theoretical basis allows other researchers to either follow the argumentation line or else reject it building on a different theory basis and provide evidence in an alternative research approach; evidence based arguing and counter-arguing being the very process of scientific research.

Developing the theory basis for case study research leading into research questions is a demanding process. Schram (2006) describes a useful procedure to clarify one's own intentions and finally come up with research questions. He suggests asking questions like 'If - what?' to clarify own ideas and assumptions about a situation. Examples related to the course example earlier mentioned in this chapter:

- If teacher students have difficulties with the notion of sustainable development as a regulative rather than a normative idea – what and how should they learn in a course on sustainable development?
- If they expect teaching materials and instructions as a guarantee for successful teaching as a teacher – how will they react on reflective rather than training approaches in the course?
- If the students have been forced so long to acquire 'proved' and unquestioned facts – what does it mean for students to dive into a culture where beliefs, values, scientific interests, 'truths' are critically reflected?

Research questions emerging from these 'if – what' might be: How do students perceive the notion of sustainable development as challenging their previous positivist knowledge and how does this have an impact on their perceived role as future teachers? And: What will learning situations look like which are evidently fruitful in giving new perspectives to the teacher students without leaving them with helplessness in view of their future teaching?

Triangulation ensured by multiple sources of evidence

Multiple sources of evidence in case study research are generally given by using documents (including official and semi-official documents, working papers, process documents like protocols, visualised outcomes of workshops, etc.), and interviews (as single oral interviews with people involved as various stakeholders, focus-groups interviews, written interviews). Depending on the research question and the methodology, observation (objective or participant) will be a useful data source for triangulation.

Chain of evidence

Yin (2013) gives a helpful analogy to demonstrate the need of a chain of evidence: In case study research, the researcher has to prove evidence of his or her findings in the same way as in criminal investigations using as many data as possible, interpreting them in a traceable way and using interpretations to prove step by step – in a chain – the final conclusion. If a case study is conducted from a phenomenological perspective with emphasis on social interaction and interpreting the social construction of meaning, or if it is rather conducted from an 'objective' observer (Chadderton and Torrance 2011): in any case the metaphor of the 'chain of evidence' is helpful as a goal for case study research. We have given an example of such a process in Kyburz-Graber (2004: 61 et seq.). Another example is given below (see: How to Conduct a Case Study Research?). An argumentatively traced chain of evidence is much more important than attempting to generalise the findings in a case study. If a traceable basis is provided the findings can be discussed and argumentatively falsified as any other research finding. The interpretation of a case study outcome may be held as long as a comparable case study does not question the findings.

Full documentation

This quality criteria is closely linked to the chain of evidence. A well founded chain of evidence is only traceable if all steps of emerging evidence are fully documented. In a publication it will not be possible to provide the reader with all documents, but the research author has to refer to existing, defined documents and provide short summaries on the nature of those sources and on aspects a reader might specifically be interested in. The research process itself, above all the procedure of data collection, data analysis and interpretation, has to be documented in adequate ways. Otherwise an unreliable basis of the findings decreases the value of the research study.

Inter-subjective validation (communicative validation)

Inter-subjective or communicative validation in every kind of qualitative research study is an indispensable procedure to ensure that data are adequately analysed and interpreted. Interview-partners have to validate if the collected data represent their view given in the particular interview situation. Data analysis and interpretation has to be validated among researchers themselves in a communicative process to make sure that they agree on data analysis procedure and interpretation of the findings. Inter-subjective validation needs extensive and rigorous discussion and exchange specifically between the researchers.

Iterative review and rewriting process

Iterative review and rewriting process is closely linked to inter-subjective validation; in fact it is actually part of it. Inter-subjective validation will lead to changes in how outcomes are described and presented. A rewriting process is indispensable until the case study research is finally presented in a way all partners involved accept to be appropriate as an adequate mirror of the situation.

How to conduct a case study research

Before starting researchers need to clarify their research intention, discussing their ideas with critical friends, experts or laypersons, to become aware of the beliefs, hidden theories and assumptions driving their interests for the research study. After such discourses the idea may more clearly emerge if case study research is an appropriate approach. As is outlined above, the decision for choosing case study research depends on ontological and epistemological reflections. Outcomes of this reflection are the research questions and decisions about the methodological approach. To make the continuing procedure in a case study research as explicative and illustrative as possible it is described in the following section with its various steps using a case study research on professional development of teachers, an example of higher (further) education for sustainable development.

Procedure of case study research illustrated by a research based in-service education project with upper secondary school teachers

The case study research in question is entitled 'The challenge of involvement in reflective teaching: Three case studies from a teacher education project on conducting classroom discussions on socio-scientific issues' (Wolfensberger *et al.* 2010).

Clarifying the research intention and the theoretical starting point

The researchers interest in inquiring the potential of a reflective teaching approach in demanding classroom situations arose from previous research studies on environmental education: After a couple of research projects on socio-ecological approaches to environmental education the research group identified the conduct of classroom discussions on complex, controversial, interdisciplinary issues at the interface between natural science and society to be crucial, particularly for questions concerning sustainable development. Earlier studies had revealed that students tend to give scientific knowledge a predominance over social knowledge, and they assigned scientists to have a higher position in democratic decision-making than other people like themselves (Wolfensberger 2008; Kyburz-Graber *et al.* 2006). The research group had noticed 'that the way in which teachers initiate and manage classroom discussions is an essential factor in promoting rich argumentative discourse in the classroom, and that there is a need for professional development in this area' (Wolfensberger *et al.* 2010: 714).

As an additional theoretical basis the research study used a reflective teaching approach (Jay and Johnson 2002). While a technical rationality in teacher education research builds on the assumption that the transmission of educational research findings leads to improving teaching competencies, the reflective rationality claims that professional development is only possible if teachers profoundly reflect on their own tacit theories and constructions of teaching and learning and on their school context (Argyris and Schön 1974). The research group assumed that the reflective teaching approach was a pathway to science teachers' professional development in conducting classroom discussions on socio-scientific issues. Hence, they aimed the research study at identifying 'paths of professional development which may meet the individual needs of teachers, respecting their values and beliefs related to their profession' (Wolfensberger *et al.* 2010: 714). The research interest was to describe, understand and explain how teachers individually experienced their professional development. That is why the researchers decided to explore the individual teaching arrangements and related experiences of the teachers as cases.

This decision takes into account that each teacher has his or her own individual background, school culture, curriculum, class and curriculum interests.

Case study design and methodological approaches

Five upper secondary school science teachers from different schools joined the project. According to the research intention they should be offered a supportive frame open enough for individual teacher planning. The frame was developed in a preliminary workshop where the teachers and the research team collaboratively agreed on 'global climate change' as a common topical frame for the classroom discussions. The teachers were free to choose their own way to prepare and conduct the classroom discussions.

The methodological approach was chosen to be narrative inquiry respecting teachers' narratives of their experiences combined with ethnographic approaches related to the way each teacher conducted classroom discussions in the given school culture.

Data collection and analysis

The teachers met with the research team six times individually and as a group to allow individual and collective reflection induced by the videotaped classroom discussions. Data were collected from semi-structured interviews, video documents, in-depth interviews and written questionnaires where the teachers described their reflection process and impact on their professional development.

Full documentation and chain of evidence

The data were analysed using naturalistic inquiry (Lincoln and Guba 1985), grounded theory procedures (Glaser and Strauss 1967) and investigator triangulation (see Wolfensberger *et al.* 2010). All data analysis steps from data collection, the raw data, the procedures of data reduction and interpretation as well as the procedure to develop working hypotheses (chain of evidence) were documented and subject to inter subjective validation.

As an outcome the researchers decided to portray the professional reflective processes of three teachers out of the five in contrasting precise case descriptions tracing the way of data analysis. For each case a chain of evidence was established based on inter-subjective validation procedures and iterative review and rewriting processes. Through those iterative processes the researchers come up with characterising the cases as 'Taking the most familiar path' (case of Vicky), 'Becoming aware of hidden concepts' (case of Silvan) and 'Getting bogged down in fundamental reflection' (case of Linus).

In a final step the researchers condensed the ways that the three teachers benefitted from the reflective teaching process and used the different styles for a cross-case perspective. They concluded that a closer individual coaching for the teachers following the concept of content-focused coaching (Staub *et al.* 2003) could increase the benefit of any of them, while strongly respecting their individual needs, backgrounds and expectations for professional development.

Cross-case analysis

As is shown in the section above, cross-case analysis is possible if single cases are founded on the same theoretical basis, if data are collected on the same case elements, and procedures of data analysis are carefully conducted on comparable aspects. Cross-case analysis is often used to build evidence on a theoretical sampling of cases: the cases are chosen with respect to some distinct differing characteristics (as for instance courses with different populations of students, varying contexts) to compare and contrast, and finally allow conclusions in the light of initial assumptions on the analysed situations. Barth and Thomas (2012) claim that more cross-case analysis should be done using the notion of meta-analysis. Cross-case analysis is sometimes looked upon as coercive for proving the general relevance of case study findings. Generalisation, though, is more a question of the quality of evidence (Chadderton and Torrance 2011) than a question of the number of cases included. Case study research outcomes are acknowledged to be generally useful in a kind of 'naturalistic generalisation' (Stake 2005) if readers recognise aspects relevant in their own experience. Yin (2013) calls it the 'replication logic' of generalisation, in distinction to a 'statistical logic' of generalisation in quantitative research studies.

An example of an elaborated cross-case analysis is given by Gough and Scott (2008). In a first part they present informative case studies. The process of data collection and analysis is not documented. But the procedure for the following cross-case analysis is extensively outlined and the conclusions of the researchers are well traceable. Two other well documented cross-case analysis are described in Barth (2013) where three distinctive patterns respecting drivers and barriers emerged, and in Ferrer-Balas *et al.* (2008).

Final remarks

Case study research is a relevant and potential methodological approach to precisely investigating, understanding and explicating complex situations of higher education for sustainable development. As a research methodology it has to be clearly distinguished from other case study attempts which may pretend to be research studies while not following distinct quality research criteria. Case study research is a strong tool supporting those transformation processes which are claimed by many actors in higher education engaged in promoting sustainable development in their institutions, because case study research involves various partners like students, educators, and technical/organisational staff. They are involved in the research as subjects with their opinions, experiences, beliefs and personal values. Case study research offers the chance to closely analyse and document boundaries and restrictions – outside and among the people concerned – which prevent higher education institutions from significantly stepping forward in the direction of sustainable development. As long as actors do not understand how and why situations in higher education function in specific ways, and as long as they do not analyse the restrictions in depth, there is little chance to step forward. Sound case study research can open eyes to what is going on in educational settings and suggest ways to transform situations, based on traceable, well documented and argumentatively interpreted findings.

References

Argyris, C. and Schön, D.A., 1974. *Theory in Practice: Increasing Professional Effectiveness*. San Francisco, CA: Jossey-Bass.

Arthur, J., Waring, M., Coe, R., and Hedges, L.V., 2012. *Research Methods and Methodologies in Education*. London: Sage.

Barth, M., 2013. 'Many Roads Lead to Sustainability: A Process-oriented Analysis of Change in Higher Education', *International Journal of Sustainability in Higher Education*, 14(2), 160–75.

Barth, M. and Thomas, I., 2012. 'Synthesising Case-study Research – Ready for the Next Step?', *Environmental Education Research*, 18(6), 751–64.

Barth, M., Godemann, J., Rieckmann, M., and Stoltenberg, U., 2007. 'Developing Key Competencies for

Sustainable Development in Higher Education', *International Journal of Sustainability in Higher Education*, 8(4). 416–30.

Baumgartner, E. and Zabin, C.J., 2008. 'A Case Study of Project-based Instruction in the Ninth Grade: A Semester-long Study of Intertidal Biodiversity', *Environmental Education Research*, 14(2), 97–114.

Biedenweg, K., Monroe, M.C., and Oxarart, A., 2013. 'The Importance of Teaching Ethics of Sustainability', *International Journal of Sustainability in Higher Education*, 14(1), 6–14.

Bohnsack, R., 2010. *Rekonstruktive Sozialforschung. Einführung in qualitative Methoden*. Opladen and Farming Hills: Barbara Budrich.

Castillo, A., García-Ruvalcaba, S., and Martínez, L.M., 2002. 'Environmental Education as Facilitator of the Use of Ecological Information: A Case Study in Mexico', *Environmental Education Research*, 8(4), 395–411.

Chadderton, Ch. and Torrance, H., 2011. 'Case Study', in Somekh, B. and Lewin, C. (eds), *Theory and Methods in Social Research*. London: Sage, 53–60.

Chapman, D.J., 2011. 'Environmental Education and the Politics of Curriculum: A National Case Study'. *The Journal of Environmental Education*, 42(3), 193–202.

Corcoran, P.B., Walker, K.E. and Wals, A.E.J., 2004. 'Case Studies, Make-your-case Studies, and Case Stories: A Critique of Case-study Methodology in Sustainability in Higher Education', *Environmental Education Research*, 10(1), 7–21.

Darke, P., Shanks, G. and Broadbent, M., 1998. 'Successfully Completing Case Study Research: Combining Rigour, Relevance and Pragmatism', *Information Systems Journal*, 8(4), 273–89.

Dillon, J. and Reid, A., 2004. 'Issues in Case-study Methodology in Investigating Environmental and Sustainability Issues in Higher Education: Towards a Problem-based Approach?', *Environmental Education Research*, 10(1), 23–37.

Evans, N., Whitehouse, H. and Gooch, M., 2012. 'Barriers, Successes and Enabling Practices of Education for Sustainability in Far North Queensland Schools: A Case Study', *The Journal of Environmental Education,* 43(2), 121–38.

Ferrer-Balas, D., Adachi, J., Banas, S., Davidson, C.I., Hoshikoshi, A., Mishra, A., Motodoa, Y., Onga, M. and Ostwald, M., 2008. 'An International Comparative Analysis of Sustainability Transformation across Seven Universities', *International Journal of Sustainability in Higher Education*, 9(3), 295–316.

Fisher, M.R., 2003. 'Applying ISO 14001 as a Business Tool for Campus Sustainability: A Case Study from New Zealand', *International Journal of Sustainability in Higher Education*, 4(2), 138–50.

Gerring, J., 2006. *Case Study Research: Principles and Practices.* Cambridge: Cambridge University Press.

Glaser, B.G. and Strauss, A.L., 1967. *The Discovery of Grounded Theory: Strategies for Qualitative Research.* New York: de Gruyter.

Gough S. and Scott, W., 2008. *Higher Education and Sustainable Development: Paradox and Possibility.* London: Routledge.

Hancock, D.R. and Algozzine, R., 2006. *Doing Case Study Research: A Practical Guide for Beginning Researchers.* New York: Teachers College Press.

Hirsch Hadorn, G. and Brun, G., 2007. 'Ethische Probleme nachhaltiger Entwicklung', in Schweizerische Akademie der Geistes- und Sozialwissenschaften (eds), *Nachhaltige Entwicklung. Nachhaltigkeitsforschung. Perspektiven der Sozial- und Geisteswissenschaften.* Bern: Schweizerische Akademie der Geistes und Sozialwissenschaften, 235–53 [online]. www.sagw.ch/dms/sagw/nachhaltige_entwicklung/publikationen/publi_nachhaltigkeit/publ_nachhaltigkeit.pdf [accessed 20 March 2014].

James, M. and Card, K., 2012. 'Factors Contributing to Institutions Achieving Environmental Sustainability', *International Journal of Sustainability in Higher Education*, 13(2), 166–76.

Jay, J.K. and Johnson, K.L., 2002. 'Capturing Complexity: A Typology of Reflective Practice for Teacher Education', *Teaching and Teacher Education*, 18(1), 73–85.

Jones, P., Selby, D. and Sterling, S.R., eds., 2010. *Sustainability Education: Perspectives and Practice across Higher Education.* London: Routledge.

Karim, S., Sriskandarajah, N. and Heiter, Å, 2013. 'Systems Study of an International Master's Program: A Case from Sweden', in Johnston, L.F. (ed.), *Higher Education for Sustainability. Cases, Challenges, and Opportunities from Across the Curriculum.* London: Routledge, 63–78.

Kopnina, H., 2013. 'An Exploratory Case Study of Dutch children's Attitudes toward Consumption: Implications for Environmental Education', *The Journal of Environmental Education*, 44(2), 128–44.

Kreber, C., 2001. 'Learning Experientially through Case Studies? A Conceptual Analysis', *Teaching in Higher Education*, 6(2), 217–28.

Kyburz-Graber, R., 2004. 'Does Case-study Methodology Lack Rigour? The Need for Quality Criteria for Sound Case-study Research, as Illustrated by a Recent Case in Secondary and Higher Education', *Environmental Education Research*, 10(1), 53–65.

Kyburz-Graber, R., 2013. 'Socioecological Approaches to Environmental Education and Research. A Paradigmatic Response to Behavioral Change Orientations', in Stevenson, R.B., Brody, M., Dillon, J. and Wals, A.E.J. (eds), *International Handbook of Research on Environmental Education*. New York: Routledge, 23–32.

Kyburz-Graber, R., Hofer, K. and Wolfensberger, B., 2006. 'Studies on Socio-ecological Approach to Environmental Education: A Contribution to a Critical Position in the Education for Sustainable Development Discourse', *Environmental Education Research*, 12(1), 101–14.

Lamnek, S., 2010. *Qualitative Sozialforschung*. Weinheim: Beltz.

Leite, S., Freitas, M. and Séneca, A., 2005. 'Promoting Education for Sustainable Development through Communitarian Problem Solving: A Case Study in the National Park of Peneda-Gerês'. in Leal Filho, W. (ed.), *Handbook of Sustainability Research*. Frankfurt: Peter Lang, 595–622.

Lincoln, Y.S. and Guba, E.G., 1985. *Naturalistic Inquiry*. Beverly Hills, CA: Sage.

Lundholm, C., 2004. 'Learning about Environmental Issues in Engineering Programmes: A Case Study of First-year Civil Engineering Students' Contextualisation of an Ecology Course', *International Journal of Sustainability in Higher Education*, 5(3), 295–307.

Lundholm, C., 2005. 'Learning about Environmental Issues: Postgraduate and Undergraduate Students' Interpretations of Environmental Contents in Education', *International Journal of Sustainability in Higher Education*, 6(3), 242–53.

Mayring, P., 2002. *Einführung in die qualitative Sozialforschung*. Weinheim: Beltz.

Mayring, P., 2003. *Qualitative Inhaltsanalyse. Grundlagen und Techniken*. Weinheim: Beltz.

Merriam, S.B., 1998. *Qualitative Research and Case Study Applications in Education*. San Francisco, CA: Jossey-Bass Publishers.

Morrison, K., Manion, L. and Cohen, L., 2011. *Research Methods in Education*.

Abingdon: Taylor & Francis.

Muhar, A., Vilsmaier, U., Glanzer, M. and Freyer, B., 2006. 'Initiating Transdisciplinarity in Academic Case Study Teaching: Experiences from a Regional Development Project in Salzburg, Austria', *International Journal of Sustainability in Higher Education*, 7(3), 293–308.

Newman, P., 2005. 'Regional Sustainability: Principles and Practices with a Case Study on Western Australia', in Leal Filho, W. (ed.), *Handbook of Sustainability Research*. Frankfurt: Peter Lang, 439–57.

Nohl, A.-M., 2012. *Interview und dokumentarische Methode. Anleitungen für die Forschungspraxis*. Wiesbaden: Springer VS.

O'Leary, Z., 2010. *The Essential Guide to Doing Your Research Project*. Reprinted edition. London: Sage Publications.

Posch, A. and Scholz, R.W., 2006. 'Guest editorial. Transdisciplinary Case Studies for Sustainability Learning', *International Journal of Sustainability in Higher Education*, 7(3), 221–25.

Posch, A. and Steiner, G., 2006. 'Integrating Research and Teaching on Innovation for Sustainable Development', *International Journal of Sustainability in Higher Education*, 7(3), 276–92.

Raudsepp, M., 2002. 'Environmentalism as a Regulative Idea: Social Psychological Analysis'. Dissertation. Tallinn: Pedagogical University.

Raudsepp, M. and Heidmets, M., 2005. 'Sustainability as a Regulative Idea and Norm of Behaviour: Social and Psychological Aspects', in Leal Filho, W. (ed.), *Handbook of Sustainability Research*. Frankfurt: Peter Lang, 205–34.

Raudsepp, M. and Tamm, G., 2004. 'Sustainable Development as an Indeterminate Regulative Idea: A Qualitative Study in Estonia'. Paper presented at the 2nd International Conference of JTET Sustainable Development, Culture and Education, April 2004, Tallinn.

Sanusi, Z.A. and Khelghat-Doost, H., 2008, 'Regional Centre of Expertise as Transformational Platform for Sustainability: A Case Study of Universiti Sains Malaysia, Penang', *International Journal of Sustainability in Higher Education*, 9(4), 487–97.

Scholz, R.W., Lang, D.J., Wiek, A., Walter, A.I. and Stauffacher, M., 2006. 'Transdisciplinary Case Studies as a Means of Sustainability Learning: Historical Framework and Theory', *International Journal of Sustainability in Higher Education*, 7(3), 226–51.

Schram, Th. H., 2006. *Conceptualizing and Proposing Qualitative Research*. Upper Saddle River, NJ: Pearson Education, Inc.

Simons, H., 2009. *Case Study Research in Practice*. London: Sage.

Somekh, B. and Lewin, C., 2011. *Theory and Methods in Social Research*. London: Sage.

Stake, R., 1995. *The Art of Case Study Research*. Thousand Oaks, CA: Sage Publications.
Stake, R., 2005. 'Qualitative Case Studies', in Denzin, N.K. and Lincoln, Y.X. (eds), *The SAGE Handbook of Qualitative Research*. Thousand Oaks, CA: Sage, 443–66.
Stark, S. and Torrance, H., 2005. 'Case Study', in Somekh, B. and Lewin, C. (eds), *Research Methods in the Social Sciences*. London: Sage Publications, 33–40.
Staub, F.C., West, L. and Bickel, D.D., 2003. 'What is Content-focused Coaching?', in West, L. and Staub, F.C. (eds), *Content-Focused Coaching: Transforming Mathematics Lessons*. Portsmouth, NH: Heinemann, 1–17.
Stauffacher, M., Walter, A.I., Lange, D.J., Wiek, A. and Scholz, R.W., 2006. 'Learning to Research Environmental Problems from a Functional Socio-cultural Constructivism Perspective: The Transdisciplinary Case Study Approach', *International Journal of Sustainability in Higher Education*, 7(3), 252–75.
Svanström, M., Palme, U., Knutson Wedel, M., Carlson, O., Nyström, T. and Edén, M., 2012. 'Embedding of ESD in Engineering Education: Experiences from Chalmers University of Technology', *International Journal of Sustainability in Higher Education*, 13(3), 279–92.
Tavers, M., 2001, *Qualitative Research through Case Studies*. London: Sage.
Thomas, G., 2011. 'A Typology for the Case Study in Social Science following a Review of Definition, Discourse, and Structure', *Qualitative Inquiry*, 17(6), 511–21.
Thomas, I., 2004. 'Sustainability in Tertiary Curricula: What is Stopping it Happening?', *International Journal of Sustainability in Higher Education*, 5(1), 33–47.
Togo, M. and Lotz-Sisitka, H., 2013. 'Exploring a Systems Approach to Mainstreaming Sustainability in Universities: A Case Study of Rhodes University in South Africa', *Environmental Education Research*, 19(5), 673–93.
Tormey, R., Liddy, M., Maguire, H. and McCloat, A., 2008. 'Working in the Action/Research Nexus for Education for Sustainable Development: Two Case Studies from Ireland', *International Journal of Sustainability in Higher Education*, 9(4), 428–40.
Van Petegem, P., Blieck, A. and Van Ongevalle, J., 2007. 'Conceptions and Awareness Concerning Environmental Education: A Zimbabwean Case-study in Three Secondary Teacher Education Colleges', *Environmental Education Research*, 13(3), 287–306.
Wals, A.E.J., Stevenson, R.B., Brody, M. and Dillon, J., 2013. 'Tentative Directions for Environmental Education Research in Uncertain Times', in Stevenson, R.B., Brody, M., Dillon, J. and Wals, A.E.J. (eds), *International Handbook of Research on Environmental Education*. New York: Routledge, 542–7.
Whyte, W.F., 1993. *Street Corner Society: The Social Structure of an Italian Slum*. Chicago, IL: The University of Chicago Press.
Wolfensberger, B., 2008. 'Über Natur, Wissenschaft und Gesellschaft reden. Eine empirisch-qualitative Untersuchung von Klassengesprächen über Themen im Schnittbereich von Naturwissenschaften, Umwelt und Gesellschaft'. Dissertation, Zurich: University of Zurich. ['Classroom Discussion on Socioecological Issues: Three Case Studies from Secondary School', www.research-projects.uzh.ch/p7434.htm].
Wolfensberger, B., Piniel, J., Canella, C. and Kyburz-Graber, R., 2010. 'The Challenge of Involvement in Reflective Teaching: Three Case Studies from a Teacher Education Project on Conducting Classroom Discussions on Socio-scientific Issues', *Teaching and Teacher Education*, 26(3), 714–21.
Yin, R.K., 2013. *Case Study Research: Design and Methods*. Thousand Oaks, CA: Sage Publications.

10

SYNTHESIS OF RESEARCH IN HIGHER EDUCATION FOR SUSTAINABLE DEVELOPMENT

Mark Rickinson and Alan Reid

Introduction

As this Handbook readily demonstrates, the last 10–15 years have seen the emergence of higher education for sustainable development as a vibrant field of policy, practice and research. Over a similar time span, research synthesis has become far more prominent in debates around enhancing the quality of education research and strengthening its influence on education policy and practice (e.g. Davies 2000; Oakley 2002; Gough *et al.* 2013; Hattie *et al.* 2014; Alton-Lee 2014). The purpose of this chapter is to explore whether and how these two trends might be connected, focusing on the role that research synthesis has played in the field of higher education for sustainable development thus far, and the roles it could play in the future.

The chapter, however, is not a guide about how to do research synthesis (see, for example, Cooper and Hedges 1994; Petticrew and Roberts 2006; Sandelowski and Barroso 2007; Borenstein *et al.* 2009; Major and Savin-Baden 2010a; Gough *et al.* 2012). Nor does it provide a synthesis of previous research (or previous research syntheses) in the field of higher education for sustainable development. Rather, it draws on selected examples of methodological writing about research synthesis and explores their relevance to synthesising research about higher education for sustainable development, in order to highlight how the latter might be better informed by the former. Our aim then, is to show how future research in this field could benefit from greater involvement with and targeted investment in research synthesis. In so doing, we highlight the need for research and researchers in higher education for sustainable development to consider:

- strategic commissioning of synthesis projects
- varied types of synthesis projects and methodologies
- fuller involvement of research users in synthesis projects
- targeted uses of synthesis to inform policy, practice and research.

After this brief introduction, the remainder of the chapter is organised into four main sections. The first section outlines the growth of interest and activity around research synthesis that has been seen in education and other social sciences over the last 10–15 years. The next section then examines the knowledge base about research synthesis that has been generated by this interest and activity, including the development of different approaches to research synthesis and insights into the practice of conducting synthesis projects. Against the backdrop of these wider developments, the third section focuses specifically on higher education for sustainable development and explores the role that research synthesis has (and has not) played in the field to date. The recurring theme is that the field has seen little or no investment in research synthesis. Finally, with an eye to the future, the concluding section explores how better research synthesis is critical to the development of research in higher education for sustainable development.

The growth of research synthesis in education

Research synthesis involves bringing together the findings of a number of different research studies on a similar topic. More specifically, it requires systematic and careful review of the findings and quality of a variety of research studies, undertaken in light of the possibility that their legitimate combination will enrich current and critical understandings of a particular topic. While most closely associated with studies of the effects of interventions in the fields of health and medical research (e.g. Chalmers 2003), research synthesis has become increasingly important within education and education research for several reasons.

First, there is the argument that in light of the fact that research questions can be answered by many different types of research, deeper insights and more powerful conclusions may be possible through the pooling and integration of numerous studies as opposed to the reporting of studies individually. As Finfgeld (2003: 894) explains in relation to the synthesis of qualitative evidence, the typical goal 'is to produce a new and integrative interpretation of findings that is more substantive than those resulting from individual investigations'. A second appeal is that research synthesis provides a means to make sense of existing, accumulated knowledge about a topic 'as distinct from undertaking yet more primary research' (Boaz *et al.* 2004: 3). Third, research synthesis is seen as a way to improve the accessibility and power of research to end-users. To quote Foster and Hammersley (1998: 610): 'The main channel of communication between researchers and [research users] ought to be reviews of whole fields of research, rather than reports of single studies.' Or as Suri and Clarke (2009: 395) put it: 'Research syntheses play an important role in disseminating research knowledge and in shaping further research, policy, practice, and public perception.'

Looking back, the practice of bringing together the findings of existing studies has long been a feature of scholarly work in the social sciences, with techniques such as 'meta-analysis' dating back to developments in the 1970s (e.g. Glass 1976, 1978). What is different, though, is that the last 10–15 years have seen a marked growth of interest and activity around research synthesis within the social sciences. In the field of education, this growth has been exemplified in a number of ways.

First, a particular conception of research synthesis popular in medicine and health, namely systematic review, has become more prevalent (and contested) within education (e.g. Davies 2000; Oakley 2003; Gough *et al.* 2012). Proponents of systematic review argue that traditional reviews of research 'commonly [use] a selective, opportunistic and discursive approach to identifying and interpreting relevant literature' (Oakley 2003: 23). Systematic review, by contrast, involves 'synthesising the findings of many different research studies in a way which is explicit, transparent, replicable, accountable and (potentially) updateable' (Oakley 2003: 23). However, responses to the introduction of such approaches within education have been decidedly mixed, revealing a wide range of perspectives and underlying commitments on these matters. For example, the model of systematic review has been challenged on various grounds, such as being 'empiricist' and/or 'positivistic' in nature, limited to questions about 'what works', and a form of political control of educational research (e.g. Elliott 2001; Hammersley 2001). As discussed recently by Biesta (2014) and Scriven (2014), a focus on (primarily quantitative) evidence of 'what works' and 'randomized control trials as the gold standard' is not always possible or desirable for educational matters. One outcome of these ongoing debates has been the development of an increasing variety of methodological approaches for synthesising different kinds of evidence for adoption and adaptation within the field of education (see, for example, Noblit and Hare 1988; Bushman and Wells 2001; Walsh and Downe 2005; Sandelowski and Barroso 2007; Hattie 2008; van der Knaap *et al.* 2008; Barnett-Page and Thomas 2009; Harden and Thomas 2010; Major and Savin-Baden 2010a; Campbell *et al.* 2011; Noyes *et al.* 2011b; Potts 2013).

A second development, closely connected with the emergence of systematic review techniques and programmes, has been the establishment of a whole series of new institutions dedicated specifically to the accumulation and communication of educational research evidence. A good example is the Evidence for Policy and Practice Information and Co-ordination (EPPI) Centre in England (Oakley 2002). Key to its work has been a focus on 'developing methods and tools for systematic reviews' in ways that help answer the questions of policy makers, practitioners and service users (Gough 2007: 63). Other international examples of similar developments include the What Works Clearinghouse in the USA, the Iterative Best Evidence Synthesis Programme in New Zealand, the Canadian Council on Learning in Canada, the Knowledge Clearinghouse in Denmark, the Knowledge Chamber in the Netherlands (for details on each of these, see OECD 2007). All of these organisations have been informed by wider work, typically associated with the Cochrane Collaboration (e.g. Higgins and Green 2011; Noyes *et al.* 2011a) and the Campbell Collaboration (e.g. Hammerstrøm *et al.* 2010; van der Knaap *et al.* 2008).

Thirdly, in terms of research funding, there has been a clear increase in support for research synthesis from funding organisations of all kinds even as funding for primary research has seen a relative decline. In terms of the key drivers for this, as Boaz *et al.* (2004: 3) noted a decade ago for the UK: 'In recent years reviews of existing research have been increasingly commissioned by government agencies, research charities, research councils and others'. While more recently, Major and Savin-Baden (2010b: 127) noting the relative inaccessibility of many research findings and communications, have observed: 'In short, stakeholders want transparent processes, clear synthesised findings, and solid recommendations for research, policy, and practice as a result of these findings'.

Fourthly, there is now a growing literature around many different aspects of research synthesis in education. In particular, there has been an increase in publications:

(i) *providing guidance on how to do different kinds of research reviews* (e.g. Cooper and Hedges 1994; Petticrew and Roberts 2006; Sandelowski and Barroso 2007; Borenstein *et al.* 2009; Major and Savin-Baden 2010a; Gough *et al.* 2012; 2013).
(ii) *investigating and reflecting on the process of conducting research synthesis projects* (e.g. Best 2003; Rickinson 2003; Reid and Nikel 2003; Andrews 2004; Boaz *et al.* 2004, 2007; Rickinson and May 2009); and
(iii) *exploring and problematising the role of different approaches to research synthesis, particularly the notion of systematic review and evidence-based agendas* (e.g. Foster and Hammersley 1998; Davies 2000; Elliott 2001; Evans and Benefield 2001; Hammersley 2001; Gough and Elbourne 2002; Oakley 2002; MacLure 2005; Torrance and Sebba 2007; Littell 2008).

Taken together, it is clear that the discourse and landscape of education-focused research synthesis has changed dramatically over the last 10–15 years. These changes have come as a result of a range of influences that are part of much larger trends across social policy development, evaluation and critique. As summarised in Figure 10.1, the growth of interest in research synthesis can be attributed to a range of factors, most notably, critiques of social science research (e.g. Oancea 2005), evidence-based policy and practice agendas (e.g. Oakley 2002), and knowledge mobilization efforts (e.g. Levin and Cooper 2012).

Different approaches and practices of research synthesis

The increased emphasis on research synthesis within education and social research has led to a rich array of different approaches and methods, and a growing knowledge base around the process of conducting reviews in practice. Both of these developments, as explained below, represent a powerful resource for researchers of education interested in exploring the evidence and trends in studies on specific topics and research questions. It is important, therefore, that researchers and research users who are interested in conducting and commissioning research synthesis projects recognise that there is now an extensive knowledge base to inform their work. This is particularly so in the field of higher education for sustainable development, as to date (and as will be argued later), there appears to have been little engagement with this wider research synthesis knowledge base.

Different approaches to research synthesis

There is a variety of well-established approaches to research synthesis and it is important to understand how and why these differ. Three contrasting examples of well-established approaches (meta-analysis, meta-ethnography, realist synthesis) are outlined in Table 10.1. They differ in a number of respects, including in relation to:

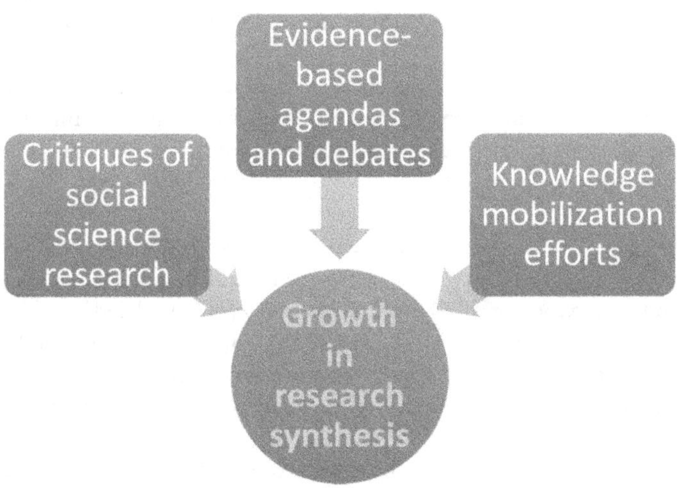

Figure 10.1 Factors influencing the growth of interest in research synthesis in education

(i) *the type of synthesis questions to which they are* suited – meta-analysis is appropriate for questions that concern the outcome or effect of a particular intervention; meta-ethnography is useful for open questions about experiences, meanings and interpretations; while realist synthesis focuses on questions about which interventions works for whom, in what circumstances, in what respects, and how they work;
(ii) *the type of research evidence that they draw upon* – meta-analysis requires quantitative studies to enable the calculation of effect sizes; meta-ethnography works with ethnographic and other suitable qualitative studies; while realist synthesis draws on relevant pieces of evidence from varied types of studies; and
(iii) *the process by which the research evidence is drawn together or synthesised* – meta-analysis uses statistical analysis to aggregate the findings of previous studies; meta-ethnography uses interpretive translation processes to identify and then re-conceptualise key metaphors from prior studies; while realist synthesis uses a developing theoretical framework to locate, integrate, and compare and contrast relevant empirical evidence in an iterative manner.

One way to make sense of the differences and overlaps in approach is to consider whether the core synthesis processes are about *aggregation* (i.e. adding up findings from multiple similar studies) or *configuration* (i.e. organising findings from previous studies). Gough *et al.* (2012: 8) characterise the difference between aggregative and configurative approaches as follows:

> *Aggregative* reviews often answer tightly specified questions using quantitative pre-specified methods to test theory using empirical observation (a deductive method). *Configurative* reviews are more likely to ask open questions that are answered with qualitative data and more iterative methods that interpret specific examples of things to address questions about experiences and meaning to generate and explore theory (an inductive method).
>
> *(Emphasis added)*

In terms of the approaches included in Table 10.1, *meta-analysis* is a prime example of an aggregative approach, *meta-ethnography* is a classic example of a configurative approach, while *realist synthesis* is an example of a mixed synthesis method that both configures and aggregates prior findings.

Thinking about research synthesis projects in terms of the extent to which they are concerned with aggregating findings, configuring findings, and/or aggregating *and* configuring findings can be helpful in making sense of the range of approaches that are available. In light of this, Gough *et al.* (2012) recommend:

- *aggregative approaches* are appropriate where key concepts are well defined in advance, data sources are numerical/categorical, and the purpose of the synthesis will be to test whether and how the key concepts are related
- *configurative approaches* are appropriate where key concepts are less well defined in advance, data sources are textual, and the purpose of the synthesis is to explore how key concepts are perceived and related, and how salient, important or valuable they are
- *mixed approaches* are appropriate where some but not all key concepts are well defined in advance, there is already a partial understanding of how they relate to each other in terms of theory or policy intentions, data sources are both numerical and textual, and/or the purpose of the review is both to assess quantitatively

Table 10.1 Examples of contrasting approaches to research synthesis

Approach	*Description*	*Key Features*	*Examples*
Meta-analysis	'the statistical analysis of a large collection of analysis results from individual studies for the purpose of integrating the findings' (Glass 1976: 3) 'the basics include finding a sample of studies, developing a single underlying continuum on which to compare results, using a metric to place effects or studies along this continuum (effect-sizes), and using moderators to explore in more detail the implications of these effects' (Hattie *et al.* 2014: 198)	• example of an *aggregative* approach • appropriate for questions concerning the outcome or effect of a particular intervention • requires quantitative studies that will enable the calculation of effect sizes • uses statistical analysis to aggregate the findings of previous studies	Hattie (2008) Denson and Seltzer (2011)
Meta-ethnography	'seeks to go beyond single accounts' through being interpretive rather than aggregative, that is constructing interpretations not analyses and by 'revealing the analogies between accounts' (Noblit and Hare 1988: 13) aims to avoid 'defaulting to an aggregative logic' in three main ways: by moving 'the synthesis from the level of data to the level of interpretation'; by proposing 'a particular theory of explanation, that social explanation is translation'; and by saying that 'there were multiple possible forms for metaethnographic synthesis: reciprocal, refutation and line of argument' (Noblit, in Thorne *et al.* 2004: 1347–8)	• example of a *configurative* approach • useful for open questions about experiences, meanings and interpretations • works with ethnographic and other qualitative studies • uses interpretive translation processes to identify and then re-conceptualise key metaphors from prior studies	Rice (2002) Savin-Baden *et al.* (2008)
Realist synthesis	'an approach to synthesising research evidence on complex social interventions, which provides an explanatory analysis of how and why they work (or don't work) in particular contexts or settings' (Pawson *et al.* 2004: iv) A realist synthesis is used 'to articulate underlying programme theories and then to interrogate the existing evidence to find out whether and where these theories are pertinent and productive. Primary research is examined for its contribution to the developing theory.' Pawson (2006: 74)	• example of a *mixed method* (aggregative and configurative) approach • focuses on questions about what interventions works for whom, in what circumstances, in what respects, and how • draws on relevant pieces of evidence from varied types of studies • uses a developing theoretical framework to locate, integrate and compare and contrast relevant empirical evidence in an iterative manner	McCormack *et al.* (2007) Rycroft-Malone *et al.* (2012)

> the strength of a causal relationship and to explore qualitatively the nature and dynamics of the relationships.
>
> (*Gough* et al. *2012: 74–5)*

Insights into the practice of conducting research synthesis

Alongside the development of different approaches to research synthesis, a literature has also developed around the *practices and outcomes of conducting research synthesis*. Boaz *et al.* (2004; 2007), for example, undertook in-depth analysis of the ways in which 28 social science research synthesis projects published in the UK in the early 2000s had been commissioned and undertaken. Rickinson and May (2009) carried out a similar comparative study of eight higher education-focused research synthesis projects funded by the Higher Education Academy in the UK in the mid 2000s. Other education-specific comparative examples include Foster and Hammersley (1998), and Torrance and Sebba (2007). There have also been reflexive accounts of people's experiences of reviewing and synthesising research that have shed light onto various aspects of the process, such as quality criteria related to triangulation processes, funnel analysis, member checking, and peer analysis of sources, data and interpretations (e.g. Grant and Graue 1999; Best 2003; Rickinson 2003; Andrews 2004; Major and Savin-Baden 2010b).

Taken together, the common message emanating from these studies is to recognise the complexity of research synthesis as a practice. More specifically, they help to highlight four key ideas about conducting research synthesis projects:

- clarity about questions and purposes is critical
- openness to tailoring methods is important
- transparency about appraising quality and synthesising primary studies is key
- working in teams and engaging users is essential.

(i) Clarity about questions and purposes is critical

Boaz *et al.* (2007: 17) argue that 'the purpose that a [synthesis] serves is crucial'. They stress the need for potential purposes to be seen as much wider than simply 'what works?'-type questions: 'There may be questions about the effectiveness of policy interventions, but equally they may be questions about the nature of phenomena, trends and patterns, contexts and comparisons or many other aspects of human behaviour' (Boaz *et al.* 2007: 17). Along similar lines, Torrance and Sebba (2007: 3) emphasise the importance not only of delineating scale and scope, i.e. the boundedness of the study, but also 'justifying synthesis projects in terms of purpose, audience, and significance'. Also in relation to scope, both Boaz *et al.* (2004) and Rickinson and May (2009) highlight the importance of question formulation at the start of projects (e.g. between project teams, commissioning bodies and relevant stakeholders) and, crucially, during their undertaking (e.g. as new knowledge about the nature and scale of the research literature emerges). The general message here is that clarification of purposes and questions is central to effective research synthesis.

(ii) Openness to tailoring methods is important

A second key message from studies of research synthesis projects is recognising the methodological complexity of this type of work and the need for approaches to be developed and adapted rather than selected and adopted. The following quotes from studies of the conduct of research synthesis projects in education and other social sciences illustrate this point well:

> reviewing 'on the hoof' tends to be a messier business than any typology [of review approaches] might imply.
>
> *(Torrance and Sebba 2007: 3)*

> explicit choices of methodology at the start of work were rare, and the methodology usually evolved as work proceeded.
>
> *(Boaz* et al. *2004: 13)*

> [there was] adaptation and tailoring of approaches throughout the review process, even where established review methodologies were being used.
>
> *(Rickinson and May 2009: 58)*

Clearly, established approaches to research synthesis are important to engage with and draw upon, but they often need to be used in tailored rather then off the peg ways.

(iii) Transparency about appraising quality and synthesising primary studies is key

Boaz *et al.* (2004: 19) report that while 'there is a growing desire to undertake syntheses in a more systematic manner', in many cases 'actual practice falls far short' of these aspirations. The first limiting factor is that any research synthesis is dependent on the quality of the primary studies included, and relatedly, how these are documented in ways that allows for their possible 're-use' via synthesis principles and protocols. Boaz *et al.* argue that a secondary problem emerges regarding the lack of transparency about the choices that have been made about 'what to include, how to judge its quality and how to synthesise results' (Boaz *et al.* 2004: 19). Similar issues are raised by Rickinson and May (2009: 59) in relation to: *evidence appraisal* ('tended to be dealt with in more inductive ways as part of the analysis, synthesis and reporting stages rather than through the application of explicit quality criteria during the selection of included studies'); and *evidence synthesis* ('predominance of narrative style synthesis … as distinct from other [established] modes of synthesis' [ibid.]). What these studies suggest is that being systematic in research synthesis projects needs to encompass not just explicit inclusion/exclusion criteria, but also a well-justified approach to the robust and critical appraisal of the primary research, including clearly-explained methods for synthesising and interpreting the findings of individual studies collected together for secondary analysis.

(iv) Working in teams and engaging users is essential

As introduced above, there is now widespread recognition that research synthesis is a demanding undertaking, suited as a task to a team rather than individuals, for pragmatic as well as conceptual reasons. Rickinson and May (2009: 57) found that 'team processes' featured in all stages of the synthesis projects and were 'aided by opportunities for regular face-to-face dialogue, careful allocation of roles and responsibilities … and drawing in of specialist expertise from beyond the team'. On the question of expertise, Boaz *et al.* (2007: 17) emphasise how 'familiarity with a field of research is a necessary but not sufficient qualification', and hence needs to be supplemented with 'methodological awareness, work planning, team work, project management and communication skills'. Also important is the potential for research synthesis to include 'multiple inputs from diverse stakeholders' including different kinds of policy-makers, practitioners and service users (Torrance and Sebba 2007: 3). The basic point is simply that, as with discussions about user engagement in educational research more generally (Rickinson *et al.* 2011), the 'who' of research synthesis is as important as the 'what', the 'how' and the 'why' (Suri and Clarke 2009; Salanti 2012; Rees and Oliver 2012).

The role of research synthesis in higher education for sustainable development

Given the significant developments in research synthesis that have taken place in education and the social sciences more generally, we now consider their implications for higher education for sustainable development.

Our first point is that, to date, there are only a few examples of research synthesis in the field of higher education for sustainable development. Our own searches and experience with the research literature suggest that the main type of synthesis is based on fairly standard literature review techniques. For example, these typically involve analysis (and not necessarily synthesis) of topic areas, such as 'Educational Research in Sustainability in Post-secondary Education' (Vaughter *et al.* 2013), the 'Evolving Roles and Contributions of Universities to Education for Sustainable Development' (Karatzoglou 2013), and 'Factors which Influence Sustainability in Higher Education Institutions' (Velazquez *et al.* 2005). Another clear type is conceptual synthesis, focused around, for example, 'Key Competencies in Sustainability' (Wiek *et al.* 2011) and 'Competencies for Interdisciplinarity in Higher Education' (Parker 2010).

However, when seen against developments in education and social research more widely, there are no clear indications that research synthesis is playing a strategic role in the development of research on higher education for sustainable development at present. For example, the syntheses projects that have been carried out do not draw explicitly on methods, approaches or ideas from the wider research synthesis literature (see Table 10.2 for comments on two examples). Furthermore, it is not evident that the existing syntheses are 'identifying and describing the relevant research', 'critically appraising reports in a systematic manner' *and* 'bringing together the findings into a coherent statement' (Gough *et al.* 2012: 5). We also note that, to the best of our knowledge, up until 2014, there have been no examples of strategic development of synthesis work relating to higher education for sustainable development, such as through journal special issues, commissioned projects, or research programmes. Furthermore, work on higher education for sustainable development has not featured explicitly in the outputs of research synthesis organisations such as the EPPI Centre (UK) or the What Works Clearinghouse (US).

There is, then, great potential for research synthesis to play a clearer, stronger and more strategic role in the development of research in higher education for sustainable development. Drawing together insights and issues from recent developments in research synthesis and the current nature of research in higher education for sustainable development, we want to suggest that more could be done in four key areas:

- the development of specific and worthwhile synthesis questions
- the use of established and emerging approaches to research synthesis
- the analysis and synthesis of research findings
- the use of mixed teams with diverse expertise.

Table 10.2 Key features of examples of research syntheses on aspects of higher education for sustainable development

Feature	*Wiek* et al. *(2011) – example of a literature review paper*	*Vaughter* et al. *(2013) – example of a conceptual synthesis paper*	*Research synthesis notes*
Focus of synthesis	'key competencies in sustainability'	'comparative [i.e. multi institutional] empirical research on sustainability in post-secondary education'	*Both studies readily afford aggregative and configurative synthesis goals, but these possibilities are not explored, reported or rationalised in the account of the design*
Purpose of synthesis	'to identify the relevant literature on key competencies, to synthesise identified competencies into a coherent framework and to identify critical gaps in the conceptualization of these key competencies' 'to support the relatively young academic programs in sustainability in HE'	'to disentangle some of the existing threads of comparative research examining sustainability in post-secondary education institutions, so as to provide a review of the topic and possible directions for further research'	*Neither study is focused specifically on analysing the evidence base in terms of what is known and not known about their selected topic*
Sources for synthesis	28 peer-reviewed journal articles with a significant focus on competencies in sustainability	117 empirical comparative articles and reports from eight leading education-related journals	*Scoping of the literature base excludes grey literatures and that from cognate fields, e.g. competencies in citizenship and social change scenarios*
Approach to synthesis	Interpretive clustering and synthesis of competencies guided by a developing integrated framework	Grounded content analysis to generate categories of types of comparative empirical studies that have examined sustainability in post-secondary education	*In both cases, synthesis processes are framed in terms of qualitative data analysis techniques but not qualitative research synthesis techniques*
Findings/conclusions of synthesis	Presents a coherent framework of sustainability research and problem-solving competence. Several gaps/issues highlighted e.g. lack of empirical evidence for key competencies.	Three themes identified and clustered on: research comparing sustainability curricula across institutions, research comparing campus operations policies and practices, and research on how best to measure audit approaches and outputs.	*Findings and discussion are not linked to explicit problem formulation or 'solution criteria' in either study, while general research recommendations are offered rather than specific policy and practice implications*

(i) Development of specific and worthwhile synthesis questions

The literature on systematic reviews is very clear about the importance of synthesis being driven by carefully formulated, worthwhile questions. Gough *et al.* (2012: 6), for example, argue that: 'Just as primary research is undertaken to answer specific questions, reviews of existing research can be productively focused on answering questions rather than addressing topic areas'. A question-based approach can also be helpful methodologically, particularly in terms of highlighting the need for synthesis methods to be selected and developed on the basis of the questions asked, and not vice versa.

Moreover, thinking carefully about what kinds of questions and sub-questions are worth investigating – and can be addressed through research synthesis – can provide a helpful way to engage different players and stakeholders in identifying priorities. Rickinson and May's analysis of six HE synthesis projects, notes how the project teams scoped their work by asking three meta-level questions ('What is needed? What is meaningful? What is practical?' [Rickinson and May 2009: 55]). The first of these focuses attention on what would be worthwhile, as in designing the study so that 'the kind of review and review outputs … would be useful and worthwhile in the light of recent developments in policy and practice and trends in relevant research and literature reviews' (Rickinson and May 2009: 42). Along similar lines, Hattie *et al.* (2014) point out that meta-analysis is only valuable if 'there is a worthwhile problem that underlies the synthesis'.

Thus far in the field of higher education for sustainable development, we have seen little in the way of strategic efforts to identify and debate what topics and questions represent 'worthwhile problems' for research synthesis as distinct from suggesting or recommending further empirical or theoretical inquiry. This situation represents an important weakness within the field that needs serious attention in future. What's important though, is that efforts to address this weakness do not need to start from scratch; as shown above, there is a wide-ranging methodological literature on research synthesis that can be drawn upon and a growing number of examples of research syntheses in education that can inform future work in higher education for sustainable development (see Table 10.3 for examples of how existing syntheses in higher education might inform future synthesis in higher education for sustainable development).

(ii) Use of established and emerging approaches to research synthesis

As outlined earlier, there is also a well-developed methodological literature on approaches to research synthesis and the practice of reviewing research. However, within the field of higher education for sustainable development, engagement with such work still seems to be limited. On the one hand, there are signs that some ideas and practices associated with systematic reviewing are being addressed. The examples in Table 10.2 provided a clear articulation of their literature search strategies, inclusion/exclusion criteria, and (to some extent) scope and timescale. They also describe and explain the process by which included studies were analysed and, ideally, synthesised. However, as in our observational notes in Table 10.2, there are few references to any wider literature on research synthesis methodology, and crucially, its application and development. Thus, for example, the synthesis processes are framed in terms of qualitative data analysis technique (e.g. Mayring's inductive category development is cited by Vaughter *et al.* 2013 and Karatzoglou 2013) but not qualitative research synthesis (e.g. Thorne *et al.* 2002; Greenhalgh *et al.* 2005; Heyvaert *et al.* 2013).

These observations suggest that there would be some advantage to the field if future research synthesis were to draw more explicitly on established and emerging approaches to research

Table 10.3 Examples of research synthesis in HE, and possible repurposing in HE for SD

Synthesis topic in HE	*Example study*	*Possibilities in HE for SD?*
Teaching and learning in interdisciplinary higher education	Spelt *et al.* 2009	• Refocus on ESD provision? • Compare and contrast the trajectory of ESD with other interdisciplinary themes?
Methods to improve student learning	Gough *et al.* 2003	• Focus on effect size of ESD interventions? • Consider realist synthesis approach – what needs improving – teaching and/or learning, and how does ESD contribute?
Non-individualised conception of academic achievement	Wilder 2014	• Aggregate claims and evidence to test whether ESD contributes distinctively to graduate attributes? • Follow Hattie (2008) and consider achievements over lifespan, and significance of SD-focused activities?
Professional identity development	Trede *et al.* 2012	• Configure studies on ecoliteracy interventions, subjectivity models, and evidence of initial and continuing professional development, to consider correlations, and identify lines of further inquiry? • Examine possibilities and lines of argument that serve to refute current professional development priorities from HE for SD perspectives?
Interactions and effects of gender on grant proposals	Marsh *et al.* 2009	• Undertake systematic review of grant awards, publications, supervisions, networks, institutions and demographics within and beyond HE for SD? • Contribute to meta-analysis on gender studies and academia?
Interventions to increase academic publication rates	McGrail *et al.* 2006	• Conduct critical interpretative synthesis on publication practices of HE for SD practitioners? • Compare meta-ethnographies of HE for SD publication practices with citation and impact data, and user engagement?

synthesis. One way in which this could be helpful is providing synthesis teams with a clearer appreciation of the different options and stages of synthesis projects. Investigations into the conduct of research reviews have flagged up the quite different methodological challenges that can arise at different stages in the process. Rickinson and May (2009), for example, highlighted the different ways in which six review teams negotiated the scoping, searching, selecting, analysing, synthesising and reporting of their synthesis. This and other similar studies into the conduct of review teams (Boaz *et al.* 2004; 2007) could prove informative to future synthesis projects in higher education for sustainable development.

A second potential benefit is in terms of the use and development of approaches to synthesis. While some guidance on systematic reviewing can give the impression that there are established approaches that should be used (cf. Table 10.1), the reality in practice is that synthesis projects often involve 'bespoke rather than off-the-peg approaches' (Boaz *et al.* 2007: 17). As Rickinson and May (2009) found, while there were some teams that used specific named approaches such as 'meta-ethnography' or 'best evidence synthesis', there were others that sought to develop new approaches such as 'grounded practitioner review' and/or combine existing approaches with some form of empirical investigation. The implication here is that future research synthesis for this field could draw on approaches not only in terms of straightforward adoption of techniques but also in terms of developing innovative approaches.

Connected with this idea of adapting (rather than adopting) synthesis approaches is a deeper recognition of the central role that interpretation plays in the synthesis process. In other words, research synthesis is much more than the brute application of a method or technique. In the context of meta-analysis, for example, Hattie *et al.* (2014: 201) talk about how:

> effect sizes are but summary statistics awaiting an interpretation. They need to be interpreted as part of a story that addresses the problem to be solved. They need to be as rich and contextualized as any literature review in educational research. Many of the earlier meta-analyses were summaries of data without an accompanying story.

In terms of the field of higher education for sustainable development, we identify a two-fold implication: there is a clear need for more explicit use of established and emerging approaches to research synthesis from education and social science research, *and* the generation of 'a story that transcends and make sense of the body of evidence' (Hattie *et al.* 2014: 204).

(iii) Analysis and synthesis of research findings

Where synthesis projects have been undertaken on higher education for sustainable development, as with Table 10.2, we note these have tended to focus on reporting the kinds of research that have been undertaken as opposed to critically discussing the kinds of findings that have been generated. In other words, they seem to have been driven by a desire to get clear about what research has been carried out but not the quality, extent and status of the evidence that research has generated. As such, their conclusions are likely to be helpful for researchers working on higher education for sustainable development but less useful for policy-makers and practitioners. Guidance on systematic reviewing, however, talks about reviews not only 'identifying and describing the relevant research' and 'critically appraising research reports in a systematic manner' but also 'bringing together the findings into a coherent statement' (Gough *et al.* 2012: 5). In our view, insufficient progress has been made against this third dimension, that is, of synthesising findings into coherent statements that can inform future policy and practice as well as future research.

Take, for example, Vaughter *et al.*'s (2013) review of educational research on 'sustainability in post-compulsory education'. This presents the literature in terms of the three main foci of previous studies ('curricula, campus operations and measuring sustainability') and draws conclusions about what research needs to be done ('gaps in the research') (Vaughter *et al.* 2013: 2265). It, therefore, 'offers a "lay of the land" for those engaged in research on furthering sustainability through post-secondary education' (Vaughter *et al.* 2013: 2266). Similarly, Karatzoglou's (2013) review of research on 'the evolving roles and contributions of universities to ESD' focuses on the characteristics of the identified literature (regions, journals, year, topics, methodologies and so on), while conclusions are drawn largely about how future reporting of case-study research might be improved.

When seen against the backdrop of the examples and developments in research synthesis outlined above, it looks as if there has not yet been a concerted effort to examine research in higher education for sustainable development as an *evidence* base (cf. Rickinson 2001: 208). As noted above, synthesis work in the field has not emphasised the identification of key messages emerging from current available evidence in ways that might be useful for research users as well as researchers. Hence, we suggest that the potential for reviews to 'inform [research users and researchers] about what is known, how it is known, how this varies across studies [and] what is not known from previous research' (Gough *et al.* 2013: 4) has not yet been realised in the field of higher education for sustainable development. Addressing this shortcoming remains a key challenge for the field.

(iv) Use of mixed teams with diverse expertise

Across education and social research, an approach we are increasingly familiar with is the widespread appreciation of the importance of involving research users in and with research (Rickinson *et al.* 2011). Very similar developments have been seen in relation to the conduct of research synthesis projects. The calls for research synthesis to be carried out by mixed teams comprising different kinds of researchers and non-researchers with varied types of expertise have been plentiful:

> Familiarity with a field of research is a necessary but not sufficient qualification for reviewers. Substantive expertise needs to be combined with methodological awareness, work planning, teamwork, project management and communication skills for successful reviewing.
>
> *(Boaz* et al. *2007: 17)*

> I would suggest that future reviews of environmental education research evidence may well benefit from being undertaken by a number of researchers working collaboratively, rather than by single individuals working in relative isolation.
>
> *(Rickinson 2003: 263)*

> Review team working was aided by opportunities for regular face-to-face dialogue, careful allocation of roles and responsibilities within the team and drawing in of specialist expertise from beyond the team.
>
> *(Rickinson and May 2009: 55)*

In relation to higher education for sustainable development then, it would seem that there is much to be gained by thinking broadly and flexibly about who undertakes future research synthesis projects, *and* who authors *and* communicates the process and final reports. In particular, we would emphasise the potential for diversity in terms of: *institutional settings* (different kinds of higher education institutions engaging with sustainable development, e.g. research intensive universities, teaching only colleges, networked institutions such as AASHE, Copernicus, Talloires signatories, etc.); *professional roles* (insiders and outsiders to higher education for sustainable development across senior leaders, practitioners, policy-makers, researchers, and service users such as students and supply chain members); and *sectoral backgrounds* (policy-making, civil society, knowledge generation, knowledge mediation/communication, etc.).

The future development of research synthesis in higher education for sustainable development

This chapter has sought to highlight the ways in which research synthesis has become an integral part of the evolution of the research landscape over the last 10 to 15 years. The commissioning, conduct, communication and critique of different kinds of research syntheses is now very much part of the mainstream of many areas of social policy and social research. As the chapter has shown, there is a rich methodological and conceptual literature relating to research synthesis, a plethora of approaches and frameworks for synthesising different types of evidence in different kinds of ways, and a number of organisations dedicated to the support and communication of high-quality syntheses. Also, as pointed out at the outset in Figure 10.1, these achievements have been part of wider developments associated with critiques of social science research, agendas around evidence-based policy and practice, and efforts to support knowledge mobilisation. In short, research synthesis has become one of the key ways in which researchers, research users and research funders have sought to enhance the quality, impact and usefulness of education and social research.

Turning to the field of higher education for sustainable development though, to date we see no clear signs of strategic involvement or investment in research synthesis. While there are some examples of research syntheses relating to aspects of higher education for sustainable development, these are few in number, have tended to ask questions about the kinds of research that has been conducted rather than the kinds of findings that have been generated, and have not drawn explicitly on any of the approaches, debates or concepts in the wider literature around research synthesis. We see this absence of strategic research synthesis as particularly problematic for a field like higher education for sustainable development because:

- It is a new and growing area of research, practice and policy, and so the field has much to gain from taking stock and looking forwards through effective research synthesis.
- It is a diverse field of research spanning many genres, disciplines and sub-fields, and so it could become better connected and more powerful through well-conducted synthesis.
- It is a field centred on a big picture strategic challenge – sustainability – and so its members should be able to make a strong case for well-targeted, strategic research synthesis.
- It is a field focused on a part of society – higher education – that is at the heart of evidence production and use, and so its members should be well placed to demonstrate the value of regular research synthesis.
- It is a field that has questions about the limits of knowledge and knowing at its core, and so its members should be able to draw upon and contribute to the growing understanding and diversity of approaches to research synthesis.

So, as we see it, there is much to be gained by the stakeholders of this field paying more serious attention to the role that research synthesis could play in its future development. This, of course, should not be as a development in isolation, but alongside and in tandem with high quality primary research, robust theoretical inquiry, innovative practical innovation, and sustained knowledge brokerage/mobilisation. In other words, research synthesis needs to be developed in connection with (rather than instead of or in isolation from) other parts of the knowledge generation, mediation and utilisation picture (Levin 2004; Sharples 2013). For this to happen within the field of higher education for sustainable development, we see a clear need for:

- strategic investment in research synthesis projects around collaboratively agreed priorities and questions
- a willingness to draw upon the tools, methods, frameworks and insights that now exist
- an enthusiasm to use, and further develop, existing approaches to synthesising different kinds of research evidence

- an openness to the role that research synthesis can play in informing policy, influencing practice and developing research
- an embracing of the expertise and contribution that varied stakeholders and types of researchers can play in research synthesis.

In relation to social science research more generally, Gough *et al.* (2012: 11) argue that all researchers and research users need to consider 'whether their needs, roles and responsibilities are best met by the current balance … between primary research and [syntheses] of that research'. Our response to this consideration for the field of higher education for sustainable development is unequivocal: the current balance between primary research and research synthesis indicates way too little attention being given to the latter. Why does this matter? As we hope this chapter has shown, however diverse and vibrant higher education for sustainable development is as a field, it will always be limited in its quality, power and reach if its leaders, innovators, students and communicators continue to overlook the potential of research synthesis to develop, critique and (re)direct their efforts and priorities.

References

Alton-Lee, A., 2014. 'Using Educational Research as a Resource for Continuous Improvement in Education: The Best Evidence Syntheses', in Reid, A.D., Hart, E.P. and Peters, M.A. (eds), *A Companion to Research in Education*. Dordrecht: Springer, 209–13.

Andrews, R., 2004, 'Between Scylla and Charybdis: The Experience of Undertaking a Systematic Review in education', in Thomas, G. and Pring, R. (eds), *Evidence-based Practice in Education*. Maidenhead: Open University Press, 65–76.

Barnett-Page, E. and Thomas, J., 2009. 'Methods for the Synthesis of Qualitative Research: A Critical Review', *BMC Medical Research Methodology* 9, 59.

Best, R., 2003. 'Educational Research, Useful Knowledge and Evidence-Based Practice – the Experience of Undertaking a Critical Review'. Paper presented at: Annual Conference of the British Educational Research Association, 11–13 September, Heriot-Watt University, Edinburgh.

Biesta, G., 2014. 'Evidence Based Practice in Education: Between Science and Democracy', in Reid, A.D., Hart, E.P. and Peters, M.A. (eds), *A Companion to Research in Education*. Dordrecht: Springer, 391–400.

Boaz, A., Solesbury, W. and Sullivan, F., 2004. *The Practice of Research Reviewing 1. An Assessment of 28 Review Reports*. London: ESRC UK Centre for EBPP.

Boaz, A., Solesbury, W. and Sullivan, F., 2007. *The Practice of Research Reviewing 2. Ten Case Studies of Reviews*. London: ESRC UK Centre for EBPP.

Borenstein, M., Hedges, L.V., Higgins, J.P.T. and Rothstein, H.R., 2009. *Introduction to Meta-Analysis*. Chichester: Wiley.

Bushman, B.J. and Wells, G.L., 2001. 'Narrative Impressions of Literature: The Availability Bias and the Corrective Properties of Meta-analytic Approaches', *Personal and Social Psychology Bulletin*, 27(9), 1123–30.

Campbell, R., Pound, P., Morgan, M., Daker-White, G., Britten, N., Pill, R., Yardley, L., Pope, C. and Donovan, J., 2011. 'Evaluating Meta-ethnography: Systematic Analysis and Synthesis of Qualitative Research', *Health Technology Assessment*, 15(43), 1–164.

Chalmers, I., 2003. 'Trying to do More Good than Harm in Policy and Practice: The Role of Rigorous, Transparent, Up-to-date Evaluations', *The ANNALS of the American Academy of Political and Social Science*, 589(1), 22–40.

Cooper, H. and Hedges, L., 1994. *The Handbook of Research Synthesis*. New York: Russell Sage Foundation.

Davies, P., 2000. The Relevance of Systematic Reviews to Educational Policy and Practice', *Oxford Review of Education*, 26(3&4), 365–78.

Denson, N. and Seltzer, M.H., 2011. 'Meta-analysis in Higher Education: An Illustrative Example using Hierarchical Linear Modelling', *Research in Higher Education*, 52, 215–44.

Elliott, J., 2001. 'Making Evidence-based Practice Educational', *British Educational Research Journal*, 27(5), 555–74.

Evans, J. and Benefield, P., 2001. 'Systematic Reviews of Educational Research: Does the Medical Method Fit?', *British Educational Research Journal*, 27(5), 527–41.

Finfgeld, D.L., 2003. 'Metasynthesis: The State of the Art – So Far', *Qualitative Health Research*, 13(7), 893–904.

Foster, P. and Hammersley, M., 1998. 'A Review of Reviews: Structure and Function in Reviews of Educational Research', *British Educational Research Journal*, 24(5), 609–28.

Glass, G.V., 1976. 'Primary, Secondary, and Meta-analysis of Research', *Educational Researcher*, 5, 3–8.

Glass, G.V., 1978. 'Integrating Findings: The Meta-analysis of Research', *Review of Research in Education*, 5, 351–79.

Gough, D., 2007. 'The EPPI-Centre', in OECD (eds), *Research and Evidence in Educational Policy-making: New Challenges*. Paris: OECD, 63–9.

Gough, D. and Elbourne, D., 2002. 'Systematic Research Synthesis to Inform Policy, Practice and Democratic Debate', *Social Policy and Society*, 1(3), 225–36.

Gough, D., Kiwan, D., Sutcliffe, K., Simpson, D. and Houghton, N., 2003. *A Systematic Map and Synthesis Review of the Effectiveness of Personal Development Planning for Improving Student Learning*. London: EPPI-Centre, Social Science Research Unit, Institute of Education, University of London, Research Evidence in Education Library.

Gough, D., Oliver, S. and Thomas, J., 2012. *An Introduction to Systematic Reviews*. London: Sage.

Gough, D., Oliver, S. and Thomas, J., 2013. *Learning from Research: Systematic Reviews for Informing Policy Decisions: A Quick Guide*. London: Nesta.

Grant, C.A. and Graue, E., 1999. '(Re)Viewing a Review: A Case History of the "Review of Educational Research"', *Review of Educational Research*, 69(4), 384–96.

Greenhalgh, T., Robert, G., Macfarlane, F., Bate, P. Kyriakidou, O. and Peacock, R., 2005. 'Storylines of Research in Diffusion of Innovation: A Meta-narrative Approach to Systematic Review', *Social Science and Medicine*, 61(2), 417–30.

Hammersley, M., 2001. 'On Systematic Reviews of Research Literatures: A Narrative Response to Evans and Benefield', *British Educational Research Journal*, 27(5), 141–61.

Hammerstrøm, K., Wade, A. and Jørgensen, A.-M.K., 2010. 'Searching for Studies: A Guide to Information Retrieval for Campbell Systematic Reviews'. www.campbellcollaboration.org/lib/download/969/ [accessed 2 March 2015].

Harden, A. and Thomas, J., 2010. 'Mixed Methods and Systematic Reviews: Examples and Emerging Issues', in Tashakkori, A. and Teddlie, C. (eds), *Handbook of Mixed Methods in the Social and Behavioral Sciences, 2nd Ed*. London: Sage, 749–74.

Hattie, J., 2008. *Visible Learning: A Synthesis of Over 800 Meta-Analyses Relating to Achievement*. London: Routledge.

Hattie, J., Rogers, H.J. and Swaminathan, H., 2014. 'The Role of Meta-analysis in Educational Research', in Reid, A.D., Hart, E.P. and Peters, M.A. (eds), *A Companion to Research in Education*. Dordrecht: Springer, 197–207.

Heyvaert, M., Maes, B. and Onghena, P., 2013. 'Mixed Methods Research Synthesis: Definition, Framework, and Potential', *Quality and Quantity*, 47(2), 659–76.

Higgins, J.P.T. and Green, S., eds., 2011. *Cochrane Handbook for Systematic Reviews of Interventions, Version 5.1.0*. Oxford, UK: The Cochrane Collaboration. http://handbook.cochrane.org [accessed 2 March 2015].

Karatzoglou, B., 2013. 'An In-depth Literature Review of the Evolving Roles and Contributions of Universities to Education for Sustainable Development', *Journal of Cleaner Production*, 49, 44–53.

van der Knaap, L.M., Leeuw, F.L., Bogaerts, S. and Nijssen, L.T.J., 2008. 'Combining Campbell Standards and the Realist Evaluation Approach: The Best of Two Worlds?', *American Journal of Evaluation*, 29(1), 48–57.

Levin, B., 2004. 'Making Research Matter More', *Education Policy Analysis Archives*, 12(56), 1–20.

Levin, B. and Cooper, A., 2012. 'Theory, Research and Practice in Mobilizing Research Knowledge in Education', in Fenwick, Y. and Farrell, L. (eds), *Knowledge Mobilization and Educational Research*. Abingdon: Routledge, 17–29.

Littell, J.H., 2008. 'Evidence-based or Biased? The Quality of Published Reviews of Evidence-based Practices', *Children and Youth Services Review*, 30(11), 1299–1317.

McCormack, B., Wright, J., Dewar, B., Harvey, G. and Ballantine, K., 2007. 'A Realist Synthesis of Evidence Relating to Practice Development: Findings from the Literature Analysis', *Practice Development in Health Care*, 6(1), 25–55.

McGrail, M.R., Rickard, C.M. and Jones, R., 2006. 'Publish or Perish: A Systematic Review of Interventions to Increase Academic Publication Rates', *Higher Education Research & Development*, 25(1), 19–35.

MacLure, M., 2005. '"Clarity Bordering on Stupidity": Where's the Quality in Systematic Review?', *Journal of Education Policy*, 20(4), 393–416.

Major, C.H. and Savin-Baden, M., 2010a. *An Introduction to Qualitative Research Synthesis: Managing the Information Explosion in Social Science Research*. London: Routledge.

Major, C. and Savin-Baden, M., 2010b. 'Exploring the Relevance of Qualitative Research Synthesis to Higher Education Research and Practice', *London Review of Education*, 8(2), 127–40.

Marsh, H.W., Bornmann, L., Mutz, R., Daniel, H.-D. and O'Mara, A., 2009. 'Gender Effects in the Peer Reviews of Grant Proposals: A Comprehensive Meta-analysis Comparing Traditional and Multilevel Approaches', *Review of Educational Research*, 79(3), 1290–1326.

Noblit, G.W. and Hare, R.D., 1988. *Meta-Ethnography: Synthesizing Qualitative Studies*. London: Sage.

Noyes, J., Popay, J., Pearson, A., Hannes, K. and Booth, A., 2011a. 'Cochrane Handbook for Systematic Reviews of Interventions', in Higgins, J.P.T. and Green, S. (eds), *Qualitative Research and Cochrane Reviews*. Version 5.1. The Cochrane Collaboration. www.cochrane-handbook.org [accessed 2 March 2011].

Noyes, J., Popay, J., Pearson, A., Hannes, K. and Booth, A., 2011b. 'Qualitative Research and Cochrane Reviews', in Higgins, J.P.T. and Green, S. (eds), *Qualitative Research and Cochrane Reviews*. Version 5.1.0. The Cochrane Collaboration. www.cochrane-handbook.org [accessed 2 March 2011].

Oakley, A., 2002. 'Social Science and Evidence-based Everything: The Case of Education', *Educational Review*, 54(3), 277–86.

Oakley, A., 2003. 'Research Evidence, Knowledge Management and Educational Practice: Early Lessons from a Systematic Approach', *London Review of Education*, 1, 21–33.

Oancea, A., 2005. 'Criticisms of Educational Research', *British Educational Research Journal*, 31(2), 157–83.

OECD, 2007. *Evidence in Education. Linking Research and Policy*. Paris: OECD.

Parker, J., 2010. 'Competencies for Interdisciplinarity in Higher Education', *International Journal of Sustainability in Higher Education*, 11(4), 325–38.

Pawson, R., 2006. *Evidenced-Based Policy: A Realist Perspective*. London: Sage.

Pawson, R., Greenhalgh, T., Harvey, G. and Walshe, K., 2004. *Realist Synthesis: An Introduction*. ESRC Research Methods Programme. RMP Methods, 2. Manchester: University of Manchester.

Petticrew, M. and Roberts, H., 2006. *Systematic Reviews in the Social Sciences: A Practical Guide*. Oxford: Blackwell.

Potts, H.W.W., 2013. 'The Meta-narrative Review: Systematic Reviewing Across Different Paradigms'. Presented at Mixed Method Evidence Synthesis: How to Combine Quantitative and Qualitative Evidence in Systematic Reviews workshop, 12 March, University of Manchester/NICE Evidence Synthesis Network, Manchester.

Rees, J. and Oliver, S., 2012. 'Stakeholder Perspectives and Participation in Reviews', in Gough, D., Oliver, S. and Thomas, J. (eds), *Introduction to Systematic Reviews*. London: Sage, 17–34.

Reid, A.D. and Nikel, J., 2003. 'Reading a Critical Review of Evidence: Notes and Queries on Research Programmes in Environmental Education', *Environmental Education Research*, 9(2), 149–65.

Rice, E.H., 2002. 'The Collaboration Process in Professional Development Schools. Results of a Meta-Ethnography, 1990–1998', *Journal of Teacher Education*, 53(1), 55–67.

Rickinson, M., 2001. 'Learners and Learning in Environmental Education: A Critical Review of the Evidence', *Environmental Education Research*, 7(3), 207–320.

Rickinson, M., 2003. 'Reviewing Research Evidence in Environmental Education: Some Methodological Reflections and Challenges', *Environmental Education Research*, 9(2), 257–71.

Rickinson, M. and May, H., 2009. *A Comparative Study of Methodological Approaches to Reviewing Literature*. York: Higher Education Academy.

Rickinson, M., Sebba, J. and Edwards, A., 2011. *Improving Research through User Engagement*. London: Routledge.

Rycroft-Malone, J., McCormack, B., Hutchinson, A.M., DeCorby, K., Bucknall, T.K., Kent, B., Schultz, A., Snelgrove-Clarke, E., Stetler, C.B., Titler, M., Wallin, L. and Wilson V., 2012. 'Realist Synthesis: Illustrating the Method for Implementation Research', *Implementation Science*, 7(33), 1–10.

Salanti, G., 2012. 'Indirect and Mixed-treatment Comparison, Network, or Multiple-treatments Metaanalysis: Many Names, Many Benefits, Many Concerns for the next Generation Evidence Synthesis Tool', *Research Synthesis Methods*, 3(2), 80–97.

Sandelowski, M. and Barroso, J., 2007. *Handbook for Synthesizing Qualitative Research*. New York: Springer.

Savin-Baden, M., McFarland, L. and Savin-Baden, J., 2008. 'Learning Spaces, Agency and Notions of Improvement: What Influences Thinking and Practices about Teaching and Learning in Higher Education? An Interpretive Meta-ethnography', *London Review of Education*, 6(3), 211–27.

Scriven, M., 2014. 'The Logic of Causal Investigations', in Reid, A.D., Hart, E.P. and Peters, M.A. (eds), *A Companion to Research in Education*. Dordrecht: Springer, 163–71.

Sharples, J., 2013. *Evidence for the Frontline*. London: Alliance for Useful Evidence.

Spelt, E.J.H., Biemans, H.J.A., Tobi, H., Luning, P.A. and Mulder, M., 2009. 'Teaching and Learning in Interdisciplinary Higher Education: A Systematic Review', *Educational Psychology Review*, 21(4), 365–78.

Suri, H. and Clarke, D., 2009. 'Advancements in Research Synthesis Methods: From a Methodologically Inclusive Perspective', *Review of Educational Research*, 79(1), 395–430.

Thorne, S., Joachim, G., Paterson, B. and Canam, C., 2002. 'Influence of the Research Frame on Qualitatively Derived Health Science Knowledge', *International Journal of Qualitative Methods*, 1(1), 1–9.

Thorne, S., Jensen, L., Kearney, M.H., Nobilt, G. and Sandelowski, M., 2004. 'Qualitative Metasynthesis: Reflections on Methodological Orientation and Ideological Agenda', *Qualitative Health Research*, 14(10), 1342–65.

Torrance, H. and Sebba, J., 2007. *Reviewing Reviews: Towards a Better Understanding of the Role of Research Reviews* (Teaching and Learning Research Briefing). London: TLRP. www.tlrp.org/pub/documents/Rev%20Rev%20RB30%20FINAL.pdf [25 June 2014].

Trede, F., Macklin, R. and Bridges, D., 2012. 'Professional Identity Development: A Review of the Higher Education Literature', *Studies in Higher Education*, 27(3), 365–84.

Vaughter, P., Wright, T., McKenzie, M., and Lidstone, L., 2013. 'Greening the Ivory Tower: A Review of Educational Research on Sustainability in Post-secondary Education', *Sustainability*, 5(5), 2252–71.

Velazquez, L., Munguia, N. and Sanchez, M., 2005. 'Deterring Sustainability in Higher Education Institutions: An Appraisal of the Factors which Influence Sustainability in Higher Education Institutions', *International Journal of Sustainability in Higher Education*, 6(4), 383–91.

Walsh, D. and Downe, S., 2005. 'Meta-synthesis Method for Qualitative Research: A Literature Review', *Journal of Advanced Nursing*, 50(2), 204–11.

Wiek, A., Withycombe, L. and Redman, C.L., 2011.' Key Competencies in Sustainability: A Reference Framework for Academic Program Development', *Sustainable Science*, 6, 203–18.

Wilder, S., 2014. 'Effects of Parental Involvement on Academic Achievement: A Meta-synthesis', *Educational Review*, 66(3), 377–97.

11

CHANGING FROM WITHIN

An Action Research perspective for bringing about sustainability curriculum change in higher education

Fiona Wahr and Barbara de la Harpe

Keeping going

Curriculum change for sustainability has been slow to happen in university contexts with few accounts of wholesale reformation or transformation reported (Holdsworth *et al.* 2006; Wals 2014). As Wals (2014: 11) points out 'despite the early signs of a transition in some parts of the academic community, sustainability by and large is still largely external to the student, academic faculty member and administrator within higher education'. Ferrer-Balas *et al.* (2008: 298) conclude that 'while there are undoubtedly some universities that are already on their way to embodying some of these ideals [of a sustainable institution], achieving change at the majority of universities around the world will require tremendous effort'.

Notwithstanding, there is overwhelming agreement that in order to address growing concerns about the future viability of life on Earth, teaching university students about sustainability and to act more sustainably in their chosen professions is a necessary part of a university education (Corcoran and Wals 2004; Wals 2009). Essentially, university curricula which encompass learning outcomes, learning activities and assessment tasks for the award/degree as a whole, as well as for each of its components, should 'make students aware of the values that are present in the professional's work and options for their own role in global challenges' (Mulder 2007: 155).

There continues to be considerable discussion across the higher education sector worldwide about how best to support the integration of sustainability into the curriculum (Sterling and Thomas 2006; Gough and Scott 2007), to achieve at the minimum reformation and at best transformation outcomes. In order to achieve *reformation* sustainability related content is integrated into the curriculum using 'a critically reflective, adaptive response or second-order change', while *transformation requires* that the entire curriculum is redesigned reflecting a paradigm change underpinned by 'new meaning-making and examination of existing assumptions' (Sterling 2004b: 55). In fact, for systemic transformation outcomes, a redesign of not only the curriculum in totality (whole of degree) but also the generative education system is required.

While achieving either reformation or transformation of the higher education curriculum is not straight forward, it remains critical that universities play their part in moving society to a more sustainable world by finding ways to encourage and support at the very least the reformation of university curricula so that graduates leave university prepared to make a difference through their chosen fields. No longer is it possible to depend on individual and isolated ad hoc academic efforts since,

> relying on individual change to lead to systemic change commits the error of 'methodological individualism'; it exaggerates the power of agency over that of structure, seeing individual actors as the prime movers and shakers in social change. Individuals are important, of course, but policies based on methodological individualism do not automatically lead to institutional change.
>
> *(Trowler and Bamber 2005: 84)*

It is imperative that those who are both deeply committed to higher education sustainability learning and those who recognise the need for reformation and transformative change make a significant effort to unite and champion from within, in ways that are sympathetic to the diversity of sub-cultures, in order to lead and bring about the curriculum and systemic changes that are so desperately required. As Wals and Blewitt (2012: 64) point out,

> mainstreaming cannot be prescriptive and so requires a participatory process of co-definition as to what can or ought to be integrated and how this might best be done in different [disciplines], universities, countries and other institutional frameworks.

Rather it 'requires permeability between disciplines, the university and wider community and between cultures, along with the competence to integrate, connect, confront and, as much as possible, reconcile multiple ways of looking at the world' (Wals and Blewitt 2012: 70).

Another look

Action Research is a research approach aimed at bringing about change, as well as creating knowledge and theory. It aims to bring about deep, lasting and meaningful change and improvements to individuals, organisations and society.

It is underpinned by a 'practical, participative, empowering, interpretive, tentative and critical' (Schmuck 2006: 28) philosophy. It is characterised by multiple cycles of critical inquiry (planning, acting, observing, critically reflecting, adapting) that are iterative, flexible and 'messy', aimed at addressing an issue or solving a problem in order to improve situations for the better (Hammond and Wellington 2013). Action Research is often concerned with questioning social, cultural and/or political practices, including democratic participation and emancipation. According to Burns (2000: 453), those involved in Action Research become more aware of 'the relationship between problems and situation and contextual factors' which 'places them in a stronger position to influence the policies which shape their practice'.

> Good action research emerges over time in an evolutionary and developmental process, as individuals learn skills of inquiry, as communities of inquiry develop, as understanding of the issues deepens, and as practice grows and shifts changes over time. Emergence means that the questions may change, the relationships may change, the purposes may change, and what is important may change. This means action research cannot be programmatic and cannot be defined in terms of hard and fast methods.
>
> *(Reason 2006: 197)*

An Action Research approach is in contrast to traditional research approaches that generally focus on generating theoretical knowledge (Coghlan and Brannick 2010).

Types and levels of Action Research

A number of types of Action Research are outlined in the literature, including Technical (Burns 2005; Kemmis 2006), Practical (Lodico *et al.* 2010), Collaborative (Somekh 1989), Participatory (Kemmis and McTaggart, cited in Reyes 2011), Community-based (Stringer 1999; Stringer 2004) and Critical/Emancipatory Action Research (Carr and Kemmis 1986). All fall within the Action Research family. While there is considerable overlap in the literature around the naming of Action Research types, a synthesis of the specific or major focus and outcomes of each of the types is provided in Table 11.1.

As indicated in Table 11.1, *Technical Action Research* focuses on 'functional improvement measured in terms of … success in changing particular outcomes of practices' (Kemmis 2006: 95), with change outcomes focusing on cause and effects and being value-free (Burns 2005).

Table 11.1 Types of Action Research highlighting focus, ethos and outcome

Type	*Focus*	*Ethos*	*Outcome*
Technical Action Research	Changes that improve functions and/or processes	Value-free	Leads to function or process changes
Practical Action Research	Changes that improve local level practice and understanding of associated meanings to assist in practical practitioner decision-making	Value-relative	Leads to personal individual changes in practice at local level
Participatory Action and/or Collaborative Action Research	Changes that improve group practices with participants working collaboratively on a shared issue	Value-relative	Leads to group level changes
Community-based Action Research	Changes that improve a community social problem (political, social and/or economic) at the local or small-scale level to extend understanding of the situation and its resolution	Value-relative	Leads to community level changes of a specific social problem in a specific situation
Critical and/or Emancipatory Action Research	Changes that improve a social problem that affects an underserved community to bring about emancipation and liberation of/for those who are oppressed or exploited by critiquing underlying causes	Value-relative	Leads to ongoing emancipation and freedom from oppression

Source: Adapted from: Burns 2005; Carr and Kemmis 1986; Coghlan and Brannick 2010; Creswell *et al.*, 2007; Hammond and Wellington 2013; Kemmis 2006; Lodico *et al.* 2010; Manfra 2009; McKernan 1991; Somekh 1989; Stringer 1999.

Practical Action Research focuses on 'everyday practice and typically focuses on making small changes at the local level' (Lodico *et al.* 2010: 333) as well as on discovering the 'meanings people make of actions' (Burns 2005: 58) in order to 'inform practical decision-making of practitioners' (Kemmis 2006: 95). This type of Action Research is less advocacy-oriented and has a more practical orientation. *Participatory Action and/or Collaborative Action Research* focuses on 'a social situation, involving the participants themselves as researchers, with a view to improving the quality of action within it' (Somekh 1989: 164). It is 'collaborative learning for the sake of the individual and collective self-formation, realised by groups of people who join together in changing the practices through which they interact in a shared social world' (Kemmis *et al.* 2014: 20). *Community-Based Action Research* focuses on 'the problems of a group, a community, or an organisation ... to assist people in extending their understanding of the situation and, thus, in resolving problems that confront them' (Stringer 1999: 10). It is about localised and small-scale theorising to resolve specific social problems in specific situations. Finally, *Critical and/or Emancipatory Action Research* focuses on a social problem that significantly affects an underserved community by critiquing underlying causes in order to bring about emancipation and liberation of/for those who are 'marginalised or who lack the power to improve their own lives' (Lodico *et al.* 2010: 332). It is aimed at producing social change to improve the conditions of the oppressed and exploited (Carr and Kemmis 1986; Creswell *et al.* 2007). Participants 'not only ... search out the interpretive meanings that educational actions have for them but to organize action to overcome constraints' (McKernan 1991: 24). Action focuses on 'political, social and economic constraints to improved conditions ... [in order to] understand what impedes more democratic and equal practices' (Burns 2005: 56). In this process 'change is value-relative and leads to ongoing emancipation' (Burns 2005: 56).

As shown above, Action Research can focus at the first, second and third person levels based on the focus of the change. Bradbury and Reason (2006: 345) differentiated first-person practice as 'work for oneself', second-person as 'work for partners', and third-person as 'work for people in the wider context'.

First-person Action Research focuses on change at the individual level. As Coghlan and Brannick (2010: 5) point out, first-person Action Research 'is typically characterized as a form of inquiry and practice that one [Action Researcher] does on one's own and so addresses the ability of the individual to foster an inquiring approach to his/her own life, to act out of awareness and purposefully'.

Second-person Action Research focuses on change at the common/shared issue/problem level. It is typically characterised as a form of inquiry and practice that an Action Researcher or Action Researchers do with a group of people to address or solve an issue or problem using a collaborative inquiry approach. Thus, as Coghlan and Brannick (2010: 6) point out, second-person Action Research addresses inquiry into and working 'with others on issues of mutual concern through face-to-face dialogue, conversation and joint action'.

Third-person Action Research focuses on change at the macro or wider community level, with the intent of significantly shifting policymaking. It is a form of inquiry that an Action Researcher or Action Researchers undertake aimed at 'collectives too large to be able to engage in direct communication' (Heen 2005: 265). It is objective and detached, resulting in more generalisable findings (Coghlan and Brannick 2010).

Thus, first-person Action Research focuses on a single person working on and for themselves, second-person focuses on bringing people together in cooperative inquiry to work as partners on an issue or problem of mutual concern, and third-person is about impacting the wider socio-political context, including large collectives, communities or policies (Heen 2005; Burgess 2006). Kemmis (2006: 95) points out that Action Research can focus on 'assisting practitioners to arrive at a critique of their social or educational work and work settings ... intervening in the cultural, social and historical processes of everyday life to reconstruct not only the practice and the practitioner but also the practice setting ... the work, the worker and the workplace'.

In summary, as discussed above Action Research can be successful in transforming individual practice, as well as transforming practices, processes, systems and policies in multiple settings at the group, intergroup, organisational, inter-organisational, as well as community and societal levels (Carr and Kemmis 1986; Kember 2000; Manfra 2009; Coghlan and Brannick 2010; Hammond and Wellington 2013).

Fundamental principles

All forms of Action Research involve critique, participation, action and research:

1. Critique

The adoption of a critical stance underscores every aspect of Action Research. Critique includes questioning assumptions and actions, pointing out the shortcomings of systems and questioning the inherent power structures within social contexts that create existing practices (Alvesson and Deetz 2000). The purpose of critique is to empower individuals and/or groups to develop a critical praxis and bring about meaningful change for the better. Critique can take an emancipatory purpose, with the goal of liberating 'human beings from the circumstances that enslave them' (Horkheimer in Hammond and Wellington 2013: 37). Critique involves close examination and 'interrogation, deconstruction and decentring ... [and] ... higher-order questioning' (McNiff and Whitehead 2010: 17), all necessary for bringing about transformation in complex situations.

2. Participation

Incorporating feedback and input from others, including from broad ranging stakeholders and/or other Action Researchers working democratically and collaboratively, is fundamental to the Action Research process. As Coghlan and Brannick (2010: 5) point out, 'the central idea is that action research uses a scientific approach to study the resolution of important social or organizational issues together with those who experience these issues directly'. The insights, skills, approaches and knowledge that others bring are seen as important in enabling better understanding of the issue or problem and its resolution (Wadsworth 1998). The underpinning belief is that 'capturing multiple and diverse interpretations adds to a deeper, richer picture of the issue at hand and holds the key to more effective resolution for the long term' (Coghlan and Brannick 2010: 57). Participation may take different forms, with variation in roles and levels of involvement amongst those involved. Participation can involve 'jointly defin[ing] research objectives and political goals, co-construct[ing] research questions, pool[ing] knowledge, hon[ing] shared research skills, fashion[ing] interpretations and performance texts that implement specific strategies for social change, and measure[ing] validity and credibility by the willingness of local stakeholders to act on the basis of the results of the action research' (Denzin and Lincoln 2011: 21). At a minimum, participation involves input to the creative visioning, planning and design of the project, as well as remaining collaborative in some way as the cycles are implemented (Reason 1988). Participation is a democratic, open process relying on trust (Burns 2000; Zuber-Skerritt 2002; McNiff and Whitehead 2010) and the creation of environments that allow for the admittance of ignorance or failure and in which critique, reflection and action are encouraged and accepted (Zuber-Skerritt 2002).

3. Action

At the core of Action Research is solving practical problems or addressing issues situated in, or arising from, local practice using data collected and analysed in iterative cycles of action and reflection in order to bring about transformation (Zuber-Skerritt and Fletcher 2007). Issues or problems are always important, non-trivial and complex; that is, there is no single, obvious or simple solution. They are located in dynamic and messy contexts (Kember 2000) and contribute to 'social and cultural transformation' (McNiff and Whitehead 2010: 20). They can include real-life authentic problems in the workplace, the community or in society at large where improvement to practice (Zuber-Skerritt and Fletcher 2007) or the development of 'practical judgment' about practice is sought (Burns 2000). Thus, 'building democratic, participative, pluralist communities of inquiry is central to the work of action research; action research is only possible with, for, and by persons and communities for political, moral, and epistemological reasons' (Reason 2006: 193).

4. Research

Contributing to the body of knowledge in the field of inquiry by making outcomes publicly available so that they can be subjected to critical peer review and further development is a key outcome of Action Research. The overarching goal is to integrate prior knowledge with purposeful and informed action, in order to create new knowledge and changed practice (Robottom and Hart 1993). Thus, the research process is an inductive one, where issues are explored and theories developed through action, rather than setting out to prove or disprove existing hypotheses or theories (Gravett 2004; Fletcher and Zuber-Skerritt 2008). Action Research contributes to theory development by either reinforcing or identifying exceptions to existing theory and in so doing creates new knowledge (Greenwood and Levin 2008). Given this context based nature of Action Research, it is not intended nor likely that the research is replicated in a precise form, but rather that results from the research are applied (Burns 2000). Action Research generates 'living theory since concepts are understood by how they are enacted in practice' (McNiff and Whitehead 2010: 18).

In the sections that follow the cyclical process in which the principles are enacted are outlined. The significance of critique, the need to engage with various stakeholders, taking action and making outcomes public are highlighted; as well as the role of the researcher in the research process.

Enacting the principles

Action cycles

In Action Research, the four principles of critique, participation, action and research are enacted in iterative cycles comprising a number of stages. As shown in Figure 11.1, the stages are typically planning, acting, observing and reflecting (Kember 2000; Kemmis and McTaggart 2008), however in the literature, there is variation in nomenclature and number of stages. For example Coghlan and Brannick (2010) refer to construct, plan action, take action and evaluate action, while Stringer *et al.* (2010) use plan, act, check. Regardless, Action Research cycle stages are fluid, overlapping and non-linear. After a cycle has been completed it is determined if the intended outcomes have been achieved and if a further cycle is required (Creswell 2005). This cyclic process provides 'a logical approach to testing and development' (Kember 2000: 27)

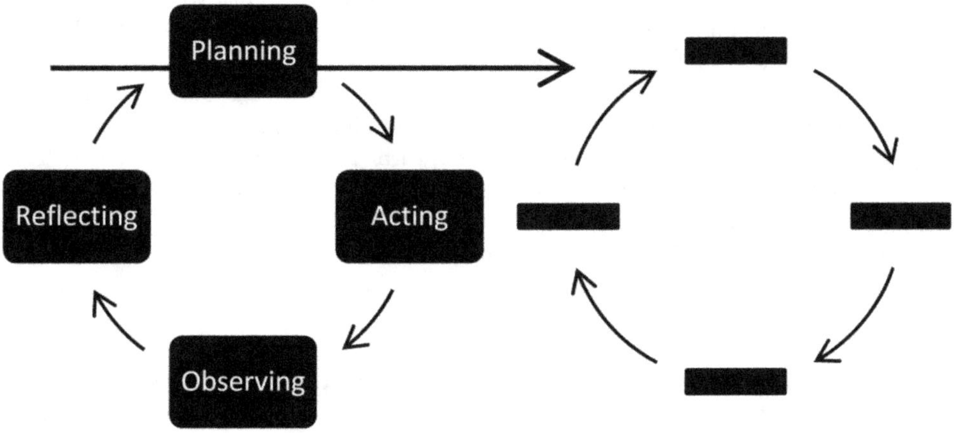

Figure 11.1 Typical action research cycles

allowing for a shift in thinking, emphasis or approach about the issue or problem over multiple cycles.

Each stage of the cycle provides opportunities for experiential learning from/through participation. Based on this, insights and understandings are gained, and decisions to take further action continue or not, and if so how, are made using reflection and judgement (Coghlan and Brannick 2010).

Stage 1: Planning

In this stage the problem to be solved or issue to be addressed is considered and clarified from both theoretical and practical perspectives. The problem or issue is critically reviewed within its context through close questioning and exploration (Burns 2000); and in so doing clarification, deep understanding and ownership of the problem or issue results.

Most important is seeking input from stakeholders. Identifying who needs to be involved in the Action Research process is critical to successful outcomes. Involvement of the broadest representation of external stakeholders brings diverse knowledge and perspectives to the problem or issue and combined with specific locally owned and understood insights and contextual knowledge, supports greater innovation of issue resolution and problem solving (Greenwood and Levin 2008). While the ongoing expectation of full and equal participation of all stakeholders in Action Research is the ideal (Reason 1988), where this level of participation is not possible, the creation of new practices will have broader acceptance when, at least, the views and perspectives of stakeholders have been incorporated into the process (Kemmis and McTaggart 2008).

In this stage, an action plan to solve the problem or address the issue is developed, which is then implemented in the next (action) stage (Cherry 1999; Burns 2000; Coghlan and Brannick 2010). The plan can be loose (allowing for emergent adaptation based on what occurs or unfolds in the action stage) or it can be more detailed and specific (as per an intervention that is implemented in the action stage), but not tightly defined (Coghlan and Brannick 2010;

Townsend 2013). The plan should include the criteria and standards that will be used to judge both achievement of outcomes and their quality (Burns 2000; Ives *et al.* 2009; Coghlan and Brannick 2010; McNiff and Whitehead 2010).

This stage also includes determining the most appropriate data gathering method to evidence changes and outcomes. Methods can range from highly quantitative (for example pre and post questionnaires) to highly qualitative (self or participant observation, interviews). These are determined based on the nature of the problem or issue (Burns 2000; Creswell 2005) and which will be most relevant to generate authentic data that is compelling and will contribute to the process of change (Mattsson and Kemmis 2007).

Stage 2: Acting

In this stage of the action cycle the action plan is implemented and data gathered. The goals at this stage aim for second order or transformational change, change that is irreversible and addresses underlying causes rather than symptoms, as well as to develop local theories which are validated through further cycles of action and reflection (Burns 2000). This iterative approach supports deeper and richer exploration which reveals new insights. Creating ongoing opportunities to question existing insights and to share and challenge ideas is critical throughout this stage (Burns 2000). Honest feedback in an environment that encourages open discussion and trusting relationships is important in contributing to successful outcomes (Kemmis and McTaggart 2008; Priestley 2011). According to Priestley (2011) promoting dialogue enhances the quality of relationships which underpin successful change. Facilitation of the action project has been identified as a key component in successful change outcomes (Tilbury *et al.* 2004; Fletcher and Zuber-Skerritt 2008; Kemmis and McTaggart 2008). However, those involved as a facilitator or 'skilled helper' must bring a distinctive set of qualities to the role. Facilitators who are able to be critical friends and trusted colleagues, and who have not only technical abilities but also human relationship and interpersonal qualities and skills, as well as time, energy and the ability to reflect on and change their own practice as well as supporting others to do the same are the most effective (Day 1993: 88). Expert facilitation has been found to foster deeper, more critical, reflection shifting from descriptive self-reflection (at the level of action) to analytical reflection (characterised by practical theorising and conscious ethical justification) which is a necessary condition for healthy professional self-critical, self-reflecting communities (Fletcher and Zuber-Skerritt 2008; Thornton and Yoong 2011).

In relation to the role of the Action Researcher, the notion of 'Action Researcher' has changed over time and amongst Action Research proponents (Kemmis and McTaggart 2008). Earlier interpretations required all participants to be labelled Action Researchers, emphasising the belief that and requirement for all those involved in the Action Research project to evidence a change in practice or in bringing about a change (Burns 2000). More recently, and more authentically, the title of Action Researcher has shifted to only those who carry the responsibility for initiating, conducting and reporting research findings (Kemmis and McTaggart 2008; Coghlan and Brannick 2010). In addition, in Action Research, the perspective(s) of the Action Researcher(s) is/are not hidden unlike in more traditional forms of research. Rather, researcher perspectives are seen as having value for the resolution of the issue or problem in terms of their commitment and expertise (Fletcher and Zuber-Skerritt 2008), while the issue of the subjectivity of the Action Researcher is addressed through critical dialogue.

Stage 3: Observing

In this stage the data (both formative and summative) is analysed to determine what has or has not been achieved (Fletcher and Zuber-Skerritt 2008; Townsend 2013). This stage involves time and stepping back from the data, which is not possible to do during the day to day work of the action cycle stage (Zuber-Skerritt and Fletcher 2007). Data is used to help determine how well the plan of action was implemented, whether or not it was successful, and to identify any 'unintended effects' or consequences, as well as to inform the need for a further Action Research cycle (Burns 2000). It is necessary for the data to be collected and analysed in-situ and in a timely way as the action cycles are worked through (Burns 2000; Coghlan and Brannick 2010), since analysis informs the reflecting stage, as well as the planning stage of the next Action Research cycle (Dick 1993). Evaluation in-situ facilitates those involved to critique what has occurred, judge its efficacy and reframe as needed, in order to guide the research forward in ways that are worthwhile for those involved.

Stage 4: Reflecting

In this stage reviewing actions and changes and contextual theorising about these changes takes place. Critical reflection on both the process and outcomes takes place in order to guide future decision-making and action, as well as to contribute to theory building. Learning is gained from reviewing both the 'intended and unintended' outcomes of changes and actions undertaken (Coghlan and Brannick 2010: 5). Learning from previous experiences is required to improve practice and reflexivity is needed to achieve learning. By reflection and looking for alternative explanations, participants engage in creating new understandings (Burns 2000). Critical reflection involves actively thinking about past or current experiences in order to improve future performance and is the central mechanism that facilitates intellectual growth and change and involves questioning what is known (content), how things are done (process) and why it is believed (premise). According to Mezirow (1990: 1), such reflection facilitates the adjustment of 'distortions in our beliefs and errors in problem-solving' and underpins learning which is 'the process of making a new or revised interpretation of the meaning of an experience, which guides subsequent understanding, appreciation and action'. In terms of theoretical outcomes, 'the validity of the "theories" generated depends not so much on "scientific" tests of truth, but on their usefulness in helping people function more intelligently and skilfully' (Burns 2000: 443). Critical self-awareness, analysis of experiences and evaluation of their meaning contributes to planning further action (Taylor 2008).

Publishing outcomes

Action Researchers write up and publish findings for three audiences and purposes. These include sharing research with participants involved in the Action Research for them to discuss and reflect on findings and outcomes; with others seeking to engage in local change for them to learn from and apply aspects to their own circumstances; and/or with other groups more widely in order to disseminate findings and to act as a prompt for reflection (Townsend 2013).

According to Guiffrida *et al.* (2011), publishing accounts of Action Research follows the same process as that used for other research, with a few additional requirements. As with all research publications, a rationale is presented along with a review of the relevant literature and an explanation of the gap that the study addresses.

For Action Research specifically, publication also requires rich descriptions of both the context of the Action Research and the process adopted in order to assist readers to fully understand the nature and context of the study, as well as to interpret and relate it to their own situations or local contexts. In relation to context, details about the make-up of the group, a description of how the group saw the issue or problem to be addressed and how the group collaborated during the project is required. In relation to the process, ethical considerations, interventions undertaken, as well as how the data was collected and analysed are fully described. In addition, the Action Researcher's experience and learning is included, along with any implications for his/her practice arising from the study. Finally, outcomes are described and discussed in relation to the evaluation plan and alternative explanations provided (Levin 2012).

Quality and rigour

Ensuring quality and rigour are important aspects of conducting Action Research in order to avoid any chance of Action Research being seen as an inferior form of research (Kember 2000). Since Action Research begins with everyday experience and is concerned with the development of living, situational knowledge, the process of inquiry is as important as the specific outcomes (Reason 2006: 193). This is in line with the aims of Action Research, which unlike more traditional research are about making a contribution to both change as well as theory (Burns 2000). It is, therefore, critical that quality and rigour are demonstrated in both the conduct of the Action Research project and in the reporting of the process and outcomes (Zuber-Skerritt and Fletcher 2007).

Thus, in order to demonstrate quality and rigour, the conduct of the project and publication of findings must align with the Action Research principles outlined earlier (McNiff and Whitehead 2010: 32). Core to quality determinations and judgments are the significance of critique, social relevance, participation, and practical outcomes and research publications (Creswell 2005; Reason 2006). As Reason points out,

> although concrete practical concerns may well be the starting point, our sense of quality must reach wider than simply 'does it work?' It must include whether we have helped the development of an effective community of inquiry among participants, whether questions of power have been addressed, whether the inquiry has been emancipatory and deepened the experiential basis of understanding, and so on. In this way, we can avoid being trapped in a heroic, agentic vision of Action Research: It is not just about solving the immediate problem but of articulating the subtle ways in which the inquiry is affecting our world.
>
> *(Reason 2006: 193)*

In terms of data, rigour includes focussing on 'how the data are generated, gathered, explored and evaluated, and how events are questioned and interpreted through multiple Action Research cycles' (Coghlan and Brannick 2010: 14). This involves 'prolonged engagement, persistent observation, triangulation, peer debriefing, negative case analysis, referential adequacy (selecting representative data), [and] member checks' (Cresswell 2003: 300) (Burns 2000; Creswell 2005; Zuber-Skerritt and Fletcher 2007; McNiff and Whitehead 2010). Inherent rigour comes from making decisions consciously through on-going critique of the way the evaluation is conducted, including 'rigorous analysis and assessment of both the intended and unintended outcomes' (Lennie 2006: 28; Coghlan and Brannick 2010).

Thus, quality and rigour are demonstrated when the Action Research project: empowers participants (Creswell 2005); achieves input from and respectful collaboration with others

(Creswell 2005) and maintains participant engagement (Greenwood and Levin 2008); is informed by valid evidence through the collection and analysis of appropriate data in support of deep theorising and critique (Creswell 2005; Reason 2006); develops skills and knowledge (Burns 2000: 445); leads to action and change (Greenwood and Levin 2008); shows evidence of Action Researcher reflection and the researcher increasingly applying their new understandings to their practice (McNiff and Whitehead 2010); includes dissemination of the Action Research outcomes that include rich descriptions of the case so that a holistic view of the research can be formed enabling the reader to interpret the work for themselves (Kincheloe and McLaren 2002).

Criticisms of Action Research

A number of criticisms exist around Action Research methodology and its application. These are outlined next and a counter point provided for each.

Lacking in quality and rigour

Action Research has been criticised as lacking rigour and being less scientific than other research methodologies (Burns 2005; Creswell 2005). This perception that Action Research is less rigorous may emanate from many studies being reported as Action Research when on closer examination the research methodology applied is more aligned to case study research (Hammond and Wellington 2013). However, when Action Research is implemented in a way consistent with its methodological principles and practices, it inherently demonstrates quality and rigour (Townsend 2013). Core to this is the inclusion of a strong evaluation strategy, including multiple data gathering methods within each Action Research cycle.

Non generalisable

The findings of Action Research are often considered unable to be transferable to other contexts (Zuber-Skerritt 2002). While the first aim of Action Research is to produce findings in the form of local theories and knowledge for participants within the particular context of the study (Zuber-Skerritt 2002; Zuber-Skerritt and Fletcher 2007), transferability and general theorising can result (Townsend 2013). Others may observe alignment between individual study findings and their own contexts, supporting the transferability and generalisability of findings (Zuber-Skerritt 2002). When findings are related to the extant literature and meta-analyses conducted, generalisations to other contexts can be explored (Lodico *et al.* 2010). Thus, Action Research, as with many other forms of research that are contextually dependent, produces emergent themes of relevance to other contexts, as well as the possibility of formal transferability.

Overly demanding

Action Research is seen by many as more demanding than other forms of research (Dick 1993). This perception is mainly attributed to the dual purposes of undertaking research while at the same time attempting to bring about change. While this might be true when compared to some forms of more traditional research, notably literature or secondary source based in the humanities and social sciences, this is not the case for all. Research approaches which involve extended and multiple data collections, fieldwork or interventions, as well as those that require substantial coordination, development of multi-pronged and complex statistical analysis, for example in the areas of biochemistry, physiology and molecular genetics, may be equally or even more complex, albeit in differing ways. As Townsend (2013) points out, no research attempting change is simple regardless of methodology. Thus, Action Research, like any good research, is demanding but not more so than engaging in other forms of rigorous research.

Too time consuming

Action Research is perceived by some as onerously time consuming (Harland and Staniforth 2000). While the types of change that are suited to Action Research study are complex and, therefore, require time (Ferreira *et al.* 2009), this time commitment may be no more demanding than that required using other methodologies, for example a rigorous long-term naturalistic ethnographic or longitudinal quantitative study. The overall time commitment for each may be similar, however, the time commitment may be directed at different activities, for example, individual support in Action Research versus managing and manipulating large data sets in quantitative studies. Thus, Action Research like any form of ambitious and comprehensive research will require time, regardless of methodology.

Cannot bring about large scale change

Action Research is seen by some to only be suitable for enacting small scale change in local contexts, rather than being able to support larger and system wide change. Unfortunately, Action Research is often misunderstood and misrepresented as first-person research that is as 'an experiment or innovation undertaken by a practitioner … [or] … as everyday practitioner inquiry' (Hammond and Wellington 2013: ix). As Townsend (2013) points out, this individual practitioner or personal professional development view is only one interpretation of Action Research. He goes on to caution that new researchers may miss its concern for understanding and developing social and working contexts and the practices associated with them (Townsend 2013: 1).

The extent of change achieved by Action Research is not limited by this scale and scope, since the principles and practices of Action Research may be applied in varying degrees and in different types of contexts. In, fact, third-person Action Research is aimed at bringing about change at the policy and political levels. Thus, while Action Research like any form of research aimed at bringing about large scale change is challenging, it is able to bring about change in large scale contexts. This level of change is what is required to ensure that graduates are equipped to respond to conditions that have resulted in the world's unsustainable path.

In the next section, the strong philosophical alignment between Higher Education related sustainability curriculum change and Action Research is highlighted.

Alignment with sustainability curriculum change

A strong philosophical alignment exists between sustainability related curriculum change in higher education and Action Research (Benn and Dunphy 2009; Ferreira *et al.* 2009; Winter and Cotton 2012).

Sustainability curriculum change aims to make 'a better world for this generation and future generations of all living things on the planet Earth' by ensuring graduates leave university in a position to be able to contribute to this goal (UNESCO nd: para 1). Action Research is an ideal method for bringing about such deep, lasting and meaningful or transformative change that improves the lives of individuals for the better and contributes to social and cultural transformation. It aims to transform individual practice, as well as transforming practices, processes, systems and policies in multiple settings at the group, intergroup, organisational, inter-organisational, as well as community and societal levels, with the intent of significantly shifting policymaking.

The alignment between sustainability curriculum change and Action Research principles, and what is fundamental and common to both is outlined next. The strong alignment points to Action Research being an ideal methodology for bringing about sustainability related curriculum change, as well as contributing to the sustainability literature.

Critique is common to both

Sustainability curriculum change challenges the existing status quo and in so doing is underpinned by an ethic of critique and emancipation (Wals 2011). Achieving sustainability curriculum change requires that existing individual academic perspectives, as well as university cultures and policies are challenged (Jones *et al.* 2008). This involves identifying, questioning and reflexive critique in order to transform perspectives, cultures and policies (Sterling and Witham 2008; Cranton 2009; Wals 2010; Winter and Cotton 2012; Wahr *et al.* 2013). Critique is also core to Action Research, since the approach requires the questioning of assumptions and actions, pointing out shortcomings of systems and questioning inherent power structures that create existing practices and the status quo. Action Research is concerned with questioning social, cultural and/or political and/or moral, and/or epistemological practices, including democratic participation and emancipation. This involves close examination and interrogation, deconstruction, decentering and higher order questioning and in so doing empowers individuals to develop a critical praxis and influence the policies which shape practice. Critical and/or Emancipatory, as well as Community-based Action Research are emancipatory, aiming to liberate individuals from circumstances that enslave them. Finally, an ethic of social justice and equity are fundamental to both sustainability curriculum change and Action Research.

Participation is common to both

Sustainability curriculum change involves participatory approaches that value the democratic sharing of ideas and social learning approaches, that lead to transformative learning and curriculum change (Wals 2010). As Wals (2010: 146) points out, 'pluralism of thought' through dialogue and debate is necessary to bring about sustainability curriculum change. Thus, sustainability curriculum change requires the incorporation of a range of alternative and multiple stakeholder perspectives and expertise (Hadgraft *et al.* 2004; Tilbury 2004; Wals and Blewitt 2012). Similarly, core to Action Research is participation, with those involved working democratically and collaboratively in a social constructivist process fostering relationships that are based on trust and mutual respect. The approach involves the inclusion of input and feedback from others, including from broad ranging stakeholders and/or other Action Researchers. Most importantly to solving the problem or addressing the issue is the involvement of the persons and/or communities affected.

Action orientation is common to both

Sustainability curriculum change is underpinned by an action orientation since it is concerned with bringing about transformative change so that graduates leave universities with 'the necessary skills to be able to take positive action to address a range of sustainability issues' (Tilbury *et al.* 2005: 1). Sustainability curriculum change is complex in that it requires making sense of a contested, multi-faceted concept (Lourdel *et al.* 2007) at the same time as responding to the pedagogical challenges associated with integrating it into disciplinary frameworks in messy dynamic contexts (Wals and Jickling 2002; Sterling 2004a). Achieving sustainability curriculum requires deliberate and significant action at an individual academic, group, as well as systemic policy levels within universities. Therefore, outcome-focussed approaches are required to drive the local and systemic changes needed to bring about sustainability transformation in higher education contexts (Huckle 2004; Sterling 2004b; Tilbury and Cooke 2005). Additionally, for transformative engagement to occur, which as mentioned is characteristic of sustainability learning and curriculum change, an open ended, experiential, reflective approach which requires support, time and space is needed. Such an approach requires opportunities for those involved in bringing about sustainability learning to 'learn from experience, identify what is significant and develop new insights, which both confirm the veracity of the initial account and contribute to future educational work' (Blewitt 2005: 174).

Action Research is directly aligned, since it is also action oriented and focused on bringing about deep, lasting and meaningful transformative change and improvements for individuals, organisations and society, with the involvement of those who experience the problem or issue directly. It aims to solve real practical problems or address issues situated in, or arising from, practice in the workplace, the community or in society at large. The method pays significant attention to past and present practice using recursive, dialectical cycles of planning, acting, observing and reflecting, in contrast to observing in order to inform and change the future. Action Research is also ideal for responding to important, non-trivial and complex problems or issues, in dynamic and messy contexts since it is adaptable, flexible, responsive and emergent. It is therefore able to accommodate the multidimensionality and interconnectedness inherent in sustainability curriculum change (Joseph 2010).

Research is common to both

Advancing sustainability requires significant research. As Waas *et al.* (2010: 630) point out 'given the pressing need for sustainability, [universities] should consider research for sustainable development [including for higher education for sustainable development] not merely as an "academic exercise" but instead as a "vital response" to a rapidly evolving crisis which should be at the top of its research agendas'. Similarly, Hirsch Hadorn *et al.* (2006: 119) suggest that 'research for sustainable development has to be issue oriented and reflect the diversity, complexity and dynamics of the processes involved as well as their variability between specific problem situations. Furthermore, the knowledge of people involved and their needs and interests at stake have to be taken into account.' Research is seen as an inherent adjunct to sustainability learning and curriculum change. Thus, sustainability curriculum change is supported by undertaking research which will contribute to further understanding and inform various aspects of sustainability learning, as well as how to embed it systemically within university contexts (Barth 2013).

Action Research is concerned with contributing to the body of knowledge in the field of inquiry, integrating prior knowledge with purposeful and informed action in order to create new knowledge at the site of change. Hence, the required research outcomes of Action Research will directly support and strengthen sustainability curriculum change.

In summary, Action Research responds directly to the aspects essential to achieve sustainability related curriculum change. As observed by Moore (2005: 552), using an Action Research methodology promotes sustainability curriculum change 'by creating spaces at the university where collaboration is practiced and encouraged, academics can move away from the current structures of competition, towards processes connected with the values of sustainability'. Moreover, engaging in the Action Research process increases 'commitment and the competence and propensity for participants to continue to act for change' (Ferreira *et al.* 2009: 3).

Potential of Action Research

Action Research is suited to contexts where bringing about transformative change is sought, where participants engage in projects where a need for change is perceived. Action Research when applied and enacted appropriately in line with the principles of critique, participation, action and research outlined above, is a methodology which results in multiple worthwhile outcomes, including changes that are owned by those engaged in the process, as well as contributing to theory about change more broadly. It is an ambitious form of research since participant willingness and ongoing involvement is required. It is also an open ended process, the success of which relies on the quality of facilitation and the quality of the evidence-based reflection undertaken by participants. As such, Action Research is particularly well suited to research higher education sustainability related curriculum change since such change seeks to provide insights, skills and capabilities necessary to bring about transformations of the curriculum and teaching, as well as building a body of knowledge more widely as to how this can best be achieved. According to Johnston (2006: 60), 'taking action and studying its consequences for student learning is the hallmark of action research. The action is intended to create change for the better and the study is intended to find out if it does.' Action Research promotes classroom change, initiated by careful self-examination and planning. Similarly, Schmuck and Stevenson (2010) point out that Action Researchers working in higher education contexts are

> concerned with intervention for improvement … to foster development and self-renewal of their own practice, College or University … concerned with meaningful local planned change … [striving] to reach beyond their own limited points of view by collecting data of multiple perspectives from significant higher education participants … concerned with obtaining trustworthy data from the right people within their own higher education setting … [working] by themselves or joining with colleagues … to increase local effectiveness in their own classroom, College or University.
>
> *(Shmuck and Stevenson 2010: 18–19)*

An external evaluation of 90 Action Research projects overseen by Kember (2000) points to an array of impressive outcomes of using Action Research in bringing about higher education curriculum transformation and reformation, making the use of this research approach compelling. In fact, the evaluation confirmed that Action Research was successful and a cost effective means for building the capacity of academics in learning and teaching improvement (including critical self-reflection) and enhancing educational quality. The external evaluators observed that having over 50 per cent of participants engaging in reflection on their teaching and the assumptions that underpinned effective practice 'is impressive, and should lay to rest doubts about the effectiveness of Action Learning [used interchangeably with Action Learning and Action Research] in Hong Kong' (Biggs and Lam 1997: 80).

Kember (2000: 23), drawing from his extensive experience with Action Research in higher education contexts worldwide, suggests that one of the greatest strengths of Action Research is that it is a quite straightforward practical approach for higher education practitioners to use when tackling issues of curriculum and pedagogical change.

In terms of change for higher education sustainable development specifically, two successful examples of whole of curriculum transformative change are described below.

The embedding of education for sustainable development in initial teacher training Professional Graduate Certificate in Education/Certificate in Education to support learners in becoming sustainable citizens used a democratic and participative approach that resulted in the participants

> supporting each other in developing the necessary knowledge, experience and values to confidently introduce sustainability to our trainee teachers … Recognizing the importance of encouraging a more radical, transformative approach, we opened ourselves up to the importance of embarking on a journey with our trainee teachers.
>
> *(Summers and Turner 2011: 465)*

The inclusion of sustainability issues in the Master of Business Administration program in a way that students could see the relevance of sustainability in the context of each discipline area (each field of study), resulted in

> the intrinsic interest to the researchers of seeing their passionate commitment to sustainability principles being translated into practice, the project also produced published article and case studies, strengthened working relationships with key executives and yielded other course materials gathered incidentally in the research process.
>
> *(Benn and Dunphy 2009: 293)*

Extensive research has shown that the most successful curriculum change approaches that foster academic engagement are those that do not alienate or disempower academics by inadvertently imposing hegemonic notions of academic learning and embrace negotiated rather than imposed collaboration (Smyth 2003: 57). Action Research is consistent with this philosophy.

Conclusion

This chapter has outlined the characteristics of Action Research. It has shown that it is an approach that is underpinned by questioning; is participatory and collaborative; is practically focused, is able to address real and complex issues; is democratic and emancipatory; is values oriented; is reflexive, recursive and dialectical; is evidence based; and is transformative of both theory and practice (Kemmis and McTaggart 2008). It has argued that it is an ideal approach for bringing about change that is meaningful and complex, given the focus on ethics and values, on opportunities to learn with and from peers, on the establishment of high trust relationships, and on facilitation.

It has pointed out that the open-endedness of engaging in the Action Research cycles allows for learning and theorising based on what is actually occurring in authentic settings without pre-empting outcomes (Zuber-Skerritt and Fletcher 2007). It has demonstrated that that Action Research brings new ideas into practice, via meaning-making experiences, rather than didactic research about practice, and that engaging in the Action Research process leads to greater empowerment and structural change – that is bottom up as well as top-down change.

Most importantly, given the strong alignment with sustainability curriculum change it has shown that Action Research is ideally suited to bring about the necessary ongoing attitudinal and meaningful structural change required from within. As Kember's (2002) reflection on the successful use of an Action Research approach to support large scale educational change points out, in many cases the journey appeared to be as important, or even more so, as reaching the final destination. The abilities and attitudes acquired on the way left the travellers well equipped to travel down similar paths in the future and keen to do so. There seemed to be some evidence that it was those who had the more troublesome journeys who developed the most on the way. The tribulations of meeting rocky or winding paths caused a rethinking of what the journey was about. These longer-term outcomes are important.

(Kember 2002: 92)

References

Alvesson, M. and Deetz, S., 2000. *Doing Critical Management Research*. London: Sage Publications Ltd.

Barth, M., 2013. 'Many Roads Lead to Sustainability: A Process-oriented Analysis of Change in Higher Education', *International Journal of Sustainability in Higher Education*, 14(2), 160–75.

Benn, S. and Dunphy, D., 2009. 'Action Research as an Approach to Integrating Sustainability into MBA Programs', *Journal of Management Education*, 33(3), 276–95.

Biggs, J.B. and Lam, R., 1997. 'Enhancing Teaching through Action Learning: Helping Innovation in Hong Kong', *New Horizons in Education*, 38, 76–84.

Blewitt, J., 2005. 'Education for Sustainable Development, Governmentality and Learning to Last', *Environmental Education Research*, 11(2), 173–85.

Bradbury, H. and Reason, P., 2006. 'Broadening the Bandwidth of Validity: Issues and Choice-points for Improving the Quality of Action Research', in Reason, P. and Bradbury, H. (eds), *Handbook of Action Research*. London: Sage Publications Ltd, 343–51.

Burgess, J., 2006. 'Participatory Action Research: First-person Perspectives of a Graduate Student', *Action Research*, 4(4), 419–37.

Burns, A., 2005. 'Action Research: An Evolving Paradigm?', *Language Teaching*, 38(2), 57–74.

Burns, R.B., 2000. *Introduction to Research Methods*. French Forest, NSW: Pearson Education Australia.

Carr, W. and Kemmis, S., 1986. *Becoming Critical: Education, Knowledge and Action Research*. Geelong: Deakin University.

Cherry, N., 1999. *Action Research: A Pathway to Action, Knowledge and Learning*. Melbourne: RMIT University Press.

Coghlan, D. and Brannick, T., 2010. *Doing Action Research in your Own Organization*. London: Sage Publications Ltd.

Corcoran, P.B. and Wals, A.E.J., 2004. *Higher Education and the Challenge of Sustainability: Problematics, Promise and Practice*. Dordrecht: Kluwer Academic Publishers.

Cranton, P., 2009. 'Transformative Learning and AVE for Social Sustainability', in Willis, P., Mckenzie, S. and Harris, R. (eds), *Rethinking Work and Learning. Adult and Vocational Education for Social Sustainability*. Dordrecht: Springer, 93–105.

Creswell, J.W., 2003. *Research Design: Qualitative, Quantitative and Mixed Method Approaches*. Thousand Oaks, CA: Sage.

Creswell, J.W., 2005. *Educational Research. Planning, Conducting, and Evaluating Quantitative and Qualitative Research*. Upper Saddle River, NJ: Pearson Education Inc.

Creswell, J.W., Hanson, W.E., Plano, V.L.C. and Morales, A., 2007. 'Qualitative Research Designs Selection and Implementation', *The Counseling Psychologist*, 35(2), 236–64.

Day, C., 1993. 'Reflection: A Necessary but not Sufficient Condition for Professional Development', *British Educational Research Journal*, 19(1), 83–93.

Denzin, N.K. and Lincoln, Y.S., 2011. *The SAGE Handbook of Qualitative Research*. Thousand Oaks, CA: Sage.

Dick, B., 1993. 'You Want to do an Action Research Thesis?' www.scu.edu.au/schools/gcm/ar/art/arthesis.html [accessed 7 August 2006].

Ferreira, J., Ryan, L., Davis, J., Cavanagh, M. and Thomas, J., 2009. *Mainstreaming Sustainability into Pre-service Teacher Education in Australia*. Canberra: Australian Research Institute in Education for Sustainability, Macquarie University.

Ferrer-Balas, D., Adachi, J., Banas, S., Davidson, C.I., Hoshikoshi, A., Mishra, A., Motodoa, Y., Onga, M. and Ostwald, M., 2008. 'An International Comparative Analysis of Sustainability Transformation across

Seven Universities', *International Journal of Sustainability in Higher Education*, 9(3), 295–316.
Fletcher, M.A. and Zuber-Skerritt, O., 2008. 'Professional Development through Action Research: Case Examples in South African Higher Education', *Systemic Practice and Action Research*, 21(1), 73–96.
Gough, S. and Scott, W., 2007. *Higher Education and Sustainable Development. Paradox and Possibility.* Abingdon: Routledge.
Gravett, S., 2004. 'Action Research and Transformative Learning in Teaching Development', *Educational Action Research*, 12(2), 259–72.
Greenwood, D. and Levin, M., 2008. 'Reform of the Social Sciences and of Universities through Action Research', in Denzin, N. and Lincoln, Y. (eds), *The Landscape of Qualitative Research*. 3rd ed,. Thousand Oaks, CA: Sage Publications, Inc., 57–86.
Guiffrida, D.A., Douthit, K.Z., Lynch, M.F. and Mackie, K.L., 2011. 'Publishing Action Research in Counseling Journals', *Journal of Counseling & Development*, 89(3), 282–7.
Hadgraft, R., Muir, P., Jollands, M., Goricanec, J., Brown, A. and Bunting, A., 2004. 'Shifting the Ground – Sustainable Engineering at RMIT', in Holdsworth, S. and Caswell, T. (eds) *Protecting the Future: Stories of Sustainability from RMIT University.* Melbourne: CSIRO Publishing, 31–51.
Hammond, M. and Wellington, J.J., 2013. *Research Methods: The Key Concepts.* Abingdon: Routledge.
Harland, T. and Staniforth, D., 2000. 'Action Research: A Culturally Acceptable Path to Professional Learning for University Teachers?', *Educational Action Research*, 8(3), 499–514.
Heen, H., 2005. 'About Feelings in Action Research An Experiment in First-person Inquiry', *Action Research*, 3(3), 263–78.
Hirsch Hadorn, G., Bradley, D., Pohl, C., Rist, S. and Wiesmann, U., 2006. 'Implications of Transdisciplinarity for Sustainability Research', *Ecological Economics*, 60(1), 119–28.
Holdsworth, S., Bekessy, S., Mnguni, P., Hayles, C. and Thomas, I., 2006. 'Beyond Leather Patches (BELP): Sustainability Education at RMIT University', in Filho, W.L. and Carpenter, D. (eds), *Sustainability in the Australasian University Context.* Frankfurt am Main: Peter Lang, 107–28.
Huckle, J., 2004. 'Critical Realism: A Philosophical Framework for Higher Education for Sustainability', in Corcoran, P.B. and Wals, A.E.J. (eds), *Higher Education and the Challenge of Sustainability.* Dordrecht: Kluwer Academic Publishers, 33–47.
Ives, C., Mcalpine, L. and Gandell, T., 2009. 'A Systematic Approach to Evaluating Teaching and Learning Initiatives in Post-secondary Education', *Canadian Journal of Higher Education*, 39(2), 45–76.
Johnston, M., 2006. 'The Lamp and the Mirror. Action Research and Self Studies in the Social Studies', in Barton, K.C. (ed.), *Research Methods in Social Studies Education. Comtemporary Issues and Perspectives. A Volume in Research in Social Education*. Greenwich: Information Age Publishing, 57–83.
Jones, P., Trier, C.J. and Richards, J.P., 2008. 'Embedding Education for Sustainable Development in Higher Education: A Case Study Examining Common Challenges and Opportunities for Undergraduate Programmes', *International Journal of Educational Research*, 47(6), 341–50.
Joseph, P., 2010. 'Holistic Curriculum', in Kridel, C. (ed.), *Encyclopedia of Curriculum Studies.* Thousand Oaks, CA: Sage Publications, Inc., 446–8.
Kember, D., 2000. *Action Learning and Action Research. Improving the Quality of Teaching and Learning.* London: Kogan Page Ltd.
Kember, D., 2002. 'Long-term Outcomes of Educational Action Research Projects', *Educational Action Research*, 10(1), 83–104.
Kemmis, S., 2006. 'Exploring the Relevance of Critical Theory for Action Research: Emancipatory Action Research in the Footsteps of Jurgen Habermas', in Reason, P. and Bradbury, H. (eds), *Handbook of Action Research.* London: Sage Publishers, 94–105.
Kemmis, S. and McTaggart, R., 2008. 'Participatory Action Research: Communicative Action and the Public Sphere', in Denzin, N. and Lincoln, Y. (eds), *Strategies of Qualitative Inquiry.* 3rd edn. Thousand Oaks, California: Sage Publications, Inc., 269–330.
Kemmis, S., McTaggart, R. and Nixon, R., 2014. *The Action Research Planner: Doing Critical Participatory Action Research.* Singapore: Springer Singapore.
Kincheloe, J.L. and McLaren, P., 2002. 'Rethinking Critical Theory and Qualitative Research', in Zou, Y. and Trueba, E.T. (eds), *Ethnography and Schools: Qualitative Approaches to the Study of Education.* Lantham, MD: Rowman and Littlefield, 87–138.
Lennie, J., 2006. 'Increasing the Rigour and Trustworthiness of Participatory Evaluations: Learnings from the Field', *Evaluation Journal of Australasia*, 6(1), 27–35.
Levin, M., 2012. 'Academic Integrity in Action Research', *Action Research*, 10(2), 133–49.
Lodico, M.G., Spaulding, D.T. and Voegtle, K.H., 2010. *Methods in Educational Research: From Theory to*

Practice. San Francisco, CA: Wiley.

Lourdel, N., Gondran, N., Laforest, V., Debray, B. and Brodhag, C., 2007. 'Sustainable Development Cognitive Map: A New Method of Evaluating Student Understanding', *International Journal of Sustainability in Higher Education*, 8(2), 170–82.

Manfra, M., 2009. 'Action Research: Exploring the Theoretical Divide between Practical and Critical Approaches', *Journal of Curriculum and Instruction*, 3(1), 32–46.

Mattsson, M. and Kemmis, S., 2007. 'Praxis-related Research: Serving Two Masters?', *Pedagogy, Culture & Society*, 15(2), 185–214.

McKernan, J., 1991. *Curriculum Action Research: A Handbook of Methods and Resources for the Reflective Practitioner.* London: Kogan Page.

McNiff, J. and Whitehead, J., 2010. *You and Your Action Research Project*. New York: Routledge.

Mezirow, J., 1990. 'How Critical Reflection Triggers Transformative Learning', in Mezirow, J. (ed.), *Fostering Critical Reflection in Adulthood*. San Francisco, CA: Jossey-Bass, 1–18.

Moore, J., 2005. 'Barriers and Pathways to Creating Sustainability Education Programs: Policy, Rhetoric and Reality', *Environmental Education Research*, 11(5), 537–55.

Mulder, K., 2007. 'Don't Preach. Practice! The Acceptability of Normative Statement in Academic Sustainability Education', in Leal Filho, W., Manolas, E., Sotirakou, M. and Boutakis, G. (eds), *Higher Education and the Challenge of Sustainability: Problems, Promises and Good Practice*. Soufli, Greece: Environmental Education Centre of Soufli, 155–66.

Priestley, M., 2011. 'Schools, Teachers, and Curriculum Change: A Balancing Act?', *Journal of Educational Change*, 12(1), 1–23.

Reason, P., 1988. 'Introduction', in Reason, P. (ed.), *Human inquIry in Action: Development in New Paradigm Research*. London: Sage Publications Ltd, 1–17.

Reason, P., 2006. 'Choice and Quality in Action Research Practice', *Journal of Management Inquiry*, 15(2), 187–203.

Reyes, W.S., 2011. *Exploring a Collaborative-participatory Process in Developing a Multicultural Teacher Education Curriculum*. Adelaide: Flinders University.

Robottom, I. and Hart, P., 1993. *Research in Environmental Education: Engaging the Debate*. Geelong, Victoria: Deakin University.

Schmuck, R.A., 2006. *Practical Action Research for Change*. California: Corwin Press.

Schmuck, R.A. and Stevenson, J.M., 2010. *Action resEarch for Higher Education: Collaborative Principles and Practices for Positive Change*. Palo Alto, CA: Academica Press.

Smyth, R., 2003. 'Concepts of Change: Enhancing the Practice of Academic Staff Development in Higher Education', *International Journal for Academic Development*, 8(1/2), 51–60.

Somekh, B., 1989. 'Action Research and Collaborative School Development', in Mcbride, R. (ed.), *The In-service Training of Teachers: Some Issues and Perspectives*. London: The Falmer Press, 160–72.

Sterling, S., 2004a. 'An Analysis of the Development of Sustainability Education Internationally: Evolution, Interpretation and Transformation', in Blewitt, J. and Cullingford, C. (eds), *The Sustainability Curriculum: The Challenge for Higher Education*. London: Earthscan, 43–62.

Sterling, S., 2004b. 'Higher Education, Sustainability, and the Role of Systemic Learning', in Corcoran, P.B. and Wals, A.E.J. (eds), *Higher Education and the Challenge of Sustainability: Problematics, Promise and Practice*. Dordrecht: Kluwer Academic Publishers, 49–70.

Sterling, S. and Thomas, I., 2006. 'Education for Sustainability: The Role of Capabilities in Guiding University Curricula', *International Journal for Innovation and Sustainable Development*, 1(4), 349–70.

Sterling, S. and Witham, H., 2008. 'Pushing the Boundaries: The Work of the Higher Education Academy's ESD Project', *Environmental Education Research*, 14(4), 399–412.

Stringer, E., 1999. *Action Research*. Thousand Oaks, CA: Sage Publications.

Stringer, E., 2004. *Action Research in Education*. Upper Saddle River, NJ: Pearson Education.

Stringer, E., McFadyen Christensen, L. and Baldwin, S., 2010. *Integrating Teaching, Learning and Action Research: Enhancing Instruction in the K-12*. Thousand Oaks, CA: Sage Publications, Inc.

Summers, D., and Turner, R., 2011. 'Outside the Green Box: Embedding Education for Sustainable Development through Cooperative Inquiry', *Educational Action Research*, 19(4), 453–68.

Taylor, E.W., 2008. 'Transformative Learning Theory', *New Directions for Adult and Continuing Education*, 119, 5–15.

Thornton, K. and Yoong, P., 2011. 'The Role of the Blended Action Learning Facilitator: An Enabler of Learning and a Trusted Inquisitor', *Action Learning: Research and Practice*, 8(2), 129–46.

Tilbury, D., 2004. 'Rising to the Challenge: Education for Sustainability in Australia', *Australian Journal of*

Environmental Education, 20(2), 103–14.
Tilbury, D. and Cooke, K., 2005. *Frameworks for Sustainability. A National Review of Environmental Education and its Contribution to Sustainability in Australia – Key Findings.* Canberra: Australian Government Department of the Environment and Heritage and Australian Research Institute in Education for Sustainability (ARIES).
Tilbury, D., Podger, D. and Reid, A., 2004. *Action Research for Change towards Sustainability: Change in Curricula and Graduate Skills towards Sustainability. Final Report.* Canberra: Australian Government Department of the Environment and Heritage and Macquarie University.
Tilbury, D., Keogh, A., Leighton, A. and Kent, J., 2005. *A National Review of Environmental Education and its Contribution to Sustainability in Australia: Further and Higher Education – Key Findings.* Canberra: Australian Government Department of the Environment and Heritage and Australian Research Institute in Education for Sustainability (ARIES).
Townsend, A., 2013. *Action Research: The Challenges Of Understanding And Changing Practice.* Maidenhead, Berkshire: Open University Press, McGraw-Hill Education.
Trowler, P. and Bamber, R., 2005. 'Compulsory Higher Education Teacher Training: Joined-up Policies, Institutional Architectures and Enhancement Cultures', *International Journal for Academic Development*, 10(2), 79–93.
UNESCO, nd. *Three Terms One Goal.* Paris: UNESCO. www.unesco.org/new/en/education/themes/leading-the-international-agenda/education-for-sustainable-development/three-terms-one-goal/ [accessed 24 October 2011].
Waas, T., Verbruggen, A. and Wright, T., 2010. 'University Research for Sustainable Development: Definition and Characteristics Explored', *Journal of Cleaner Production*, 8(7), 629–36.
Wadsworth, Y., 1998. *What is Participatory Action Research?* Action Research International. www.aral.com.au/ari/p-ywadsworth98.html [accessed 20 May 2007].
Wahr, F., Underwood, J., Adams, L. and Prideaux, V., 2013. 'Three Academics' Narratives in Transforming Curriculum for Education for Sustainable Development', *Australian Journal of Environmental Education*, 29(1), 97–116.
Wals, A.E.J., 2009. *Decade for Education for Sustainable Development, Review of Contexts and Structures for Education for Sustainable Development.* Paris: UNESCO.
Wals, A.E.J., 2010. 'Mirroring, gestaltswitching and Transformative Social Learning: Stepping Stones for Developing Sustainability Competence', *International Journal of Sustainability in Higher Education*, 11(4), 380–90.
Wals, A.E.J., 2011. 'Learning our Way to Sustainability', *Journal of Education for Sustainable Development*, 5(2), 177–86.
Wals, A.E.J., 2014. 'Sustainability in Higher Education in the Context of the UN DESD: A Review of Learning and Institutionalization Processes', *Journal of Cleaner Production*, 62, 8–15.
Wals, A.E.J. and Blewitt, J., 2012. 'Third Wave Sustainability in Higher Education: Some (Inter) National Trends and Developments', in Sterling, S. (ed.), *Sustainability Education: Perspectives and Practice across Higher Education.* Hoboken, NJ: Earthscan, 55–74.
Wals, A.E.J. and Jickling, B., 2002. '"Sustainability" in Higher Education: From Doublethink to Newspeak to Critical Thinking and Meaningful Learning', *International Journal of Sustainability in Higher Education*, 3(3), 221–32.
Winter, J. and Cotton, D., 2012. 'Making the Hidden Curriculum Visible: Sustainability Literacy in Higher Education', *Environmental Education Research*, 18(6), 783–96.
Zuber-Skerritt, O., 2002. 'A moDel for Designing Action Learning and Action Research Programs', *The Learning Organization*, 9(4), 143–9.
Zuber-Skerritt, O. and Fletcher, M., 2007. 'The Quality of an Action Research Thesis in the Social Sciences', *Quality Assurance in Education*, 15(4), 413–36.

12

GENDER AND DIVERSITY IN RESEARCH ON HIGHER EDUCATION FOR SUSTAINABLE DEVELOPMENT

Angela Franz-Balsen

Gender matters – diversity is cultural reality

To include gender aspects in the design of research projects is increasingly becoming a common standard of quality research and an issue of political correctness, which is regulated by funding policies. That such progress can be observed in academic contexts worldwide is due to the strategy of Gender Mainstreaming (GM). GM goes back to the development context where it aimed at securing gender equality in development projects. The UN then made it a UN policy instrument of general application and global outreach, endorsed in the Beijing Platform for Action from the United Nations Fourth World Conference on Women 1995. In an official definition dating from 1997 GM is defined as

> the process of assessing the implications for women and men of any planned action, including legislation, policies or programmes, in all areas and at all levels. It is a strategy for making women's as well as men's concerns and experiences an integral dimension of the design, implementation, monitoring and evaluation of policies and programmes in all political, economic and societal spheres so that women and men benefit equally and inequality is not perpetuated. The ultimate goal is to achieve gender equality.
>
> *(United Nations 2002: 1)*

The mainstreaming strategy is implemented in somewhat different ways in areas like research, policy development, technical assistance or education; there is no blueprint that can be applied in every context. Therefore a first important step of this contribution is to illustrate what GM means for the design of research projects, ensuring that conceptual frameworks and methodologies capture the different and unequal situations of women or men, that androcentrism or gender-blindness in some sectors of science is overcome and that 'conscious subjectivity' of the researcher (acknowledging his/her gender role, class, race etc.) replaces the 'value-free objective' of traditional research (Marchbank and Letherby 2007: 24). In a second step it will be illustrated what a 'gender-sensitive' approach could look like in research on HESD.

Key terms have to be clarified in order to do so. 'Gender' stands for the socially determined difference of cultural norms and expectations linked to the biological differences between the sexes. These social constructions of gender vary in time and place and between cultures (European Commission 2009: part 1.2). 'Sex' is determined by biological characteristics such as anatomical, reproductive and chromosomal attributes. Until recently, in most cultures a binary code was applied to classify human beings regarding sex (either male or female). This binary system was mirrored in traditional gender systems: either masculinity or femininity were and still are major norms to guide the personal development and social learning processes of an individual. In this respect it is important to mention that gender systems usually are dominance systems, often devaluating and subordinating non-masculine gender groups.

With the knowledge generated over past decades in both natural and social sciences, the issue of sex and gender has become more complex, if not to say complicated: Both sex and gender cannot be seen as binary systems any more. It is undeniable that the categories male and female represent only the endpoints of a continuum of possible biological expressions, whereas the gender norms masculinity and femininity are not opposing, mutually exclusive choices for an individual any longer. The latest state of art is partly covered by the term 'diversity' (Thomas 1995; Cox 2001). The diversity-concept recognises that each individual is unique and tolerates and accepts individual profiles along the dimensions of gender (including sexual orientation), race, ethnicity, socio-economic status, age, physical ability, beliefs and more. The fact that gender is not a stand-alone category regarding the position of individuals in society, but always interwoven with the above-mentioned aspects of a singular person or a group, is captured in the term 'Intersectionality' (Crenshaw 1988). Intersectionality is a US-related concept originating from an anti-discriminatory context.

'Gender equality' is another key term in Gender Mainstreaming. It refers to the situation where individuals of all gender groups are free to develop their personal abilities. The different behaviours, aspirations and needs of women, men and others are considered, valued and favoured equally (equality in difference) (European Commission 2009: part 1.2). In contrast to this the term 'equal opportunities' indicates the absence of barriers to economic, political and social participation on the grounds of sex, based on the rationale that a whole range of actions are necessary to redress sex- and gender-based inequities (European Commission 2009: part 1.2). As important as these political concepts that brought a lot of progress over the last two decades are the changes that took place at the same time in academic discourse, more precisely in theoretical debates within women's and gender studies.

A short history of gender research

Gender research began as Feminist Studies, embedded in the feminist movement. In the 1970s and 1980s, more gender equality in society was the political aim of this advocatory research. The introduction of female perspectives into an androcentric scientific system was the contribution of a branch which was summarised as 'feminist critique of science' (Keller 1985; Harding 1986; Haraway 1991; Schiebinger 1999; Marchbank and Letherby 2007: 24). Feminist Studies were complemented by Women's Studies when the relevance of this research became gradually acknowledged and a distinction was made between academic and political spheres (Marchbank and Letherby 2007: 14). Women remained the core of this research, however, until Men's Studies came up as an analogy (Brod 1987; Connell 1995; Marchbank and Letherby 2007: 100), followed by Queer Studies (Kulick 1998; Prieur 1998). Based on the theses of the social construction of gender identities (Oakley 1972; Butler 1990), the gender discourse shifted from the dualism of women vs. men to concepts of masculinity and femininity as well as diverse gender identities, a level of abstraction that allowed for a certain distance to the objects of research which had been missing before. Nevertheless, it took a long time before it was generally understood that gender research is no longer confined to women's issues. Today, research is confronted with a diversity of gender identities in addition to other demographic features of individuals or groups (Intersectionality). Table 12.1 offers an overview of the most important forms or stages of gender studies (here used as an umbrella term), as characterised by their research subjects or objects and their respective ideological or academic approaches:

In the context of this book the strand called 'ecofeminism' is of special importance. The term was frequently misunderstood as representing any kind of gender-oriented research on environmental issues. Such a simplification ignores the very special history and the multitude of approaches of ecofeminism, ranging from women's projects in countries of the global South (which were typical of the early years of ecofeminism) to a number of very distinct academic, often philosophical discourses from 1990 onwards on various continents. There is no coherent theory of ecofeminism and any effort to systematise the diversity of approaches is doomed to fail (Warren 2004; Katz 2013). A more neutral phrase like 'gender, environment and sustainable development' (Nieves Rico 1998) is recommended to cover the great amount of research carried out over the last 25 years on the diverse links between gender, environmental problems and sustainable development.

Altogether the diverse streams of gender studies generated an enormous and enlightening body of evidence that today serves to underpin the benefit of Gender Mainstreaming in science. After many years of very little progress and much resistance, mainly in male connotated

Table 12.1 Development of gender studies from 1970s to 2010

Research Object	*Name of Research*	*Approach*
Women vs. patriarchalism	Feminist Studies *1970 and 1980s*	Advocacy in research, women friendly
Scientific system	Feminist critique of science *1970 and 1980s*	Epistemological
Women/femininity	Women's Studies *1980s onwards*	Academically integrated, less political than Feminist Studies
Women/nature/environment	Ecofeminism *1980s onwards*	Starting from social movements, turning into academic research
Masculinity/masculinities	Men's Studies *Starting around 1986*	Analogy to Women's Studies, partly advocatory
Femininity/masculinity and gender relations	Gender Studies *Starting around 1990*	Gender-sensitive in a broad sense
Diverse sexual identities	Queer Studies *Starting in early 1990s*	Gender-sensitive in a broad sense, advocatory for gay movement, transgender, etc.
Complex interplay of gender, ethnicity, class, age, religion, abilities, etc.	Gender and Diversity or Intersectionality *Starting around 2005*	Gender only one of several categories of analysis; anti-discriminatory aspects

Source: Franz-Balsen 2014: 1978

disciplines like engineering, natural sciences or information and computer science (Ernst 2010), since 2010 a breakthrough for GM in research is tangible.

Gender as a mark of excellence – new standards in quality research

Innovations in research can be imposed and implemented via funding policies. The progress of GM in research activities is in part due to such top-down strategies applied by governments, e.g. via US National Science Foundation (NSF), German Research Foundation (DFG), Austrian Science Fund (FWF), etc., or by international bodies like the European Commission. Starting in 2011 the European Commission organised annual Gender Summits which involved partner organisations from other continents and gathered experts and policy makers from all over the world to discuss ways of making research gender-sensitive and to define standards of gender in science. The following summary is based on documents and wordings used in these occasions (European Commission 2009; genSET 2010).

From gender-bias and gender-blindness to gender-competence

> Science is supposed to be the paradigm of objective, rational and critical thought. For many people it is still the ideal model of modernity, social progress and even of enlightened civilization itself insofar as it confronts customary biases and superstitions. So its continued refusal to examine critically its own gender prejudices, where this occurs, damages that reputation these days.
>
> *(Harding 2001)*

In academic institutions prejudices have existed against women with regard to certain disciplines (Barone 2011) and to leadership, and quite generally against the relevance of the gender dimension. To combat gender-bias and gender-blindness in research a dual strategy is needed, relating both to equal opportunities of men and women in research and to the gender dimension of research:

a. Equal opportunities for men and women in research means creating the best possible team which is a mixed team. Working conditions and culture should allow men and women to have equally fulfilling careers.
b. Addressing the gender dimension of research content means using gender as a key analytical and explanatory variable in research.

The gender-sensitive research cycle (see Figure 12.1 below) shows how step by step the research process can be gendered. Prerequisite in order to understand the relevance of each single step is gender-competence or gender-diversity-competence of the researcher, or sex and gender-competence in medicine, health sciences or engineering (Schiebinger *et al.* 2011–2013). Capacity building (gender training, gender consulting, gender coaching) is needed to discover gender in one's discipline and to apply the tools of gender-analysis. Gender competence can be defined as gender expertise (awareness of the social construction of gender and understanding the complexity of gender relations) in combination with methodical skills and the ability to apply all this in professional contexts. Gender-diversity-competence includes skills of corporate diversity management (anti-discrimination, culture of respect and esteem).

There is consensus among experts and policy makers that gender is becoming a mark of quality: 'If relevant gender issues are missed or poorly addressed, research results will be partial

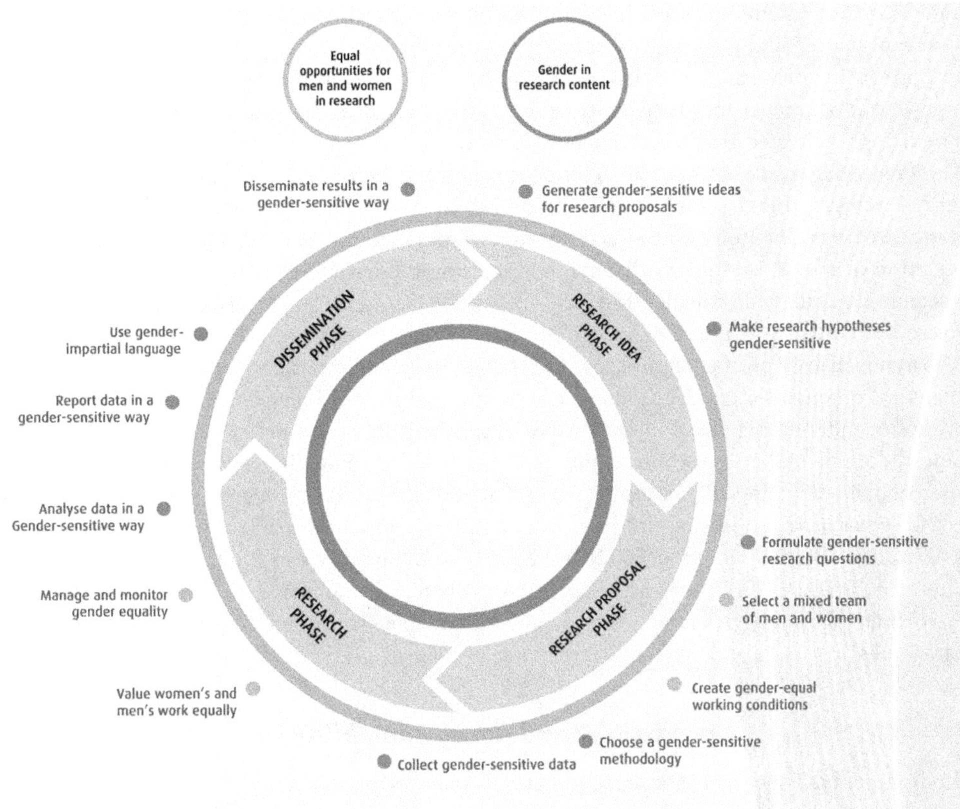

Figure 12.1 Gender-sensitive research at all stages of the research cycle

Source: European Commission 2009: part 2.1

and potentially biased. Gender can thus be an important factor in research excellence' (European Commission 2009: part 1.4). In the sustainability context it is also a normative obligation, derived from the sustainability concept.

Gender and diversity in ESD and in research on HESD

In this main part of the chapter links are finally drawn between gender and sustainable development, between (H)ESD and Gender Mainstreaming and consequences for research on HESD. A clear mandate was imposed on ESD and HESD to integrate gender in all activities by the Bonn Declaration, the final document of the UNESCO World Conference on Education for Sustainable Development 2009, setting the course for ESD worldwide (UNESCO 2009). 'ESD should actively promote gender equality, as well as create conditions and strategies that enable women to share knowledge and experience about social change and human well-being' (UNESCO 2009: paragraph 15 m). It is great progress that the document repeatedly and prominently draws attention to gender issues in ESD. On the other hand, a very traditional understanding of gender shines through: gender is reduced to gender equality with focus on women and girls only. Blake gives an overview of more policy documents calling for empowerment of women and diagnoses a 'mismatch between the primacy given to gender in high-level documents and the paucity of discussions within ESD discourses' (Blake 2007: 418). The latter is reflected by the lack of publications discussing gender and (H)ESD (Blake 2007: 419; Franz-Balsen *et al.* 2011: 120). This goes well together with the results of an experts' delphi on research priorities for HESD (Wright 2007a): the role of gender in sustainable development was one of very few items considered not important (Wright 2007a). However, in a later interpretation of the data set it says that via cross-cutting themes like inclusiveness or social change research projects could include 'research on gender, class, race, and marginalization in sustainable development' (Wright 2007b: 40). But focusing alone on marginalisation is a limited view. Apparently, the scientific community of HESD researchers has not been familiar with the analytical potential of gender as a research category in sustainability issues, e.g. explaining why groups or individuals behave in sustainable or unsustainable ways or – on a macro-level – why unjust dominance structures rule the globalised world. This, however, demands a holistic approach, investigating all gender constructions and all demographic groups. Only few authors ask for what has been missing in the gender and development discourse (Martine and Villareal 1997; Cornwall 2000; Ruxton 2002) and equally in the gender and ESD context (Casimir and Dutil 2003; Blake 2007; Franz-Balsen 2014): Where are the men? To reveal links between masculinity, femininity, gender relations and sustainable development is the aim of the next paragraphs.

Gender and (un)sustainability

Environmental issues are not gender-neutral, and today this formerly surprising fact has become an integral aspect of other fields of socio-ecological research. The first findings were gathered more or less unintentionally in the early 1990s, when in empirical studies on risk perception, environmental awareness and environmental behaviour of national populations in Europe and the United States data was segregated along the gender variable just as a routine procedure. From this, consistent and reproducably significant differences between the categories 'male' and 'female' showed up: health care and consumption patterns, waste management, transportation, risk awareness and political engagement – all these fields of environmental attitudes and behaviour seemed to be highly gendered. The differences found in risk awareness along the variables gender and race (Flynn *et al.* 1994; Finucane *et al.* 2000) were stunning: white male probands showed comparatively little fear of anthropogenic environmental risks.

Emerging research on gender and environment discovered blind spots in disciplines like planning (Moser 1993), transport studies (Polk 1998; Spitzner 2009; genderSTE 2015), the study of consumption patterns (Casimir and Dutilh 2003; Schultz and Stieß 2009), energy (Rukato 2001; Röhr 2001), agriculture (The World Bank/FAO/IFAD 2009) or economy (Buckingham-Hatfield 2000; Biesecker and Hofmeister 2010). Confronted with problems of global scope, it has to be kept in mind that in different parts of the world the relationships between gender/diversity issues and questions of sustainability can be very different, ranging from structural inequality of certain groups of population to individual behaviour in professional and private contexts, ranging from poverty/malnutrition problems to the impacts of luxury lifestyles and exaggerated meat consumption. In the global South, the tradition of developmental studies foresaw to integrate gender aspects in research on key issues of sustainable development: gender equality and human rights, education, participation, land use, food security, access to water and sanitation, etc. Today, a new area of investigation is shared by researchers both from global North and South: gender and climate change (Röhr 2007; Schiebinger *et al.* 2011–2013). What makes gender such an important factor for Sustainable Development?

Understanding the conflict of norms

Gender norms, the social constructs of masculinity and femininity serving as cultural guidelines, have been identified as factors inhibiting sustainable development (Eisler 1994; Blake 2007; Rogers 2008; Franz-Balsen 2014). The culturally defined, symbolic norms of masculinity vs. femininity (macro-level) are intruding every aspect of our lives. They shape the expectations that society has towards our individual appearance and performance (micro-level) which are supported by societal infrastructures and legislations (meso-level). Both the norms of masculinity and femininity are in tension with some principles and implications of sustainable development.

Connell's concept of 'hegemonic masculinity' (Connell 1995) explains the constraints that the masculine role comprises in western civilisation: the 'ideal man' is a working man, competitive and successful, thus able to support a family; he tries to be better than others and to acquire power. A culture of domination (Eisler 1994), exploitation and social inequality is thus sustained by this norm, which in economic contexts and business has become a global standard of behaviour. Gender as an analytical category equally helps to understand phenomena like the financial crisis, the male resistance against gender equality or the cult around powerful cars.

If one looks at the ethics and values of sustainable development, as they have been operationalised in the Earth Charter (The Earth Charter Initiative 2000), the conflict of norms between sustainable development and the norm of hegemonic masculinity is obvious:

1. Respect and care for the community of life (e.g., long-term thinking; respect of human rights);
2. Ecological integrity (e.g., by a precautionary approach);
3. Social and economic justice (equitable distribution of wealth within nations and among nations; elimination of discrimination in all its forms);
4. Democracy, nonviolence and peace (e.g., participation in decision-making).

In conclusion, it can be said that sustainable development is a threat to prevailing gender concepts of masculinity, which give competiveness and short-term success on the individual or corporate scale highest priority (Eisler 1994; Rogers 2008; Franz-Balsen 2014).

The norms of femininity show more differences between cultures and are less easy to generalise. Quite ubiquitous, however, is the norm of the good, caring mother, responsible for nutrition, health, education and well-being of a family. In many societies, until today, it has confined women to the reproductive sphere and the role of the housewife who does not need more than basic education, because she keeps out of politics, other public affairs and the majority of professions. Wherever the full burden of domestic work is assigned to the female part of population (with growing numbers of employed women who carry a double burden), it seems that women have a long way to go before meeting the great expectations that we find in documents, e.g. Agenda 21, chapter 2 4 (UNCED 1992) on the importance of women for sustainable development. Sustainable development counts on empowerment and active participation of women, but traditional norms of femininity don't encourage them to look beyond the familial or local context.

Prevailing gender norms, it can be concluded, contribute more to unsustainability than to sustainability. But social norms gradually change when social and cultural reality changes, which is the case in many regions of the world. Education, training and communication are drivers of change, and higher education in particular is a space where paradigms are questioned and future-oriented concepts are developed.

Consequences for research on higher education for sustainable development

The aim of research on Higher Education for Sustainable Development should be to develop, foster and monitor gender and diversity-oriented HESD. Personality development is a key element of HESD, and gender, ethnicity, age or class have proved to be key analytical and explanatory variables for individuals in the sustainability context. Consequently, areas of research on HESD could be:

At university level

- *Curriculum:* analysis of content and gender/diversity-sensitive curriculum development; assessment of gender/diversity-competence of teaching staff;
- *Research design:* including gender analysis (data segregation and interpretation) in all empirical studies on students or staff or other interest groups; avoiding bias and stereotyping; mixed research teams (see also Figure 12.1);
- *Audience research:* measuring gender-specific attitudes, interests, capacities and behaviour on campus (before and after interventions), drawing consequences from the results regarding gender/diversity-sensitive communication and content of courses;
- *Organizational culture:* focus G & D policies in sustainability reporting (equal opportunities, work-life balance, inclusion, etc.)

At international level

- Survey of state of art (gender in HESD) worldwide; systematic search for best practice, existing models and tools;
- International, comparative studies;
- Meta-analysis of existing studies;
- Theoretical, conceptual studies, aiming at integration of G & D in HESD.

To date, research and development projects explicitly focusing on gender and diversity in HESD are rare, as a review of recent literature shows. The following trends were found when searching the small number of research papers that include gender aspects:

If gender-analysis was carried out at all, in the majority of cases it focused on certain target groups, usually students, sometimes academic staff (Cotton *et al.* 2007) or non-academic staff (Davis *et al.* 2009). Studies were carried out in order to assess either beliefs and attitudes (Cotton *et al.* 2007), knowledge (Tuncer Teksoz *et al.* 2014) or both (Tuncer Teksoz *et al.* 2014; Franz-Balsen and Heinrichs 2007), as well as risk awareness (Krause-Steger and Roski 2014), environmental behaviour (Davis *et al.* 2009) or participation (Franz-Balsen and Heinrichs 2007; Stevenson and Clegg 2012; Tudor and Dutra 2014; Rose 2008). Measurement of HESD learning outcomes (Burek and Bonwick 2010; Gordon 2015; Tuncer Teksoz *et al.* 2014; Myers and Beringer 2010) present data before and after pedagogical interventions.

Most of the papers do report of gender differences: usually these are not spectacular; other studies don't find significant gender differences (e.g. Cotton *et al.* 2007, Myers and Beringer

2010). Most results confirm the kind of 'stereotype' reaction of female probands: attitudes closer to SD, higher risk awareness, pro-sustainable lifestyle, hesitating in extra-curricular engagement (Franz-Balsen and Heinrichs 2007; Stevenson and Clegg 2012; Tudor and Dutra 2014). The overall results indicate (not at all surprisingly) that the cultural gap and the gender divide between scientific domains (humanities vs. technology) reinforce gender-specific approaches to SD.

Considering this impact of disciplines in combination with gender, the following example was chosen to illustrate what gender-sensitive research on HESD could look like. It is clearly structured and illustrates how HESD implementation can profit from gender-sensitive research. And it shows that – whereas all the documents talk of empowerment of women – male students are the biggest challenge for HESD.

Box 12.1 The project 'SUPER' at Bochum University of Applied Sciences, Germany

The Development of a Sustainable Perception Index regarding Gender and Diversity Aspects (Steger and Roski 2014)

At Bochum University of Applied Sciences a perception index was created concerning personal relations of students to sustainability issues, in order to adapt future educational offers accordingly. At male dominated technical universities this is of major importance.

Research questions:

- Which aspects of SD are known?
- Which cohorts could be drivers for sustainability on campus?
- Do female students have special access to SD?
- How can the results be taken up by the university?

For the perception index **three levels of perception** were chosen:
Knowledge (12 questions regarding ecological, economic and social sustainability)
Evaluation (evaluating issues of SD by relevance)
Emotional response (reaction to Fukushima accident)
plus info on personal lifestyle and demographic data (incl. age, discipline, migrational background)
An online survey is complemented by qualitative research (15 in-depth interviews).

Results of online survey:

Number of female respondents proportionally higher; female participants scoring higher in knowledge, especially regarding the social dimension of SD; male respondents evaluated sustainability issues as less import than females; the emotional response to the Fukushima accident showed that the majority of students is worried, but again female participants expressed greater fears. No female person, but 17 per cent of males gave the answer that they do not feel anything about the incident in Fukushima. Females also scored higher regarding sustainable lifestyle.

Conclusion: The gender dimension led to the most significant differences in the quantitative data. Different needs of gender groups will be considered in gender-sensitive educational concepts. In these economic and social sustainability topics will be increased.

Gender mainstreaming in HESD

Regarding the fact that HESD experts to date have considered gender and diversity aspects of minor importance (Wright 2007a, 2007b), this contribution argues for the necessity of Gender Mainstreaming in HESD.

It is evident that Gender Mainstreaming in higher education institutions is an enormous task that demands an overall strategy, consisting of parallel initiatives in the areas of research and teaching (science knowledge making process) and the area of administration and infrastructure (organisational culture and structure) of the college or university. Whereas gender equity policies have a tradition at many universities worldwide, gendering the domains of research and teaching is still a novel approach. Here the combined strategy of 'Integrative Gendering' is recommended, developed at German universities from 2004 onwards (Jansen-Schulz 2008). It is based on an integrative, holistic concept of education which is very close to the idea of a sustainable university. Integrative gendering is competence-oriented and targets awareness, knowledge and behaviour of people in the first step, resulting in an increasing integration of the gender dimension in knowledge production and transfer in the second. Target groups are professors, researchers and teaching staff, the presidential committee and employees in service management as well as students. Integrative gendering considers gender and diversity aspects of teaching and research from planning to execution and evaluation. In order to institutionalise such a new culture in teaching and research the following instruments can be applied for capacity building:

- Lecture series (addressing academic staff)
- Synopsis of gender-relevant modules
- Gender training
- Gender consulting (groups, individuals)
- Coaching for gender-diversity in teaching
- Support for gender-diversity in teaching (online resources, gender-packages)
- Gender-check for project proposals
- Workshops, conferences.

Neither Gender Mainstreaming policies nor the processes of introducing sustainability management at universities are welcomed by all members of the institution. The recommendations given in the following are a fusion of the 'Expert to Expert Approach', which is part of 'Integrative Gendering' and the 'Individual Interaction Method' which was developed at Delft Technical University (Peet *et al.* 2004). What both approaches have in common, is that they establish individual contact to the researcher and/or lecturer and link capacity building to their current projects and seminars. Intriguing about the 'Individual Interaction Method' is that it is unobtrusive and invites members of the target group to make propositions on how their discipline could contribute to sustainable development. The authors report that cooperation was possible in most cases afterwards. Likewise one could start personal dialogues about gender, stereotypes, intersectionality, discrimination, etc. within the discipline or institute and encourage colleagues to talk frankly about scepticism or bias.

Conclusion: bridging the gap

Higher education for sustainable development and research on higher education for development need to catch up on the integration of sex, gender and diversity aspects into all their projects and activities. Capacity building for all university members (directors, researchers, teaching staff, administrative staff, students) is the first indispensable step. Judging from today's state of art, it seems clearly a missed chance for both that Gender Mainstreaming and sustainability mainstreaming have not been brought together, but co-exist as parallel worlds at most universities. Sustainability programs could have complemented and reinforced the changes initiated by Gender Mainstreaming or even initiated GM where it was missing. It is a challenge for research on HESD to explore ways that this can happen and to monitor problems and progress.

References

Barone. C., 2011. 'Some Things Never Change. Gender Segregation in Higher Education across Eight Nations and Three Decades', *Sociology of Education*, 84(2), 157–76.

Biesecker, A. and Hofmeister, S., 2010. 'Focus: (Re)productivity: Sustainable Relations both between Society and Nature and between the Genders', *Ecological Economy*, 69(8), 1703–11.

Blake, J., 2007. 'Missing Links: Gender and Education for Sustainable Development', *International Journal of Innovation and Sustainable Development*, 2(3/4), 414–32.

Brod, H., ed., 1987. *The Making of Masculinities: The New Men's Studies*. Boston, MA: Allen and Unwin.

Buckingham-Hatfield, S. (2000) *Gender and Environment*. London: Routledge.

Burek, C. and Bonwick, G., 2010. 'A Novel Example of Cross Discipline Education for Sustainable Development in Higher Education in UK: Gender Differences'. University of Chester. www.ifuw.org/wp-content/uploads/2014/01/burek1.pdf [accessed 20 March 2015].

Butler, J., 1990. *Gender Trouble*. London: Routledge.

Casimir, G. and Dutilh, C., 2003. 'Sustainability: A Gender Studies Perspective', *International Journal of Consumer Studies*, 27(4), 316–25.

Connell, R., 1995. *Masculinities*. Berkeley, CA: University of California Press.

Cornwall, A., 2000. 'Missing Men? Reflections on Men, Masculinities and Gender in GAD', *IDS Bulletin*, 31(2), 18–25.

Cotton, D.R.E., Warren, M.F., Maiboroda, O. and Bailey, I., 2007. 'Sustainable Development, Higher Education and Pedagogy. A Study of Lecturers' Beliefs and Attitudes', *Environmental Education Research*, 13(5), 579–97.

Cox, T., 2001. *Creating the Multicultural Organization: A Strategy for Capturing the Power of Diversity*. Business School Management Series. Michigan: University of Michigan.

Crenshaw, K.W., 1988. 'Race, Reform and Retrenchment: Transformation and Legitimation in Antidiscrimination Law', *Harvard Law Review*, 101(7), 1331–87.

Davis, G., O'Callaghan, F. and Knox, K., 2009. 'Sustainable Attitudes and Behaviours amongst a Sample of Non-academic Staff', *International Journal of Sustainability in Higher Education*, 10(2), 136–51.

Eisler, R., 1994. 'From Domination to Partnership: The Hidden Subtext for Sustainable Change', *Journal of Organizational Change Management*, 2(4), 32–46.

Ernst, W., ed., 2010. *Geschlecht und Innovation. Gender Mainstreaming im Techno-Wissenschaftsbetrieb*. Berlin: LIT Verlag.

European Commission, 2009. 'Gender in EU-funded Research. Toolkit'. www.yellowwindow.be/genderinresearch/ [accessed 4 June 2014].

Finucane, M.L., Slovic, P., Mertz, C.K., Flynn, J. and Satterfield, T.A., 2000. 'Gender, Race, and Perceived Risk: The "White Male" Effect', *Health, Risk & Society*, 2(2), 159–72.

Flynn, J., Slovic, P. and Merz, C.K., 1994. 'Gender, Race, and Perception of Environmental Health Risks', *Risk Analysis*, 14(6), 1101–8.

Franz-Balsen, A., 2014. 'Gender and (Un)Sustainability – Can Communication Solve a Conflict of Norms?', *Sustainability*, 6(4), 1973–91.

Franz-Balsen, A. and Heinrichs, H., 2007. 'Managing Sustainability Communication on Campus: Experiences from Lüneburg', *International Journal of Sustainability in Higher Education*, 8(4), 431–45.

Franz-Balsen, A., Mat Isah, N. and Lai, W.T., 2011. 'Merging Gender Mainstreaming and Sustainability Strategies: A Win-Win Approach', in Barth, M., Rieckmann, M. and Sanusi, Z.A. (eds), *Higher Education for Sustainable Development. Looking Back – Moving Forward*. Bad Homburg: Verlag für Akademische Schriften, 118–34.

genderSTE, 2015. Why Transport? www.genderste.eu/i_transport01.html [accessed 20 March 2015].

genSET (2010) 'Recommendation for Action on the Gender Dimension in Science'. <www.genderinscience.org/index.php/downloads/cat_view/10-genset-project-publications> [accessed 6 June 2014].

Gordon, N., 2015. 'Sustainable Development as a Framework for Ethics and Skills in Higher Education Computing Courses', in Leal Filho, W., Brandli, L., Kuznetsova, O. and do Paco, A.M.F. (eds), *Integrative Approaches to Sustainable Development at University Level.* World Sustainability Series. Cham, Switzerland: Springer International Publishing AG, 345–57.

Haraway, D., 1991. *Simians, Cyborgs and Women. The Reinvention of Nature.* New York: Routledge.

Harding, S., 1986. *The Science Question in Feminism*, 1st edn, Ithaca, NY: Cornell University Press.

Harding, S., 2001. 'How can Women's Standpoint Advance the Growth of Scientific Knowledge?', in European Commission (ed.), *Gender & Research*, Conference Proceedings, Brussels, 8–9 November, 316–22.

Jansen-Schulz, B., 2008. 'Integrative Gendering. A Strategy for Teaching, Research and University Structures'. www.gender.hu-berlin.de/publikationen/gender-bulletins/texte-34/texte34pkt4.pdf [accessed 6 June 2014].

Katz, C., 2013. 'Ökofeminismus', in Hofmeister, S., Katz, C. and Mölders, T. (eds), *Geschlechterverhältnisse und Nachhaltigkeit.* Berlin and Toronto: Barbara Budrich, 79–85.

Keller, E.F., 1985. *Reflections on Gender and Science.* New Haven, CT: Yale University Press.

Krause-Steger, S. and Roski, M., 2014. 'The Development of a Sustainable Perception Index regarding Gender and Diversity Aspects', in EDUCON 2014 Conference Book, IEEE Global Engineering Education Conference, 3–5 April 2014, Istanbul, Turkey. http://educon-conference.org/educon2014/ [accessed 20. March 2015].

Kulick, D., 1998. *The Gender of Brazilian Transgendered Prostitutes.* Chicago, IL: University of Chicago Press.

Marchbank, J. and Letherby, G., 2007. *Introduction to Gender: Social Science Perspectives.* Harlow: Pearson Education Limited.

Martine, G. and Villareal, M., 1997. 'Gender and Sustainability: Re-assessing Linkages and Issues'. FAO Women and Population Division. www.fao.org/sd/wpdirect/wpan0020.htm [accessed 2 January 2014].

Moser, C.O.N., 1993. *Gender Planning and Development: Theory, Practice and Training.* London: Routledge.

Myers, O.E. and Beringer, A., 2010. 'Sustainability in Higher Education: Psychological Research for Effective Pedagogy', *Canadian Journal of Higher Education*, 40(2), 51–77.

Nieves Rico, M., 1998. *Gender, the Environment and Sustainability of Development.* Santiago de Chile: United Nations, Women and Development Unit.

Oakley, A., 1972. *Sex, Gender and Society.* London: Maurice Temple Smith.

Peet, D.J., Mulder, K. and Bijma, A., 2004.' Integrating SD into Engineering Courses at the Delft University of Technology: The Individual Interaction Method', *International Journal of Sustainability in Higher Education*, 5(3), 278–88.

Polk, M., 1998. 'Gendered Mobility: A Study of Women's and Men's Relations to Automobility in Sweden'. Humanekologiska Skrifter, 17, Goeteborg: Goeteborg Universitet.

Prieur, A., 1998. *Mema's House. On Transvestites, Queens, and Machos.* Chicago, IL: University of Chicago Press.

Röhr, U., 2001. 'Gender and Energy in the North'. Background paper for the Expert Workshop 'Gender Perspectives for Earth Summit 2002: Energy, Transport, Information for Decision-making'. Berlin, Germany, 10–12 January 2001. www.earthsummit2002.org/workshop/Gender%20%26%20 Energy%20N%20UR.pdf [accessed 15 January 2015].

Röhr, U., 2007. *Gender, Climate Change and Adaptation. Introduction to the Gender Dimensions.* Berlin: Genanet – Focal Point Gender, Environment, Sustainability. www.unep.org/roa/Amcen/ Projects_Programme/climate_change/PreCop15/Proceedings/Gender-and-climate-change/ Roehr_Gender_climate.pdf [accessed 15 January 2015].

Rogers, R.A., 2008. 'Beasts, Burgers and Hummers: Meat and the Crisis of Masculinity in Contemporary Television Advertisements', *Environmental Communication*, 2(3), 281–301.

Rose, G., 2008. 'Encouraging Sustainable Campus Travel: Self-Reported Impacts of a University TravelSmart Initiative', *Journal of Public Transportation*, 11(1), 85–108.

Rukato, H., 2001. 'Gender and Energy in the South: A Perspective from Southern Africa'. Background paper for the Expert Workshop 'Gender Perspectives for Earth Summit 2002: Energy, Transport, Information for Decision-making', Berlin, Germany, 10–12 January 2001.

www.earthsummit2002.org/workshop/Gender%20%26%20Energy%20S%20HR.pdf [accessed 23 March 2015].

Ruxton, S., 2002. 'Gender Equality and Men'. Oxfam Publications. www.xyonline.net/sites/default/files/Ruxton,%20Gender%20equality%20and%20men.pdf [accessed 23 March 2015].

Schiebinger, L., 1999. *Has Feminism Changed Science?* Cambridge, MA: Harvard University Press.

Schiebinger, L., Klinge, I., Sánchez de Madariaga, I., Schraudner, M. and Stefanick, M., eds, 2011–2013. *Gendered Innovations in Science, Health & Medicine, Engineering, and Environment.* http://genderedinnovations.stanford.edu [accessed 5 June 2014].

Schultz, I. and Stieß, E., 2009. 'Gender Aspects of Sustainable Consumption Strategies and Instruments'. Europe Working Paper 1. Frankfurt am Main: ISOE. <www.eupopp.net/docs/isoe_wp1.1sum.pdf> [accessed 5 June 2014].

Spitzner, M., 2009. 'How Global Warming is Gendered', in Salleh, A. (ed.), *Eco-Sufficiency and Global Justice. Women write Political Ecology*. London: Pluto Press, 218–29.

Steger, S. and Roski, M., 2014. 'The Development of a Sustainable Perception Index regarding Gender and Diversity Aspects'. IEEE Global Engineering Education Conference (EDUCON), 3–5 April, Conference Proceedings, 586–91.

Stevenson, J., and Clegg, S., 2012. 'Who Cares? Gender Dynamics in the Valuing of Extra-curricular Activities in Higher Education', *Gender and Education*, 24(1), 41–55.

The Earth Charter Initiative, 2000. *The Earth Charter.* www.earthcharterinaction.org/content/pages/Read-the-Charter.html [accessed 5 June 2014].

The World Bank, FAO and International Fund for Agricultural Development, 2009. *Gender in Agriculture. Sourcebook.* Washington, DC: The World Bank. www.fao.org/docrep/011/aj288e/aj288e00.htm [accessed 23 March 2015].

Thomas Jr, R.R., 1995. 'A Diversity Framework', in Chemers, M., Oskamp, S. and Costanzo, M.A. (eds), *Diversity in Organisations*. Thousand Oaks, CA: SAGE Publications.

Tudor, T. and Dutra, C., 2014. 'Understanding Student Engagement with Social Entrepreneurship: A Case Study of the University of Northampton', *Enhancing the Learner Experience in Higher Education*, 6(1), 4–20.

Tuncer Teksoz, G., Boone, J.W., Yilmaz Tuzun, O. and Oztekin, C., 2014. 'An Evaluation of the Environmental Literacy of Preservice Teachers in Turkey through Rasch Analysis', *Environmental Education Research*, 20(2), 202–27.

UNCED, 1992. *Agenda 21.* Rio de Janeiro: UNCED.

UNESCO, 2009. *Bonn Declaration.* Bonn: UNESCO. www.esd-world-conference-2009.org/fileadmin/download/ESD2009_BonnDeclaration.pdf [accessed 5 June 2014].

United Nations, 2002. *Gender Mainstreaming – An Overview*, New York: Office of the Special Adviser on Gender Issues and Advancement of Women. www.un.org/womenwatch/osagi/pdf/e65237.pdf [accessed 6 June 2014].

Warren, K., 2004. 'Sustainable Development and Sustainable Development Education: An Eco-feminist Philosophical Perspective on the Importance of Gender', in Blewitt, J. and Cullingford, C. (eds), *The Sustainability Curriculum*. London: Earthscan, 104–25.

Wright, T., 2007a. 'Higher Education for Sustainability: Developing a Comprehensive Research', *Journal of Education for Sustainable Development*, 1(1), 101–6.

Wright, T., 2007b. 'Developing Research Priorities with a Cohort of Higher Education for Sustainability Experts', *International Journal of Sustainability in Higher Education*, 8(1), 34–43.

13

POSTCOLONIAL PERSPECTIVES IN RESEARCH ON HIGHER EDUCATION FOR SUSTAINABLE DEVELOPMENT

Vanessa de Oliveira Andreotti

'thank you'
for **developing**
my labor, my intellect, my people
my language, my self-image,
my sensibilities, and my dreams
into a poor caricature of yourself

essential intervention
for **sustaining**
your dominance, your affluence,
your futurity, your legacy,
your innocence, your arrogance, and
your fantasy of humanitarian imperialism

Postcolonial studies is a heterogeneous field that, rather than offering a cohesive theory as such, raises an important set of questions about the production of knowledge and its social and political effects, particularly in privileged spaces of knowledge production such as higher education. These questions complicate and complexify conversations about sustainable development by making visible the choices and silences inherent in conceptualisations and interventions related to sustainability (see for example Banerjee 2003; Munshi and Kurian 2005; Chakravartty and da Silva 2012), to international development (see for example Cooke and Kothari 2001; Baaz 2005; Bhambra 2007; Kapoor 2008; McEwan 2008; Biccum 2010) and to the geo-political politics of knowledge production in higher education (see for example Altbach 1977; Nandy 1988; Russell 2005; Hay 2008). Postcolonial studies focus on analyses of representations and engagements with the 'Other' of Western humanism: those who have been considered not fully human, capable or intelligent, whose culture and traditions have not been accorded the status of knowledge of worth, and who have been victims of continuous epistemic and material violence through exploitation, dispossession, destitution and genocide (Andreotti 2011). These analyses illuminate precisely the relational construction of peoples in modern States in the 'global North'[1] (defined as exceptional people 'heading humanity') in relations to those in the 'global South' (defined as lacking, lagging behind, and 'dragging' human evolution). They outline implications for knowledge production in the 'global North', especially knowledge produced about 'Others' and about collective futures.

This chapter starts with a brief introduction to key postcolonial analyses that outline the problems of naming the world from a specific geo-political location, focusing on the works of Walter Mignolo, Gayatri C. Spivak and Ananya Roy. The second part outlines a differentiated praxis that recognises complicity while trying to subvert the imperialistic tendencies inherent in conservative and liberal institutions framed by Western modernity. The third part of the chapter explores implications of taking these analyses seriously when doing research related to sustainable development in higher education. The conclusion proposes the concept of social accountability in research as a form of self-reflexivity that keeps the politics, violences and implications of chosen stories of the past, the present and the future firmly in view.

The Darker Side of Western Modernity: Walter Mignolo

The idea of sustainable development is used to mobilise desires of engineered harmony, security and enjoyment, often grounded in the dominant market logic that has become the hallmark of late modernity (Munshi and Kurian 2005; Gunder 2010). A critical examination of the structures of meaning and affect that animate these desires can shed light on the unsustainable nature of this construction and of the very project of modernity. Walter Mignolo (2000a; 2011) offers a useful metaphor for this critique that makes visible the violence of modernity's stories about engineered futures. Mignolo suggests that the 'light' side of Western modernity, represented in assumed ideals of seamless progress, shared humanity, environmental and urban planning, continuous economic growth, secularised civility, individual freedom, Nation States as a basis for membership and organisation, and representational democracy, are only made possible through modernity's dark side of continuous colonialism, imperialism, over-exploitation (of so-called human and environmental 'resources'), war, epistemic racism, dispossession, destitution and genocide. Mignolo affirms that the dark side of modernity is not an unpleasant effect of modernity that can be remedied with more modernity, but the very condition of modernity's existence. However, the dark side of modernity needs to be *continuously denied* in order to legitimise the circulation of meaning and affect that secure people's investments in desires for modern teleologies, innocent heroic agency, and totalising forms of knowledge production (Andreotti 2014). In other words, those (of us) who inhabit the 'shiny' side of modernity have been taught to continuously deny its 'shadow', the fact that we systematically and necessarily have had and still have to inflict violence on other people in order to continue to believe in the notions of territory, time, history, human nature and progress that place us ahead of humanity, above criticism, and at the centre of the world.

This violence is articulated through what Mignolo calls coloniality (a concept borrowed from Quijano 1999). Coloniality is conceptualised as a system that defines the organisation and dissemination of epistemic, moral and aesthetic resources in ways that mirror and reproduce modernity's imperial project. Coloniality ensures the forgetting of spaciality (expansionist control of lands), of epistemic racism (elimination and subjugation of difference) and of the geopolitics of knowledge production (epistemic violence) that is constitutive of modernity (Maldonado-Torres 2007). Mignolo argues that coloniality is both 'the hidden face of modernity and the condition of its possibility' (2000b: 772). Modernity's shadow of coloniality is necessarily 'foreclosed'. Coloniality is foreclosed in modernity's ontological choices of anthropocentric, Cartesian, and universalising reasoning, and in its desires for a teleological future of consensual unanimity (Andreotti 2011, 2014). This foreclosure means that the link between deep modern investments and their role in the systemic production of exploitation, discrimination and inequalities *inevitably* has to be negated so that we can continue to believe that we are good altruistic people moving 'ahead' in linear time and history towards a homogeneous better future of rational consensual unanimity, regardless of our political affiliation or skin colour.

Worlding the world as West: Gayatri Spivak

Gayatri Spivak exposes the epistemic and material implications of this foreclosure in the production of unequal divisions of wealth and labour grounded in a political economy of knowledge production that 'worlds the world as West' producing 'First' and 'Third World', 'developed' and 'developing' categories (see for example Spivak 1995, 1999, 2004, 2012). A glimpse of the complexity and depth of her work can also be represented through a metaphor. An adaptation of Galshiot's sculpture 'Justitia: the Western Goddess of Justice' offers a visual narrative of modernity's foreclosures at work in knowledge production, which is emphasised in Spivak's scholarship. In Galshiot's sculpture, a very heavy white woman is being carried by a skinny black man. She has her eyes closed and is carrying a scale (representing justice) in one hand and a staff in the other. She is saying: 'I'm sitting on the back of a man. He is sinking under the burden. I would do anything to help him. Except stepping down from his back.'

Spivak's work is best represented through a few modifications of this visual image where gender relations are reverted: a gagged black woman carries a blindfolded heavy white man who holds the scales of justice in one hand and has a free hand to dispense alms, to hug poor children, to offer 'assistance' and to build schools; he says 'I will do anything to help you except what would really change the historical conditions of our relationship'. Spivak's analyses of foreclosures are represented in the several unexamined injustices made more visible in this image, such as, for example, the racialised and gendered exploitative division of labour that 'finances' the undeserved accumulation of capital, and racialised notions of cultural supremacy and exceptionalism that ground the justifications of privilege. The scale held by the man can represent the epistemic violence of the positionality that defines what counts as normal, legal and just. The man's statement can represent the complicity in violence of seemingly benevolent trusteeship. From the perspective of those who are being carried, the disadvantage of the Other is rationalised as a deficit of knowledge, reason, work ethic, education, civilisation and trustworthiness. While the (universal) self has knowledge and technology; the (local) other has culture, tradition and beliefs. While the self is represented as a superior, developed, civilised, future oriented, global knowledge producer and rights and aid dispenser; the Other is represented as inferior, underdeveloped, uncivilised, traditional, living in the past and dependent on aid, knowledge, rights and education handouts.

The image highlights processes of knowledge production that foreclose the historical complicity of the reproduction of unequal relations of power through knowledge itself. Despite claims of globality and inclusion, the absence of analyses of power relations, knowledge production and complicity in harm often results in practices that unintentionally reproduce hegemonic, ethnocentric, ahistorical, depoliticised, simplistic, uncomplicated and paternalistic patterns of engagement and representation which tend to pathologise, trivialise and/or misrepresent difference (Andreotti 2006, 2011, 2012). The image also opens a possibility beyond it: the possibility of naming the dynamics of complicity in violence and of facing the paradoxes and double binds of working the system from within in the hope of transforming this picture.

Ananya Roy expresses the complexities and difficulties of this task through an articulation of the doubleness of Empire in the context of higher education.

Liberal complicities in imperialism: Ananya Roy

Drawing on Spivak's work, Roy (2006) describes how the time of Empire is a time of doubleness – both a time of war and of reconstruction, of military and humanitarian and educational apparatuses, of rule through coercion and violence, but also education and consent, and of a mandate to annihilate, but also to protect, to rebuild and to preserve. She claims that the (interested) benevolence of empire poses difficult dilemmas for those professionally entangled with imperial enterprises. Drawing on Roy's scholarship on planning, higher education can be conceptualised as tied in empire's present history, having its ethical autonomy constantly constrained by its complicity with the imperialism inherent in the expansion of global capitalism, an expansionism undertaken by, and on behalf of, different ruling classes, an alignment that can be theorised as a collusion of religious and market fundamentalisms (Ali 2002).

Roy argues that imperial hegemony can be best understood in an examination of empire's benevolent face of liberalism, particularly in terms of notions of 'postmodern imperialism' sustained through human rights and cosmopolitan values that present force as a vehicle for peace and right (Hardt and Negri 2000). Liberal interventions are presented as benevolent actions to ease suffering, and their connections with what 'creates suffering' is foreclosed. This can be observed in different moments of the (recent) history of international development: both in its earlier promise of modernisation and trickle-down growth, and the neoliberal promise of the free market. Roy affirms that both expressions of liberal imperialism, grounded on a trusteeship of development, continue the 'civilising mission' of nineteenth-century colonialism, where the duty and capacity to intervene are framed and exercised in the name of justice, peace and civilisation, foreclosing the violence, coercion, expansion and exploitation also at the heart of the same imperialist project (e.g. the Justitia sculpture described before).

In professions and disciplines that are involved in practices aligned with the reconstructive and humanitarian 'band-aid' faces of liberal empire (e.g. education and research), disavowal and refusal of imperialism becomes difficult – who would refuse to raise research capacity and bring education to the 'rest of the world'? Is it necessary to align with empire to be able to do good? Can an innocent educator/researcher be dissociated from the political regime that frames her work? Roy affirms that both band-aid approaches and the desire for professional innocence create dilemmas where it is difficult to tell what is complicity and what is subversion. This becomes even more complicated in an environment of increasing corporatisation of higher education, where state support is being substituted for private funds, where 'fund-raising entrepreneurship is lauded as academic success' **(12)**, and where 'improvements' are translated into technical programs that aim to impose linear narratives of problems, interventions and results onto complex contexts and messy conjunctures, in ways that make political-economic relations invisible (Li 2007; Rankin 2010).

Postcolonially as differentiated praxis: Roy, Scott and Sousa Santos

I outline possibilities for a differentiated praxis based on questions raised in postcolonial studies through the works of Roy (2006), Scott (1999, 2004) and Sousa Santos (2007). Roy (2010) affirms that postcolonial perspectives can recalibrate the temporal dimension of modernity's empire by shifting the modern focus on 'present futures' towards 'present pasts' (Gregory 2004: 7) and reconfigure spatial dimensions of our professional and disciplinary work. Scott (2004) proposes a form of strategic critical praxis that moves beyond the rationalist desire for mastery, certainty and the imposition of universal meanings. He conceptualises it as a reading of past, present and future imaginaries that aspires to unlock a new vocabulary of possibilities for future futures that can re-animate the present and generate unexpected horizons of transformative possibilities. Similarly, Sousa Santos (2007) proposes epistemological pluralism as a way of countering the historical elimination of differently articulated possibilities (i.e. epistemicides) that have happened as a result of the universalist drives of Western modernity.

Roy borrows from Harvey (2000) the idea of insurgent praxis, a praxis that is not the platform for the 'agent of freedom', a praxis that recognises its agent as a historically constructed figure, as an embodied person, an agent of change and a member of the professional elite: 'a cog in the wheel of global capitalism, as much constructed by as constructor of the process' (Roy 2006: 237). This praxis recognises the forms of epistemic and symbolic violence at work even in the most well-meaning forms of education and research. Roy speaks of an ethics of doubleness where doubleness is signification and signification is a double-voiced articulation that 'put[s] to use hegemonic discourses, while imbuing them with a signal difference, deferential yet disruptive' (Roy 2006: 23). She states that: 'the ethics of doubleness is a provisional and improvisional praxis, one … which cannot claim professional innocence' (Roy 2006: 23). Roy evokes Spivak's distinction of 'responsibility for' Others (as a 'civilizing mission') versus 'responsibility towards' Others as answerability for complicity in violence (Spivak 1994: 22). Roy suggests the term 'accountability' as a way of distancing 'responsibility for' from 'responsibility towards'.

From Scott's perspective, any ideal of social accountability needs to emphasise the 'worth' of difference and of peaceable and creative dissensus in the refashioning of futures. The strategic praxis that Scott proposes requires a strategic criticism that is consciously bound to a 'problem space' where questions and answers are historicised and their dynamic contingency acknowledged (i.e. their commitment to current crises as much as to critiques of prior analyses), building a genealogy of the present as the construction of the colonial modern. Scott (1999) affirms that this requires both a revitalisation of the political sphere, a reconceptualisation of community, and the idea of visionary memory that connects past, present and future and that alters the concept of horizon (beyond teleology and progressivisms). He explains what this could look like:

> A displacement of the nationalist-modern vision of the postcolonial state that has sought to integrate individuals around a single conception of the good and of the citizen-subject by a vision of an ethical-political field of pluralisations of identity/difference; an agonistic field of differently constituted vernacular public spheres in which different ways of being-in-common, different modes of flourishing, are practiced.
>
> *(Scott 1999: 219–20)*

Sousa Santos argues that epistemological resistance is necessary in the struggle for global cognitive justice. This resistance calls not for 'more alternatives' but for an '*alternative thinking about alternatives*' (2007: 10) based on a *sociology of emergences* (2004) which involves 'the symbolic amplification of signs, clues, and latent tendencies that, however inchoate and fragmented point to new constellations of meaning as regards both to the understanding and the transformation of the world' (2007: 10). Santos explores the implications of a commitment to an 'ecology of knowledges' based on a recognition of the 'plurality of heterogeneous knowledges (one of them being modern science) and on the sustained and dynamic interconnections between them without compromising their autonomy' (Sousa Santos 2007: 11). In Sousa Santos' ecology of knowledges, knowledges and ignorances intersect: 'as there is no unity of knowledge, there is no unity of ignorance either' (2007: 12). Given the interconnection of knowledges and ignorances, he proposes the creation of 'inter-knowledges' where engaging with other knowledges does not mean forgetting one's own (Sousa Santos 2007).

Sousa Santos argues that a commitment to an ecology of knowledges leads to 'pluralistic, propositional thinking' (2007: 12), where the limits and value of knowledges are attributed according to the notion of 'knowledge-as-intervention-in-reality' and not 'knowledge-as-a-representation-of-reality' (Sousa Santos 2007: 13). He states that the credibility of knowledge construction should be measured by the type of past, present and future it has/can enable(d) or render(ed) impossible. This requires not only a break from the mono-epistemicism of seamless constructions of sustainability, progress and development, but an active affirmation of 'radical co-presence', or the 'conflation of contemporaneity with simultaneity, which involves the abandonment of the notion of linear time' (Sousa Santos 2007: 11) and 'the cultivation of a spontaneity that refuses to 'deduce the potential from the actual' (17). Santos argues that: 'The ecology of knowledges is a destabilizing epistemology to the extent that it engages in a radical critique of the politics of the possible without yielding to an impossible politics' (Sousa Santos 2007: 17).

The idea of egalitarian simultaneity is based on an acknowledgement of incompleteness: 'since no single type of knowledge can account for all possible interventions in the world, all of them are incomplete in different ways [hence] each knowledge is both insufficient and interdependent on other knowledges' (Sousa Santos 2007: 17). Santos's propositions de-naturalise the certainty and arrogance often associated with normative modes of knowledge production:

> It is in the nature of the ecology of knowledges to establish itself through constant questioning and incomplete answers. This is what makes it a prudent knowledge. The ecology of knowledges enables us to have a much broader vision of what we do not know, as well as of what we do know, and also to be aware that what we do not know is our own ignorance, not a general ignorance.
>
> *(Sousa Santos 2007: 18)*

Roy's critical emphasis on the liberal complicity of higher education in the project of imperialism, Scott's praxis of historicity, dissensus and agonism for interrupting the comforts of modern forms of being, belonging and organisation, and Santos's proposition of an epistemology that is plural, equivocal, incomplete and insufficient, can form the basis for a project of social accountability in higher education. Drawing on an on-going international research project focusing on higher education, the last section of this chapter presents examples of how these insights can be operationalised in a potential conceptual framework to inform discussions about research on sustainable development.

Mapping the terrain: making accountable research choices and claims

Roy's (2006) analyses raise the question: if we can't be neutral, and if we can't just refuse to participate in the (seemingly) benevolent dimension of imperialism, how can we do it differently? The first part of this chapter outlined a few partial answers, including the need to make visible social (discursive and affective) dynamics of reproduction of harm; to acknowledge our complicity as researchers in the doubleness of Empire; to historicise questions and answers and to affirm co-presence in order to foster ecologies of knowledge.

Drawing on the questions raised in this discussion, the project 'Ethical Internationalism in Higher Education in Times of Crises' (EIHE) has taken up the challenge of operationalising provisional answers through conceptualisations and practices that enact emergent forms of postcolonial ethics. These emergent ethics offer a reading of past, present and future imaginaries that aspire to unlock new vocabularies of possibilities for future futures that can re-animate the present and generate unexpected horizons of transformative possibilities, as Scott (2004) proposes.

EIHE is an inter-disciplinary, international mixed-methods research project funded by the Academy of Finland from 2012 to 2015 that involves more than 20 universities in ten countries in five continents. This project examines ethical issues in internationalisation processes in higher education, with a focus on representations of and engagements with 'epistemic difference'. The data includes both policy documents and qualitative and quantitative data collected through surveys, interviews and ethnographies in 20 university sites. Research partners in these institutions have agreed to address key questions using the same methods of data collection to create a common dataset that can be used in comparisons.

Shared questions at the heart of the study include: How is the role of the university, faculty and graduates perceived in terms of global ethics and social accountability ideals? How is diversity/plurality perceived in internationalisation policies and initiatives at participating universities? What kinds of educational policies and processes have the potential to resist and disrupt dominant patterns of knowledge production that restrict possibilities for ethical relationalities and solidarities in local and global academic spaces? This research collective is interested in testing relationships between, on the one hand, ideas of the role of the university in relation to individual and collective imaginaries (geographical, cultural, linguistic and economic), and, on the other hand, ideas of global citizenship, interdependence, global change and social accountability mobilised in higher education institutions.

Drawing on the methodology of social cartographies (Pauslton 1999, 2000), EIHE aims to create a socially accountable cartography of shifting imaginaries of higher education and of trends in internationalisation. According to Paulston (2000), social cartographies work as heuristic devices to visualise differences within and between discursive orientations and to help clarify and compare perspectives and underlying onto-epistemological choices. They help identify unexamined macro abstractions that condition thinking and practices at a micro level. Social cartographies allow for a multiplicity of ways of seeing and visual regimes to be contemplated, and for the partiality of positions, including the position of the map-maker to be acknowledged without compromising conviction or imposing a demand for immediate consensus. The conceptual framework of the EIHE project presents a heuristic of three major discursive orientations in higher education and four areas of interface. These orientations are used as a basis for interpreting policies, perceptions and practices in HE. The main discursive orientations are: neoliberal, liberal and critical.

A neoliberal discursive orientation is made more visible in the context of public sector austerity and state defunding of higher education, which animates a corporate imaginary of the university (Barnett 2013) and practices of academic capitalism (Slaughter and Rhoades 2004). This discursive orientation commodifies knowledge, research, teaching and service, framing the core 'business' of the university as a provider of credentials, expert services, and commercial innovations. Students are framed as rational clients/customers in a transactional relationship with instructors, and knowledge of worth is evaluated in terms of its exchange value. This discursive orientation operates within an economy of prestige where international rankings define measures of success. Income generation and branding become cornerstones of institutional survival, where the buzz words of 'sustainable development' are deployed both as an opportunity for business and for public relations discourses that add value to the university brand.

A liberal discursive orientation is located within a civic university imaginary that is accountable to the State. This orientation frames education as having an inherent value in the formation of national citizens committed to a singular ideal of progress, conceptualisation of humanity and vision of the future. Research is framed as a form of problem solving that provides answers for society. This orientation promotes representational democracy, equity, inclusion and access as the extension of membership to marginalised actors in society in established institutions. Connections between the material and epistemic violence of economic development (through exploitation, destitution, dispossession) and the sustainability of the 'First World' state through the unequal international distribution of wealth and labour that produce the 'Third World' are often foreclosed. Sustainable development is perceived as a benevolent extension of a single story of (civic and economic) progress to be dispensed as social responsibility 'for' the Other, rather than accountability towards the Other.

A critical discursive orientation seeks to interrupt violent patterns of power and knowledge. It highlights capitalist exploitation, processes of racialisation, and other forms of oppression at work in seemingly benevolent normalised patterns of thinking and behaviour. This configuration is also located within the civic university imaginary, emphasising the need for the inclusion of other voices, and for radical forms of democracy. However, rather than reproducing singular and homogeneous narratives of the State (like the liberal orientation), it aims to transform, pluralise or replace these narratives through critiques of systemic patterns of oppression. This orientation tends to see the university as an elitist space, an ivory tower, and call for its accountability towards marginalised populations, emphasising the public role of the university and its mandate in relation to the public good. This discursive orientation problematises common conceptualisations of sustainable development and can re-deploy it often with a focus on environmental sustainability and post-development, reflexive, participatory or alternative development frameworks (see for example Pieterse 1998).

The interfaces between these different configurations are: neoliberal-liberal; liberal-critical; critical-neoliberal; and all three configurations at once (see Figure 13.1). These interfaces are spaces of ambivalence where signifiers are deployed with multiple strategic meanings. The neoliberal-liberal interface is often used in economic rationalisations of former civic processes and meanings. The liberal-critical interface shows a deeper recognition of injustices, but advocates for institutional change based on personal (rather than systemic) choice or transformation. The critical-neoliberal interface deploys critical strategies to defend interests framed in economic terms, i.e. framing the economy as the common good, or the protection of entitlements of 'clients' and stakeholders (ranked by institutional investments and risks) as the promotion of fairness and justice. The fourth interface is where signifiers that appeal to all three discursive orientations are deployed.

As an illustration of a critical exercise that can be used in sustainable development research in higher education, the signifiers 'sustainability' and 'international development' were used as examples of analyses of different discursive configurations through this framework. The first analysis shows that the idea of sustainability can be understood differently depending on the discursive orientation used to interpret its meaning in policies and practices in higher education. From a neoliberal discursive orientation, sustainability can be tied to institutional interests of fiscal continuity, organisational efficiency, and ecological branding. From a liberal discursive orientation, sustainability can be interpreted as initiatives to improve the environment through individual self-improvement, captured in the phrase: 'reduce, reuse, recycle'. From a critical discursive orientation, where the focus changes from individuals to systemic change, systems

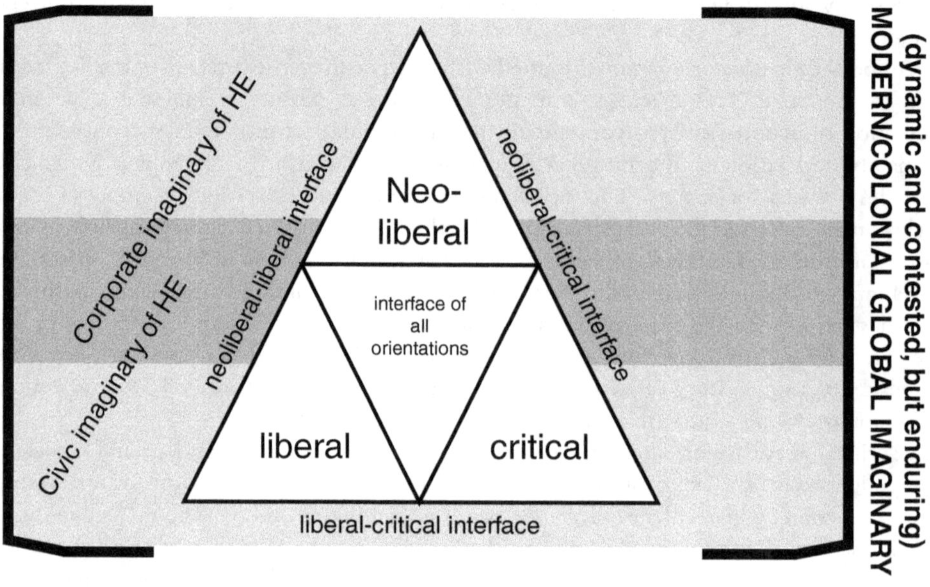

Figure 13.1 EIHE conceptual framework

thinking (e.g. cradle-to-cradle approaches) is often evoked to show that individual choices are not enough to change structural issues. Webster (2004) has suggested the slogan 'rethink, refuse, reduce' as a substitute for 'reduce, reuse, recycle' to highlight this difference; however, in recent years, it has been common to find the two slogans combined in education.

What is interesting to note in this example is that, although the critical orientation has a more rigorous analysis of the mechanisms and impact of global capitalism, it is similar to the other two orientations in its ontology. All three orientations propose (different) solutions that rely on the same grammar and desires of modernity, which can be observed in strong attachments: to modern teleologies (e.g. a seamless notion of progress in linear time); to anthropocentric Cartesian conceptualisation of agency; and to totalising forms of knowledge production as a means to solve problems created by totalising forms of knowledge production (Andreotti 2014). The latter is captured in the sentiment that 'if only we had more correct knowledge/research, we would be able to engineer a perfect solution/society/space for social relationships'. Part of the problem we face in knowledge production in this area is that these unacknowledged attachments and the teleologies they imply often calibrate the analyses that are possible in higher education institutions, reproducing the denials and foreclosures that both Mignolo and Spivak highlight in their work.

A critical orientation to sustainability can also question some of these attachments. In environmental movements, it is common to question anthropocentrism and the idea of development as capitalist hyper-consumption. In this case, indigenous cultures are often presented as sources of answers to environmental questions. However, this stance is problematic for two important reasons. First it homogenises and idealises indigenous cultures, which are living, heterogeneous and changing cultures. Second, it tends to juxtapose indigenous epistemologies onto non-indigenous ontologies, recasting a way of being as a way of knowing and missing the 'gift' that may be offered by indigenous cultures in terms of 'being' differently (see Kuokkanen 2007; Souza 2011; Andreotti *et al.* 2011; Andreotti *et al.* 2012).

A similar pattern can be observed when (international) development is used in this exercise. From a neoliberal discursive orientation, development represents the expansion of global capitalism, often proposing more capitalism as a solution to the problems that capitalism has created – as an opportunity for business that is mutually beneficial. From a liberal discursive orientation, development is interpreted as the imperative to 'help' (Heron 2007) by dispensing access to knowledge, education, values, governance systems, planning and medical care considered to be of universal worth and perceived to be lacking in the recipient communities. A critical discursive orientation would question a singular story of development and implement alternative, participatory or post-development initiatives that would be more attentive and respectful to local contexts and local voices.

It is important to note here that this conceptual framework is used as a pedagogical cartography to prompt further discussions, rather than a normative or moral guide. All orientations are related to contextual dynamics and all orientations enact contradictions and paradoxes. This conceptual framework is presented as a tool that can generate new vocabularies for the discussion and clarification of differences, dilemmas and difficulties in designing and conducting research on sustainable development in higher education.

Conclusion

In my conclusion I offer a table of common problematic patterns of engagements and representation with marginalised communities, and questions that can assist those involved in research projects related to sustainable development to identify and possibly address those patterns. This instrument was originally developed in response to the difficulties of problematising benevolence (Jefferess 2008) in development education initiatives (Andreotti 2012). The 'HEADS UP' table helps identify seven problematic patterns of representation and engagement related to epistemological, ontological and metaphysical dominance, and to ask questions that may help start to address those.

It is important to recognise that in any funded research project it will be very difficult to move completely beyond the problematic patterns identified in this table. This is due to the historical, social and systemic nature of the reproduction, naturalisation and normalisation of representations of poverty and development through education, institutional structures, media exposure, and socialisation. This also illustrates how higher education institutions have been part and parcel of the structure of colonialism and imperialism. In this sense, naming these problems and asking these questions can help those involved with research on sustainable development in higher education to work through the doubleness of their positions, to historicise their questions and answers, and to transform unexamined complicity into more subversive forms of praxis that can shed light on and potentially disrupt cognitive and existential injustices in practices of research and education.

Note

1 The terms global North and global South are used strategically to represent unequal flows of knowledge and divisions of labour, resources and human value. For a historical and more complex exploration of the use of these terms, I recommend McGregor and Hill (2009).

Table 13.1 HEADS UP 'sustainable development'

Historical pattern of engagement and representation	*Whose teleology of development/ sustainability/the future?*	*Whose template for 'being' and for knowledge production?*
Hegemony (justifying dominance and supporting domination)	What assumptions and imaginaries inform the ideal of development and sustainability [in this project]?	Who is perceived to be 'heading' humanity [in this project]?
Ethnocentrism (projecting one view as universal)	What is being projected as ideal, normal, good, moral, natural or desirable?	How is dissent addressed? How are dissenting groups framed?
Ahistoricism (forgetting historical legacies and complicities)	Does the project recognise the complicity of 'problem solvers' in the formulation of problems and solutions?	How is the historical connection between dispensers and receivers of knowledge framed?
Depoliticisation (disregarding power inequalities and ideological roots of analyses and proposals)	What is this project's analysis of unequal power relations between the parties involved?	Does the project recognise itself as ideologically motivated or potentially deaf to important alternative views?
Salvationism (framing help as the burden of the fittest)	Does this project present marginalised peoples as helpless and those who intervene as benevolent, innocent, heroic and indispensible global leaders?	Does the project acknowledge that the arrogance and violence of a single story of development has been a fundamental part of the problem of 'unsustainability'?
Uncomplicated solutions (ignoring complexity and epistemological, ontological and metaphysical dominance)	Does this project offer simplistic analyses and answers that do not invite people to engage with complexity or recognise complicity in harm?	Does this project focus on quick fixes that make those (individuals and/or institutions) intervening feel and look good?
Paternalism (seeking affirmation of superiority through the provision of help)	Does this project expect those at the receiving end of sustainable development to be grateful for the 'help' they receive?	Does this initiative acknowledge the legitimate right of less powerful partners to disagree with the formulation of problems and solutions in this initiative?

Source: Adapted from: HEADS UP preface (Andreotti 2012).

References

Ali, T., 2002. *The Clash of Fundamentalisms: Crusades, Jihads and Modernity*. London: Verso.

Altbach, P., 1977. 'Servitude of the Mind? Education, Dependency, and Neocolonialism', *The Teachers College Record*, 79(2), 187–204.

Andreotti, V., 2006. 'Soft Versus Critical Global Citizenship Education', *Policy and Practice: Development Education Review*, 3(Autumn), 83–98.

Andreotti, V., 2011. *Actionable Postcolonial Theory in Education*. New York: Palgrave MacMillan.

Andreotti, V., 2012. 'Editor's preface: HEADS UP', *Critical Literacy: Theories and Practices*, 6(1), 1–3.

Andreotti, V., 2014. 'Conflicting Epistemic Demands in Poststructuralist and Postcolonial Engagements with Questions of Complicity in Systemic Harm', *Educational Studies: A Journal of the American Educational Studies Association*, 50(4), 378–97.

Andreotti, V., Ahenakew, C. and Cooper, G., 2011. 'Epistemological Pluralism: Challenges for Higher Education', *AlterNative Journal*, 7(1), 40–50.

Andreotti, V., Ahenakew, C. and Cooper, G., 2012. 'Towards global citizenship education "otherwise"', in de Oliveira Andreotti, V. and de Souza, L. (eds), *Postcolonial Perspectives on Global Citizenship Education*. New York: Routledge, 221–38.

Baaz, M., 2005. *The Paternalism of Partnership: A Postcolonial Reading of Identity in Development Aid*. London: Zed Books.

Banerjee, S. B., 2003. 'Who Sustains whose Development? Sustainable Development and the Reinvention of Nature', *Organization Studies*, 24(1), 143–80.

Barnett, R., 2013. *Imagining the University*. New York: Routledge.

Bhambra, G.K., 2007. *Rethinking Modernity: Postcolonialism and the Sociological Imagination*. New York: Palgrave Macmillan.

Biccum, A., 2010. *Global Citizenship and the Legacy of Empire: Marketing Development*. New York: Routledge.

Chakravartty, P., and da Silva, D.F., 2012. 'Accumulation, Dispossession, and Debt: The Racial Logic of Global Capitalism – an Introduction', *American Quarterly*, 64(3), 361–85.

Cooke, B., and Kothari, U., eds., 2001. *Participation: The New Tyranny?* London: Zed Books.

Gregory, D., 2004. *The Colonial Present*. Cambridge: Blackwell.

Gunder, M., 2010. 'Planning as the Ideology of (Neoliberal) Space', *Planning Theory*, 9(4), 298–314.

Hardt, M. and A. Negri., 2000. *Empire*. Cambridge, MA: Harvard University Press.

Harvey, D., 2000. *Spaces of Hope*. Berkeley, CA: University of California Press.

Hay, I., 2008. 'Postcolonial Practices for a Global Virtual Group: The Case of the International Network for Learning and Teaching Geography in Higher Education (INLT)', *Journal of Geography in Higher Education*, 32(1), 15–32.

Heron, B., 2007. *Desire for Development: Whiteness, Gender, and the Helping Imperative*. Waterloo, ON: Wilfrid Laurier University Press.

Jefferess, D., 2008. 'Global Citizenship and the Cultural Politics of Benevolence' *Critical Literacy: Theories and Practices*, 2(1), 27–36.

Kapoor, I., 2008. *The Postcolonial Politics of Development*. New York: Routledge.

Kuokkanen, J., 2007. *Reshaping the University: Responsibility, Indigenous Epistemes, and the Logic of the Gift*. Vancouver: UBC Press.

Li, T.M., 2007. *The Will to Improve: Governmentality, Development, and the Practice of Politics*. Durham, NC: Duke University Press.

McEwan, C., 2008. *Postcolonialism and Development*. New York: Routledge.

McGregor, A. and Hill, D., 2009. 'North/South', in Kitchin, R. and Thrift, N. (eds), *International Encyclopedia for Human Geography Volume 1*. Oxford: Elsevier, 473–80.

Maldonado-Torres, N., 2007. 'On the Coloniality of Being: Contributions to the Development of a Concept 1', *Cultural Studies*, 21(2–3), 240–70.

Mignolo, W., 2000a. *Local Histories/Global Designs: Essays on the Coloniality of Power, Subaltern Knowledges and Border Thinking*. Princeton, NJ: Princeton University Press.

Mignolo, W., 2000b. 'The Many Faces of Cosmo-polis: Border Thinking and Critical Cosmopolitanism', *Public Culture*, 12(3), 721–48.

Mignolo, W., 2011. *The Darker Side of Western Modernity: Global Futures, Decolonial Options*. Durham, NC: Duke University Press.

Munshi, D., and Kurian, P., 2005. 'Imperializing Spin Cycles: A Postcolonial Look at Public Relations, Greenwashing, and the Separation of Publics', *Public Relations Review*, 31(4), 513–20.

Nandy, A., ed., 1988. *Science, Hegemony and Violence. A Requiem for Modernity*. Delhi: Oxford University Press.

Paulston, R., 1999. 'Mapping Comparative Education after Postmodernity', *Comparative Education Review*, 43(4), 438–63.

Paulston, R., 2000. 'A Spatial Turn in Comaprative Education? Constructing a Social Cartography of Difference', in Schriewer, J. (ed.), *Discourse Formation in Comparative Education*. New York: Peter Lang, 297–354.

Pieterse, J.N., 1998. 'My Paradigm or Yours? Alternative Development, Post-development, Reflexive Development', *Development and Change*, 29(2), 343–73.

Quijano, A., 1999. 'Colonialidad del poder, cultura y conocimiento en América Latina', *Dispositio*, 24(51), 137–48.

Rankin, K.N., 2010. 'Reflexivity and Post-colonial Critique: Toward an Ethics of Accountability in Planning Praxis', *Planning Theory*, 9(3), 181–99.

Roy, A., 2006. 'Praxis in the Time of Empire', *Planning Theory*, 5(1), 7–29.

Russell, C.L., 2005. '"Whoever Does Not Write is Written": The role of "Nature" in Post-post Approaches to Environmental Education Research', *Environmental Education Research*, 11(4), 433–43.

Scott, D., 1999. *Refashioning Futures: Criticism after Postcoloniality*. Princeton, NJ: Princeton University Press.

Scott, D., 2004. *Conscripts of Modernity: The Tragedy of Colonial Enlightenment*. Durham, NC: Duke University Press.

Slaughter, S. and Rhoades, G., 2004. *Academic Capitalism and the New Economy: Markets, State, and Higher Education*. Baltimore, MD: Johns Hopkins University Press.

Sousa Santos, B., 2004. 'A Critique of Lazy Reason: Against the Waste of Experience', in Wallerstein, I. (ed.), *The Modern World-system in the Longue Durée*. Boulder, CO: Paradigm Publishers, 157–97.

Sousa Santos, B., 2007. 'Beyond Abyssal Thinking: From Global Lines to Ecologies of Knowledges', *Review*, 30(1), 45–89.

Souza, L., 2011. 'Engaging the Global by Resituating the Local: (Dis)locating the Literate Global Subject and his View from Nowhere', in Andreotti, V. and de Souza, L. (eds), *Postcolonial Perspectives on Global Citizenship Education*. New York: Routledge, 68–83.

Spivak, G., 1994.' Responsibility', *Boundary 2*, 21(3), 19–64.

Spivak, G., 1995. *The Spivak Reader: Selected Works of Gayati Chakravorty Spivak*. New York: Routledge.

Spivak, G., 1999. *A Critique of Postcolonial Reason: Toward a History of the Vanishing Present*. Cambridge, MA: Harvard University Press.

Spivak, G. 2004. 'Righting wrongs', *The South Atlantic Quarterly*, 103(2/3), 523–81.

Spivak, G.C., 2012. *An Aesthetic Education in the Era of Globalization*. Cambridge, MA: Harvard University Press.

Webster, K., 2004. *Rethink Refuse Reduce: Education for Sustainability in a Changing World*. Preston Montford: Field Studies Council Publications.

14

A REVIEW OF THREE GENERATIONS OF CRITICAL THEORY

Towards conceptualising critical HESD research

Heila Lotz-Sisitka

Introduction

The project of researching and coming to understand environment and sustainability education and social change in higher education (also referred to as higher education for sustainable development, HESD) is deeply intertwined with coming to not only understand, but also to deepen democracy, social justice and human emancipation. This in turn, involves undertaking critical forms of research that can tease out, model and realise possible transformative acts of democracy, social justice and human emancipation in and through research.

Adopting a critical research trajectory is, however, not a simple matter, as there are a range of different *critical theories* that have emerged over time, and critical theory itself has undergone several generational changes. Then there is the 'post-critical' and discussions on critical theory lacking an adequate politics that also need to be considered, and there are recent moves in critical realist social theory that move towards developing a reconstructive social theory. These generational changes in critical theory have, and are influencing HESD research as will be discussed below.

To discuss critical theory influences in HESD research it is necessary to firstly provide some history of critical theory, to differentiate critical theory from other theories, and to consider the emergence of a critical theory research tradition in HESD research, which, as explained below, emerges via the uptake of critical research traditions in educational research and in environmental education (EE) research (a precursor to research on education for sustainable development, ESD) in the late 1980s and early 1990s.

While critical theory is recognised as sharing a core of philosophical concerns, it is also recognised as being immensely diverse with individual thinkers differing substantively (Held, 1980). Despite this, critical theory has been described as having three fairly distinct 'generations' starting in the 'first generation' with the work of early Frankfurt School theorists led by Horkheimer, Marcuse and Adorno (among others) (Rush 2004; Held 1980). Later Jürgen Habermas was a key figure in the emergence of a second generation of critical theory, where he differentiated knowledge interests, and developed his theory of communicative action and deliberative democracy (Held 1980; Rush 2004). Responding to critiques of some of the assumptions of the Habermasian theory of communicative rationality in critical theory, are a third generation of critical theorists (Axel Honneth, Seyla Benhabib and others) who are seeking to strengthen the emancipatory intentions and outcomes of critical theory via a deeper theorising of representation and deliberation, including agonistic approaches. Canaday (2003) explores how critical theory has also been deliberated within feminist critical theories, where the complex process of maintaining some commitments to universal objectives while also recognising particularity have been a key point of debate. These approaches are discussed in more detail below.

Critical theory is a vast and complex arena of theorising and it is not possible to include all of the details of this field here; these have been covered in publications such as that produced by Held (1980), McCarthy (1981), Poster (1989), and Rush (2004) among others. The focus in this chapter is on how it has been taken up in earlier forms of EE/HESD research, what can be learned from this for HESD research, and what some implications of the different generations of critical theory may be for conceptualising a critical HESD research programme or agenda today.

Held (1980) and Rush (2004) provide useful overviews of the history of the genesis of the critical research tradition, and of Horkeimer, Marcusse, Adorno, Hegel, Marx and other 'first generation' influences in and on the 'Frankfurt School'. Explaining many detailed nuances in the uptake of ongoing theorising of critical theory, Rush also explains the key difference between critical theory and traditional theory as follows:

> Traditional theory includes rationalist idealism and reductive materialism, wed as they are to universalistic nonhistoricism and to an instrumental concept of reason. The scientific model that it believes to have universal application across theoretical and historical boundaries, is, in fact, related to a very specific historical form of human organization – the economic form of capitalism constitutive of and expressed in bourgeois self-understanding [which some have said is a key underlying cause of sustainability issues] … Critical theory attempts to rescue from idealism a conception of reason as *unified in its practical and theoretical employment*, coupled with a dialectical and materialist account of human flourishing … The point upon which the rehabilitation turns is Hegel, though Hegel tempered in a Kantian way. Marx is also pivotal, but not the Marx that can be made into a form of materialism that joins hands with instrumental thought, but rather the 'humanistic' Marx of the 1844 *Manuscripts.*
>
> *(Rush 2004: 25; my emphasis)*

Early encounters with critical theory in our HESD research

In the early 1990s when I started in HESD research (my research was in the field of environmental education and teacher education research, which I refer to here as EE/HESD[1] research) I, like others in environmental education interested in the relationship between environmental education and social change, worked mostly with Frankfurt School Critical Theories, these being dominant at the time (Lotz 1995). These approaches were adopted by a range of environmental educators involved in teacher professional development research (EE/HESD research) at the time, such as Robottom (1987, 1991), Fien (1993), and Huckle (1993), who in turn found inspiration in the critical educational theorising of educational theorists such as Apple (1982), Giroux (1988) and Kemmis *et al.* (1983). These educational theorists, in turn, drew on theories of Horkheimer, Adorno, Marcuse, Hegel, Gramsci, and post-Marxian theories of communicative action and rationality that were developed mainly through the work of

Habermas (1972, 1984, 1987). While these influences were strongly present in the critical educational research and theorising of EE/HESD researchers at the time, Lather (1995) suggests that critical educational theorising was constructed out of *a combination* of Frankfurt School critical theory, Gramscian counter-hegemonic practice and Freirian conscientisation, which can also be seen in the EE/HESD theoretical texts of the time.

Importantly though, these critical theory influences opened up critical and participatory approaches to EE/HESD research. The move towards uptake of critical research traditions in EE/HESD is best documented in Mrazek's (1993) edited monograph text on *Alternative Paradigms in Environmental Education Research*, which captures debates on this issue held at a North American Association of Environmental Education (NAAEE) conference. The associated research methodology text written by Robottom and Hart (1993) titled *Research in Environmental Education* also consolidates the influence of critical theory in environmental education (EE/HESD) research, where it was seen as an important 'alternative paradigm', more consistent with the political and social change objectives of EE/ESD than positivist or hermeneutic forms of research. The influence of critical theory was especially evident in the uptake of an interest in praxis-oriented research, which manifested mainly in action research designs and projects, some of which were undertaken as HESD research programmes. Examples include the works of Elliot (1991), Posch (1991), Stapp and Wals (1993), O'Donoghue (1990) and my own work at the time (Lotz 1995).

The text written by Robottom and Hart in 1993, and the Mrazek debate (1993) captured in the NAAEE monograph were, in particular, strongly influenced by 'second generation' critical theory in the form of Habermas's (1972) work on knowledge interests which outlined the differences between practical, technical and critical knowledge interests in and for research and his subsequent work on communicative action (Habermas 1984, 1987). This resonated strongly with participatory action research approaches[2] in EE/HESD, as this methodology allowed for participatory interaction and deliberation of change oriented praxis, a theme which continues today in many forms ESD/HESD research (Stevenson *et al.* 2013) (see also Wahr/de la Harpe in this Handbook).

It is also the influence of this early critical educational research theorising that gave rise to the emergence of a differentiation between education *in*, *about* and *for* environment (Fien 1993).[3] It is these historical antecedents in the emergence of critical research and pedagogy traditions in the field of environmental education that later also shaped the discourse on education *for* sustainable development (ESD), which was taken up into official policy circles and practices in and through the UN Decade of Education for Sustainable Development which has been running since 2005.[4] This Decade has shaped and influenced an international HESD movement, which reflects similar commitments to education *for* sustainable development (UNESCO 2014).

Through these early engagements with Frankfurt School critical theory and associated works in education and EE/HESD theory and research praxis, we realised that our methodologies, methods and practices were never a-political and that somehow we were all implicated in politics (Robottom and Hart 1993; Fien 1993; Huckle 1993). We learned that it was possible, through our research methodologies and approaches, to strive for universally accepted democratic norms and practices as captured in concepts such as democracy, social justice and sustainability.

At the time, South Africa was emerging from 300 years of colonial rule and a vicious period of apartheid oppression, and there was a strong need to work with theories and methodologies that explicitly engaged with social transformation. Critical theory appeared to offer the best alternative at the time, especially because critical theory offered a strong alternative to positivist social science, which had been predominant in the social engineering efforts of the colonial and apartheid states. There was no hesitation at the time in adopting critical theory's normative agenda. As said by Chambers, critical theory stated 'its interest is the emancipation of humanity from injustice' (2004: 221). The original 'content' of critical theory and its normative agenda still have relevance to the HESD research programmes today, as can be seen from the citation below, especially if one reflects that the injustices referred to still prevail, particularly when viewed from sustainability perspective,

> Critical theory's 'content is the transformation of the concepts which dominate the economy into their opposites: fair exchange into deepening of social injustice, a free economy into monopolistic control, productive work into rigid relationships which hinder production, the maintenance of society's life into the pauperization of the people's'.
>
> *(Chambers 2004: 221–2, citing Horkeimer 1975)*

It would be possible to 'rest here' and simply adopt this critical theory normative commitment and content agenda for designing a HESD research programme. However, there is need to probe the unfolding of critical theory in more detail to develop a fuller understanding of the potential for informing a critical theory-led HESD research programme.

Second generation critical theory and emerging doubts

A young, idealistic and somewhat naïve researcher at the time caught up in the possibilities of a society in rapid transformation in the mid-1990s, it is not surprising that it took some years for me to come to fully understand the foundational tenets of the Frankfurt School/Habermasian form of critical theory, most notably its reliance on historically constituted and trans-boundary effective reason (Rush 2004). Understanding the implications of this for educational research (and the HESD research that I was doing in teacher education) was not an easy matter. A key and very influential text that offered some early disruptions to a somewhat blind allegiance to critical theory research traditions was the work of Ellsworth (1989) who pointed to the paradoxes inherent in emancipatory assumptions of critical theory research. As Lather (1995) commented a few years later, when reviewing the reception of the Ellsworth paper: ' too often [critical theory inspired] pedagogies [and by implication action research attempts] have failed to probe the degree to which "empowerment" becomes something done "by others" "to" or "for" the as-yet-unliberated, the object upon which is directed the "emancipatory" actions' (Lather 1995: 169, citing Ellsworth 1989).

Ellsworth's critique was against the 'violence of rationalism against its "Others"'.[5] She suggested shifting attempts from creating a dialogical community after Habermas's communicative action to 'sustained encounters with apparently oppressive formations and power relations', which led many critical theorists to the work of Foucault and the power of deconstruction (Ellsworth 1989: 304). In 1995, as I was finalising my thesis on participatory approaches to EE/HESD in teacher education, I found myself saying this in the final chapter of my thesis:

> The situatedness within the discourse of critical theory and socially critical environmental education, together with the challenge of responding to the environmental crisis through environmental education in ways that do not re-enact the grand narratives of modernism, has presented enormous challenges within this research project.

> This chapter reveals an internal and tentative critique of the preceding pages and attempts to move the research and pedagogy done in the name of liberation, democracy and transformation beyond the contemporary horizons of critical traditions which have, according to Lather (1991: 155) 'become trapped in their own limitations'.
>
> *(Lotz, 1995: 262)*

Under the influence of socio-historical research traditions, and the emerging linguistic turn and post-modern research, colleagues in South Africa were also beginning to doubt the usefulness of critical theory research in and for environmental education. This was reflected in wider debates such as that offered by Nancy Fraser (1995) when she questioned 'What's Critical about Critical Theory?' in a seminal paper. At the time, O'Donoghue (1994), also working in the field of environmental education in southern Africa, argued for the mobilisation of doubt about the 'ideological trajectory of critical theory' and warned against adherence to an ahistorical critical tradition, which 'takes on a life of its own to give identity and power to people and institutions' (1994: 23, 30). He critiqued the critical theory tendencies in environmental education research at the time, suggesting that they were leading to reification of the critical theory tradition, and posits that,

> [a] more recent feeding frenzy around a somewhat convoluted inversion of modernist social engineering which idealises the critical facilitative engineering of self liberation may merit particular attention ... [so that we may clarify trends in social theory and] ... stop simply bobbing in the wake of mainstream education discourse.
>
> *(O'Donoghue 1994: 28)*

Important to conceptualising critical HESD research is the insight that Habermas himself, relatively early on in his work, recognised that the idea of emancipation from oppression could no longer be found in a unified version of the history of the species. The same question arose in EE/HESD research, framed by the Ellsworth and Lather critiques, and the Fraser work referred to above, which made us self-consciously ask 'Who were "*we*" to be anticipating the enlightenment of "Other's" anyway, even if we were using participatory and assumed-to-be democratic pedagogical approaches?'

Following this critique of first and second generation critical theory research in our earlier EE/HESD research, transboundary 'enlightenment' intentions changed form and universal ambitions shrunk into contexts of cultural pluralism. This was reflected in a new influence coming from poststructuralist research processes influencing educational research, and soon there were many examples of critical educational researchers working with poststructuralist principles (e.g. Lather 1995). This led to an emphasis on context (Poster 1989; Canaday 2003) and consequently the particularism of the contextual also shaped a new emphasis on *social methodologies*, strongly influenced by the linguistic turn, and the emergence of post-structural and post-modern forms of social critique, which have also been defined as 'post-critical' (e.g. Lather, 1995). This led to ongoing debates amongst critical feminist scholars as to the relationship between universality and particularity (Canaday, 2003). Lather (1995) suggested at the time that the critical project could continue under the banner of deconstruction (which she referred to as an orientation in post-critical research). She provided a deliberation on the Ellsworth critique of critical theory's embedded assumptions and stated that instead of continued reliance on somewhat instrumental efforts to emancipate the other, there is a need to focus on self-reflexivity in which the researcher can 'foreground how her construction of herself as privileged inscribes as well as subverts, in essence deconstructing her own self-legitimation' (Lather 1995: 175). This has implications for how the critical HESD researcher would position herself in the research process and it is no surprise that I ended my doctoral HESD research with a commitment to this form of reflexivity in research (Lotz 1995).

Lather further stated that, 'Such a move would have added another textual dimension to the Foucauldian suspicion of every operation that seeks to centre a subject who is in a position to know' (1995: 175). She suggested that bringing a 'feminist suspicion' to the 'largely male' discourses of critical theory via deconstruction can help to provide a means of *resituating* our emancipatory work. This, Lather said, brings to the fore the Foucauldian tenet that 'nothing is innocent' (1995: 178). She further suggested that such an approach to working with critical theory in research does not position liberatory pedagogies or educational research practices as 'logical unfoldings towards a desired goal', but rather that such work 'explores their contradictions and contingencies, their tensions and internal resistances to their own 'forward' movement' (Lather 1995: 178).

This suggests foregrounding the exclusions, limitations and constraints placed on practice in HESD research. Applied to the framing of an HESD research agenda, following this period of doubt in critical theory, it would be possible to suggest critical HESD research that explores the contradictions and contingencies, tensions and internal resistances, exclusions and limitations that are placed on the HE practices of academics and stakeholders engaged with sustainability concerns.

However, we may also look critically at the 'era' of post-critical deconstruction in EE/HESD research. In this time it became difficult to identify the unity of a single rationality, leading to problems of relativism and performative contradiction, lacking ways of enabling action (Price 2007). Critical HESD researchers (such as myself) thought that if only we could get our forms of deconstruction and representation 'right' and if only we could reason more explicitly with each other in our communicative actions, emancipation would emerge. We became good at analysing each other's discourses, and pointing out what was wrong, who was being racist, or fascist, or unsustainable; we could exercise an 'in your face' power – the power of 'showing up' the other even if we ourselves were guilty of the same. We thought that if we could reason our way to understanding our structural constraints and if we could 'enlighten others' from their 'false consciousness' with enough depth and critique, then we would achieve emancipatory outcomes. Ah, the dream!

Third generation critical theory – are our standards of rationality the problem?

One of the difficulties emerging from this period, is that critical theory at the time tended to project societal problems as a 'social pathology of reason' (Honneth 2004), and to see the main cause of a negative state of society in a deficit of social rationality. However, reason is embedded in complex realities and the separation of mind/body may not be 'as easy as Descartes imagined' (ibid.). Norrie (2010), Bhaskar (1993), Honneth (2004), Rancière (2006) and others all show that the ethical core of the initial hypotheses of social criticism remains overlaid or actualised through anthropological premises. Norrie (2010) points out so well how ideals of justice and well-being, for example, are actualised in less than perfect ways through anthropological processes. Democracies do not function as they are rationally thought to. Rancière's (2006) discussion on a 'hatred of democracy' lays bare exactly how far democracies have strayed from their ideational foundations (see below). The rational universal of democracy, meant to lead to an 'intact' form of social life for all, strays, and the actual organisation of society falls short of the standards of rationality. The same can be said of sustainability as rational ideal, as so many environment and sustainability reports continue to show (e.g. the recent IPCC 2014 reports on climate change). These often provide foundational narratives for HESD research so this point may be worth reflecting on in and for a HESD research programme.

It is not surprising that critical theorists have tried to respond to this insight emerging from second generation critical theory. Critical theorists such as Honneth (2004) and Benhabib (2002), in what has been termed a 'third generation' of critical theory have vigorously debated the standards and processes of attaining rationality. With the influence of the postmodern, *aesthetic praxis* became a medium of social integration for subjects to satisfy their social needs, and ever more rigorously debated notions of communicative agreement or deliberation became the form of establishing democracy and sustainability. This has had an influence on HESD pedagogical research, which can be seen in 'deliberative' pedagogies and social learning approaches that accommodate dissonance (e.g. Wals 2007). Within this generation of critical theory, the potential of more rigorously constituted forms of discursive rationality have gained increased acceptance and have started to shape research and pedagogical practices. Highly valued are forms of linguistic agreement, debate and deliberation. The rational universal remains central for the possibility of self-actualisation of society, but via communicative interactions that are deliberative. The methodological form of achieving the rational universal of democracy/sustainability changes to participation in discursive acts, rather than a reasoning and/or emergent practice out of history as proposed by critical realists (Bhaskar 1998; Norrie 2010).

This form of critical theory also gives rise to social pathologies that are not so much the fault of our reasoning (as in second generation critical theory) but are more related to losses in inter-subjective self-actualisation. In this framing of critical theory, the goal of cooperative self-actualisation in a community of free human beings becomes the rational universal (Honneth 2004). As Honneth (2004: 341) stated, for Habermas in his later work, the goal of communicative agreement became a 'rational form of a successful mode of socialization'. In response, Honneth (1996, 2004) suggested theorising of identity formation and recognition, which he proposed could become the means to achieve communicative agreement, while Benhabib (2002) argued for a recognition of contingency, pluralism and recognising dissonance in forms of deliberative democracy. Here the 'universal' [scare quotes] ideal still remains intact. Honneth (2004: 342) explains that in this period of critical theory, the rational universal otherwise often known as 'the common good' becomes more embedded in the self-actualisation of the individual, whom, it is assumed, will act in agreement with others cooperatively. This ethical idea places utmost value on a form of '*common praxis* in which subjects can achieve cooperative self-actualisation' (Honneth 2004: 342; my emphasis).

However, as shown in the IPCC findings of 2014 and as reflected in more recent HESD research that we have undertaken (to map university responses to climate change in southern Africa) (Urquart *et al.* 2014), it is not easy to work out how such a 'common praxis' is to emerge in a globalising world where pluralism [often shaped by 'market democracy'] is now foregrounded as the most valued common form of cultural praxis. Climate change and other sustainability concerns as experienced in southern African higher education contexts and associated communities appear to require more than *assumptions* that a common praxis will emerge that will ensure emancipation from climate change impacts in southern African countries. In our most recent HESD research, the vulnerabilities of southern African citizens are clearly articulated by higher education researchers in the region and elsewhere, and by global studies such as the IPCC reports, which indicate that southern Africa is likely to face approximately a 6 degree temperature rise by 2100 with severe consequences for food and water security, health, well-being and livelihoods (Urquart *et al.* 2014). And as the extensive continuities of poverty and 'structured underdevelopment' on the African continent show (ibid.; Bond, 2006), university HESD researchers should not be naïve when considering possible critical theory orientations to their research. We cannot just assume that a 'common good' praxis will emerge.

Significant for HESD research are insights from some of the major critiques of the status quo (e.g. Bond 2006; Graber 2013; Pikkety 2013), which show that it is increasingly obvious that the spread of liberalism and neo-liberalism do not allow for the degree of intersubjective agreement that would be required for the forms of common good praxis to emerge that a more just and sustainable society seems to require. Critical theory presupposes a normative ideal of society that is incompatible with the individualistic premises of the liberal tradition and of so-called neo-liberal democracies. Value judgements, or normative pluralism, thus come into focus, still based on the actualisation of reason within a framework of common good praxis. It may well be that it is for this reason that Sayer (2000) states that it is not surprising that in times of struggle, ethics come to the fore and that social learning theorists promote 'struggle' and discontinuities in learning interactions (Wals 2007).

Struggle seems to be an ever-more present concept in third generation critical theory, and in discussions on democracy and sustainability, with interesting implications for HESD research. For example, Mouffe (2000), in describing the 'democratic paradox' begins to discuss *agonism* as a form of social methodology for democratic process and practice. Interesting, for deliberating the possibility of a critical theory informed HESD research programme, is the continued focus on social methodology for achieving the aims of social criticism and democratic practice. Mouffe (2000) emphasises politics in democracy, and brings in a shift from *antagonism* to *agonism*, being more political, and allowing people not to seek consensus, but to 'agree to disagree' as the primary social methodology. This translates into a foregrounding of discontinuity and understanding adversity and divergent viewpoints in HESD research. This brings into focus a need for framing, deframing and reframing in and through HESD research where such research begins to also be *a process of reflexive learning*, as proposed by Wals (2007).

A loss of engagement with the structural?

Along with changes in critical theory and democracy, with its increased consciousness of a plurality of cultures and the engaging of experiences of diverse value positions, individual actors and social methodology, is a disembedding of social critique from longer term historically formed social structures and from the 'collective' historical process itself (Honneth 2004). We could pause here to ask whether this has, together with a host of other factors such as the marketisation of life, paradoxically lowered the expectations of what social criticism and democracy ought to be, or could be? As Honneth stated as early as 2004:

> Generally speaking, there is prevalent today a liberal conception of justice that utilizes criteria for the normative identification of social injustice without the desire to explicate further the institutional framework for the injustice as embedding it within a particular type of society.
>
> *(Honneth 2004: 337)*

This problem can be seen in a reflexive reading of the most recent HESD research we have undertaken – a climate change mapping study involving an analysis of climate change conditions and university responses across 12 countries (Urquart *et al.* 2014) where the discussion is mainly on the problems of climate change, the impacts of climate change, and how universities could/should be responding, the deficiencies that exist in these universities, and what kind of cooperative research agenda can be framed. In reflecting critically on this study, it would seem that the HESD research we have done (ibid.) fails to more explicitly locate the problems of climate change in southern Africa within the wider neo-liberal, global-capitalist world order where carbon emissions are yet to be halted by developed nations and transnational corporations, and mitigation policy attempts have simply failed to produce any kind of meaningful solution. The report fails to articulate the global injustices of climate change clearly and strongly (ibid.). It does not fully articulate the type of society in which the problem exists and has its paradoxical impacts, as suggested by Honneth's (2004) critique.

In the setting described by Honneth (2004) above and given the reflexive example I have mentioned above from our own research (Urquart *et al.* 2014), it would therefore seem possible to be critical and undertake critical theory research without concerning ourselves too much about what kind of society we are being critical in. In and through the way we do our HESD research, we can be critical, deconstruct and politely or agonistically discuss climate change or other sustainability issues in southern Africa and elsewhere, and come to understand the complex and diverse viewpoints and diverse cultural contexts, and structural constraints. But, at the same time, we can fail in our capacity to provide substantive insight into the deep seated underlying generative mechanisms that hold the problems in place, and we can fail to provide substantive insight into 'doing anything' about the underlying causes and structural factors shaping the problem we are being critical about at a more surface level.

Turning to the question: 'what is to be done'?

Chambers (2004) offers useful insights into these problems when she suggests that critical theory tends to lack politics when defined by the question 'What is to be done?' She traces back to the critical theory of Horkeimer and Adorno, suggesting that their critical theory had no politics because its diagnosis of the times was so pessimistic that it made any political action 'or any attempt to break out of the logic of instrumental reason, futile' (Chambers 2004: 219). She explains that, subsequently, critical theorists such as Marcuse, as well as later thinkers such as Habermas and Honneth, sought to address this political deficit within the *Dialectic of Enlightenment,* but goes on to say that 'Despite these attempts, the accusation of weak or non-existent politics persists until today' (Chambers 2004: 219). She explains further that,

> Critical theory was born in the conviction that social theory should embrace normative, and pursue moral ends. Thus for every evaluation of an 'is', critical theory suggests an 'ought'. What critical theory has not always been good at is suggesting how we get from the 'is' to the 'ought'.
>
> *(Chambers 2004: 219–20)*

Chambers goes on to suggest that critical theory set itself an immensely complex task of using the 'interconnectedness of knowledge and experience to break out of the given and project normative goals and ends', a process which she says has been 'stymied' by critical theory's own analysis of the contradictions of modernity (2004: 221). She explicates the paradox within critical theory in which, through the negative dialectic, critique is generated that provides new understandings of the object (in the case of the climate change HESD research programme referred to above one could develop new critiques of the cause of climate change, for example). This understanding is meant to open up the possibility for real change, but that change is 'again only articulated in the negative' (Chambers 2004: 222). As such, 'Critical theory does not propose positive programmes for change' (Chambers 2004: 222). Chambers suggests that it is a reliance on negative dialectics that has undermined the possibility of a path towards a positive programme of change as 'All action *in* the world is immediately contaminated *by* the world' (2004: 222). Marcuse (1964) in his *One Dimensional Man,* offered a somewhat pessimistic perspective on this, suggesting that all that was possible was participation in the negative analysis and 'personal moral rectitude of the Great Refusal' (Chambers 2004: 224). Chambers goes on to say that Marcuse's idea of transformation entailed only an unimaginable but hoped for 'rupture' with the present, and that this would set 'agents of the revolution free from existing institutions' to bring about 'the rational society through untainted means' (2004: 224).

In discussing later generations of critical theory's ability to overcome the pessimism and lack of politics in the first generation of critical theory, Chambers (2004) suggests that Habermas saw his work as corrective to the immobility of first generation critical theory. Habermas re-envisioned emancipation as a process of identifying those forces within the Enlightenment that could be put into the service of emancipation and autonomy, hence his interest in the reform of democratic institutions and democratic practice. However, critiques of Habermasian politics (his procedurally centred approach to deliberative democracy) is that it is not radical enough, and that by placing consensus at the centre of his democratic vision, he effectively transcended or displaced politics (Chambers 2004). In HESD research programmes, one may potentially also naïvely make the mistake here of following the Habermasian trajectory of deliberative democracy which,

> involves taking the liberal state as it stands now in most western democracies and expanding the public sphere as to involve citizens to a greater degree in public opinion and will formation ... The idea is to take citizens out of the narrow competitive model of politics and place them in a deliberative politics where their opinions are formed in critical concert with others.
>
> *(Chambers 2004: 231)*

The assumption being that 'Not only do collective opinions epistemically benefit from rational debate, but citizens are also empowered through public sphere participation' (Chambers 2004: 231). However, as has been noted, these conditions include certain levels of equality and respect and make up the content of a well ordered public sphere which is not often present in southern African states (or elsewhere) as impacts of colonialism and persistent poverty or the excesses and structural inequalities inherent in neo-liberal market-based economics and associated patterns of thought and practice dominate most forms of public engagement, despite apparent commitments to democracy. Habermas is also critiqued for not giving adequate attention to social justice in his political theorising (Chambers 2004), and his assumption is that this will come about through a well ordered deliberative democracy. Chambers suggests that at the end of the day, Habermas' critical theory is hampered by the fact that he is a 'committed empirical proceduralist' (2004: 231).

More recent forms of critical theory seek to address this problem, and here democracy is not seen as being tied to the *demos,* but rather to strategies that can hold institutions, elites and governments accountable to the plurality of voices joined together by issues or causes rather than culture or history (Chambers 2004). This form of 'decentered democracy' involves recognition of the role of grassroots activists and forces that engage in global and local campaigns and change practices or engage in 'discursive harrying', as Chambers puts it (2004: 234). Mouffe's (2000) work on 'agonistic democracy' suggests that our aim should be to transform 'antagonism' into 'agonism', a process that forces us to keep the democratic constellation alive.

Honneth (1996) in his work on a 'politics of recognition', suggests that there is a need to develop our sense of self, self-worth and capability to engage in inter-subjective relations with others. For any critical theory HESD research programme, this would mean that the research programme should foreground identity formation, and develop capabilities to engage inter-subjectively with other players in sustainability or climate change relations (see Wiek *et al.* in this Handbook).

Honneths' insistence on engaging with violation of the body (e.g. through continued and expanding poverty and impacts of drought, heat stress etc.), denial of rights (e.g. rights to life, food, water, education, health – all of which will be exacerbated by climate change in southern Africa), and denigration of ways of life (climate change will fundamentally change the ways of life of southern African citizens) creates a strong agenda for HESD research inspired by critical theory. The IPCC (2014) projects extreme forms of distortion of ways of life from climate change, and this, drawing on Honneth's perspectives, could potentially rise to prominence in our HESD research. Chambers says that Honneth's critical theory suggests that 'personal integrity (wholeness) and undamaged development are essential for leading the emancipated life' (2004: 238). However, she suggests that while Honneth's work raises important dynamics of a potential programme of action, like other critical theorists, his programme offers 'vague' insights for political action. He still fails to adequately answer the question 'what is to be done'? (Chambers 2004: 238).

Linking with Honneth's (1996; 2004) work in third generation critical theory is the work of Benhabib (2002), who suggests that struggle, contestation, contingency and partiality characterise all situations, decisions and rulings. However, she does not adopt a relativist stance, and suggests instead that is it possible to criticise decisions and rulings if people affected are not given a chance to speak and have their claims and objectives heard (Chambers 2004). Benhabib rejects Habermas's view that moral laws can be articulated in terms of dialogue amongst 'generalised others'. She sees this as a disembedded and disembodied view (Canaday 2003). Benhabib envisions moral selves who are both 'generalized others', and 'concrete others' (Benhabib 1992: 169). Canaday (2003: 50) suggests that in doing this, Benhabib 'attempts to resuscitate universalism, making it responsive to difference and contextualism' not unlike other feminist critical researchers such as Nancy Fraser (1995), and critical realists who describe the 'concrete universal' (Hartwig 2007). Benhabib therefore offers a more concrete way of theorising emancipation through enhancing practical approaches to democratic procedures, conditions and institutional reforms. However, despite these advances in critical theory, Chambers suggests that third generation critical theory is 'in the same bind as the first generation and second generation critical theory … In giving up vanguardism for democracy, critical theory will always be limited by democratic will' (Chambers 2004: 243).

Perhaps it is this democratic paradox that ultimately needs to become a focus of critical HESD research. Allowing the ultimate democratic paradox of democratic failure to exist is perhaps the most substantive research question to engage with when we consider critical HESD research programmes.

Rancière (2006) notes that this paradoxical failure is happening in all of our societies where we have the perverse effect of allowing democracies that are in effect forms of oligarchy to exist, and that this brazenly creates unchecked climate change, 'the spread of democracy' through war mongering, and governance through fear of terror and immigrants. It also pushes up the Gini coefficient, practices massive exploitation of resources and leaves children and future generations to face the consequences of climate change, ongoing environmental degradation and social injustice. Texts such as the *Millennium Ecosystem Assessment* (UN 2000), Bauman's *Wasted Lives* (Bauman 2004) and Ferguson's (2006) text on Africa describing illegal and immoral forms of multinational hopping, land grabbing and 'sustainable development', all describe the current democratic paradox, as do the findings of the IPCC (2014), albeit not in so many words. For academics seeking to develop a critical theory research agenda for HESD in southern Africa or elsewhere, this may well be an appropriate place to start thinking, i.e. to start with a re-interpretation of sustainable development issues as representing a failure of democracies the world over.

As we have seen across three generations of EE/HESD research that draws on critical theory, it is possible to have critical forms of educational research that do not challenge us to be 'too critical' and that fail to lead to real transformation. While I too have been involved in these types of critical theory inspired HESD research projects (from early on in the 1990s until recently as explained above), it is sobering to think that these forms of critical theory inspired research may well be inadequate for the challenges of our times. We may need to turn anew to the question of 'What is to be done?'

HESD research as democratic acts based on egalitarian relations and dialectical 'pulses of freedom'

Price, in her environmental education research, expresses a frustration with positivist and post-modern methodologies alike, as they fail to provide a means of theorising action (Price 2007; 2012/2013). Instead, she turns, not to traditional critical theory in its various generations, but to Critical Realism, that via Bhaskar's (2008) theorising of critical naturalism develops a possibility for action that is ontologically realist, yet epistemologically relativist. It also allows for judgemental rationality and a differentiating between transitive and intransitive realities (Sayer 2000).

Rancière (2006) in the conclusions of his book on *Hatred of Democracy* also suggests another form of engagement. He suggests we should carefully and clearly identify those structural factors that promote a 'hatred of' or disfiguring of democracy, and that we should reclaim democracy and 'rediscover the singular power that is specific to it' (2006: 96). Democracy, he says, 'is neither a form of government that allows oligarchies to rule in the name of the people, nor is it a form of society that governs the power of commodities' (2006: 96). Democracy, Rancière says, is '*the action* that constantly wrests the monopoly of public life from oligarchic governments, and the omnipotence over lives from the power of wealth' (2006: 96; my emphasis). Rancière also states that there should be no paradox, but a 're-discovery of the singularity of democracy', and *'an awareness of its solitude'* (2006: 96; my emphasis). He further states that 'Unequal society does not carry any equal society in its womb. Rather, egalitarian society is only ever the set of egalitarian relations that are traced here and now *through singular and precarious acts* (2006: 96; my emphasis). Democracy, and we could argue sustainability, social justice and climate resilient development, is entrusted to 'the constancy of its specific acts' (Rancière 2006: 96–7). Žižek goes further to suggest that such democratic acts ought to be disruptive or brave acts. They should allow disruption for 'the refusal to risk a gesture of disruption is the surest bulwark against change'. (Johnston 2008: 116)

From this we could suggest that we should risk radical breaks in and through our HESD research and practice, in other words, embrace a more activist stance, one that is oriented towards transformative praxis. Reading from the above, we could also ask how HESD research processes can be constituted as singular and precarious acts of democracy based on egalitarian relations that can embrace disruption and 'risk breaks' from the present, past and future projections? And what methodological guidance might we find for this kind of critically inspired HESD research?

Bhaskar's (1998) work on an onto-axiological dialectic (not an epistemological (rational) dialectic as per Hegel's dialectical legacy which shaped the 'Dialectic of Enlightenment' referred to above) provides some social methodological guidance for emancipatory practice as argued for by Rancière (2006). Bhaskar (1998) suggests the 'absenting of absences', i.e. the planned and structured removal of absences and 'ills' or constraints on freedom to flourish in diverse contexts.[6] This can emerge through forms of social critique that take history, structural factors, judgmental rationality, and emancipatory possibility into account, *and* through participation in ongoing practices that continue the mobilisation of agency for transformative praxis in what Bhaskar describes as an onto-axiological chain of 'being and becoming' constituted in tensed socio-temporal time-space configurations. Unlike Marcuse (1964), who suggested that people could not act, and second and third generation critical theorists who suggested that we need to rationalise possibilities for action in more or less deliberative or agonistic ways, Bhaskar (1998) suggests that people need to be involved in action to act. As Bhaskar states, when we act, we absent, and it is what we absent and why that is at issue. Furthermore, unlike in first generation critical theory, there is a need to act now, we are always implicated in action. For a critical HESD research agenda we may then ask 'what action, what constraints on our freedom can be absented by our actions, and why is our action necessary'? In engaging such a critical research framework in HESD research, we will still need to engage in structural critique; we will still need to deliberate and debate emancipatory possibilities; we will still need ethical engagement to show care for the kind of society that we are acting in; *however* we also need to be involved in creating transformative relational movements that emerge in and from actions and acting in the world.

This approach to critical HESD research differs from social and educational processes that involve 'realising a false consciousness' or 'agreeing to disagree' or 'deliberating alternatives' or 'critiquing social structures' (it may include all such social methodologies of earlier critical, democratic forms of pedagogy, but it is more than this). Ethics and an understanding of well-being or the flourishing of all, and social methodologies that foster participation remain at the core, as does an ongoing commitment to the transboundary notions of freedom, sustainability, solidarity and democracy. According to Norrie (2010: 241), 'Judgment as a human act always retains an irreducible element of choice, but it is nonetheless grounded in a naturally and socially developed conception of freedom'. He suggests further, however, that our conceptions of freedom operate 'alongside a socio-historical critique of how freedom is actualized under different sets of social relations' (ibid.). People have the capability to make judgements and to act. It is how this is oriented, validated and supported in and through generative forms of HESD research (as well as other societal processes) that is at issue here.

Bhaskar (2008) encourages us, in and through our research efforts, to create examples of how our HESD research and teaching work can contribute to what he calls 'pulses of freedom' that contribute to human and non-human flourishing, and how these may open up participation in transformative sustainability and social-justice-oriented praxis. The phrase 'pulses of freedom' has a commitment to situated, action oriented transformational processes that addresses the question 'what is to be done'. As Bhaskar says:

> Degrees of freedom consist of agentive freedom, formal legal freedom, negative freedom from, positive freedom to, emancipation from specific constraints, autonomy, rational autonomy, universal human autonomy, well being, flourishing, progressively dependent on the positive generalization of the concept of freedom to include needs and possibilities for development as rights.
>
> *(Bhaskar 2008: 398)*

Norrie's (2010) discussion of Bhaskar's work on solidarity and freedom reminds us that Bhaskar's work encompasses a dialectical relationship between abstract, ideal ethics (freedom and solidarity) and a situated, structurally grounded, historically embedded conception of realist dialectics. Norrie (2010) explains that these fit together within Bhaskar's view of eudamonia, which is based on a view that 'the free flourishing of each is the condition of the free flourishing of all' (Bhaskar 2008: 98). This is a dialectical, relational notion of freedom and solidarity – where the freedom of each must always be related to the freedom of all. Bhaskar's critical theory includes 'a Kantian moment of freedom alongside a substantive ethics of human flourishing', co-articulated with 'a constellated, structural and historical account of their emergence' (Norrie 2010: 124). In my view, this potentially offers us a 'fourth generation' of critical theory that is rooted in transformative praxis acts, where 'what is to be done' is the central question to focus on, not in a superficial manner, but informed by the many lessons of earlier generations of critical theory.

Conclusion

This chapter has considered the influence of three generations of critical theory on HESD research. It has outlined the origins of critical theory research, and core tenets of the different generations of critical theory research. It has considered how these have been applied in EE/HESD research through accounts of such HESD research praxis in southern Africa, where I, together with other colleagues have been involved in reflexive critical theory research for the past 20 or more years. The chapter has shown that in each generation of critical theory, questions have come to the fore that have shaped subsequent generations of critical theory research, and that all of these have implications for how we might work with critical theory in HESD research today.

The final section of the chapter argues for a more situated, action-oriented and generative form of critical HESD research in the face of increasingly complex and intractable sustainability issues – climate change being one that we have also recently engaged with in our HESD research – as outlined above. The sustainability challenges of our time, persistent poverty and climate change included (including their nexus), indicates the need for massive social transformation, and points to the need for carefully constituted forms of critical HESD research. *How* we might tackle the sustainability concerns of our times via our HESD research drawing on the historical and conceptual tools provided by various generations of critical theory has been the subject of this chapter.

Notes

1 Note that in the early 1990s ESD discourse had not risen to power. However, in southern Africa we used EE in very similar ways to the way in which mainstream ESD researchers work as our interest was at the intersection of environment-development-economy and social justice and societal transformation following years of apartheid in social-ecological injustice (Lotz 1995). I use EE/ESD or EE/HESD to signal both the time period, and the relational way in which we have worked with EE and ESD concepts in our research programme over time.

2 Perhaps noteworthy here is that action research approaches are seeing a revival under the banner of transdisciplinary research approaches which are newly emergent HESD research approaches (Hirsch Hadorn *et al.* 2008).

3 With the *for* being seen as a commitment to critical and action-oriented approaches to environment and sustainability education.

4 This development was not uncontested (see for example Jickling 1992).

5 This critique of uncritical assumptions of empowering 'others' has been raised in the development literature, where at times an uncritical allegiance to participatory approaches have become a 'tyranny',

or a new form of social engineering (O'Donoghue 1994; Rahnema 1992; Cooke and Kothari 2001).

6 Note that I am not using freedom here in the same sense as it is used in neo-liberal economics. I am using it here in the sense as it is used by Bhaskar (1998) when he suggests that the freedom of one is closely related to the freedom of all (he couples freedom with solidarity and truth).

References

Apple, M.W., ed., 1982. *Cultural and Economic Reproduction in Education: Essays on Class, Ideology and the State*. London: Routledge and Kegan Paul.

Bauman, Z., 2004. *Wasted Lives: Modernity and its Outcasts.* Cambridge: Polity.

Benhabib, S., 1992. *Situating the Self: Gender, Community and Postmodernism in Contemporary Ethics* New York: Routledge.

Benhabib, S., 2002. *Claims of Culture: Equality and Diversity in the Global Culture,* Princeton, NJ: Princeton University Press.

Bhaskar, R., 2008. *Dialectic: The Pulse of Freedom,* 2nd edn. Abingdon: Routledge.

Bond, P., 2006. *Looting Africa: The Economics of Exploitation*. Pietermaritzburg: University of Kwazulu Natal Press.

Canaday, M., 2003. 'Promising Alliances: The Critical Feminist Theory of Nancy Fraser and Seyla Behabib', *Feminist Review*, 74, 50–69.

Chambers, S., 2004. 'The Politics of Critical Theory', in Rush, F. (ed.), *The Cambridge Companion to Critical Theory.* Cambridge: Cambridge University Press, 219–47.

Cooke, B. and Kothari, U., 2001. *Participation: The New Tyranny.* London: Zed books.

Elliot, J., 1991. *Action Research for Educational Change.* Milton Keynes: Open University Press.

Ellsworth, E., 1989. 'Why Doesn't this Feel Empowering? Working through the Repressive Myth of Critical Pedagogy', *Harvard Educational Review*, 59(3), 297–324.

Ferguson, J., 2006. *Global Shadows. Africa in the Neo-liberal World Order.* Durham, NC and London: Duke University Press.

Fien, J., 1993. *Education for the Environment. Critical Curriculum Theorizing and Environmental Education.* Geelong, Victoria: Deakin University Press.

Fraser, N., 1995. 'What's Critical about Critical Theory?', in Meehan, J. (ed.), *Feminists read Habermas: Gendering the Subject of Discourse.* London: Routledge, 21–55.

Giroux, H., 1988. *Schooling for Democracy: Critical Pedagogy in the Modern Age.* London: Routledge and Kegan Paul.

Graber, D., 2013. *The Democracy Project: A History. A Crisis. A Movement.* London: Penguin.

Habermas, J., 1972. *Knowledge and Human Interests.* London: Heinemann.

Habermas, J., 1984. *The Theory of Communicative Action, Vol 1: Reason and the Rationalisation of Society.* Boston, MA: Beacon.

Habermas, J., 1987. *The Theory of Communicative Action, Vol. 2: Lifeworld and System: A Critique of Functionalist Reason.* Boston, MA: Beacon.

Hartwig, M., 2007. *Dictionary of Critical Realism.* Routledge: New York.

Held, D., 1980. *Introduction to Critical Theory: Horkeimer to Habermas.* California: University of California Press.

Hirsch Hadorn, G.H., Hoffmann-Riem, H., Biber-Klemm, S., Grossenbacher-Mansuy, W., Joye, D., Pohl, C., Wiesmann, U. and Zemp, E., eds., 2008. *Handbook of Transdisciplinary Research.* Dordrecht: Springer.

Honneth, A., 1996. *The Struggle for Recognition: The Moral Grammar of Social Conflicts.* Cambridge, MA: MIT Press.

Honneth, A., 2004. 'A Social Pathology of Reason: On the Intellectual Legacy of Critical Theory', in Rush, F. (ed.), *The Cambridge Companion to Critical Theory.* Cambridge: Cambridge University Press, 336–60.

Horkeimer, M., 1975. *Critical Theory.* New York: Continuum.

Huckle, J., 1993. 'Environmental Education and Sustainability: A View from Critical Theory', in Fien, J. and Trainer, T. (eds), *Environmental Education: A Pathway to Sustainability.* Geelong, Victoria: Deakin University Press, 43–68.

Intergovernmental Panel on Climate Change (IPCC), 2014. *Climate Change 2014: Impacts, Adaptation, and Vulnerability. Part A: Global and Sectoral Aspects. Working Group II Contribution to the Fifth Assessment Report of the Intergovernmental Panel on Climate Change.* Cambridge: Cambridge University Press.

Jickling, B., 1992. 'Why I Don't Want my Children to be Educated for Sustainable Development', *Journal*

of Environmental Education, 23(4), 5–8.
Johnston, A., 2008. *Žižek's Ontology: A Transcendental Materialist Theory of Tubjectivity.* Evanston, IL: Northwestern University Press.
Kemmis, S., Cole, P. and Suggett, D., 1983. *Orientations to Curriculum and Transition: Towards the Socially Critical.* Melbourne: Victorian Institute of Secondary Education.
Lather, P., 1991. *Getting Smart. Feminist Research and Pedagogy within the Post-modern.* New York: Routledge.
Lather, P., 1995. 'Post-critical Pedagogies: A Feminist Reading', in McLaren, P. (ed.), *Postmodernism, Post-colonialism and Pedagogy.* Albert Park, Australia: James Nicholas Publishers, 167–86.
Lotz, H.B., 1995. 'The Development of Environmental Education Resource Materials for Junior Primary Education through Teacher Participation: The Case of the We Care Primary Project'. Unpublished D.Ed thesis, University of Stellenbosch, South Africa.
McCarthy, T. 1981. *The Critical Theory of Jurgen Habermas.* Cambridge, MA: The MIT Press.
Marcuse, H., 1964. *One Dimensional Man.* Boston, MA: Beacon Press.
Mouffe, C., 2000. *The Democratic Paradox.* London: Verso.
Mrazek, R., ed., 1993. *Alternative Paradigms in Environmental Education Research.* Ohio: NAAEE.
Norrie. A., 2010. *Dialectic and Difference. Dialectical Critical Realism and the Grounds of Justice.* London: Routledge.
O'Donoghue, R., 1990. 'An Action Research Case Study of the Action Ecology Project, 1984–1990'. Unpublished M.Ed thesis, University of Natal, Pietermaritzburg.
O'Donoghue, R., 1994. *Free-wheeling Figurations: A Report on a Conference and Research Trip to Europe.* Pietermaritzburg: Natal Parks Board.
Pikkety, T., 2013. *Capital in the Twenty First Century.* Harvard, MA: Harvard University Press.
Posch, P., 1991. *Environment and School Initiatives: Background and Basic Premises of the Project.* Paris: OECD.
Poster, M. 1989. *Critical Theory and Poststructuralism: In Search of a Context.* New York: Cornell University Press.
Price, L., 2007. *A Transdisciplinary Explanatory Critique of Environmental Education.* Unpublished Doctoral dissertation, Rhodes University, South Africa.
Price, L., 2012/2013. 'Think Piece. Naked Science: Avoiding Methodolatry in an Environmental Education Context', *Southern African Journal of Environmental Education*, 29, 10–24.
Rahnema, M., 1992. 'Participation', in Sachs, W. (ed.), *The Development Dictionary. A Guide to Knowledge and Power.* London: Zed Books, 116–31.
Rancière, J., 2006. *Hatred of Democracy.* London: Verso Books.
Robottom, I., 1987. *Environmental Education: Practice and Possibility.* Geelong, Victoria: Deakin University Press.
Robottom, I., 1991. 'Technocratic Environmental Education: A Critique and some Alternatives', *Journal of Experiential Education*, 14(1), 20–6.
Robottom, I. and Hart, P., 1993. *Research in Environmental Education.* Geelong: Deakin University Press.
Rush, F., 2004, 'Conceptual Foundations of Early Critical Theory', in Rush, F. (ed.), *The Cambridge Companion to Critical Theory.* Cambridge: Cambridge University Press, 6–39.
Sayer, A., 2000. *Realism and Social Science.* London: SAGE.
Stapp, W. and Wals, A.E.J., 1993. 'An Action Research Approach to Environmental Problem-solving', in Fien, J. and Spork, H. (eds), *Trends and Issues in Environmental Education: Study Guide and Reader.* Victoria, Geelong: Deakin University Press, 170–9.
Stevenson, R., Brody, M., Dillon, J. and Wals, A., eds., 2013. *International Handbook of Research on Environmental Education.* New York: AERA/Routledge.
UNESCO (2014). *Shaping the Future we Want.* UN Decade of Education for Sustainable Development (2005–2014). Final report. Paris: UNESCO.
United Nations (UN), 2000. *Millennium Ecosystem Assessment.* www.millenniumassessment.org/documents/document.356.aspx.pdf [accessed 8 August 2014].
Urquhart, P., Lotz-Sisitka, H.B., Kruger, B. and Naudé, J., 2014. *SARUA Climate Change Counts Mapping Study, Vol. 1 Knowledge Co-production Framework.* Johannesburg: SARUA.
Wals, A.E.J., 2007. *Social Learning: Towards a Sustainable World.* Wageningen: Wageningen Academic Press.

15

EVALUATION AND EDUCATION FOR SUSTAINABLE DEVELOPMENT

Navigating a shifting landscape in regional centres of expertise

Rob O'Donoghue

Deriving a perspective on evaluation

The expert-mediated evaluation of change and impact found in the education literature was primarily framed in the structural functionalist conventions of modernity that emerged within education as an emancipatory process of mediated social control in the education project of the twentieth century (Popkewitz 2008). Evaluation in Education is characterised by tensions across empirical analytical, constructivist and socially critical perspectives that have been hotly contested over the years. The emergence of Critical Realism after Bhaskar (2008 [1978]) has latterly come to provide some useful tools for resolving much of the ambivalence in the social sciences of the 1980s and 1990s when appreciative enquiry (Cooperrider and Srivastva 1987) and developmental evaluation (Patton 1994) began to emerge and were applied in the evaluation of schooling, community and development projects. Drawing on the Critical Realism oeuvre, the works of Pawson and Tilley (1997) are notable for signalling the advent of a realist turn in evaluation research that brought some order to a diverse and contested landscape at the close of the twentieth century.

Within these emergent trajectories of expansion and realignment, evaluation has primarily remained the realm of experts who are commonly contracted to mediate the steering and summative evidence demanded by the structural functionalist conventions of state and international environment and sustainability institutions. Quinn Patton vividly illustrates the expert position of the evaluator and the balancing act between working with participants and undertaking assessments for funding agencies by noting:

> Indeed, in my own work, I prefer to facilitate the generation of recommendations by my clients and primary users. I rarely formulate independent recommendations. However, in the developmental evaluation process, part of my value to a design team is that I bring a reservoir of knowledge (based on 25 years of practice) about what kinds of things tend to work and where to anticipate problems.
>
> *(Patton 1994: 316)*

The evaluation of Education for Sustainable Development (ESD) has, more recently, been one of the expert-mediated and contested terrains, particularly as mid-decade reporting emerged and as the United Nations Decade of Education for Sustainable Development (UNDESD) was coming to a close. Here the tension has been between the participatory imperatives for ESD in civil society movements like Regional Centres of Expertise (RCEs) and the institutional need for evidence of tangible change desired by international convention networks. Within this arena, and following earlier work on evaluation with the Australian Research Institute for Environment and Sustainability (ARIES), Tilbury (2007) produced one of the early framings for the evaluation of education for sustainability and has played a coordinating role in much of the United Nations Economic Commission for Europe (UNECE 2011) framing of evaluation work to review the DESD.

In a time of fascination with the competence framing of education processes, some notable work was undertaken to develop concepts and competence specifications (de Haan 2010; Wiek *et al.* 2011) to constitute ESD as a measured and measurable processes of learner-led, reflexive, social learning and change. This work served not only to more firmly frame the field but did so in ways that might make curricula more coherent and learning/change more readily assessed. It is thus no surprise that UNECE published *Learning for the Future: Competencies in Education for Sustainable Development* by 2011 as the imperatives to evaluate the effectiveness of the UNDESD began to emerge.

A review of competence perspectives must remain beyond the scope of this chapter but it is important to note that inscriptions of competence and implicit theories of change here became infused into ESD curriculum discourses and the practices and perspectives of social movements amidst imperatives to undertake some form of evaluation of activities and impacts in the reviews of the UNDESD. The processes examined here are primarily centred on some of the challenges in the evaluation of RCEs and co-engaged ESD activities where measures of change had long been established as the gold standard.

Measuring change entrenched as the 'gold standard' in programme assessment

From early on, expanding Education for Sustainability initiatives (EE and ESD) sought reliable measures of change. These measures were the 'gold standard' or the 'holy grail' (Moore 2012) for assessing impact as behaviour change. Measuring values/attitudes and behaviour were combined in the concept of pro-environmental behaviour as a trustworthy approach for the assessment of change brought about by education as a process centred on the production of new environmental behaviour (Hungerford and Volk 1990). The shift to more participatory approaches and a socially critical trajectory in the 1990s led to behavioural measures becoming less prominent (O'Donoghue 2014). Courtenay-Hall and Rogers (2002) note fundamental tensions between a 'behaviour modelling' commitment to measuring impact as evidence of behavioural change, and participatory approaches that commit to stakeholder engagement in learner-led change practices. Towards the close of the UNDESD, the resolution of this contradiction in favour of the latter (participation) shaped a shift from an emphasis on measures of behaviour change to environmental literacy (Hollweg *et al.* 2011), with the measurement of change remaining an often, elusive ideal.

Today there is a proliferation of measures ranging from institutions that survey behavioural patterns in their target communities (see, for example Department for Environment Food and Rural Affairs 2008 and Moore 2012), to rapidly expanding batteries of tests for environmental knowledge/literacy (Hollweg *et al.* 2011) along with diverse contexts where consultant groups produce measurement instruments (metrics[1]) for the assessment of specified attributes (competences) and impact. Evaluative measures of environmental literacy and indicators of competence and change are now found in global-level metrics for initiating, tracking, steering and evaluating education programmes directed at enabling global citizenship for a sustainable future (O'Donoghue 2014b).

Education to foster the literacy and competences necessary to bring about a necessary re-orientation in a changing world and the search for evidence-based assessment of change has continued to be a challenge in RCEs as an expanding field of multiple stakeholder engagement in the escalating global risk to future sustainability. Here, measures of behaviour change and proxy measures that reflect the attributes for the necessary change-orientated dispositions (competences) remain a key concern in most large-scale, survey instruments that have an evaluative dimension (UNESCO 2013a, 2014a). When these programme and evaluation processes are read with care, it is apparent that education processes and assessment are seldom meshed with sufficient coherence. There has thus always been a search for refinements for the more effective and reliable evaluation of programmes and the assessment of change. In the latter part of the UNDESD, where calls for evidence-based assessment became pressing, the production and measurement of change included:

- contouring the necessary attributes (competences) for change to a more sustainable world;
- literacy (knowledge-led agency) in relation to sustainability concerns; and
- social learning practices to bring about the desired change (sustainable development).

Here the expert mediation of metrics to generate reliable evidence of change and established conventions for expert-mediated evaluation are developing into global-scale collaborative process in systems design evaluation (UNESCO 2014a). This is particularly evident in the criterion-referenced framing of initiatives in Global Citizenship Education (UNESCO 2013a) where there is a notable shift to own-assessment as expert in context but within the earlier established cultural conventions of measured changes in practices/behaviour. These developments have brought new challenges to higher education research and evaluation practices conceptualising and appraisal of ESD.

ESD as evaluation that needs reflexive evaluation and expected to produce value

Without a clear grasp of ESD as a critical process of evaluative enquiry and learning-to-change in relation to unsustainable patterns of human conduct, to propose that an appraisal of an ESD initiative as 'an evaluation of an evaluation' suggests tautology. However, praxiological enquiry as an evaluation process is at the heart of ESD as a process undertaken as a deliberative process with the intention of reimaging more sustainable ways of doing things. Here the educative processes of evaluative enquiry are centred on ESD as a review of human conduct and its effects. Processes of learning and change such as this are dialectical in character (deliberative across differences) and are centred on exploratory processes of learning-to-change (reflexivity). For an appraisal of evaluative learning such as this, an emerging culture of evaluation in RCE contexts came to be conceptualised and approached as three intermeshed processes:

- Evaluation as an implicit ESD process (praxiological enquiry)
- Evaluation in ESD processes of co-engaged learning (strategic enquiry)
- Evaluation of ESD as a process with more sustainable outcomes (emerging outputs and impacts).

The evaluation of ESD would commonly be directed at outputs and impacts so differentiating and enacting these intermeshed dimensions of evaluation as, in and of ESD necessitated an expansion of earlier more expert mediated framings of evaluation practice. The expansion developed over an extended period of deliberative work on evaluation in the multi-stakeholder contexts of many RCEs.

Clarifying a cultural context for evaluation in RCEs

A relatively undifferentiated collaborative and participatory framing of evaluation in RCEs was prevalent at mid UN Decade, and pressure for more measured assessments of impact and change escalated. As noted above, differences between what one might call participatory perspectives and more empirical/impact assessment approaches that sought tangible measures of change were not easily reconciled and it became clear that the necessary expertise in evaluation was not always to hand in RCE contexts. The ARIES (2007) handbook on evaluating Education for Sustainability in local government contexts presented evaluation as a review of a programme where:

> As part of the planning or review of your programme you will have identified **the needs of your participant groups.** Deciding **whether you have met these needs** has to be part of your evaluation. You will also **have identified clear objectives**. Part of the process of setting objectives is to agree desired outcomes (including **learning outcomes) that will be measurable** to varying degrees. These will help define what you are trying to achieve and **the information you need to collect to measure what has actually been achieved**.
>
> *(My bold to accentuate the expert-mediated educational conventions of the time: ARIES 2007: 147)*

Here, an expert disposition is clearly evident along with the prevailing structural functionalist and behaviourist education research conventions of the time. In response to the framing of evaluation in this way, the United Nations University – Institute for Advanced Studies (UNU-IAS) initiated a deliberative process and a concept paper to decode much of the complexity was developed out of the Tongyoeng Global RCE Conference in 2011. A consultative process followed in The Netherlands where a working group on evaluation was constituted. The process emerging here involved clarifying the constituting and practices of RCEs and trying to develop principles for the assessment of RCE processes and the impact of our diverse change practices. This work drew on some early evaluation that was undertaken by Geoff Scott in RCE Western Sidney and perspectives emerging in RCE Graz (Clemens Mader) and in the work of RCE European Advisor, Jos Hermans. This work was undertaken in a rapidly evolving field of diverse evaluation practices and is now being extended into the Global Action Plan (UNESCO 2013b).

Many other RCEs, including those in an emerging African regional network of RCEs coordinated through the SADC Regional Environmental Education Centre in Howick, participated in the deliberation on evaluation. This engagement became a testing ground for diverse approaches and a consensus-seeking process on perspectives for suitable evaluation practices in RCEs. For example, one of the early propositions was that of establishing a baseline from/against which an evaluation could be conducted. Other perspectives were centred on the importance of collaborative review so that all interest groups in an RCE were included in an evaluation process. The latter received positive responses that exemplified participatory approaches and appreciative enquiry emerged as an important constituent of evaluation in RCEs as collaborative civil society initiatives. Alongside this, a clarifying of the strategic purpose of RCEs emerged as a priority and it was noted that some tangible baseline data, appreciative records and a strategic assessment would lend themselves to some sort of meta-analysis of RCEs that would be necessary for reporting the outcomes and impact of the global network of Regional Centres of Expertise in ESD.

The UNU-IAS working document became a reference point for the development of an evaluation process by southern African RCEs following the preliminary evaluation processes that were undertaken in Goa, and in other contexts in India in early 2013 (UNU-IAS 2013).

Towards a situated framework for evaluating RCEs

With the RCEs in the region having emerged at differing times within the UN DESD and with them taking many forms (some being centred on cities whilst others having a regional or small country character), the idea of a baseline for an evaluation process became a concern for the development of contextual profiling data. Contextual profiling had emerged as a situating methodology for much of the environment and sustainability research in the SADC region along with the need for a grasp of the way in which each RCE had been constituted. 'Constitutive evaluation' thus became an opening deliberation in an evaluation framework that was to be developed for site-based collaborative evaluation across the RCEs of the region. Drawing on the earlier evaluation work done in Goa, this opening move was then broken down into a framing of an RCE as:

- *A platform for dialogue* on concerns and practices among RCE stakeholders.
- *A local resource base* to support ESD work.
- *A networking structure for enabling ESD* in local school and community initiatives.

This allowed each RCE to begin an appreciative review of how the collaboration had been constituted in a particular context but did not provide an adequate model of process for evaluative data generation that resonated with the evaluation literature. An associated problem was that much of the sophistication demanded by the professionalised evaluation literature in higher education research was not accessible to the constituency wanting to undertake evaluation initiatives as RCEs. Evaluation work was thus most commonly mediated by a university academic or by an expanding network of experts who held sway over the conventions demanded for evaluation in the environment and sustainable development sector. Navigating these complexities was not an easy matter as the evaluation discourses were complex and contested, with tightly held conventions where each interest group had sought to package all of the elements necessary for undertaking an evaluation.

The emergence of a hybrid framework for evaluation in RCEs

Appreciative inquiry approaches to evaluation, after Cooperrider and Srivastva (1987), Coghlan *et al.* (2003) and Cooperrider *et al.* (2008), reflect the participatory and collaborative dimensions necessary for work in RCEs but are orientated towards common sense consensus within constructivist conventions. Deference to collective consensus around their 4D model and five guiding principles for a positive critical engagement process can often fall short of a demand for robust empirical data on impact or overlook the less positive side of things, for example.

Literature on what has been broadly termed developmental evaluation (Gamble 2008) emerged alongside much of this work to partially resolve some of these tensions but, in our reading, was less amenable to collaborative approaches and orientated towards expert mediation, particularly for processes of extended formative and summative review using a tool like the Panarchy Loop. This was developed by Holling for the evaluation of complex economic, ecological and social system contexts (Holling 2001) and for reviewing social innovation processes (Westley *et al.* 2007).

Appreciative and developmental approaches to evaluation are not dissimilar in many ways but each, like most framings of evaluative processes, demands allegiance to a set of inscribed perspectives and processes. Ignoring some of the peripheral inscriptions and working with the essences of the perspectives, we began to draw on both, the former for a positive, co-engaged roadmap and the latter for a more in-depth strategic review of emergent evidence and a probing of underlying 'theory of change' (Gamble 2008: 48; Blamey and Mackenzie 2007).

With evaluation practices becoming more diverse and variously informed, we elected to construct a hybrid start-up tool for framing co-engaged evaluation processes in RCEs. Figure 15.1 summarises the perspectives that we have drawn on to construct a framework tool for situating a positive, co-engaged and developmental evaluation framework that can enable participants to probe practices, to generate evidence of impact and also begin to assess value creation within the RCE network in the SADC Region. The remainder of this chapter reports an initial implementation of this open-ended evaluation start-up process that can be expanded and deepened by drawing on the constituent perspectives as evaluation capabilities emerge and are enhanced in capacity development initiatives.

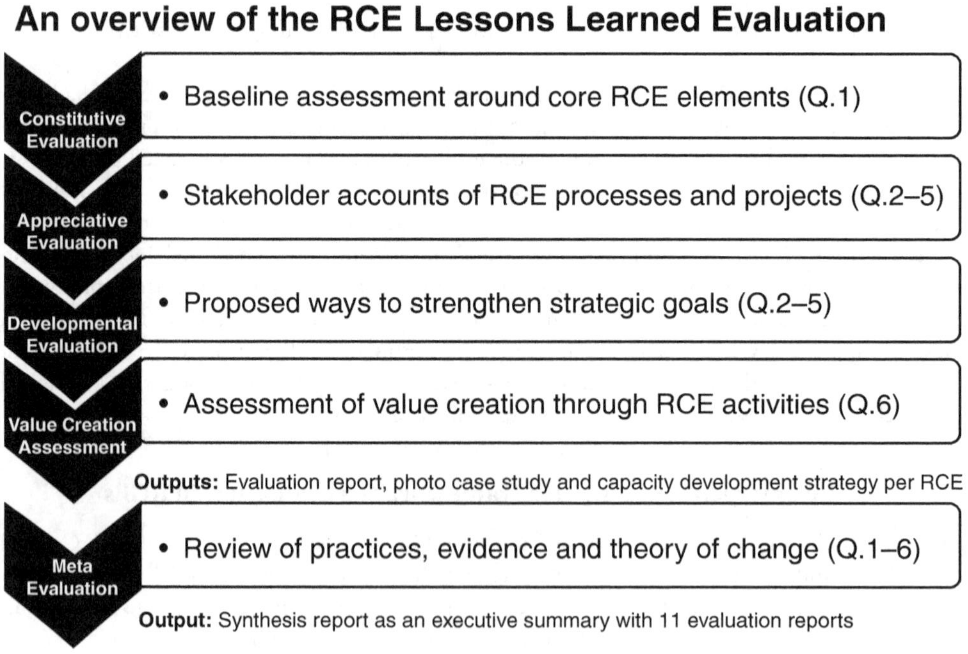

Figure 15.1 Overview of the evaluation tool kit developed for SADC RCEs

The evaluation process started with the development of an evaluation toolkit as a hybrid instrument that, as outlined above, draws on a range of evaluation traditions that can be adapted to differing needs and contexts. These include: Constitutive, Appreciative and Developmental Evaluation, and Value Creation Assessment.

The start-up tool kit opens with a review of documentary evidence on how the RCE was constituted. It then develops as an unfolding review of 'The RCE Journey'. The opening development is an appreciative picture of how the RCE evolved and the six-stage process is guided by questions (see Appendix 15.1). This is designed to provide key reference points or a baseline around which the participants can probe the core elements of the emerging RCE activities and practices.

The evaluation is approached as a deliberative process of appreciative[2] inquiry with developmental evaluation dimensions designed to prompt expansion of successes related to:

1. How the RCE developed as an ESD coordination and networking structure
2. The activities undertaken and their effects
3. A review of initiatives producing transformations and enhanced sustainability
4. Strategic focus areas and the links established for these to be effective
5. Collaboration with and support from the RCE Global Service Centre
6. The assessment of value creation within the RCE and its activities

The focus areas and questions in the each of the stages are intended to loosely frame an evaluative concern to prompt appreciative conversations that generate evidence and developmental inferences that can be built on these.

The evaluation concludes with an open-ended assessment of value creation (Wenger *et al.* 2011), which describes how communities of practice produce value in their work cycles of activity. Value creation starts with a sense of something that is of immediate value that might be seen to have a wider potential for value creation. The aspiration to create value is then initiated through applied work that affirms and creates value, often producing change that is realised in context and can involve a positive reframing of what is of value and worth achieving. Looking back into the document record and the appreciative data of an RCE, it is possible to work with the evidence to undertake an assessment of value creation in the emerging story of the RCE as an active learning community producing value through the work that they have done and continue to do together.

The focus areas outlined above were used to produce a question framework for the toolkit (Questions 1–6) that scaffolds an appreciative review process to inform and to strengthen an RCE. The appreciative and developmental story of an RCE can be used in a meta-evaluation of emerging ESD activities and practices across regional RCEs. This wider picture of the practices, evidence of impact and theory of change will be useful for understanding and informing our continuing RCE work.

Case study of work with the hybrid evaluation framework in Makana RCE

The RCE Evaluation Toolkit was used over a three-day review workshop with 12 participants in the Makana RCE involved in education activities related to:

- water (Water for Dignity group),
- energy (St Mary's Development and Care Centre staff)
- waste and sanitation (Makana Youth group)

- cleaning and compost gardens (Inqaba Yegolide organisation).
- an education exhibit on water (Albany Museum education staff)

Used in a primarily discursive process of six stages of scaffolded questions, as outlined above, and with a field visit to develop case stories of situated practice, the workshop was seen as a preliminary evaluation around which other evaluation focus areas, instruments and strategies could be developed as increasing capacity in evaluation practice emerged.

Groups unable to attend the review process that was convened by Makana Municipality as the new host of the RCE secretariat were subsequently interviewed using the same framework tool (Cowie Catchment Campaign, Eco-Schools, Umthathi, Fundisa for Change, RU Green and Galela Amanzi). The interview process allowed these groups to reflect on the outcomes of the evaluation and to provide their input into the process. This was not ideal but was a necessary adaptive move that illustrated how the RCE is a 'moveable feast' of partners/activities that, as affiliates, have tended to move in and out of the RCE structure over the years. Here it was notable that social movements from poorer communities tend to be facilitated by more formal structures like Makana Municipality (Makana Youth and *Inqaba Yegolide*) and the Rhodes University Water Research Institute (Water for Dignity)

The Makana RCE was identified as a structure for collaboration where 'people meet and work together' or 'meet – talk – act' in a local context. The Water Research Institute is exploring 'a new paradigm of transdisciplinary research' that interfaces university researchers, civil society organisations and state service institutions. These approaches were noted with appreciation as they meant that local issues could be addressed. The following positive features were recorded:

- beginning to communicate through water forums and by forming cooperatives (Water for Dignity)
- supporting small gardens with composting and then seedlings (*Inqaba Yegolide*)
- hot bags being made and shared to save electricity costs (St Mary's DCC)
- stories of water and change-choice-practices are in the museum education programs (Albany Museum)
- sanitation practices are changing and problems are decreasing in Extension 6 and Extension 10 (Makana Youth)

1. Appreciative review of context, coordination and networking

The opening appreciative summaries emerging from the initial interest group discussions illustrate that the Makana RCE is a mix of university, NGO and municipal community-engaged projects that are independently active across civil society, youth and community service organisation structures. All are funding-dependent and most focus areas are reflected in the Local Environmental Action Plan (LEAP) that was a core focus in the constituting of the RCE. Project implementation has been small-scale but uneven, although there has been an Environmental Education (EE) and awareness strategy and there is now more provision for LEAP projects within the municipal Integrated Development Plan (IDP) with some funding having been allocated to projects by Makana Municipality and with the municipal counsellors having tried to establish and maintain a Makana Environmental Forum for collaboration and reporting on environmental problems and activities. This structure has become more of a complaints space than a project development structure. The coordination and networking has thus moved to many groups acting on their own and with the University Community

Engagement structure and other independent organisations initiating and managing projects outside and critical of the municipal services framework that is not operating effectively in most sectors.

After the opening appreciative conversation and a scoping of the coordination and networking processes in play, the appreciative exploration continued in relation to activities and their positive effects (appreciative) that could be built on to strengthen (developmental) what was being done and valued by the groups participating in the evaluation.

2. Review of activities and their effects

This review process was once again developed around the success stories but it probed the collaborative processes within which the learning and change emerged and then developed to examine possible up-scaling, mainstreaming and widening collaboration within the RCE and with other structure across the region.

Notable here were:

- Eco-school support – primarily gardening and curriculum initiatives.
- Waste communication – pilot projects at the household level.
- School water materials and exhibition at the museum.
- An emergency water proposal being advanced by civil society and the university Water Research Institute.
- The identification of training priorities – LEAP and IDP.
- Health and service data collection and reporting to the municipality.
- Hot bag distribution to save money and with follow-up to provide counselling and support to families suffering unemployment.

It was noted that working in and with small structures can be rewarding and effective but it was found to be difficult to scale-up activities to work effectively with big structures. This insight pointed to a gap where there was a need for the training of community facilitators. By chance, a training manual had recently been developed by the Environmental Science Department and the Community Engagement unit of the University was running its first course across town. This activity was discussed as an initiative that would strengthen the work of civil society initiatives. More community facilitators would strengthen work within small structures emerging in and in support of those suffering from environmental problems and training makes it possible for RCE initiatives to work better with the big structures of municipal governance and service delivery. Here it was notable that whereas many initiatives were being undertaken and having an effect, these could be strengthened by the RCE operating as a more formal structure supporting collaboration and community-engaged initiatives.

The next stage of the evaluation probed emerging 'flagship initiatives' in more depth to assess positive transformation and processes that are strengthening sustainability as a project impact.

3. Evidence of transformation and sustainability

It was at this stage that the evaluation participants went on a field trip to review flagship initiatives by developing picture narratives that would inform the evaluation process. The projects selected were:

- Health and service delivery data collection (WfD)

- Hot bag saving and family support services (DCC)
- The Umthathi SUS Garden (Makana Municipality)
- Youth Cleaning and Composting (Inqaba Yegolide)
- Waste awareness communicating (Makana Youth)
- Blue Planet Gallery water education exhibit (Albany Museum)

The objective was to scope the scale of knowledge and practice transformation and to examine how the mobilisation of resources and patterns of governance might be contributing to the successes being experienced by those involved. This was to be extended to the identification of barriers and how these might be overcome to sustain and strengthen the work being done.

The photo narrative approach was successful to a point, particularly for representing what was being done. This will need to be extended, with more time allowed, to probe for depth data and to source wider participant accounts that can be examined in relation to patterns of resource use and governance that are contributing to learning and change. These questions of practice and effectiveness were probed in more depth when strategic areas and linkages were reviewed the next day.

4. Strategic areas and linkages

Although it was noted that the 'RCE structures enable projects to link strategically on and around local issues' this was seldom realised and most projects worked independently, particularly community/civil society initiatives that tended to work directly with a particular university or municipal structure. The key outcome from the review was that 'the RCE should be formalised as a platform for key stakeholders to meet and engage around local environmental issues and initiatives'.

The key outcome of this focus was the deliberation of a strategy for capacity development training and to strengthen the RCE by establishing a platform for co-engaged ESD with the Makana Municipality structures and projects working on problem solving and change in the area.

Capacity development for community facilitators and decision-makers in the city hall was identified as the priority with partners working to:

- Get reliable data together on health and basic services.
- Develop pilot projects on key interventions that reduce risk, notably the idea of 'one street one tank' to ensure potable water when the system breaks down.
- Have water forum meetings where residents will have a voice and access change practices that have immediate and tangible benefits.
- Train museum, project staff and community facilitators to support co-engaged education initiatives.
- Expand communication and resourcing to the house-to-house engagement of youth in problem solving related to waste, water and sanitation.

5. RCE and global service centre

The university-based RCE structure has been little more than a forum and staging post for small-scale initiatives that have come and gone in cycles of activity and inactivity over the years. What was noted as necessary is core funding to maintain and manage the RCE as a platform for capacity development and collaboration. The RCE has also been too far removed from the municipal structures and has not had the capacity to mobilise and initiate anything more than small-scale pilot initiatives. These have been useful and have built some small-scale success stories that could now be scaled up to make an impact beyond the few participants involved. The RCE has, however been critical for supporting community-based initiatives that would not have emerged or not have been sustained without RCE training support. It will be important to strengthen both the training support and operate in ways that are more closely tied to and better aligned with the municipality.

Being recognised as an RCE initially produced some momentum in key areas but this has not been sustained or scaled-up sufficiently. Participation in regional conferences has enabled a sharing of ideas but a more strategic platform is needed to work up wider engagements and benefits. This evaluation report will be shared with other RCEs through the Global Service Centre and it will also be used to bring projects together under the municipality as the secretariat for the RCE as is the case in many other RCEs in the region.

6. Assessment of value creation

The focus here was on 'what value creation would not otherwise have happened if it was not for our initiatives'. This was not an easy matter to assess because many of the initiatives reviewed would probably have happened through university programs and community engagement initiatives or municipal project funding without an RCE that had been an open voluntary and informal structure over the years of the UN Decade of Education for Sustainable Development. However, many of the small-scale initiatives in co-engaged innovation would not have happened without the social learning commons project that was established within the RCE at the Environmental Learning Research Centre.

The most meaningful activities, of self-evident value to participants in the evaluation process, were:

- The collection and sharing of data on health issues and water problems.
- A realisation that Makana Municipality had many problems to deal with.
- That the RCE was providing a platform in which small-scale community-based projects could emerge and flourish.
- The use of hot bags had high value for the electricity savings that they bring.
- There is a potential value in collaborative work but this is not yet being realised as projects tend to work independently.
- The evaluation process gave participants support to begin to think systematically about their activities.

The output could be more fully developed as value creation case stories (Rivers 2014) and these could be developed from the photo narratives generated on the field trip. Here it was felt that flagship projects, for example, could be drawn together with the support of some capacity development training within the RCE.

Overall, the review of value creation was somewhat surface and centred on what participants were getting out of the evaluation exercise. This was said to help 'getting around mental road blocks by working from what is appreciated and practically available'.

Finally the outcomes were all drawn together into a vision for the RCE, a shared image of tangible value in relation to the context and priorities for capacity development and training. These are summarised in the evaluation record images and associated summaries below:

Strategic Platform

An affirming perspective on the RCE as a civil society platform enabling diverse structures for and processes of co-engaged learning and change in Makana

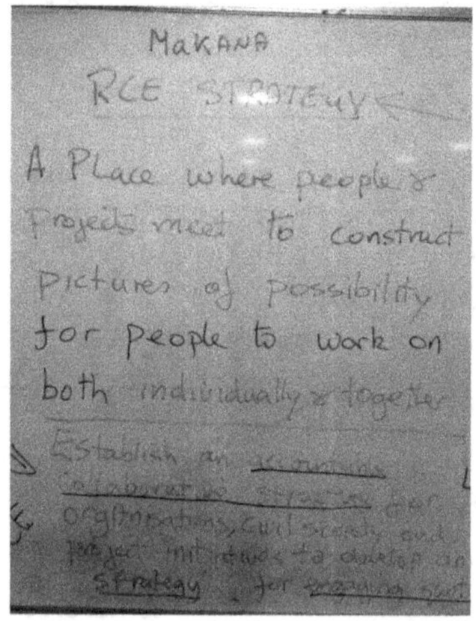

RCE Vision

This schematic diagram summarised how both the improvement of service delivery and management could be supported alongside work on change-choice-practices

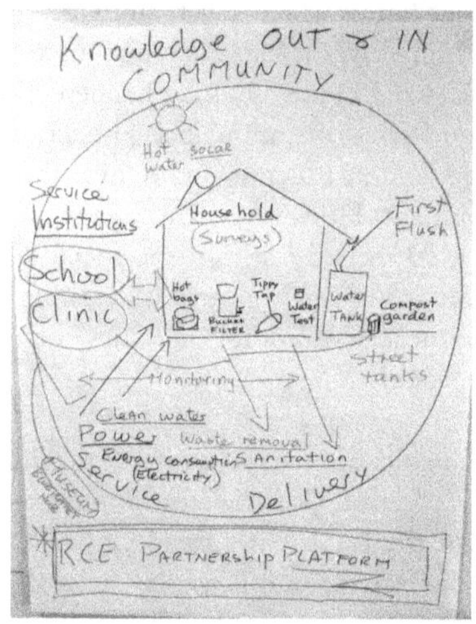

RCE Capacity Development

Training priorities includes community facilitation as well as technical skills and evaluation practices as a key strategy in the strengthening of local RCE initiatives

Figure 15.2 Evalution record images

Concluding synthesis

The above case record of an initial deliberative evaluation by community project partners in Makana RCE reflects how it was possible to draw on key features of evaluation practice to produce a hybrid evaluation framework for a participatory review of an RCE as a collaborative process of co-engaged social learning. The evaluation had high local relevance and was a step towards approaching ESD as an evaluative process as well as supporting capacity development in RCEs as sites of co-engaged, transformative social learning for the common good.

Notes

1 It is notable that metric-based assessment is an a priori process where the measures and proxy criteria for evaluation are pre-inscribed. This is useful for achieving clarity and projective certainty but not where outcomes are not wholly predictable or are open, variable and even unknown in diverse contexts of change.

2 It is notable how the opening trajectory of 'what positive things people appreciated' came to shape 'narrative appreciations of how things are' (informed critical appraisals) that entered conversations towards developmental possibilities to strengthen RCE activities. (See evidence of this in the record that follows.)

References

Australian Research Institute for Environment and Sustainability (ARIES), 2007. *Education for Sustainability in Local Government: Handbook*. Canberra: Australian Government.

Bhaskar, R., 2008 [1975]. *A Realist Theory of Science*. London: Routledge.

Blamey, A. and Mackenzie, 2007. 'Theories of Change and Realistic Evaluation: Peas in a Pod or Apples and Oranges?', *Evaluation*, 13(4), 439–55, http://evi.sagepub.com/content/13/4/439.

Coghlan, A. Preskill, H. and Tzavaras, T., 2003. 'An Overview of Appreciative Inquiry in Evaluation', *New Directions for Evaluation*, 100 (Winter), 5–22.

Cooperrider, D.L. and Srivastva, S., 1987. 'Appreciative Inquiry in Organizational Life', in Woodman, R.W. and Pasmore, W.A. (eds), *Research. In: Organizational Change and Development, Vol. 1*. Stamford, CT: JAI Press, 129–69.

Cooperrider, D.L., Whitney, D. and Stavros, J.M., 2008. *Appreciative Inquiry Handbook*. Brunswick, OH: Crown Custom Publishing.

Courtenay-Hall, P. and Rogers, L., 2002. 'Gaps in Mind: Problems in Environmental Knowledge-behaviour Modelling Research', *Environmental Education Research*, 8(3) 284–97.

de Haan, G., 2010. 'The Development of ESD-related Competencies in Supportive Institutional Frameworks', *International Review of Education*, 56(2/3), 315–28.

Department for Environment Food and Rural Affairs, 2008. *A Framework for Pro-Environmental Behaviours*. London: DEFRA, Business Resource Efficiency and Consumers Division.

Gamble, J.A., 2008. *A Developmental Evaluation Primer*. Canada: The J.W. McConnell Family Foundation.

Holling, C.S., 2001. 'Understanding the Complexity of Economic, Ecological, and Social Systems', *Ecosystems*, 4(5), 390–405.

Hollweg, K.S., Taylor, J.R., Bybee, R.W., Marcinkowski, T.J., McBeth, W.C., and Zoido, P., 2011. *Developing a Framework for Assessing Environmental Literacy*. Washington, DC: North American Association for Environmental Education. https://www.naaee.net/sites/default/files/framework/DevFramewkAssessEnvLitOnlineEd.pdf [accessed 23 March 2015].

Hungerford, H.R. and Volk, T.L., 1990. 'Changing Learner Behaviour through Environmental Education', *Journal of Environmental Education*, 21(3), 8–21.

Moore, J., 2012. *Social and Behavioural Aspects of Climate Change: Ireland's Climate Change Challenge: Final Report of the NESC Secretariat: Connecting 'How Much' with 'How To'*. Ireland: National Economic and Social Council.

O'Donoghue, R., 2014a. 'ThinkPiece: Re-thinking Education for Sustainable Development as Transgressive Processes of Educational Engagement with Human Conduct, Emerging Matters of Concern and the Common Good', *Southern African Journal of Environmental Education*, 30, 7–26.

O'Donoghue, R., 2014b. 'ESD and the Framing of Transformative Social Learning in RCEs', in Fadeeva, Z., Payyappallimana, U., Tabucanon, M. and Chhokar, K. (eds), *Building a Resilient Future through Multistakeholder Learning and Action: Ten Years of Regional Centres of Expertise in Education for Sustainable Development*. Tokyo: United Nations University Institute for the Advanced Study of Sustainability, 129–40.

Patton, M.Q., 1994. 'Developmental Evaluation', *Evaluation Practice*, 15(3), 311–19.

Pawson, R. and Tilley, N., 1997. *Realistic Evaluation*. London: SAGE.

Popkewitz, T., 2008. *Cosmopolitanism and the Age of School Reform: Science, Education, and Making Society by Making the Child*. London and New York: Routledge.

Rivers, N., 2014. 'Summary Report on Methodology used to Construct Value-Creation Stories'. Project Report: Environmental Learning Research Centre, Rhodes University.

Tilbury, D., 2007. 'Monitoring and Evaluation during the UN Decade of Education for Sustainable Development', *Journal of Education for Sustainable Development*, 1(2), 239–54.

United Nations Educational, Scientific and Cultural Organization (UNESCO), 2013a. 'Outcome Document of the Technical Consultation on Global Citizenship Education: Global Citizenship Education: An Emerging Perspective'. http://unesdoc.unesco.org/images/0022/002241/224115E.pdf [accessed 20 March 2015].

United Nations Educational, Scientific and Cultural Organization (UNESCO), 2013b. *Proposal for a Global Action Programme on Education for Sustainable Development as a follow-up to the United Nations Decade of Education for Sustainable Development (DESD) after 2014*. Paris: UNESCO General Conference, 37th Session, Resolution 37 C.

United Nations Educational, Scientific and Cultural Organization (UNESCO), 2014a. 'Towards Universal Learning: Implementing Assessment to Improve Learning'. UNESCO Institute for Statistics and Centre for Universal Education at Brookings, Report No.3 of 3, Learning Metrics Task Force, June 2014.

United Nations Educational, Scientific and Cultural Organization (UNESCO), 2014b. *Global Citizenship Education: Preparing Learners for the Challenges of the Twenty-first Century*. Paris: UNESCO.

United Nations Economic Commission for Europe (UNECE), 2011. *Learning for the Future: Competencies in Education for Sustainable Development*. Paris: UNESCO Publishing.

United Nations University – Institute for Advanced Studies (UNU-IAS), 2013. *RCE Assessment Experience: RCE Goa*. Tokyo UNU-IAS: Case Study Report.

Wenger, E., Trayner, B. and de Laat, M., 2011. *Promoting and Assessing Value Creation in Communities and Networks: A Conceptual Framework*. The Netherlands: Ruud de Moor Centrum.

Westley, F., Zimmerman, B. and Patton, M., 2007. *Getting to Maybe*. Canada: Random House.

Wiek, A., Withycombe, L. and Redman, C.L., 2011. 'Key Competencies in Sustainability: A Reference Framework for Academic Program Development', *Sustainability Science*, 6(2), 203–18.

Appendix

Appendix 15.1 Guiding questions of the six stage process of RCE development

Question 1: **RCE Coordination and Networking**

The RCE Journey:

A review of how the RCE was constituted and how it is functioning to enable learning and change.

- How did the RCE evolve?
- How has membership changed?
- How are local issues being addressed?
- What ESD initiatives have been undertaken?
- a) What can be done to improve RCE work, and b) How?

Question 2: **RCE Activities and Their Effects**

- How has the portfolio of activities of the RCEs evolved?
- What have been the best/most successful RCE activities and why?

- Give examples of how successful collaboration/decision making is producing the effects that are being achieved?
- How can useful activities be up-scaled and mainstreamed?
- How could better work be achieved?
  - In the RCE? (inward looking)
  - In the region? (collaboration and outward looking)

Question 3: **Transformation and Sustainability**

- What **flagship initiatives** reflect the successes of the RCE?
- The **scale of knowledge and practice transformation** has been involved:
  - Summarise what has happened in key focus areas over a period 12, 24, 36 months etc.
  - What has changed and how is the change evident?
- What **resources and governance** have enabled success?
- What, besides funding, can be done to **overcome barriers** and **sustain the work** of the RCE

Question 4: **Strategic Areas and Linkages**

- What **strategic focus** areas, partnerships, activities have been key to the successes of the RCE?
- What could be done to **improve learning and effectiveness** (e.g. partnerships, resourcing and scale)?
- How can existing linkages, processes and programs be strengthened?
- What new strategic links and capacity development could be explored?

Question 5: *RCE* **Global Service Centre**

- What have been the benefits of being acknowledged as an RCE?
- How are you interacting with the RCE Service Centre?
- How are you working with other RCEs and what are some of the activities, successes and challenges?
- How has your RCE participated in regional and global RCE conferences and undertaken follow-up activities?
- How could regional and global RCE activities be improved to strengthen your RCE work?

Question 6: **Review of Documents and Conclude with a Value Creation Assessment**

- Comment on **documents** available for review: RCE application, articles in the RCE bulletin, RCE publications, project documents, other publications, audio visual materials etc.
- What **value creation** does the appreciative evidence reflect?
  - What were the most meaningful RCE activities discussed?
  - What of potential value are the RCE activity producing?
  - What difference has this made that would not happen otherwise
  - What difference has it made to the ability of the RCE to produce what matters through its ESD projects?
  - What has produced new understandings of what produces value in RCE work?

PART 3

Issues and themes of research on higher education for sustainable development

16

OPERATIONALISING COMPETENCIES IN HIGHER EDUCATION FOR SUSTAINABLE DEVELOPMENT

Arnim Wiek, Michael J. Bernstein, Rider W. Foley, Matthew Cohen, Nigel Forrest, Christopher Kuzdas, Braden Kay and Lauren Withycombe Keeler

Introduction

The civil war raging in Syria at the time of this writing demonstrates the devastating effects of converging extreme drought, population growth and corrupt governance on natural, human and economic systems (Friedman 2013). A recent study on childhood and adult obesity in the United States concludes that prevalence of obesity has not changed significantly over the past ten years, remaining at more than 33 per cent of adults and 17 per cent of youth (Ogden *et al.* 2014). The detrimental effects of obesity on American society include the cost of individual illnesses, public health and financial burdens, lost worker productivity, and environmental degradation. Climate change has begun to impact cities and regions worldwide through storms and associated flood damages, extensive droughts, sea-level rise, and other disruptions; with impacts expected to increase in frequency and/or severity (Melillo *et al.* 2014). The above are but a few of the challenges that pertain to sustainability and display features of significant harm, complexity, urgency and contestation.

Throughout this chapter, we adhere to the following definition of sustainability (and by extension of sustainable development and sustainability problems) set forth in the literature (e.g. WCED 1987; Kates *et al.* 2001; Wiek *et al.* 2012): *Sustainability is the collective willingness and ability of a society to reach or maintain its viability, vitality, and integrity over long periods of time, while allowing other societies to reach or maintain their own viability, vitality, and integrity.* Sustainability challenges do not seem tractable to business-as-usual solutions; novel approaches are needed, for example, solution-oriented and transformational sustainability research efforts (Lang *et al.* 2012; Sarewitz *et al.* 2012; Wiek *et al.* 2012; Miller *et al.* 2014). Similarly, a large-scale educational transformation is needed to equip a new generation of professionals (not only *sustainability* professionals!) to address sustainability challenges through problem-solving approaches that integrate systems thinking, structured anticipation, value-laden deliberation, evidence-supported strategies, and strong collaboration across government, businesses and civil society (Wiek *et al.* 2011a).

Sustainability programmes in higher education institutions are supposed to convey these competencies in sustainability and enable graduates to make contributions to resolving challenging societal problems and building a sustainable future.[1] Competencies in this context entail far more than just topical or issue-related knowledge, for instance, on the global water cycle, or consumption patterns in the US, or distributional injustices in developing countries. We define competence as 'a functionally linked complex of knowledge, skills, and attitudes that enable successful task performance and problem solving'; applied to competencies *in sustainability*, these are 'complexes of knowledge, skills, and attitudes that enable successful task performance and problem solving with respect to real-world sustainability problems, challenges, and opportunities' (Wiek *et al.* 2011b: 204). Competencies, as defined here, accommodate the topical knowledge required for successful problem solving in a particular context. We propose a fairly smooth transition from competencies to learning objectives/outcomes – the former being more generalised and abstract, the latter being more detailed and specific. More details on the concept and definition of (key) competencies can be found in Barth and Michelsen (2013).

Competencies have received increasing attention as critical reference points for the development of curricula and courses. There are some differences across competencies concepts, ranging from minor terminological to more substantive differences (Wiek *et al.* 2011b; De Kraker *et al.* 2014). We focus here on moving forward with a converging set of key competencies in sustainability, supported by a variety of scholars (de Haan 2006; Sterling and Thomas 2006; Barth *et al.* 2007; Wiek *et al.* 2011b; Frisk and Larson 2011; Rieckmann 2012; Steiner 2013; Thomas and Day 2014). These key competencies are (Wiek *et al.* 2011b):

- Systems thinking competence
- Futures thinking (or anticipatory) competence
- Values thinking (or normative) competence
- Strategic thinking (or action-oriented) competence
- Collaboration (or interpersonal) competence

However, these competencies are rarely operationalised as specific learning objectives for different educational levels. The majority of proposals remain generic, with few exceptions that attempt to specify different levels of competence for graduate and undergraduate programmes (Roorda 2010; von der Heidt and Lamberton 2011). This lag behind conceptualisation offers one explanation for why incorporation of sustainability competencies into curricula and courses has been slow (Thomas and Day 2014).

In this chapter, we first present a consolidated and integrated set of operationalised competencies in sustainability. We differentiate the competencies into novice, intermediate and advanced levels, which in turn can translate to high school, undergraduate and graduate levels of sustainability education. We then present three case studies on how we have designed and taught courses at the School of Sustainability (Arizona State University) and elsewhere to convey the integrated delivery of competence-based education on the three levels. There are many more courses that convey key competencies individually, but here we focus on integrated problem-solving courses that allow for a comprehensive approach to delivering the suite of key competencies.

This chapter does *not* present a review of sustainability competencies concepts. This has been done elsewhere, as indicated above. The objective of this chapter is depth (operationalising competencies!). There are plenty of books and articles available that discuss different competencies concepts, but little on how to operationalise them for use in curricula and courses.

The operationalisation of competencies is the *first* step of curriculum and course design, delivery and assessment, following backward design (Wiggins and McTighe 2005), or constructive alignment (Biggs and Tang 2007). We touch upon appropriate pedagogies to convey key competencies, and in passing touch on measuring/assessing the acquisition of competencies. Elsewhere we have published a series of articles on problem- and project-based learning (Brundiers and Wiek 2011; Brundiers and Wiek 2013; Wiek *et al.* 2014), on solution-oriented sustainability learning (Wiek and Kay 2015), as well as on international sustainability education (Wiek *et al.* 2013) as prominent pedagogical approaches to support competence-based education in sustainability. The operationalised competencies can be applied in undergraduate and/or graduate programmes, and even in efforts to prepare high school students for sustainability programmes in higher education institutions, as demonstrated by the subsequent case studies.

Key competencies in sustainability

Wiek *et al.* (2011b) undertook a broad literature review of sustainability competencies in higher education and synthesised a set of five key competencies in sustainability education, namely: systems thinking competence, anticipatory competence, normative competence, strategic competence, and interpersonal competence. Implicitly, the authors also suggest a critical *sixth* competence, namely the meta-competence of meaningfully using and integrating the five key competencies for solving sustainability problems and fostering sustainable development (Wiek *et al.* 2011b).

In the following, we present dense profiles of these six competencies by providing: a definition of the competence (through overarching learning objectives); selected concepts entailed; selected methods entailed; specifications of the competence for novice, intermediate and advanced levels; and finally, selected key readings for learning more about the competence. Delineations among levels of proficiency were determined, at this stage, by the authors' collective experiences with sustainability education at high school, undergraduate, graduate and professional levels. We note that although the progression from 'novice' to 'advanced' appears linear, our experiences suggest that it is an iterative process. Additional research is needed to verify and further examine this iterative competence acquisition process; we present select elements of such a research approach in the discussion section.

Systems thinking competence

Definition through learning objectives

Graduates competent in systems thinking are able to analyse sustainability problems cutting across different domains (or sectors) and scales (i.e. from local to global), thereby applying systems concepts including systems ontologies, cause-effect structures, cascading effects, inertia, feedback loops, structuration, etc.

Graduates are also able to describe the need for systemic thinking in sustainability problem solving, for example, for anticipating future trajectories from a systems perspective, for identifying intervention points and critical actors, and for testing transition strategies. Finally, graduates are able to describe how different professional activities contribute to, or solve/mitigate sustainability problems.

Selected Concepts (Students are able to explain and apply concepts of ...)

- Systems and problem ontologies

- Variables/indicators, clusters, sub-systems
- Cause-effect chains, cascading effects, feedback loops, delays
- Tipping points, resilience, adaptation
- Structures and dynamics across/multiple scales: local to global
- Structures and dynamics across multiple/coupled domains (e.g. society, environment, economy, technology, culture)
- Values, needs, perceptions, actions, tactics
- Institutions (e.g. rules, rights, decision-making processes), power relations, structuration

Selected Methods (Students are able to generate and interpret results using …)

- Qualitative system analysis (e.g. structural analysis, cognitive mapping)
- Quantitative modelling (e.g. system dynamics or statistical modelling)
- Institutional analysis
- Causal problem analysis (e.g. causal chain analysis, root cause analysis)
- Social and agent network analysis
- Participatory systems approaches (e.g. participatory modelling)

Specifications for novice, intermediate, and advanced levels

See Table 16.1.

Futures thinking or anticipatory competence

Definition through learning objectives

Graduates competent in futures thinking are able to anticipate how sustainability problems might evolve or occur over time (scenarios), considering inertia, path dependencies and triggering events; as well as create and craft sustainable and desirable future visions, considering evidence-supported alternative development pathways.

Graduates are also able to describe the need for futures thinking in sustainability problem-solving, for example, for informing strategy building, including prevention, mitigation, and adaptation responses (responding to scenarios), as well as actively pursuing visions; further, for exercising precaution in decision making, and motivating change. Finally graduates are able to anticipate how one's job might evolve over time (career trajectory) and how one's professional activities might contribute to, or mitigate future sustainability problems.

Selected Concepts (Students are able to explain and apply concepts of …)

- Temporal terms, phases, states, continuity and non-linearity (conceptualised differently in different cultures)
- Possibility, plausibility, probability and desirability
- Inertia, path-dependency and non-intervention features
- Consistency and coherence
- Quality criteria of visions (e.g. visionary, tangible, plausible, shared)
- Risk, precaution and intergenerational equity

Table 16.1 Systems thinking learning objectives at different levels of mastery (acquired competence level)

Novice level	*Intermediate level*	*Advanced level*
Graduates are able to: • Create basic systems diagrams of sustainability problems, using some empirical data to illustrate elements of the problem (e.g. adverse effects) • Understand how sustainability problems have emerged (historical perspective) • Understand that different intervention points are relevant for sustainability problem-solving • Understand how modifications of the problem constellation (interventions in drivers) play out • Describe some functions of systems thinking in sustainability problem-solving • Describe in principle how different professional activities contribute to, or solve/mitigate sustainability problems	Graduates are able to: • Perform all activities on the novice level • Define all steps of problem and system analysis methods • Apply these methods to construct advanced conceptual problem models that incorporate feedback loops and other advanced systems features, with empirical data for all elements of the problem, as well as some evidence for selected links between effects and causes (tracing back) (e.g. using basic STELLA models) • Analyse (conceptually) how sustainability problems have emerged (historical perspective) • Identify different intervention points relevant for sustainability problem-solving • Analyse conceptually how modifications of the problem constellation (interventions in drivers) play out • Describe all functions of systems thinking in sustainability problem-solving • Describe in detail how different professional activities contribute to, or solve/mitigate sustainability problems	Graduates are able to: • Perform all activities on the intermediate level • Construct dynamic systems and problem models that allow simulating dynamic developments of systems and problems (e.g., using advanced STELLA models) • Simulate how sustainability problems have emerged (historical perspective) • Analyse model-based and in detail how modifications of the problem constellation (interventions in drivers) play out (intended and unintended consequences)

Selected Methods (Students are able to generate and interpret results using …)

- Scenario construction/analysis methods (qualitative and quantitative)
- Forecasting from statistical and simulation models
- Visioning methods, including the first module of backcasting
- Participatory anticipatory approaches (e.g. Delphi)

Specifications for novice, intermediate, and advanced levels

Table 16.2 Futures thinking learning objectives at different levels of mastery (acquired competence level)

Novice level	*Intermediate level*	*Advanced level*
Graduates are able to: • Understand different concepts about the future, including long-term, short-term; possible, probable, plausible and desirable • Understand cultural differences in concepts of time and the future • Describe intergenerational equity and its importance for sustainability • Describe the basic structure of scenario construction, forecasting, and visioning; link these methods with the types of knowledge they generate • Outline basic scenarios and visions for their own lives and for familiar systems (like their school) on different timescales • Describe some functions of futures thinking in sustainability problem-solving • Anticipate in principle how one's job might evolve over time (career trajectory) and how one's professional activities might contribute to, or mitigate future sustainability problems	Graduates are able to: • Perform all activities on the novice level • Define all steps of scenario construction, forecasting and visioning methods, respectively • Apply these methods to generate basic scenarios (e.g. using scenario axis technique; using simple STELLA models), basic forecasts, and visions related to sustainability problems • Develop basic narratives (e.g. day-in-the-life) and visuals (e.g. pictures and diagrams) that illustrate scenarios, forecasts or visions • Describe all functions of futures thinking in sustainability problem-solving • Anticipate in detail how one's job might evolve over time (career trajectory) and how one's professional activities might contribute to, or mitigate future sustainability problems	Graduates are able to: • Perform all activities on the intermediate level • Construct advanced scenarios, forecasts and visions related to complex sustainability problems over long time periods (50–100 years) • Simulate how modifications of the problem constellation (interventions) play out in the future • Appraise scenarios, forecasts, or visions for their consistency, plausibility, saliency, and other quality criteria

Values thinking or normative competence

Definition through learning objectives

Graduates competent in values thinking are able to specify, compare, apply, reconcile and negotiate sustainability values, principles, goals and targets, informed by concepts of justice, fairness, responsibility, etc., in various processes, including visioning, assessment and evaluation.

Graduates are also able to describe the need for values thinking in sustainability problem solving, for example, for providing normative orientations to problem analysis, futures thinking activities and strategy building. Finally, graduates are able to assess the sustainability effects/impact of one's job activities and envision a sustainable future for one's profession.

Selected Concepts (Students are able to explain and apply concepts of ...)

- Sustainability, sustainable development
- Viability, vitality, liveability, (social-ecological) integrity, etc.
- Sustainability principles, goals, targets, thresholds, tipping points, etc.
- Justice, fairness, responsibility, etc.
- Risk, harm, damage, etc.
- Ethical and moral claims
- Resource stewardship, fair use and conservation
- Tradeoffs and 'win-win' synergies

Selected Methods (Students are able to generate and interpret results using ...)

- Sustainability assessment and appraisal methods
- Multi-criteria assessment methods (e.g. MCA, cost-benefit analysis)
- Impact assessment methods (e.g. LCA, SIA)
- Risk analysis
- Visioning methods
- Participatory normative methods (e.g. negotiation methods, consensus conference)

Specifications for novice, intermediate, and advanced levels

See Table 16.3.

Strategic thinking or action-oriented competence

Definition through learning objectives

Graduates competent in strategic thinking are able to develop and test systemic interventions, transformational actions and transition strategies toward sustainability, accounting for unintended consequences and cascading effects. They are able to develop plans that leverage assets, mobilise resources, and coordinate stakeholders to overcome systemic inertia, path dependencies and other barriers to reach envisioned outcomes.

Graduates are also able to describe the need for strategic thinking in sustainability problem-solving, for example, in designing and carrying out plans, interventions and actions to mitigate sustainability problems and make progress toward sustainability visions. Finally, graduates are able to position job activities in a way that contributes to sustainability transitions.

Selected Concepts (Students are able to explain and apply concepts of ...)

- Intentionality and decision making
- Theories of change (e.g. behaviour change, social transformations)
- Strategies, action programmes, transition agendas and systemic interventions
- Adaptation and mitigation strategies

Table 16.3 Values thinking learning objectives at different levels of mastery (acquired competence level)

Novice level	*Intermediate level*	*Advanced level*
Graduates are able to: • Understand concepts of justice, fairness, and responsibility as part of the overarching concept of sustainability • Understand the influence of values on stakeholder actions and activities • Explore their own values, preferences and norms (self-discovery) • Identify value differences and trade-offs, e.g. among different courses of actions • Empathise with others • Describe the basic structure of sustainability assessments and visioning; link these methods with the types of knowledge they generate and their use in sustainability problem-solving activities • Describe some functions of values thinking in sustainability problem-solving • Exemplarily assess the sustainability effects/impact of one's job activities and envision a sustainable future for one's profession	Graduates are able to: • Perform all activities on the novice level • Partly operationalise sustainability principles • Define all steps of sustainability assessments • Conduct basic sustainability assessments of problems, scenarios, visions and strategies (interventions) • Construct visions that draw upon sustainability values and principles • Describe all functions of values thinking in sustainability problem-solving • Fully assess the sustainability effects/impact of one's job activities and envision a sustainable future for one's profession	Graduates are able to: • Perform all activities on the intermediate level • Fully operationalise sustainability principles • Perform advanced sustainability assessments related to complex sustainability problems, scenarios, visions and strategies (interventions) • Conduct advanced visioning processes, based on sustainability criteria

- Quality criteria including, success factors, viability, feasibility, effectiveness
- Barriers including obstacles, inertia, path dependencies
- Carriers including incentives, assets and resources, roles and responsibilities
- Stakeholder networks and alliances
- Power, politics, authority in strategy building and change (vested interests in the status quo)

Selected Methods (Students are able to generate and interpret results using …)

- Intervention design (e.g. constructive governance design, policy design)
- Programme planning and evaluation

- Decision support (e.g. tools, techniques)
- Organisational change management approaches
- Behavioural change approaches (e.g. behavioural economics)
- Transition management approaches (e.g. strategies, tactics)
- Reflexive learning (e.g. socio-technical integration research)

Specifications for novice, intermediate, and advanced levels

Table 16.4 Strategic thinking learning objectives at different levels of mastery (acquired competence level)

Novice level	*Intermediate level*	*Advanced level*
Graduates are able to: • Understand basic concepts of intentionality and decision-making • Understand basic theories of change (e.g. behaviour change, social transformations) • Understand basic concepts of barriers, assets, roles, effectiveness, etc. as part of the overarching concepts of sustainability transitions, social learning and organisational change • Describe the basic structure of building strategies for change (transitions, interventions) towards sustainability • Identify factors that affect the success or failure of transitions and interventions • Create basic transition strategies that intervene in a defined system or problem constellation • Describe some functions of strategic thinking in sustainability problem-solving • Explore strategies how to position one's job activities in a way that it contributes to sustainability transitions	Graduates are able to: • Perform all activities on the novice level • Understand advanced theories of change • Understand advanced concepts of barriers, assets, roles, effectiveness, etc. • Define all steps of building transition strategies as well as designing and testing interventions • Build basic transition strategies as well as design and test basic interventions (transition experiments) • Describe all functions of strategic thinking in sustainability problem-solving • Partly operationalise quality criteria to select intervention points that acknowledge conflicting values and priorities (link to normative competency) • Describe all functions of strategic thinking in sustainability problem-solving • Consolidate strategies how to position one's job activities in a way that it contributes to sustainability transitions	Graduates are able to: • Perform all activities on the intermediate level • Craft complex transition strategies as well as design and test complex interventions (transition experiments) • Link intervention assessment to the implementation as a feedback mechanism to assess distance-to-target and adapt strategy

Collaboration or interpersonal competence

Definition through learning objectives

Graduates with interpersonal competence are able to initiate, facilitate and support different types of collaboration, including teamwork and stakeholder engagement, in sustainability efforts (as described in the previous four competencies). They are able to incorporate and complement the experiences and expertise of others when working in or leading teams in professional settings; in addition, they are able to successfully collaborate with various stakeholders from government, business and civil society. In these functions, graduates are skilful in communication, pluralist (trans-cultural) and empathetic understanding, deliberation, negotiation and leadership.

Graduates are able to describe the need for teamwork and stakeholder engagement in professional sustainability efforts and how teamwork and stakeholder engagement equally apply to the four competencies described above. Graduates are able to articulate the roles, responsibilities and contributions of different stakeholder groups to effective sustainability problem solving.

Selected Concepts (Students are able to explain and apply concepts of …)

- Cooperation and empathy (e.g. benefits, limits, types)
- Effective verbal and written communication criteria
- Team work, including its functions, types, dynamics, roles, etc.
- Stakeholder engagement, including its functions, types, dynamics, roles, etc.
- Project (group) management
- Cross-cultural collaboration and empathy
- E-communication
- Leadership styles and attributes
- Solidarity, ethnocentrism, nationalism, etc. (impacts of culture and perspective on collaboration and participation)

Selected Approaches (Students are able to facilitate team work and stakeholder engagement using …)

- Effective communication, listening, inquiry
- Trust building, including non-judgmental interactions
- Empathy including perspective taking and immersive experiences
- Effective negotiation, conflict resolution
- Stakeholder workshops (including planning, dry-runs, volunteer selection and training, recruitment, execution, follow-up, etc.)
- Project management techniques
- Group facilitation techniques including active listening, rapport building, managed conflict, consensus building
- Peer- and self-evaluation techniques

Specifications for novice, intermediate, and advanced levels

Table 16.5 Collaboration learning objectives at different levels of mastery (acquired competence level)

Novice level	*Intermediate level*	*Advanced level*
Graduates are able to: • Understand general concepts critical to interpersonal interactions, including listening, communication, negotiation, conflict resolution, teamwork, stakeholder engagement, etc. • Describe the basic types, phases and techniques of teamwork and stakeholder engagement in sustainability projects • Work effectively and respectfully in teams on simple projects • Identify different groups of stakeholders relevant to a particular project • Conduct stakeholder interviews to build understanding of different perspectives and values • Understand the basic benefits of listening, communication, teamwork, stakeholder engagement, and other interpersonal skills for one's professional job	Graduates are able to: • Perform all activities on the novice level • Participate in or lead team work with stakeholder engagement in simple projects • Consistently foster team success by peer-mentoring, building upon strengths, and overcoming weaknesses • Resolve internal team conflicts with and without external mediation • Initiate and maintain stakeholder contacts • Incorporate diverse and/or conflicting stakeholder input into sustainability problem-solving activities • Serve a diversity of roles in stakeholder engagement activities, including presenter, station facilitation, note-taking, etc. • Fully assess the need for and gaps associated with teamwork and stakeholder engagement for one's job activities and profession	Graduates are able to: • Perform all activities on the intermediate level • Seek out and experiment with novel approaches of working in teams and engaging stakeholders • Foster and facilitate team and individual growth through advanced goal setting activities, evaluation and reflexive practices • Coordinate work across multiple teams working in concert on complex sustainability problem-solving activities • Conduct stakeholder engagement in complex/high-risk settings that require negotiation and conflict resolution activities • Communicate to diverse audiences, in written and oral formats, the results of sustainability-problem solving efforts

Integrated problem-solving competence

Definition through learning objectives

Graduates competent in integrated problem-solving are familiar with and able to apply different problem-solving frameworks to complex sustainability problems and develop viable solution options. This capacity enables graduates to meaningfully integrate problem analysis, sustainability assessment, visioning and strategy building.

Graduates are also able to describe the need for integrated problem-solving activities and how the different competencies enable this effort to foster sustainability (this is complementary to the ability to articulate the individual contributions of the previous five competencies to sustainability problem-solving).

Selected Concepts (Students are able to explain and apply concepts of …)

- Transitions and transformations (and other change dynamics)
- Roadblocks and barriers
- Triggers and supporting factors
- Social movements and organisational change (learning)
- Power, politics, authority in transition processes

Selected Procedural Frameworks (Students are able to generate sustainable solution options using …)

- Transition management/governance
- Organisational change management
- Intervention research methodology
- Integrated foresight and backcasting
- Transformational planning methodology

Specifications for novice, intermediate, and advanced levels

Table 16.6 Integrated problem-solving learning objectives at different levels of mastery (acquired competence level)

Novice level	*Intermediate level*	*Advanced level*
Graduates are able to: • Understand general concepts of transition, transformation, etc. • Describe prominent cases of social movements and organisational change • Apply one problem-solving framework to defined sustainability problems • Describe how sustainability problem-solving competence integrates the five other competencies • Understand how sustainability problem-solving competence is critical in professional jobs	Graduates are able to: • Perform all activities on the novice level • Understand advanced concepts of transition, transformation, etc. • Refer to and utilise a larger pool of prominent cases of social movements and organisational change • Apply one problem-solving framework to a sustainability problems of their interest • Describe and compare different frameworks of sustainability problem-solving • Utilise sustainability problem-solving competence in internships and other semi-professional settings	Graduates are able to: • Perform all activities on the intermediate level • Apply different problem-solvings framework to sustainability problems • Utilise sustainability problem-solving competence in professional settings

Case examples

In this section, we present three case studies to exemplify how a competencies approach can be operationalised for and integrated in different educational settings. We have selected cases at the high school, undergraduate and graduate levels to demonstrate course design at the three levels of acquired competence – respectively novice, intermediate and advanced – introduced above. In addition, cases were selected for being the kind of exemplary, integrated problem-solving courses that facilitate a comprehensive approach to delivering the suite of key competencies. The cases are distinct, and connected only by the faculty and pedagogy; students in the cases did not progress from the high school to the graduate level (although students in the graduate level course had received prior coursework as part of their graduate training).

Novice level – Bioscience High School, Phoenix, Arizona

Located in downtown Phoenix, Arizona, Bioscience High School is a 300-student school that specializes in science, technology, engineering and mathematics (STEM) education and attracts diverse students from across the city (Kay *et al.*, 2012). Graduate students from ASU's School of Sustainability have worked at Bioscience since 2009 (through the NSF-funded grant 'Sustainability Science for Sustainable Schools'), developing an approach to teaching sustainability competencies that is now a core of the school's pedagogy. During the 2011–12 academic year, Bioscience implemented a competence-based problem-solving programme that allowed students to work on solutions to real-world sustainability challenges. Freshmen students spent some 45 hours in the spring term, and upper class students worked some 90 hours over the course of the year. Students applied a five-step problem-solving framework, worked in teams, and collaborated with stakeholders (Kay *et al.* 2014).

We present here the steps used by a group of students aiming to improve urban vibrancy and indicate the relevant competencies that were being built. The student group developed solution options to the problem of economic decline, urban decay and lack of social cohesion in a neighbouring arts district [Integrated Problem-Solving].

Step One – Identifying Sustainability Challenges: Business owners, residents and community leaders visited classes and discussed neighbourhood history and recent occurrences of urban decay and declining economic development with students [Systems Thinking: understand how sustainability problems have emerged]. The stakeholders described challenges such as vacant lots and trash, lack of mobility options and low engagement of youth and minority populations. During this step, students formed teams to address these challenges in concert (not separately) [Collaboration: team building].

Step Two – Analysing Sustainability Challenges: Students identified upstream drivers, downstream impacts and relevant stakeholders for the identified challenges. They collected data about vacant lots and local businesses through interviews, Internet, local media and walking audits [Collaboration: identify stakeholder groups; interview individuals; learn diverse perspectives]. They represented this analysis through simple problem models [Systems Thinking: create basic systems diagrams]. One team interviewed residents and police on teenagers' impact on perceptions of public safety and blight. They identified low attendance and interaction with youth as well as trash from public events as problem drivers [Systems Thinking: understand different intervention points]. Their solution was a game that turned trashcans into basketball hoops, making trash removal fun and motivating teenagers to help clean at public events.

Step Three – Visioning: Students created future visions in which the analysed problems no longer existed [Futures Thinking/Values Thinking: construct basic visions]. These visions blended the views of multiple stakeholders [Values Thinking: identify value differences] and were crafted to conform to sustainability principles such as intergenerational equity [Values Thinking: integrate foundational concepts of justice]. The urban vibrancy group created the following vision (Kay *et al.* 2012):

> Our vision for the vacant lots around Roosevelt Row will be a place where you'll find a thriving safe and clean cultural centre which includes a large variety of foods, independent bands, small business boutiques and an opportunity to connect with developing local artists, while still being a place where all ages can hang out in a comfortable shaded area, converse and be a part of a growing urban community.

Step Four – Strategy Building and Intervention Planning: Students brainstormed interventions leading from their analysed challenges to their visions of a thriving, inclusive arts district. They developed a long-term plan, starting with small-scale outreach and culminating in mature organisations managing festivals and community centres [Strategic Thinking: articulate key phases of transitions]. Teams designed early-stage interventions, paying attention to achievability [Strategic Thinking: describe general barriers and carriers; describe general assets and resources]. One intervention was a website to engage young Latinos in arts and cultural events [Strategic Thinking: create transition strategies]. Students established a plan to create the website, develop content, and spread information [Strategic Thinking: create basic action plans].
Step Five – Implementation, Evaluation and Revision: A team addressing mobility challenges in automobile-centric Phoenix implemented a bicycle rental programme for Art Walk events to raise awareness and promote cycling. They partnered with local bicycle shops [Collaboration: identify and develop new opportunities for collaboration]. The students reviewed rentals with the bike shops after operations began and realised the programme depended on volunteer workers [Strategic Thinking/Values Thinking: monitor and evaluate outcomes]. They recommended future students advocate for a permanent citywide bike-share solution that is now being implemented.

Intermediate level – undergraduate course 'society and sustainability'

This undergraduate course, with an average enrolment of 50–60 sustainability major students, intends to build students' sustainability problem-solving competence through training in using tools (including concepts and procedures), each of them designed for a specific phase of the problem-solving process (Wiek 2014). Students met in class for three hours per week, with an expected additional workload of six hours per week over 15 weeks, for a total of 135 hours. The students applied these tools and demonstrated competence acquisition through a series of essays, addressing a sustainability problem of their interest. At the same time, the course built students' critical-thinking capacity by making clear that 'solving' sustainability problems is a daunting task. Students became aware that it takes coordinated efforts, reflection and reconsideration, learning from failure, goal revision, negotiations, convincing people in power, smart fundraising, forging unconventional alliances, continuously motivating partners, and strategically utilising windows of opportunity. The tools conveyed in this course are more fundamental than life-cycle assessment or cost-benefit analysis – they are basic aides and structures of thinking, on which other tools rest. In support of the real-world orientation of the course, we integrated problem- and project-based learning elements, including field trips and real-world sustainability problem case studies (Wiek *et al.* 2014).

The brief introductory part of the course (two sessions) familiarised students with the basics of sustainability problem solving, exemplary case studies, and the most critical ingredients [Integrated Problem-Solving]. It built the stage on which the main course components were played.

The first main part of the course trained students in reliably *identifying and framing* problems as *sustainability* problems. It built students' expertise in differentiating between sustainability problems and other problems [Values Thinking]. Students were encouraged to select for their essay a problem that was relevant to them (to motivate students) and to link their work to an on-going initiative, program, or project on- or off-campus [Collaboration]. Most students responded positively to class activities that allowed them to contribute to the mitigation of real-world sustainability problems. Students were familiarised with using a tool for identifying and framing sustainability problems. Students learned how to describe features of sustainability problems, including: being significantly harmful over the long term, applying basic sustainability principles [Values Thinking]; being urgent/irreversible in the short term; having adverse effects that spread across different sectors and spatial levels; being driven by causes that are manifold and often indirect [Systems Thinking]; being controversially discussed and even wilfully obscured. Students also identified the need for sustainability problem-solving through determining to what extent legitimate stakeholders recognise and judge this situation as negative or adverse, in terms of sustainability, on justifiable grounds; to what extent stakeholders are honestly interested in doing something to resolve and mitigate this situation [Collaboration]; and to what extent there is a demonstrable lack of intervention capability to develop and implement a solution that mitigates or resolves the identified problem.

The second part of the course was devoted to the skill set necessary to reliably *analyse* sustainability problems. Students were familiarised with a second tool that allowed them to reveal and visualise the basic cause-effect structure of the sustainability problems they identified in the first part and first essays [Systems Thinking]. Students worked through a sequence of issues, starting with adverse effects and affected stakeholders (summarising who is significantly harmed through dispersed effects); continuing with causing actions, activities, actors, in conjunction with technologies (linking the adverse effects back to actions, activities, behaviour, as well as the used technologies and infrastructure); then spelling out benefits and benefiting stakeholders (positive effects attached to the identified actions, activities, behaviour, and, who is benefitting from those); finally, analysing upstream drivers of the problem, including motives, needs, and preferences; enabling and constraining social rules and norms; available knowledge and capacity; and available resources. Students learned how to visualise such cause-effect structures through system diagrams.

The third part of the course focused on building students' capacity in *developing sustainable solution visions*. Students were trained in envisioning future states where the analysed problems have been solved – again, using a tool they can apply to any given or chosen problem [Futures Thinking/Values Thinking]. Students started with a systemic exploration going from the mitigated negative effects and the enhanced beneficial effects, and then work backwards to the root causes of the vision [Systems Thinking]. Students learned how to make visions tangible (real locations and people), how to craft vision narratives, and how to use systems diagrams to visualise the causal structure of the envisioned future states (similar to the problem maps). Students also learned how to justify that visions are sustainable by applying sustainability principles [Values Thinking]. Students were also trained in justifying the plausibility of visions by providing a real-world example from the past, or from somewhere else, or through another source of evidence (proof of concept, extended peer review, simulations). Finally students were encouraged to engage stakeholders in crafting their vision, learning what makes visions compelling to stakeholders and how shared visions are more likely to get pursued than purely expert-based visions [Collaboration: engagement with non-academic stakeholders].

The fourth and final part of the course trained students in building sustainable solution strategies for transitioning from the problems analysed to the vision crafted [Strategic Thinking: create transition strategies]. The strategy-building tool provided to the students allowed them to identify the point(s) of intervention referring back to the analysed problem (where does one plan on intervening); the transition actions (steps), their sequence (what comes first, next, etc.), their timeline (how much time needed for each action/step), and their intermediate and final outcomes (from 'where we are now' to 'where we would like to be'); the roles of different stakeholders (who is doing what) in the transition actions (for each step) [Collaboration: engagement with non-academic stakeholders]; the resources (time, funding, material, etc.) required for the transition actions and the sources for those; and finally potential barriers (resistance, institutional inertia, etc.) that might be encountered during the problem solving process – and how you propose overcoming these barriers.

Advanced level – graduate studio 'sustainable solutions for Phoenix'

This sustainability graduate studio aimed to develop a collaborative tree and shade intervention to mitigate negative effects of urban sprawl in the Sky Harbor Neighborhood (SHN) of Phoenix, Arizona (Bernstein *et al.* 2014). The studio involved four students and two faculty, as well as community representatives, city staff, and non-profit organisations. Students spent an average of 15 hours per week over 15 weeks working on the project, for a total of 225 hours, plus additional follow-up with community partners after the course ended.

The students' first task was to build a functioning team with assigned roles and responsibilities, a code of conduct, a work plan, as well as project benchmarks and goals [Collaboration: teamwork involving phases of teamwork and best practices]. Throughout the project, the team coordinated activities with city officials, community stakeholders, and non-profit representatives [Collaboration: stakeholder engagement in complex, high-levels of public exposure]. Over the course of the 14-week term, the team met more than 30 times, organised three public workshops, and delivered a final report for non-academic partners.

After team building, the team began to select a particular problem to target with an intervention. To do so, the team held a community-based, participatory workshop with 20 participants [Collaboration: engagement with non-academic stakeholders]. The predominant issues of interest to the community were walkability and safety. These results were fed into a subsequent community meeting [Collaboration: stakeholder engagement leveraging existing relationships] in which residents chose a tree and shade intervention [Strategic Thinking: considering key problem and vision inputs; selected based on previous community success with block watch and alley clean up programmes] to address the aforementioned challenges. As part of this first workshop, members of the research team also elicited stakeholder visions using visual and narrative methods [Futures Thinking/Values Thinking: plausibility and desirability of possible futures] anchored in sustainable development concepts including intergenerational justice, environmental stewardship and social cohesion [Values Thinking: diverse values]. The elicited visions for a walkable, safe, beautiful neighbourhood aligned with those of the targeted intervention [Strategic Thinking/Collaboration: co-creation of a plan to foster buy-in and account for community inputs].

Independently and to assist with intervention design, the research team developed a systemic perspective to contextualise the low walkability and perceptions of unsafe transportation [System Thinking: problem analysis and system map]. Phoenix struggles with various challenges, including urban sprawl, water stress and childhood obesity. These problems, made worse by automobile dependence, have negative impacts on public health, social equity and public safety. Low-income neighbourhoods, like the Sky Harbor Neighborhood of the study, are particularly afflicted by these negative outcomes.

Based on problem and vision inputs, the research team drafted a general intervention programme [Strategic Thinking]. This general programme was fed into a second community-based participatory workshop [Collaboration] to develop a neighbourhood-specific tree acquisition and maintenance plan with the input of city, community and non-profit representatives [Strategic Thinking]. Following an intervention design template, the workshop participants discussed topics including key steps, barriers and coping strategies, costs, timelines and definitions of success [Collaboration/Strategic Thinking].

After synthesising the results of the intervention design workshop and additional research on best practices, the team produced two intervention manuals: a longer, technical resource, and a shorter, resident-friendly primer [Strategic Thinking]. The primer, reviewed in multiple drafts by the community and expert partners [Collaboration], provided tailored suggestions for the community to plant and care for trees to enhance neighbourhood walkability, safety and pride – addressing community problems and striving after the community vision [Integrated Problem-Solving].

In such real-world sustainability projects, students' competence is built by coping with various challenges. Exemplary challenges were: reconciling preferences of the community with broader principles of justice, environmental integrity, and social cohesion; compromising between high-impact intervention upstream in the problem constellation (building community capacity for future organisation and problem-solving) and the resulting tree and shade project as a downstream intervention in the near term (planting trees to mitigate urban heat island and promote walkability and pride); recruiting stakeholders to workshops, a challenge despite local canvassing efforts aided by the neighbourhood association president; coping with fast-pace, high-pressure project situations which placed novel stressors on students' project management and conflict resolution capacities. Overall, the students persevered and adapted to deliver a high-quality product to community partners, developing solid experience in sustainability problem-solving.

Discussion and conclusions

We present in this chapter a novel synthesis and operationalisation of key competencies in sustainability at novice, intermediate and advanced levels. Despite these advances, illustrated by the case studies presented above, the sustainability competencies framework still offers many opportunities for future research and practice. One such vital area of sustainability competencies research relates to the demarcation among the levels. Additional research could be conducted to more quantitatively establish competence profiles across levels, as well as approximate study hours associated with proficiency at each level.

Another area of research is in assessment of competence acquisition. As indicated above, at this stage, our account of integrated sustainability problem-solving courses is qualitative and thus only suggestive of reasons for continuing this line of pedagogy. A research agenda in competence acquisition is needed to empirically investigate issues such as: returns of the competence over status-quo approaches in sustainability education; how interdependencies among competencies and reflection and iteration in the learning process shape competence acquisition; how competence acquisition relates to the complexity of the topic and stakeholders involved in a given project; and, through longitudinal investigations, how the professional trajectories of graduates in sustainability may be influenced by the competence pedagogy. Such a research agenda would benefit from an institutionally and culturally diverse set of cases, as well as the inclusion of benchmark, non-competence-based course cases for comparison. Outcomes of competence- and non-competence-based cases could be systematically assessed to ascertain advantages and disadvantages of the competence approach. This research could be *prospective*, involving course design; *contemporary*, involving implementation with currently available courses; and/or *retrospective*, involving review of past courses.

Central to competence-based sustainability education is the practice of coordinating and aligning courses across the curriculum. In the School of Sustainability at Arizona State University, this is underway at the undergraduate level. Student progress will be tracked and courses will be reorganised and sorted based on the competencies framework presented here. Many other programmes across the world have adopted the framework and are currently in the process of refining and aligning their curricula. Comparisons across these programmes may yield valuable insights on more efficient ways to support students in the acquisition of sustainability competencies. A student-empowered approach to competence acquisition is critical as many degree programmes elsewhere will face the challenge of integrating undergraduate or graduate students who may have no prior exposure to competence-based sustainability education. Further, such a student-empowered approach enables students not trained in all competencies to find and build teams capable of applying the suite of competencies necessary for sustainability problem-solving.

Universities, units and individual professors attempting to adopt similar approaches should be aware of the unique attributes of organisational setting that may hinder or enable the adoption of competence-based education (Wiek *et al.* 2011a). Arizona State University is a progressive higher education institution open to, supportive of, and flexible with novel pedagogies (with inevitable growing pains) (Crow and Dabars 2015). At the School of Sustainability, the university is adopting a problem-based and solution-oriented approach to higher education, a paradigm that lends itself well to the sustainability competencies framework. These conditions may not exist where others attempt competence-based sustainability education.

Two institutional issues in particular are critical to address. The first relates to faculty training, and the second pertains to institutional incentives for professors (e.g. tenure guidelines and departmental norms about pedagogies). Concerted efforts to train faculty in the design of competence-based courses allow adoption across the curricula. Courses designed with sustainability competencies in mind are not necessarily more difficult to create, but there are fixed costs associated with learning about the competencies, how they are operationalised, and how to teach more project and problem-based courses (for example, coordinating learning activities with stakeholder partners). At present, we provide faculty-training workshops and prepare teaching materials to be distributed to interested institutions. Faculty themselves may find it challenging to adopt sustainability competencies approaches to coursework if the incentives of their home institution or academic unit directly oppose the pursuit of innovative pedagogies. Current tenure paradigms are conservative, risk-averse and biased toward research outcomes (Belkin 2014). Universities with sustainability units should assess the call made by sustainability scholars for problem-based, solution-oriented work, and reconsider tenure guideless accordingly. Guidelines need not be relaxed, but rather reorganised away from ill-fitting, one-size-fits-only-some approaches.

For sustainability problem-solving to take off, it must, obviously, expand beyond the halls of academia. Scaling sustainability competencies for societal benefit will require creating professional profiles that, in essence, operationalise sustainability competencies for different professional activities. Research on the adaptation of sustainability competencies for professional profiles would help elaborate the constraints, trade-offs and advantages of operationalisation in professional versus educational settings. In scoping the competencies for professional settings, one can imagine, for example, how the profile of an urban planner, refined through the lens of sustainability competencies, may place greater emphasis on values-thinking competence (accounting for sustainability, alongside the diverse interests competing for city resources) and collaboration competence (collaborating with relevant stakeholders to learn and incorporate diverse values). As another example, the professional profile of an investment banker, refined through the lens of sustainability competencies, may place greater emphasis on systems and values thinking (considering the cascading consequences of profit maximisation at the expense of societal and environmental values). These are just two of hundreds of professional profiles augmented with a sustainability competencies approach – aspirations for students, graduates and society at large.

Note

1 For additional perspectives on, critiques of, and approaches to, competence-based educational approaches, see Lansu *et al.* (2013).

References

Barth, M. and Michelsen, G., 2013. 'Learning for Change: An Educational Contribution to Sustainability Science', *Sustainability Science*, 8(1), 103–19.

Barth, M., Godemann, J., Rieckman, M. and Stoltenberg, U., 2007. 'Developing Key Competences for Sustainable Development in Higher Education', *International Journal of Sustainability in Higher Education*, 8(4), 416–30.

Belkin, D., 2014. 'Design for a New College – Arizona State's President Says It's Time to Rethink Tenure and Other Academic Traditions' [Interview with Michael Crow], *The Wall Street Journal*, 9 March 2014.

Bernstein, M.J., Wiek, A., Brundiers, K., Pearson, K., Minowitz, A., Kay, B. and Golub, A., 2014. 'Mitigating Urban Sprawl Effects – A Collaborative Tree and Shade Intervention in Phoenix, Arizona, USA', *Local Environment* (in press).

Biggs, J. and Tang, C., 2007. *Teaching for Quality Learning at University*, 3rd edn. Maidenhead: Open University Press.

Brundiers, K. and Wiek, A., 2011. 'Educating Students in Real-world Sustainability Research – Vision and Implementation', *Innovative Higher Education*, 36(2), 107–24.

Brundiers, K. and Wiek, A., 2013. 'Do we Teach what we Preach? An International Comparison of Problem- and Project-based Learning Courses in Sustainability', *Sustainability*, 5(4), 1725–46.

Crow, M.M., and Dabars, W.B., 2015. *Designing the New American University*, Baltimore, MD: Johns Hopkins University Press.

de Haan, G., 2006. 'The BLK "21" Programme in Germany: A "Gestaltungskompetenz"-Based Model for Education for Sustainable Development,' *Environmental Education Research*, 12(1), 19–32.

De Kraker, J., Corvers, R. and Lansu, A., 2014. 'E-learning for Sustainable Development: Linking Virtual Mobility and Transboundary Competence', in: Azeiteiro, U.M., Leal Filho, W. and Caeiro, S. (eds.), *E-Learning and Education for Sustainability*. Frankfurt am Main: Peter Lang, 29–46.

Friedman, T.L., 2013. 'Without Water, Revolution', *The New York Times*, 18 May, SR1.

Frisk, E. and Larson, K.L., 2011. 'Educating for Sustainability: Competencies & Practices for Transformative Action', *Journal of Sustainability Education*, 2, 1–20.

Kates, R.W., Clark, W.C., Corell, R., Hall, J.M., Jaeger, C.C., Lowe, I., McCarthy, J.J., Schellnhuber, H.J., Bolin, B., Dickson, N.M., Faucheux, S., Gallopin, G.C., Grübler, A., Huntley, B., Jäger, J., Jodha, N.S., Kasperson, R.E., Mabogunje, A., Matson, P.A., Mooney, M., III, B.M., O'Riordan, T. and Svedin, U., 2001. 'Sustainability Science', *Science*, 292(5517), 641–2.

Kay, B., Boyd, T. and Schurgurensky, D., 2012. 'Where do we Start? Initiating Local Transition Processes through Urban High Schools', *Arizona State University: Working Paper, School of Sustainability.*

Kay, B., Wiek, A., Cohen, M. and Forrest, N., 2014. 'Transformational Sustainability Learning – The 5-Step Framework', *Arizona State University: Working Paper, School of Sustainability.*

Lang, D.J., Wiek, A., Bergmann, M., Stauffacher, M., Martens, P., Moll, P., Swilling, M. and Thomas, C., 2012. 'Transdisciplinary Research in Sustainability Science – Practice, Principles and Challenges', *Sustainability Science*, 7(1), 25–43.

Lansu A., Boon, J., Slop, P.B. and van Dam-Mieras, R., 2013. 'Changing Professional Demands in Sustainable Regional Development: A Curriculum Design Process to Meet Transboundary Competence', *Journal of Cleaner Production*, 49(4), 123–33.

Melillo, J.M., Terese, R. and Yohe, G.W., eds., 2014. *Highlights of Climate Change Impacts in the United States: The Third National Climate Assessment*. Washington DC: US Global Change Research Program.

Miller, T.R., Wiek, A., Sarewitz, D., Robinson, J., Olsson, L., Kriebel, D. and Loorbach, D., 2014. 'The Future of Sustainability Science: A Solutions-oriented Research Agenda', *Sustainability Science*, 9(2), 239–46.

Ogden, C.L., Carroll, M.D., Kit, B.K. and Flegal, K.M., 2014.' Prevalence of Childhood and Adult Obesity in the United States, 2011–2012', *Journal of the American Medical Association*, 311(8), 806–14.

Rieckmann, M., 2012. 'Future-oriented Higher Education: Which Key Competencies should be Fostered through University Teaching and Learning?', *Futures*, 44(2), 127–35.

Roorda, N., 2010. 'Sailing on the Winds of Change – The Odyssey to Sustainability of the 10 Universities of Applied Sciences in the Netherlands'. PhD Thesis, Maastricht University, The Netherlands.

Sarewitz, D., Clapp, R. Crumbley, C., Kriebel, D. and Tickner, J., 2012. 'The Sustainable Solutions Agenda', *New Solutions*, 22(2), 139–51.

Steiner, G., 2013. 'Competences for complex real-world problems: Toward an integrative framework', *Working Paper Series No. 13- 0002*. Cambridge, MA: Harvard University, Weatherhead Center for International Affairs.

Sterling, S. and Thomas, I., 2006. 'Education for Sustainability: The Role of Capabilities in Guiding University Curricula', *International Journal of Innovation and Sustainable Development*, 1(4), 349–70.

Thomas, I. and Day, T., 2014. 'Sustainability Capabilities, Graduate Capabilities, and Australian Universities', *International Journal of Sustainability in Higher Education*, 15(2), 7–17.

von der Heidt, T. and Lamberton, G., 2011. 'Sustainability in the Undergraduate and Postgraduate Business Curriculum of a Regional University: A Critical Perspective', *Journal of Management and Organization*, 17(5), 670–90.

Wiek, A., 2014. 'Solving Sustainability Problems – Tools for a New Generation of Sustainability Professionals', *Arizona State University: Working Paper, Sustainability Transition and Intervention Research Lab, School of Sustainability*.

Wiek, A., Withycombe, L., Redman, C.L. and Banas Mills, S., 2011a. 'Moving Forward on Competence in Sustainability Research and Problem Solving', *Environment: Science and Policy for Sustainable Development*, 53(2), 3–12.

Wiek, A., Withycombe, L. and Redman, C.L., 2011b. 'Key Competencies in Sustainability – A Reference Framework for Academic Program Development', *Sustainability Science*, 6(2), 203–18.

Wiek, A., Ness, B., Brand, F.S., Schweizer-Ries, P. and Farioli, F., 2012. 'From Complex Systems Analysis to Transformational Change: A Comparative Appraisal of Sustainability Science Project', *Sustainability Science*, 7(1), 5–24.

Wiek, A., Bernstein, M., Laubichler, M., Caniglia, G., Minteer, B. and Lang, D.J., 2013. 'A Global Classroom for International Sustainability Education', *Creative Education*, 4(4a), 19–28.

Wiek, A. and Kay, B., 2015. 'Learning while Transforming – Solution-oriented Learning for Urban Sustainability in Phoenix, Arizona', *Current Opinion in Environmental Sustainability*, 16, 29–36..

Wiek, A., Xiong, A., Brundiers, K. and van der Leeuw, S., 2014. 'Integrating Problem- and Project-based Learning into Sustainability Programs – A Case Study on the School of Sustainability at Arizona State University', *International Journal of Sustainability in Higher Education*, 15(4), 431–49.

Wiggins, G.P. and McTighe, J., 2005. *Understanding by Design*. Alexandria, VA: Ascd.

World Commission on Environment and Development (WCED), (1987). *Our Common Future*, Oxford and New York: Oxford University Press.

17

INDIVIDUAL CHANGE

Researching educational outcomes achieved by higher education for sustainable development

Kerry Shephard

Introduction

This chapter is intended for two categories of institution. Some will be committed to ESD and will wish to advocate for sustainability to achieve sustainability-related educational outcomes as a normative objective. They may have in place assessment or evaluation regimes to ensure that that each individual named graduate does indeed have all of the outcomes that they require. These institutions will also, it is hoped, wish to understand what their students' personal perceptions of sustainability are in circumstances where they are anonymous and where their qualifications do not depend on how they answer the questions. The chapter is also intended for another type of institution. These do not currently educate *for* sustainability but may wish to explore the impact of their 'higher education' on the developing worldviews of their students. These institutions do not impose normative expectations on their students, with respect to sustainability, but will, nevertheless, be pleased to learn more about how their students' worldviews are developing.

On the nature of ESD outcomes

We start by considering the nature of the outcomes of ESD and address the idea that for ESD to be considered successful, students should graduate from the process with a range of personal attributes compatible with sustainable development and emphasising their personal roles within this. In many situations, perhaps in most, students will change. In an educational context this change is identified as 'learning' and changes in personal attributes as 'learning outcomes'. ESD researchers (see, for example, Shephard 2010) often look to Agenda 21 (UN Conference on Environment and Development 1992: Chapter 36) for guidance about what ESD seeks.

> Both formal and non-formal education are indispensable to changing people's attitudes so that they have the capacity to assess and address their sustainable development concerns. It is also critical for achieving environmental and ethical awareness, values and attitudes, skills and behaviour consistent with sustainable development and for effective public participation in decision-making.

In the context of ESD, and for the purposes of this chapter, Agenda 21 provides clarity about ESD objectives and prescribes some underlying assumptions for our present purposes. First, the changes anticipated by ESD generally apply to all students, not just to those who voluntarily enrol in programmes for which sustainability is already integrated. This chapter is about the former group of students and not, necessarily, the latter. Second, Agenda 21, in the context of higher education, may be rather blunt in asserting that teaching will change people's attitudes, but it does, at least, emphasise that teaching is about achieving change. This chapter is about change and assumes that readers will be interested in change. Third, even readers who do not engage with educational theory will identify diversity in the nature of the educational outcomes incorporated in Agenda 21. Change in 'awareness' is different from change in 'skills'; both are different from change in 'values and attitudes'; and all of these are somehow less than change in 'behaviour'. Intuitively educators realise that some ESD outcomes are more challenging to teach, and learn, than others. Indeed, this chapter assumes that teaching awareness of, or knowledge of, sustainability is not a particular problem that need concern us here. From this point onwards, the chapter selectively focuses on values, attitudes, dispositions and behaviours and on related skills, abilities and competencies.

On the nature of research, assessment and evaluation as applied to ESD outcomes

Readers may be confused by the juxtaposition here of the three terms research, assessment and evaluation, perhaps mostly because these terms do have broadly different meanings in everyday usage. In higher education, however, the terms assessment and evaluation are used in diverse and occasionally in interchangeable ways. Compare, for example, the advice given to academic colleagues in one university in the USA (Duke University 2014) where *assessment* 'is an interactive process between students and faculty that informs faculty how well their students are learning what they are teaching' and yields information that is 'learner-centered, course based, frequently anonymous, and not graded'; with that given in another university on the other side of the Atlantic Ocean (University of Bath 2014) about *evaluation*, providing similar underpinning and also emphasising the anonymity of students in the process. In general, for each institution, country or discipline, where students are anonymous in an evaluation, they are not anonymous in the equivalent assessment, and visa-versa, as most educational institutions feel the need to link aspects of 'performance', with individual, named students. This author uses the term assessment to relate to the measured achievement of a set of learning outcomes by individual and identified students. Evaluation is then the process used to make an overall judgement on the quality of education provided by a programme or institution. In all cases the data used for evaluation in this sense is anonymous. Nevertheless, such is the confusion in the literature about these terms, and the need to bring clarity to this discourse, this author tends to, where possible, abandon both and instead admits to *researching educational outcomes* rather than *assessing* or *evaluating* them; hence the title of this chapter.

On anonymity

Human nature and the power relationships present within higher education between students and teachers, professors or assessors lead us to be wary of any assessment, or evaluation, that asks students to say what their core values and attitudes are and what their future behaviour might be. Rational behaviour, in responding to these questions in a way that fits best with likely positive outcomes in degree and career, may be different from the kinds of behaviour that would otherwise result from deeply held values and attitudes. Bloom at al. (1971) in considering learning in the affective domain of values, attitudes and behaviours, described how anonymity can be used to gather information about affective objectives. As described by Bloom *et al.*, 'it is possible to evaluate a curriculum's affective objectives both formatively and summatively without grading an individual's private and personal affective behaviour' (Bloom *et al.* 1971: 228). We should be wary of research that claims to identify or otherwise measure the values, attitudes, dispositions or self-reported behaviours (or other considerations that are themselves dependent on or underpinned by these qualities) of individual students, where such measurements could conceivably be traced back to the individuals concerned. Subject anonymity is vital to any form of research emphasised in this chapter.

On other challenges involved in researching ESD outcomes

Several features related to ESD make researching its educational outcomes, at the level of affect, particularly challenging. Perhaps most significant amongst these is that ESD is just one part of a broad range of sustainability-related educational missions that individually stem from different longstanding or recently-developed research and education paradigms. These include environmental education (EE), environmental studies (ES), and more recently 'education for sustainable development (ESD)' and 'education for sustainability (EforS)'. For the purposes of this publication ESD is highlighted but readers need to be aware that not all involved in sustainability education (SE) fully appreciate others' educational objectives, perhaps particularly in relation to the student subsets to whom they are applied and the outcomes intended. Some researchers (Jickling and Wals 2008; Shephard 2008, 2010, as examples) express concern about the extent to which education is asked to influence not only what students learn about a topic, but what they think about it and how they will behave in relation to it. These objectives are somehow incongruous with the liberal traditions of higher education. This issue will reappear later in this chapter.

In line with different modes of SE, and their different educational philosophies, higher education institutions also use different educational processes to reach students. Some (see, for example, Katherine 2008) have embarked on systematic 'greening of the curriculum' to enable students in every discipline to experience sustainability concepts. Others (see, for example, California State University 2014) extend traditional liberal studies approaches to ensure that many, most, or all students can benefit from a sustainability-inclusive curriculum. No doubt other SE strategies exist.

Overall, the aims, objectives and approaches present in this broad area of SE vary widely but in general terms do include the hope, up front or unspoken, that higher education will contribute to social change towards sustainability, via changes in choices that graduates will make (i.e. changes in behaviour). Such aspirations for social change, reconfigured as educational outcomes, will always be challenging to research. Research is, by and large, an exacting pursuit. To research ESD outcomes we need to be specific about what they are, from an educational and theoretical perspective.

On addressing the challenges in ESD outcome research

One approach that helps us to conceptualise the nature of the learning changes anticipated in various forms of SE is to consider what students *know*, what *skills* they have to put this knowledge to effect and what they might *choose* to do with the knowledge and skills that they learn in higher education (a model that draws heavily from the ideas of Bloom and Krathwohl;

differentiating between cognition and affect, in learning; Bloom *et al.* 1971; Krathwohl *et al.* 1964). In this model, knowledge and skills are addressed within the cognitive domain of learning, but what graduates might choose to do with their knowledge and skills are described as affective attributes in a hierarchy. Students learn, sequentially, to listen, to respond, to value, to organise and to characterise. Each stage in the hierarchy can be described by a range of typical actions. At the highest level of the affective domain, learners acquire a particular worldview and behave in relation to this. There are strong links between progression up the affective domain hierarchy and equivalent progressions within the cognitive domain of learning, as certain affective characteristics underpin particular cognitive abilities (Bloom *et al.* 1971) such as critical thinking (Facione 1990).

There have been other attempts to combine notions of *choice* with those of *ability*, *skill* or *competence*. Choice is central to the ideals of democratic education and links to the competency debate via the concepts of 'action competence' (Jensen and Schnack 2006; Mogensen and Schnack, 2010) and 'key competencies' (Barth *et al.* 2007; Wiek *et al.* in this Handbook); but nonetheless is challenging to fit within conventional higher educational processes. Action competence has been described simply as an 'ability to act' (Jensen and Schnack 2006; emphasising, in Bloom's terminology, a skill to be learned and therefore an educational outcome to be researched using conventional educational processes). But with more explanation, 'competence' acquires additional meaning; 'Competence' is associated with being able, and willing, to be a qualified participant (Jensen and Schnack 2006: 473). With this meaning there is clear combination of literal and every-day meanings of '*ability*' and '*willingness*'. To be *willing* is essentially the same as making the *choice to be*, and this interpretation of educational outcome as action competence suggests combination of Bloom's cognitive and affective domains of learning.

Barth *et al.* (2007) have researched the development of many competencies, described as key competencies, and they emphasise 'qualitative extension that points out the special significance of certain competencies' (Barth *et al.* 2007: 417). These competencies are 'characterised as dispositions' and 'are reflected in successful actions' (Barth *et al.* 2007: 417). The application of key competencies to this debate has been developed further by Rieckmann (2012) with respect to sustainability, and by Fischer and Barth (2014) with respect to sustainable consumption. These latter authors identify that 'competencies deal with complex demands that necessitate the interplay of cognitive, emotional and motivational dispositions' (Fischer and Barth 2014: 194) and that 'each [key competency] consists of cognitive and non-cognitive dispositions' (Fischer and Barth 2014: 196; see also Barth *et al.* 2007).

For this author, and for the purposes of this chapter, expressions of emotional, motivational and non-cognitive dispositions are, in essence, paraphrases of affect and so relate to what learners choose to do with their knowledge and skills. It seems likely that the cognitive skills, action competencies and key competencies that are so critical to sustainability behaviour, and so legitimately sought as ESD outcomes, are themselves underpinned by and dependent on affective learning. For this author, our tour of affect, action competence and key competencies has gone full circle to suggest that education for sustainability, for sustainable development, and for sustainable consumption, are fundamentally quests for affective outcomes (as proposed by Shephard 2008). Other outcomes may be sought, but they are probably either relatively educationally-straightforward (such as knowledge and understanding), or fundamentally dependent on affective change (as described by Fischer and Barth, 'on the level of underlying dispositions, where such motivational dispositions to engage with sustainable consumption or attitudes towards sustainable consumption inform and shape the nature of literally every key competency' [Fischer and Barth 2014: 197]). In researching educational outcomes achieved by ESD, we do need to address affect; and maintain a focus on the anonymity of students in the process.

Researching affect-laden educational outcomes relevant to ESD

Research into affective educational outcomes relevant to sustainability has a substantial history. Dunlap and Jones, for example, attempted to clarify the meaning of 'environmental concern' from a historical perspective (Dunlap and Jones 2002). In doing so they confirmed that by 1978 more than 300 research studies had been established about understanding peoples' environmental concern. It is apparent that environmental concern is just one of many themes important for our interest in sustainability outcomes (Buissink-Smith *et al.* 2011). The full repertoire of research papers focusing on sustainability outcomes would number many thousands and many of these identify the development and use of research instruments relevant to this chapter. It is also apparent, historically, that researchers have understood the complexity of the issues involved. Stern (1992) described the multiple attempts to make measurements in this field as 'anarchy of measurement'. Even the word 'measurement' as applied to educational outcomes as complex as those that result from sustainability education causes problems, but it should be noted that '*We cannot improve at scale what we cannot measure*' is one of six core principles for educational improvement adopted by the Carnegie Foundation (Carnegie 2015).

Taking into account preceding paragraphs, this chapter argues that researching sustainability outcomes relevant to ESD-promoted educational change requires us to work systematically with respect to four resolutions:

1. finding approaches that *measure* outcomes (assuming that higher education does want to 'improve at scale' its impact on the sustainability attributes of its students), and
2. seeking *outcomes that can be measured* (emphasising that not all objectives are measurable, so some compromise may be necessary), and
3. focussing on *affect* (as all the knowledge and skill in the world may not be enough if our graduates choose not to utilise them to sustainability ends), and
4. being cautious about researching individuals unless they are *anonymous* in the process (as even the most enlightened amongst us may be motivated by self-interest, some of the time).

It seems likely that no simple research instrument or approach could possibly address all four requirements. Before we jump to this conclusion, however, we might seek assistance from an unlikely source and emphasise that we are, at this stage, working systematically towards something greater.

The revised New Ecological Paradigm scale (NEP)

The New Environmental Paradigm scale was developed by Dunlap and van Liere in 1978. It resurfaced in 2000 as the Revised New Ecological Paradigm scale (Dunlap *et al.* 2000) and it has been extensively used for classifying the views that people have about the natural environment (styled as ecological worldview by Dunlap *et al.* 2000). The NEP includes 15 statements that relate to limits to growth, the position of humans in the environment, the fragility of nature, and the imminence of ecocrisis that alternate between pro and anti-stances on the issues. Respondents are asked to record their agreement with these items on 5-point Likert-like scales. The validity of the construction of the NEP and its ability to accurately represent environmental attitudes have been repeatedly tested (Dunlap 2008; Harraway *et al.* 2012). The worth of the NEP has been discussed on many occasions during its more than 30 year history. Researchers worry about its simplicity, the difficulty of understanding exactly what it measures, whether it relates to belief or attitude and what 'worldview' or environmental attitude means in the context of ESD (most recently, for example by Noblet *et al.* 2013). For the purposes of this chapter, focussed as it is on ESD outcomes, the NEP is, of itself, insufficient. Yes, the NEP is a measurement instrument (at its simplest it allocates a number between 1 and 5 to each individual) and, certainly, it can be used for anonymous individuals in groups (matching Resolutions 1 and 4). But the educational objectives of ESD relate to far more than environmental attitude or ecological worldview. Perhaps we can forgive this deficiency in the spirit of Resolution 2 (as there seems little doubt that the NEP does measure something at least related to sustainability). In pursuance of Resolution 3, there is no doubt that the NEP does address affect, be it worldview (at the highest level of the affective hierarchy, Bloom *et al.* 1971), or something more modest such as attitude (Hawcroft and Milfont 2010).

It seems inevitable that a better instrument than the NEP will be developed for our purposes but the NEP has been so widely used already that its continued use seems assured. Following an extensive review of its use over a 30-year period, Hawcroft and Milfont (2010) concluded that 'until a gold-standard EA [environmental attitude] measure has been widely accepted, it is probably advisable for researchers to continue using the NEP scale as a standardised measure of EA'. The 15 item revised NEP scale is described in Table 17.1. We should use the NEP as a tool to help us work systematically towards something better.

Using the NEP to research ESD outcomes

Most often the NEP is used to benchmark the environmental worldviews of discrete populations or to compare different populations (for example, student groups enrolled into different programmes as in Shephard *et al.* 2009). Some comparative data is provided in a meta-analysis of the use of the NEP (Hawcroft and Milfont 2010). Used in this way NEP does enable researchers to discriminate between different groups to identify which group has the greatest environmental worldview. Conventional parametric and non-parametric statistical analysis may

Table 17.1 The 15 item revised New Ecological Paradigm scale. Respondents are asked to agree or disagree with each statement on a 5 point Likert-like scale. Note that alternate statements express pro- or anti-environmental/sustainability sentiments.

1	We are approaching the limit of the number of people the earth can support.
2	Humans have the right to modify the natural environment to suit their needs.
3	When humans interfere with nature it often produces disastrous consequences.
4	Human ingenuity will ensure that we do not make the earth unliveable.
5	Humans are severely abusing the environment.
6	The earth has plenty of natural resources if we just learn how to develop them.
7	Plants and animals have as much right as humans to exist.
8	The balance of nature is strong enough to cope with the impacts of modern industrial nations.
9	Despite their special abilities humans are still subject to the laws of nature.
10	The so-called 'ecological crisis' facing humankind has been greatly exaggerated.
11	The earth is like a spaceship with very limited room and resources.
12	Humans are meant to rule over the rest of nature.
13	The balance of nature is very delicate and easily upset.
14	Humans will eventually learn enough about how nature works to be able to control it.
15	If things continue on their present course we will soon experience a major ecological catastrophe.

Source: Adapted by the author from Dunlap *et al.* 2000

be used in these circumstances as described by Harraway *et al.* (2012). It is notable that numerous studies have found significant relationships between responses to the NEP and various types of behavioural intentions, self-reported and observed behaviours (Dunlap *et al.* 2000).

Research on change

Measuring change in the value of a complex construct is a more challenging task than simply measuring the construct at a single point in time. Even where appropriate research or measurement instruments are available to determine, say, the environmental concern or attitudes of students, identifying change in these things presents additional problems.

- Institutions may need to grapple with these questions at the individual and cohort level.
- They may involve many individuals, multiple test points, extended time periods and multiple overlapping cohorts.
- The subjects of this enquiry, students, may be volunteers in the research, unreliable attendees and move between cohorts as they pass, fail and retake courses and change programmes.

The process of monitoring such a dynamic entity is fraught with statistical complexity. The following account focuses on research that has used the NEP, but could be adapted to use almost any instrument with quantitative numerical outputs.

Before and After analysis

Perhaps most simply, the NEP and paired statistical tests may be used in a 'before and after' format on a single cohort of anonymous individual students (see as examples, Anderson *et al.* 2007; Harraway *et al.* 2012). From a statistical perspective it is important that paired formats are used, as in many other formats samples must be independent from one another for valid statistical inference. In most cases comparisons are made between NEP scores averaged over all 15 items (reversing the scores of alternate NEP items) (see for example Harraway *et al.* 2012). In some cases, subsets of NEP items are compared, for example as in Harraway *et al.* (2012), using NEP items grouped as tendencies (to conserve, to recycle, to respect plant and animal rights and to be cautious about the future) as described initially by Shephard *et al.* (2009). Students should always be anonymous in these surveys. They can be tracked by using a code that is calculated from their date of birth and name but that cannot be traced to them by the university administration (Harraway *et al.* 2012).

Matched data t-tests are generally used to investigate differences in the overall NEP mean scores and subsets of NEP items. Wilcoxon Signed Rank tests are used to investigate differences in medians for the scores on the individual items at two time points. (The Wilcoxon test is appropriate for discrete, non-normal data, which arises from the individual items measured on Likert-like scales. T-tests are appropriate for normally distributed data, which arises when individual items are combined into multi-item scales.)

Of general importance in this form of analysis is the acceptance that where change may be recorded, we cannot necessarily identify its cause. In particular, and from an educational perspective, it would be good to be able to say that change was associated in some way with the educational efforts of the institutions' teachers. Generally we can make no such claim.

Cross sectional analysis

An alternative approach for modelling change is to analyse data in a cross-sectional manner, rather than sequentially in relation to time. At any one time, students exist in several cohorts and these can be compared. Teisl *et al.* (2011) used three logistic regression models to investigate changes in environmental attitudes in response to different courses and teachers. Jowett *et al.* (2014) developed an alternative multinomial logistic regression (MLR) model to explore differences between cohorts. The MLR was developed because of its improved efficiency (only one model is fitted) and because it is easier to interpret the results than using separate logistic regression models.

Use of this model does, as with all other models, have some limitations. In particular this form of modelling anticipates that each cohort arrives at the institution with approximately the same measured characteristics, that their experiences whilst at the institution are approximately the same each year, and that the demographic characteristics of each cohort do not change as it passes from one year to the next. Differences between say first year students and second year students at any particular time may therefore reflect their experiences within the intervening year. A particular problem for some universities is that students may be selected for moving from one year to another. In this situation, perhaps the less academically able students will not move forward, making the second year cohort effectively a different group from the first year cohort. Modelling is always problematic where collinearity between variables such as age, gender, academic success and programme of study occur.

Longitudinal modelling approaches to analysis

'Before and after' analyses and 'cross sectional' analyses both operate with identified cohorts of students on specified occasions. It is challenging, particularly from a statistical point of view, to incorporate additional data at different time points. In general, and hopefully in the long term, those higher education institutions that adopt ESD will wish to step back from detailed analysis of particular cohorts and answer the much more general questions 'Do our students, in general and over extended time periods, change? And if they do, to what degree and how?' These are similar questions to those posed by epidemiologists who might ask about the development of particular diseases in a population over extended time periods. Longitudinal modelling approaches make optimum use of data available from dynamic systems over extended time periods. Shephard *et al.* (2012) report on the development of a longitudinal analysis using a 'linear mixed-effects model' (LME), suitable for use with the NEP, that tracks an individual cohort of students over several years. Students record their ecological worldview anonymously at several points in time during the course of their undergraduate studies. The approach is robust in that it allows for missing data (some students attend regularly and contribute more than one NEP record but some students miss some opportunities). The approach also allows for the NEP surveys to be used at different times of the year to suit the university teachers who administer them. Students are anonymous in the survey. The approach has been extended to allow multiple cohorts of students taking different programmes of study to be incorporated into the analysis (Shephard *et al.* 2014).

What the NEP data shows us

Extensive research using the NEP in the author's own institution demonstrates the efficacy of this instrument and the approaches used in distinguishing between the worldviews of different groups of students (Shephard *et al.* 2012, 2014; Harraway *et al.* 2012). Year after year students arrive at this institution with worldviews already mapped to their chosen discipline; with zoology students, for example, generally holding more pro-environmental worldviews than do, for example, surveying students. But research with the NEP does not yet suggest that students change their worldviews as they experience higher education.

Beyond the NEP

Institutions that use the NEP to explore their students' ecological worldviews, either within an ESD framework or within some other research framework, such as the exploration of environmental literacy as described by Shephard *et al.* (2013a), may discover much about themselves that will be valuable should they proceed seriously to seek ESD outcomes. As described above, the educational challenges involved in changing people's attitudes and behaviours are considerable, as indeed are the challenges of demonstrating that attitudes truly have been changed. Although representatives of more than 470 universities in more than 50 countries have signed the Talloires Declaration (ULSF 2014) agreeing to create an institutional culture of sustainability and to educate for environmentally responsible citizenship, it is not clear how these institutions have validated these claims. They could choose to research the learning outcomes achieved by their students as described in this chapter using the NEP or any of many other instruments. They could in particular use the longitudinal model described here, and it is notable that these processes could easily fit into the routine evaluation process that many higher education institutions undertake to explore or validate the quality of their teaching.

The NEP can also be combined with other instruments to research a wider range of educational outcomes in student groups. The North American Association for Environmental Education (NAAEE) has developed instruments to assess environmental literacy (EL) and a framework within which EL could be measured (McBeth and Volk 2009; Hollweg *et al.* 2011). It is important to note that the development of an instrument in this complex domain provides not just a means to measure but also the opportunity to more tightly define, and understand, the nature of what is being measured. NAAEE researchers include, within their instrument, knowledge (including knowing about social, cultural and political systems), dispositions (including attitudes, concern, worldview and personal responsibility), competencies (clusters of skills and abilities that may be called upon and expressed for a specific purpose such as the ability to evaluate and make personal judgments about environmental issues), and environmentally responsible behaviour (self-reported) all of which are expressed in particular contexts. The NAAEE EL instrument represents a 'strong' interpretation of EL (Stables and Bishop 2001); one that encompasses far more than 'environmental concern', extending as it does to a wide range of sustainability issues; and one that includes what students know about the environment (knowledge), what skills they have to put this knowledge to effect (competence) and what they might choose to do with this knowledge and skill (dispositions or affect) (Shephard *et al.* 2013a). The NAAEE EL Instrument inspired researchers in New Zealand to produce the Environmental Literacy Evaluation Instrument (ELEI) for use in higher education (Shephard *et al* 2013a) and to incorporate the NEP to address affect. The publication includes the ELEI itself and these authors also produced comprehensive guidelines on its use (Shephard *et al.* 2013b). To date in the author's own institution, one department (Human Nutrition) has used these guidelines to adapt the ELEI to make it highly relevant to that discipline and to the needs of its teachers. The ELEI is designed specifically to enable a higher education institution that sets out to foster, or develop, the environmental literacy of its students to research the extent to which it achieves its objectives.

Beyond ESD

Even if readers of this chapter accept that ESD is primarily a quest for affective educational outcomes (Shephard 2008) and that these outcomes can be researched at the level of anonymous individuals (as described in this chapter), there remains the critical question of where ESD fits within higher education. Agenda 21 objectives may seem reasonable to those inside or outside of higher education who embrace 'sustainable development as a normative framework for selecting key competencies' (Barth *et al.* 2007: 417) and for whom 'acquiring relevant competencies within and by academic work cannot be a private concern of faculty, staff or administration' (Barth *et al.* 2007: 416), but university teachers have differing views on what should be taught in higher education, how it should be taught and assessed, and what their personal role is in doing these things (Shephard and Furnari 2013). Shephard (2008) identified this conundrum and suggested that interpreting sustainability-related outcomes as affective outcomes in a hierarchy enables university teachers to address the acceptability of their approaches to their profession, their institution and to the liberal traditions of higher education. The emphasis here is on diverse interpretations of what ESD currently is, and could be. Using research instruments like the NEP, with all of its imperfections and limitations, with anonymous students, may allow the widest possible range of sustainability-minded educational practitioners, with their diverse interpretations of ESD, to converge to research something that all may agree underpins the diversity of SE objectives. Above all, higher education institutions and their practitioners who claim to educate for sustainable development do need to substantiate their claims by demonstrating, to all higher education practitioners, the nature and magnitude of their impact on student outcomes. Failure to do so may place the wider projects of ESD, and EforS, in jeopardy.

References

Anderson, M., Criner, G., Teisl, M., Smith, H., Hunter, M., Norton, S. and Bicknell, E., 2007. 'Attitude Change of Undergraduate Students in General Education Courses', *Journal of General Education*, 56(2), 149–68.

Barth, M., Godemann, J., Rieckmann, M. and Stoltenberg, U., 2007. 'Developing Key Competencies for Sustainable Development in Higher Education', *International Journal of Sustainability in Higher Education*, 8(4), 416–30.

Bloom, B.S., Hastings, J.T. and Madaus, G.F.. 1971. *Handbook on Formative and Summative Evaluation of Student Learning*. New York: McGraw-Hill.

Buissink-Smith, N., Mann, S. and Shephard, K., 2011. 'How Do We Measure Affective Learning in Higher Education?', *Journal of Education for Sustainable Development*, 5(1), 101–14.

California State University, 2014. 'Liberal Studies Sustainability Track'. www.csun.edu/sustainability/curriculum/liberal-studies-sustainability-track/ [accessed 13 February 2015].

Carnegie (Foundation for the Advancement of Teaching), 2015. 'Community Engagement Classification'. www.carnegiefoundation.org/our-ideas/six-core-principles-improvement/ [accessed 16 June 2015].

Duke University, 2014. 'What is the Difference between Assessment and Evaluation?' http://duke.edu/arc/documents/The%20difference%20between%20assessment%20and%20evaluation.pdf [accessed 13 February 2015].

Dunlap, R.E., 2008. 'The New Ecological Paradigm Scale: From Marginality to Worldwide Use', *Journal of Environmental Education* 40(1), 3–18.

Dunlap, R.E. and van Liere, K.D., 1978. 'The New Environmental Paradigm', *Journal of Environmental Education*, 9(4), 10–19.

Dunlap, R.E. and Jones, R.E., 2002. 'Environmental Concern: Conceptual and Measurement Issues', in Dunlap, R.E. and Michelson, W. (eds), *Handbook of Environmental Sociology*. Westport, CT: Greenwood Press, 482–524.

Dunlap, R., van Liere, K., Mertig, A. and Jones, R., 2000. 'New Trends in Measuring Environmental

Attitudes: Measuring Endorsement of the New Ecological Paradigm: A Revised NEP Scale', *Journal of Social Issues*, 56(3): 425–42.
Facione, P.A., 1990. 'Executive Summary: Critical Thinking: A Statement of Expert Consensus for Purposes of Educational Assessment and Instruction'. Millbrae, CA: The California Academic Press. www.insightassessment.com/CT-Resources/Expert-Consensus-on-Critical-Thinking/Delphi-Consensus-Report-Executive-Summary-PDF [accessed 13 February 2015].
Fischer, D. and Barth, M., 2014. 'Key Competencies for and beyond Sustainable Consumption: An Educational Contribution to the Debate', *Gaia*, 23(S1), 193–200.
Harraway, J., Broughton-Ansin, F., Deaker, L., Jowett, T. and Shephard, K., 2012. 'Exploring the Use of the Revised New Ecological Paradigm Scale (NEP) to Monitor the Development of Students' Ecological Worldviews', *The Journal of Environmental Education*, 43(3), 177–91.
Hawcroft, L.J. and Milfont, T., 2010. 'The Use (and abuse) of the New Environmental Paradigm Scale over the Last 30 Years: A Meta-analysis', *Journal of Environmental Psychology*, 30(2), 143–58.
Hollweg, K., Taylor, J., Bybee, R., Marcinkowski, T., McBeth, W. and Zoido, P., 2011. 'Developing a Framework for Assessing Environmental Literacy'. Washington, DC: North American Association for Environmental Education. www.naaee.net/framework [accessed 13 February 2015].
Jensen, B.B. and Schnack, K., 2006. 'The Action Competence Approach in Environmental Education', *Environmental Education Research*, 12(3/4), 471–86.
Jickling, B. and Wals, A.E.J., 2008. 'Globalization and Environmental Education: Looking Beyond Sustainable Development', *Journal of Curriculum Studies*, 40(1), 1–21.
Jowett, T., Harraway, J., Lovelock, B., Skeaff, S., Slooten, L., Strack, M. and Shephard, K., 2014. 'Multinomial-regression Modelling of the Environmental Attitudes of Higher Education Students based on the Revised New Ecological Paradigm Scale', *Journal of Environmental Education*, 45(1), 1–15.
Katherine, A., 2008. 'What is "Greening the Curriculum"'. www.smc.edu/ACG/AcademicSenate/Documents/Environmental_Affairs_Committee/GreeningtheCurriculum9-09.pdf [accessed 13 February 2015].
Krathwohl, D., Bloom, B. and Masia, B., 1964. *Taxonomy of Educational Objectives, Handbook II: The Affective Domain*. New York: David McKay Co.
McBeth, W. and Volk, T., 2009. 'The National Environmental Literacy Project: A Baseline Study of Middle Grade Students in the United States', *The Journal of Environmental Education*, 41(1), 55–67.
Mogensen, F. and Schnack, K., 2010. 'The Action Competence Approach and the "New" Discourses of Education for Sustainable Development, Competence and Quality Criteria', *Environmental Education Research*, 16(1), 59–74.
Noblet, C.L., Anderson, M. and Teisl, M.F., 2013. 'An Empirical Test of Anchoring the NEP Scale in Environmental Ethics', *Environmental Education Research*, 19(4), 540–51.
Rieckmann, M., 2012. 'Future-oriented Higher Education: Which Key Competencies should be Fostered through University Teaching and Learning?' *Futures*, 44(2), 127–35.
Shephard, K.L., 2008. 'Higher Education for Sustainability: Seeking Affective Learning Outcomes', *International Journal of Sustainability in Higher Education*, 19(1), 87–98.
Shephard, K., 2010. 'Higher Education's Role in "Education for Sustainability"', *Australian Universities Review*, 52(1), 13–22.
Shephard, K. and Furnari, M., 2013. 'Exploring what University Teachers think about Education for Sustainability', *Studies in Higher Education*, 38(10), 1577–90.
Shephard, K., Mann, S., Smith, N. and Deaker, L., 2009. 'Benchmarking the Environmental Values and Attitudes of Students in New Zealand's Post-compulsory Education', *Environmental Education Research*, 15, 571–87.
Shephard, K., Harraway, J., Lovelock, B., Skeaff, S., Slooten, E., Strack, M. and Jowett, T., 2012. 'Monitoring Changes in the Sustainability Attributes of Higher Education Students in a New Zealand University', in Leal, W. (ed.), *Sustainable Development at Universities: New Horizons*. Frankfurt: Peter Lang, 117–27.
Shephard, K., Harraway, J., Lovelock, B., Skeaff, S., Slooten, L., Strack, M., Furnari, M. and Jowett, T., 2013a. 'Is the Environmental Literacy of University Students Measurable?', *Environmental Education Research*, 20(4), 476–95.
Shephard, K., Harraway, J., Lovelock, B., Skeaff, S., Slooten, L., Strack, M., Furnari, M. and Jowett, T., 2013b. 'Environmental Literacy Evaluation Instrument: Departmental Guidelines'. www.otago.ac.nz/council/committees/committees/otago059689.pdf [accessed 13 February 2015].
Shephard, K., Harraway, J., Jowett, T., Lovelock, B., Skeaff, S., Slooten, E., Strack, M. and Furnari, M., 2014. 'Longitudinal Analysis of the Environmental Attitudes of University Students'. *Environmental Education*

Research. www.tandfonline.com/doi/full/10.1080/13504622.2014.913126 [accessed 13 February 2015].

Stables, A. and Bishop, K., 2001. 'Weak and Strong Conceptions of Environmental Literacy: Implications for Environmental Education', *Environmental Education Research*, 7(1), 89–97.

Stern, P.C., 1992. 'Psychological Dimensions of Global Environmental Change', *Annual Review of Psychology*, 43(1), 269–302.

Teisl, M., Anderson, M., Noblet, C., Criner, G., Rubin, J. and Dalton, T., 2011. 'Are Environmental Professors Unbalanced? Evidence from the Field', *The Journal of Environmental Education*, 42(2), 67–83.

ULSF – University Leaders for a Sustainable Future, 2014. *Talloires Declaration Institutional Signatory List*. www.ulsf.org/programs_talloires_signatories.html [accessed 12 January 2015].

United Nations Conference on Environment and Development, 1992. 'Agenda 21 Chapter 36'. www.un-documents.net/a21-36.htm [accessed 13 February 2015].

University of Bath, 2014. 'Unit Evaluation'. www.bath.ac.uk/learningandteaching/surveys/unit-evaluation/index.html [accessed 13 February 2015].

18

STUDENT ENGAGEMENT AND LEADERSHIP IN HIGHER EDUCATION FOR SUSTAINABILITY

Daniella Tilbury

Introduction

As higher education policy, funding and practice become increasingly student-centred, research into higher education is also being challenged to rethink its dominant paradigm. The narrative on student engagement provides the backdrop to understanding much of what is currently happening across the sector globally and provides alternative frames from which to review studies of higher education for sustainable development.

Recent writings capture how student engagement has become the focus of global academic conversations and the basis for exploring the new edges around practice in universities and colleges of higher education (GUNI 2014). The catch-phrase 'placing student at the heart of the higher education system' underpins UK policy on higher education (Department for Business, Innovation and Skills [BIS] 2011); with similar phrasing found in Australian higher education frameworks (Marginson 2013). Few would dispute the need to improve student engagement levels in higher education given the often exclusive[1] and mostly transmissive[2] approaches adopted by higher education institutions (Alvares and Faruqi 2012).

The student engagement narrative resonates deeply with proponents of sustainable development who seek to engage students in real world issues, reframe the teacher-learner relationships, promote participatory and active learning and embed responsibility into professional education outcomes (Bartlett and Chase 2013; Ryan and Cotton 2013; Sterling *et al.* 2013; Scott *et al.* 2012; Tilbury 2011). These transformative learning ambitions, often associated with education for sustainable development, have not translated well into empirical research work. The contextual dynamics of institutions and narrow interpretations of the principle of 'student engagement' have led to a fixation on studies to establish student satisfaction levels rather than on research to improve participation levels or outcomes. In Australia and New Zealand, for example, the administration of an Australasian Survey of Student Engagement (AUSSE) has helped institutions collect information that increases understanding of student satisfaction levels. Similar major evidence-based collection of data on student engagement (aka satisfaction levels) are in use in the United States[3] and UK.[4] These sector responses point to the difficulty of embedding deeper conceptions of student engagement and the challenges of shifting paradigms that currently serve the higher education sector. Genuine student engagement is hard to practice across a system that currently regards students as recipients rather than co-creators of knowledge.

This chapter identifies the tensions captured by, as well as reflected in, the research literature around student engagement. It takes a focus on sustainable development research contrasting the ambitions of student empowerment, participation and change agency with the research themes and methodologies that focus on students as receivers of knowledge, respondents of attitudinal surveys or subjects in the testing of behaviour change theories.

The writing is informed by a UNESCO commissioned research study that assessed progress in reorienting higher education toward sustainable development (Tilbury 2014). The UNESCO report reviewed evidence from literature published between 2005 and 2014,[5] as well as key indicators such as the emergence of student associations with a primary focus on sustainable development, case studies captured in international journals and data from national student surveys. Supplementing documentation analysis was an expert review of trends and data arising from regional consultations undertaken by UNESCO during 2013.

Student engagement for sustainable development

Fredricks *et al.* (2004) define student engagement as a 'meta-construct' which draws together diverse threads of research that seek to improve the quality of educational processes, experiences or outcomes. Kuh (2009) goes as far as suggesting that student engagement now acts as a proxy for quality in education; whist Trowler (2010) concludes that the significance and value of student engagement is no longer questioned as an educational force for change. This literature offers a diversity of definitions to clarify what is meant by 'student engagement' and common to most is the term 'participation' as well as association between the active involvement in the educational experience and learning that is more meaningful and enduring (Bomia *et al.* 1997).

This narrative of student engagement is strong across discourses on sustainable development and highly visible in the UN literature. The Rio+20 outcomes document *The Future We Want* (UN 2012) is a prime example of this with the terms 'engagement' and 'participation' appearing across almost all paragraphs. The International Union for the Conservation of Nature and Natural Resources (IUCN) publication *Engaging People in Sustainability* (Tilbury and Wortman 2004) defines a pedagogical framework for engagement and proposes experiences where learners are: envisioning more positive futures; developing critical reflective and systemic skills which help them actively interpret scenarios; and, participating in decision-making skills that support their effective engagement with real issues. Similarly, the UN Economic Commission for Europe (UNECE) offers an Education for Sustainable Development Competences Framework (UNECE 2011) to help educators reframe the learning experience to be more engaging and participatory. It mirrors the active learning pedagogical principles proposed by the IUCN publication that can help students understand the world in which they live, act on this understanding and address the complexity of and interconnectedness of sustainability issues.

Ambitions of empowerment underpin the human rights based approaches to education for sustainable development. The United Nations Population Fund (UNFPA 2012) argues that only engaged learning approaches can help realise equality, achieve access to education and health services, develop active citizens and protect people from exploitation. Faith-based organisations, such as Soka Gakkai International (SGI), also interpret deep learner engagement as key to improving wellbeing and livelihoods, and critical to the creation of more sustainable futures (SGI 2012).

Learner empowerment is capturing fresh interest in higher education circles as flexible pedagogies gain in importance across policy circles. The Higher Education Academy of the UK explicitly promotes the creation of flexible learning opportunities that enable the learner to choose place, pace and mode of learning. These discussions are often Information and Communication Technology (ICT) flavoured with advances in this area opening up the HE environment and extending learning access to new stakeholder groups as well as offering more 'flexible' patterns of participation. In their recent research review, Ryan and Tilbury (2013) frame flexible pedagogies within an education for sustainable development perspective, drawing attention to how learner empowerment can be developed through education that is future-facing, promotes social learning, decolonises the curriculum, crosses disciplinary boundaries and actively seeks to develop transformative capabilities.[6]

The multiple studies examined as part of the UNESCO review suggested that the student engagement narrative has a strong presence across sustainable development scholarly and policy debate and especially in the literature that call for transformative outcomes in higher education. Box 18.1 defines student engagement making explicit connections to sustainable development.

From behaviour change to empowerment

Kahu (2011) reminds us that although student engagement in higher education is well articulated across various frames of reference and widely endorsed by stakeholder groups, research has made a limited contribution to translating these goals into practice. This, he argues, results from the dominance of behavioural and psychological studies in this area. An analysis of research studies into higher education, published over the last ten years, reveals that sustainability researchers have focused primarily on student behaviour change, attitudinal shifts and the sharing of experiences in this area.[7] The literature review uncovered a multitude of studies that assess levels of student understanding or their adoption of sustainable behaviours, using underlying models that treat students not in terms of their potential contribution to sustainability, or as co-generators of knowledge, but more as objects of study.

Azapagic *et al.* (2005), for example, in a special issue on education for sustainable development in the *European Journal of Engineering Education*, undertakes a worldwide survey of engineering students to assess their level of knowledge and understanding of sustainable

Box 18.1 Defining student engagement

Traditional definitions of student engagement refer to the degree of responsiveness (attention, curiosity, interest, optimism and/or passion) that students show when they are learning, or are being taught (Fletcher 2014; Trowler 2010).

Student engagement in this chapter is seen through the sustainable development lens as defined by Tilbury and Wortman (2004). It draws attention to i) power threads in education (or research) activity, and ii) authentic participation opportunities where students inform and influence that activity. Student engagement, in this sense, is committed to student empowerment and supports the development of action competence and leadership capability. It also leads to alternative research processes and inquiries.

development. The survey results suggest that, overall, the level of understanding is not satisfactory and that significant knowledge gaps exist. Kagawa, in her 2007 research paper on 'Dissonance in Students' Perceptions of Sustainable Development and Sustainability: Implications for Curriculum Change' reports on the findings of an online questionnaire that captures University of Plymouth students' perceptions and understandings of, and attitudes towards, sustainable development. She uses SPSS tools and cross tabulates coded responses to identify emerging themes that 'facilitate students' pro-sustainability behaviours'. Whannall *et al.*'s (2012) inquiry into tertiary students' attitudes to the bicycle community in Australia published in the same journal, *International Journal of Sustainability in Higher Education*, administers another survey to assess the likelihood that participants would use a bicycle to commute to university and the factors which influenced the decision to bicycle commute. A survey also underpins Emanuel and Adams' (2011) study from the US of 406 college students' perceptions of campus sustainability in Alabama and Hawaii that establishes there are no significant differences between college students in these two US States.

Most popular are the use of Environmental Attitude Scales (EAS) as a means of conducting studies *on* students. In Turkey, for example, Tuncer (2008) gathers data through the administration of a modified version of the standard EAS and conducts a two-way Analysis of Variance (ANOVA). The results published in the *International Journal of Geographical and Environmental Education Research* revealed that while there was a statistically significant mean difference between males and females with respect to perception on sustainable development, there was no difference between students who enrolled in an environment-related course and those who did not. Along similar lines is McMillan *et al.*'s 2004 Canadian study into the 'Impact of a University-Level Environmental Studies Class on Students' Values'. Interviews and questionnaires were used to determine whether values changed or developed after an introductory university-level environmental studies class on environmental values. Questionnaires were administered in a pre-test and post-test fashion and accompanied by unstructured interviews conducted throughout the academic year. The students were found 'to deepen their environmental values after taking the class, becoming more ecocentric, and less homocentric' (McMillan *et al.* 2004: 19).

Studies of this kind dominate the research literature and unwittingly reproduce prevailing views of students as subjects of research into sustainability in higher education. One of the most obvious patterns in the evidence, which stands out as a real obstacle to deeper student engagement, is the tendency to view students as empty vessels, ready to be filled with the ideas about sustainability from the 'experts' around them. This contrasts with the student engagement based on critical-democratic principles which underpin sustainable development discourses and which support research with students as co-producers of research. Indeed, initiatives that seek to assess students' levels of understanding or literacy appear to be on the rise, as are research studies that identify factors that influence students' behaviour towards sustainability.[8]

Research into Business Studies students seems to dominate much of literature. Prime examples of this work include: Reid *et al.*'s (2009) study into business students' conceptions of sustainability, and Thomas' (2005) study into measuring business students' attitudes toward the legitimacy of sustainability. A similar trend is emerging in engineering, with students being the subject of various interventions to assess changes in knowledge or receptivity to sustainability. Watson *et al.*'s (2013) assessment of Georgian student perceptions from the integration of sustainability into engineering courses is an example of this. This work highlights the importance of educating engineers on the attainment of sustainable development and identifies how sustainability is being taught, and how this can be improved.

On occasion, research texts identify the skills students need to address sustainable development issues or prepare themselves for challenging future scenarios – from the perspective of staff working in the sector. For example, Barth *et al.*'s (2007) study, draws attention to the process of acquiring key competences for sustainable development and provides an expert review of what and how competences are acquired. Stubbs and Cocklin's (2008) study into 'Teaching Sustainability to Business Students: Shifting Mindsets' describes a framework used to help MBA students understand and reconcile the different sustainability perspectives. It argues that for the most part MBA students have only been exposed to neoclassical economic thinking within the other MBA subjects. The aim of the sustainability framework is to develop students' thinking skills by engaging with sustainability from different perspectives.

Case studies can be sourced of meaningful student participation in sustainability issues such as Tappeser's (2014) brief report on student-led experiences for sustainability at the Maastricht University. Tappeser recounts how the University's Green Office, a student-led department that develops sustainability projects, has supported students to help shape and transform universities as part of their learning journey towards sustainability. Examples such as this are rarely found in international peer-reviewed journals although they do have a presence on local and regional media.[9] Analytical case studies or meta-analysis of case studies on student-led change for sustainable development in higher education are also absent from the international peer-reviewed literature.

Are HE students interested and engaged with sustainability?

Key informants advising the UNESCO global study into higher education for sustainability explained that student leadership in sustainable development remains an aspiration rather than a trend (Tilbury 2014). They suggest that the absence of student leadership studies or indeed the student voice in research results from a lack of student engagement with sustainability in higher education. To validate this argument there is a need to look to other indicators. Research compiled for the UNESCO review confirms that the last ten years have seen the rise of several national and regional student organisations with a primary remit of engaging with sustainable development (Tilbury 2014). These new entities have focused their attention on practical initiatives, demonstration projects and sometimes on academic activities, and they have forged partnerships with opinion leaders and higher education agencies, to advocate for a healthier, greener and more just future. Table 18.1 presents examples of these groups and the range of green as well as social enterprise projects they are engaged in.

The table also documents their relatively low membership numbers, which may reflect the fact that most of these associations have only recently been established. An alternative interpretation, however, is that these low overall numbers point to the lack of broader student practical engagement with this agenda.

J. Benayas del Almo, Executive Secretary of the Commission of Spanish Rectors (CADEP) special working groups on Sustainable Development, Environment and Risk (CRUE) explains:

> The key problem with student associations is their lack of continuity. On average, a student remains at the University between 3–5 years. Over time they become more involved with sustainability projects and initiatives but then they leave the University. This means that associations which are very active one year may stop existing the following year. This is the main reason why there are no strong or stable student-led organisations in Spain.
>
> *(Benayas del Almo, personal correspondence to author, 16 May 2013)*

Table 18.1 Examples of higher education student-led organisations (and) groups with a primary focus on sustainable development

Network/Group (national or regional)	*Established*	*Scale*	*Focus*	*Flagship Projects*	*Numbers*
World Student Community for Sustainable Development www.wscsd.org	2002 Established in Switzerland and Uganda	International (100 countries)	Student engagement in multi-disciplinary activities that improve lives and communities around the world	Nyakongo Water and Sanitation projects Adopt a river Adopt a forest Youth encounter on Peace	Estimated at 10,000
Sustainable Living Ambassadors	2009 Established at Hamad bin Khalida University, Qatar	National	Educating students in the residence halls	Recycle Mania Green Cleaning Education Sustainable Building Tours	600
PRISM ***Postgraduate Researchers Interested in Sustainability Matters*** www.glos.ac.uk/prism	2008 Established in UK	International (mostly European membership)	Research and alternative research methods	Student Summer camps Conferences Sharing of Information via elists	90
GeoJunvenil ***Youth organisation involving HE students***	Unconfirmed	Latin America and the Caribbean	Awaiting info	Summer camps and practical activities	400
OIKOS International www.oikos-international.org	1987 Established in Switzerland	Global (mostly European membership)	Oikos is an international student-driven organisation for sustainable economics and management	Oikos Winter school Oikos Future Lab Oikos PhD Fellowship Programme Oikos Development Academy	1,000

Table 18.1 continued

Network/Group (national or regional)	*Established*	*Scale*	*Focus*	*Flagship Projects*	*Numbers*
Rootability www.rootability.com	2012 Established in Holland	European Union	Social Enterprise in HE Establishing and supporting student-driven sustainability teams and projects	Coaching of student-driven change projects and programmes Workshops and seminars	100
Teens Turning Green Youth organisation involving HE students	2002 Established in the US	US	To educate and inspire young adults to promote environmentally conscious and socially responsible choices To mobilise peers to advocate for a healthy and just planet	Project Green Challenge http://projectgreenchallenge.com Green University, the Conscious College Road Tour www.teensturninggreen.org/programs/pgc-conscious-college-road-tour/ The Conscious Kitchen www.teensturninggreen.org/the-conscious-Kitchen/	15,000
Sneep – student network for ethics and economics in practice	2003 Established in Germany	Germany	To support sustainable practices in theory and management	Sneep academy, summer academy and autumn meetings	27

Table 18.1 continued

Network/Group (national or regional)	*Established*	*Scale*	*Focus*	*Flagship Projects*	*Numbers*
REFEDD (French student's network for sustainable development) www.refedd.org	Established in 2007	France	A sharing, supporting and promotional platform of HE students initiatives in SD	National meeting To support students with their projects by offering them free tools and training 'Campus d'avenir/Campus of the future' initiative – students envision the campus in 2050. Bi-annual surveys of students' perceptions	7,000 (subscribed through 105 associations)

These indicators lean towards relatively low levels of genuine student involvement in a sector where the volume and growth of student numbers could be the source for real change. Current estimates circle around 150 million students currently enrolled in higher education internationally – an increase of more than 50 per cent in the past decade alone.[10] The potential impact of widespread student involvement with sustainability is therefore highly significant, particularly through coordinated efforts at the national level and through mainstream student associations.

Further investigation has identified rare examples of research studies that sought to create spaces for student voices, support student empowerment and/or engage students in the research act itself. These studies challenged the dominant paradigm and engaged students as co-researchers shifting away from research *on* students to research *with* students. Interestingly, this work is yet to make its way to internationally peer-reviewed journals but can be found in university libraries that collect PhD studies. One example is El Zoghabi's (2013) work on 'Youth Engagement with Climate Change and Wellbeing: A study of Dutch and South African University Students'. This doctoral researcher took a different perspective, engaging students in envisioning exercises and creating spaces for university students to reflect and articulate their engagement options in relation to climate change issues. The study also identified how universities should respond to their positions and concerns. Podger's (2009) doctoral thesis into Bahai-inspired service learning and sustainable development principles generated a values framework for supporting student learning as an alternative to the prevalent capabilities and competencies models. Most importantly, the study adopted participatory inquiry approaches where learners were able to shape the direction as well as the outcomes of the research. It challenged traditional conceptions of research and questioned the division between the researcher and the researched.

Students as leaders and agents of change: turning tides?

The evidence collected by this study reveals that there have been blind spots with regards to research into student engagement for sustainability, representing a significant missed opportunity. Narrow interpretations of the principle of 'student engagement' have led to a fixation on studies to establish student satisfaction levels and the testing of behaviour change strategies rather than on research to improve participation or empowerment level. In addition, most of the examples cited refer to institutional or student development with an absence of studies relating to national programmes or pathways for student engagement in sustainability. One exception stands out as a path-finding example of how research has been used to inform and support student leadership for sustainability in higher education at this level. This work promotes student agency and has been led by the National Union of Students (NUS) in the UK.

The NUS is a confederation of 600 student unions composed of over 7 million students in tertiary education: 2.35 million of these are in higher education across the UK. The NUS has had student engagement for sustainability in its sights for over a decade. Its early work focused primarily on promoting pro-environmental behaviours amongst students (for example, Student Switch-Off[11]) and supporting student unions to 'green' their operations (for example, Green Impact Scheme[12]) and later moved towards assessing student attitudes and capturing expectations (see Box 18.2) reflecting the dominant trends captured in the literature review reported in this chapter.

Despite a sustained effort and investment in behaviour change projects over a period of nine years, NUS found that it was struggling to impact on student engagement. It commissioned a study in 2012 that suggested that student commitment to sustainability was lower than that among the general UK population, supporting the view that engagement is overall far less effective when attempting to promote behaviour change in sustainability. Its *Lifting the Lid* study (NUS 2013a) concluded that 54.8 per cent of students recycle whilst 75 per cent of the general population in the UK are actively engaged in this activity. Around 10 per cent of students participating in the study did not recycle at all and around half of these (47.5 per cent) were first year students. This finding agreed with reports from University Green Officers who have pointed to the challenge of engaging first year students in sustainable practice despite the increasing interest from employers and local communities in this agenda.[13]

The NUS learnt from its experience and in 2013, it redirected its energies to a fresh programme underpinned by an action research model that seeks to build student leadership capability and scale up change across the UK through strategic partnerships (Tilbury 2014).

The 2013 Green Fund Scheme arose out of a partnership between the NUS and the Higher Education Funding Council for England (HEFCE). Over £5 million has been provided to student unions through a competitive bidding process for student-led environmental sustainability projects around four key themes: student participation, partnership, impact and legacy. Twenty-five student hubs have been funded for two years at a cost of c. £50,000–£150,000 per year. The hubs implement a broad mix of sustainability projects which include developing: grass roots student activism through sustainability (UCLan); student-led food-growing projects on campus (Universities of Lancaster and Roehampton); green audits for student homes; social enterprise companies (University of Gloucestershire) and greening local businesses (University of Southampton); and developing an institution-wide team of Green Course Ambassadors supporting the embedding of ESD into the curriculum (University of Liverpool). The projects are an interesting mix of conventional, innovative and transformative projects, including the first UK pilot of the Maastricht Green Office model (University of Exeter) and pilot local

Box 18.2 Understanding student commitment and expectations

Several small scale studies existed, but no substantial data was available to indicate the potential interests of students in sustainability in their university experience, whether practical or educational. This was addressed by a series of NUS national studies commissioned by the UK Higher Education Academy. The research surveyed first year students over three years, finding consistently that 85 per cent of student respondents believe that universities should actively promote sustainable development and that 60 per cent want to learn more about sustainability (base c.11,100; see Figure 18.1).

The most recent study surveyed third year students and results replicated those for first year students, showing their belief that universities should be responsible for actively incorporating and promoting sustainable development to prepare their students for graduate employment. The research highlights a range of recommendations and calls for universities and colleges to focus their efforts where they can be most effective, particularly on education and the curriculum, not just the institution's carbon footprint.

These results have provoked much interest and debate across UK universities, with the overall conclusion that students are committed to sustainability at a professional level, as they are aware of employer expectations and can see the importance of this agenda for future life prospects. This insight goes some way to explaining why only smaller groups of students tend to engage in demonstration or action projects at universities (see below), as many more are now studying whilst undertaking paid employment to meet recent increases in university fees.

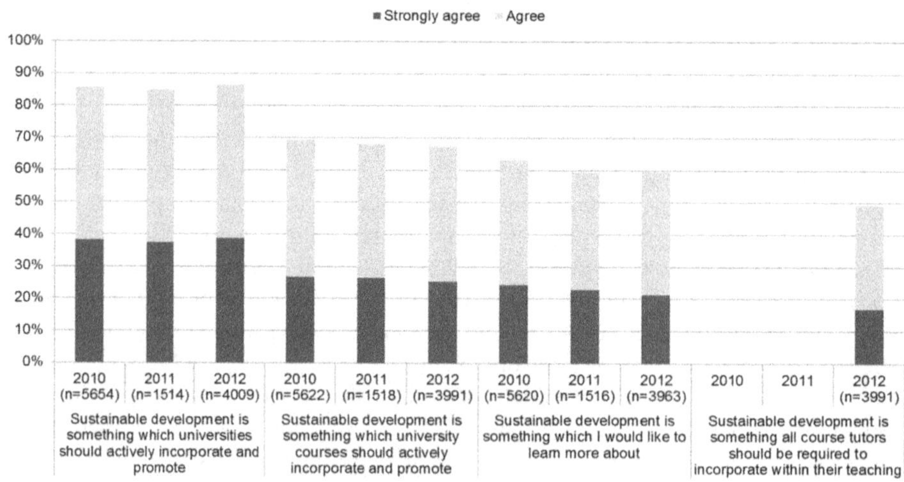

Figure 18.1 Understanding student commitment and expectations

Source: Drayson *et al.* 2014, published with permission from the Higher Education Academy

Green Funds (University of Leeds). As well as managing the Fund, the NUS add value by developing the skills of student and change agency abilities of student unions throughout the process, from application to delivery and evaluation.

The Green Fund Scheme follows the stages of the action research cycle using the experience of planning, action, critical reflection and evaluation as key frames for the development of this national initiative. A mid-point evaluation at the end of 2014 will gather data and help construct an understanding of change for sustainability in higher education as well as capture the effectiveness of the Fund (Agombar 2014). It is expected that collectively, the projects will engage 352,000 students in sustainability over the next two years, equivalent to about 15 per cent of students in English higher education. The NUS expects that the actual student activities will also collectively save at least 4,000 tCO_2/year, making a strong contribution towards the sector's carbon targets (NUS 2013b).[14]

Final words

The UK example cited in this chapter shows that more can be done to incentivise student engagement in sustainability, and in ways that are underpinned by more democratic and participatory models of research. Just as there is a need to challenge the paradigms that shape higher education to support sustainability and to exemplify alternatives (Hargraves and Fink 2006), there is also a need for fresh research frames that lead to new questions and to methodologies that view students as agents of change and not recipients of knowledge or expertise. Indeed, research into student engagement, seen via the critical-democratic lens often associated with sustainable development, offers a different research landscape to that currently reflected in international peer-reviewed journals. Thematic entry points would also be more diverse extending from the 'green' waste and energy reduction agendas to embrace issues such as decolonisation of the curriculum. Student empowerment studies would gain in prominence as would research studies that actively engage students in the design, data capture and data analysis of the research.

Genuine student engagement in research would have a dual effect. Firstly, it is likely to change the research questions being asked, the way the research is undertaken, and results are applied. It challenges traditional conceptions of research: Podger's (2009) and El Zoghabi's (2013) work, cited earlier in the text, show how this can manifest in practice. Taking this further, national policy research on higher education supported by student engagement would see:

1. students and student bodies working with academic colleagues identifying research questions;
2. students and student bodies working with academic colleagues framing research design, methodology and data capture;
3. students and student bodies working with academic colleagues in undertaking data analysis and/or validating findings; and,
4. students and student bodies playing a role in communicating the research, and where possible, applying research findings.

In addition, it would build research and action competence in students as well as leadership capabilities such as those defined by the UNECE ESD competence framework (UNECE 2011). Efforts in this area would shift the emphasis from research *on* students to research *with* students and *for* the benefit of students.

As Radloff and Coates (2013) suggest, unless students are engaged in research, tertiary participation has little value except to reduce unemployment numbers.

Notes

1 Limited access and low participation rates from minority and low income groups in HE is an issue which plagues the sector.
2 Knowledge transmission dominates higher education practice despite research confirming that participatory approaches to learning improve learning outcomes.
3 National Survey of Student Engagement.
4 National Satisfaction Survey.
5 The review undertaken in October 2013 was informed by publicly available government and NGO reports as well as academic publications written in UN official languages (English, Spanish and French) and released between January 2003 and September 2013.
6 The term 'transformative capabilities' is used here to reflect the dynamic and engaging ESD competencies promoted by UNECE 2011. These competences support critical reflection and agency.
7 See note 5.
8 The UNESCO review (Tilbury 2014) identified the following themes dominating the academic literature on students in higher education for sustainability. They appear in rank order: 1. Assessment of students' behaviour or attitudes and identification of factors which influence these; 2. Evaluation of sustainability literacy levels and needs; 3. Defining student learning outcomes, competences and/or graduate attributes; 4. Case studies of engaging students in practical sustainability initiatives.
9 Media reports have captured individual examples of student enterprise and involvement, particularly with regard to the green agenda (see for example Schuetze 2013).
10 www.timeshighereducation.co.uk/features/trouble-with-numbers/413555.article (UniversitiesUK 2012).
11 *Student Switch Off* – an inter-dormitory energy-saving competition that is run through Facebook: www.nus.org.uk/studentswitchoff.
12 Green Impact – An environmental accreditation and award scheme for student unions which has been extended across university administrative and academic departments:. www.nus.org.uk/greenimpact.
13 Environmental Association of Universities and Colleges, UK (EAUC 2011), personal communications that took place at the 2011 EAUC National Conference, University of York, 11 April.
14 These are examples of research studies for students by students and using methodologies which empower students themselves to lead changes in higher education policy and practice.

References

Agombar, J., 2014. 'NUS HEFCE Green Fund Mid-Term Report' (unpublished). NUS.

Alvares, C. and Faruqi, S., eds., 2012. *Decolonising the University: The Emerging Quest for Non-eurocentric Paradigm*. Pulau Pinang: Penerbit Universiti Sains Malaysia.

Azapagic, A., Perdan S. and Shallcross, D., 2005. 'How Much do Engineering Students Know about Sustainable Development? The Findings of an International Survey and Possible Implications for the Engineering Curriculum', *European Journal of Engineering Education*, 30(1), 1–19.

Barth, M., Godemann, J., Rieckmann, M. and Stoltenberg, U., 2007. 'Developing Key Competencies for Sustainable Development in Higher Education', *International Journal of Sustainability in Higher Education*, 8(4), 416–30.

Bartlett, P. and Chase, G., eds, 2013. *Sustainability in Higher Education: Stories and Strategies for Transformation*. Cambridge, MA: MIT Press.

Bomia, L., Beluzo, L., Demeester, D., Elander, K., Johnson, M. and Sheldon, B., 1997. *The Impact of Teaching Strategies on Intrinsic Motivation*. Champaign, IL: ERIC Clearing House on Elementary and Early Childhood Education, 294–9.

Department for Business, Innovation and Skills (BIS), 2011. *Higher Education: Students at the Heart of the System*. London: White Paper, BIS.

Drayson, R., Bone, E., Agombar, J. and Kemp, S., 2014. *Student Attitudes Towards and Skills for Sustainable Development*. York: Higher Education Academy.

El Zoghabi, M., 2013. 'Youth Engagement with Climate Change and Well-Being. A Study of Dutch and South African University Students'. PhD thesis, University of Gloucestershire, UK.

Emanuel, R. and Adams, J.N., 2011. 'College Students' Perceptions of Campus Sustainability', *International Journal of Sustainability in Higher Education*, 12(1), 79–92.

Fletcher, A., 2014. 'Defining Student Engagement: A Literature Review'. www.soundout.org/student-engagement-AF.pdf [accessed 13 February 2015].

Fredricks, J., Blumenfeld, P. and Paris, A., 2004. 'School Engagement: Potential of the Concept and State of the Evidence', *Review of Educational Research*, 74(1), 59–109.

Global Universities Network for Innovation (GUNI), 2014. *Higher Education in the World 5 Knowledge, Engagement and Higher Education's Contribution to Social Change*. London: Palgrave Macmillan.

Hargraves, A. and Fink, D., 2006. *Sustainable Leadership*. San Francisco, CA: Jossey-Bass Wiley.

Kagawa, F., 2007. 'Dissonance in Students' Perceptions of Sustainable Development and Sustainability: Implications for Curriculum Change', *International Journal of Sustainability in Higher Education*, 8(3), 317–38.

Kahu, E., 2011. 'Framing Student Engagement in Higher Education', *Studies in Higher Education*, 23(5), 758–73.

Kuh, G.D., 2009. 'The National Survey of Student Engagement: Conceptual and Empirical Foundations', *New Directions for Institutional Research*, 141, 5–20.

Marginson, S., ed., 2013. 'Tertiary Education Policy in Australia'. University of Melbourne: Centre for the Study of Higher Education, July 2013. www.cshe.unimelb.edu.au/research/policy_dev/docs/Tert_Edu_Policy_Aus.pdf [accessed 16 February 2015].

McMillan, E., Wright, T. and Beazley, K., 2004. 'Impact of a University-Level Environmental Studies Class on Students' Values', *Journal of Environmental Education*, 35(30), 19–26.

National Union of Students (NUS), 2013a. *Lifting the Lid: Student Attitudes and Behaviours towards Recycling and Waste*. Maidenhead: NUS.

National Union of Students (NUS), 2013b. 'Students' Green Fund Business Plan'. www.green-impact.org.uk/wp-content/uploads/2013/04/20130121-Students-Green-Fund-Business-plan-non-confidential.pdf [accessed 16 February 2015].

Podger, D., 2009. 'Contribution of a Faith Organisation to Education for Sustainability: Infusing Spirituality into Learning for Sustainability'. PhD thesis, Macquarie University, Australia.

Radloff, A. and Coates, H., 2013. 'Monitoring and Improving Student Engagement', in Marginson, S., (ed.), *Tertiary Education Policy in Australia*. University of Melbourne: Centre for the Study of Higher Education, July 2013, 21–30. www.cshe.unimelb.edu.au/research/policy_dev/docs/Tert_Edu_Policy_Aus.pdf [accessed 16 February 2015].

Reid, A., Petocz, P. and Taylor, P., 2009. 'Business Students' Conceptions of Sustainability', *Sustainability*, 1(3), 662–73.

Ryan, A. and Cotton, D., 2013. 'Times of Change: Shifting Pedagogy and Curricula for Future Sustainability', in Sterling, S. Maexy, L. and Luna, H. (eds), *The Sustainable University: Progress and Prospects*. Abingdon: Earthscan Routledge, 151–67.

Ryan, A. and Tilbury, D., 2013. *Flexible Pedagogies: New Pedagogical Ideas*. York: Higher Education Academy.

Schuetze, C., 2013. 'How Green is your School', *New York Times online*, March 2013. www.nytimes.com/2013/03/27/education/how-green-is-youruniversity.html?pagewanted=all&_r=2&%20.%20N& (accessed 24 September 2014).

Scott, G., Tilbury, D., Deane, E. and Leith, S., 2012. *Turnaround Leadership for Sustainability in Higher Education*. Sydney: Australian Office of Learning and Teaching.

Soka Gakkai International (SGI), 2012. 'Sustainability: Learning for Empowerment'. www.sgiquarterly.org/feature2012Apr-1.html [accessed 16 February].

Sterling, S., Maxey, L. and Luna, H., 2013. *The Sustainable University: Progress and Prospects*. Abingdon: Earthscan, Routledge.

Stubbs, W. and Cocklin, C., 2008. 'Teaching Sustainability to Business Students: Shifting Mindsets', *International Journal of Sustainability in Higher Education*, 9(3), 206–21.

Tappeser, V., 2014. 'Empowering Students for a More Sustainable University'. www.guninetwork.org/resources/he-articles/empowering-students-for-a-more-sustainable-university [accessed 16 February 2015].

Thomas, T.E., 2005. 'Are Business Students Buying It? A Theoretical Framework for Measuring Attitudes toward the Legitimacy of Environmental Sustainability', *Business Strategy in the Environment*, 14(3), 186–97.

Tilbury, D., 2011. *Higher Education for Sustainability: A Global Overview of Commitment and Progress in Global University Network for Innovation (GUNI), 2011. Higher Education's Commitment to Sustainability: From Understanding to Action*. World in Higher Education Series No.4 Barcelona. Spain: GUNI.

Tilbury, D., 2014. *Education for Sustainability in Higher Education*. Report Commissioned by UNESCO

ESD Secretariat to inform the 3rd Global DESD Assessment. Paris: UNESCO.

Tilbury, D. and Wortman, D., 2004. *Engaging People in Sustainability.* Gland: IUCN.

Trowler, V., 2010. 'Student Engagement Literature Review York: Higher Education Academy'. www.heacademy.ac.uk/sites/default/files/StudentEngagementLiteratureReview_1.pdf [accessed 16 February 2015]

Tuncer, G., 2008. 'University Students' Perception on Sustainable Development: A Case Study from Turkey', *International Research in Geographical and Environmental Education,* 17(3), 212–26.

United Nations (UN), 2012. *The Future We Want: Rio+20 Outcomes Document,* 49. www.un.org/en/sustainablefuture/ [accessed 16 February 2015].

UN Economic Commission for Europe (UNECE), 2011. *Learning for the Future: Competences in Education for Sustainable Development.* UNECE Strategy for Education for Sustainable Development. www.unece.org/fileadmin/DAM/env/esd/ESD_Publications/Competences_Publication.pdf [accessed 16 February 2015].

United Nations Population Fund (UNFPA), 2012. 'Empowering People to Ensure a Sustainable Future for All'. http://eudevdays.eu/sites/default/files/UNFPA%20Post%202015%20Position%20Paper%20Final%2021%20October.pdf [accessed 16 February 2015].

UniversitiesUK, 2012. 'The Trouble with Numbers', *Times Higher Education,* 12.

Watson, M.K., Lozano, R., Noves, C. and Rodgers, M., 2013. 'Assessing Curricula Contribution to Sustainability more Holistically: Experiences from the Integration of Curricula Assessment and Students' Perceptions at the Georgia Institute of Technology', *Journal of Cleaner Production,* 61(15), 106–16.

Whannell, P., Whannell, P. and White, R., 2012. 'Tertiary Student Attitudes to Bicycle Commuting in a Regional Australian University', *International Journal of Sustainability in Higher Education,* 13(1), 34–45.

19

TOWARDS A SCHOLARSHIP OF CURRICULUM CHANGE

From isolated innovation to transformation

Kathryn Hegarty and Sarah Holdsworth

Curriculum content and practice in Higher Education (HE) is commonly seen as the central wellspring of change for the diffusion of sustainability throughout HE. In the light of a nearly complete UN Decade it is timely to consider the learnings of the sustainability education movement. With more than a decade of initiatives, we may well stop to reflect on the various approaches to recalibration of higher education (HE) towards sustainability. One important aspect of this is to consider the various and flourishing curriculum initiatives which have emerged the world over under the ESD banner.

This chapter offers context and theorisation of the means by which we might revisit notions of curriculum, *effective* change and design for the researches to identify these. We will evaluate the terrain by which we arrived at this point in the ESD project, consider common (tacit) assumptions which have underpinned work in ESD and explore ways to respond. We will capture and consider implications of the learnings gained through consideration of curriculum work undertaken over the last, UN, decade in key ESD journals.

In our canvas of the key journals for the period of the UN Decade on ESD, we bring eclectic lenses to bear. These include *deep* interdisciplinarity, as all approaches to and framings of curriculum are then equally valued at the point of entry, regardless of differences in focus and professional field (Hegarty 2009). We bring a constructivist ontology to our scholarly practice, seeking to engage the authentic narratives of peers in ESD, which we argue is a hallmark practice of interdisciplinarity. Our methodology in this instance is thus grounded theory, which allows us to theorise 'what's going on' as it emerges from the chosen methods of enquiry (Dawes and Larson 2011).

The authors note that there has been some debate about nomenclature in the environmental education and ESD literature over the period of the UN DESD. As scholars and practitioners, we bring varied understandings of sustainability education to our work, as do many academics. Nonetheless, we have determined to use ESD throughout this chapter. This decision was taken in the interests of clarity and in recognition that ESD is arguably the dominant term applied in Europe. The literature consulted for this chapter reflects the range of nomenclature used in sustainability education domains.

Towards ontologies for curriculum change research

Such a comprehensive reflective project as this, begs certain assumptions. Much ESD activity has occurred, and while the ESD community is well able to capture the common themes, learnings and approaches that emerge from this action, it is the key argument of this chapter that we have *not yet determined* which approaches have the most efficacy for long term change and diffusion. We are not even yet able to identify the measures by which diffusion and embeddedness will be recognised.

We consider, in our experience as front-line ESD practitioners, that there often exists in ESD curriculum literature an epistemology which is positivist in its nature. While this may reflect the plethora of originating disciplines, it has not best fitted to the ESD sub-discipline or project, for the difficult and pragmatic task ahead of it, one that we describe as unapologetically teological in nature (Hegarty 2008). That is, ESD was constituted to lead diffusion of sustainability content in all higher education disciplines' and professions' curriculum. Recognition of the role of academics was underscored, both as providers and deliverers of recast curricula. As Kumar *et al.* famously said in 2005, 'Sustainability is incumbent on academics' (218). But how did the ESD community *interpret* this exhortation?

It would seem, based on a ten year review of academic journals, that the response was a call to action. And much was learned. This approach may have been necessary as a point of entry to ESD. It is premature to attempt to capture what are termed the 'methodologies' for curriculum change research (and this is an assumption we do not share, that these methodologies have been developed and tested in the scholarly sense of the word). Consequently, *we must lay the scholarly foundations* which make this possible. Rigour and validity are the hallmarks of academic excellence and these must characterise the next stage of ESD activity if we are to win hearts and minds across all disciplinary endeavours, much less those outside academe. There are 'epistemological tensions' in this process, identified by Whiteford and Pereira (2012). These authors suggest that science disciplines needs to 'read into' their own constructions. There seems to be an assumption of 'normativity' amongst some sections of the ESD community, that the styles of writing in our fields will be uniform, usually to the sciences or engineering. Disciplinary identity is a key organising principle in the cultures of universities (Hegarty 2008; Trowler *et al.* 2012). It impacts the choice of epistemologies employed and the ways in which methodologies are devised. We wish to propose an approach which allows to revisit these assumptions, thereby welcoming all approaches to knowledge and scholarship in higher education into the ESD community.

We agree with Kumar *et al.* and we recognise that the keenest point in the HE trajectory is the site of curriculum, *where decisions are made about what knowledge is needed and the skills to apply that knowledge in the world*. Change must occur at key focal points. It is our argument that the mechanisms for making such decisions have been flawed and inadequate, lacking in the scholarly conversations which are crucial to rigour in research, not to mention to young academics' development and growth within their identities as ESD practitioners.

Situating curriculum change in ESD

The term 'curriculum' is used in Higher Education Institutions (HEI) (and beyond) to mean many things to many people. This reflects the intensity of the varied but always steadfast policy and funding focus on what goes on in classrooms. Pinar *et al.* (1995), under the banner 'curriculum studies', has defined curriculum as the 'active force of human educational endeavour'. Schubert (1986) demonstrates the assumption that curriculum is a politicised practice, through the title of his influential work, *The Curriculum: Perspective, Paradigm, and Possibility*. Indeed, the social movements of the 1960s and 1970s showed a profound interest in the content of curriculum across the sectors of formal education, emulating their Emersonian cousins some century before (Freire 1972; Shor and Freire 1987). Durkheim (1961) famously coined the term 'hidden curriculum', exhorting educators to be conscious of world views and epistemological assumptions that embed both the material chosen and their delivery of it. Durkheim's argument, that curriculum is moral in nature and that this needs to be explicit, rather than largely unstated, underpins much contemporary debate on HEI curriculum (Sund and Öhman 2014; Mulder 2010).

We define curriculum as all content, learning materials and activities, including formal assessment, which may also encompass interactions *between* learners, or *from* learner to teacher *adding a dynamism* to what is often perceived as a singular, linear process. Curriculum is generally understood as situated within the various subcultures of education (Phenix 1962; Hegarty 2009). We all bring to it and project onto it, world views and priorities, not to mention differences of discipline and professional field. It is not uncommon in HE to find ourselves using common terms and yet, meaning very different things by them. The notion of 'theory' is a case in point. In cultural studies, it will refer to applications of critical work, such as that of Foucault. In construction management, it may refer to formulas for materials' stability or the application of environmental sustainability measures such as water tanks and double glazing (Hayles and Holdsworth 2008; Holdsworth *et al.* 2006). Localised, particularised notions of terms express an authenticity of disciplinary concerns and needs which are paramount and which must be supported, no matter that this adds layers of considerable challenge to our project (Jacobs 1990).

We argue that these wide-ranging, disciplinary-based local usages and inflections must be *welcomed and valued* within ESD. But to do this we must hold a deep ethic of interdisciplinarity and this throws into relief a specific scholarly challenge to the ESD project. This challenge is repeated in relation to the many key terms which recur in the various considerations of the goals of the ESD project. These terms are arguably ESD 'bread and butter'; they describe our key objectives and intention in the work that we do. They characterise the majority of publications around curriculum, change, teaching, learning and even, occasionally, campus operations. They include (but are not limited to) terms like: embedded, diffused, innovation, novel, recalibration, competences, leadership. We use these terms constantly and sometimes interchangeably. But they remain *unvalidated* in a scholarly sense. We use them, heavy with local meanings and, often, a singular ontological assumption. We have had too little scholarly dialogue, *in the context of ESD curriculum [change] instances*, about what these terms mean and what their realisation might look like. It may be argued, that the curriculum change processes we have examined through key ESD journals demonstrate a lack of cohesion or comparability, much less transferability. And this is a major impediment to diffusion.

Diffusion has been much discussed in the ESD literature but we are not really able as a field to identify effective measures or determinants of progress on this goal. In seeking to understand the extent and processes of curriculum change for ESD, our review of the key journals over the UN DESD mapped a range of categories of curriculum change, by driver or underpinning ethos.

Contexts for change: a review of a decade of ESD curriculum development and change

The evolution of ESD curriculum development and change is best understood by reviewing the contemporary literature. This section of the chapter presents a review of the ESD curriculum work published from 2005, the launch of the UN Decade on Education for Sustainable

Development, until 2013. It has been limited to the *International Journal of Sustainability in Higher Education*, *Environmental Education Research*, *Journal of Cleaner Production* and *Journal of Environmental Education*. These journals were selected as they have provided a peer review platform for the communication and dissemination of work in the area of sustainability and education. The review sought to identify curriculum activity in ESD within HEIs, and consider these under a set of identified cascading curriculum themes, which emerged from the literature review. These curriculum themes frame common beliefs or assertions about effective diffusion of sustainability education across higher education endeavours and reflect approaches to, beliefs about and understandings of what curriculum actually is and what is involved in doing it in HE contexts. Three categories of curriculum change have been identified and can be described as:

1. Historical/structural readjustment – increasingly reflected in government interventions in both HE curriculum and evaluation/scrutiny measures.
2. Governance/regulation/university policy – whole of institution or faculty endeavours. These may be very broad or quite specific and prescriptive.
3. Contemporary theoretical concerns and even fashions – these are likely led by disciplines or professional fields.

The review recognised all initiatives that use the word curriculum, sustainability, sustainable development, in abstract, key words or body, even if not consistent with the definition above. The only papers then not considered were those focused *outside* formal higher education learning spaces.

Cascading theme 1. Historical structural readjustment through government

The international community has responded to the growing recognition of sustainability issues with the initiation of, and signatory to, a number of international treaties and conventions. These specifically focused on education to encourage the development of environmental and, more recently, sustainability education. Governments have responded to these signatory agreements through the development of national, state and local policies, and institutions to support, encourage and facilitate ESD across all levels of education. The review of the literature suggests the approach adopted nationally has little global consistency, reflected in the varying approaches to ESD.

The literature review identified much published on the UK's national approach to ESD. The governments of the United Kingdom recognised the imperative to embed SD into education within HE in the 1990s, and commissioned the Toyne Report (DfEE, Welsh Office 1993), established the Sustainable Development Education Panel (2003), developed the DfES Sustainable Development Action Plan (DfES 2005) and the policy paper 'Sustainable Development in Higher Education' (HEFCE 2005) (Sterling and Witham 2008). In 2004 the Higher Education Academy (HEA) was established to bring together the functions of the Institute for Learning and Teaching in Higher Education, the Learning and Teaching Support Network and its subject centres, a network of 24 different disciplinary centres. The HEA was expected to help deliver HEFCE's sustainable development strategy and action plan and in 2004/05 funded a program of work to the value of £100,000 in preparation for activity over the following five years. In 2005, the HEA subject centres initiated an ESD project in response to HEFCE's request that HEA should take the lead in efforts to embed ESD in the HE curriculum (Sterling and Scott 2008). One strand of activity was the funding of individual subject centre projects to,

- build awareness and understanding of the principles of sustainable development (SD) in the context of each discipline,
- research current ESD practice,
- unearth existing and/or develop new learning and teaching resources, and
- identify opportunities for further development and propose outline work programmes for 2005/06 and beyond.

HEFCE also funded two 'Centres for Excellence in Teaching and Learning' with five-year programmes to advance SD within and beyond their institutions; the Centre for Sustainable Futures (CSF) at the University of Plymouth and the Centre for Sustainable Communities Achieved through Professional Education (C-SCAIPE) at Kingston University, London.

The policy directives and organisational support have contributed significantly to advancing the acceptance and integration of sustainability into the curriculum within the UK's HEIs (Katayama and Gough 2008, Sterling and Witham 2008). Research undertaken to determine how UK HEI's have embraced these policy initiatives identified more than 1,600 courses or programmes containing sustainable development related to teaching as problem-oriented, responsibility-oriented, creativity-oriented or skills oriented (Katayama and Gough 2008). While there has been a significant response to ESD, the authors noted, only a few HEIs were explicitly committed to the concept across their operations, that research into the impact of the national policy approach is limited, it is difficult to generalise about the sector, and it is even harder to do so about individual institutions, programmes and courses (Katayama and Gough 2008). Much of the work at the local level has been decoupled into areas of activity in the development of skills, literacies, curriculum content or delivery methods. The result is that the scholarship of learning and teaching in the development and dissemination of ESD, has been reduced to isolated components. Subsequently, research into these areas at the national level focuses on methods required for the collection of what curriculum or course has been developed, how to communicate information to educators and the best approach to providing support.

Additionally, research evaluating the approach to systemic policy development, as a vehicle for change in ESD, argues that it must be practical and contextually relevant to the sector and to the academic audience (Sterling and Witham 2008). How this influences, informs and is understood and evaluated by ESD practitioners is yet to be understood (Rode and Michelsen 2008). Rode and Michelsen (2008) argue that while there exist indicators and frameworks to assess the success of ESD in higher education, there is a need to develop a systemic approach. However, this assumes that the speed with which ESD is introduced into courses is convergent with a systemic, multi-sector and integrated approach.

Cascading theme 2. Governance/regulation/university policy – whole of institution or faculty endeavours

The literature review identified that engagement with ESD varies significantly across HEIs and disciplines. This is not an issue of alignment of SD to disciplinary context, but an 'educator's willingness or ability to engage' (Hopkinson *et al.* 2008: 437). Katayama and Gough (2008) recognised that commitment to sustainable development at the university level does not guarantee academic commitment to ESD or vice versa; however, it does provide leaderships and capacity to encourage and support change. This is reflected in the proportion of curriculum developed in HEIs adopting such an approach.

The University of Gloucestershire is an example of such of an institution. An institution-wide intervention informed the development of ESD, and was encouraged by a supportive and collegial environment including senior management and interested academic staff (Roberts and Roberts 2008). Undergraduate and postgraduate courses in environmental issues were initiated in the 1980s. By 2005, Gloucestershire University had become the first English university to achieve ISO14001 Environmental Management accreditation. To maintain ISO14001 certification continuous improvement in all areas including the formal curriculum delivery must be achieved. This resulted in the establishment of academic development activities to encourage the continual development of sustainability in the curriculum. Much of the work in this area resulted in support for staff through the incitation and facilitation of collaborative activities, predominately the development, sharing and publishing of teaching case studies (Roberts and Roberts 2008). How research and the type that informed this approach was not found within the literature sample.

The University of Luneburg has addressed ESD by adopting an intuitional approach; specifically, the 'Agenda 21 and the University of Luneburg' (1999–2001) and 'Sustainable University – Sustainable Development in the Context of University Remits' (2004–2007) initiatives, as well as through the UNESCO Chair of Higher Education for Sustainable Development (Barth *et al.* 2007). The whole of institution change approach integrated SD into all areas of operation. This resulted in a restructuring and development of curriculum within the bachelor and master's qualifications, framed by its mission and curriculum guidelines of action orientation (Handlungsorientierung), personal development (Humanismus), and a volunteering option (Projekt Ehrenamt) (Barth *et al.* 2007; Barth and Godemann 2006; Beringer 2007; Beringer and Adomßent 2008; Adomßent and Michelsen 2006). Curriculum and student opportunities included a compulsory, for all students, first year project-based sustainability learning within a semester-long subject. The approach recognises that combined expertise in organisational leadership and management, operations and academic research and scholarship and education are required to fulfil Sustainability in Higher Education (SHE) synergies (Beringer 2007). A research outcome associated with ESD was the identification of a set of ESD competencies (Barth and Godemann 2006); however, research into how to integrate these into curriculum and learning outcomes was not found in the literature review.

In 2005 the University of Bradford launched its whole of institution policy under the umbrella term 'Ecoversity' to address two key objectives: 1) sustainable development across the operations and culture of the University, and 2) ESD in the learning and living experience of all students (Hopkinson *et al.* 2008). Three curriculum models were developed and described in the literature; however, detailed research into these programmes has not been identified within the parameters of this literature review.

Curriculum work identified under this cascading theme suggests that education renewal for SD is directly connected to a whole of institution approach. Through the establishment of ESD policy ESD curriculum is more likely to become embedded within formal curriculum and in turn increase student engagement with SD. While these institution-wide ESD initiatives have been successful in the promotion of ideas and developing momentum, if we focus more deeply on the curriculum component, within the literature surveyed, it can be identified that there is simply an analysis of what has been undertaken to date, and the categorisation of work into key themes often in relation to skills. There is a decoupling of the development of skills, learning objectives and content itself. There is little published that explores or evaluates how the educator and their assumptions have connected to the documented process (Hopkinson *et al.* 2008; Adomßent and Michelsen 2006).

Cascading theme 3. Contemporary theoretical concerns (fashions) – led by discipline/professional-led changes

Within the literature there is a significant amount of theoretical work published on the key principles that characterise ESD curriculum (Baud 2004; Fien 2001; Holdsworth *et al.* 2006a; Parker *et al.* 2004). For example Fien (2001) argues that four interdependent systems underpin the sustainability paradigm: biophysical, economic, social and cultural, and political, and that some understanding of these systems is required so that relevant content can be embedded into existing and new curriculum. Additionally, there are some commonalities in the contemporary approach including: respecting learners' values and prior learning; investigation into sustainability issues; recognition and interpretation of issues from other perspectives; construct of the meaning of their experience; and informed decision making (Baud 2004; Fien 2001; Holdsworth *et al.* 2006b; Parker *et al.* 2004). However, limited research has been carried out into the scholarship of learning and teaching and its relationship to curriculum development and delivery in ESD, and this has resulted in unevenness in the extent to which is it embedded or evident (Dawe *et al.* 2005; HEFCE 2008; Roberts and Roberts 2008).

Within the literature reviewed there is a significant body of knowledge in the areas of literacy and skills for ESD. This is particularly dominant within the UK and draws from the initial work undertaken by Forum for the Future (2004) and Parkin *et al.* (2004). Research into sustainability literacies has evolved with work undertaken by Forster (2006), StudentForce for Sustainability for the Higher Education Academy (Cade 2008) and the UK Sustainable Development Commission (2007) (Hopkinson *et al.* 2008). Consequently, ESD is increasingly being reflected in the development of literacies within Higher Education Institutions which equip students to live and work in a rapidly changing and complex world (Sen 1992, 1999; Walker 2010).

However, literacies and their use in ESD curriculum are predominately focused in the debate around which literacy or skill is characteristic of a sustainability able individual. There is little consensus within the literature of which literacies or skills best characterises a sustainability literate graduate; Hopkinson *et al.* argue that they 'diverge almost as much as they converge' (Hopkinson *et al.* 2008: 437). Selecting a set of literacies may not be possible, and the diversity in understanding and application of sustainability in education is part of the problems discussed earlier. However, Hopkinson *et al.* argue that the value of literacies or skills has been the recognition of 'developing knowledge, skills/capabilities and values' (Hopkinson *et al.* 2008: 438). Yet, there is limited research investigating how individual or sets of literacies or skills inform the development of curriculum, meeting learning outcomes etc. We are a long way from identification of measures to evaluate the efficacy of these proposed skills and literacies.

Additionally, the literature review identified that there has been much published in understanding the value of the student experience or the impact on student behaviour associated with completing an ESD course. Predominately this has been researched using case study methodology (Brody and Ryu 2006; Meyers 2006). This research method, descriptive and advocacy-oriented research, has been criticised as lacking rigourous research design, in particular detailed discussion on data collection procedures, data analysis and issues of validity (Corcoran *et al.* 2004; Fien 2002; Meyers 2006). Corcoran *et al.* (2004) undertook an analysis of 54 journal articles on sustainability in higher education, and found case studies methodology to be *lacking in detailed analysis* of the research methods and simply relied on *anecdotal* evidence to support their main claims. While these instances may be of interest to ESD practitioners, they cannot helpfully inform the development of methodologies for curriculum change research.

A number of single ESD-focused courses have been cited within the literature. The University of Bristol developed an optional undergraduate 'open unit' in sustainable development. The development and delivery has been situated in an action research methodology; consisting of documentation and feedback from within the teaching team and enrolled students. However, the research focus was limited to process; the philosophy underpinning the process was not explored (Hoare *et al.* 2008). The University of Cambridge Engineering Department developed a program-wide approach to the development of ESD. The department included all levels of education, and recognised the need to educate a diversity of skills and values to empower engineering graduates to transcend the traditional approach to practice. The department developed new pedagogies and connected these to the construction of curriculum; however, the reporting of their experience is limited to teaching methods employed in the classroom and associated case study activities (Fenner *et al.* 2005). In Australia a national survey was undertaken within the field of industrial design to determine the scope of ESD in HE courses. While this provides a snapshot of what educators were teaching, there was no insight into how curriculum was understood in relation to the scholarship of learning and teaching, or how it was constructed (Ramirez 2006). At RMIT University, the authors and their colleagues explored the learning outcomes in a 'bolt on' core subject in ESD (Hegarty *et al.* 2011).

In a number of special issues across the decade, *Journal of Cleaner Production* (JCP) captured a profoundly diverse range of curriculum approaches, locations and instances, although these continue in mainstream issues also. Discussions of ways forward both for, and in, higher education around the world, abound. Yet these instances are still, at best, ad hoc or omit the basis by which diffusion is claimed to occur. The breadth of the JCP remit creates an opportunity for the next 'meta' stage of ESD scholarship that we propose. (Special issues Vols 18(7), 2010; 4(8) 2013; 61, 2013; 62(1), 2014.)[1]

ESD curriculum change: methods, methodology, future research directions

Reflecting on the work undertaken, it is clear that one of the epistemological assumptions which underpins a key hypothesis about curriculum change is that a preexisting 'method[ology]' may be drawn into play, to assist in the identification of the most effective change processes and the research into them. From the literature, we would argue this approach is yet to be created; indeed, we are not yet in a position to frame it. Karatzoglou notes,

> that the published ESD research covers a wide range of regions, topics, methodologies, and findings. The prevailing methodological approaches include theoretical and case-study articles. Yet, the former suffer from a *rigourous conceptual framework deficiency* while the latter are characterised by their descriptive nature which can be inspiring and encouraging for future peer efforts but of limited added value to theory development.
>
> *(Karatzoglou 2013: 44; emphasis added)*

How might the ESD project respond? We offer some points of entry to such a conceptualisation in this chapter. Initially, we need to identify the contemporary curriculum platforms (for ESD) which exist in the peer-reviewed literature. These do not easily lend themselves to classification. We are not entirely in agreement with Karatzoglou; without 'rigourous conceptual frameworks', it is our view that methodologies are merely methods, lacking any generalisability.

It is our argument that the many excursions into curriculum – to develop it, change it, renew it or inflect it with localised themes of ESD – reflect what might be determined the *ad hoc* (Stubbs and Schapper 2011) approach to ESD, or more importantly, the ways in which bottom-up (local, field-specific) approaches vary in reflecting the needs, concerns and contexts of their disparate disciplines, locations and professional concerns.

In designing an approach to assess the learnings from curriculum 'change' for higher education, the intention was that we would seek to develop a scholarly narrative of the 'methodologies' which offered the most efficacy in these change instances. As we move out of the UN Decade, as we seek to review curriculum change practice in ESD for the last decade, with a view to identification of effective methodologies, we need to question ourselves. Denzin and Lincoln (1998) remind us that post-positivist, or constructivist, approaches to enquiry are important conceptualisations of that enquiry. By definition, we must recognise that the underpinning assumptions – the ontologies – need reflection, problematisation and theorisation. They *must* be identified and debated amongst ESD scholars. Such a debate is imperative as a platform for conceptualisations of change. In this way, we will more strategically situate the many reports of innovations and activities and to begin to theorise rigourous researches into curriculum change.

We see the misuse of the term 'methodologies' which causes confusion when all meanings – scholarly and generalised – are projected onto it. The world over, examiners of doctoral theses receives guidelines advising them to evaluate the situatedness of the research contained in a dissertation *to its field of knowledge*. This is how validation occurs. When we see claims made in a journal paper for the efficacy of a curriculum approach, we must look for the evidence for this efficacy. How was its impact measured? Why that way? What are our objectives? We need to revisit and debate the processes of developing our lenses for scholarly enquiry; whilst these may differ as markedly as does the ESD field, the rigour that may only be enabled this way is imperative to change leadership and credibility. As Hammersley (1995) has noted, research is never value 'free', nor neutral. Sund and Öhman (2014) argue we need to *repoliticise* sustainability education.

> For decades, attention has been drawn to the normativity of an environmental and sustainability education (ESE) that bases its understanding on, and embraces, universal aspects and ethical ideals. The problem with universal values and how to address them is neither new nor unique for the field of ESE.
>
> *(Sund and Öhman 2014)*

Where is the dialogue about this notion in the ESD curriculum literature? Whereas Mulder (2010) cautions ESD educators against any necessity for prescriptive teaching of values, arguing that SD is a normative concept: the responsibility for future generations and for the poor and underprivileged of this world is a normative choice (Mulder 2010). This is surely a precursive, or at the very least, concurrent responsibility with and contributor to the development of curriculum, not to mention research into its effective diffusion.

We do not argue that this conversation has *not* occurred in ESD or any of its other incarnations. What we have seen, in our own experience as scholars and in our literature work for this chapter and more generally, is a lack of *situatedness*, of reflective connection back to the important and formative work done by eminent leaders in our field (Sterling 2004; Fisher *et al.* 2007; Lundegård and Wickman 2007; Wals 2010). It is our experience (anecdotally) that this is attributed to differences in discipline, which is ironic when we consider the imperative of deep interdisciplinarity crucial to ESD. Scholarly rigour must be universal. Reductionist appeals to shallow, value-free scientificity have been well disrupted in post-positivist critiques (Hassan and Hanapi 2013). There is also some irony in the scientifist obsession with empirical data, given so few claims in the ESD literature have been validated or tested. This reductionism functions to *exclude many disciplines* from the ESD community. Hay argues for recognition of contesting perspectives:

> greater ontological and epistemological awareness and, indeed, reflexivity can, and perhaps should *first*, be justified in their own terms – as a necessary, but of course not in itself sufficient, condition of being able both to *recognise* and to adjudicate between *contending theoretical perspectives.*
>
> *(Hay 2007: 116; emphasis added)*

If we are about to move to the identification of effective methodologies, we will do so through the deepest of scholarly discourses on the various underpinning assumptions which attend our epistemological practice. We have not done so.

A summary in point

Clearly, there is considerable diversity in educational approaches and research foci under the remit of ESD, and these are based on different epistemological paradigms. As a consequence of its interdisciplinary nature, clear conceptualisation of the theory, practice and findings in relation to knowledge in the areas of ESD is problematic and this limits research-based advice to inform praxis (Meyers 2006; Disinger 2001). While there is much practice to guide educators in relation to classroom activities and content, there is little research into the epistemological foundations that inform the fundamental conceptualisations of ESD. ESD requires research and understanding in the area of educational theory as it informs practice, and this includes the need to better understand research methodologies and methods to help identify what is important to learn about learning, and how this informs practice and content (Meyers 2006). Further, we need to recognise and explore the epistemological foundations which inform the breadth of approaches to ESD and how these might evolve. The literature suggests that research is required in the areas of our understanding of the nature of knowledge, how we understand and standards used to identify it. Recognition of epistemological commonalities and differences, and understanding how the strengths and weaknesses of different notions of knowledge inform educational development is required (Dewey 1916; Gutek 1997; Meyers 2006).

These areas of further research are important as they influence how decisions are made in relation to engaging with learners, and the development and selection of curriculum. Theoretical awareness situated within practice is central to our understanding of our praxis (Dewey 1966 [1916]). As argued by Meyers (2006: 322) if 'theory is not understood or is disconnected from practice, it is not pragmatic', and this is critical, as it tacitly guides our decision-making about the content and teaching methodology that need to be considered in lesson and curriculum planning (Dewey 1966 [1916]; Meyers 2006).

Additionally, learning and teaching are both political and cultural (Freire 1972). Politically, what is taught, how it is taught, assessed, constructed, and the values brought to the education process, by student and teacher, shape the learning process and outcomes. As such, the development of literacies, skills and/or capabilities that reflect a sustainability paradigm are predetermined by the social and economic context that is embodied by the educator and/or institution. An understanding of theory is central to educational praxis and the resultant types of curriculum developed and learning and teaching methods employed. How sustainability is understood and practiced by the educator will influence the curriculum content that is considered relevant to disciplinary knowledge and practice (Fien 2001; Kemmis and Smith 2008). The educational practice or praxis will then be predetermined in the practitioner's resulting pedagogy, learning and teaching methods and identified curriculum. Freire (1972) argued that we are 'beings of praxis' and hence capable of transforming the world; this will only occur in education, if we are able as individuals 'to see' or 'become aware' of the inherent links between pedagogy, learning and teaching approaches, curriculum and the assumptions that we bring to these.

Much of the research that does exist within the literature is developed by individuals or those who are part of a broader institutional push to further the ESD agenda. The indicator of success is the development of curriculum, as a sustainability unit or course within an HEI. This is dominated by case study analysis and while this is useful for those wanting to engage in the development of ESD, the conceptual and theoretical challenges discussed here are highlighted in relation to comparing and interpreting such research. Meyers (2006) argues that there is the need to develop better methods for interpreting the generalisability of results and recommendations based on them. Additionally, these approaches are predominately constructivist in approach, informed by teaching methods such as identification and exploration of issues, participatory and action research and critical reflection. How this is taught by academics with conflicting ideological and epistemological paradigms is an area where further research is required.

Clearly there is need for ESD practitioners to recognise and engage with epistemological and methodological frameworks to improve the evidentiary base. At the heart of scholarly enquiry lies the ontology-epistemology-methodology triumvirate, which we need to engage directly if we are to validate and diffuse the wide ranging instances of innovation we have seen summarised here. This model is the means by which scholars have always enabled the deepest scrutiny and interrogation, and therefore raised the bar on the means of socially and meaningfully distributing the fruits of their researches.

A summarising meta-analysis of extensive curriculum instances, and the changes needed to undertake and embed these, will assist ESD communities to inform, develop and debate a situated approach to scholarly enquiry. As Sterling argued in Huckle *et al.* (1996) some years ago, education itself *must be transformed* if it is to be transforming, which is, of course, the promise of education for sustainability.

Note

1 *Journal of Cleaner Production*, editor in chief Professor D. Huisingh, www.journals.elsevier.com/journal-of-cleaner-production.

References

Adomßent, M. and Michelsen, G., 2006. 'German Academia Heading for Sustainability? Reflections on Policy and Practice in Teaching, Research and Institutional Innovations', *Environmental Education Research*, 12(1), 85–99.

Barth, M. and Godemann, J., 2006. 'Study Programme Sustainability – A Way to Impart Competencies for Handling Sustainability?', in Adomßent, M., Godemann, J., Leicht, A. and Busch, A. (eds), *Higher Education for Sustainability: New Challenges from a Global Perspective*. Frankfurt/M.: Verlag für Akademische Schriften, 198–207.

Barth, M., Godemann, J., Rieckmann, M. and Stoltenberg, U., 2007. 'Developing Key Competencies for Sustainable Development in Higher Education', *International Journal of Sustainability in Higher Education*, 8(4), 416–30.

Baud, R., 2004. 'Y.E.S. – Student Education in Sustainability Public Education in a Knowledge Society: Creativity, Content, and Delivery Mechanisms'. New Delhi, India: Delhi Sustainable Development Summit, February 2004.

Beringer, A., 2007. 'The Luneburg Sustainable University Project in International Comparison: An Assessment against North American Peers', *International Journal of Sustainability in Higher Education*, 8(4), 446–61.

Beringer, A. and Adomßent, M., 2008. 'Sustainable University Research and Development: Inspecting Sustainability in Higher Education Research', *Environmental Education Research*, 14(6), 607–23.

Brody, S. and Ryu, H., 2006. 'Measuring the Educational Impacts of a Graduate Course on Sustainable Development', *Environmental Education Research*, 12(2), 179–99.

Cade, A., 2008. 'Employable Graduates for Responsible Employers. Student Force for Sustainability/HE Academy'. https://www.heacademy.ac.uk/sites/default/files/esd-employable-graduates-responsible-employers.pdf [accessed 16 February 2015].

Corcoran, P.B., Walker, K.E. and Wals, A.E.J., 2004. 'Case Studies, Make-your-case Studies, and Case Stories: A Critique of Case-study Methodology in Sustainability in Higher Education', *Environmental Education Research*, 10(1), 7–21.

Dawe, G., Jucker, R. and Martin, S., 2005. 'Sustainable Development in Higher Education: Current Practice and Future Developments'. Higher Education Academy. http://thesite.eu/sustdevinHEfinalreport.pdf [accessed 16 February 2015].

Dawes, N.P. and Larson, R., 2011. 'How Youth get Engaged: Grounded-theory Research on Motivational Development in Organized Youth Programs', *Developmental Psychology*, 47(1), 259–69.

Denzin, N.K. and Lincoln, Y.S., 1998. *The Landscape of Qualitative Research: Theories and Issue*. London: SAGE Publications.

Dewey, J., 1966 [1916]. *Democracy and Education: An Introduction to the Philosophy of Education*. New York: Macmillan.

DfEE, Welsh Office, 1993. *Environmental Responsibility – An Agenda for Further and Higher Education. Report of a Committee on Environmental Education in Further and Higher Education, Toyne Report*. London: DfEE.

DfES, 2005. 'Sustainable Development Action Plan for Education and Skills'. www.dfes.gov.uk/ about us/sd/actionplan.shtml [accessed 16 February 2015].

Disinger, J., 2001. 'K-12 Education and the Environment: Perspectives, Expectations and Practice', *Journal of Environmental Education*, 33(1), 4–11.

Durkheim, E., 1961. *Moral Education*. New York: The Free Press.

Fenner, R., Ainger, C., Cruickshank, H. and Guthri, P., 2005. 'Embedding Sustainable Development at Cambridge University Engineering Department', *International Journal of Sustainability in Higher Education*, 6(3), 229–41.

Fien, J., 2001. 'Education for Sustainability: Reorientating Australian Schools for a Sustainable Future', *Tela Papers*, 8. Melbourne: ACF.

Fien, J., 2002. 'Advancing Sustainability in Higher Education: Issues and Opportunities for Research', Higher Education Policy, 15(2), 43–52.

Fischer, J., Manning, A.D., Steffen, W., Rose, D.B., Daniell, K., Felton, A. and Wade, A., 2007. 'Mind the Sustainability Gap', *Trends in Ecology & Evolution*, 22(12), 621–4.

Freire, P., 1972. *Pedagogy of the Oppressed*. Harmondsworth: Penguin.

Forster, J., 2006. 'Sustainable Literacy: Embedding Sustainability into the Curriculum of Scotland's Universities and Colleges'. Report for the Scottish Funding Council.

Forum for the Future, 2004. *Learning and Skills for Sustainable Development: Developing a Sustainability-literate Society, Guidance for Higher Education Institutions*. London: Scottish Funding Council.

Gutek, G., 1997. *Philosophical and Ideological Perspectives in Education*. Needham Heights, MA: Allyn and Bacon.

Hammersley, M., 1995. *The Politics of Social Research*. London: SAGE, 100.

Hassan, S.A. and Hanapi, M.S., 2013. '"Scientificity" of Social Research: Its Challenges and Implications', *Academic Journal of Interdisciplinary Studies*, 2(9), 62–7.

Hay, C., 2007. 'Does Ontology Trump Epistemology? Notes on the Directional Dependence of Ontology and Epistemology in Political Analysis'. *Politics*, 27(2), 115–18.

Hayles, C.S. and Holdsworth, S.E., 2008. 'Curriculum Change for Sustainability', Journal *for Education in the Built Environment*, 3(1), 25–48.

HEFCE, 2005. 'Sustainable Development in Higher Education – Statement of Policy'. Higher Education Funding Council for England. www.hefce.ac.uk/pubs/hefce/2005/05_28/ [accessed 16 February 2015].

HEFCE, 2008. *Sustainable Development in Higher Education: Consultation on 2008 Update to Strategic Statement and Action Plan*. London: Higher Education Funding Council for England.

Hegarty, K., 2008. 'Shaping the Self to Sustain the Other: Mapping Impacts of Academic Identity in Education for Sustainability', *Environmental Education Research*, 14(6), 681–92.

Hegarty, K., 2009. 'Sustaining Collegiality through the Imperative of Interdisciplinary Practice', *London Review of Education*, 7(1), 83–90.

Hegarty, K., Thomas, I., Kriewaldt, C., Holdsworth, S. and Bekessy, S., 2011. 'Insights into the Value of a "Stand-alone" Course for Sustainability Education', *Environmental Education Research*, 17(4), 451–69.

Hoare, A., Cornell, S., Bertram, C., Gallagher, K., Heslop, S., Lieven, N., MacLeod, C., Morgan, J., Pickering, A., Wells, S. and Willmore, S., 2008. 'Teaching Against the Grain: Multi-disciplinary Teamwork Effectively Delivers a Successful Undergraduate Unit in Sustainable Development', *Environmental Education Research*, 14(4), 469–81.

Holdsworth, S., Bekessy, S., Hayles, C., Mnguni, P. and Thomas, I., 2006a. 'Beyond Leather Patches Project for Sustainability Education at RMIT', in Filho, W.L. and Carpenter, D. (eds), *University Sustainability in the Australasian University Context*. Frankfurt: Peter Lang Scientific Publishers, 107–28.

Holdsworth, S., Bekessy, S., Hayles, C., Mnguni, P. and Thomas, I., 2006b. 'Beyond Leather Patches: Sustainability Education at RMIT University, Australia', in Filho, W.L. (ed.), *Innovation, Education and Communication for Sustainable Development*. Frankfurt: Peter Lang Scientific Publishers, 153–76.

Holdsworth, S., Bekessy, S. and Thomas, I., 2009. 'Evaluation of Curriculum Change at RMIT: Experiences of the BELP Project', *Reflecting Education*, 5(1), 51–72.

Hopkinson, P., Hughes, P. and Layer, G., 2008. 'Sustainable Graduates: Linking Formal, Informal and Campus Curricula to Embed Education for Sustainable Development in the Student Learning Experience', *Environmental Education Research*, 14(4), 435–54.

Jacobs, H.H., 1990. 'The Growing Need for Interdisciplinary Curriculum Content', in Jacobs, H.H. (ed.), *Interdisciplinary Curriculum Design and Implementation*. Alexandria, VA: Association for Supervision and Curriculum Development, 1–11.

Karatzoglou, B., 2013. 'An In-depth Literature Review of the Evolving Roles and Contributions of Universities to Education for Sustainable Development', *Journal of Cleaner Production*, 49(June), 44–53.

Katayama, J. and Gough, S., 2008. 'Developing Sustainable Development within the Higher Education Curriculum: Observations on the HEFCE Strategic Review', *Environmental Education Research*, 14(4), 413–22.

Kemmis, S. and Smith, T.J., 2008. *Enabling Praxis: Challenges for Education*. Rotterdam, The Netherlands: Sense Publishers.

Kumar, V., Haapala, K., Rivera, J. and Hutchins, M., 2005. 'Infusing Sustainability Principles into Manufacturing/Mechanical Engineering Curricula', *Journal of Manufacturing Systems*, 24(3), 215–26.

Lundegård, I. and Wickman, P.O., 2007. 'Conflicts of Interest: An Indispensable Element of Education for Sustainable Development', *Environmental Education Research*, 13(1), 1–15.

Meyers, R.B., 2006. 'A Pragmatic Epistemology for Free-choice Learning', *Environmental Education Research*, 113(3), 309–20.

Mulder, K.F., 2010. 'Don't Preach. Practice! Value Laden Statements in Academic Sustainability Education', *International Journal of Sustainability in Higher Education*, 11(1), 74–85.

Parker, J., Wade, R. and van Winsum, A., 2004. 'Citizenship, and Community from Local to Global; Implications for Higher Education of a Global Citizenship Approach', in Blewitt, J. and Cullingford, C. (eds), *The Sustainability Curriculum: The Challenge for Higher Education*. London: Earthscan, 63–77.

Parkin, S., Johnston, A., Buckland, H., Brookes, F. and White, E., 2004. 'Learning and Skills for Sustainable Development – Developing a Sustainability-Literate Society, Guidance for Higher Education Institutions'. Cheltenham Higher Education Partnership for Sustainability/Forum for the Future.

Phenix, P.H., 1962. 'The Use of the Disciplines as Curriculum Content', *The Educational Forum*, 26(3), 273–80.

Pinar, W.F., Reynolds, W.M., Slattery, P. and Taubman, P.M., 1995. *Understanding Curriculum: An Introduction to the Study of Historical and Contemporary Curriculum Discourses*. Counterpoints: Studies in the Postmodern Theory of Education, Vol. 17. New York: Peter Lang.

Ramirez, M., 2006. 'Sustainability in the Education of Industrial Designers: The Case for Australia', *International Journal of Sustainability in Higher Education*, 7(2), 189–202.

Roberts, C. and Roberts, J., 2008. 'Starting with the Staff: How Swapshops can Develop ESD and Empower Practitioners', *Environmental Education Research*, 14(4), 423–34.

Rode. H. and Michelsen, G., 2008. 'Levels of Indicator Development for Education for Sustainable

Development', *Environmental Education Research*, 14(1), 19–33.
Schubert, W., 1986. *The Curriculum: Perspective, Paradigm, and Possibility*. New York: Macmillan.
Shor, I. and Freire, P., 1987. 'What is the "Dialogical Method" of Teaching?', *Journal of Education*, 169(3), 11–31.
Sen, A., 1992. *Inequality Re-examined*. Oxford: Oxford University Press.
Sen, A., 1999. *Development as Freedom*. New York: Alfred Knopf.
Sterling, S., 2004. 'Higher Education, Sustainability, and the Role of Systemic Learning', in *Higher Education and the Challenge of Sustainability*. Netherlands: Springer, 49–70.
Sterling, S. and Scott, W., 2008. 'Higher Education and ESD in England: A Critical Commentary on Recent Initiatives', *Environmental Education Research*, 14(4), 386–98.
Sterling, S. and Witham, H., 2008. 'Pushing the boundaries: the work of the Higher Education Academy's ESD Project', *Environmental Education Research*, 14(4), 399–412.
Stubbs, W. and Schapper, J., 2011. 'Two Approaches to Curriculum Development for Educating for Sustainability and CSR', *International Journal of Sustainability in Higher Education*, 12(3), 259–68.
Sund, L. and Öhman, J., 2014. 'On the Need to Repoliticise Environmental and Sustainability Education: Rethinking the Postpolitical Consensus', *Environmental Education Research*, 20(5), 639–59
Sustainable Development Education Panel, 2003. 'Learning to Last'. www.dcsf.gov.uk/aboutus/%20sd/docs/LearningtoLast03.doc [accessed 18 February 2015].
Toyne, P., 1996. 'The Toyne Review', cited in British Government Panel on Sustainable Development Third Report 1997. www.sd-commission.org.uk/panel-sd/ panel3/10.htm [accessed 16 February 2015].
Trowler, P., Saunders, M. and Bamber, V., 2012. *Tribes and Territories in the 21st Century: Rethinking the Significance of Disciplines in Higher Education*. International Studies in Higher Education. London: Routledge.
Walker, M., 2010. 'Critical Capability Pedagogies and University Education', *Educational Philosophy and Theory*, 42(8), 898–917.
Wals, A.E., 2010. 'Between Knowing What is Right and Knowing that is it Wrong to tell others What is Right: On Relativism, Uncertainty and Democracy in Environmental and Sustainability Education', *Environmental Education Research*, 16(1), 143–51.
Whiteford, G.E. and Pereira, R.B., 2012. 'Occupation, Inclusion and Participation', in Whiteford, G.E. and Hocking, C. (eds), *Occupational Science: Society, Inclusion, Participation* Oxford: Wiley-Blackwell, 185–207.

20

ORGANISATIONAL CHANGE AND ORGANISATIONAL LEARNING FOR PROMOTING HIGHER EDUCATION FOR SUSTAINABLE DEVELOPMENT

Paul Sylvestre and Tarah Wright

Introduction

Realising organisational transformation for sustainability in higher education is a complex process fraught with resistance and ambiguity. While there are signs of promise in the proliferation of declarations for Higher Education for Sustainable Development (HESD), the growth in sustainability related courses and research, and the efforts taken by a number of campuses to green their operations (Hopkinson and James 2013; Luna and Maxey 2013; Sylvestre *et al.* 2013a; Wals 2014), HESD scholars and advocates criticise what they view as a 'bolt-on' approach to sustainability rather than a fundamental commitment to organisational transformation (Ferrer-Balas *et al.* 2010; Lotz-Sisitka 2004; Sterling 2004; Sterling 2010; Wals 2014). It is one thing for a university to become a signatory to a declaration, develop new course offerings or revamp pre-existing courses to incorporate sustainability related content, and undertake a series of energy efficiency retro-fits; it is another matter altogether to make concrete the forms of radical, whole institution transformations implied in the language of the HESD declarations and called for by many scholars in the field (Jickling and Wals 2008; Lozano 2006a; Sterling 2010; Velazquez *et al.* 2006). The former entails change that fits within pre-established norms of the institution, while the latter necessitates a complete re-envisioning of the fundamental norms and structural relations that in many ways culturally define contemporary universities (Cortese 2003; Sterling 2013; Tilbury 2013).

Whole institution transformation necessitates more than asserting claims to a moral high ground, a little gumption, and good deal of elbow grease. Transforming a university from merely using HESD rhetoric, into an institution that truly engages in concrete pro-sustainability change activities requires a serious commitment to understanding how universities as organisations learn and change (Kezar 2005; Kezar and Eckel 2002, Sterling 2013). This assertion is in no way novel. Over a decade ago, Corcoran *et al.* (2004) called for the scholarship of HESD to move beyond cases reporting on individual, campus-based SHE projects and to move toward more meta-analyses and a theoretical commitment to organisational theory as a body of scholarship. Wright (2007) echoed this in her report on research priorities for the HESD field, highlighting consensus around the perceived importance of greater engagement with the scholarship of organisational studies. Despite this, there are few examples of HESD studies grounding their work in a robust theorising of organisational learning and change (with a few notable exceptions: Cebrián *et al.* 2013; Stephens and Graham 2010).

The relationship between organisational learning (OL) and organisational change (OC) is complex. Whether learning is conceptualised as a cognitive process which underpins and leads to change (as it is for Senge 1990 and Argyris and Schon 1978), or as practical and collective action where the distinction between learning and change is dissolved (see for example Caldwell 2012 or Gherardi 2009), the importance of working toward understanding the nature of learning in an organisation cannot be sufficiently underscored. In this chapter, we present a review of several trajectories of thought concerning how OL is thought to facilitate and drive change, placing these in the context of sustainability in higher education. The scholarship and practice of OL is a jargon-laden, interdisciplinary field whose divergent threads draw from a diversity of ontological and epistemological positions which translates into a high level of contention regarding even the most basic premises related to the nature of knowledge and agency within an organisation (Friedman *et al.* 2005). Given that different ways of conceptualising the relationship between organisations and individuals, and learning and change, necessarily lead to different ideas on how to promote learning for the purpose of creating effective and sustained change, drawing lessons from the OL and change literature that are applicable to the context of HESD is important, not only for creating successful change but also for understanding past failures.

This chapter is divided into two sections. In the first section we offer an overview of four broad typologies of OL theory and how these construct concepts of change, learning and the relationship between individuals and organisations. We will then highlight the unique nature of universities as organisations and discuss which theoretical frameworks are best suited to dealing with the inherent complexity of promoting organisational transformation for sustainability within higher education.

In the second section we identify three areas of inquiry that show great potential for advancing our understanding of how institutions of higher education learn while concomitantly promoting learning and transformation for sustainability. We discuss the importance of developing a deep understanding of the institutional contexts where change initiatives will be implemented. We discuss approaches and reasons for constructing culturally appropriate change strategies rooted in institutional histories and the lived experiences of stakeholders prior to deploying change initiatives. Following this, we explore the processual conceptions of change and how strategies for collaborative and dialogically driven methodologies for promoting learning and change can be effectively employed to achieve buy-in around sustainable transformation among a multiplicity of constituencies. Finally, we discuss examples of promising structural developments that can act as an institutional substrate for leaning and change. Specifically, we discuss the importance of developing effective assessment tools for measuring and reporting progress while possessing the requisite sophistication to adequately engage with a pluralistic and transformative conceptualisation of sustainability. In addition, we describe institutional mechanisms developed elsewhere that can give a transformative process a foothold so that it can be sustained for the long term.

Organisational change and learning

Given the breadth of the field of OL and OC, a comprehensive review is clearly beyond the scope of this chapter. Many scholars of the field have noted how the diversity of theoretical perspectives tends to obfuscate rather than clarify what is meant by even the most basic questions, such as what is learning in an organisational context and how does it relate to change (Friedman *et al.* 2005; Lipshitz *et al.* 2002; Shipton 2006). However, broad typologies and dichotomies have been suggested to exist (Bapuji and Crossan 2004; Cook and Yanow 2011; Shipton 2006) that allow for a cursory thematic examination of the state of the field that could act as an entry point for HESD practitioners and scholars seeking to embed their research in the field. Though using 'disciplinary' boundaries to frame a discussion of OL and OC is helpful for coherently navigating the diversity of perspectives, it is important note, as Bapuji and Crossan (2004) and Shipton (2006) suggest, that these distinctions are largely academic and in 'real world' contexts often require a cross-cutting approach. It is equally important to note that although we introduce concepts of change and learning separately in order to explore what is being said about them in more depth, as discussed above the relationship between change and learning is complex and framed differently by various groups of experts.

Deep change and learning are viewed synergistically throughout the literature surveyed for this chapter. Understanding the nature of change in an organisation is helpful in being able to comprehend how learning may be constructed. OC is often framed as a process of action informed by reflection which leads to further action and reflection represented in the literature through chains of action-oriented verbs (e.g. unfreezing, moving, refreezing [Lewin 1951]; consulting, engaging, deliberating [Lichtenstein 2000]) in which learning is implied at every stage.

Orders of change

Generally speaking, OC is the movement of an organisation from one state to another in response to some internal or external stimulus (Levitt and March 1988; By 2005). Scholars and practitioners of OC tend to conceptualise change as existing along a continuum. At one end of the continuum we find change that occurs within the pre-established social norms of an organisation which does not require an examination or alteration of the tacit assumptions and processes that underpin the organisation's current set of practices. This is sometimes referred to as first-order change (Argyris and Schön 1996), incremental change (Boonstra 2004), strategic change (Denis *et al.* 2001), or adaptive change (Friedman *et al.* 2005; Senge 1990). Change thusly conceived is characterised by strategic or incremental adjustments aimed at addressing questions of efficiency, where errors are detected and corrected (Argryis and Schön 1996) and is driven by linear, cause and effect forms of learning that seek to create small behavioural adjustments, which are typically easy to achieve. In the context of HESD an example would be seeking to increase waste diversion rates on campus by implementing a four-bin waste system. To date the majority of change for sustainability in higher education concerned with the diffusion and institutionalisation of particular innovations have largely engaged with teleological, first order, models of change whereby change is rational, linear and adaptive (Albrecht *et al.* 2007; Beringer and Adomβent 2008; Kezar 2001; Sylvestre *et al.* 2013b).

By contrast, the other end of the continuum hosts higher-order change, which is required when the underlying assumptions (beliefs that drive action), often referred to as mental models (Senge 1990), 'theories in use' (Argyris and Schön 1996), or histories of practice (Caldwell 2012) can no longer adequately contend with either internal or external pressures exerted on the organisation. At this point a transformation of the basic premises under which the organisation operates is needed. In the OC literature this is often referred to as fundamental change or radical change (Lichtenstein 2000), second-order change (Argyris and Schön 1996; Boonstra 2004), generative change (Senge 1990), and whole institution transformation (Kezar 2001;

Sterling 2013). Change of this order is multi-dimensional, meaning that higher-order OC must necessarily engage a morass of cultural, structural and cognitive realities which produce the current state of institutional inertia.

Whereas first-order change tends to be teleological in nature, it is far more amenable to prescriptive sets or recommendations. By contrast, the inherent complexity and scale of higher order change makes it far more difficult to plan and implement (Kezar 2001). Nevertheless, given that whole institution change for sustainability in higher education involves a fundamental rethinking of pedagogy and curriculum (Lambrechts *et al.* 2013; Lidgren *et al.* 2006; Sterling 2010; Wals 2014); a (re)shaping of epistemological and ontological commitments that result in socio-ecological degradation through teaching (Foster 2001; Huckle 2010) and research (White 2013); and a (re)envisioning of the organisational structures that limit an institution's ability to engage more deeply with sustainability (Blewitt 2013; Higher Education Treaty Circle, 2012), it is clear that change for sustainability requires a fundamental transformation of the organisation.

This is likely not a novel idea to HESD practitioners and scholars. Excellent work has already been done in articulating visions for sustainability in higher education (see for example Velazquez *et al.* 2006; Lukman and Glavič 2007; Sterling 2013; Higher Education Treaty Circle, 2012); in outlining the role and qualities of the kind of leadership necessary to bring universities in line with such visions (see for example Scott *et al.* 2012); and how such change may be managed (see for example Mader *et al.* 2013; Stephens and Graham 2010). While much of the aforementioned HESD OC literature is sensitive to developing a deep and collaborative understanding of the context in which change initiative will be deployed, it is the authors' experience that concepts of OL within these OC frameworks tend to be under theorised or assumed.

Equally important is an explicit awareness that the majority of OL and OC literature has been theorised in a business context. In contrast to most business organisations, institutions of higher learning are loosely coupled, pluralistic systems with diffuse and often informal decision-making structures (Boyce 2003; Denis *et al.* 2007; Sporn 1996); their goals are many and often ambiguous, and they focus on people rather than profits (Sherren 2010). Like most pluralistic systems they are highly adaptive and can readily undertake adaptive change. However the diversity of values and cultures present within the university acting in tandem with the complexity of organisational practices and routines makes whole institution transformation far more difficult (Birnbaum 2000; Sporn 1996; Sylvestre *et al.* 2013b). In fact, it is shown that a deep understanding of the varying contexts on which OC and OL strategies are to be applied is essential for long term success (Kezar 2001; Keup *et al.* 2001; Kezar and Eckel, 2002). As a result, process-oriented approaches to OC and OL which focus on participation and collaboration of the multiplicity of university constituencies is essential for successful long-term change (de la Harpe and Thomas 2009; Denis *et al.* 2007; Hopkinson and James 2013; Lichtenstein 2000; Moore *et al.* 2005). As noted above, what follows is a broad review of a number of OL typologies which are significant for developing change strategies toward OC for sustainability in higher education and how these relate to some current efforts.

Organisational learning in the context of organisational change

The nature of change will dictate the form of learning required for change to be both effective and sustained (Boyce 2003). Much like the OC literature, the OL literature often presents learning as dichotomous. For instance, Argyris and Schön (1996) distinguish between what they refer to as single-loop and double-loop learning, whereas Senge (1990) frames learning in terms of adaptive and generative learning. Simply put, lower level learning can be understood as problem solving, wherein an action which does not produce a desired outcome is reflected upon and altered in such a way to produce the desired outcome. This level of learning is the motor mechanism that drives first-order change. Since higher order change necessitates the re-examination of values, beliefs, assumptions and practices that underpin organisational objectives, the reflexive processes that comprise this re-examination are understood as higher level learning (Argyris and Schön 1996). Given the way in which we have framed OC for sustainability the following discussion will exclusively concern itself with what constitutes higher level OL and ways in which it can be promoted.

Navigating the OL theory literature is a challenging task. Many have noted a lack of cohesion within the field and how the proliferation of papers on the topic has added, rather than reduced confusion around the concept (Cook and Yanow 2011; Shipton 2006, Tosey *et al.* 2011). To begin our discussion we shall employ Kezar's (2005) distinction between prescriptive and descriptive approaches; where prescriptive approaches seek to describe and implement sets of best practices to promote organisational learning as an essential component of planned change and are heavily favoured by practitioners and managers. Descriptive approaches, on the other hand, represent a diverse collection of scholarly work concerned with exploring and understanding the mechanisms by which learning is thought to occur in an institution.

Prescriptive approaches to organisational learning: from best-practices to management fads

Prescriptive approaches to OL tend to draw heavily on the cognitive models of learning, discussed in more detail below, where learning is a function of the mind and the goal is to embed individuals with novel cognitive frames more suited to a new vision for the organisation (Argyris and Schön 1996; Senge 1990; Shipton 2006). Much of this research is centred on identifying and recommending best-practices for achieving transformative forms of learning (such as double-loop learning or generative learning) and situating these with a multi-phase change strategy designed to be broadly applicable across a number of organisational contexts. Popular examples that have been implemented in higher education are management trends like Total Quality Management (Birnbaum 2001), the learning organisation (Garvin 1993; Senge 1990), and the transition management framework (Stephens and Graham 2010). These change strategies offer step-by-step processes to promote the dissemination of new knowledge and practices that promise to revitalise one's organisation in which OL is a central theme.

However, in practice, some have noted that prescriptive approaches to organisational learning generally do not deliver the sort of results that their adherents claim. As a result, retrospectively, many such trends are pejoratively lumped in with a growing list of failed management fads once the initial excitement wanes and the shortcomings of the approach become evident (Birnbaum 2000; Kezar 2005). Nevertheless, many such trends can possess kernels of wisdom that if applied properly can provide useful insights for promoting OL. It is a matter of understanding how to apply them judiciously (Kezar 2005). For instance, in discussing the usefulness of the Transition Management Framework in promoting change for sustainability in higher education, Stephens and Graham (2010) admit its inability to cope with the diversity of organisational cultures present at a university, while highlighting its sensitivity to the multiplicity of levels where learning must necessarily occur for successful transformation toward sustainability. The challenge then becomes gaining enough insight into the nature of one's university to be able to discern what aspects of particular management fads are appropriate and applicable (Birnbaum 2000; Kezar and Eckel 2002).

Descriptive approaches to organisational learning: cognitive and cultural perspectives

Rather than championing strategies for promoting OL, descriptive literature is more concerned with understanding the mechanism that creates learning and where learning is thought to occur (Argyris and Schön 1996; Caldwell 2012; Crossan *et al.* 1999; Kezar 2005; Shipton 2006). Beyond this high level alignment of cause exists a significant amount of contention regarding questions of whether learning occurs at an individual or organisational level, what is to be considered knowledge and where it is thought to reside. Conflict around basic ontological and epistemological assumptions makes synthesising broad recommendations for practice much more challenging as commitment to divergent conceptualisations of OL necessarily lead to significantly different ways of promoting learning. Nevertheless, we contend that a more robust awareness of how learning is thought to occur can aid change agents in planning change strategies geared toward their particular contexts.

Argyris and Schön (1996) (whose work as noted above underpins many prescriptive approaches) pose the question 'what is an organization that it may learn?', seemingly answering in the affirmative that organisations as entities can indeed learn. However, their focus on single and double-loop learning implies a cognitive stance to OL where individuals are the focal point for learning and the locus of change. As alluded to above a cognitive standpoint frames learning as the transfer of explicit, objectified knowledge rather than tacit or relational forms of knowing (Crossan *et al.* 1999; Shipton 2006) and, as a result, agency is often separated from organisational systems and structures (Caldwell 2012). In other words, knowledge is an artefact of the mind and all forms of learning are working to 'change' or 'replace' the knowledge in people's heads with new and better knowledge. Examples of this theoretical position tend to dominate the HESD literature in terms of discussing barriers to change in the form of lack of knowledge or not seeing the relevance of sustainability to one's discipline on the part of university stakeholders (Cotton *et al.* 2007; Dawe *et al.* 2005; de la Harpe and Thomas 2009; Lozano 2006a; Velasquez *et al.* 2006), and in practice, for example, through identifying the importance of staff development initiatives as a means of promoting and sustaining successful change (Barth and Rieckmann 2012), or behavioural change interventions (Beringer and Adomβent 2008), and in evaluation by developing outcomes-based indicators to measure success (Brody and Ryu 2006; Tilbury 2007).

However, for Caldwell (2012) and Gherardi (2009) to conceive of learning in an organisation in such a way is to reify both knowledge and organisations. They adopt a relational ontology, arguing that objectifying both knowledge and organisations is to fundamentally misunderstand how learning occurs and how people come to know in an organisational context. As proponents of a practice-based (PB) conception of OL, organisations are not entities in and of themselves, rather they are a 'texture of interrelated practices which extend to form an action-net sustained by a knowing-in-action which renews itself and transforms itself into being practiced' (Gherardi 2009: 357). In addition, knowledge (and learning by association) is situated, emergent and embedded in practices, routines, objects, artefacts and social environments, and is expressed through relationships of practice, be those social or technical. Therefore 'learning and knowing are processes of doing and saying that are enacted in practice rather than cognitive attributes of mind' (Caldwell 2012: 160) and bound up in the relationship between people and things. This extends into a discussion of organisational culture, where the culture of an organisation is not a cognitive artefact, but a net of expectations (re)produced by the relationships between groups of individuals and between individuals and their organisational environments (Cook and Yanow 2011). In contrast to a cognitive stance, learning and change become a question of negotiated meanings, sense-making and understanding the discourses embedded in the (re)production of tacit knowledge (where tacit knowledge is understood as the knowledge embedded in objects and routines) in order to understand how change and learning emerge out of the routines and practices of the social environment rather than giving individuals the 'right' knowledge and expecting them to act accordingly (Denis *et al.* 2007).

Such a stance necessarily leads to different modes of action when considering how to foster learning for the purpose of change in an organisation. While it is useful to conceive of organisational knowledge as relational and embedded in 'doing' (in that it shifts the locus of learning from individual minds to developing new forms of social practices), the PB literature offers little in the way of clear guidance in strategising OL for the purpose of change. However, recent HESD projects have shown sensitivity to such an approach, though without making explicit reference to PB studies as a theoretical stance. Hopkinson and James (2013) found it highly beneficial to engage with social practice as a unit of analysis when planning learning for their institution during their attempt at whole institution transformation at the University of Bradford. They argue that such an approach is instrumental in coming to understand the multiplicity of pressures, contexts and histories that form a contemporary university. Similarly, Sutherland Olsen (2009) describes interdisciplinary projects within technological firms as a phenomenon that establishes new forms of practice-based learning. This echoes the HESD stance on the importance of transdisciplinarity as an essential component of both research and learning for sustainability in higher education (Gaziulusoy *et al.* 2013; Mader *et al.* 2013). These examples highlight parallel research trajectories between HESD and OL scholarship in which potential synergies ought to be identified and parsed. In the following section we will highlight methods and strategies geared to organisational inquiry focusing on three themes: learning about your organisation, learning with your organisations, the learning of your organisation. We advance these as three mutually supported approaches that can be embedded into a greater reflexive process of promoting organisational learning for the purpose of creating and sustaining 'change' for sustainability in higher education

Methods and strategies geared to organisational inquiry and learning

Initial inquiry: learning about the organisation

Commitment to a process-oriented conceptualisation of change in higher education requires awareness and sensitivity to organisational cultures and the tacit knowledge in which they are rooted. Context-based information is essential to developing knowledge about how best to promote learning for change in one's organisation (Kezar and Eckel 2002). This is difficult to achieve given that developing a deep understanding of the cultural norms of any group lends itself to sets of methodologies (e.g. ethnography, thick description) that are suited to very small populations, while more wide scale data collection efforts generally lack the sensitivity to give great insight into the nature of culture.

Understanding the cultural networks of large institutions with hundreds of departments and thousands of individuals presents a challenge. Kezar and Eckel (2002) offer some insight by drawing on the work of Bergquist (1992) and Tierney (1991) to develop frameworks for understanding broad institutional cultures. Bergquist (1992) postulated four organisational archetypes in higher education through which the culture and behaviour of a university can be understood: collegial culture, managerial culture, developmental culture, and negotiating culture. Tierney (1991) identified six dimensions which could be assessed to explore the complex nature of institutional cultures: environment, mission, socialisation, information, strategy, and leadership. Kezar and Eckel (2002) combine Bergquist's four archetypes with Tierney's six institutional dimensions to develop an a priori framework through which to study change processes at several universities. Similarly, Sporn (1996) presents a biaxial vision of university cultures on a spectrum from weak to strong institutional cultures and external to internal orientations to suggest four overarching 'types' of culture. For instance, according to Sporn, an institution may have a weak, internally focused culture where institutional values, beliefs and norms are divergent and dominated by cultural sub-groups implying little to no institutional identity, while concomitantly being inward looking and poorly receptive to environmental pressures. By contrast, an institution with a strong, externally focused culture will have fewer divergent cultural sub-groups as most of the constituencies at the institution share a collective vision of the institution's direction and identity. Their external focus makes them more sensitive to environmental stimuli. These sorts of frameworks, while being overly general, can provide a good starting point for thinking about one's institution.

High level cultural probes, such as the preceding examples applied to higher education, echo similar studies conducted on successful higher order change in other loosely coupled organisations (see Lichtenstein 2000 and Denis *et al.* 2001) and illustrate the importance of developing a strong sensitivity to culture for promoting a culture of learning with a view to sustaining change. This is likely to be all the more important when trying to promote organisational transformation for sustainability, as contestation around the concept of sustainability itself adds another layer of complexity to facilitating change (Sylvestre *et al.* 2014). Analytical frameworks and typologies like these can help develop clarity around an institution's culture by situating them in broad, empirically derived categories that seek to anticipate successful change strategies (Bartell 2003; Sporn 1996) but they do not provide the sort of fine grained information required to answer questions like, where is power situated and how is it wielded; how and by whom are decisions made, and who or what is informally influential in this process; what is considered knowledge (Kezar and Eckel 2002; Moore *et al.* 2005; Smith and Parker 2005).

Case study research has been a hallmark of HESD scholarship (Barth and Thomas 2012; Corcoran *et al.* 2004) and is an approach that could be highly effective for developing a deeply contextual understanding of an organisation. However, care should be taken in selecting methodological approaches to support such research. The existence of multiple distinct cultures within an organisation is likely to produce multiple, localised realities based in the different lived experiences of communities of practice (Hosking 2004). Therefore, we suggest using a 'sense-making' approach, drawing on methods such as narrative inquiry (Connelly and Clandinin 1990), appreciative inquiry (Hammond 2013), or dialogic inquiry (Ash 2003; Wells 2009), which are conceptually well placed to draw out and explicate important differences rather than muting or diminishing them. This is an important first step in adopting a 'different but equal relations' among various constituencies, and as an approach to OL can be used to support a truly collaborative change process (Hosking 2004: 268).

Collaborative and action inquiry: learning with the organisation

Meaningful and collaborative stakeholder engagement that empowers people to take ownership over a change initiative by incorporating their lived experience into a strategy for change in a fundamental way is an effective means of promoting successful and sustained change (Boyce 2003; de la Harpe and Thomas 2009; Lichtenstein 2000; Mader 2012; Moore *et al.* 2005) (see also Wahr and de la Harpe in this Handbook). Collaborative inquiry, participatory action research, and co-inquiry methodologies can be used as both a form of and tool for OL

(Boonstra 2004; Hosking 2004). Enabling institutional stakeholders to infuse the change process with their knowledge and experience of the organisation creates a substrate from out of which new ideas can emerge (Cebrián *et al.* 2013; Gravenhorst and Veld 2004; Lichtenstein 2000). In addition, given that visions of transformation for sustainability at universities often call for promoting social learning, transdisciplinary forms of inquiry, and other forms of collaborative knowledge creation (Cebrián *et al.* 2013; Mader 2012; Sterling 2013; Wals 2014), having a strategy for a process-oriented approach to change rooted in a commitment to collaboration and dialogue demonstrates a deep commitment to those values. Moreover, as Wegner (1998: 234) contends: 'no community can fully design the learning of another; no community can fully design its own learning'. Therefore, collaborative effort during the change process, though difficult to maintain (Denis *et al.* 2001; Moore *et al.* 2005) will likely make change more culturally self-referential and can help to identify pre-existing structures that can help to advance the process (Lichtenstein 2000; Boyce 2003). Such approaches are described, for example, by Hopkinson and James (2013) and Taylor (2013) in their discussion of transformation at the University of Bradford and Kingston University respectively. However, given the context-dependent nature of what an effective and appropriate collaborative learning and change strategy ought to look like, hard set rules or detailed frameworks are difficult to come by.

Our review of the literature yielded little in the way of readily applicable approaches and rather sought to underscore the importance of truly collaborative processes as an important conceptual starting point. For instance, as Denis *et al.* (2007) discuss, committing to this form of approach is taking the long view of organisational transformation where 'patience, persistence, and subtlety' on the part of the agents seeking to create change are a necessity but avoid making any specific recommendations. Lichtenstein (2000) adds to this by suggesting that although long term incremental change can lead to organisational transformation it is important to be sensitive enough to your organisation climate to be 'creatively opportunistic' and push collaboratively developed sets of recommendations at times of institutional upheaval, but offers little insight into how to promote 'collaborative development'. This may seem of questionable use to practitioners seeking methods that are readily applicable. However, we argue that developing and administering collaboratively processes for the context of sustainability at the university, based on an iterative and continuous cultural and organisational probing, is an area of fruitful inquiry for HESD.

Assessment and communication: learning of the organisation

Despite using OL to develop culturally appropriate and/or collaborative change initiatives, if change is not adequately institutionalised or successes go unnoticed change efforts are likely to fail (Boyce 2003; Smith and Parker 2005). The 'learning of the organisation' constitutes finding ways to turn ideas and thoughts generated within the two steps outlined above into tangible sets of new practices and or structures. Assessment tools, capacity development, and embedding change through deploying new practices (e.g. changing reward structures) are all conventional and popular approaches that are well represented among the efforts taken by HESD scholars and practitioners to promote OC and OL for sustainability (AASHE 2013; Barth and Rieckmann 2012; Lozano and Peattie 2011; Mader 2012). Such approaches, *if applied properly*, can give nascent, yet promising organisational changes initiative the foothold they require to persist in a meaningful way.

For instance, the importance of developing the sustainability capacity of university faculty and staff is often cited as essential to any change strategy (Barth and Rieckmann 2012; Dahle and Neumayer 2001; Dawe *et al.* 2005; Lieberman 2005; Lozano-Garcia *et al.* 2008). However, given the culture of universities, programmes aimed at educating staff and faculty are often met with resistance (Kezar 2005). Boyce (2003) suggests (in a manner which mirrors our discussion on collaborative approaches) approaching campus-wide learning from the perspective of creating a learning community and engaging in pedagogical approaches that distribute power and are less transmissive. Imbuing capacity development strategies with a more dialogic or participative commitment could conceivably overcome cultural impediments to their being viewed as useful and can be considered an important first step in developing new sets of practice such as commitments to pedagogical approaches in the classroom that are more aligned with the goals of sustainability.

Deploying effective assessment can enable one to systematically assess performance, to correct actions as needed, and to make visible the positive effects of a change process (Kezar 2005). SHE scholars have long since understood the importance of developing and implementing these sorts of tools (AASHE 2013; Lukman and Glavič 2007; Rode and Michelsen 2008), if we are to move away from goal-oriented change strategies (planned change) to a more process-oriented idea of continuous change for sustainability rooted in cultural sensitivity and collaboration. Process oriented, multi-stakeholder, holistic assessment tools such as the Graz Model of Integrative Development (GMID), the Graphical Assessment of Sustainability in Universities (GASU), or the Sustainability Tool for Assessing University's Curricula Holistically (STAUNCH™) may be a means of promoting OL while concomitantly highlighting where and how change has been effective and where to further focus one's efforts (Lozano and Peattie 2011; Lozano 2006b; Mader 2012) (see also Rammel *et al.* in this Handbook).

Conclusions

This chapter has attempted to provide a broad overview of prominent trajectories and approaches in OL literature, relevant to the context of higher education, so that HESD scholars seeking to embed their work in this body of scholarship can identify areas that align with their needs. This is not meant to be a comprehensive treatment of the diversity of thought on the nature of change and learning in organisations. Rather, it is an introduction to elements that could be of great value in guiding future HESD research. Although many of the theoretical approaches described in the first section may seem familiar to individuals who work in sustainability, we have found little evidence to suggest they are being explicitly articulated when being applied to the promotion of whole institution transformation for sustainability in higher education.

Fundamental to our framing of organisational transformation and learning for sustainability is that change and learning be viewed as mutually reinforcing processes rooted in cycles of reflection and action and not a series of linearly conceived, outcomes-oriented initiatives focused on engineering 'appropriate' behaviours. This is not to say that first-order or incremental change projects and small victories are not important, only that they need to be explicitly embedded into a long-term, collaboratively constructed commitment to organisational development.

Change for sustainability is just one of many changes that are currently called for in higher education (others include economic/fiscal change, and internationalisation). By framing the transformation we wish to see for sustainability in a way that resonates with the various cultures of our respective institutions, while at the same time mirroring the very principles that we espouse as sustainability scholars (collaboration, transdisciplinarity, transformative pedagogies, etc.), we may stand a better chance of embedding change for sustainability within the DNA of the institution in a manner which will be self-referential and therefore sustained. Given that

HESD research has been criticised for being atheoretical and case study based (Barth and Thomas 2012; Corcoran *et al.* 2004; Fien 2002), we advance that future research ground itself theoretically in a far more robust manner into much of the ongoing and highly relevant scholarship within the field of OL and OC. We envision a commitment beyond simply deploying prescriptive management fads as they emerge, but rather developing a robust theoretical discussion which steps back from the immediacy of questions of best practice around change management, goal setting, and measurable outcomes to ask more fundamental questions about the nature of the changes we are proposing and how the way in which we frame our discussion of change and learning locks us into specific courses of action and where these courses will take us.

References

Albrecht, P., Burandt, S. and Schaltegger, S., 2007. 'Do Sustainability Projects Stimulate Organisational Learning in Universities?', *International Journal of Sustainability in Higher Education*, 8(4), 403–15.

Argyris, C. and Schon, D.A., 1978. *Organizational Learning*. Reading, MA: Addison-Wesley.

Argyris, C. and Schön, D.A., 1996. *Organisational Learning II: Theory, Method and Practice*. Reading, MA: Addison-Wesley.

Ash, D., 2003. 'Dialogic Inquiry in Life Science Conversations of Family Groups in a Museum', *Journal of Research in Science Teaching*, 40(2), 138–62.

Association for the Advancement of Sustainability in Higher Education (AASHE), 2013. 'STARS a program of AASHE'. https://stars.aashe.org/ [accessed 16 February 2015].

Bapuji, H. and Crossan, M., 2004. 'From Questions to Answers: Reviewing Organizational Learning Research', *Management Learning*, 35(4), 397–417.

Bartell, M., 2003. 'Internationalization of Universities: A University Culture-based', *Higher Education*, 45(1), 43–70.

Barth, M. and Rieckmann, M., 2012. 'Academic Staff Development as a Catalyst for Curriculum Change Towards Education for Sustainable Development: An Output Perspective', *Journal of Cleaner Production*, 26, 28–36.

Barth, M. and Thomas, I., 2012. 'Synthesising Case-study Research: Ready for the Next Step ?', *Environmental Education Research*, 18(6), 751–64.

Beringer, A. and Adomßent, M., 2008. 'Sustainable University Research and Development: Inspecting Sustainability in Higher Education Research', *Environmental Education Research*, 14(6), 607–23.

Bergquist, W.H., 1992. *The Four Cultures of the Academy: Insights and Strategies for Improving Leadership in Collegiate Organizations*. San Francisco, CA: Jossey-Bass.

Birnbaum, R., 2000. 'The Life Cycle of Academic Management Fads', *The Journal of Higher Education*, 71(1), 1–16.

Birnbaum, R., 2001. *Management Fads in Higher Education: Where They Come From, What They Do, Why They Fail*. San Francisco, CA: Jossey-Bass.

Blewitt, J., 2013. 'Efs: Contesting the Market Model of Higher Education', in Sterling, S., Maxey, L. and Luna, H. (eds), *The Sustainable University: Progress and Prospects*. New York: Routledge, 17–50.

Boonstra, J.J., 2004. 'Introduction', in Boonstra, J.J. (ed.), *Dynamics of Organizational Change and Learning*. Chichester: Wiley, 1–21.

Boyce, M.E., 2003. 'Organizational Learning Is Essential to Achieving and Sustaining Change in Higher Education', *Innovative Higher Education*, 28(2), 119–36.

Brody, S.D. and Ryu, H., 2006. 'Measuring the Educational Impacts of a Graduate Course on Sustainable Development', *Environmental Education Research*, 12(2), 179–99.

By, R.T., 2005. 'Organisational Change Management: A Critical Review', *Journal of Change Management*, 5(4), 369–80.

Caldwell, R., 2012. 'Systems Thinking, Organizational Change and Agency: A Practice Theory Critique of Senge's Learning Organization', *Journal of Change Management*, 12(2), 145–64.

Cebrián, G., Grace, M. and Humphris, D., 2013. 'Organisational Learning Towards Sustainability in Higher Education', *Sustainability Accounting, Management and Policy Journal*, 4(3), 285–306.

Connelly, F.M. and Clandinin, D.J., 1990. 'Stories of Experience and Narrative Inquiry', *Educational Researcher*, 19(5), 2–14.

Cook, S.D.N. and Yanow, D., 2011. 'Culture and Organizational Learning', *Journal of Management Inquiry*, 20(4), 362–79.

Corcoran, P.B., Walker, K.E. and Wals, A.E.J., 2004. 'Case Studies, Make-your-case Studies, and Case Stories: A Critique of Case-study Methodology in Sustainability in Higher Education', *Environmental Education Research*, 10(1), 7–21.

Cortese, A.D., 2003. 'The Critical Role of Higher Education in Creating a Sustainable Future', *Planning for Higher Education*, 31(3), 15–22.

Cotton, D.R.E., Warren, M.F., Maiboroda, O. and Bailey, I., 2007. 'Sustainable Development, Higher Education and Pedagogy: A Study of Lecturers' Beliefs and Attitudes', *Environmental Education Research*, 13(5), 579–97.

Cotton, D., Bailey, I., Warren, M. and Bissell, S., 2009. 'Revolutions and Second-best Solutions: Education for Sustainable Development in Higher Education', *Studies in Higher Education*, 34(7), 719–33.

Crossan, M.M., Lane, H.W., White, R.E. and White, E., 1999. 'Learning from Intuition to Framework', *The Academy of Management Review*, 24(3), 522–37.

Dahle, M. and Neumayer, E., 2001. 'Overcoming Barriers to Campus Greening: A Survey among Higher Educational Institutions in Lond', *International Journal of Sustainability in Higher Education*, 2(2), 139–60.

Dawe, G., Jucker, R. and Martin, S., 2005. 'Sustainable Development in Higher Education : Current Practice and Future Developments'. York: Higher Education Academy.

de la Harpe, B. and Thomas, I., 2009. 'Curriculum Change in Universities: Conditions that Facilitate Education for Sustainable Development', *Journal of Education for Sustainable Development*, 3(1), 75–85.

Denis, J., Lamothe, L. and Langley, A., 2001. 'The Dynamics of Collective Leadership and Strategic Change in Pluralistic Organizations', *The Academy of Management Journal*, 44(4), 809–37.

Denis, J., Langley, A. and Rouleau, L., 2007. 'Strategizing in pluralistic contexts: Rethinking Theoretical Frames', *Human Relations*, 60(1), 179–215.

Ferrer-Balas, D., Lozano, R., Huisingh, D., Buckland, H., Ysern, P. and Zilahy, G., 2010. 'Going Beyond the Rhetoric: System-wide Changes in Universities for Sustainable Societies', *Journal of Cleaner Production*, 18(7), 607–10.

Fien, J., 2002. 'Advancing Sustainability in Higher Education: Issues and Opportunities for Research', *International Journal of Sustainability in Higher Education*, 3(3), 243–53.

Foster, J., 2001. 'Education as Sustainability', *Environmental Education Research*, 7(2), 153–65.

Friedman, V.J., Lipshitz, R. and Popper, M., 2005. 'The Mystification of organizational learning', *Journal of Management Inquiry*, 14(1), 19–30.

Garvin, D., 1993. 'Building a Learning Organization', *Harvard Business Review*, 71(4), 78–91.

Gaziulusoy, a. ., Boyle, C. and McDowall, R., 2013. 'System Innovation for Sustainability: A Systemic Double-flow Scenario Method for Companies', *Journal of Cleaner Production*, 45, 104–16.

Gherardi, S., 2009. 'Knowing and Learning in Practice-based Studies: An Introduction', *The Learning Organization*, 16(5), 352–9.

Gravenhorst, K.B. and Veld, R., 2004. 'Power and Collaboration: Methodologies for Working Together in Change', in Boonstra, J.J. (eds.), *Dynamics of Organizational Change and learNing*. Chichester: Wiley, 317–41.

Hammond, S.A., 2013. *The Thin Book of Appreciative Inquiry*. New York: Thin Book Publishing.

Higher Education Treaty Circle, 2012. 'The People's Treaty on Higher Education for Sustainable Development'. www.copernicus-alliance.org [accessed 16 February 2015].

Hopkinson, P. and James, P., 2013. 'Whole Institution Change towards Sustainable Universities', in Sterling, S., Maxey, L. and Luna, H. (eds), *The Sustainable University: Progress and Prospects*. New York: Routledge, 235–55.

Hosking, D.M., 2004. 'Change Works: A Critical Construction', in Boonstra, J.J. (ed.), 'Dynamics of Organizational Change and Learning'. Chichester: Wiley, 259–78.

Huckle, J., 2010. 'ESD and the Current Crisis of Capitalism: Teaching beyond Green New Deals', *Journal of Education for Sustainable Development*, 4(1), 135–42.

Jickling, B. and Wals, A.E.J., 2008. 'Globalization and Environmental Education: Looking beyond Sustainable Development', *Journal of Curriculum Studies*, 40(1), 1–21.

Keup, J.R., Astin, H.S., Lindholm, J.A. and Walker, A.A., 2001. 'Organizational Culture and Institutional Transformation', in Higher Education Research Institute (eds), *Transforming Institutions: Contexts and Processes*. Los Angeles, CA: University of California Press, 17–40.

Kezar, A.J., 2001. 'Understanding and Facilitating Organizational Change in the 21st Century: Recent Research and Conceptualizations', ASHE-ERIC Higher Education Report, 28(4), 1–153.

Kezar, A., 2005. 'What Campuses Need to Know about Organizational Learning and the Learning Organization', *New Directions for Higher Education*, 131, 7–22.

Kezar, A.J. and Eckel, P.D., 2002. 'The Effect of Institutional Culture on Change Strategies in Higher Education: Universal Principles or Culturally Responsive Concepts?', *The Journal of Higher Education*, 73(4), 435–60.

Lambrechts, W., Mulà, I., Ceulemans, K., Molderez, I. and Gaeremynck, V., 2013. 'The Integration of Competences for Sustainable Development in Higher Education: An Analysis of Bachelor Programs in Management', *Journal of Cleaner Production*, 48, 65–73.

Levitt, B. and March, J. 1988. 'Organizational Learning', *Annual Review of Sociology*, 14, 319–40.

Lewin, K., 1951. *Field Theory in Social Science: Selected Theoretical Papers*. New York: Harper and Brothers.

Lichtenstein, B.B., 2000. 'Self-organized Transitions: A Pattern Amid the Chaos of Transformative Change', *Academy of Management Executive*, 14(4), 128–41.

Lidgren, A., Rodhe, H. and Huisingh, D., 2006. 'A Systemic Approach to Incorporate Sustainability into University Courses and Curricula', *Journal of Cleaner Production*, 14(9–11), 797–809.

Lieberman, D., 2005. 'Beyond Faculty Development: How Centers for Teaching and Learning can be Laboratories for Learning', *New Directions for Higher Education*, 131, 87–98.

Lipshitz, R., Popper, M. and Friedman, V.J., 2002. 'A Multifaceted Model of Organizational Learning', *Journal of Applied Behavioural Science*, 38(1), 78–98.

Lotz-Sisitka, H., 2004. 'Stories of Transformation', *International Journal of Sustainability in Higher Education*, 5(1), 8–10.

Lozano, R., 2006a. 'Incorporation and Institutionalization of SD into Universities: Breaking through Barriers to Change', *Journal of Cleaner Production*, 14(9–11), 787–96.

Lozano, R., 2006b. 'A Tool for a Graphical Assessment of Sustainability in Universities (GASU)', *Journal of Cleaner Production*, 14(9–11), 963–72.

Lozano, R. and Peattie, K.E.N., 2011. 'Assessing Cardiff University's Curricula Using the STAUNCH (RTM) System INTRODUCTION', *Journal of Education for Sustainable Development*, 5(1), 115–28.

Lozano-García, F.J., Gándara, G., Perrni, O., Manzano, M., Hernández, D.E. and Huisingh, D., 2008. 'Capacity Building: A Course on Sustainable Development to Educate the Educators', *International Journal of Sustainability in Higher Education*, 9(3), 257–81.

Lukman, R., and Glavič, P., 2007. 'What are the Key Elements of a Sustainable University?', *Clean Technologies and Environmental Policy*, 9(2), 103–14.

Luna, H. and Maxey, L., 2013. 'Towards a Green Academy', in Sterling, S., Maxey, L. and Luna, H. (eds), *The Sustainable University: Progress and Prospects*. New York: Routledge, 281–303.

Mader, C., 2012. How to Assess Transformative Performance towards Sustainable Development in Higher Education Institutions. Journal of Education for Sustainable Development, 6(1), 79–89.

Mader, C., Scott, G. and Razak, D.A., 2013. 'Effective Change Management, Governance and Policy for Sustainability Transformation in Higher Education', *Sustainability Accounting, Management and Policy Journal*, 4(3), 264–84.

Moore, J., Pagani, F., Quaylle, M., Robinson, J., Sawada, B., Spiegelman, G., and van Wynsberghe, R., 2005. 'Recreating the University from Within : Collaborative Reflections on the University of British Columbia's Engagement with Sustainability', *International Journal of Sustainability in Higher Education*, 6(1), 65–80.

Olsen, D.S., 2009. 'Emerging Interdisciplinary Practice: Making Nanoreactors', *The Learning Organization*, 16(5), 398–408.

Rode, H. and Michelsen, G., 2008. 'Levels of Indicator Development for Education for Sustainable Development', *Environmental Education Research*, 14(1), 19–33.

Scott, G., Tilbury, D., Leith, S. and Deane, E., 2012. 'Turnaround Leadership for Sustainability in Higher Education', Learning and Teaching Excellence Division, DEEWR, Australian Government, Canberra, 1–101.

Senge, P.M., 1990. *The Fifth Discipline: The Art and Practice of the Learning Organization*. New York: Doubleday/Currency.

Sherren, K., 2010. 'The Pieces We Have', *Environments*, 37(2), 51–9.

Shipton, H., 2006. 'Cohesion or Confusion? Towards a Typology for Organizational Learning Research', *International Journal of Management Reviews*, 8(4), 233–52.

Smith, D.G. and Parker, S., 2005. 'Organizational Learning: A Tool for Diversity and Institutional Effectiveness', *New Directions for Higher Education*, 131, 113–25.

Sporn, B., 1996. 'Managing University Culture: An Analysis of the Relationship between Institutional

Culture and Management Approaches', *Higher Education*, 32, 41–61.

Stephens, J.C. and Graham, A.C., 2010. 'Toward an Empirical Research Agenda for Sustainability in Higher Education: Exploring the Transition Management Framework', *Journal of Cleaner Production*, 18(7), 611–18.

Sterling, S., 2004. 'Higher Education, Sustainability, and the Role of Systemic Learning', in Corcoran, P.B. and Wals, A.E.J. (eds), *Higher Education and the Challenge of Sustainability*. Dordrecht, Netherlands: Kluwer Academic Publishers, 49–70.

Sterling, S., 2010. 'Transformative Learning and Sustainability: Sketching the Conceptual Ground', *Learning and Teaching in Higher Education*, 5, 17–33.

Sterling, S., 2013. 'The Sustainable University', in Sterling, S., Maxey, L. and Luna, H. (eds), *The Sustainable University: Progress and Prospects*. New York: Routledge, 17–50.

Sylvestre, P., McNeil, R. and Wright, T., 2013a. 'From Talloires to Turin: A Critical Discourse Analysis of Declarations for Sustainability in Higher Education', *Sustainability*, 5(4), 1356–71.

Sylvestre, P., Wright, T. and Sherren, K., 2013b. 'Exploring Faculty Conceptualizations of Sustainability in Higher Education: Cultural Barriers to Organizational Change and Potential Resolutions'. *Journal of Education for Sustainable Development*, 7(2), 223–44.

Sylvestre, P., Wright, T. and Sherren, K., 2014. 'A Tale of Two (or more) Sustainabilities: A Q Methodology Study of University Professors' Perspectives on Sustainable Universities', *Sustainability*, 6(3), 1521–43.

Taylor, R., 2013. 'Bottoms Up for Sustainability: The Kingston Experience', in Sterling, S., Maxey, L. and Luna, H. (eds), *The Sustainable University: Progress and Prospects*. New York: Routledge, 256–80.

Tierney, W., 1991. 'Organizational Culture in Higher Education: Defining the Essentials', in Peterson, M. (ed.), *ASHE Reader on Organization and Governance*. Needham Heights, MA: Ginn Press, 126–39.

Tilbury, D., 2007. 'Monitoring and Evaluation during the UN Decade of Education for Sustainable Development', *Journal of Education for Sustainable Development*, 1(2), 239–54.

Tilbury, D., 2013. 'Another World is Desirable', in Sterling, S., Maxey, L. and Luna, H. (eds), *The Sustainable University, Progress and Prospects*. New York: Routledge, 17–50.

Tosey, P., Visser, M. and Saunders, M.N., 2011. 'The Origins and Conceptualizations of "Triple-loop" Learning: A Critical Review', *Management Learning*, 43(3), 291–307

Velazquez, L., Munguia, N., Platt, A. and Taddei, J., 2006. 'Sustainable University: What can be the Matter?', *Journal of Cleaner Production*, 14, 810–19.

Wals, A.E.J., 2014. 'Sustainability in Higher Education in the Context of the UN DESD: A Review of Learning and Institutionalization Processes', *Journal of Cleaner Production*, 62, 8–15.

Wegner, E., 1998. *Communities of Practice: Learning, Meaning, and Identity*. Cambridge, MA: Cambridge University Press.

Wells, G., 2009. 'Dialogic Inquiry as Collaborative Action Research', in Nofke, S. and Somekh, B. (eds). *The Sage Handbook of Educational Action Research*. London: SAGE, 50–61.

White, R., 2013. 'Sustainability Research: A Novel Mode of Knowledge Generation to Explore Alternative Ways for People and Planet', in Sterling, S., Maxey, L. and Luna, H. (eds), *The Sustainable University: Progress and Prospects*. New York: Routledge, 168–91.

Wright, T.S., 2007. 'Developing Research Priorities with a Cohort of Higher Education for Sustainability Experts', *International Journal of Sustainability in Higher Education*, 8(1), 34–43.

21

HIGHER EDUCATION FOR SUSTAINABLE DEVELOPMENT IN THE COMMUNITY AND THROUGH PARTNERSHIPS

Debra Rowe and Krista Hiser

Introduction

This chapter highlights the importance of student learning in the context of community-based projects and partnerships, with an emphasis on real world project-based research, learning, and sustainability competency acquisition. Action research, community engaged research, and indigenous research methodologies as they are currently used in education and public health fields are suggested as frameworks to be integrated with engaged pedagogies for Higher Education for Sustainable Development (HESD). By learning through authentic, reciprocal community partnerships, students attain the interpersonal skills and proactive problem solving that 21st century employers are requesting, and that the development of sustainable systems and improved quality of life requires.

Undergraduate education has not yet integrated Higher Education for Sustainable Development fully into the curriculum; attention remains focused on graduation, career identification and disciplinary specialisation over a values-driven paradigm of sustainability. The annual Cooperative Institutional Research Program (CIRP) Freshman Survey conducted at hundreds of American colleges and universities discerns trends in student values, such as their reasons for attending college. Since the 1980s, 'Being well off financially' has been the top value for students, while 'developing a life philosophy' ranks fifth (Astin 1998). In the 1960s, those values were reversed, and students attended college with a less careerist point of view. Statistics are frequently disseminated that link college degrees to increases in income, and indeed a new measure in the Obama administration's college rating plan for US institutions includes post-graduation income as an indicator of college effectiveness (Pryor *et al.* 2007). Perhaps this values reversal is a response to the increasing income inequality in the US and the accompanying increase in the percentage of jobs that are less secure and less well paid, creating more concerns about future income among students. Such a trend connotes a more urgent need for the triple bottom line of sustainability that includes access to sustainable livelihoods.

However, given parallels today to the 1960s movements in social justice, civic engagement and environmental protection, it is likely that these trends could once again reverse. The Princeton Review (2014) created its 'Green Rating' as a criterion for evaluating colleges, because 62 per cent of students said that a college's commitment to the environment would influence their choice. *The Democracy Project* of the American Association of State Colleges and Universities (AASCU) and the Association of American Colleges & University's *Crucible Moment* report have generated real momentum in turning (or returning) the core values of higher education to civic engagement and social responsibility, with a priority of moving from 'partial transformation to pervasive civic and democratic learning and practices' (National Task Force on Civic Learning and Engagement 2012: 42). HESD is both a result and a catalyst for the shifting values that may be anticipated in the next 40-year analysis of what students seek in a college education.

Even though a promising career is the top reason for attending college, Pryor (2014 cited in Lawlor Group 2014), a Senior Research Scientist with Gallup Education, reported that only 34 per cent of college seniors said they are 'very satisfied with the relevance of their coursework to their future career plans'. At the same time, faculty claim to prioritise workforce needs in their learning outcomes. Pryor argued that there is a 'mismatch between what faculty mean by learning goals and what employers mean' (Lawlor Group 2014: para. 3). This mismatch may also reflect the context in which faculty teach these skills, or the way in which students demonstrate them. A promising trend in HESD is to include real-world problem-solving assignments that also build a student's skills for solving global sustainability challenges. Real-world assignments teach practical skills such as teamwork and proactive problem solving which are valuable in both the work setting and in the solving of societal problems. In this chapter, the authors argue that HESD can reconcile the values of students, the wants of employers, and the needs of communities through integration of active, engaged service, research and pedagogy with community partnerships. This chapter provides suggestions for next steps in delivering sustainability competencies in higher education in the context of community partnerships, and then describes a variety of action research frameworks from related fields, and their benefits for community-based learning. The chapter concludes with suggestions for further research and applications.

Change agent skills

College students confront a lot of bad news: social issues, population thresholds, economic injustice and the multifaceted planetary emergency. It is imperative that sustainability curricula also give students opportunities for positive action in a real-world context, in order to develop the hopeful and empowered mindset of a change agent for sustainable development. A pervasive finding in the literature on sustainability curricula is a 'dissonance' between what students claim to value, and what they actually do (Kagawa 2007). Dissonance results within everyday life when habits, peer pressure and costs of behaviour change do not support sustainable choices. The dissonance continues in college when doom and gloom facts are given in the classroom without a focus on practical solutions, or when proposed solutions do not match the scale of the issue being studied, or when what is being taught in the classroom is not what is experienced on campus or in the community (Hiser 2012). HESD can reduce this dissonance and empower students to be systemic thinkers and change agents by involving them in real-world projects that contribute to sustainability solutions. Such experiential learning 'especially facilitates the development of action competencies' (Dohmen 2001 cited in Barth *et al.* 2007: 421).

Change Agent skills are the understandings, motivation and abilities needed to create a sustainable future; as such, they should be at the core of sustainability curricula. Svanström *et al.* (2008) compared the United States, Mexico and Sweden's efforts at education for sustainable development as well as international declarations; their findings emphasised the need for students to develop change agent skills – to move beyond thinking to the intellectual and affective skills for effective action. A literature has developed regarding what the sustainability competencies should be (Barth *et al.* 2007; Rieckmann 2012; Wiek *et al.* 2011). All of this work has moved the field forward and is discussed in another chapter in this Handbook (see Wiek *et al.*). However the most effective pedagogies and assessments are still being developed.

Three of the important next steps in this area that relate to assessment of community-based learning will be: 1) to assess whether the learning of these competencies produces graduates capable of building a more sustainable society, locally and globally; 2) to establish which pedagogies are most effective for teaching these layers of sustainability competencies; and 3) to include that competencies have to go beyond skills and knowledge to the development of a long-term mind-set, a self-concept that contains: an understanding of the potentials to build a future of sustainable abundance, a commitment to creating solutions to societal problems, and an ability to implement the strategies for systemic change (Rowe *et al.* 2014; Rieckmann 2012). Additionally, it is important to create and use institutional level assessments which ensure that the typical selections or requirements of both course and co-curricular experiences for undergraduates provide the combination of learning opportunities to cover the acquisition of these key sustainability competencies.

At the same time, colleges must remain attuned to workforce needs, both in technical skills and in affective qualities. HESD remains a value paradigm that may not be embraced by all university stakeholders, entering students, or their families. Sustainability still takes some students by surprise, yet the educational agenda of HESD is of vital importance for the survival of the planet and the future of communities. Higher Education Institutions (HEIs) can learn to synthesise sustainability competencies with the qualities that employers want – the businesses, agencies, schools, establishments where students obtain jobs are, in the end, the same settings where sustainable solutions will be created and implemented. Quality sustainability education creates students who plant and nurture the seeds of change in all jobs, not just those labelled as 'green workforce' jobs (Rowe 2013).

Table 21.1 compares personal qualities engendered by a list of Change Agent skills for sustainability with a list of workforce skills taken from *10 Things Employers Want you to Learn in College* by Coplin (2012), a book written for a student audience.

These skills and qualities can be aligned by designing problem-based research and real-world experiences through pedagogies of service learning, active learning, problem-based learning, community-based learning, and civically engaged learning with action research frameworks: participatory action research, community-based research, indigenous research methodologies and community-engaged research. Research with community partners can be at the graduate student level within research oriented institutions with faculty conducting scholarly and scientific investigation (and with accompanying institutional support for such research) and also at the level of undergraduate research in all of higher education (an increasingly emphasised High Impact Practice at two- and four-year colleges across the United States) (Kuh 2008).

Table 21.1 Change agent skills vs. 10 things employers want you to learn in college

Change Agent Skills for a Sustainable Future	*10 Things Employers Want you to Learn in College*
assertive, persuasive, empathetic, authentic, ethical, self-aware, competent, curious, resilient, optimistic, tenacious, committed, passionate, patient and emotionally intelligent,communicate ideas clearly, concisely, and precisely both orally and in writing, creatively and collaboratively solve problems...	taking responsibility, developing physical skills, communicating verbally, communicating in writing, working directly with people, influencing people, gathering information, using quantitative tools, asking and answering the right questions, and solving problems

Service learning and community partnerships

The rich history and literature around service learning and community partnerships can inform HESD, and effective strategies for blending service learning and sustainability pedagogies are beginning to emerge. Adomßent *et al.* (2014) state that 'Service learning occurs when there is a balance between learning goals and service outcomes' (74). Service learning is grounded in reciprocity, social justice and real-world problem-solving. It counteracts dissonance by giving equal emphasis to theory and practice, study and application. Muller-Christ *et al.* (2014) share a synthesis of roundtable dialogues on 'campus', 'curriculum' and 'community' held on the last day of the UNESCO Conference on HESD in 2011. One key point was that 'universities should opt for a more collaborative development of knowledge by initiating a society-wide dialogue with other key players that also reflects their visions and ethical considerations' (135). In the US., Franco *et al.* (2014) synthesised the best practices in integrating service learning and sustainability shared at several conferences over a two year period, and discerned five areas where service learning and HESD overlapped in practice: campus as a living laboratory; campus and community resilience and disaster preparedness; inter- and transdisciplinary integration across the curriculum; direct service on and off campus; and student-driven change initiatives including legislation, programmes and college governance and policy. The point is that there is a vibrant dialogue occurring internationally about integrating community, campus and classroom through engaged research methodologies for real-world problem-solving.

National Campus Compact, a consortium of community-engaged colleges and universities in the United States, has advocated the contextualising of faculty research and scholarship in community partnerships since 1999. Campus Compact's 1999 Presidents' Fourth of July Declaration on the Civic Responsibility of Higher Education, in part, reads, 'We also challenge higher education to become engaged, through actions and teaching, with its communities' (cited in Berberet 2002: 93). HESD, combined with action-oriented research and service, can help colleges and universities to 'develop and leverage tactics that have social and intellectual multiplier effects in teaching, research, and service' (Franco 2014). Exploring questions that matter to both community-partners and academic researchers (which can be faculty or undergraduates) begins with a commitment to the community partner.

Both faculty and students can provide service, contributing significantly to local economies through much-needed labour. This service helps the academic participants to understand the community partner, whether it is a non-profit organisation, a school, a government entity or a neighbourhood board, while building skills that will serve them in their multiple adult roles. For example, students at Kapi'olani Community College in Hawai'i participated with neighbourhood schools to remove over 3 million pounds of invasive algae from nearby Maunaloa Bay. The algae was removed by handfuls, manually weeded, and recycled into compost at local farms. As part of a National Science Foundation-funded grant project, the college students worked with scientists to monitor the cleared areas and track regrowth. This is an excellent example of integrated HESD service (providing much needed labour and direct economic benefit to communities) and research (meeting learning outcomes of the students and faculty of the area community college) (Mālama Maunalua 2014).

Successful service learning experiences must be effectively designed, using a model such as IPARDE: Investigation, Preparation, Action, Reflection, Demonstration and Evaluation (GenerationOn n.d.). When implemented with committed and community partners, this service-cycle teaches practical academic concepts in the field, as well as creating affective learning, breaking down stereotypes, and stimulating civic and moral responsibility. When designed poorly, however, or without strong community partnerships, service learning can reinforce a 'charity' mindset that hinders systemic change and can be demeaning to community recipients of the service. As HEIs continue to integrate sustainability curriculum with service learning and community engagement, institutions must be mindful of the same concerns, and of the importance of critical self-reflection among all stakeholders to solidify and articulate knowledge, skills and attitudes that are learned. Figure 21.1 illustrates the Active Citizen continuum, which defines the depth of impact that service projects can have on the student participants, from the community 'member', to the 'volunteer', to the 'conscientious citizen', to the 'active citizen', for whom 'community becomes a priority in values and life choices' (Break Away 2014). Assessing the impact of community service and community-engaged research is essential.

When done effectively, education with community partnerships can develop 'active citizens', students with a sense of personal accountability and a desire to participate in civic life. Colby, *et al.* (2000), in the introduction to *Civic Responsibility and Higher Education,* wrote that

> A morally and civically responsible individual recognizes himself or herself as a member of a larger social fabric and therefore considers social problems to be at least partly his or her own; such an individual is willing to see the moral and civic dimensions of issues, to make and justify informed moral and civic judgments, and to take action when appropriate.
>
> *(xxvi)*

There are many examples of HEIs engaging in community partnerships to help society move toward sustainability. 127 UN Regional Centres of Expertise (RCE), a global network, exist to support such work. An RCE is

> a network of existing formal, non-formal and informal education organisations, mobilised to deliver education for sustainable development (ESD) to local and regional communities … RCEs aspire to achieve the goals of the UN Decade of Education for Sustainable Development (DESD, 2005–2014), by translating its global objectives into the context of the local communities in which they operate.
>
> *(United Nations University 2013: 1)*

There are networks made up of, or working with, HEIs focusing on community engagement, including but not limited to the following examples: the ACU University Extension and

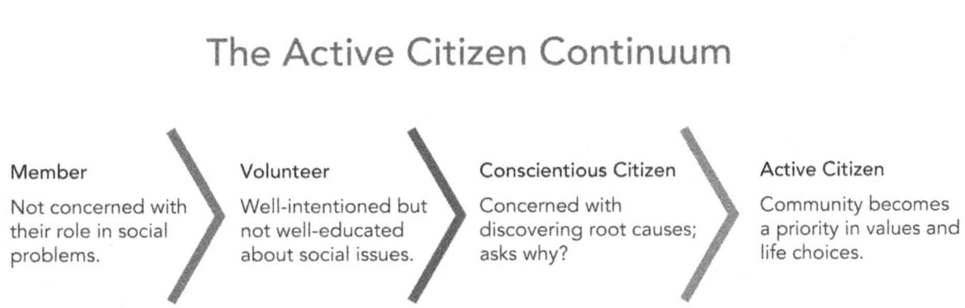

Figure 21.1 The Active Citizen continuum

Source: Break Away 2014

Community Engagement Network; the Global Alliance of Community Engaged Research; the Global Universities Network for Innovation, PASCAL International Observatory; Centro Boliviano de Estudios Multidisciplinarios; the Society for Participatory Research in Asia, and the international Transition Town movement.

The Oberlin Project, led by David Orr, is an example of HESD that started on campus and expanded to the local community, with goals derived in sustainability and its improvement of quality of life: making community and campus climate positive, supporting local business ventures in food and energy, conserving green space, integrating sustainability across all levels of schooling, developing affordable and energy-efficient housing, creating an arts district, and serving as a model that can be replicated in other communities. Similarly, Portland State University reconceived its Sustainability Institute as an Ecodistricts collaboration with the City & County of Portland (Portable Sustainability Institute 2010). Around the world, partnerships between colleges and universities and their local communities are being redefined and catalysed by sustainability transformation in higher education.

In the US, with its 4,000+ colleges and universities, the Higher Education Associations Sustainability Consortium (HEASC), a network of mainstream higher education associations, including presidents, business officers, students affairs, facilities directors and others, have created a call to action to use the 'campus and regional communities as a living lab for sustainability' (Williamson 2012), with an emphasis on real-world community-based projects. HEASC members called for the Sustainability Tracking and Rating Systems, a self-reporting mechanism to track sustainability performance from the Association for the Advancement of Sustainability in Higher Education (2010) that gives credit for community partnerships with student civic engagement learning and research projects. The American Association of Community Colleges' produced the Green Genome (2012) self assessment tool and the new Climate Resiliency Guide (2014). Both frameworks stress the importance of community-based learning and stakeholder engagement. The recent US Department of Education funded project entitled *Sustainability Improves Student Learning* (2013) included the empowerment of students to be systemic change agents in the community as a key component of quality sustainability assignments and provided a beginners' toolkit and learning activities resources for educators.

The UN multimedia teacher education programme *Teaching and Learning for a Sustainable Future* (2010) has a focus on learning outside the classroom. It focuses on the eight steps for community problem solving and makes the connections to service learning and the learning of civic engagement skills and attitudes. In Europe there are multiple examples of students driving the curricula, moving institutions to more transdisciplinary work and deep engagement in the creation of real-world solutions to our shared sustainability challenges. For example, the Centre for Environment and Development Studies (CEMUS) offers unique student-led interdisciplinary education and a transdisciplinary research school (CEMUS n.d.). Another example is the work of the Higher Education Academy (HEA) in support of students as partners in the creation of curricula. HEA (2014) has created 'students as partners' guidance documents, including a framework for partnership in learning and teaching in higher education.

The International Institute for Sustainable Communities and the Urban Sustainability Directors' Network are creating community projects for higher education, often using the needs of the city/region as the starting point for a multi-stakeholder approach that builds into ongoing partnerships, with students working on long-term projects that are passed on to new groups of students in subsequent semesters. The goal of a longer term view is to help create, nurture and connect both community and higher education sustainability champions to develop quality community partnerships that further both real-world sustainability and student learning.

HEIs and their communities are linked by sustainability goals and challenges such as climate change, transportation, energy, waste, economic disparities and cultural displacement. The urgency of these goals are creating a trend of new collaborations that build student experiences, knowledge, skills and ongoing commitments to help create solutions to our sustainability challenges. Through a combination of community projects, students can and should learn how to create systemic shifts through both cultural and policy changes.

> Community partnerships for sustainability create a win-win structure, building student skills while helping implement solutions to our urgent societal challenges … Through community-learning projects centered on sustainability, higher education meets its objectives of education and outreach, and communities gain valuable labor capacity and knowledge.
>
> *(Williamson 2013: 1)*

An understanding of research frameworks for working with community partnerships, including action research and related methodologies, as well as their alignment with teaching and service is an important next step for HESD. For example, Bodorkos and Pataki (2009) integrated Participatory Action Research (PAR) with service learning and regional sustainability initiatives in Hungary. They describe 'science shops' and their North American equivalent, 'community research centres' (1124). They note that 'It is not enough that universities as producers of knowledge educate students … but they should take the responsibility to engage with local communities through answering their research questions and (thus) contribute to solving various local problems' (1124). In the US, George Mason University integrated sustainability programmes with undergraduate research to create a 'three-level' pyramid to scaffold student-driven research in sustainability. The foundational level is 'Discovery of Scholarship'; the core of the pyramid is 'Scholarly Inquiry'; and the pinnacle is 'Creation of Scholarship', which is completed through an action-research project designed in a capstone course, Sustainability in Action (Sklarew and Wingfield 2014). An example of community-based research in a region is in southeast Michigan, where students at multiple colleges and universities work to develop the city of Detroit's green economy in collaboration with local green businesses, the US Green Building Council's local Emerging Professionals group, and economic and workforce development non-profits. Over several semesters, students from multiple local colleges and universities gathered data on green businesses and non-profits to develop a Detroit Green Skills Alliance and a Detroit Green Map. The projects are now multi-year and have utilised research data on green economy shared business issues and facilitation of solutions, and the results of social marketing efforts to increase awareness of the local green economy. Both business owners and students have shared that this work builds their skills for systemic real-world problem solving and connects employers to potential employees (Rowe 2012).

The Council on Undergraduate Research just published a special issue on sustainability and undergraduate research and many of the articles are about community based projects (CUR Quarterly 2014). The next section outlines action research frameworks from public health and education that can be used to design HESD projects in the community.

Action research, participatory action research and youth-led participatory action research

All community-based or community-engaged research is a form of action research. Action research is understood as the 'systematic collection of information that is designed to bring about social change' (Bogdan and Biklen 1992: 223). Action research is defined more by principles than methodology; it is an approach that emphasises reciprocity and continual improvement towards social and systemic change. Action research can be seen as a 'family' of research (McCutcheon and Jung 1990). Differences in methodology are seen as 'cousins' related on the family tree of action research.

In the primary and secondary schools, action research, also called participatory action research (PAR), is used by teachers to improve their practice by designing research within their classroom setting, simultaneously teaching and observing the class in order to answer a compelling question. Different epistemologies may be used to describe reality, relationships, the nature of understanding, the role of value and the purposes of research (McCutcheon and Jung 1990). What defines PAR in the K-12 setting is a desire to improve education for all.

Youth-led participatory action research (YPAR) 'is a change process that engages students in identifying problems that they want to improve, conducting research to understand the nature of the problems, and advocating for changes based on research evidence' (Ozer and Wright 2012: 268). For example, one study included elementary students in an evaluation of recess behaviours, and the school stakeholders worked together to define problems on the playground and move towards changing them (Ren and Langhout 2010). In another example, university graduate students in counselling psychology worked with high school students in a PAR model exploring creativity and relationship building (Goessling and Doyle 2009). In this model, information, solutions and change flow freely and quickly between researchers, communities and individuals, as opposed to the one-way nature of traditional academic research. At Maastricht University, students co-created the Green Office that houses a Community Project Coordinator to help identify and publicise sustainability projects. The model of PAR and YPAR has particular applications for college campuses utilising the 'campus and the community as a living [learning] lab for sustainability' model (Williamson 2013: 127), in which students experiment to solve problems and make campuses and surrounding communities energy positive, zero waste, food sovereign, and inclusive of social and cultural sustainability.

Community-based and community-engaged research

Public health research has increasingly shifted its emphasis from *subject-oriented* research with the randomised double-blind trial as its 'gold standard' to more *participant-based* research, which is intended to expedite the information flow from the community, to the research institution, and back to the community in a usable form. This type of public health research is most often called community-based research, one of the cousins of action research. Israel *et al.* (1998) synthesised eight key principles in community-based health research, which are here cited and explored as a model for developing change agent skills and attitudes through Community Engaged HESD research that includes phases of Observe, Serve and Change. This model is then described as the Change Agent Portfolio.

1. Community is the unit of identity:

'Communities of identity may be centered on a defined geographic neighbourhood or a geographically dispersed ethnic group with a sense of common identity and shared fate' (Israel *et al.* 1998: 178). For HESD, the defined community is often a geographic area of physical proximity to the college or university: a neighbourhood, a district, a county or a state/province. Research is defined by common ground, which in this case may be literally the common ground of shared streams, species or natural resources; common economies; shared fate in climate-related disaster preparedness. Of course, community interdependence and impacts often have a regional, national or international component, and systemic change requires thinking on multiple geographic levels. Additionally, some countries have weak higher education systems, and community-based projects targeted in their communities via collaborations with distant higher education institutions can address urgent human and ecosystem needs. Defining a community of identity through observation and self-reflection is the first step to becoming a change agent, and to conducting HESD in a community context.

2. Builds on strengths and resources within the community:

Community-engaged research starts by identifying not only issues and problems in the community, but also positive assets in that challenged community. Strengths and assets 'may include skills and assets of individuals, networks of relationships characterised by trust, cooperation and mutual commitment, and mediating structures within the community' (Israel *et al.* 1998: 178). Researchers coming from an HESD perspective can employ this principle in needs assessment through qualitative and quantitative research conducted via observation, interview and survey methods. What type of community networks exist? Who are the formal and informal leaders in the community who can become drivers for sustainability and what do they have to say? What are the strongest assets that can be utilised to design sustainable communities? Community assets can be economic, social, cultural or environmental.

3. Facilitates collaborative partnerships in all phases of the research:

Community-based public health research retains a commitment that all parties at all times 'participate as equal members and share control over … the research process, e.g. problem definition, data collection, interpretation of results, and application of the results to address community concerns' (Israel *et al.* 1998: 179). It is as vital that community partners play an equal role, in defining research questions and in designing sustainability research and service initiatives. HEIs must balance their own research agendas and personal needs (whether for faculty publication or undergraduate learning outcomes) with the real, stated needs and interests of the community. Food systems are often a starting point of mutual interest: disaster preparedness, educational equity, violence prevention, sustainable economic development and climate action plans are other examples of starting points. In other words, HESD researchers must listen to the community before designing or generating change and throughout the process of implementation. Meaningful service and labour are excellent ways to listen and discover how sustainable solutions might work in specific local contexts.

4. Integrates knowledge and action for mutual benefit of all partners:

'Community-based research may not always incorporate a direct action component, but there is a commitment to the integration of research results with community change efforts' (Israel *et al.* 1998: 179). Community-engaged HESD research shifts the focus of academic labour to creating tangible change in the community, and does include an action component, either through direct action, application of course concepts and skills, or leadership. Academic products – discoveries, theories, inventions or skills – are practiced or applied in the community, for mutual benefit. The target community must understand the academic product in order for it to be usable, which requires the practice of rhetorical principles such as audience analysis, ethos, logos and pathos.

5. Promotes a co-learning and empowering process that attends to social inequalities (Israel et al. 1998):

Community-based health research focuses on equalising social, physical and structural barriers to health. Sustainability is sometimes seen as a luxury concern; for example, organic produce with its higher cost is not a priority for low-income communities. However, community-engaged HESD must view sustainability as an equity issue. Many of the problems that sustainability solutions address have inequality at their core, and HEIs have a civic and moral responsibility to address such issues in the classroom and in the community. Initiatives such as 'grow local' movements can create an inclusive local economy and job base that empowers communities.

6. Involves a cyclical and iterative process (Israel et al. *1998):*

A cyclical process implies a commitment to the community, a long-term, reciprocal research and sustainability agenda that evolves over time. Institutionalised community partnerships and coalition-building develops assets in the community, and likewise, an iterative process should inform sustainability-related competencies and learning outcomes in college. A coordinator can help with institutionalising community partnerships and coalition building, project identification and management, and facilitation of communication between students, faculty and community stakeholders, freeing students and stakeholders to learn from each other as they focus on project work (Brundiers and Wiek 2010).

While the students may have information to share with the community about urgent sustainability challenges that can help reduce community blind spots and science denial, the best teachers of sustainable solutions (farmers, for example) may not have advanced degrees, but have real-world practices to teach. A component of community-engaged HESD should be to include community wisdom and experience.

7. Is holistic:

Community-engaged research, from a public health perspective, 'addresses health from both positive and ecological perspectives … that encompasses biomedical, social, economic, cultural, historical, and political factors' (Israel *et al.* 1998: 180). These principles from public health are congruent with the holistic approach that HESD should take with community partners; in fact, the concept of holistic health is represented in what is sometimes called the 'four pillars' definition of sustainability and usually includes culture, economics, social justice and the environment. Sustainability itself is holistic. HESD, and higher education in general, should seek to develop the student as a 'whole' person with a self-concept that includes a long-term commitment to help solve our shared sustainability challenges.

8. Disseminates findings and knowledge gained to all partners:

In community-based research there are frequent member checks of data, perspectives and interpretations on what is discovered, and what is planned, and all knowledge is shared with community partners (Israel *et al.* 1998). Just as reflection is an essential part of the learning process, this form of iteration is essential to community-engaged HESD research. All minds are needed to inform sustainable solutions; no one person, group, organisation or institution can possess information or ideas; the flow of information must be frequent, rich and timely.

Additionally, the lessons learned and tools developed from such projects can be shared more widely by including results in an online repository. The US Partnership for Education for Sustainable Development has called on academic libraries to create online repositories searchable across institutions for faculty identified, quality student sustainability projects and research that would otherwise not be published.

Indigenous research

Indigenous research methodologies take the core principle of reciprocity to an even deeper level. 'An indigenous paradigm comes from the fundamental belief that knowledge is relational, is shared with all creation, and therefore cannot be owned or discovered' (Wilson 2001: 176). While a full exploration of indigenous research methodologies is beyond the scope of this chapter, it is clear that sustainability research must also interact with indigenous epistemologies, since indigenous practitioners may be the very sources of solutions to problems of sustainability. When partnering with indigenous communities, key features of the work echo the principles of all action research, including respect, collaboration, active participation and meeting needs (de Crespigny *et al.* 2004).

While each of these action research frameworks has specific guidelines and methodological considerations, what they share is a 'collaborative approach to research that equitably involves all partners in the research process and recognizes the unique strengths that each brings' (Kellogg Health Scholars 2014: 2). Research in Sustainability science is, by nature and definition, problem-based, interdisciplinary and transdisciplinary; all of which create barriers for academic research (Clark 2007: 1737). A review of transdisciplinary research in sustainability science found that while researchers do exchange information with community practitioners, stakeholder empowerment is rare. Research that generates information alone, without change, as is seen in the case of climate change, does not move forward quickly enough to realise a sustainable future (Brandt *et al.* 2013). Using action research, community-engaged research and indigenous research models in HESD can lead to greater reciprocity and accelerated change in not only what is taught, but how.

Assessing sustainability competencies: the change agent portfolio

Sustainable communities start from sustainable mind-sets. Apathy and cynicism will only make our societal problems worse. In order to develop the appropriate attitudes, skills and behaviours needed to solve problems and create necessary transformation at the community level, HEIs can integrate the learning of sustainability competencies, including change agent skills, into both curricular and co-curricular activities, and students can track and improve their learning through the use of portfolios. Portfolios help students solidify their learning through reflection, and also provide them with examples of specific skills to show prospective employers.

Figure 21.2 depicts a roadmap for integrated sustainability research, pedagogy and service in the community. The portfolio could be for a class project, a larger capstone project in which students act as researchers of their own change process, or as a personal roadmap that students receive at freshman orientation and utilise throughout their higher education experience. Learning outcomes can be assessed, including measures of self-concept (Markus and Wurf 1987) and commitment to ongoing participation in the creation of sustainable solutions to

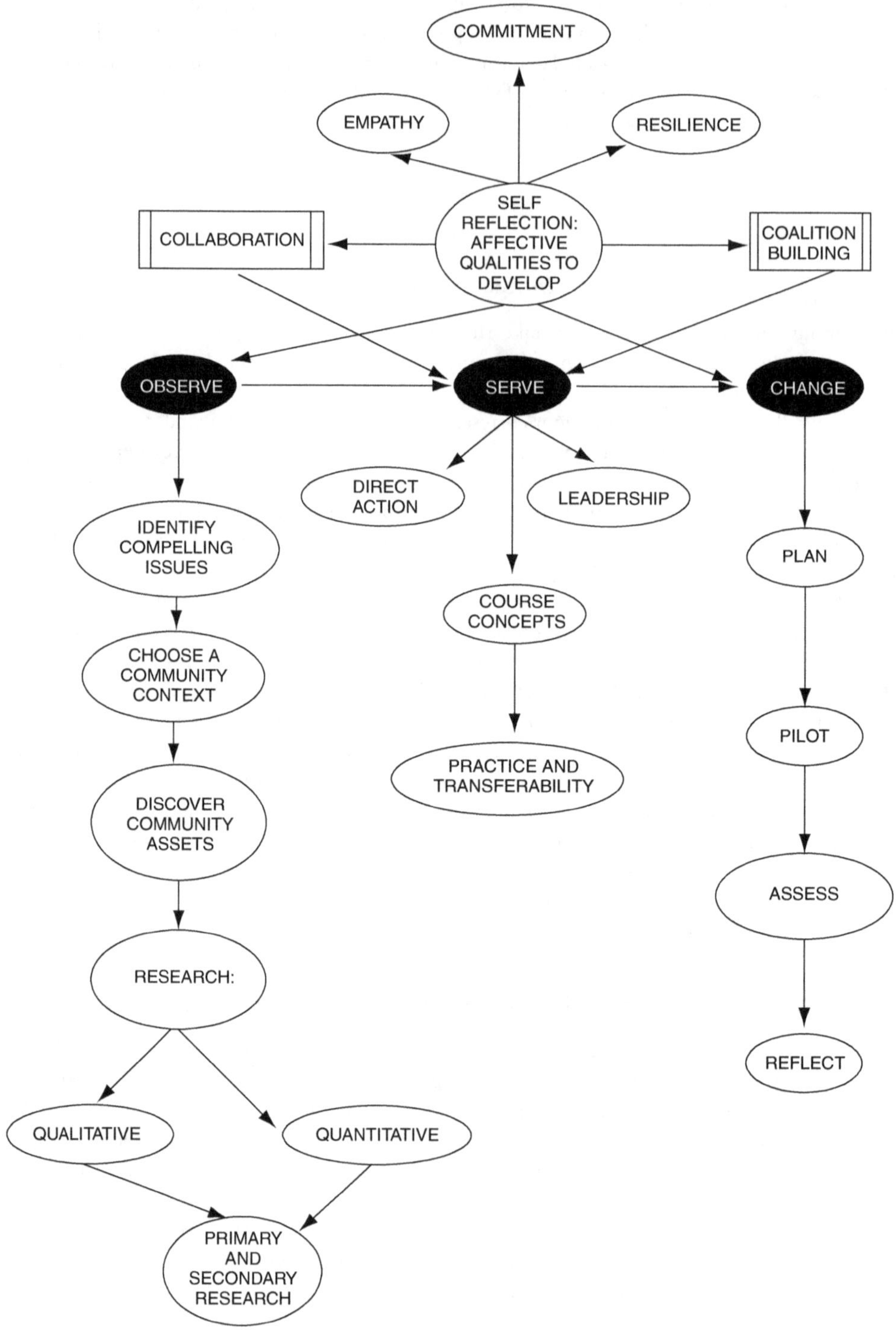

Figure 21.2 The change agent portfolio

societal problems. Through real-world experiences and guided self-reflection, students develop the skills and the self-concept for ongoing sustainability engagement and learn to express and apply them towards community challenges.

With the institution's community partners, students practice creating systemic solutions, including collaboration and coalition building through well-designed service experiences that may take the form of direct action, policy advocacy, and application of specific course concepts. During or after their service, students and community members can design research together that identifies and addresses compelling issues in the defined community. With assistance from university librarians or faculty members, and utilising campus resources, students learn to use qualitative and quantitative research methodologies within the frameworks of action research, community-engaged research and indigenous research. Such research and problem-solving skills have been identified as part of the top skills employers seek from college graduates. Research is reviewed and strengthened by input from faculty and community members, locating the college student 'within an ecosystem of knowledge production' (Saltmarsh *et al.* 2009: 10).

To implement a sustainable solution that emerges from the research, students learn to plan, pilot and assess impact on a small scale. In a cycle of self-reflection and dialogue with community partners, and by sharing their work via national and international higher education networks focused on sustainability and social media, they can take next steps towards scaling the solution to the societal level. This step is often left out of course assignments but is required to help move society toward sustainability.

Action research projects with community partners are designed and implemented in a cycle that integrates theoretical learning, community input and problem solving, with a continuous emphasis on student self-reflection. Barth *et al.* (2007) mention two key challenges for teaching sustainability competencies: one is interdisciplinarity, which we have discussed, and the other is the need for students to become much more self-directed learners, in both formal and informal, curricular and co-curricular settings. Integrating community engaged research changes the dynamic, the context and the culture of academic learning, and a portfolio, or electronic portfolio, can help students navigate how both their curricular and co-curricular experiences contribute to their learning. Barth *et al.* (2007) also note that such implementation of HESD is congruent with the needs of twenty-first-century employers, and 'aims at a personal development that enables individuals to cope with complex situations, to be able to act and to decide reflectively, to take responsibility, to consider ethical criteria while acting and to be able to envision consequences' (2007: 428).

The perceived mismatch between what students learn in college and what employers perceive in them can be solved by having students themselves document and share their work with all stakeholders: community partners, academic researchers, teachers and workforce employers. Colleges and universities with existing civic engagement, service learning, and sustainability initiatives can coordinate and integrate these programmes with undergraduate research initiatives. Faculty are responsible for crafting these learning opportunities, and can do so with: more integrated community liaisons; greater recognition of sustainability science and community engaged research as not only valid, but valiant forms of scholarship; and professional development to effectively implement engaging, active pedagogies and portfolio assessment of real-world problem solving. Systematic international collaboration is needed, to share promising practices that improve higher education as well as improve community project outcomes for the implementation of sustainable solutions.

The structure of the Change Agent portfolio will be refined by the ongoing work on sustainability learning outcomes. Whatever form it takes, it can demonstrate skills that have been of direct service to communities, and can be transferred to the workplace. Along with those skills, students will take with them embedded change agent values, a sense of civic responsibility, and energy to participate in sustainability transformations and challenges that will persist across their lifetimes.

Conclusions

The international growth of HESD and its use of community-based learning is promising but insufficient. Educators need to include more experiential learning with community partners, coupled with reflection, to help students develop a lifelong self-concept that they can and want to participate in the creation of solutions to our sustainability challenges on the individual and systemic levels. The application of research frameworks used in the fields of public health and education, combined with tested pedagogies such as service learning, can inform an integrated strategy for HESD. More educational research will be needed to better validate which types and combinations of community partnerships and pedagogies are best at serving both the community and the development of the student's knowledge, skills and self-concept.

More work is needed to identify key competencies that lead to the development of both sustainability leaders and active citizens. Assessing changes in affective qualities and action-oriented competencies, and incorporating holistic dimensions such as self-concepts into academic contexts are a leading edge of outcomes assessment work. Courses, programmes and degrees coupled with co-curricular activities need to be reoriented and regularly assessed to assure the attainment of sustainability competencies.

Formal and informal educators, indeed, all stakeholders in the academic setting, will need to attain their own sustainability competencies alongside their students. The framing of sustainability competencies as valuable for employment can help ramp up HESD in institutions not already oriented to sustainability. Portfolios can help with both student learning and communication to potential employers. In addition, the campus itself can be examined as a community with its own internal partnerships to be developed. Lastly, more research needs to be done to explicitly link pedagogies for sustainability to mechanisms to share and scale up to systemic levels the implementation of solutions for a sustainable future.

References

Adomßent, M., Barth, M., Fischer, D., Richter, S. and Rieckmann, M., 2014. 'Learning to Change Universities from Within: A Service-learning Perspective on Promoting Sustainable Consumption in Higher Education', *Journal of Cleaner Production*, 8(4), 72–81.

American Association of Community Colleges, 2012. 'Green Genome Self Assessment'. http://theseedcenter.org/GreenGenome [accessed 15 January 2015].

American Association of Community Colleges, 2014. 'Climate Resiliency Guide'. http://theseedcenter.org/ClimateResiliencyGuide [accessed 15 January 2015].

Association for the Advancement of Sustainability in Higher Education, 2010. *Sustainability Tracking and Rating System*. https://stars.aashe.org/ [accessed 15 January 2015].

Astin, A., 1998. 'The Changing American College Student: Thirty-year Trends, 1966–1996', *The Review of Higher Education*, 21 (2), 115–35.

Barth, M., Godemann, J., Rieckmann, M. and Stoltenberg, U., 2007. 'Developing Key Competencies for Sustainable Development in Higher Education', *International Journal of Sustainability in Higher Education*, 8(4), 416–30.

Berberet, J., 2002. 'Nurturing an Ethos of Community Engagement', *New Directions in Teaching and Learning*, 90, 91–100.

Bodorkos, B. and Pataki, G., 2009. 'Linking Academic and Local Knowledge Community-based Research and Service Learning for Sustainable Rural Development in Hungary', *Journal of Cleaner Production*, 17, 1123–31.

Bogdan, R. and Biklen, S.K., 1992. *Qualitative Research for Education: An Introduction to Theory and Methods*. 2nd edn. Boston, MA: Allyn & Bacon.

Brandt, P., Ernst, A., Gralla, F., Luederitz, C., Lang, D., Newig, J., Reinert, F., Abson, D. and von Wehrden, H., 2013. 'A Review of Transdisciplinary Research in Sustainability Science', *Ecological Economics*, 1(92), 1–15.

Break Away, 2014. *Learn More*. www.alternativebreaks.org/wp-content/uploads/2014/06/Active-Citizen-Continuum-2014.pdf [accessed 15 January 2015].

Brundiers, K. and Wiek, A., 2010. *Educating Students in Real-world Sustainability Research: Vision and Implementation*. Springer: Innovative Higher Education, DOI 10.1007/s10755-010-9161-9.

CEMUS, n.d. 'About CEMUS'. www.csduppsala.uu.se/cemus/about/ [accessed 17 February 2015].

Clark, W.C., 2007. 'Sustainability Science: A Room of its Own', *Proceedings of the National Academy of Science*, 104(6), 1737–8.

Colby, A. *et al.*, 2000. 'Higher Education and the Development of Civic Responsibility', in Ehrlich, T. (ed.), *Civic Responsibility and Higher Education*. Westport, CT: Oryx Press, xxi–xliii.

Coplin, B., 2012. *10 Things Employers Want You To Learn In College: The Skills you Need to Succeed*. New York: Ten Speed Press.

CUR Quarterly, 2014. 'Undergraduate Research in Support of Sustainability'. Council on Undergraduate Research Fall 2014 Edition. www.cur.org/publications/curq_on_the_web/ [accessed 29 September 2014].

de Crespigny, C., Emden, C., Kowanko, I. and Murray, H., 2004. 'A Partnership Model for Ethical Indigenous Research', *Collegian*, 11(4), 7–13.

Franco, R., 2014. 'Decades Past, Decades Future: Weaving Colleges, Universities, and Partnerships for Resilient Communities'. Keynote address at the 17th Annual Continuums of Service Conference, Western Campus Compact, Honolulu, HI.

Franco, R., Hiser, K. and Hasager, U., 2014. 'A Community of Practice for Advanced Practitioners in Service and Sustainability Learning'. Scottsdale AZ: Paper presented at the Community College National Center for Community Engagement conference (CCNCCE), 17th Annual Continuums of Service Conference, Honolulu, HI, 2–14 April.

GenerationOn, n.d.. 'IPARDE: Stages of Service-learning'. www.generationon.org/educators/lessons-resources/iparde [accessed 8 September 2014].

Goessling, K. and Doyle, C., 2009. 'Thru the Lenz: Participatory Action Research, Photography, and Creative Process in an Urban High School', *Journal of Creativity in Mental Health*, 4(4), 343–65.

Higher Education Academy, 2014. 'Students as partners'. https://www.heacademy.ac.uk/workstreams-research/themes/students-partners [accessed 8 September 2014].

Hiser, K., 2012. 'Sustainability: Perspectives of Students as Stakeholders in the Curriculum'. PhD, University of Hawai'i at Manoa, ProQuest, UMI Dissertations. www.aashe.org/files/aashe2012-materials/hiser_dissertation_0.pdf [accessed 8 September 2014].

Israel, B.A., Schulz, A.J., Parker, E.A. and Becker, A.B., 1998. 'Review of Community-based Research: Assessing Partnership Approaches to Improve Public Health', *Annual Review of Public Health*, 19(1), 173–202.

Kagawa, F., 2007. 'Dissonance in Students' Perceptions of Sustainable Development and Sustainability', *International Journal of Sustainability in Higher Education*, 8(3), 317–38.

Kellogg Health Scholars, 2014. 'Community Track'. www.kellogghealthscholars.org/about/community.cfm [accessed 8 September 2014].

Lawlor Group, 2014. '"Alignment" as the Next Higher Education Frontier'. www.thelawlorgroup.com/pov/focus/1402-%E2%80%9Calignment%E2%80%9D-next-higher-education-frontier [accessed 8 September 2014].

Mālama Maunalua, 2014. Mālama Maunalua. http://malamamaunalua.org/ [accessed 8 September 2014].

Markus, H. and Wurf, E., 1987. 'The Dynamic Self-Concept: A Social Psychological Perspective', *Annual Review of Psychology*, 38 (February), 299–337.

McCutcheon, G. and Jung, B., 1990. 'Alternative Perspectives on Action Research', *Theory into Practice*, 29(3), 144–51.

Muller-Christ, G., Sterling, S., Van Dam-Mieras, R., Adomßent, M., Fischer, D. and Rieckmann, M., 2014. 'The Role of Campus, Curriculum, and Community in Higher Education for Sustainable Development – A Conference Report', *Journal of Cleaner Production*, 8(3), 134–7.

National Task Force on Civic Learning and Democratic Engagement, 2012. 'A Crucible Moment: College Learning and Democracy's Future' [pdf]. www.aacu.org/sites/default/files/files/crucible/Crucible_508F.pdf [accessed 8 September 2014].

Oberlin Project, n.d. David Orr ed. www.oberlinproject.org/ [accessed 8 September 2014].

Ozer, E. and Wright, D., 2012. 'Beyond School Spirit: The Effects of Youth-led Participatory Action Research in Two Urban High Schools', *Journal of Research on Adolescence*, 22(2), 267–83.

Portland Sustainability Institute, 2010. 'Gateway Ecodistrict Pilot Study'. www.pdx.edu/sites/www.pdx.edu.usp/files/gateway_ecodistrict_pilot_study_final_report.pdf [accessed 8 September 2014].

Princeton Review, 2014. 'The Princeton Review's Guide to 332 Green Colleges'. http://centerforgreenschools.org/PrinRevGdGreenCols_2014Edn.pdf [accessed 19 February 2015].

Pryor, J., Hurtado, S., Saenz, V., Santos, J.L. and Korn, W., 2007. 'The American Freshman: Forty Year Trends: 1966–2006'. www.heri.ucla.edu/PDFs/pubs/TFS/Trends/Monographs/TheAmerican Freshman40YearTrends.pdf [accessed 8 September 2014].

Ren, J. and Langhout, R., 2010. 'A Recess Evaluation with the Players: Taking Steps Toward Participatory Action Research', *American Journal of Community Psychology*, 46(1/2), 124–38.

Rieckmann, M., 2012. 'Future-oriented Higher Education: Which Key Competencies should be Fostered through University Teaching and Learning?', *Futures*, 44(2), 127–35.

Rowe, D., 2012. 'Business and Student Project Evaluations'. Unpublished data.

Rowe, D., 2013. 'Green and Sustainability Jobs and Career Resources', *Career Convergence Magazine*, National Career Development Association, Broken Arrow, OK. www.ncda.org/aws/NCDA/pt/sd/news_article/83053/_PARENT/layout_details_cc/false [accessed 8 September 2014].

Rowe, D., Gentile, S. and Link, T. (eds), 2014. 'Preface', in *Achieving Sustainability: Visions, Principles, and Practices*. Detroit, MI: Macmillan, ix–xiv.

Saltmarsh, J., Hartley, M. and Clayton, P., 2009. 'Democratic Engagement White Paper'. www.ncat.edu/research/civic-engagement/nerche-paper.pdf [accessed 8 September 2014].

Sklarew, D. and Wingfield, A., 2014. 'Up the Pyramid, Around the Loop – Action Research Cultivates Sustainability Scholars to Green the Campus'. CUR Quarterly: Undergraduate Research in Support of Sustainability. www.cur.org/publications/curquarterly/ [accessed 28 September 2014].

Sustainability Improves Student Learning (SISL), 2013. http://serc.carleton.edu/sisl/ [accessed 8 September 2014].

Svanström, M., Lorenzo-Garcia, F. and Rowe, D., 2008. 'Learning Outcomes for Sustainable Development in Higher Education', *International Journal of Sustainability in Higher Education*, 9(3), 339–51.

UNESCO, 2010. 'Teaching and Learning for a Sustainable Future: Community Problem Solving'. www.unesco.org/education/tlsf/mods/theme_d/mod27.html? [accessed 8 September 2014].

United Nations University, 2013. 'Regional Centres of Expertise'. http://archive.ias.unu.edu/sub_page.aspx?catID=1849&ddlID=183 [accessed 8 September 2014].

Wiek, A., Withycombe, L. and Redman, C.L., 2011. 'Key Competencies in Sustainability: A Reference Framework for Academic Program Development', *Sustainability Science*, 6(2), 203–18.

Williamson, S., 2012. 'HEASC: Higher Education Associations Sustainability Consortium'. http://heasc.aashe.org/sites/heasc1.drupalgardens.com/files/HEASC%20-%20Relationship.png [accessed 8 September 2014].

Williamson, S., 2013. 'Community Partnerships: A Key Component of Sustainability'. http://heasc.aashe.org/sites/heasc1.drupalgardens.com/files/201307/F%20Partnership_Op_Ed_June_2013.pdf [accessed 8 September 2014].

Wilson, S., 2001. 'What is an Indigenous Research Methodology?', *Canadian Journal of Native Education*, 25(2), 175–9.

22

SUSTAINABILITY ASSESSMENT IN HIGHER EDUCATION INSTITUTIONS

What and how?

Christian Rammel, Luis Velázquez and Clemens Mader

Introduction

Universities play a crucial role in promoting sustainability principles and should contribute to a paradigm shift towards a more sustainable society. They are essential drivers of education for sustainable development (ESD) and constitute fundamental vehicles to explore, test, develop and communicate conditions for transformative change (Disterheft *et al.* 2013; Leal Filho 2012). But before universities can really promote and drive sustainable development (SD), their sustainability activities must extend a still prevailing narrow perception of sustainability, limited to environmental issues or the simple integration of sustainability topics into existing curricula (Wals 2014; Leal Filho 2009). In order to incorporate SD into the daily life of universities, sustainability has to become mainstream and cannot be implemented as a simple 'add-on'. This mainstreaming or institutionalising is only achieved, when the idea of SD is accepted and integrated into a universities' culture and its day-to-day operations (Lozano 2006a). In short, SD must become an integrative and structural element of all aspects of higher education institutions (HEI) (Tilbury 2011). Without a whole-institution approach that aims at real change and a holistic integration of SD, university are caught in a crossfire of greenwashing, reductionist models and the increasing demand to produce knowledge and students simply for an economy based on unchallenged economic growth.

Even this necessary mainstreaming process is still difficult to identify on a broader scale (Wals 2014), there are the first signs of a paradigm shift and several small milestones of change became visible during the last decade. Among others, the recent debate of integrating SD into exiting approaches of quality management at HEI is one of these milestones, which have the potential to deliver deep change into the very core of higher education (Fadeeva *et al.* 2014; Mader 2014). On the contrary to the general perception of quality management at HEI as a tool for ranking systems, compliance or marketing, quality assurance can be a fundamental tool for transitions, and as such should be seen as crucial for sustainability at our universities. Especially newer quality assurance approaches such as the quality culture model and its related shift towards more development-oriented and value-based aspects (Vettori 2012) exhibit promising linkages to ESD and sustainability at HEI. Herein, the process of mainstreaming SD could be enhanced by bridging the quality culture concept with ESD and reframe sustainability principles as part of a university's overall quality goals and procedures (Vettori and Rammel 2014). This strategy would not only help ESD processes at university to become structurally anchored, it would also provide the institutional quality assurance system with a constructive orientation beyond the generation of static performance data and evaluation cycles. Besides different priorities and perspectives of linking SD with the quality management system of HEI, all approaches exhibit one crucial benefit for mainstreaming SD: if they succeed, sustainability would be embedded in the structural and institutional setting of the university management and development. This means, SD is not seen any longer as an additional cost or perceived as one among many different competing issues, projects and initiatives.

Complimentary to recent developments around quality assurance and ESD, sustainability assessment in HEI can be seen as another milestone for enhancing the mainstreaming process of SD. Recently, an increasing body of literature emphasises sustainability assessment as strong support for implementing sustainability in HEI (Zwickle *et al.* 2014; Cairo *et al.* 2013; Remington-Doucette *et al.* 2013). For the challenge to incorporate sustainability in the management and continuous improvement of the university, assessing the performance and achievements is seen as one essential aspect of 'sustainable universities'.

Subsequently, there are a growing number of assessment tools for sustainability in HEI, ranging from environmental driven approaches, assessing sustainability within the curricula to more integrative and holistic approaches (Cairo *et al.* 2013; Remington-Doucette *et al.* 2013; Lozano 2011). Among them, there are many promising and effective approaches, which provide potentially useful insights for different audiences and address important challenges of a 'sustainable university'. Nevertheless, the majority of existing assessment tools in HEI still apply a narrow focus on particular aspects of sustainable development and are often locked into the shortfalls of pure economic numbers or a predominant accentuation on issues of eco-efficiency (Cairo *et al.* 2013; Lozano 2006b; Shriberg 2002). Therefore, while stressing the need for an integrative and dynamic assessment, we want to address existing conceptual gaps of sustainability assessment at HEI. Hereby, we aim at clarifying two basic questions: '*what do we want to assess?*' and '*how do we assess?*' These questions might seem to be trivial or even superfluous, but we argue, that many universities have transferred or modified existing sustainability assessment approaches without asking themselves these questions in relation to the specific demands of sustainable higher education, before.

We start this chapter by addressing the first question of '*what do we want to assess?*'. This question is deeply linked with the ongoing debate about how we define sustainability or sustainability principles at universities. The sustainability approach adopted by a HEI determines, to a large extent, the process, direction and outcomes of any sustainability assessment. Following the recent debate on the fundamentals of a 'sustainable university', we argue in this section that sustainability at HEI reflects a transformative learning process rather than a concrete final state. Consequently, we must look out for guiding principles that help us to assess the quality of this process. Building on this, we suggest to orientate the assessment process at core principles of SD and ESD, which are expressed in key documents of the United Nations and several international treaties on higher education. The section that follows deals with the question '*how do we assess?*' SD at HEI. Here, we argue that a principal weakness of many sustainability assessment models at universities is their clear prioritisation of predefined performance improvement and the related top-down, expert driven assessment, where the focus is more on outputs and states than on processes and change. As we deal with context-dependent educational institutions that must transform themselves to be transformative, universities are facing an internal dynamics, which is characterised by renewal, testing, errors and open outcomes. Consequently, sustainability assessment at HEI must focus more on supporting this internal learning process rather than aiming at simple measurements of fixed performance indicators. The next section tries to answer both questions by providing a list of conceptual corner stones and attributes of assessing sustainability at HEI. The chapter finishes with some concluding remarks about sustainability assessment at HEI and related conflicts.

What do we want to assess?

Sustainable universities

In general, sustainability assessment in higher education starts from the assumption that if you cannot measure sustainability, you can neither manage nor improve it. But the principle understanding of sustainability or SD, which shall be implemented by a university, determines largely the process, direction and outcomes of any sustainability assessment. Thus, we must take a closer look of how sustainability is reflected in the context of HEI. Despite the growing popularity of SD, we face a great variety of conflicting ideological, conceptual and terminological aspects of this concept, which is already discussed in the literature on a broad scale (Sneddon *et al.* 2006; Rammel and van den Bergh 2003; Folke *et al.* 2002). Even though there are still interpretations of SD, that neither see the concept's inherent demand for radical change nor its integrative and procedural characteristics, a growing body of literature emphasises SD as an open and undetermined process, driven by improved understanding, integration and co-evolving dynamics on socio-ecological systems (Rammel *et al.* 2007). There is also an increasing consensus about the general principles that underpin the concept of SD such as intra-and intergenerational equity, participation, normativity and acknowledging natural limits or justice (UNCED 1992; Commission of the European Communities 2005), which are also reflected within the key characteristics of ESD (UNESCO 2006). The ongoing discourse about SD launched the debate about the concept of a 'sustainable university' and the general role of HEI to initiate and enhance sustainable change. To highlight one among many definitions, Velazquez *et al.* (2006: 812) define a sustainable university as a

> higher education institution, as a whole or as a part, that addresses, involves and promotes, on regional or global level, the minimization of environmental, economics, societal, and health negative effects in the use of their resources in order to fulfill its main functions of teaching, research, outreach & partnership, and stewardship among other as a way to helping society make the transition to sustainable life styles.

Sustainability processes at universities are being initiated by a variety of key players, in different institutional settings with different interests and backgrounds. Consequently, there are varying conceptions of a 'sustainable university' (Velazquez *et al.* 2006).

Nevertheless, most of these conceptions, which apply an integrative focus, emphasise several key characteristics of our subject of assessment, sustainability at HEI:

- First, sustainability at HEI covers various interlinked dimensions of a university, such as teaching, research, management or outreach (Velazquez *et al.* 2005; Cortese 2003).
- Second, there is no final state of sustainability at universities, rather there is an open learning process towards a more sustainable educational institution (Lozano 2006a).
- Third, sustainability at HEI has also a strong transformative aspect, that encourages the involvement of individuals in the transition towards a more sustainable society (Disterheft *et al.* 2013).
- Fourth, to be transformative, HEI must transform itself (Mader *et al.* 2013).

In short, sustainability at HEI reflects a transformative learning process that bridges different functions and values along with the stewardship for performing those functions and participation of stakeholders from inside and outside the university. The degree of change driving this transformational process is enormous, the implications for the daily life of universities radical (Thomas 2009). Authors such as Lozano (2006a) understand this process as radical innovation which, while facing many existing barriers, shall be incorporated incrementally and must develop along the lines of concrete and standardised quality criteria.

SD and ESD principles

According to these characteristics, assessing sustainability at HEI is assessing the quality of an integrative process where a possible 'end-state' or outcome is not known in advance. Consequently, this shifts the weight from general assessment objectives aiming at particular preferred outcomes based on fixed performance indicators towards a stronger focus on the quality of a dynamic change process and its related quality criteria. Notably, we use here the term criteria and not indicator. A criterion is a standard by which something is judged. Moreover, a criterion gives operationally and concrete meaning to a guiding principle or 'something we want to achieve' without itself being a direct measure of performance. Thus, criteria can be seen as the intermediate points of an assessment process to which the data provided by indicators can be integrated and where an interpretable assessment crystallises. In contrast, an indicator is any variable that is used to infer the status of a particular criterion. Indicators should provide a single meaningful message and define what information is delivered to evaluate the criteria (Siemer *et al.* 2006; Pokorny and Adams 2003). Together, criteria and indicators represent a form of communication network and are designed to deliver transparent information sets that are required to implement, monitor and assess sustainability processes (Prabhu *et al.* 1998). Fundamental to the use of criteria and indicators for sustainability assessment is the rule that no single criterion or indicator reflects, by itself, a complete measure of sustainability (Lanckner and Nijkamp 2000). It is the interwoven dynamics and relations between all criteria and indictors that provide us with an integrative picture that reflects the quality of the process we want to assess.

As stated before, criteria provide operationally and concrete meaning to a principle. In an assessment process, a principle reflects a common consensus about particular values, key objectives or normative regulations that form the basis of reasoning or action and provides the justification for the criteria and indicators (Pokorny and Adams 2003). Hence, the task of defining guiding principle and objectives at the very start of any assessment is critical as a foundation for designing appropriate criteria and indicators (Kates *et al.* 2001). If the quality of a sustainability process is assessed, we have to ask how successful core principles of SD have been put into practice. Hence, for the context of higher education, we must define core principles that serve as fundamental focal points for 'sustainable universities', and act as actual objectives of the overall assessment. For defining guiding principles for sustainability processes at HEI, we see two important aspects: First, the need for comparability and benchmarking of sustainability assessments at HEI calls for the use of standardised principles, which are principles that that are based on a strong international consensus and widely in use. Second, as HEI comprise a dichotomy of an integrative institution that reflects a socio-ecological setting as well as an educational/research dimension we must look for SD as well as ESD principles, both of which must drive the assessment of sustainability at HEI.

SD core principles that form the conceptual foundation of SD are reflected by a vast body of literature within sustainability research and are explicitly stated in a number of key documents of the United Nations or the European Union (UNCED 1992; Commission of the European Communities 2005). They are widely known, generally accepted and to a varying extent already underpin many sustainability assessment approaches (Singh *et al.* 2012). The concept of SD and its core principles emerged out of the need to tackle complex sustainability challenges we are facing at global scale and gave rise to a new field of sustainability science. Subsequently, ESD and its guiding principles were born to provide a new educational concept complementary to sustainability science (Wiek *et al.* 2011) that shall initiate a radical change in how we see our world accompanied by enhancing our competencies to shape actively a more sustainable society. During the last decade, the development of ESD key principles described a shift from education characterised by issues such as the reductionist view of disciplinary knowledge or a deficit view of the learner (testing and competition) towards a transformative view of pedagogy and participative learning (Sterling 2010).

A number of declarations and treaties highlight ESD principles in the context of higher education (Lozano *et al.* 2013, Disterheft *et al.* 2013). These university-specific landmark documents deal with the duties related to universities for SD. By analysing their contents, it is possible to identify their fundamental characteristics. First of all, they are voluntary statements of commitment that encourage sustainability leaders in HEI to establish a plan of actions to promote sustainability in the range of operations that are being carried out by them. While some declarations need to be endorsed either by individuals representing institutions or academic departments, groups, other statements only ask to follow their principles. Consistently, these documents translate a series of general ESD principles (such as listed in Table 22.1) into the dimensions of HEI: research, education, management and outreach (Cortese 2003).

Table 22.1 Key characteristics of ESD named in the International Implementation Scheme

Education for sustainable development will aim to demonstrate the following features:
Interdisciplinary and holistic: learning for sustainable development embedded in the whole curriculum, not as a separate subject;
Values-driven: it is critical that the assumed norms – the shared values and principles underpinning sustainable development – are made explicit so that they can be examined, debated, tested and applied;
Critical thinking and problem solving: leading to confidence in addressing the dilemmas and challenges of sustainable development;
Multi-method: word, art, drama, debate, experience, … different pedagogies which model the processes. Teaching that is geared simply to passing on knowledge should be recast into an approach in which teachers and learners work together to acquire knowledge and play a role in shaping the environment of their educational institutions;
Participatory decision-making: learners participate in decisions on how they are to learn;
Applicability: the learning experiences offered are integrated in day to day personal and professional life;
Locally relevant: addressing local as well as global issues, and using the language(s) which learners most commonly use. Concepts of sustainable development must be carefully expressed in other languages – languages and cultures say things differently, and each language has creative ways of expressing new concepts.

Source: UNESCO 2006

Among the most recent of these treaties is the 'Rio+20 Treaty on Higher Education'. It was developed by more than 30 higher education networks and institutions gathered under the leadership of the COPERNICUS Alliance, the International Association of Universities and the United Nations University – Institute of the Advanced Studies for Sustainability. Stressing a holistic and transformative perspective to sustainable higher education the treaty promotes the following eight principles:

1. To be transformative, higher education must transform itself
2. Efforts across the higher education system must be aligned
3. Partnership underpins progress
4. Sustainable development is an institutional and sector-wide learning process
5. Facilitating access to the underprivileged
6. Inter- and transdisciplinary learning and action
7. Redefining the notion of quality higher education
8. Sustainable development as a whole-of-institution commitment. (COPERNICUS Alliance 2012)

Obviously, there are more HEI relevant ESD principles than stated in the Rio+20 Treaty, but it would already make a big difference to incorporate these principles into ongoing sustainability assessment procedures and shift the focus from economic numbers and environmental parameters toward more holistic and process-oriented assessment approaches. The key issue here is the processual and transformative understanding of a 'sustainable university' and the related focus on assessing the quality of this process by using international agreed core principles of SD and ESD.

Putting the compliance with ESD and SD principles at the forefront of sustainability assessment at HEI, is a possible answer to our first question 'what do we want to assess?'. We argue that it is also a first major step towards incorporating assessment models into a sustainability-orientated governance model of universities. The second step goes along the line of answering the second question and is about choosing an appropriate assessment framework that can tackle sustainability at HEI as a transformative learning process.

How do we assess?

Sustainable assessment approaches

After we have defined sustainability at universities as an open and transformative process, whose quality should be assessed by using core principles of SD and ESD, we have to focus on the appropriate sustainability assessment framework for HEI. We start this by proving a short overview about recent trends of sustainability assessment outside and inside of HEI. Over the last decade, sustainability assessment has received an enormous amount of attention among the academic community (Morrison-Saunders *et al.* 2014; Ness *et al.* 2007; Pope *et al.* 2004). Introducing the notion of sustainability science, Kates *et al.* (2001: 642) identify two crucial questions which implicitly describe the common ground for sustainability assessment:

> How can today's operational systems for monitoring and reporting on environmental and social conditions be integrated or extended to provide more useful guidance for efforts to navigate a transition towards sustainability?

> How can today's relatively independent activities of research planning, monitoring, assessment, and decision support be better integrated into systems for adaptive management and societal learning?

Beside methodical differences and varying priorities, most of the sustainability assessment tools in use share the common understanding that for a necessary transition towards a more sustainable society, particular objectives and achievements must be assessed. All the existing assessment models try to tackle the need of individuals, institutions and societies to find metrics, models and tools for analysing and communicating the unsustainability in current activities and processes (Bebbington *et al.* 2007). An issue – especially one as complex as SD – that cannot be measured will be difficult to improve. Subsequently, assessment tools were developed and applied for a wide range of contexts and provide us with data, case study experiences, assessment guidelines and most of all concrete suggestions for decision makers (Ness *et al.* 2007).

Regarding the evolving diversity of sustainability assessment, we define the purpose of sustainability assessment along the lines of Ness *et al.* (2007: 499) 'to provide decision makers with an evaluation of global to local integrated nature-society systems in short and long term perspectives in order to assist them to determine which actions should or should not be taken in an attempt to make society more sustainable'.

Besides the common understanding of the purpose of sustainability assessment, there is no common consensus about how to categorise tools for sustainability assessment. Existing overviews of assessment tools have shown that they can be categorised based on factors such as temporal characteristics (ex-post or descriptive vs. ex-ante or change-oriented and long term vs. short term), the focus/objectives, or the level of integration (Kates *et al.* 2001; Finnveden and Morberg 2005). Ness *et al.* (2007) divide sustainability assessment tools into three general categorisation areas:

- *Indicator and indices*: Indicators are seen as simple measures, mostly quantitative and present a particular state of economic, social and/or environmental development in a defined region or context. An index consists of aggregated indicators. In applying a retrospective point of view indicators and indices are continuously measuring and monitoring in order to allow timely identification of longer sustainability trends.
- *Product related assessment tools*: Related to regional flow indicators, these tools focus on flows in relation with consumption and production of goods and services. Product related assessment tools are mainly focusing on environmental aspects and do not apply an integrative perspective on socio-ecological dynamics; and
- *Integrated assessment tools*: Integrated assessment tools aim at supporting decisions related to a project, management or policy in a defined region or context. They are often based on system analysis approaches and use scenario methods. These tools all apply an ex-ante focus.

In their comparison of these three categories Ness *et al.* (2007) emphasise that only integrated assessment tools are capable to tackle the multi-dimensionality of integrating socio-ecological facets. In contrast, indicator/indices and product related assessment approaches have a too narrow focus on environmental parameters as well as expressing a strong retrospective perspective for analysing the past and are not optimally designed for assessing long-term sustainability processes.

Other authors such as Morrison-Saunders *et al.* (2014) are drawing on the original model of Pope *et al.* (2004) and distinguish between three different conceptual models of integrative sustainability assessment:

- Environmental Impact Assessment (EIA)-driven integrated assessment: The tools within this category aim at minimising negative environmental, social and economic (ESE) impact within acceptable limits;
- Objective-led integrated assessment: This approach is focusing on maximised positive ESE outcomes; and
- Contribution for sustainability: Tools applying this approach are aimed at delivering positive outcomes (such as the objective-led integrated assessment model), but do not apply a separate ESE or triple bottom line perspective and assess whether a proposal makes a sufficient contribution for sustainability.

Arguing for a holistic approach to sustainability assessment, which is outlined by authors such as Gibson *et al.* (2005), Morrison-Saunders *et al.* (2014) criticise the first two approaches for their simplistic and reductionist 'triple bottom line' model. In their description of the contribution for sustainability assessment approach, the authors underline three core aspects of a holistic sustainability assessment, which are also highly significant for any sustainability assessment approach at HEI:

First, the notion of *trade-offs*, which means the evaluation and management of trade-offs, which will inevitable emerge out of the assessment (Morrison-Saunders and Pope 2013). As a quality defining key feature of an assessment process, the evaluation and tackling of trade-offs cannot achieved by an objective analysis, but will require a critical and participative judgment by the involved stakeholders. The consideration of trade-offs is stressing the context specific character of an integrated sustainability assessment as well as the need for transparent values, participative learning and decision making. The second notion is *interdisciplinarity*, which is already described as a core principle of good impact assessment practice almost 50 years ago (Senate and House of Representatives of the United States of America 1969). Morrison-Saunders *et al.* (2014) state that compared to other already applied assessment approaches, only the contribution for sustainability approach implies the need for interdisciplinarity as the orientation of the assessment towards sustainability principles embodies a multi-dimensional range of inter-related issues. The third notion highlighted by the authors is the focus on a *participatory ex-ante assessment process*. Similar to Ness *et al.* (2007), they argue that due to the intergenerational mandate and the changing dynamics of expectations and impacts, any top-down, expert driven ex-post assessment and its related assumptions of unchanging conditions and maximised outcomes are invalid from an integrative sustainability perspective.

The obvious demand for holistic and integrated assessment, and the necessity to tackle trade-offs, interdisciplinarity or a participatory ex-ante assessment process already prepare the conceptual ground for transferring the idea of sustainability assessment into the context of HEI. Consequently, universities should only consider assessment models that are able to tackle the dynamic, integrative and open characteristics of SD, which limits the range of potential candidates to integrative assessment models such as the contribution for sustainability assessment approach.

Sustainability assessment at HEI

A growing number of sustainability assessment tools are trying to embrace the specific context of sustainable higher education (Cairo *et al.* 2013; Glover *et al.* 2011, Lozano 2011; Shriberg 2002). Tools such as AISHE, AUA, STAR, STAUNCH or GASU are among the most prominent and successful assessment pioneers and have been specifically developed and applied at various universities around the globe (Urbanski and Rowland 2014; Lambrechts and

Ceulemans 2013; AUA 2011; Glover *et al.* 2011; Lozano 2006b; Roorda 2004). Herein, the usefulness of assessment tools can vary, depending on a number of factors such as size and complexity of the HEI as well as the scope of its sustainability initiatives to be assessed. Among the great variety of existing tools, we have chosen the following three sustainability assessment tools to provide a brief glance at the different ways to assess a 'sustainable university'. For a more comprehensive work on the existing tools see Cairo *et al.* (2013).

A good example for an assessment tool that could provide an initial starting point for an internal learning process towards a 'sustainable university' is the Assessment Instrument for Sustainability in Higher Education (AISHE). AISHE was one of the first assessment tools for sustainability at HEI and was developed by the Dutch Committee on Sustainable Higher Education (CDHO) in 2000–01. After the tool was tested and applied by universities mainly in Europe, a second version of the tool – AISHE 2.0 was developed in 2009 by a consortium of researchers from the Netherlands, Austria, Sweden and Spain. The conceptual framework of AISHE consists of five modules – covering the five functions of universities – and six related criteria to each module. The criteria are described by five development stages (activity-oriented, process-oriented, system-oriented, chain-oriented, society-oriented), which should reflect the process of mainstreaming sustainability. According to those development stages, the institution is assessing its state of development and developing strategies on how to achieve higher stages (Roorda *et al.* 2009). Notably, the self-assessment part of AISHE 2.0 shows that the success of any sustainability assessment at a university depends strongly on involving stakeholders from all the different areas or dimensions of a university. However, besides AISHE 2.0 strong accentuation on qualitative and processual aspects, its application at two Austrian universities in 2014 (one of the authors was involved in both assessment processes) also showed the need for assessment tools that can be adapted and modified to the particular context and put a stronger focus on the interactions between the particular criteria and the actual criteria development.

A different approach of linking sustainability assessment with internal learning is applied by the Alternative University Appraisal (AUA). AUA was launched in 2009 as an initiative by the members of ProSPER.Net (Promotion of Sustainability in Postgraduate Education and Research Network). This is an Asia-Pacific network coordinated by the United Nations University – Institute for the Advanced Studies of Sustainability (UNU-IAS) focusing on the integration of Education for Sustainable Development principles among academic institutions. AUA was introduced in 2009 as a learning initiative to introduce ESD or advance current ESD initiatives among ProSPER.Net members, as well as to create a community of learning in which HEIs can identify their own strengths and weaknesses, learn from one another and share good practices in their own area of interest (AUA 2011). The AUA model is based upon three main pillars: education, research and governance. Outreach and transformation are seen as overarching criteria that need to be reflected in each of the three main pillars. AUA is providing a ready questionnaire catalogue that is used for self-reflection or peer reflection. Alongside this reflection and peer consultation AUA aims at supporting a learning process among participating institutions. This shall support institutions in their progress of integrating sustainability into their education, research and governance activities. Furthermore, the questions are taking stock on initiatives that have already been taken (such as mission planning, educational programs or research projects and groups) and provide this information to ProSPER.Net members through community exchange opportunities

Out of the need to track sustainability performance in higher education, the Sustainability Tracking, Assessment and Rating System (STARS) was developed by the Association for the Advancement of Sustainability in Higher Education based in the US. STARS is a transparent, self-reporting framework that provides colleges and universities with a platform for measuring their sustainability performance. The system covers areas of higher education including curricula and research, student and public engagement, campus operations as well as investment and administration (Urbanski and Rowland 2014). After a development phase, the system was officially launched in 2009. By 2014 more than 300 institutions across the US and Canada have participated and applied the STARS system, and as international demand has grown, STARS pilots were also developed for higher education institutions outside US and Canada. STARS is built upon an online reporting tool. Participating institutions upload their evaluation materials and receive a rating ranging from Bronze to Platinum, depending on their performance and points they get. Through the online reporting, actors can also get access to the online information system and receive feedback or further information from the growing community of applicants (Urbanski and Rowland 2014). Clearly STARS is a learning tool that facilitates capacity building through the self and peer-assessment process.

In spite of these promising developments, many existing sustainability assessment tools, which are applied in HEI are still locked into the shortfalls of pure economic numbers or into a predominant accentuation on issues of eco-efficiency (Wals 2014; Shriberg 2002). The reason for this undesired situation can often be found in the existing orientation towards an entrepreneurial model of universities (Yarime *et al.* 2012), which serve as knowledge factories for economic growth and often follow traditional old mechanistic mental frames of education (Lozano *et al.* 2013). Therefore, we argue that without switching from the business-as-usual approach to the imperative of substantial change, a simple transfer of existing sustainability assessment models into the context of higher education could easily face dead ends. We also have already shown, that among the great variety of existing sustainability assessment models, only a few express an integrative and participative assessment approach that can tackle the dynamics of a multi-dimensional sustainability process over time. Moreover, all the holistic assessment tools were developed for corporations, regions or countries and neither include a focus on ESD nor do they encompass the different functions of HEI (Lozano 2006a). Thus, HEI have two options: either to develop their own sustainability assessment tools or to modify already existing ones. Whichever option is chosen, the applied assessment tool must be designed according to the specific context of a 'sustainable university' and ESD. Obviously, we have to raise the subsequent question: what is this specific context, and what does it mean for the conceptual cornerstones of sustainability assessment?

As already described before, universities are multi-dimensional institutions that reflect a socio-ecological setting as well as an educational and research dimension. The socio-ecological aspects of HEI are not substantially different from the socio-ecological aspects of other institutions or organisations, and do not constitute the uniqueness of universities. Nevertheless, they present an important part of the overall sustainability process at HEI and should be tackled through an integrative and participative assessment process and be guided by SD principles. When it comes to the educational and research dimension, the situation is different. Compared to other institutions, these two functions of HEI are unique and do not fit into regular sustainability assessment models. Nevertheless, both functions are also essential elements of the overall sustainability process at HEI and can be assessed similar to socio-ecological elements by using ESD principles. In the process of developing or modifying a new sustainability assessment tool for a university, we would start from both sets of principles. The next conceptual steps would be the development/modification of related sets of criteria, which would provide operationally and concrete meaning to the principles. Subsequently, appropriate indicators need to be designed to measure the status of the particular criterion.

However, we have already emphasised that in the very heart of sustainability assessment at

HEI, there is assessing the quality of an integrative process where a possible 'end-state' or outcome is not known in advance. We have defined this process as institutionalised transformative learning. This is of major importance for the conceptual framework of developing or modifying appropriated assessment tools. The importance of transformative learning for ESD has been stated elsewhere by authors such as Sterling (2010) or Thomas (2009). In the context of a 'sustainable university', transformative learning addresses the need of change at two different levels. First, it has a strong pedagogic perspective on teaching and emphasises that 'teaching approaches must focus on elements relating to the process of learning, rather than the accumulation of knowledge … which provides students with the opportunities to learn to think, specifically "how to think" rather than "what to think"' (Thomas 2009: 245). Along similar lines, Sterling (2010: 19) defines transformative learning as follows: 'It refers essentially to a qualitative shift in perception and meaning making on the part of the learner in a particular learning experience such as the learner questions or reframes his/her assumptions or habits of thought.'

The second level is the level of the overall institutions and reflects learning, innovation and improvement across the whole institution, which provides the dynamic setting for mainstreaming SD at a university. To overcome existing barriers and prejudices, the institutionalisation of SD and the related paradigmatic shift across all functions of a HEI need to be implemented in a participative and incremental way (Lozano 2006b). Transformative learning at this level is an opportunity to change radically but to achieve it in a sensible and step-by-step process. As an institutional learning process, it has the power to overcome old paradigms, internalise new values, skills and behaviour and brings the change from individual mindsets towards integration towards successful institutionalisation. Without this paradigm shift, learning at university level would be limited to cosmetic change and efficiency gains. It would be concerned primarily with doing things (even if unsustainable) better, but not with doing better things, which would be improvement but no transformation. As stressed by Sterling (2010: 23): 'The case for transformative learning is that learning within paradigm does not change the paradigm, whereas learning that facilitates a fundamental recognition of paradigm and enables paradigmatic reconstruction is by definition transformative'.

Consequently, sustainability assessment at HEI must establish the institutional setting to initiate, monitor and assess the quality of this internal transformative learning process. Cleary, this excludes any assessment tools based on top-down, expert-driven approaches and stresses the importance of context-dependent self-assessment as a learning instrument. An appropriate sustainability assessment tool for HEI provides a sound balance between standardised elements that aim at comparable outcomes and flexible structures that give enough room to all members of the university to learn, communicate and collect together the mosaic patterns of their 'sustainable university'. Clearly, it is useful to apply already existing and standardised quantitative indicators when it comes to environmental management aspects. We also argue for using the four dimensions of a university as reference points of the process, as well as existing ESD and SD principles as focal points of the assessment process. Besides such standardised specifications, context-dependency and heterogeneity within and between universities underline the need for universities to also design their own specific criteria and indicator settings. Although, this requires more effort, this part of a self-assessment depends on the understanding of the sustainability process itself in order to reach the acceptation of various interest groups on campus.

Answering the questions

In the beginning of this chapter, we raised the questions of 'what do we assess?' and 'how do we assess?'. To frame the setting of these two questions, we have highlighted the processual and transformative characteristics of a 'sustainable university' and defined it as a transformative learning process that bridges different functions and values along with the stewardship for performing those functions, and participation of stakeholders from inside and outside the university. To answer both questions, we have built on existing work within the literature of sustainability assessment and cast a glance at existing sustainability assessment approaches at HEI. At the end of this chapter, we want to sum up the issues we have raised and present a basic conceptual frame for sustainability assessment tools at universities. Hereby, we are following Shriberg's (2002) approach of attributes of an 'ideal assessment tool', and summarise our answers as conceptual corner stones of assessing sustainability at HEI in Table 22.2.

Table 22.2 reflects our general conceptual view on sustainability assessment at HEI. Our focus on assessing sustainability as the quality of internal learning processes should provide university stakeholders with guidance to develop or modify an adequate assessment approach for their own contextual settings. Nevertheless, we are aware that by putting the quality of the assessment process in the centre of the debate, we risk excluding or marginalising the outcomes of the sustainability (assessment) processes themselves. Usually, sustainability pioneers at HEI do not convince decision-makers to implement sustainability assessment through normative or conceptual arguments. Clearly, without communicating concrete benefits or cost-savings, many sustainability processes at our universities would not have ever started (Vogtländer *et al.* 2002). To name only a few, benefits such as increased resource-efficiency, decreased CO_2 emissions, a greater transparency of internal decision-making, improved communication patterns, enhanced

Table 22.2 Key attributes of sustainability assessment at HEI

Sustainability assessment at HEI should reflect the following attributes:
Measures the quality of a sustainability process and not particular states: Sustainability at HEI reflects a transformative learning process that bridges different functions and values along with the stewardship for performing those functions and participation of stakeholders from inside and outside the university. Thus, assessing sustainability at HEI is assessing the quality of this process.
Applies a holistic and integrative perspective: Only a holistic and integrative assessment approach can tackle the multi-dimensionality of the different functions of HEI and their socio-ecological setting.
Reflects the compliance with SD and ESD principles: SD and ESD principles shall serve as concrete focal points for the assessment process. Evaluating their actual compliance is at the forefront of the assessment.
Initiates an institutional learning process towards a more sustainable university: The main objective of the assessment process is initiating an institutional learning process that reflects a sustainable transformation.
Is participative: The assessment must have a strong participatory aspect reflected in the learning process as well as in the related decision making (e.g. the management and weighting of related trade-offs).
Is interdisciplinary: Interdisciplinarity must be an integrative aspect of the assessment process, as the orientation of the assessment towards sustainability principles embodies a multi-dimensional range of inter-related issues.
Is comparable: The assessment must integrate processes and outcomes into a comparable, understandable and calculable framework to support benchmarking and the identification of good practice.
Emphasises transparency and comprehensibility. Sustainability assessment tools must be transparent and comprehensible to stakeholder inside and outside of HEI.

cooperation with sustainability-oriented business, and many other aspects could be highlighted and explained in more detail as outcomes of sustainability (assessment) processes at universities (Maiorano and Savan, 2015).

The reason why we did not put much accentuation on concrete sustainability outcomes is that outcomes such as increased eco-efficiency or bigger cost-savings are already reflected by most existing assessment approaches. Transformative learning or a holistic and participative assessment, however, is reflected in only a few existing approaches. To change or extend an already existing assessment tool, which is mostly limited to a predominant accentuation on a few concrete outcomes like eco-efficiency, is a real challenge. By contrast, we think that starting from an integrative conceptual framework should provide the base for an assessment process that can tackle both: the requirements of ESD and SD principles, as well as the subsequent need for concrete benefits as outcomes of the sustainability (assessment) process. When applying a participative self-assessment process, which is driven by continuous internal learning and improvement, concrete benefits like cost savings or resource-efficiency will follow. We even argue that participation and the ability to link with internal learning processes – both major aspects for increasing the quality of a sustainability assessment at HEI – do not only provide a much more comprehensive picture of the actual sustainability process at a university. Bringing together different stakeholders with different backgrounds and ideas from all university areas has the potential to assess the status quo more accurately than integrating only the perspectives of a few 'experts'. The integration of various university stakeholders in the assessment process provides more creative and more efficient sustainability measures, as the process itself can draw on many insights from a range of university areas, disciplines and professional backgrounds. Subsequently, the actual measures, strategies or initiatives that emerge out of the assessment process are supported by a greater number of stakeholders across the particular institutional levels.

Conclusions

As old mental models and reductionist perceptions of SD prevail, sustainability assessment at HEI is still more concerned with economic numbers or fixed performance indicators based on efficiency gains and international rankings. Therefore, it is of uttermost importance to apply integrative and participative assessment models that enhance the mainstreaming of a 'sustainable university' through initiating an institutionalised and transformative learning process. The degree of change driving this process is enormous, the implications for the culture of universities radical and obviously there will be conflicts and resistance. As mainstreaming sustainability is opposing the current neo-liberal setting at many HEI, these conflicts are necessary and must be dealt with in a transparent and sensible way during an assessment. Integrative and participative assessment tools provide an institutional learning process that is shaped by an open dialogue of the various stakeholder groups. This dialogue about values, interpretations of SD or about the fundamental purpose of education itself offers a promising setting to tackle these conflicts in a way that sustainability as radical innovation is implemented incrementally and guided by social learning, participation and empowerment. A continuous accentuation of sustainability assessment tools on operational eco-efficiency does not support sustainable change at HEI. On the contrary, this creates the impression that we need no change at HEI at all, as sustainability would be only a matter of technological control and can be tackled sufficiently by the already existing structures and patterns of our universities. At the end of the day, HEI will only be able to drive sustainable development and contribute to a paradigm shift towards a more sustainable society if they succeed in overcoming their own internal inertia and transform themselves.

References

AUA, 2011. 'Alternative University Appraisal Model for ESD in Higher Education Institutions (Vers. 1.1 as of Feb. 2011)', ProSPER.Net. 29.

Bebbington, J., Brown, J. and Frame, B., 2007. 'Accounting Technologies and Sustainability Assessment Models', *Ecological Economics*, 61, 224–36.

Cairo, S., Leal Filho, W., Jabbour, C. and Azeiteiro, U., eds, 2013. *Sustainability Assessment Tools in Higher Education Institutions: Mapping Trends and Good Practices Around the World.* Switzerland: Springer.

Commission of the European Communities, 2005. *Declaration on Guiding Principles for Sustainable Development.* Brussels: Communication from the Commission to the Council and the European Parliament.

COPERNICUS Alliance, 2012. 'Rio +20 Treaty On Higher Education'. United Kingdom: COPERNICUS Alliance Secretariat. http://hetreatyrio20.com/wordpress/wp-content/uploads/2013/06/treaty_rio.pdf [accessed June 2015].

Cortese, A.D., 2003. 'The Critical Role of Higher Education in Creating a Sustainable Future', *Planning for Higher Education*, 31(3), 15–22.

Disterheft, A., Cairo, S., Azeiteiro, U. and Leal Filho, W., 2013. 'Sustainability Science and Education for Sustainable Development in Universities: A Way for Transition', in Cairo, S., Leal Filho, W., Jabbour, C. and Azeiteiro, U. (eds), *Sustainability Assessment Tools in Higher Education Institutions: Mapping Trends and Good Practices Around the World.* Switzerland: Springer.

Fadeeva, Z., Galkute, L., Mader, C. and Scott, G., 2014. *Sustainable Development and Quality Assurance in Higher Education.* Houndmills: Palgrave Macmillan.

Finnveden, G. and Moberg, Å., 2005. 'Environmental Systems Analysis – An Overview', *Journal of Cleaner Production*, 13(12), 1165–73.

Folke, C., Carpenter, S., Elmqvist, T., Gunderson, L., Holling, C.S. and Walker, B., 2002. 'Resilience and Sustainable Development: Building Adaptive Capacity in a World of Transformations', *Ambio*, 31(5), 437–40.

Gibson, R., Hassan, S., Holtz, S., Tansey, J. and Whitelaw, G., 2005. *Sustainability Assessment Criteria, Processes and Applications.* London: Earthscan.

Glover A., Peters, C. and Haslett, S.K., 2011. 'Education for Sustainable Development and Global Citizenship', *International Journal of Sustainability in Higher Education*, 12(2), 125–44.

Kates, R.W., Clark, W.C., Corell, R., Hall, M.J., Jaeger, C.C., Lowe, I., McCarthy, J.J., Schellnhuber, H.J., Bolin, B., Dickson, N.M. *et al.*, 2001. 'Sustainability Science', *Science*, 292(5517), 641–2.

Lambrechts, W. and Ceulemans, K., 2013. 'Sustainability Assessment in Higher Education. Evaluating the Use of the Auditing Instrument for Sustainability in Higher Education (AISHE) in Belgium', in Cairo, S., Leal Filho, W., Jabbour, C. and Azeiteiro, U. (eds), *Sustainability Assessment Tools in Higher Education Institutions: Mapping Trends and Good Practices Around the World.* Switzerland: Springer.

Lancker, E. and Nijkamp, P., 2000. 'A Policy Scenario Analysis of Sustainable Agricultural Development Options: A Case Study for Nepal', *Impact Assessment and Project Appraisal*, 18(2), 111–24.

Leal Filho, W. (ed.), 2009. *Sustainable Development at Universities – Opportunities, Challenges and Trends.* Frankfurt: Peter Lang.

Leal Filho, W. (ed.), 2012. *Sustainable Development at Universities.* Frankfurt: Peter Lang.

Lozano, R., 2006a. 'Incorporation and Institutionalization of SD into Universities: Breaking though Barriers to Change', *Journal of Cleaner Production*, 14(9–11), 787–96.

Lozano, R., 2006b. 'A Tool for a Graphical Assessment of Sustainability in Universities (GASU)', *Journal of Cleaner Production*, 14(9–11), 963–72.

Lozano, R. 2011. 'The State of Sustainability Reporting in Universities', *International Journal of Sustainability in Higher Education*, 12(1), 67–78.

Lozano, R., Lukman, R., Lozano, F.J., Huisingh, D. and Lambrechts, W., 2013. 'Declarations for Sustainability in Higher Education: Becoming Better Leaders, through Addressing the University System', *Journal of Cleaner Production*, 48(June), 10–19.

Mader, C., 2014. 'The Role of Assessment and Quality Management in transformations towards Sustainable Development: the nexus between Higher Education, Society and Policy', in Fadeeva, Z. Galkute L., Mader, C. and Scott G. *Sustainable Development and Quality Assurance in Higher Education: Transformation of Learning and Society.* Houndsmill: Palgrave Macmillan.

Mader, C., Scott, G. and Razak, D.A., 2013. 'Effective Change Management, Governance and Policy for Sustainability Transformation in Higher Education', *Sustainability Accounting, Management and Policy*

Journal, 4(3), 264–84.

Maiorano, J. and Savan, B., 2015. 'Barriers to Energy Efficiency and the Uptake of Green Revolving Funds in Canadian Universities', *International Journal of Sustainability in Higher Education* 16(2), 200–16.

Morrison-Saunders A. and Pope J., 2013. 'Conceptualising and Managing Trade-offs in Sustainability Assessment', *Environmental Impact Assessment Revue*, 38(January), 54–63.

Morrison-Saunders, A., Pope, J., Bond, A. and Retief, F., 2014. 'Towards sustainability assessment follow-up', *Environmental Impact Assessment Review*, 45(February), 38–45.

Ness, B., Urbel-Piirsalu, E., Anderberg, S. and Olsson, L., 2007. 'Categorising Tools for Sustainability Assessment', *Ecological Economics*, 60(3), 498–508.

Pokorny, B. and Adams, M., 2003. 'What do Criteria and Indicators Assess? An Analysis of Five C&I Sets Relevant for Forest Management in the Brazilian Amazon', *International Forestry Review*, 5(1), 20–8.

Pope, J., Annandale, D. and Morrison-Saunders, A., 2004. 'Conceptualising Sustainability Assessment', *Environmental Impact Assessment Review*, 24(6), 595–616.

Prabhu, R., Ruitenbeek, H., Boyle, T. and Colfer, C., 1998. 'Between Voodoo Science and Adaptive Management: The Role and Research Needs for Indicators of Sustainable Forest Management'. Paper presented at the IUFRO Conference, Melbourne, 24–28 August.

Rammel, C. and van den Bergh, J., 2003. 'An Evolutionary Perspective on Sustainable Development Policies: Adaptive Flexibility and Risk Minimising', *Ecological Economics*, 47(2–3), 121–33.

Rammel, C., McIntosh, B. and Jeffrey, P., eds, 2007. '(Co)evolutionary Approaches to Sustainable Development – Special Issue', *International Journal of Sustainable Development and World Ecology*, 4(1).

Remington-Doucette, S., Connell, K., Armstrong, C. and Musgrove, S., 2013. 'Assessing Sustainability Education in a Transdisciplinary Undergraduate Course Focused on Real World Problem Solving', *International Journal of Sustainability in Higher Education*, 14(4), 404–33.

Roorda, N., 2004. 'Developing Sustainability in Higher Education using AISHE', in Corcoran, P. and Wals, A. (eds), *Higher Education and the Challenges of Sustainability Problematics, Promise, and Practice*. Dordrecht: Kluwer, 5–18.

Roorda, N., Rammel, C., Waara, S. and Fra Paleo, U., 2009. *AISHE 2.0 Manual*. Tilburg: AISHE.

Senate and House of Representatives of the United States of America, 1969. 'The National Environmental Policy Act of 1969'. www.nepa.gov/nepa/regs/nepa/nepaeqia.htm [accessed 17 February 2015, not found].

Shriberg M., 2002. 'Institutional Assessment Tools for Sustainability in Higher Education', *International Journal of Sustainability in Higher Education*, 3(3), 254–70.

Siemer, S., Rammel, C. and Elmer, S., 2006. *Pilotstudie zu Indikatoren einer Bildung für nachhaltige Entwicklung*. Vienna: Bundesministerium für Bildung, Wissenschaft und Kultur.

Singh, R., Murty, H. Gupta, S. and Dikshit, A., 2012. 'An Overview of Sustainability Assessment Methodologies', *Ecological Indicators*, 15(1), 281–99.

Sneddon, C., Howarth, R. and Norgaard, R., 2006. 'Sustainable Development in a Post-Brundtland World', *Ecological Economics*, 57(2), 253–68.

Sterling, S. 2010. 'Transformative Learning and Sustainability: Sketching the Conceptual Ground', *Learning and Teaching in Higher Education*, 5(5), 17–33.

Thomas, I., 2009. 'Critical Thinking, Transformative Learning, Sustainable Education, and Problem-based Learning in Universities', *Journal of Transformative Education*, 7(3), 245–64.

Tilbury, D., 2011. 'Higher Education for Sustainability: A Global Overview of Commitment and Progress', in GUNI (ed.), *Higher Education in the World 4. Higher Education's Commitment to Sustainability: From Understanding to Action*. Barcelona: Palgrave, 1–21.

UNCED, 1992. *Rio Declaration on Environment and Development*. Brazil: United Nations Publication.

UNESCO, 2006. *Framework for the UNDESD International Implementation Scheme*. Paris: UNESCO Education Sector.

Urbanski, M. and Rowland, P., 2014. 'STARS as a Multipurpose Tool for Advancing Campus Sustainability in US', in Fadeeva, Zinaida, Galkute, L., Mader, C. and Scott G., *Sustainable Development and Quality Assurance in Higher Education – Transformation of Learning and Society*. Houndsmill: Palgrave Macmillan, 153–83.

Velazquez, L., Munguia, N. and Sanchez, M., 2005. 'Deterring Sustainability in Higher Education Institutions: An Appraisal of the Factors which Influence Sustainability in Higher Education Institutions', *International Journal of Sustainability in Higher Education*, 6(4), 383–91.

Velazquez, L., Munguia, N., Platt, A. and Taddei, J., 2006. 'Sustainable University: What can be the Matter?', *Journal of Cleaner Production*, 14(9–11), 810–14.

Vettori, O., 2012. *A Clash of Quality Cultures? Conflicting and Coalescing Interpretive Patterns in Austrian Higher Education*. Vienna: University of Vienna.

Vettori, O. and Rammel, C., 2014. 'Linking Quality Assurance and ESD: Towards a Participative Quality Culture of Sustainable Development in Higher Education', in Fadeeva, Z., Galkute, L., Mader, C. and Scott, G., *Sustainable Development and Quality Assurance in Higher Education – Transformation of Learning and Society*. Houndsmill: Palgrave Macmillan, 49–65.

Vogtländer, J., Bijma, A. and Brezet, A., 2002. 'Communicating the Eco-efficiency of Products and Services by Means of the Eco-costs/Value Model', *Journal of Cleaner Production*, 10(1), 57–67.

Wals, A., 2014. 'Sustainability in Higher Education in the Context of the UN DESD: A Review of Learning and Institutionalization Process', *Journal of Cleaner Production*, 62(January), 8–15.

Wiek, A., Withycombe, L. and Redman, C., 2011.' Key Competencies in Sustainability. A Reference Framework for Academic Program Development', *Sustainability Science*, 6(2), 203–18.

Zwickle, A., Koontz, T., Slagle, K. and Bruskotter, J., 2014. 'Assessing Sustainability Knowledge of a Student Population: Developing a Tool to Measure Knowledge in the Environmental, Economic and Social Domains', *International Journal of Sustainability in Higher Education*, 15(4), 375–89.

PART 4

Examples of research on higher education for sustainable development

23

SUSTAINABLE BEHAVIOUR IN HIGHER EDUCATION INSTITUTIONS

An exploratory approach

Margarita Juárez-Nájera

Introduction

Motivations leading to this study

The objective of this study was to present the ways in which people act in the face of social dilemmas. According to J.J. Rousseau (2001), humans act based on egotism or self-interest, and altruism, which is the application of the general will of society for the welfare of others.

In order to respond to the objective of this study, sociology and psychology – academic disciplines in which behavioural change may be produced – were reviewed (Kruglanski and Higgins 2003; Myers 2007; Smith and Mackie 2007). Meanwhile, changes in behaviour which are studied from a biological perspective were not considered (Berry *et al.* 2002). Importantly, social psychology attempts to explain the behaviour of individuals by taking into account human values and moral and subjective norms. In this context values and norms appear to be key elements for attending to social dilemmas (Axelrod and Lehman 1993; Hardin 1968; Kollock 1998; Macy and Flache 2002; Rokeach 1973). In turn, social dilemmas describe situations in which the rational behaviour of an individual – defined in economic terms – leads to suboptimal outcomes from the collective standpoint (Kollock 1998). A social dilemma is a conflict in which the most beneficial action for an individual will, if chosen by most people, have a harmful effect on everyone (Aronson *et al.* 2009).

In an attempt to promote sustainable human development, the United Nations proposes to attend to social dilemmas (UNEP 2011) which affect the world in order to reduce poverty, as well as to promote health, respect for human rights, sustainable production and consumption, gender equality, environmental conservation and protection, rural transformation, and adoption of interculturalism as a path toward peace.

Education is a cornerstone for achieving sustainable development. Thus, UNESCO (2005, 2009 and 2012) launched the Decade of Education for Sustainable Development (DESD) for 2005–2014. This initiative has the potential to be transformative and emphasises aspects of learning which facilitate a transition toward sustainability as it promotes holistic educational practices intended to develop responsible citizens with critical attitudes, and who participate in economic, environmental, political and cultural spheres of society.

Behavioural psychosocial theories which attempt to explain key determinants of behaviour – such as beliefs, attitudes and values which promote or limit behaviour of individuals in society – are based on cognition (von Eckardt 1996) and on information processing (Leahey and Harris 2001). Within the field of cognitive information processing, two conceptual frameworks explain human behaviour (Kaiser *et al.* 2005); one is based on self-interest, deliberation and rational choice (Ajzen 1991, 2005); the other is based on altruism and is rooted in values and moral norms (Schwartz 1977, 1994). Some authors (Corral-Verdugo 2001; Harland 2001; Stern 2000) present social psychology models which explain behaviour in favour of the environment with a variance of approximately 40 per cent. These authors call for an attempt to increase variance in psychosocial models in order to explain such behaviour.

With these concepts as guiders, the present study used conceptual frameworks (Corral-Verdugo 2010; Corral-Verdugo and Pinheiro 2004; Gardner 2001; Hines *et al.* 1988; Stern, 2000) based on values and moral norms as these appear to explain peoples' altruism. According to the philosophers Rousseau (2001) and Neuhouser (2008), human goodness should be fomented so that the individual may continue to be human.

Following this development for the research frameworks the study process followed an additional seven stages. Figure 23.1 schematically shows these stages.

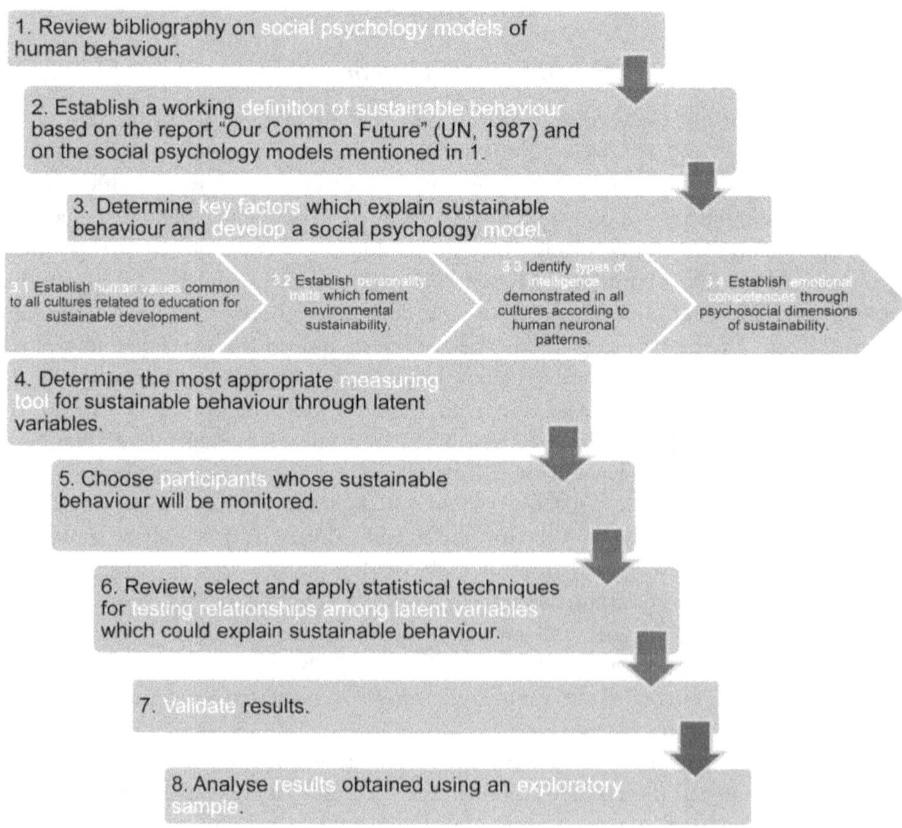

Figure 23.1 Planning of the study in eight stages

Research process

Development of a model for determining sustainable behaviour

Definition of sustainable behaviour

Virtually all conceptual schemes which have been used in psychology have been applied to behaviour. Cognitive information processing (Leahey and Harris 2001; Matthews *et al.* 2000) appears to be the most useful school of thought for explaining peoples' behaviour, as their mental operations (beliefs, attitudes and perceptions) interact with the environment and influence individual and social well-being and material security.

This notion of behaviour includes a deliberate, intentional component and supposes an action. Extending the definition of Corral-Verdugo and Pinheiro (2004) and considering the original definition of sustainable development (UN 1987), sustainable behaviour is defined in this study according to Juárez-Nájera *et al.* (2010: 687) as the 'effective, deliberate, anticipated set of actions with the objective that people accept responsibility for preventing, conserving, and preserving physical and cultural resources. These resources include animal and plant species, as well as social well-being and the security of present and future human generations'.

Conceptual frameworks for determining a model for sustainable development

Predicting sustainable behaviour is not an easy task; it appears to involve a number of variables, none of which is likely to operate without interacting with others. Therefore, it is difficult to develop a model. Some authors in social psychology (Blamey 1998; Corral-Verdugo and Pinheiro 2004; Harland 2001; Hines *et al.* 1987; Stern 2000) have used a group of latent variables in models of attitudes as a measure to identify factors which lead to a change in behaviour in favour of the environment.

With the objective of proposing a model to determine sustainable behaviour, a number of conceptual frameworks, mentioned below, were reviewed. These help to identify psychological, situational and contextual factors which explain such behaviour.

The norm-activation theory by Schwartz (1977, 1994), which ascribes a significant role to personal norms, was selected. This theory postulates that moral norms are intrinsically motivated by one's expectations regarding morally appropriate behaviour. Personal norms, if activated, are experienced by individuals as feelings of personal obligation as to whether or not they admit responsibility for the consequences of their choice of behaviour as it affects the well-being of others.

The meta-analysis conceptual framework by Hines *et al.* (1987), updated by Bamberg and Möser (2007), was also considered. Meta-analysis explains four aspects of intention involved in carrying out any individual action: recognition of the problem, knowledge of the course of action in a given situation, ability to implement strategies for action, and appropriate knowledge.

The value-belief-norm framework of Stern *et al.* (1999), tested in the United States to determine political activism, was also taken into account in this study. Such political activism is essential for social movements which seek collective well-being. Additionally, personal intelligences were considered, based on the theory of multiple intelligences by Gardner (2001), which delineates the abilities shown by humans in all cultures.

Finally, five psychological characteristics of sustainability were taken into account: effectiveness, austerity, solidarity, deliberation and anticipation, as proposed by Corral-Verdugo and

Pinheiro (2004) and Corral-Verdugo (2010). These dimensions affect or are affected by the interaction between the individual and the environment, and elucidate aspects underlying sustainable behaviour.

With the objective of determining individuals' mental processes, the theoretical framework of cognitive information processing (Leahey and Harris 2001) holds that such mental processes are impossible to observe directly. However, upon incorporating hypothetical or latent variables, individual responses may be determined as real entities which allow for exploring constructs (Bartholomew 1987; McDonald 2011), in this case sustainable behaviour.

Tool for determining sustainable behaviour

In order to prepare a questionnaire to measure latent variables, relevant literature was reviewed (Aiken 1997; Converse and Presser 1988; Henerson *et al.* 1991; Ligtvoet *et al.* 2011). An extensive 177-item questionnaire was initially prepared; nevertheless, based on previous experience, collaborators recommended reducing the size of the questionnaire, sacrificing breadth in favour of quality of participant responses. The final questionnaire consisted of 67 questions divided into five sections (see Juárez-Nájera *et al.* 2010).

The questionnaire was developed based on the work of Stern *et al.* (1999) and included four types of motivational values (self-enhancement, conservation, self-transcendence and openness to change), as mentioned by Schwartz (1994), who suggests that these values are present in humans throughout the world. The following personality traits, which incline an individual to norm activation, were included (Schwartz 1994): ascription of responsibility, which refers to people's receptiveness to act in the face of situational needs, and awareness of consequences, which refers to people's inclination to admit responsibility for consequences of their choice of behaviour directed toward others.

Twenty of 72 emotional competencies mentioned by Boyatzis *et al.* (2002) were selected among the four categories suggested by this author: self-knowledge, self-determination, understanding of others and social skills. Selected emotional competencies were adapted to the five psychological dimensions of sustainability (effectiveness, deliberation, anticipation, solidarity and austerity) mentioned by Corral-Verdugo and Pinheiro (2004) and Corral-Verdugo (2010).

The final section of the questionnaire contains eight items related to demographic aspects, as recommended by Hines *et al.* (1987). Two variables used by Stern *et al.* (1999) were omitted – the new ecological paradigm and cultural models – as they showed low confidence levels in a previous study (Kaiser *et al.* 2005).

Participants in the study

The questionnaire was applied to individuals in two universities with different cultures and economies. The first is the Universidad Autónoma Metropolitana (Autonomous Metropolitan University) in Azcapotzalco (UAMA), which is located to the north of Mexico City and is one of five UAM campuses. The UAM is a public university which in 2006 developed an Environmental Plan toward Sustainability. This plan was part of a broader programme developed by a tripartite initiative of the Mexican Ministry of Environment, the National Association of Universities and Higher Education Institutions, and the Centre for University Studies. This program, initiated in 2000, promotes a strategy for guiding HEI toward improving environmental performance in the light of the Decade of Education for Sustainable Development (Juárez-Nájera *et al.* 2006).

The second university is the Leuphana Universität Lüneburg (LUL). This public university, located 30 km from Hamburg, Germany, was honoured with the UNESCO Chair in Higher Education for Sustainable Development. The central objective of the UNESCO Chair is to promote an integrated system of research, training, information and documentation related to sustainability for university education.

At the UAMA, the questionnaire was applied directly to participants, and for the LUL via Internet.

The Mexican sample of 82 participants consisted of 15 (19 per cent) students, 40 (49 per cent) faculty members, and 27 (32 per cent) administrators. Average age was 43.7 (ranging from 20 to 78). The sample included 29 (35 per cent) women and 53 (65 per cent) men; 67 participants were born under the Roman Catholic religious denomination, 1 to Calvinists, 10 claimed to be born to non-religious parents, and 3 mentioned 'others'.

The German sample of 40 participants consisted of 30 (15 per cent) students, 7 (17.5 per cent) faculty members, and 2 (5 per cent) administrators. Average age was 27.7 (ranging from 21 to 58). The sample included 29 (72.5 per cent) women, 10 (25 per cent) men, and one participant who did not specify sex. Five participants were born under the Roman Catholic denomination, 15 under the Lutheran, 2 under the Calvinist, and 16 indicated that their parents were non-religious. Participants responded to the questionnaire in approximately 12 minutes; no credit or incentive was offered.

Statistical methods to validate the model of sustainable behaviour

Two statistical methods were used to identify significant relationships among the four latent variables: 1) principal component analysis (PCA) (Basilevsky 1994; Jolliffe 1986), and 2) the Rasch model (RM) (Maydeu-Olivares and Montaño 2013; Scheuthle *et al.* 2005; Rost 1990) based on item response theory (Embretson and Reise 2000; van der Linden 2005).

The PCA technique was used because it conserves much of the original variation of the data upon transforming them into a new group of variables – principal components – which are not correlated among each other but rather are ordered according to the first few variables which maintain the majority of the variation present in all the original variables (Jolliffe 1986). That is, PCA establishes the main factors which underlie a large number of the latent variables considered for this construct and indicates the relationships among these latent variables.

RM describes the non-linear relationship among independent variables, a person's trait score, and item difficulty, combined in an additive manner, and the dependent variable describes the likelihood of a person's response to a specific question. This method was proposed to determine whether differences exist among participants of HEI (students, faculty members and administrators) in the latent variable abilities (interpersonal – directed toward others, as well as intrapersonal – directed toward oneself) associated with the five psychological dimensions of sustainability.

Data analysis

In this study, an exploratory factorial analysis was proposed, as this method does not test the hypothesis by means of a formal significance test; instead, it explores the possibility of a factorial structure which underlies the variables. It provides a large quantity of information that the researcher may use for posterior studies of members of HEI (Brace *et al.* 2006; Gardner 2003; Landeros 2009).

Results

Results reveal a general pattern of the principal latent variables which underlie sustainable behaviour in the three types of university members. Each of the five psychological dimensions of action for sustainability shows differences between the two HEIs, UAMA and LUL, summarised in Table 23.1.

The descriptive statistics in Table 23.1, section A, indicate through the Cronbach's alpha that moderate relationships exist among the four latent variables which explain sustainable behaviour. The value expected for Cronbach's alpha is greater than 0.6 (0.643 for the UAMA and 0.779 for LUL).

The variable ascription of responsibility shows the highest value for Cronbach´s alpha for both universities (0.700 for UAMA and 0.744 for LUL). The other latent variables show moderate and contrasting Cronbach's alpha values; when the alpha in the UAMA increases, in LUL it decreases; none of the alphas is less than 0.541, except the demographic variables (0.001 for UAMA and -0.173 for LUL), which indicates lack of relationship with the other variables.

The communalities, or explicative variance, of sustainable behaviour of Table 23.1, section E, is a very promising value as it indicates values from 0.626 to 0.889 for UAMA and 0.740 to 0.939 for LUL. That is, the values obtained for the explicative variance of the proposed model in this study explain, in an exploratory manner due to the low number of participants, 70 per cent and 75 per cent of sustainable behaviour in UAMA and in LUL, respectively.

Section K of Table 23.1 summarises and highlights the results of the Cronbach's alphas and the communalities between the two universities; component 1 shows that the variable ascription of responsibility is most closely related to the latent variables values and personal intelligences in the two HEI.

Finally, section L of Table 23.1 shows the probabilities calculated with the Rasch model for the items asked of participants. Anticipation appears to be the most unlikely behaviour to be shown by students, faculty members and administrators; effectiveness appears to be the dimension most likely to be shown in universities of nations with a lower socioeconomic level, and austerity appears to be most probable for participants in universities of nations with a higher socioeconomic level. Solidarity and deliberation show intermediate patterns.

Following these results this study proposes a model (see Figure 23.2) which affords greater comprehension of those factors which tend to induce a change toward sustainable behaviour: values, personality traits, and inter- and intrapersonal intelligences. This study may have implications for public policy which influence the field of social psychology, in which contexts of intrapersonal processes and interpersonal relationships are related to intergroup and social behaviours. This study may also provide a process for establishing factors which induce sustainable behaviour in higher education institutions.

Reflections on this study

The emerging construct of sustainable behaviour is elucidated by a model based on valid conceptual frameworks which are guided by principles of Education for Sustainable Development. Importantly these conceptual frameworks reviewed provide a set of declarations which allow for constructing a structure for carrying out systematic studies which statistically determine significant relationships among factors which appear to influence intention and behavioural change in universities around the world.

The proposed model appears to be the first which allows for explaining, measuring and predicting sustainable behaviour of members of HEI, as well as understanding their determinants.

Table 23.1 Summary of outcomes for the two HEI observed

	UAMA CASE	*LULIFUK[1] CASE*
A. Descriptive statistics	Cronbach's alpha for the entire UAMA sample was 0.643, but no squared multiple correlations were found.	Cronbach's alpha for the entire LULIfUK sample was 0.779, but no squared multiple correlations were found.
	In relation to universal values: Cronbach's alpha was 0.670, R2 range was 0.370 to 0.770. Two categories of variables had values in disagreement: variable 12 (Enjoying life) within the hedonism values, variable 10 (Varied life) within the stimulation values, both in the openness to change section; and variable 2 (Influential) within the achievement values in the self-enhancement section. But the three variables are close to each other. Nine variables had values on 'totally agree' score; but the variable with the highest value was variable 9 (Prevention) within the universalism values in the self-transcendence section.	**In relation to universal values:** Cronbach's alpha was 0.732, R2 was 0.464 to 0.891. Two variables had values 'disagree' score, variable 12 (Enjoying life) within the hedonism values and variable 10 (Varied life) within the stimulation values. Both were in the openness change section. Six variables had values within the 'totally agree' score; but variable with the highest value was variable 9 (Prevention) within the universalism values in the self-transcendence section.
	With respect to awareness of consequences: Cronbach's alpha was 0.667, R2 range was 0.164 to 0.573. All variables had scores of 'very serious'. Variable 27 (c Forest plants) had the highest score with the initial factors.	**With respect to awareness of consequences:** Cronbach's alpha was 0.590, R2 range was 0.220 to 0.736. All variables had scores as very serious problem, but variable 27 (c Forestplants) had the highest score with the initial factors.
	With respect to ascription of responsibility: Cronbach's alpha was 0.700, R2 range was 0.240 to 0.705. All variables scored 'totally agree', but the variable most agreed with was 35 (Government 1) within the external locus of control.	**With respect to ascription of responsibility:** Cronbach's alpha was 0.744, R2 range was 0.189 to 0.665. All variables scored 'totally agree', but the variable most agreed with was 39 (Industry) within the external locus of control.
	With respect to personal intelligence: Cronbach's alpha was 0.715, R2 range was 0.127 to 0.728. Variable 54 (Believes capable) is very often achieved and variable 56 (Doubts own ability) is less frequent, both in the effectiveness dimension.	**With respect to personal intelligence:** Cronbach's alpha was 0.541, R2 range was 0.364 to 0.725. Variable 50 (Keeps promises), in the austerity dimension, was very often achieved, and variable 49 (Personally leads), in the anticipation dimension, was less frequent.
	With respect to demographics: Cronbach's alpha was 0.001, R2 range was 0.049 to 0.358.	**With respect to demographics:** Cronbach's alpha was -0.173. The value is negative due a negative average covariance among items.

Table 23.1 continued

	UAMA CASE	*LULIFUK[1] CASE*
B. Matrix of correlation	18 correlations were above the 0.445 cut-off.	64 correlations were above the 0.445 cut-off.
C. Kaiser-Meyer-Olkin measure and Bartlett's Test of Sphericity	KMO measure for the entire UAMA sample was 0.066. KMO for universal values was 0.602. KMO for awareness of consequences was 0.536. KMO for ascription of responsibility was 0.539. KMO for personal intelligences was 0.738. KMO for demographics was 0.481. Bartlett's test was $p<0.05$ in all cases.	No KMO for the entire LULIfUK sample. KMO for universal values was 0.561. KMO for awareness of consequences was 0.511. KMO for ascription of responsibility was 0.623. KMO for personal intelligences was 0.524. KMO for demographics was 0.645. Bartlett's test was $p<0.05$ in all cases.
D. Anti-images matrices	On–diagonal values for the anti-image correlation were very low.	No anti-image matrices. Number of participants was under 40.
E. Communalities	Three variables had values above 0.600, 28 above 0.700, and 34 above 0.800. Variable 36 (Government 2) had the highest communalities (0.889) and variable 59 (Changes strategy) the lowest (0.626).	Nine variables had values above 0.700, 39 above 0.800, and 17 above 0.900. Variable 22 (a Climate you) had the highest communalities (0.939) and variable 42 (Solicits input) the lowest (0.740).
F. Total explained variance	Explained variance was 79.78% and 21 factors were extracted.	Explained variance was 86.68% and 18 factors were extracted.
G. Scree plot	21 factors were detected in the graph.	17 factors were detected in the graph.
H. Component matrix	46 correlations (either positive or negative) were above 0.445.	64 correlations (either positive or negative) were above 0.445.
I. Matrix of residual correlation	The matrix presents 250 values (12%) which exceeded 0.05.	The matrix presents 238 values (11%) which exceeded 0.05.
J. Matrix of rotated factors	No matrix of rotated factors was obtained after 25 iterations.	No matrix of rotated factors was obtained after 25 iterations.

Table 23.1 continued

	UAMA CASE	*LULIFUK[1] CASE*
K. Pattern of components and latent variables	**Component 1:** middle values were shown for ascription of responsibility (AR) and personal intelligences (PI); lower values were shown for a mix of four latent variables: universal values (UV) and PI, AR and awareness of consequences (AC).	**Component 1:** higher values were shown for values ascription of responsibility (AR) and universal values (UV), middle values for awareness of consequences (AC) and AR, lower values for PI and UV.
	Component 2: UV and PI were mainly related to this component.	**Component 2:** higher values were shown for PI and UV, middle values for AC and UV, lower values for a mix of 4 main latent variables.
	Component 3: higher value was shown for awareness of consequences (AC), PI and UV: middle values for the same combination, and lower values for PI and demographics (D).	**Component 3:** UV and PI were mainly related to this component.
	Component 4: higher values were shown for UV, D, middle values for awareness of consequences (AC), and lower values for PI and UV.	**Component 4:** higher values were shown for demographics (D), AR, middle values for PI, UV, D and AR, lower values for PI and AR.
L. Probability of observed item and actor pattern	'Solidarity' and 'Anticipation' dimensions had the least common trait levels, and are the least likely behaviours. 'Anticipation' was the least common among the three types of participants considered. The 'Austerity' and 'Deliberation' dimension had intermediate probability values and 'Effectiveness' dimension was the most likely sustainable behaviour achieved by students (10 individuals).	'Solidarity' and 'Anticipation' had the least common trait levels, and these are the least likely behaviours. 'Anticipation' was the least likely among the three types of participants considered. 'Effectiveness' and 'Deliberation' had intermediate probability values and 'Austerity' was the most likely sustainable behaviour achieved by staff (2 individuals).

Note: 1.Leuphana Universität Lüneburg, Institute für UnweltKommunication.

This model differs from others as it takes into account the complete range of universal values found throughout the world, as well as human abilities which are found in all cultures. Critically for the first time, the five psychological dimensions of sustainable action are tested; differences are found between two HEI in different nations, albeit in an exploratory manner.

However, results of the relationships among latent variables of the PCA were lower than expected due to the fact that in calculating the matrix of correlation, the value selected (0.445) was higher than that recommended by the literature (0.300). This higher value selected lowers the confidence level. Although in future studies using the recommend value of 0.300, it could be expected that outcomes would be within the confidence level.

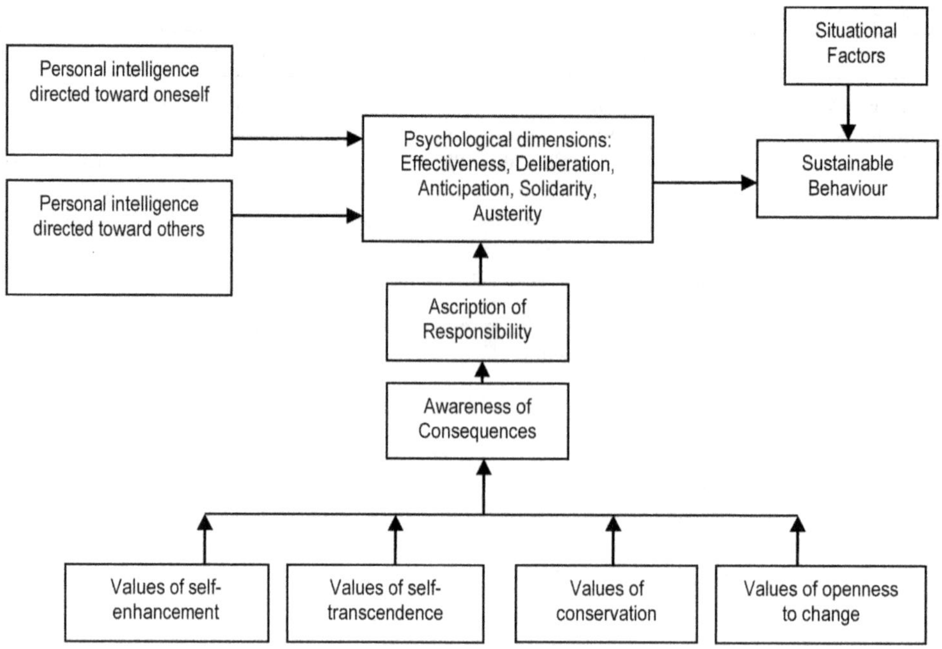

Figure 23.2 Proposed model for explaining sustainable behaviour
Source: adapted from Juárez-Nájera *et al.* 2010

Based on the two data sets the behavioural variance appears to explain sustainable behaviour of individuals around the world to a greater extent than any other study thus far, although the sample size (less than 100 in each HEI) is insufficient to be conclusive according to the literature on the topic.

Also, while this exploratory procedure seeks to identify underlying factors of correlation, additional research and analysis would be required to confirm such factors, and that research should aim to increase the number of participants as well as including participants from a larger range of HEIs.

Clearly sustainable behaviour is difficult to predict due to the multiple factors involved. Designing a model is a complex task which requires conceptual frameworks, as well as knowledge of regarding statistical tools which support the findings.

As we wish to have HEI embrace Education for Sustainable Development it is important that members of a university community should identify the determinants which induce sustainable behaviour, so as to promote programmes of teaching, research, extension, together with campus administration which promotes sustainable community development. Achieving this sort of change is not a simple task, since inducing change toward sustainable behaviour is a complex action which requires participation of the institution's community to introduce policies which facilitate psychosocial capacities to generate synergies, promote exchange of information, and create mechanisms which lead to a shared vision with common goals.

References

Aiken, L.R., 1997. *Questionnaires and Inventories: Surveying Opinions and Assessing Personalities.* New York: John Wiley and Sons.

Ajzen, I., 1991. 'The Theory of Planned Behavior', *Organizational Behavior and Human Decision Process*, 50(2), 179–211.

Ajzen, I., 2005. *Attitudes, Personality and Behavior.* 2nd Edn. London: McGraw-Hills International.

Aronson, E., Wilson, T.D., Akert, R.M. and Fehr, B., 2009. *Social Psychology*, 4th Edn. Toronto: Pearson.

Axelrod, L. and Lehman, D., 1993. 'Responding to Environmental Concerns: What Factors Guide Individual Action?', *Journal of Environmental Psychology*, 13(2), 149–59.

Bamberg, S. and Möser, G., 2007. 'Twenty years after Hines, Hungerford, and Tomera: A New Meta-analysis of Psycho-social Determinants of Pro-environmental Behavior', *Journal of Environmental Psychology*, 27, 14–25.

Bartholomew, D.J., 1987. *Latent Variable Models and Factor Analysis.* London: Charles Griffin & Company LTD; New York: Oxford University Press.

Basilevsky, A., 1994. *Statistical Factor Analysis and Related Methods. Theory and Applications.* Shewhart, W.A. and Wilks, S.S. (eds), *Wiley Series in Probability and Mathematical Statistics.* New York: John Wiley & Sons.

Berry, J.W., Poortinga, Y.H., Segall, M.H. and Dasen, P.R., 2002. *Cross-Cultural Psychology: Research and Applications*, 2nd Edn. Cambridge: Cambridge University Press.

Blamey, R., 1998. 'The Activation of Environmental Norms, Extending Schwartz's Model', *Environment and Behavior*, 30(5), 676–708.

Boyatzis, Goleman, and Hay Acquisition Co. Inc., 2002. *Inventario de competencias emocionales [Inventory of emotional competences].* New York: HayGroup.

Brace, N., Kemp, R. and Snelgar, R., 2006. *SPSS for Psychologists: A Guide to Data Analysis using SPSS for Windows Version 12 & 13.* New York: Palgrave Macmillan.

Converse, J.M. and Presser, S., 1988. *Survey Questions. Handcrafting the Standardized Questionnaire*, 2nd Printing. University Press series no. 07-063. Beverly Hills, CA: Sage.

Corral-Verdugo, V., 2001. *Comportamiento Proambiental. Una introducción al estudio de las conductas protectoras del ambiente [Pro-environmental behavior. An introduction to the study of environmental conservation behavior].* Canarias: Editorial Resma.

Corral-Verdugo, V., 2010. *Psicología de la sustentabilidad: un análisis que nos hace pro ecológicos y pro sociales [Psychology of sustainability: an analysis that makes us ecological and social pro].* Mexico: Trillas.

Corral-Verdugo, V. and Pinheiro, J., 2004. 'Aproximaciones al estudio de la conducta sustentable' [Approaches to the study of sustainable behavior], *Medio Ambiente y Comportamiento Humano*, 5(1–2), 1–26.

Embretson, S.E. and Reise, S.P., 2000. *Item Response Theory for Psychologist.* Mahwah, NJ: Lawrence Erlbaum Associates.

Gardner, H., 2001. *Estructuras de la Mente. La teoría de las inteligencias múltiples [Frames of Mind: The Theory of Multiple Intelligences]*, 2nd Edn. Mexico: Fondo de Cultura Económica.

Gardner, R.C., 2003. *Estadística para Psicología usando SPSS para Windows [Statistics for Psychology using SPSS for Windows].* Mexico: Prentice Hall.

Hardin, G., 1968. 'The Tragedy of the Commons', *Science*, 13 December, 162(3859), 1243–8.

Harland, P., 2001. 'Pro-environmental Behavior'. Doctoral Thesis. Faculteit der Wiskunde en Natuurwetenschappen en die der Geneeskunde [Faculty of Science and Medicine], Universiteit Leiden, The Netherlands.

Henerson, M.E., Morris, L.L. and Fitz-Gibbon, C.T., 1991. *How to Measure Attitudes*, 2nd Edn. New York: Sage Publication.

Hines, J.M., Hungerford, H.R. and Tomera. A.N., 1987. 'Analysis and Synthesis of Research on Responsible Environmental Behavior: A Meta-Analysis', *Journal of Environmental Education*, 18(2), 1–8.

Jolliffe, I.T., 1986. *Principal Component Analysis.* Brillinger, D., Fienberg, S., Gani, J., Hartigan, J. and Krickeberg, K. (Advisors), *Springer Series in Statistics.* New York: Springer-Verlag.

Juárez-Nájera, M., Dieleman, H. and Turpin-Marion, S., 2006. 'Sustainability in Mexican Higher Education, Towards a New Academic and Professional Culture', *Journal of Cleaner Production*, 14(9–11), 1028–38.

Juárez-Nájera, M., Rivera-Martínez, J.G. and Hafkamp, W.A., 2010. 'An Explorative Socio-psychological Model for Determining Sustainable Behavior: Pilot Study in German and Mexican Universities', *Journal of Cleaner Production*, 18(7), 686–94.

Kaiser, F.G., Hübner, G. and Bogner, F., 2005. 'Contrasting the Theory of Planned Behavior with the Value-Belief-Norm Model in Explaining Conservation Behavior', *Journal of Applied Social Psychology*, 35(10), 2150–70.

Kollock, P., 1998. 'Social Dilemmas: The Anatomy of Cooperation', *Annual Review of Sociology* 24, 183–214.

Kruglanski, A.W. and Higgins, E.T. (eds), 2003. *Social Psychology. General Reader*. New York: Psychology Press.

Landeros, R., 2009. *Estadística con SPSS y metodología de la investigación [Statistics with SPSS and research methodology]*. Reimpr. México: Trillas.

Leahey, T.H. and Harris, R.J., 2001. *Aprendizaje y cognición [Learning and Cognition]*. 4a. Edición. Madrid: Prentice Hall.

Ligtvoet, R., Van der Ark, L.A., Bergsma, W.P. and Sijtsma, K., 2011. 'Polytomous Latent Scales for the Investigation of the Ordering of Items', *Psychometrika*, 76(2), 200–16.

McDonald, R.P., 2011. 'Measuring Latent Quantities', *Psychometrika*, 76(4), 511–36.

Macy, M.M. and Flache, A., 2002. 'Learning Dynamics in Social Dilemmas', *PNAS*, 99(3) (14 May), 7229–36.

Matthews, G., Davis, R., Westman, S.J. and Stammers, R., 2000. *Human Performance: Cognition, Stress and Individual Differences*. Sussex: Psychology Press.

Maydeu-Olivares, A. and Montaño, R., 2013. 'How Should We Assess the Fit of Rasch-type Models? Approximating the Power of Goodness-of-Fit Statistics in Categorical Data Analysis', *Psychometrika*, 78(1), 116–33.

Myers, D.G., 2007. *Exploring Social Psychology*, 4th Edn. Boston, MA: McGraw-Hill.

Neuhouser, F., 2008. *Rousseau's Theodicy of Self-love. Evil, Rationality, and the Drive for Recognition*. New York: Oxford University Press.

Rokeach, M., 1973. *The Nature of Human Value*. New York: Free Press.

Rost, J., 1990. 'Rasch Models in Latent Classes: An Integration of Two Approaches to Item Analysis', *Applied Psychological Measurement*, 14(3) (September), 271–82.

Rousseau, J.J., 2001. *Discurso sobre el origen de la desigualdad entre los hombres [Discourse on the Origin and Basis of Inequality Among Men]*. Madrid: Diana.

Scheuthle, H., Carabias-Hütter, V. and Kaiser, F.G., 2005. 'The Motivational and Instantaneous Behavior Effects of Contexts: Step toward a Theory of Goal-Directed Behavior', *Journal of Applied Social Psychology*, 35(10), 2076–93.

Schwartz, S.H., 1977. 'Normative Influences on Altruism', in L. Berkowitz (ed.), *Advances in Experimental Social Psychology*. New York: Academic Press, Ch.10, 221–79.

Schwartz, S.H., 1994. 'Are There Universal Aspects in the Structure and Contents of Human Values?', *Journal of Social Issues*, 50(4), 19–45.

Smith, E.R. and Mackie, D.M., 2007. *Social Psychology*, 3rd Edn. New York: Psychology Press.

Stern, P.C., 2000. 'Toward a Coherent Theory of Environmentally Significant Behavior', *Journal of Social Issues*, 56(3), 407–24.

Stern, P.C., Dietz, T., Abel, T., Guagnano, G.A. and Kalof, L., 1999. 'A Value-Belief-Norm Theory of Support for Social Movements: The Case of Environmentalism', *Human Ecology Review*, 6(2), 81–97.

UN (United Nations), 1987. 'Report of the United Nations General Assembly. Forty-second session. Item 83 (e) of the provisional agenda. Development and International Economic Co-operation: Environment. Report of the World Commission on Environment and Development. A/42/427. Annex: "Our Common Future"'. www.un-documents.net/wced-ocf.htm [accessed 10 February 2015].

UNEP (United Nations Environment Programme), 2011. *Visions for Change: Recommendations for Effective Policies on Sustainable Lifestyles*. Nairobi: UNEP.

UNESCO (United Nations Educational, Scientific and Cultural Organization), 2005. 'Report by the Director-General on the United Nations of Education for Sustainable Development: Draft International Implementation Scheme and UNESCO'S contribution to the implementation of the Decade (2005–2014). Hundred and seventy-second session'. Paris: UNESCO August 2005. http://unesdoc.unesco.org/images/0014/001403/140372e.pdf [accessed 10 Febraury 2015].

UNESCO (United Nations Educational, Scientific and Cultural Organization), 2009. 'Bonn Declaration'. UNESCO World Conference on Education for Sustainable Development, 31 March – 2 April 2009. Bonn: UNESCO. www.esd-world-conference-2009.org/fileadmin/download/ESD2009_Bonn Declaration080409.pdf [accessed 10 February 2015].

UNESCO (United Nations Educational, Scientific and Cultural Organization), 2012. *Shaping the Education of Tomorrow: 2012 Full-length Report on the UN Decade of Education for Sustainable Development.* DESD Monitoring & Evaluation. Paris: UNESCO Education Sector.

Van der Linden, W.J., 2005. ‚Linear Models for Optimal Test Design', in Fienberg, S.E. and Van der Linden, W.J. (Advisors), *Statistics for Social and Behavioral Sciences Series.* New York: Springer Science+Business Media, Inc., 1–32.

von Eckardt, B., 1996. *What is Cognitive Science?* Cambridge, MA: The MIT Press.

24

EDUCATION FOR SUSTAINABLE DEVELOPMENT AND CURRICULAR GREENING OF UNDERGRADUATE COURSES

Trends in Brazilian research (1987–2009)

Jorge Megid Neto and Juliana Rink

Introduction

Training of teachers to act as agents in bringing about current social changes has been regarded as a worldwide priority (UNESCO 2004). Against a background of Education for Sustainable Development (ESD), there is a debate about teacher training. According to Leff (2001), ESD should feature in an interdisciplinary, cross-sectional and holistic way in both formal and non-formal education and thus become a key factor in the search for sustainability. Undergraduate courses have an important role in training professionals who will work in ESD. There are several studies dealing with environmental issues in Bachelor and Technology degree courses, including areas not traditionally linked to ESD, such as biology and geography (Kawasaki *et al.* 2009).

According to Grindsted (2011), several statements on Higher Education for Sustainable Development (HESD) were formulated. These statements have promoted progress and implementation of ESD in higher education institutions, enabling the creation of networks (Gutiérrez and González 2005) and expanding academic research (Adomßent *et al.* 2014), especially in Europe, North America and Australia (Barth and Rieckmann 2013; Stevenson *et al.* 2013). As a result, there has been a significant growth of academic research into Environmental Education (EE)[1] and this was particularly striking at the beginning of the 1990s. It is estimated that there were more than 3,000 dissertations and theses on EE produced in Brazil between 1987 and 2012 (Megid Neto 2010; Carvalho *et al.* 2013). However, such output is not studied as a whole and their findings cannot contribute to the transformation of formal or non-formal ESD. This lack of review on research in Higher Education for Sustainable Development (HESD) is also mentioned by Barth and Rieckmann (2013); and in this Handbook, Chapter 7. Thus, this research aims at analysing what has been produced on curricular greening of undergraduate courses, between 1987 and 2009. We will examine the main pedagogical and curricular trends appointed by these studies.

This research is closely linked to the *EArte Project – Environmental Education in Brazil: An*

Analysis of Academic Studies (Dissertations and Theses), developed by research groups from three Brazilian public universities: São Paulo State University (UNESP), University of Campinas (UNICAMP) and University of São Paulo (USP). The project involved a survey of theses and dissertations produced in Brazil on EE and the development of an analytical catalogue of this production together with several meta-analytical studies (Carvalho *et al.* 2013).

ESD on curricular greening of undergraduate education and theoretical framework

It is recognised that inter-governmental meetings are political and epistemological signs of the importance attached to ESD, and that these are encouraging initiatives on a global scale. For Junyent *et al.* (2003), international conferences reveal trends, and significant political and epistemological stances, which can provide guidance for agendas and international activities on Higher Education. Between 2001 and 2010, HESD began to feature more prominently in official documents (Wright 2002) and strong encouragement was given to setting up inter-institutional teams and networks.

Ibero-American universities networks – ACES,[2] OIUDSMA,[3] UNESCO Network for Reorienting Teacher Education to Address Sustainability – are some examples of these activities in HESD (Gutiérrez and Gonzáles 2005). Information made available by the REBEA[4] shows that there are more than 40 networks, some of which are specifically concerned with Higher Education. Among several initiatives referred to above, it is worth drawing attention to the ACES network.

After being set up in 2000, this network held meetings and issued publications on greening the curriculum in Higher Education with the aim of establishing mechanisms and strategies to investigate the degree to which environmental studies play a role in universities (Junyent *et al.* 2002: 10).

A capital referential built by the ACES network was ten characteristics for a study with environmental aspects, represented in a Circular Diagram which can be divided into the following components: Commitment to a change in the relations between society and nature; Complexity; Disciplinary order: flexibility and permeability; Local-global-local context; Taking account of the subject in the construction of knowledge; Considering the cognitive and affective aspects of people; Cohesion and reconstruction between theory and practice; Prospective guidance to alternative scenarios; Methodological accuracy; Space for reflection and democratic participation (Junyent *et al.* 2003: 42).

Each group within the Network can adjust the Diagram to the particular context of their own university. For example, researchers attached to UNESP restructured the ten indicators into four main groupings (Carvalho *et al.* 2003: 118):

a) Relationship between the course and complex reality (social/economic/ecological/cultural/technological): this encompasses the contextualisation of the curriculum, its guiding principles, and the inclusion of local and global problems, as well as a systematic analysis of the relationship between course and reality.
b) Structuring and organisation of the curriculum (flexibility and permeability): this covers aspects of disciplinary order such as inclusion of compulsory and optional subjects; involvement of professionals from different areas of knowledge in forming and planning of curriculum; inclusion of interdisciplinary activities; and interaction between courses and intra/extra class subjects or activities. It also encompasses the participation of the teaching staff and students in defining the content, planning and work required to complete the

course. This involves having both an ethical and aesthetic dimension in activities that are carried out.

c) Methodological accuracy (coherence and articulation between theory and practice): this involves analysing the degree of compatibility between practical work and theoretical ideas, and between institutional discourse and teaching with regard to practices carried out (assessment, teaching plans, pedagogical projects). It also covers the merging of content and methodology, as well as employing participative methodological systems.

d) Action and intervention (space for reflection and participation, commitment to a change in social and environmental relations): this provides guidance for prospective alternative scenarios (new forms of technology, and commitment to training teachers and future generations); creation of space for shared participation and collaboration between teachers and students in classroom; and lines of research aimed at including environmental issues in courses and the institution.

Thus we decided to make use of the four groupings of Carvalho *et al.* (2003) as *categories for the analysis of curricular greening* in studies selected. It was also judged to be necessary to outline the conceptions of *Environmental Education*, *Environment* and *Curriculum* that are found in these academic studies and these features have thus been included as analytical categories which will later be explored in greater detail.

Methodology and stages of research

State-of-the-art studies or bibliographical reviews have been usual in American scientific literature for several decades (Brandão 1984). In Brazil, the first state-of-the-art studies in education only began to appear in the 1970s (Megid Neto 2010). These studies consist of an evaluative kind of documentary research (Gay 1981) and allow a balance to be struck with the degree of knowledge attained in a particular area within an established period. Studies of this kind allow researchers to identify trends of the production of research, as well as factors that have not been explored and possible limitations, which might suggest the need for new areas for investigation. In short, state-of-the-art research comprises:

> descriptive-analytical and evaluative inventories of what is produced in a particular field of knowledge. It seeks to identify and describe the works selected, analyze their features and tendencies, seek evidence of any progress made in the form of contributions or unforeseen gaps in knowledge and finally to understand and assess the research field in question from a theoretical-epistemological, historical and methodological standpoint, among other factors. Depending on the ultimate goals of the investigation, the degree of depth sought by the researcher and the complexity of the object of the study, this kind of research can be shaped in way that is a more panoramic and descriptive-analytical of its main characteristics and tendencies or else in terms of the more comprehensive-evaluative nature of the chosen field of research.
>
> *(Fernandes and Megid Neto 2012: 653)*

This kind of research has been undertaken in Brazil by making use of various sources such as articles in scientific journals, abstracts or completed studies published in scientific annals, dissertations and theses. In relation to EE or ESD, Lorenzetti and Delizoicov (2007), Carvalho (2008), Kawasaki *et al.* (2009) and Rink (2009) have contributed.

It should also be stressed that analytical catalogues have acquired importance for state-of-the-art research. With regard to studies on EE, one we have come across is the project called *What we Know about Environmental Education in Brazil: An Analysis of Academic Works* compiled by Hilário Fracalanza, from the Faculty of Education at UNICAMP (Megid Neto 2010). In 2008, this work was transformed into the EArte Project.

In the light of previous considerations, the central concern of this study is to investigate which curricular greening is revealed in Brazilian dissertations and theses on EE (or ESD) that were produced between 1987 and 2009, and which investigate the initial training or courses for teachers and other professionals.

The EArte Project Catalogue is used as a main source for identifying the dissertations and theses. The search for studies to compile the catalogue was held in March 2011, directly at the database of the *Coordenadoria de Aperfeiçoamento de Pessoal do Ensino Superior* (CAPES).[5] This database contains information of the dissertations and theses, such as author, title, supervisor, institution, year of submission, abstract and keywords among other factors. Unfortunately, it does not provide the full text of the studies.

After several exploratory searches through the keywords, we decided to use the expression *educ* environment** as keyword for the search, which would cover the following set of words: *education, educative, educational or educator,* and *environment, environmental, environmentalism* among others. Owing to the historical period in which the survey was conducted, we decided to map the studies that were presented to the examining board between 1987 (the first record of theses and dissertations stored in the CAPES database) and 2009. Not all the data related to 2010 had been included in the database at the time of the consultation. In this way, 8,437 references to theses and dissertations were obtained.

Following this, we read through all the titles and abstracts with a view to eliminating any studies that did not involve conducting research into EE. The 8,437 studies were handed out to pairs of researchers who then undertook the task of inclusion or exclusion by means of a 'double-blind' system. If there were any divergences, a third researcher carried out the classification. In this way, there remained 2,151 studies.

The selection of studies which addressed the question of greening the curriculum in initial training courses for teachers and other professionals was undertaken by the authors of this study and, to start with, entailed conducting searches through the keywords based on the titles and abstracts available in the EArte Project Catalogue. The keywords used for the search were as follows: 'teacher-training', 'initial training', 'training of educators', 'training of agents', 'curricular greening' and 'curriculum'.

The search yielded 516 references although a sizeable number of these were concerned with continuous training for teachers. Following a further reading of the abstracts, 71 dissertations and 14 theses were selected, which addressed the question of curricular *environmentalisation* in initial training courses of teachers and/or environmental educators.

We configured a set of descriptors (or indicators) for the classification and analysis of 85 studies and this enabled aspects of the curricular-environmental basis of the selected works to be analysed as follows:

a) *Conception of Environment* – abiotic environment; abiotic + biotic environment without presence of mankind; integrated environment + utilitarian perspective; integrated environment: natural, social, multidisciplinary and interdependent.
b) *Conception of Environmental Education* – Conservationist; Pragmatic; Critical (Layrargues and Lima 2011).
c) *Conception of Curriculum* – Traditional; Critical; Post-critical (Silva 2004).

d) *Features of Curricular Greening* – Relation between course and complex reality; Structuring and organisation of the Curriculum; Methodological accuracy; Action and intervention (Carvalho *et al.* 2003).

The classification and analysis of the 85 studies was carried out through a reading of the full text of the studies. During the reading, we sought to detect features that had been made explicit by the respective authors of the studies and which could allow us to make a classification in accordance with the descriptors that had been laid down. To a certain extent, we employed the content analysis technique (Bardin 2011), by regarding the descriptors referred to above, as 'previous analytical categories', with their sub-descriptors being recorded as units included in areas of the text where they appear. Setting out from the use of particular applications, a number of tables, spreadsheets and graphs were created to systematise the data and obtain results with regard to the features and patterns of what was produced.

Features and patterns of the 85 research studies identified

The first studies that were retrieved were submitted to the Examination Board in 1995 and where there was an increase after 2000. These results were in accordance with the encouragement given to the environmentalism of the courses at the university which were a historical landmark; moreover, they complied with the international and national regulations of the EE, as set out in the studies of Wright (2002); Sterling and Scott (2008) and Grindsted (2011)

With regard to *modality of the course,* 50.6 per cent of the studies involve undergraduate degree courses. The bachelor degree is undertaken by slightly fewer than 40 per cent of the total number of studies.

Regarding *curricular areas*, most of the studies were developed in Biological Sciences and Pedagogy degree courses (35.3 per cent and 21.2 per cent respectively) while 16.5 per cent were in Health and 9.4 per cent in Geography.

Diagnostic studies of courses or particular subjects were found in 71 documents (83.5 per cent). These largely consist of degree courses which investigated EE in real circumstances of a course or in a set of subjects. Ten studies (11.8 per cent) were classified as *Proposition, application and evaluation of courses or subjects* and these sought to include environmental issues and discussions arising from the curriculum of the courses involved. Three studies involved a *discussion of basic theoretical-methodological principles for planning or courses* of EE in higher education.

With respect to the *conception of Environment*, most of the analysed studies address this in a view of the abiotic environment, which excludes the human kind as an integral part.

With regard to the *conception of Environmental Education*, 40 studies (47.1 per cent) had a *conservative* conception of EE by adopting the categorising system of Layrargues and Lima (2011). This is regarded as an educational practice, which aims at arousing human awareness of nature and is governed by a heightened consciousness of 'ecology'; moreover, it is linked to a conservative view of EE. Gonzales-Gaudiano (2005) states that the strongly conservative trend, which is characterised by a desire to include content, has been overvalued in the curriculum of initial training courses. This is largely because it has been regarded as easy to put into effect by making rigorous changes without any major restructuring of the Higher Education curriculum.

A *pragmatic* conception was found in 24 studies (28.2 per cent). These have an anthropocentric and behaviourist character and are concerned with resolving immediate environmental problems. They share a view that there is a close relationship between access to environmental knowledge and changes in the behaviour of professionals undergoing training.

Finally, 21 documents (24.7 per cent) were classified in the *critical* category. Here is a conception of environment that is integrated, multidisciplinary and interdependent and sets out from the assumption that mankind is a part of nature and both are intertwined.

With regard to the *conception of curriculum*, we employ the categorisation of Silva (2004). The *traditional* conception was found in a little over 95 per cent of the studies, and these include features that enable one to regard the curriculum as an expression of academic subjects, where the content material is handled in a fragmentary manner. This result is disturbing since it reveals a trend in research to treat EE as something which must be 'naturalized' in the training of environmental teachers and educators, since its importance in addressing current challenges is to endow them with legitimacy.

The *critical* conception was found in three studies (3.5 per cent). In these studies, the curriculum is often contextualised as an artefact of struggle and conflict from a perspective of power relations. These studies discuss the role of the universities, together with the profiles of their students, lecturers, directors and in some cases, the surrounding community. ESD is not regarded as a theoretical framework that is required for the professional training of the students but rather as a critical educational dimension that can foster the training of a future professional by providing a new awareness of environmental issues as representing a complex reality (Loureiro 2006).

Only one study was classified as a *post-critical* conception of curriculum. This highlights the cultural diversity of the university world and recognises it as a privileged space for the development of critical EE, including discussions about inclusion, gender, sexuality and ethnic questions.

Finally, we examined the *features of curricular greening,* where the studies were analysed in accordance with the four groupings of Carvalho *et al.* (2003).

Most of the studies which investigated degree courses and bachelor courses carried out diagnostic studies of courses and subjects. A small proportion of studies include discussions that recognise the value of the path followed by teachers in including ESD in higher education and the question of vocational aims of the university and the profile of the professionals they seek to train. Along general lines, the studies show a lack of theoretical benchmarks for the curricular field and have little discussion on training, or of the real world of the courses or universities. Unfortunately, the view of curricular greening that can be found in this documentary material treats EE as content and recommends that it should be included in specific subjects in the curriculum of courses.

In summary, the set of research studies provide evidence that there is a strong trend to treat environmental issues as a discipline in initial training courses and this reveals the restricted extent to which this incorporation takes place in Higher Education. In any event, as in Moore (2005), we also found a number of constraints linked to institutional conditional factors that definitely encourages a superficial approach. This is entirely circumscribed by a disciplinary sphere and has a technical bias together with the conservative and pragmatic perspectives of EE. This is possibly because it is difficult to establish the necessary conditions that are required to attain a critical perspective (with a collective and integrating character, complex ideas and interdisciplinarity).

Final considerations

This study reveals a panorama where: a) there has been a growth in the number of research documents on curricular greening during initial teacher-training courses, with a notable increase at the beginning of the 2000s; b) most of the papers are concerned with teacher training courses, predominantly in Biological Sciences and Pedagogy; c) most of the studies involve diagnoses of courses or specific subjects; d) few studies implement and evaluate curricular proposals; e) most ideas about curriculum still involve a conservative conception of environment; f) few studies adopt an ESD (or EE) critical perspective.

It should be pointed out that ESD research in Brazil is relatively recent and studies on curriculum and sustainable development in higher education have emerged from a scenario in which the epistemological foundations are still being established. It is possible to notice some effort from Brazilian universities to insert environmental education in undergraduate courses; however, there is a need to overcome a certain tendency to break up subjects or create courses, which can be observed in most studies discussed here.

With regard to possible difficulties faced by the state-of-the-art research underlying dissertations and theses, it is a daunting task to obtain a complete text of these kinds of academic studies. Either because the studies are relatively unknown or because they have not been made available in digital libraries, it is only possible to find a sample of research in the libraries of universities where it was carried out. This scenario has improved in the last three or four years, since it is estimates that about 70–80 per cent of the Brazilian studies are available in the internet.

Another warning is the difficulty of establishing a set of descriptors that enable deep understanding of the phenomenon of curriculum greening in higher education. A deep search in the field's literature and other state-of-the-art studies may help to make this process easier. An initial and exploratory investigation of a study's sample and further revision of the initial set of descriptors could also assist. The researcher should strive to define descriptors in the exploratory phase, in order to avoid reaching the final stage of analysis and classification of studies and be faced with the absence of a relevant descriptor. This situation would imply a return to reading again all selected documents.

For further research, we believe that it would be interesting to identify those studies that have investigated the curriculum greening across the campus (including initiatives promoted by institutions, involving teaching, research, extension and management areas). Furthermore, a comparative study of dissertations and theses about ESD in higher education in other countries would also be interesting. However, the difficulty in getting access to international material needs to be overcome.

Notes

1 In Brazil, the term 'Environmental Education' continues to be employed rather than 'Education for Sustainable Development', which has only recently become widespread. Gough (2013) points out that the change of EE to ESD caused controversy but was reinforced by the declaration of Johannesburg (2002), when the launch of the United Nations Decade on ESD occurred.

2 Rede Ambientalização Curricular no Ensino Superior [Network for Curricular Environmentalisation of Higher Education].

3 Organización Internacional de Universidades por el Desarrollo Sostenible y Medio Ambiente [International Organization of Universities for Sustainable Development and Environment].

4 Rede Brasileira de Educação Ambiental [Brazilian Network of Environmental Education].

5 CAPES is a Brazilian Federal agency that provides support of post-graduate education.

References

Adomßent, M., Fischer, D., Godemann, J., Herzig, C., Otte, I., Rieckmann, M. and Timm, J., 2014. 'Emerging Areas in Research on Higher Education for Sustainable Development – Management Education, Sustainable Consumption and Perspectives from Central and Eastern Europe', *Journal of Cleaner Production*, 62(1), 1–7.

Bardin, L., 2011. *Análise de conteúdo*. Lisboa: Edições 70.

Barth, M. and Rieckmann, M., 2013. 'A Review on Research in Higher Education for Sustainable Development'. Paper presented at the 7th World Environmental Education Congress, Marrakech, Morocco, 9–14 June. www.weec2013.org/adminweec/UserFiles/ABSTRACT/365_presentation.pdf (accessed 10 February 2015).

Brandão, C.R., 1984. *Educação Popular*. São Paulo: Brasilien, 1984.

Carvalho, I.C.M., 2008. 'Mapeando a educação ambiental desde uma pesquisa em rede', *Revista Brasileira de Educação Ambiental*, II(3), 34–49.

Carvalho, L.M. *et al.*, 2013. *Relatório do Projeto A Educação Ambiental no Brasil: análise da produção acadêmica (dissertações e teses)*. Rio Claro, SP: UNESP/UNICAMP/USP/UFSCar.

Carvalho, L.M., Cavalari, R.M.F. and Santana, L.C., 2003. 'O Processo de ambientalização curricular da UNESP-Campus de Rio Claro: diagnóstico e perspectivas', in Junyent, M., Geli, A.M. and Arbat, E. (orgs.), *Ambientalización Curricular de los Estudios Superiores, Vol. 3, Servei de Publicaciones*. Girona: Universitat de Girona, 171–207.

Fernandes, R.C.A. and Megid Neto, J., 2012. 'Modelos educacionais em 30 pesquisas sobre práticas pedagógicas no ensino de ciências nos anos iniciais da escolarização', *Investigações em Ensino de Ciências*, 17(3), 641–62.

Gay, L.R., 1981. *Educational Research: Competencies for Analysis & Application*. Columbus, OH: Charles E. Merrill Publishing.

Gonzales-Gaudiano, E., 2005. 'Interdisciplinaridade e educação ambiental: explorando novos territórios epistêmicos', in Sato, M. and Carvalho, I.C.S. (Orgs), *A educação ambiental: pesquisas e desafios*. Porto Alegre: Artmed, 119–33.

Gough, A., 2013. 'The Emergence of Environmental Education Research: A "History" of the Field', in Stevenson, Robert B., Brody, Michael, Dillon, Justin and Wals, A.E.J. (eds), *International Handbook of Research on Environmental Education*. New York: Routledge, 13–22.

Grindsted, T.S., 2011. 'Sustainable Universities: From Declarations on Sustainability in Higher Education to National Law', *Environmental Economics*, 2(2), 29–36.

Gutiérrez, J. and González, A., 2005. 'Ambientalizar la universidad: un reto institucional Para el aseguramiento de la calidad en los ámbitos curriculares y de la gestión', *Revista Iberoamericana de Educación*, 35(6), 5–66.

Junyent, M., Geli, A.M. and Arbat, E. (orgs), 2002. *Ambientalización Curricular de los Estudios Superiores*, v.2. Girona: Universitat de Girona, Servei de Publicaciones.

Junyent, M., Geli, A.M. and Arbat, E. (orgs), 2003. *Ambientalización Curricular de los Estudios Superiores*, v.3. Girona: Universitat de Girona, Servei de Publicaciones.

Kawasaki, C.S., Kato, D.S., Valdanha Neto, D., Souza, J.C.B., Oliveira, L.B. and Matos, M.S., 2009. 'A pesquisa em educação ambiental nos ENPEC: contextos educacionais e focos temáticos', *Atas do VII Encontro Nacional de Pesquisa em Educação e Ciências (ENPEC)*, Florianópolis, SC.

Layrargues, P.P. and Lima, G.F.C., 2011. 'Mapeando as macro-tendências político-pedagógicas da educação ambiental contemporânea no Brasil', *Procedures of VI Encontro Pesquisa em Educação Ambiental (EPEA): a pesquisa em educação ambiental e a pós-graduação*. Ribeirão Preto, USP, v.0, 1–15.

Leff, E., 2001. *Epistemologia Ambiental*. São Paulo: Cortez.

Lorenzetti, L., and Delizoicov, D., 2007. 'A produção acadêmica brasileira em educação ambiental', *V Congreso CEISAL*, Bruselas. www.reseau-amerique-latine.fr/index.php?act=busc&result=actu&multi=lorenzetti [accessed 10 February 2015].

Loureiro, C.F.B., 2006. 'Educação ambiental e "teorias críticas', in Guimarães, M. (org.), *Caminhos da educação ambiental: da forma à ação*. Campinas: Papirus, 51–86.

Megid Neto, J., 2010. 'Educação Ambiental como campo de conhecimento: a contribuição das pesquisas acadêmicas para sua consolidação no Brasil', *Pesquisa em Educação Ambiental*, Unesp-UFSCar-USP. 5, 67–91, janeiro/junho.

Moore, J., 2005. 'Barriers and Pathways to Creating Sustainability Education Programs: Policy, Rhetoric and Reality', *Environmental Education Research*, 11(5), 537–55.

Rink, J. 2009. *Análise da produção acadêmica apresentada nos Encontros de Pesquisa em Educação Ambiental (EPEA)*. 217p. Dissertação (Mestrado em Educação) – Unicamp, Campinas.

Silva, T.T., 2004. *Documentos de Identidade: uma introdução às teorias do currículo*. Belo Horizonte: Autêntica.

Sterling, S. and Scott, W., 2008. 'Higher Education and ESD in England: A Critical Commentary on Recent Initiatives', *Environmental Education Research*, 14(4), 386–98.

Stevenson, R., Dillon, J. and Brody, M., eds, 2013. *International Handbook of Research on Environmental Education*. New York: Routledge.

UNESCO, 2004. *O Perfil dos professores brasileiros: o que fazem, o que pensam, o que almejam*. São Paulo: Moderna.

Wright, T., 2002. 'Definitions and Frameworks for Environmental Sustainability in Higher Education', *International Journal of Sustainability in Higher Education*, 3(3), 203–20.

25

SOCIAL REPRESENTATION OF SUSTAINABLE DEVELOPMENT MODELS IN STUDENTS AT A MEXICAN PUBLIC UNIVERSITY

Antonio Fernández-Crispín and David Lara-González

Introduction

For many people, the current environmental crisis is directly related to the prevailing development model, which is unsustainable (Wals and Jickling 2002; Fernández-Crispin *et al.* 2005). This model is not only behind the divorce between humankind and nature, but also attempts to put the longest distance possible between them, generating the idea that human issues are outside nature (Gladwin *et al.* 1995). Within this nature-society confrontation, we are becoming less concerned about what nature can do to us (droughts, floods, etc.) and more concerned about what we have done to nature (Giddens 2002).

In this view of humans undergoing a break with nature, Earth is considered as a sick mother who needs to be protected. This position is taken from a modernist epistemology that cannot go beyond its own ethnocentrism (Descola and Pálsson 1996; Latour 2009).

In order to overcome the socio-environmental crisis, various alternative development models have been proposed. In this context, the term Sustainable Development (SD) appears, presenting a conceptualisation of development that is defined not only in material terms, but also in terms of the search for harmony with the environment for the benefit of future generations (Hopwood *et al.* 2005). However, sustainable development means 'different things to different people in different contexts' (Laine 2005).

The changes proposed in the process of institutionalising SD and the solutions it proposes result from three key concepts that come from areas of fundamental importance to modern society: efficacy (technical), profitability (economical) and objectivity (scientific) (Latour 2007). In this context, environmental education has been seen essentially as an environmental problem-solving and management tool to be used to ensure sustainable development (Sauvé *et al.* 2005). Development models that propose minimal adjustments (reforms) to the predominant development model, rather than substantial changes to our relationship with the environment, are known as Weak Sustainable Development (WSD) models (Haughton and Hunter 1994). Whereas development models that propose radical changes (transformation) in the way in which we relate to nature are grouped within the concept of Strong Sustainable Development (SSD) (Haughton and Hunter 1994).

Latin American environmental thinking differs from other systems of thought through its radical epistemological interpretation of the concept of the environment, and acquires its identity from the cultural heritage of its peoples and the ecological potential of its territories (Leff 2012a). This environmental rationality is framed around the deconstruction and decolonisation of North-centric knowledge in order to establish a new social appropriation of nature (Leff 2012b; Descola and Pálsson 1996). For example, some indigenous communities, while avoiding many of the common models of modernisation, which lead to specialised, unsustainable and ecologically disruptive systems of production, probably achieve the most successful designs for the utilisation of tropical forest, in terms of biodiversity, conservation, resilience and sustainability (Toledo *et al.* 2003).

Because of this diversity of focus, the aim of sustainable education (SE) would not be to impose a particular point of view, but to promote a critical and respectful dialogue (Wals and Jickling 2002).

Universities play an important role in shaping the future of world society in terms of sustainable development (Rieckmann 2012). Karatzoglou (2013) presents a broad analysis of the relevant literature about the importance of universities to SD, and emphasises the role and contribution of two leading journals in the field, the Journal of Sustainability in Higher Education and the Journal of Cleaner Production. Nevertheless, it must be noted that contemporary universities are modern institutions with complex structures that make them resistant to change (Clark 1986). The degree of change required to achieve SE is enormous because these 'rebuild, or redesign' and integrative (interdisciplinary) expectations pose a serious challenge to those academics who perceive a university's strengths to be related to its unidisciplinary structures for research and teaching (Thomas 2009).

Today, there are 63 environmental plans in place in Mexican universities (Bravo 2012). These plans comply with the Treaty on Environmental Education for Sustainable Societies and Global Responsibility held in Rio de Janeiro in 1992 (Ferreira 2002). The Benemérita Universidad Autónoma de Puebla (BUAP) has recognised the importance of this plan.

In the context of this activity in universities, the aim of this study is to analyse the influence that a Mexican public university (BUAP) can have on social representation change in the formation of critical professionals, capable of promoting sustainable development to overcome this socio-environmental crisis. In this sense, education is understood as a process of promoting critical thinking and emancipative practices.

Research paradigms that guide the research

In order to achieve our aim, this study begins with Moscovici's social representation theory and its structural approach (Moscovici 2008; Moliner 1995). Social representation (SR) is the set of ideas shared among a human community that allows it to understand and interpret the world. SR is collectively constructed and constituted by a particular logic and language, which form a kind of 'collective science' or knowledge of daily life. This knowledge can be nourished by scientific concepts; however, in this process, these are detached from their meaning, acquire new meanings and convert the unusual to the familiar. This is how what Moscovici (2008) called a 'thematic language' is constructed.

SR comprises a central core and a corresponding peripheral system (Rateau *et al.* 2012). According to Abric (1993), the central core is the medullar part of social representation, with its origin found in collective memory and group history. The peripheral system includes elements linked to the core that cover the concretion, regulation and defence functions of social representation.

Research has been carried out on social representations of the environment in Latin America since the 1990s. Among those carried out on university students, noteworthy studies include Ferreira (2002), Andrade *et al.* (2004), Amérigo and Bernardo (2007), Calixto (2008) and Lara *et al.* (2010). However, this research field is in its initial exploratory stages, requiring further studies and the application of their results in order to orient processes, practices and educative propositions toward the formation of more sustainable habits and values (González and Valdez 2012).

Research process

Method

This study was conducted in the Benemérita Universidad Autónoma de Puebla (BUAP), a public university in Puebla, Mexico. In 2004 (the year the sample was taken), the BUAP offered 54 degree courses, grouped within six areas of knowledge: Education and Humanities; Natural and Exact Sciences; Health Sciences; Social and Administrative Sciences; Engineering and Technology; and Agriculture and Livestock Sciences.

Although, in theory, all degree courses should be oriented towards sustainability, this is only the case for some. For example, at the BUAP, there are five degrees courses that were created specifically to form environmental professionals: Environmental Urban Design, Environmental Engineering, Agro-hydraulics, Agronomy and Animal Sciences, and Biology. Recently, Veterinary Medicine and Economics have incorporated sustainability as an important part of curriculum. While other faculties have departments involved in sustainability, it is not a predominant feature in their curriculum, as, for example, in the Faculty of Law.

The sample for our research included three degree courses randomly selected from each area of knowledge, with those seven degree courses, mentioned above, that are more directly related to environmental subjects referred to as the related group (RG). Subsequently, quota sampling was performed in two stages: 1) first semester students (FS); and 2) students close to graduation (CG). Of the 1,208 instruments that were applied, 637 were applied to FS students (198 to the related group), and 571 to CG students (168 to the related group).

The goal of quota sampling is to set a target number of completed interviews with specified subgroups from the population of interest. The sampling procedure then proceeds using a non-random selection mechanism, until the desired number of completed interviews is obtained (Lavrakas 2008). In this case, each quota (25–35 students) corresponded to a school group to which the questionnaire was applied in the classroom.

The research instrument included a questionnaire comprising 47 open questions that presented 'inducer-phrases' to the subjects, who had to answer with two words or short phrases (three words maximum), for example:

> I think the human being-nature relationship should be:
> __________________ and __________________

Each item belonged to one of the indicators of variable analysis that constitute the basic concepts of the socio-environmental and natural environment relationship system defined by Bifani (1997): Natural Environment, Cultural system, Social Organisation, Economy and Environment Transformation. Sustainability is seen to help make this relationship system harmonious for the benefit of future generations.

Therefore, the following hypotheses are presented:

H1: If the University exerts an influence on the SR of the development model, then the SR found in graduates will be different from that found in first semester students.

H2: There is a difference between the SR of the development model found in the students enrolled in Related Group degree courses and those from the other degree courses (Not Directly Related Group). This difference will be greater at the end of their degree.

Using a Chi square test, researchers assessed the various groups identified by this study, both RG (FS and CG) and both Not Directly Related Groups (FS and CG), in terms of whether the university in question has any influence on its students' SR. If differences were detected in the ideas expressed by these groups, a Factorial Correspondence Analysis (using Statistica.6 software) was performed on the most frequently appearing ideas in those that comprise the SR of each indicator considered.

Factorial Correspondence Analysis (CA) is a multivariate method of reducing the valid dimensions for qualitative variables at a nominal level (words instead of numbers) (Doise *et al.* 1993; Moliner *et al.* 2002). CA does not conceive of SR as statistics and consensus; on the contrary, it assumes that there is a representational field in which the groups of individuals can adopt different positions (Doise *et al.* 1993). The design of this research, in which a comparison between those students enrolled on courses that are related or less related at different stages (FS and CG), allows the observation of the dynamic components of SR.

The combination of quantitative and qualitative methods is common in SR research, allowing comparisons between groups and the interpretation of the deepest content of SR. This interpretation of the data is easier when it is conducted within an 'interpretative framework' (Wagner *et al.* 1996; Wagner and Hayes 2005).

Research outcome (results)

Description of social representation

As Table 25.1 shows, many responses to the various items comprising the central core of social representation are incommensurable (Kuhn 1962), in that they have opposite meanings, leading to the conclusion that rather than one social representation, there are, in fact, several.

The role of the university in producing environmentally aware professionals

If the university has any influence on its students' SR, it must be expected that its graduates, especially those in the RG, will have different ideas from those recently admitted to the university. On the other hand, it could also be expected that students from the RG are more aware of environmental issues, or, at least, have a greater interest in them than those students from the Not Directly Related Group (NDRG).

As Table 25.2 shows, the Chi square test revealed that there are no significant differences in the social representation of science, while significant differences were found in the SR of the other concepts.

The representation field was analysed using a correspondence analysis (CA), which enabled researchers to find a link between various components of RS as well as the membership of each individual to a group, by observing the distances between their positions on the graph (Doise *et al.* 1993). However, the CA revealed that the groups are not sufficiently far (i.e. a value above

Table 25.1 Statements within the central core of social representation that make reference to the following themes: natural environment, cultural system, social organization, economy and environment transformation

Concept	*Central core*
Natural Environment: The human being-nature relationship should be:	Respectful 212→207, close 76→48, harmonious 73→85, good 74→44, balanced 16→26, fair 14→17, mutual 13→13, friendly 15→13, cordial 10→12, human 10→8, pleasant 13→4, constant 10→7.
Environment Transformation: Technology In Mexico, technology should be:	Better 163→100, supported 86→85, advanced 107→51, higher 61→22, updated 25→28, developed 26→22, for everybody 24→21, good 23→16, extended 19→12, modern 14→13, (Mexican) owned 4→19, better used 13→7, efficient 10→9, promoted 8→8, avant-garde 5→10.
Economy: Living well means:	Health 232→199, happiness 87→81, peace 62→56, comfort 24→31, stability 16→35, money 25→20, to have the necessary 22→13, to eat 15→9, to be okay 10→15, liberty 11→12, balanced diet 7→12, decent housing 15→4, quality of life 5→14.
Social Organisation: Rule of Law Lawlessness in Mexico can be corrected by:	Work 147→160, education 77→107, government 70→53, laws 59→47, honesty 39→33, justice 33→19, culture 16→31, surveillance 33→14, firm hand 24→15, good police 23→7, support 15→12, to meet the law 8→16, bigger sentences 13→10, collaboration 12→8, unity 6→13.
Cultural system: Ethics Ethics means:	Values 179→141, respect 124→126, honesty 71→81, morality 64→41, principles 31→35, professionalism 25→22, culture 29→18, what is correct 18→25, sincerity 19→13, reasoning 12→10, loyalty 7→12, behaviour 11→7.
Cultural system: Science Science means:	Knowledge 174→197, study 94→66, technology 83→77, advancement 87→56, research 51→50, to know 47→38, help 20→21, culture 14→15, necessity 7→8.

Note: Numbers indicates responses frequencies. Arrows indicate the change in frequencies between the beginning (FS) (n=637) and end of the degree course (CG) (n=571). Words are translated from Spanish and express synthetic ideas, because the questioner demands short sentences (one to three words) to express complex concepts.

Table 25.2 Chi square test between frequencies of words presented that are found at the central core of SR: related group FS, related group CG, not directly related group FS and not directly related group CG

Concept	*Significance level*
Human being-nature relationship	$p< 0.001$
Technology in Mexico	$p< 0.001$
Living well	$p= 0.01$
How can lawlessness in Mexico be corrected	$p< 0.001$
Ethics	$p=0.04$
Science in Mexico	$p= 0.32$

0.5) from the origin (the point at which the two axes intersect) in order to be sure that there is a relationship between them and the ideas they present. The influence of the university on the SR of these issues appears minimal, at least at a central core level.

Figure 25.1 shows two factors (axis) that slightly affect the SR of the human being-nature relationship. Above the X axis, it could be seen that graduates hold more academic ideas (balanced, reciprocal, fair). The NDRG (at the right) presents either rational ideas (conscious, balanced) or emotive (careful, cordial). To the left of the graph is the RG, which prefers to use such words as *fair, mutual* and *conservative*. The distance to the origin indicates how both factors influence the group and the statements expressed by the students within it. Generally, it is accepted that values below 0.5 are not relevant which, to make this clear, is indicated by a box in the graph. In this sense, it can be seen that change by the end of the degree course (CG) is small. The words *respectful, harmonious* and *careful* are very frequent (in bold) and close to the origin, which indicates that they are shared between groups and can be considered as central core components of SR.

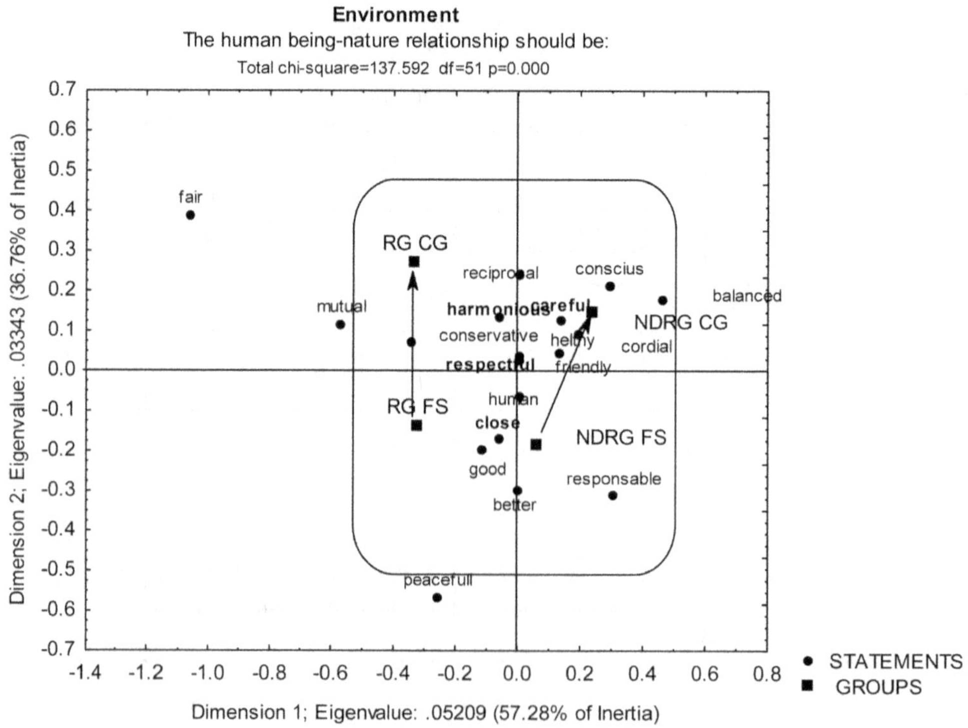

Figure 25.1 Factorial correspondence analysis that shows the social representation of the human being-nature relationship

Notes: RG FS: Related Group First Semester; NDRG FS: Not Directly Related Group First Semester; RG CG: Related Group Close to Graduation; NDRG CG: Not Directly Related Group Close to Graduation.

New knowledge (discussion)

Socio-environmental development models in social representations

Moscovici (2011) proposed nature and culture as principles for social classification and used them to anchor social representations of ethnic minorities. Following this idea, an 'interpretative framework' was constructed by identifying the degree to which responses suggest a break with the crisis in modern epistemology (not modern), an acceptance of the model (modern), or a position that is contrary to the environmental effects of modernity without breaking with it (antimodern) (Latour 2009). Under this approach, the three models of development proposed by Haughton and Hunter (1994) (Developmentalism, WSD and SSD) were used for the interpretation of the responses to the questionnaire. The interpretation framework considers to what degree the status quo (civilisation model) is accepted (acceptance, reforms or transformations), as proposed by Hopwood *et al.* (2005). As the questionnaire was applied in Spanish and the meaning of words depends on their context, Latin American literature was consulted in order to interpret the meaning of the responses.

Developmentalism (modernist)

Social Representation from the perspective of modern developmentalism is characterised by a simple reasoning (Marcuse 2013; Leff 2012b) which does not allow the perception of its socio-environmental consequences or, at the very least, conceives of them as a necessary evil in order to live more *comfortably. Comfort* as an equivalent to living well is achieved with *money* and *science* and *technology*, with the last two terms frequently and mistakenly used interchangeably (Fernández-Crispín *et al.* 2005). The human being modifies nature in order to obtain that which nature does not provide. Technology is the tool that humanity has developed to modify nature in order to satisfy its needs (Ortega and Gasset 1965). Given the importance of technology, it should be *better, advanced, avant-garde* and *major*, a perspective which is defined as technophile (Meira 2005) or technocentrist (Gladwin *et al.* 1995).

Due to an inability to understand lawlessness as the result of more structural problems such as poverty and inequality (Cálix 2007), some students considered it an issue that the *government* must solve by means of *surveillance, punishment* and the application of *a firm hand.* Surveillance and punishment are basic elements for the exercise of power by governments that, according to Foucault (1977), have evolved from violent acts, such as public executions, into the more subtle and institutionalised activities that characterise the modern state.

Weak sustainable development

The SR of Weak Sustainable Development begins with a criticism of the socio-environmental consequences of modernity without breaking with its epistemology. This anti-modern position (Latour 2012) focuses on the defence and protection of nature from the negative human effects on natural spaces without criticising the dominant socio-economic system (Leff 2012b). From this perspective, the students consider that this relationship with nature should be *careful, conscious* and *conservative.* Concerned about the 'victims of modernity', they state in the results that technology, as a solution to problems, should be *for everybody.*

Living well means taking care of the body, thus indicating why *health* and a *balanced diet* are important to some students. Liu (2006) also finds that social thinking about quality of life in

Chinese society is activated in five critical areas of life: health, family, work, social relations and the natural environment.

From a conventional moral judgment, the students believe in the application of a single 'golden rule' in each situation in life (Power *et al.* 1991). Therefore, the concept of ethics is interpreted by the students to mean having *values* and *principles* and doing *what is correct.* Furthermore, lawlessness is perceived as a problem generated by unfair social situations. The students again side with the poor and state that lawlessness can be corrected with *better salaries,* thus simplifying the matter to an economic level and assuming that delinquents are found primarily among the poor.

For the students, science means *knowledge, research* and *study.* Nevertheless, science is not the only valid and legitimate form of knowledge (Lévi-Strauss 1966).

Strong sustainable development

The Strong Sustainable Development model represents an emancipatory movement seeking to set free the potential of biological and cultural diversity (Leff 2012a), and overcome the break between society and nature proposed by modernity. Although the SR of ethics as *conscious* seems unspecific, this implies a post-conventional moral judgment (Power *et al.* 1991), since principles are not accepted as pre-established issues, and instead created from a rational judgment, which implies both an awareness of the significance of said judgement and critical thinking.

In the SR of quality of life, students mentioned *respect* and *harmony*. *Respect* and *harmony* also are manifested as the principles that should regulate the relationship between human beings and nature.

Science is no longer seen as absolute and universal knowledge, rather as a perspective that proposes a plurality of knowledge for a plural society (Ziman 2002). If science is not universal, technology is even less so. In this sense, some students responded that technology in Mexico should be *Mexican-owned,* bearing in mind the conception of self-managed development.

Implications of the key findings

In moving toward sustainable education (SE), universities start from the 'bolt-on' approach of Education about Sustainable Development (ESD), which requires minimal change to curricula, and then move on to the more radical Education for Sustainability (EfS), in which curricula are transformed to 'build-in' sustainability (Thomas 2009). The CA shows that the BUAP plays a marginal role in the formation of professionals capable of transforming, in a conscious, ethical and professional manner, the development models that have caused the current socio-environmental crisis. One explanation for this is that the BUAP currently finds itself in the ESD phase.

To operationalise SE, teaching approaches should focus on elements relating to the processes of learning, rather than the accumulation of knowledge, and skills encompassed by the pedagogy of problem-based learning. These provide students with opportunities to learn 'how to think' rather than 'what to think' potentially within the framework of sustainability (Thomas 2009). Key links here are critical thinking and emancipative practices (Caride 2005; Kearins and Springett 2003).

As the discussion of sustainability potentially brings together different groups in society, as mentioned above, the aim of SE is not to impose a particular point of view, but instead to promote a dialogue (Wals and Jickling 2002).

Reflections

Achievements of the research design

As developed by Moscovici, SR theory is related to analysis and assessment at a collective level (Wagner *et al.* 1996). However, the majority of the Latin American research on social representation of Education for Sustainable Development is realised by means of semi-structured interviews, which deeply analyse the thoughts of a few individuals (González and Valdez 2012). These are predominantly descriptive and do not go much beyond 'storytelling'. Studies should go beyond description to include a critical and theoretical analysis (Fien 2002; Adomßent *et al.* 2007).

To overcome the individual analysis, Wagner *et al.* (1996) suggest a method (based on CA) to look for structural proprieties of free word association. As in this study, the analysis is based primarily upon description, and is based only post-hoc on inferential statistics. While the descriptive focus centres on searching for the collective, frequent and interrelated responses, the inferential statistics enable the identification of differences among groups of individuals.

This study takes an opposite point of departure from those individual analyses, interpreting a group of brief responses produced by a wide group of people. In contrast with the majority of the studies carried out in the social sciences by means of questionnaires, this study does not consider groups as a collection of individuals that hold information in a static form. SR is understood here as a collective construction of meanings, a population of ideas in which different discourses dynamically interact, and in which some displace others. This perspective enables researchers to see how SRs adapt themselves to particular contexts, and how new ideas, as much individual ones as those that come from different sources (for example the university itself), incorporate themselves into SRs.

The evocation questionnaire enables the direct treatment of the data obtained from the free expression of the subjects, and is easy to apply and codify (Moliner 1995). The data can also be analysed in a descriptive and inferential manner. From the descriptive point of view, prototypical and categorical analysis allows us to investigate the way in which free associations are structured, and to identify elements both within the central core and those on the periphery (Bonnec *et al.* 2002).

Limitations

Due to its ease of use and the explicatory power of its identification of the elements of representation, the methodology used here runs the risk of it being forgotten that it is based on the assumption that the responses that occur to the respondent the most quickly have the greatest symbolic value and are, therefore, part of the central nucleus. However, this assumption has not been verified experimentally, given that it emerges as a complement to the analysis of the SR through qualitative methods (Vergès *et al.* 1994; Moliner *et al.* 2002).

The research design departs from the application of a questionnaire to a group of presumably different university students, expecting that CA could detect the structure of the SR from the influence of the groups that express views that are closer to sustainability. However the groups were more homogeneous than expected. Although this methodology enabled researchers to identify more than one model of development in the SR, the reduction of both the sample and the number of questions and the increase of the number of words in the response to a question is suggested, in line with Wagner *et al* (1996) rather than Vergès (1992). In this way, CA would give insight as to how the subjects' words structured the semantic space graph rather than the groups' (as in this work).

Recommendations

Explorative and descriptive approaches are particularly useful when researching a little known or little studied area or field. The theoretical-methodological model used here enables the researcher to analyse a university's influence on changes to social representation in the formation of critical professionals capable of promoting sustainable development in order to overcome the socio-environmental crisis. Furthermore, it is possible to identify and describe the different SRs related to the development model to which BUAP students ascribe by means of a simple and practical methodology. As the methodology enabled researchers to identify that the BUAP is currently in an ESD phase, it would be interesting to apply this methodology to a university in the EfS or SE phase.

Finally, it is advisable to complement this study with research directed at ascertaining which factors have influence on the type of development model presented, which in turn, can be translated into pedagogical proposals.

References

Abric, J.C., 1993. 'Central System, Peripheral System: Their Functions and Roles in the Dynamics of Social Representations', *Papers on Social Representations*, 2(2), 75–8.

Adomßent, M., Godemann, J. and Michelsen, G., 2007. 'Transferability of Approaches to Sustainable Development at Universities as a Challenge', *International Journal of Sustainability in Higher Education*, 8(4), 385–402.

Amérigo, M. and Bernardo, A., 2007. 'Representación social del ser humano versus naturaleza y su relación con las creencias medioambientales' (Social representation of humans versus nature and its relation with environmental believes), *Revista de Psicología Social*, 22(3), 219–33.

Andrade, M., Aguiar de Souza, M. and Brochier, J., 2004. 'Representação de educação ambiental y de educação em saúde em universitários de Brasil' (Representation of environmental education and health education in university students from Brazil: from Portuguese), *Psicología, reflexión y crítica*, 17(1), 43–50.

Bifani, P., 1997. *Medio ambiente y desarrollo* (Environmental and sustainable development: from Spanish). Guadalajara: University of Guadalajara.

Bonnec, Y., Roussiau, N. and Vergès, P., 2002. 'Categorical and Prototypical Analysis: A Study on the Quality-process in Hospital Institutions', *European Review of Applied Psychology*, 52(3/4), 213–20.

Bravo, M.T. (coord.), 2012. *Los planes ambientales institucionales en la educación superior en México: Construyendo sentidos de sustentabilidad (2002–2007)* (Institutional environmental curricula in higher education in Mexico: building sustainability senses [2002–2007]: from Spanish). México: SEMARNAT, INE, ANUIES, UNAM.

Cálix, A., 2007. 'La falacia de más policías, más penas y más cárceles: el problema de la inseguridad y el castigo desde una visión alternativa' (The fallacy of more police officers, more sentences and more prisons: the problem of insecurity and the punishment from an alternative view: from Spanish), *Revista Nueva sociedad*, 208, 40–55.

Calixto, R., 2008. *Representaciones sociales de medio ambiente en los estudiantes de licenciatura en educación primaria* (Social representations of the environment in the students of Bachelor's degree in elementary education: from Spanish). México: Universidad Pedagógica Nacional.

Caride, J.A., 2005. 'In the Name of Environmental Education: Words and Things in the Complex Territory Of Education–Environment–Development Relations', *Policy Futures in Education*, 3(3), 260–70.

Clark, B.R., 1986. *The Higher Education System: Academic Organization in Cross-national Perspective*. California: University of California Press.

Descola, P. and Pálsson, G. (eds), 1996. *Nature and Society: Anthropological Perspectives*. New York: Routledge.

Doise, W., Clémence, A. and Lorenzi-Cioldi, F., 1993. *The Quantitative Analysis of Social Representations*. Abingdon: Taylor & Francis.

Fernández-Crispín, A., Benayas-Del-Alamo, J. and Barroso-Jerez, C., 2005. 'Social Representation of the Way to Interact with Environment of the Elementary School Teachers of the Puebla's Municipality (Mexico)', *International Journal of Environment and Sustainable Development*, 4(2), 140–53.

Ferreira, R., 2002. 'Representaciones sociales de medio ambiente y educación ambiental de docentes universitarios(as)' (Social representations of the environment and environmental education of university teachers: from Spanish), *Tópicos en Educación Ambiental*, 4(10), 22–36.

Fien, J., 2002. 'Advancing Sustainability in Higher Education: Issues and Opportunities for Research', *Higher Education Policy*, 15(2), 143–52.

Foucault, M., 1977. *Discipline and Punishment*. New York: Pantheon.

Giddens, A., 2002. *Runaway World: How Globalisation is Reshaping our Lives*. London: Profile Books.

Gladwin, T.N., Kennelly, J.J. and Krause, T.S., 1995. 'Shifting Paradigms for Sustainable Development: Implications for Management Theory and Research', *Academy of Management Review*, 20(4), 874–907.

González, E. and Valdez, R.E., 2012. 'Enfoques y sujetos en los estudios sobre representaciones sociales de medio ambiente en tres países de Iberoamérica' (Approaches and subjects in studies on social representations of environment in three countries of Latin America: from Spanish), CPU- e, *Revista de Investigación Educativa*, 14, 1–17.

Haughton, G. and Hunter, C., 1994. *Sustainable Cities*. London: Kingsley.

Hopwood, B., Mellor, M. and O'Brien, G., 2005. 'Sustainable Development: Mapping Different Approaches', *Sustainable Development*, 13(1), 38–52.

Karatzoglou, B., 2013. 'An In-depth Literature Review of the Evolving Roles and Contributions of Universities to Education for Sustainable Development', *Journal of Cleaner Production*, 49(June), 44–53.

Kearins, K. and Springett, D., 2003. 'Educating for Sustainability: Developing Critical Skills', *Journal of Management Education*, 27(2), 188–204.

Kuhn, Th., 1962. *The Structure of Scientific Revolutions*. Chicago, IL: The University of Chicago Press.

Laine, M., 2005. 'Meanings of the Term "Sustainable Development" in Finnish Corporate Disclosures', *Accounting Forum*, 29(4), 395–413.

Lara, J.D., Fernández, A., Silva S. and Pérez R., 2010. 'Representación social de las causas de los problemas ambientales: el caso de la Benemérita Universidad Autónoma de Puebla' (Social representation of the causes of environmental problems: the case of the Meritorious Autonomous University of Puebla: from Spanish), *Trayectorias, revista de ciencias sociales de la Universidad Autónoma de Nuevo León*, 12(30), 40–55.

Latour, B., 2009. *Politics of Nature*. Cambridge, MA: Harvard University Press.

Latour, B., 2012. *We Have Never Been Modern*. Cambridge, MA: Harvard University Press.

Latour, B., 2007. 'The Recall of Modernity: Anthropological Approaches', *Cultural Studies Review*, 13(1), 11–30.

Lavrakas, P.J., 2008. *Encyclopedia of Survey Research Methods: AM* (Vol. 1). Thousand Oaks, CA: Sage.

Leff, E., 2012a. 'Latin American Environmental Thinking', *Environmental Ethics*, 34(4), 431–50.

Leff, E., 2012b. 'Political Ecology: A Latin American Perspective'. Encyclopedia of Life Support Systems (EOLSS). www. eolss. net.

Lévi-Strauss, C., 1966. *The Savage Mind*. Chicago, IL: University of Chicago Press.

Liu, L., 2006. 'Quality of Life as a Social Representation in China: A Qualitative Study', *Social Indicators Research*, 75(2), 217–40.

Marcuse, H., 2013. *One-dimensional Man: Studies in the Ideology of Advanced Industrial Society*. New York: Routledge.

Meira, P.A., 2005. 'In Praise of Environmental Education', *Policy Futures in Education*, 3(3), 285–95.

Moliner, P., 1995. 'A Two-dimensional Model of Social Representations', *European Journal of Social Psychology*, 25(1), 27–40.

Moliner, P., Rateau, P. and Cohen-Scali, V., 2002. *Les représentations sociales: pratiques d'études de terrain* (Social representations: study field practices). Rennes: PUR, Collection Didact Psychology Sociale.

Moscovici, S., 2008. *Psychoanalysis. Its Image and its Public*. Cambridge: Polity Press.

Moscovici, S., 2011. 'An Essay on Social Representations and Ethnic Minorities', *Social Science Information*, 50(3–4), 442–61.

Ortega y Gasset, J., 1965. *Meditación de la técnica* (Meditation about technique: from Spanish). Madrid: Colección Austral.

Power, F.C., Higgins, A., Power, C.F. and Kohlberg, L., 1991. *Lawrence Kohlberg's Approach to Moral Education*. New York: Columbia University Press.

Rateau, P., Moliner, P., Guimelli, C. and, Abric, J.C., 2012. 'Social Representation Theory', in Van Lange, P.A.M., Kruglanski, A. and Higgins, J. (eds), *Handbook of Theories of Social Psychology, Volume 2*. Thousand Oaks, CA: Sage, 477–97.

Rieckmann, M., 2012. 'Future-oriented Higher Education: Which Key Competencies should be Fostered through University Teaching and Learning?', *Futures*, 44(2), 127–35.

Sauvé, L., Brunelle, R. and Berryman, T., 2005. 'Influence of the Globalized and Globalizing Sustainable Development Framework on National Policies Related to Environmental Education', *Policy Futures in Education*, 3(3), 271–83.

Thomas, I., 2009. 'Critical Thinking, Transformative Learning, Sustainable Education, and Problem-based Learning in Universities', *Journal of Transformative Education*, 7(3), 245–64.

Toledo, V.M., Ortiz-Espejel, B., Cortés, L., Moguel, P. and Ordoñez, M.D.J., 2003. 'The Multiple Use of Tropical Forests by Indigenous Peoples in Mexico: A Case of Adaptive Management', *Conservation Ecology*, 7(3), 9. www.consecol.org/vol7/iss3/art9.

Vergès, P., 1992. 'L'evocation de l'argent: Une méthode pour la définition du noyau central d'une représentation' (The evocation of the money: A method for the definition of the central core of a representation: from French), *Bulletin de Psycologie*, 65(405), 203–9.

Vergès, P., Tyszka, T. and Vergès, P., 1994. 'Noyau central, saillance et propriétés structurales' (Central core, salience and structural properties: from French), *Papers on Social Representations*, 3(1), 3–12.

Wagner, W. and Hayes, N., 2005. *Everyday Discourse and Common Sense. The Theory of Social Representations*. Houndmills, London: Palgrave Macmillian.

Wagner, W., Valencia, J. and Elejabarrieta, F., 1996. 'Relevance, Discourse and the "Hot" Stable Core Social Representations – A Structural Analysis of Word Associations', *British Journal of Social Psychology*, 35(3), 331–51.

Wals, A.E. and Jickling, B., 2002. '"Sustainability" in Higher Education: From Doublethink and Newspeak to Critical Thinking and Meaningful Learning', *Higher Education Policy*, 15(2), 121–31.

Ziman, J., 2002. *Real Science: What It Is and What It Means*. Cambridge: Cambridge University Press.

26

THE RESEARCH PROCESS OF UNDERSTANDING BIOGRAPHICAL LEARNING PROCESSES OF SUSTAINABILITY ENTREPRENEURS

Jana Timm

Introduction to my research

The presented doctoral study is assigned to the research field of education for sustainable development (ESD). ESD is understood as a politically motivated programme, which has been supported and promoted by numerous international political conventions and agreements, such as the Halifax Declaration in 1991, Agenda 21 as a result of the Earth Summit in Rio de Janeiro in 1992 and the Decade for Education for Sustainable Development (2005–2014), led by UNESCO. ESD aims to promote learning which develops skills such as 'Gestaltungskompetenz' (de Haan 2008, 2006; Barth *et al.* 2007), 'Values, Knowing, Skills, Understanding' (Parkin *et al.* 2004), and 'Heads, Hands, and Heart' (Sipos *et al.* 2008). The ultimate objective is to help learners develop competences and skills that are conducive to social transformation processes (in terms of sustainable development) (e.g. Barth and Michelsen 2013; Wals 2010).

The focus of this chapter is to present the research process of understanding biographical learning processes of sustainability entrepreneurs (SE). SEs are understood as innovators for societal transformation, in this case within the private sector. Their work has a multiplying effect as they spread innovation through their actions (Rogers 2003). I refer to biographical learning as the life experiences that are these kinds of experiences that connect awareness of the world with self-awareness and evolve when dealing with the world (Schulze 1997). Biographical learning processes are crucial for the development of an individual biography (Schulze 2009, 2006, 2005; Ecarius 2006).

The *research question* of the study has been: 'What kinds of biographical learning processes have SEs undergone?'. Thus, my *object of research* is biographical learning processes and my *subjects of research* are sustainability entrepreneurs. I have aimed at finding out more about the process of self-awareness of the biographical subject, the individual SE, and I am doing this by means of researching their individual life narratives.

By way of introduction, I argue that SEs are attractive research subjects for ESD research as they demonstrate sustainability competence consistent with the goals of ESD. Researching their biographical learning process contributes valuable insights into sustainability-related personal development because,

1. SEs are *actors* for sustainable development, especially in the private sector. They are seen as intentionally acting and self-directed innovators (Weidinger *et al.* 2014; Schaltegger and Wagner 2011), also 'catalysts of change' (de Leeuw 1999). Thus, they represent those kinds of people often referred to as 'agents of change' who, it is argued by politicians and the ESD community, are so desperately 'needed' for a social transformation towards sustainable development (Barth and Michelsen 2013; Adomßent *et al.* 2009; Vare and Scott 2007);
2. my research assumption was that in their life history SEs have undergone *biographically relevant learning processes* (Schulze 2009, 2005) that led them to become change agents for sustainable development; and
3. studying biographical learning processes of SEs, may inform *theoretical and practical development* of ESD in economics and business education. This is becoming increasingly relevant as economics and business education scholars have begun to question their own assumptions (e.g. Müller-Christ 2013; Morsing and Rovira 2011) and have started contemplating the idea of introducing sustainability and general humanistic values into economics and business education at universities (Lourenco *et al.* 2013; Amann *et al.* 2011b; Amann *et al.* 2011a).

If the goal of ESD is to generate agents of change for a grand transformation (Barth 2015; Wals *et al.* 2010), then researching the biography of already developed and active change agents, such as SEs, may provide information on the origins and learning stages of SEs' relevant biographical learning processes. The hope is that the study contributes to the theoretical foundation of ESD theory, particularly in economics and business education. Ideally, follow-up research projects can then build on these theoretical strands to finally produce reliable results for the practical design of ESD learning and teaching.

As the aim of this contribution is to elaborate on the research process, I will present the methodological approach and reflect on limitations it brings with it.

Research process

With regard to the research objective of 'understanding SEs' biographical learning processes' the research is being conducted using the 'understanding perspective'. To make this research paradigm clearer, I would first like to briefly introduce its philosophical and theoretical background. Thereupon, I will present the methodology and the applied research design.

A brief theoretical introduction to the 'understanding paradigm'

The philosophical-sociological perspective of Critical Theory inspired the philosophical framework for the study. I based my work on the assumption that society consists largely of subjects, who, on the one hand, reproduce social structures through their behaviour and their subjectively meaningful action; on the other hand, to a certain extent they shape and create social reality. Therefore, this research can be classified neither in the purely objectivist-structural nor in the subjectivist-individual line of argument. The dichotomy between the two perspectives does not apply in this case. This is evident particularly in view of the above briefly explained understanding of SEs. In this research, I assume that SEs represent precisely those subjects who shape society deliberately in prevailing power structures, i.e. as subjects they act meaningfully.

Accordingly, the present work shows a similar epistemological perspective as Jürgen Habermas' critical theory. Habermas understands an action conducted by a subject (a person) as 'meaningful' (as it has a meaning for the subject). At the same time, this action needs to be seen as taking place within existing and emerging social structures (Habermas 1995). To answer my research question, I would like to understand how the learning processes of SEs arise and how SEs (understood as intentionally acting subjects) apply meaning construction (and action). Thus, the present research is located in the tradition of *pragmatist* procedures and is a *phenomenologically* inspired *interactionist* social scientific research. The philosophical and social scientific concepts considered significant include: social phenomenology, symbolic interactionism, pragmatism and social constructivism.

My basic paradigmatic assumptions that arise from this socio-philosophical framing, if I aim to *understand* SEs, are the following:

- Reality is (subjectively and socially) constructed. It is of no interest to what extent reality is objectively given and if the subjects look at reality in the 'right' way. Rather it seeks to understand how they interpret reality.
- Therefore, the goal is to understand the subjects' interpretations.
- This is possible through applying scientific methods of interpretation, which are conducted by me, as the researcher.
- In particular, the research is interested to identify the interpretations, which illuminate understanding of the research subject and possibly about other actors.
- The goal of a scientific interpretation is not to reproduce a simplified picture of the supposed reality. Rather, it is intended to produce an image of a different, new 'reality' and represent the inherent complexity of such reality.

Accordingly, this research is located within the *Interpretative Paradigm*, in which *understanding is the purpose* and *interpretation is a means* to this end. Hence, the goal was to find a suitable methodology for the object of research.

Methodological considerations

The research question and the object of research (i.e. SEs' biographical learning processes) already indicate that no hypotheses (that I have developed in advance followed by relevant procedures of distribution and frequency analysis) are in the foreground of this study. Rather, this study is inductive and aims to capture the *meaning making structures* within biographical learning processes.[1] It is therefore in line with the tradition of qualitative educational research (Koller 2013, 2012, 2011; Marotzki and Tiefel 2010).

A 'biographical research in educational science' is seen as a research strategy able to make a significant contribution exploring individual and collective meaning making structures that are revealed in narrations (e.g. Koller 2013; Fuchs 2012; Krüger and Marotzki 2006; Alheit and Dausien 2006; Schulze 2006; Ecarius and Friebertshäuser 2005; Kokemohr and Koller 1996; Baacke and Schulze 1979/1993). By studying life histories, biographical research in educational science sheds light on the subject and their identity-building, socialising and learning processes. This, in turn, serves as a basis for the development of educational theory. Thus, it was the aim of the study to shed light on learning processes of SEs that have showed to be biographically relevant, i.e. that have been forming their biography (Koller 2013; Schulze 2009; Marotzki 2006).

Research design

The research design of a social scientific and empirical study usually consists of two parts: data collection and data analysis. However, this study follows the interpretive social scientific paradigm: biographical case reconstruction, where data collection and analysis phases are not separated (Rosenthal 2012, 2011, 2006). Throughout the entire research process, out of the biographical-narrative interview data I formulated step by step interpretational readings, which I gradually confirmed or disproved. Moreover, the sample is selected according to the principle of theoretical sampling, which involves a gradual development of case selection during the research process (Roberts 2002).

In the next section, I present the fundamental essence of the study's data collection and data analysis methods. I discuss in more detail how the data collection procedures of the biographical-narrative interviews have been applied and how the sampling of the cases, or rather interviewees, has been carried out. Also, I will explain the method of biographical case analysis.

Data collection method

In the present research context, I have collected biographical narratives by means of *biographical-narrative interviews*. I oriented my research to the following formal structure, inspired by the narrative interview structure originally proposed by Schütze (1983), which had been expanded by Rosenthal (2011):

Phase I

I started the interview with a *narrative prompt*, which referred to the interviewee's entire life story and was:

> Please tell me your whole life story, all the experiences that you can think of. Not only directly related to your current job. Please take your time. I will not interrupt you, just take some notes, to which I will, if appropriate, come back to later.

The reason to request the entire life story, and not to choose a more limited narrative stimulus, was that after a more open narrative prompt there will be topics addressed that may be able to give additional guidance on biographical learning processes. This would not have been possible with a limited or more focused stimulus (Rosenthal 2011; Marotzki 2006).

The narrative prompt was usually followed by a longer narrative response from the interviewee. In this part I abstained from interposed or specifying questions, since according to Rosenthal (2011) the 'prevention of interposed questions or their postponement to the questioning part of the interview, the … narrative constraints have a far greater effect than in interviews that are more structured by the interviewer's questions' (own translation from: Rosenthal 2011: 156).

During the interview itself, I, as the interviewer, only conveyed 'para linguistic expressions' like 'mhm' and eye contact and communication measures known from everyday expressions that indicated my interest in the narrative. Also, to show my attention, I did nod encouragingly. 'Hold-ups in the narrative' (ibid.) were overcome by motivational stimuli questions in order to encourage the interviewee to continue her/his story, such as 'And what happened next?' So the goal was to leave the interviewee to 'spice up' her/his narrative herself/himself and to keep my influence as low as possible. Only when a 'narrative koda' (Schütze 1983), and thus a concluding sentence was set for the main part of the narrative, did the next interview phase (II) begin.

Phase II

I began Phase II by asking *questions basing on protocol-like notes* I made during the main part of the narrative. They serve to illustrate open or uncertain relaxed points in the main story. The first questioning part with respect to *already told or indicated topics* was followed by a second questioning part. This referred to *questions related to external information and theories* within the field of research, which I had brought in, and about which I had made assumptions as I reckoned them relevant for the research question, but that I had still not elaborated sufficiently.

Phase III

At the end of the interview, I asked:

> Now we have talked about a lot of things, is there anything you consider important that has not yet come up?

Answering this question, the interviewees often brought up topics that they would like to emphasise again. This indicated the importance of those topics for the interviewees. Moreover, in three cases the interviewees even picked up a new experience that they had not previously raised.

Shortly after the interview, usually on the same day, I prepared a conversation protocol. In there I wrote down my impressions to different issues regarding the conversational atmosphere and conversational dynamics. The protocol, together with the interview recording, gave a comprehensive picture of the overall interview situation that showed to be relevant for the data analysis phase. For example, the relation between the interviewee and me, as the interviewer, has showed to be crucial for *what* and *how* the interviewee told in her/his narrative. So, for example, in some cases, the atmosphere was characterised by a 'business tone'. In other cases, the interviewee and I carried out a rather private and intimate conversational style. In one case, interestingly enough, the interviewee and I created a striking imbalance of power, in comparison to the other interviews. Here probably the age difference and the personalities of the two interview partners were decisive.

Sampling

In the research I used *theoretical sampling* as the case selection method. In the theoretical sampling, the criteria for selecting relevant cases arise during the course of investigation (Schreier 2010; Glaser and Strauss 2005). The characteristics of the 'SE' arise from the identified research interest and thus from the research question.

I selected the first case by investigating some databases of individuals and firms that work in sectors that are concerned with sustainable production and consumption patterns, like food, energy, clothing and infrastructure or mobility but also with services like hair cutting, financial consultancy. At that time, the global financial crisis was still present in public discussion. Thus, I made a decision regarding the first interviewee due to up-to-date issues in society and selected a financial consultant that had been innovative in terms of financial consulting products. According to the iterative and successive procedure, I selected subsequent cases according to the findings of the previous case(s). By selecting individuals that differ greatly in comparison to the previous cases, I aimed for *contrast within the sample.* So the second interviewee I selected from a contrasting branch. My second interviewee was not a service provider like the consultant; she/he was a manufacturer, a baker. Since I was not aiming to achieve theoretical saturation, it was the *research context* and the *associated practical considerations* that informed my research practice and guided when I need to stop the sampling process (Schreier 2010).

Data analysis method

As already indicated, I applied *biographical case analysis* according to Rosenthal (2011; 2006) to analyse the audio recording and transcribe the biographical-narrative interviews. In the first analysis phase, I analysed *biographical and historical context data* of the respective case. I did this by sequentially analysing objective data (according to sociological biography research) as it has been proposed by Radenbach and Rosenthal (Radenbach and Rosenthal 2012). I have been doing this using a process of individual elaboration. First, I put data about family history into a temporal sequence and embedded it in collective historical data (Radenbach and Rosenthal 2012).

In the second analysis phase, a general *text and thematic field analysis* takes place, which I have carried out following the analysis steps described by Rosenthal (2011). I have been analysing the narrative sequences within an interpretation group as well as in individual elaboration. Narration analysis is based on the procedure originally introduced by Schütze (Kleemann *et al.* 2009; Rosenthal 2006; Schütze 1983) and I have been conducting the analysis using formal structure markers and frame switching elements, like words indicating the transfer to a new occurrence (e.g. often verbs that show different tenses in one sentence).

The *unit formation within life story narratives* occurs by examining each narrative's focus individually. For this purpose, I used the biographical learning theory as a heuristic technique to investigate whether each case showed representations of the biographical theory fields (Fuchs 2011).

Eventually, I undertook *case contrasting*, considering individual and group interpretation sessions.

The goal of the analysis is not to find generalised structures that can be found in any biography. But rather, it seeks to explore the SEs' meaning making processes, which they subjectively go through by interacting with other people and the environment. Therefore, I considered both the individual and the collective experiential space (Marotzki 2006). The research looks at individual learning processes to reveal SEs' individual meaningful worlds, life and problem-solving styles as well as their learning and orientation patterns.

Reflections on the research process

I have experienced that it is vital for me as an early career researcher to be clear about what kind of research interest I have. I needed to understand how I am viewing the world (or my own research), that is, from an objectivist-structural, a subjectivist-individual or rather from a critical point of view. Being aware of my *theoretical perspective* on the research, I was able to identify which paradigm (explaining or understanding paradigm) is useful for exploring my research objectives. This in turn provided the basis for the methodological approach. From this I needed to decide on which *methodological perspective* to take: a (post-)positivist perspective that is

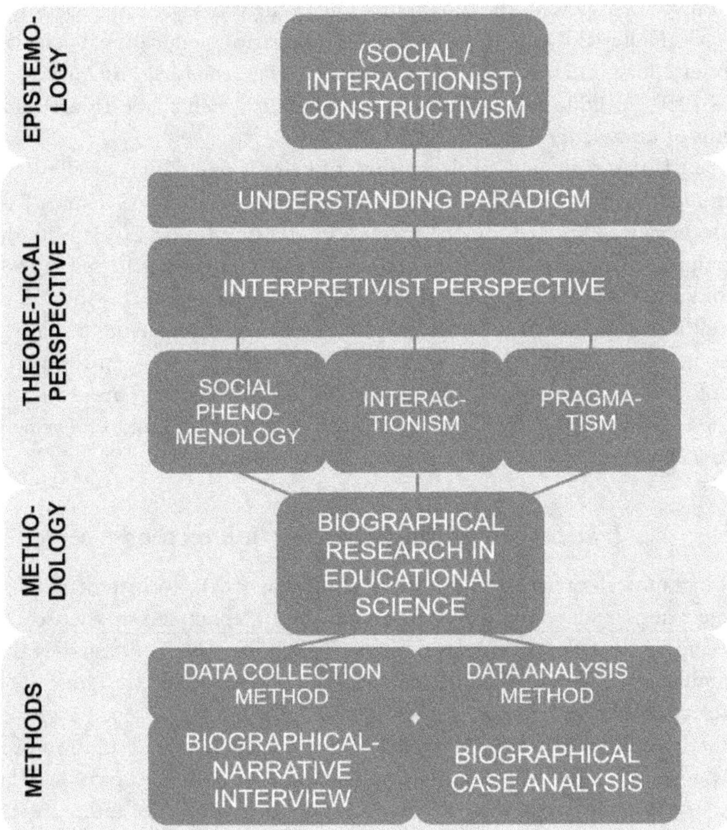

Figure 26.1 Research process

oriented to facts or evaluation procedures, or a constructivist- or interactionist-oriented research. Figure 26.1 illustrates the interconnections between the theory of knowledge informing the philosophical stance (Epistemology), the philosophical stance informing the methodology (theoretical perspective), the research strategy (methodology) informing the methods used, and the data gathering and analysing procedures or techniques (methods) that have been relevant for the presented study.[2]

Limitations of the research approach

The present study explores the biographical learning processes of SEs and is directly relevant to educational research in the area of Education for Sustainable Development. The chosen research approach is 'educational scientific biographical research', which is now an established form of empirical educational research. To be specific: in this research, I used the methodology *educational theory-based biographical research*. This term includes the two areas of educational science: educational theory and biographical research that is theory and empiricism. Often both areas are perceived as independent from each other. Educational theory defines theoretically, what is education, without empirically exploring it. Empirical educational research explores education, mainly with a view to the final result, not to the process, i.e. the focus is on the *what* and not the *how* (Koller 2011). Put simply, there are various educational-scientific types of knowledge about education: the *empirical knowledge* and *theoretical-reflexive knowledge*. In particular, since the 1960s in educational science references are often made to a conflict between these two forms of knowledge.

It is important that we recognise this conflict, to keep it open, but not allow it to become a legal or legitimation dispute (Koller 2013). Accordingly, we need 'to [express] what cannot be said in each prevailing kind of discourse' (own translation: Koller 2013: 146); that is, either in theory or empirical data alone. The issue then is about recognising the respective limitations of each type of knowledge. Accordingly Koller (2013: 145) points out, as soon as one form of knowledge – either the theoretical or the empirical – is valued as having a sole right to exist over the other, it will be of little help. He argues that a conflict between the two knowledge types, that would become some type of litigation, should be avoided. Thus, educational theory can be extended and improved by the inclusion of empirical findings. Conversely, empirical data can be conceptualised in a reflexive process about the data.

Limitations of the data collection method

The applied biographical-narrative interview method has worked out remarkably well. Thus far it is as if the research subjects were 'pulled away' by or 'entangled in' their own narratives. They actually told their life story, and consistent with Schütze (2007, 1983), they demonstrated an 'urge' to simultaneously detail, form and condense their narrations. Thus, they went into detail trying to make a logical, rounded story that was, for me as a listener, easy to follow.

At this point, I would like to make the following remark about the evolution of my research process. In my research, I began using a semi-structured interview approach. However, after evaluating the first semi-structured interview, I found that this type of interviewing produced less than adequate answers for my research goal. Accordingly, I started searching for a different data collection method that would go into more depth, and found the biographical-narrative interview. This method corresponds much more to my research focus and has proven to be far more expedient.

However, the setting affects the data: each interviewee knows that her/his statements will constitute material for a scientific project since I have told her/him; this is due to my researcher sincerity. This knowledge can lead to reactive effects. The reason is that it makes a difference whether you tell the reconstruction of your life to a partner, a friend or a stranger, who then possibly uses it for scientific purposes. These effects do not lead to a distortion, but can certainly mean difficulties in the validity of the collected data (Marotzki 2006).

The interview setting in itself is an abnormal situation of interaction, but a certain asymmetry between informant and researcher cannot be avoided (Marotzki 2006; Schulze 1997). An interview itself, but especially the biographical interview, is a special form of interaction. Particularly, in the first part of the interview unilateral verbal communication on the part of the interviewee is taking place. This is far away from everyday conversation, and thus from alternating speech acts, which occur in a dialogue between the interlocutors. Also, I, as the researcher, said little, but rather listened. This from the interaction experience is usually unknown from everyday life conversation (Rosenthal 2011; Stroobants 2005). Although it is possible to be careful to talk openly about this kind of special situation and to show a possible natural and relaxed dealing with it, in order to pre-define the role of the interview actors. However, it will hardly be possible to avoid these 'artificial' situations completely (Marotzki 2006).

During the interview, the interviewees often see themselves addressed in the role of the entrepreneur. This contributes to the fact that they, at least initially, tell their story primarily in this role, and only slowly move to their private role. Interestingly, some interviewees make no strict separation between the private and entrepreneurial person. Also, that some interviewees took longer to engage in the interview situation than others influenced how or whether at all they were narrating their life story. Often, however, they initially coped with the unfamiliar situation by simply reporting and describing their story, and then more often narrative sequences followed in their life narrations.

Limitations of the data analysis method

In the process of interpretation, I, as the researcher, am not a blank sheet of paper. Although I can try to prevent inclusion of my story and my life experiences too much into the interpretation, I will always try to understand what is said in the context and from the perspective to which I have access to (Stroobants 2005). Of course, I can, to a certain degree, control this process consciously and try to deliberately look from a certain angle at the data. However, I will not succeed in entirely leaving out my own life experiences and my social embeddedness (Schulze 2006). For this reason, qualitative research literature recommends that analysis of qualitative data is undertaken by several interpreters, ideally to analyse the data in a so-called analysis-workshop where several qualitative researchers get together in order to analyse qualitative data together. Then, if many readings and interpretations are generated and finally the most likely one is confirmed, a distortion caused by the unilateral interpretation of only one researcher can be kept as low as possible (Rosenthal 2011). According to this advice, I joined such an analysis-workshop that took place on a regular base at my university. There qualitative researchers from different disciplines (e.g. sociology, cultural studies, environmental studies) have come together to interpret their data.

Although the methodological approach presented here may seem complicated and too time-intensive to some scholars – especially if they are more used to a way of thinking and a research approach that is closer to the explaining paradigm – my choice of the understanding paradigm and methods has proven suitable for the present research interest. By exploring the application of the methodology of biographical research in educational science and its data collection and analysis methods, I gained significant new insights into two aspects. Firstly, I have obtained a comprehensive overview of methodological backgrounds and research opportunities, as well as understanding the appropriate research methods for the objective of my research. Consequently, I feel more knowledgeable and confident now when justifying my research approach. Secondly, it is becoming apparent that my selection and application of the methodological design will lead to meaningful results and thus to – at least – a little contribution to the ESD research.

My recommendations for emerging researchers

As a result of my experiences, I would like to encourage early career researchers to intensively examine their research interests, which then leads to their objective of their research. Only then will it be possible to be creative with the research design, and not just 'to play it safe' in their own research or to do research only 'by the book', i.e. applying methods that are 'frequently' applied and therefore appear as 'proven'. Rather, I think it is important for researchers to focus on their own research interests. Of course, they should keep in view the added value their research can contribute to the ESD research. Still, the most important thing is to find the most appropriate methodology and methods for their research objective. Only when their research interests and methods align, can exciting results come to light. Only if they know 'what' to do and 'why' to do it, will they become an actor in research. Early career researchers will be starting to really enjoy their own research and eventually contribute to their research field. So, they need to find their individual way of doing research. I am of the opinion that research approaches should be chosen in relation to research interests and not due to practicability. The same applies to the research interest, which should not be overly influenced by wide-spread and typically applied research methods.

Notes

1 A subject (in this case a SE) conducts a meaningful action as soon as it has a meaning for her/him. Thus, she/he acts intentionally and meaningfully. Still, her/his actions take place within existing and emerging social structures. Meaning making structures refer to subjective meaning making of an action that is related to socially (also culturally) constructed meaning structures.

2 A very good introduction to the basics of social science research I used was the Michael Crotty book *The Foundations of Social Research* (Crotty 1998). This helped me to refresh my knowledge and served as a re-introduction to the field of the paradigms and methodologies. Although it is not the latest work in this field, it is still a basic book that has lost nothing of its topicality. Rather, I see it as a good and easy introduction to this subject that, next to the books of Denzin and Lincoln (Denzin and Lincoln 2000, 2011) and a few German books (e.g. Abels 2010; Kerber 1991) have greatly helped me in navigating the jungle of philosophical backgrounds and methodologies.

References

Abels, H., 2010. *Interaktion, Identität, Präsentation: Kleine Einführung in interpretative Theorien der Soziologie* [Interaction, Identity, Presentation – A little introduction to interpretative theories in sociology], Hagener Studientexte zur Soziologie [Hagen's study texts for sociology], 5th edn. Wiesbaden: VS, Verlag für Sozialwiss.

Adomßent, M., Beringer, A. and Barth, M., eds, 2009. *World in Transition: Sustainability Perspectives for Higher Education*. Bad Homburg v.d.H.: VAS Verlag für Akad. Schriften.

Alheit, P. and Dausien, B., 2006. 'Biographieforschung in der Erwachsenenbildung' [Biographical research in adult education], in Krüger, H.-H. and Marotzki, W. (eds), *Handbuch erziehungswissenschaftliche Biographieforschung* [Handbook for educational biographical research], 2nd edn. Wiesbaden: VS, Verlag für Sozialwiss., 431–57.

Amann, W., Pirson, M., Dierksmeier, C., Kimakowitz, E.v., Khan, S. and Spitzek, H., 2011a. 'The Rise of the Humanistic Businesss Schools as the Way Forward', in Amann, W., Pirson, M., Dierksmeier, C., Kimakowitz, E.v. and Spitzek, H. (eds), *Business Schools under Fire: Humanistic Management – Education as the Way Forward*, Humanism in Business Series. Houndmills, Basingstoke: Palgrave Macmillan, 447–69.

Amann, W., Pirson, M., Spitzek, H., Dierksmeier, C., Kimakowitz, E.v. and Khan, S., 2011b. 'Humanistic Management Education – Academic Responsibility for the 21st Century', in Amann, W., Pirson, M., Dierksmeier, C., Kimakowitz, E.v. and Spitzek, H. (eds), *Business Schools under Fire: Humanistic Management – Education as the Way Forward*, Humanism in Business Series. Houndmills, Basingstoke: Palgrave Macmillan, 3–15.

Baacke, D. and Schulze, T. (eds), 1979/1993. *Aus Geschichten lernen: Zur Einübung pädagogischen Verstehens* [Learning from narratives. To practice pedagogical understanding]. Weinheim: Juventa Verlag.

Barth, M., 2015. *Implementing Sustainability in Higher Education: Learning in an Age of Transformation*, Routledge Studies in Sustainable Development. London: Routledge.

Barth, M., Godemann, J., Rieckmann, M. and Stoltenberg, U., 2007. 'Developing Key Competencies for Sustainable Development in Higher Education', *International Journal of Sustainability in Higher Education*, 8(4), 416–30.

Barth, M. and Michelsen, G., 2013. 'Learning for Change: An Educational Contribution to Sustainability Science', *Sustainability Science*, 8(1), 103–19.

Crotty, M., 1998. *The Foundations of Social Research: Meaning and Perspective in the Research Process.* London and Thousand Oaks, CA: SAGE Publications.

de Haan, G., 2006. 'The BLK "21" Programme in Germany: A "Gestaltungskompetenz"-based Model for Education for Sustainable Development', *Environmental Education Research*, 12(1), 19–32.

de Haan, G., 2008. 'Gestaltungskompetenz als Kompetenzkonzept der Bildung für nachhaltige Entwicklung' [Gestaltungskompetenz (shaping competence) as competence concept for education for sustainable development], in Bormann, I. and Haan, G. (eds), *Kompetenzen der Bildung für nachhaltige Entwicklung: Operationalisierung, Messung, Rahmenbedingungen, Befunde* [Competences of education for sustainable development: operationalisation, assessment, findings], 1st edn. Wiesbaden: VS, Verlag für Sozialwissenschaften, 23–43.

de Leeuw, E., 1999. 'Healthy Cities: Urban Social Entrepreneurship for Health', *Health Promotion International*, 14(3), 261–9.

Denzin, N.K. and Lincoln, Y.S., 2000. *Handbook of Qualitative Research*, 2nd edn. Thousand Oaks, CA: SAGE Publications.

Denzin, N.K. and Lincoln, Y.S., 2011. *The Sage Handbook of Qualitative Research*, 4th edn. Thousand Oaks, CA: SAGE.

Ecarius, J., 2006. 'Biographieforschung und Lernen' [Biographical research and learning], in Krüger, H.-H. and Marotzki, W. (eds), *Handbuch erziehungswissenschaftliche Biographieforschung* [Handbook for educational biographical research], 2nd edn. Wiesbaden: VS, Verlag für Sozialwiss., 91–108.

Ecarius, J. and Friebertshäuser, B., 2005. 'Einleitung: Literalität, Bildung und Biographie – empirische und theoretische Herausforderungen' [Introduction: Literality, education and biography – empirical and theoretical challenges], in Ecarius, J. and Friebertshäuser, B. (eds), *Literalität, Bildung und Biographie: Perspektiven erziehungswissenschaftlicher Biographieforschung* [Literality, education and biography: Perspectives of educational biographical research. Opladen: Budrich, 7–16.

Fuchs, T., 2011. *Bildung und Biographie: Eine Reformulierung der bildungstheoretisch orientierten Biographieforschung, Pädagogik* [Education and biography – A reformulation of educational theory-oriented biographical research], 1st edn. Bielefeld: transcript.

Fuchs, T., 2012. 'Bildungstheorie und Bildungsforschung – Die Etablierung von 'Annäherungsarenen' im Kontext der qualitativen Forschung' [Educational theory and educational research – The establishment of 'convergence arenas' in the context of qualitative research], in Miethe, I. and Müller, H.-R. (eds), *Qualitative Bildungsforschung und Bildungstheorie* [Qualitative educational research and educational theory]. Leverkusen: Budrich, 129–47.

Glaser, B.G. and Strauss, A.L., 2005 [1965]. *Awareness of Dying*. New Brunswick, NJ: Aldine Transaction.

Habermas, J., 1995. *Theorie des kommunikativen Handelns* [Theory of communicative action]. Frankfurt a.M.:Suhrkamp-Taschenbuch Wissenschaft, 1175, Suhrkamp.

Kerber, H. (ed.), 1991. *Soziologie: Arbeitsfelder, Theorien, Ausbildung. Ein Grundkurs* [Sociology – Fields of work, theories, education. A basic course], Orig. ed, Reinbek bei Hamburg: Rowohlt-Taschenbuch-Verl.

Kleemann, F., Krähnke, U. and Matuschek, I., 2009. *Interpretative Sozialforschung: Eine praxisorientierte Einführung, Lehrbuch* [Interpretative social research – A practice-oriented introduction], 1st edn. Wiesbaden: VS, Verlag für Sozialwiss.

Kokemohr, R. and Koller, H.-C., 1996. 'Die rhetorische Artikulation von Bildungsprozessen. Zur Methodologie erziehungswissenschaftlicher Biographieforschung' [The rhetorical articulation of educational processes. The methodology of educational biographical research], in Krüger, H.-H. and Marotzki, W. (eds), *Erziehungswissenschaftliche Biographieforschung* [Educational biographical research]. Wiesbaden: VS Verlag für Sozialwiss, 90–102.

Koller, H.-C., 2011. 'The Research of Transformational Education Processes: Exemplary Considerations on the Relation of the Philosophy of Education and Educational Research', *European Educational Research Journal*, 10(3), 375–82.

Koller, H.-C., 2012. 'Anders werden. Zur Erforschung transformatorischer Bildungsprozesse' [Becoming different. The exploration of transformational educational processes], in Miethe, I. and Müller, H.-R. (eds), *Qualitative Bildungsforschung und Bildungstheorie* [Qualitative educational research and educational theory]. Leverkusen: Budrich, 19–33.

Koller, H.-C., 2013. *Bildung anders denken: Einführung in die Theorie transformatorischer Bildungsprozesse* [Thinking education differently. Introduction into the theory of transformational learning processes]. Stuttgart: Kohlhammer Verlag.

Krüger, H.-H. and Marotzki, W., 2006. 'Biographieforschung und Erziehungswissenschaft – Einleitende Anmerkungen' [Biographical research and educational sciences – introductory remarks], in Krüger,

H.-H. and Marotzki, W. (eds), *Handbuch erziehungswissenschaftliche Biographieforschung* [Handbook for educational biographical research], 2nd edn. Wiesbaden: VS, Verlag für Sozialwiss, 7–10.

Lourenco, F., Jones, O. and Jayawarna, D., 2013. 'Promoting Sustainable Development: The Role of Entrepreneurship Education', *International Small Business Journal*, 31(8), 841–65.

Marotzki, W., 2006. 'Bildungstheorie und allgemeine Biographieforschung' [Educational theory and general biograpical research], in Krüger, H.-H. and Marotzki, W. (eds). *Handbuch erziehungswissenschaftliche Biographieforschung* [Handbook for educational biographical research], 2nd edn. Wiesbaden: VS, Verlag für Sozialwiss, 59–70.

Marotzki, W. and Tiefel, S., 2010.' Qualitative Bildungsforschung' [Qualitative educational research], in Friebertshäuser, B., Langer, A. and Prengel, A. (eds), *Handbuch qualitative Forschungsmethoden in der Erziehungswissenschaft* [Handbook for qualitative research methods in educational sciences]. Weinheim: Juventa Verlag, 73–88.

Morsing, M. and Rovira, A.S., 2011. 'Business Schools As Usual?', in Morsing, M. and Rovira, A.S. (eds), *Business Schools and their Contribution to Society*. Los Angeles, CA and London: SAGE, xviii–xxv.

Müller-Christ, G., 2013. 'Der Umgang mit Komplexität und Widersprüchen im Nachhaltigkeitsmanagement: Ein Blick auf das Prämissensystem betrieblicher Entscheidungen' [The approach to complexity and conflicts in sustainability management: A glance at the premise system operational decisions]. Wirtschaftsuniversität Wien: Paper presented at Herbsttagung der Kommission Nachhaltigkeitsmanagement, 7–8 October.

Parkin, S., Johnston, A., Buckland, H., Brookes, F. and White, E., 2004. 'Learning and Skills for Sustainable Development. Developing a Sustainability Literate Society, Guidance for Higher Education Institutions'. https://www.forumforthefuture.org/sites/default/files/project/downloads/learningandskills.pdf [accessed: 20 February 2015].

Radenbach, N. and Rosenthal, G., 2012. 'Das Vergangene ist auch Gegenwart, das Gesellschaftliche ist auch Individuell' [The past is also present, the social is also individual], *Sozialer Sinn – Zeitschrift für hermeneutische Sozialforschung*, 13(1), 3–37.

Roberts, B., 2002. *Biographical Research, Understanding Social Research*. Buckingham: Open University Press.

Rogers, E.M., 2003. *Diffusion of Innovations*, 5th edn. New York: Free Press.

Rosenthal, G., 2006. 'The Narrated Life Story: On the Interrelation Between Experience, Memory and Narration', in Milnes, K., Horrocks, C., Kelly, N., Roberts, B. and Robinson, D. (eds), *Narrative, Memory, and Knowledge: Representations, Aesthetics, and contexts*. Huddersfield: University of Huddersfield, 1–16.

Rosenthal, G., 2011. *Interpretative Sozialforschung: Eine Einführung* [Interpretative social research. An introduction], Grundlagentexte Soziologie. Weinheim [u.a.]: Juventa.

Rosenthal, G., 2012. 'A Plea for a More Interpretative, More Empirical and More Historical Sociology', in Kalekin-Fishman, D. and Denis, A. (eds), *The Shape of Sociology for the 21st Century: Tradition and Renewal*. Thousand Oaks, CA: SAGE Publications, 202–17.

Schaltegger, S. and Wagner, M., 2011. 'Sustainable Entrepreneurship and Sustainability Innovation: Categories and Interactions', *Business Strategy and the Environment*, 20(4), 222–37.

Schreier, M., 2010. 'Fallauswahl' [Sampling], in Mey, G. and Mruck, K. (eds), *Handbuch Qualitative Forschung in der Psychologie* [Handbook for qualitative research in psychology], 1st edn. Wiesbaden: VS, Verlag für Sozialwiss, 238–51.

Schulze, T., 1997. 'Interpretation von autobiographischen Texten' [Interpretation of autobiographical texts], in Friebertshäuser, B., Prengel, A. and Annedore, A. (eds), *Handbuch qualitative Forschungsmethoden in der Erziehungswissenschaft* [Handbook for qualitative research methods in educational sciences]. Weinheim: Juventa, 323–40.

Schulze, T., 2005. 'Strukturen und Modalitäten biographischen Lernens. Eine Untersuchung am Beispiel der Autobiographie von Marc Chagall' [Structures and modalities of biographical learning. An exploration using the example of Marc Chargall's autobiography], *Zeitschrift für qualitative Sozialforschung*, 1, 43–64.

Schulze, T., 2006. 'Biographieforschung in der Erziehungswissenschaft – Gegenstandbereich und Bedeutung' [Biographical research in educational sciences – subject area and meaning], in Krüger, H.-H. and Marotzki, W. (eds), *Handbuch erziehungswissenschaftliche Biographieforschung* [Handbook for educational biographical research], 2nd edn. Wiesbaden: VS, Verlag für Sozialwiss, 35–57.

Schulze, T., 2009. 'Annäherung an eine Theorie komplexer und längerfristiger Lernprozesse' [Approaching a theory of complex and long-term learning processes], in Strobel-Eisele, G. and Wacker, A. (eds), *Konzepte des Lernens in der Erziehungswissenschaft: Phänomene, Reflexionen, Konstruktionen,*

Klinkhardt Forschung [Concepts of learning in educational sciences: phenomena, reflections, constructions]. Bad Heilbrunn: Klinkhardt, 56–69.

Schütze, F., 1983. 'Biographieforschung und narratives Interview' [Biographical research and the narrative interview], *Neue Praxis*, 13(3), 283–93.

Schütze, F., 2007. 'Biography Analysis on the Empirical Base of Autobiographical Narratives: How to Analyse Autobiographical Narratives Interviews. Part 1', in *Biographical Counselling in Rehabilitative Vocational Training*. Magdeburg: Universität Magdeburg.

Sipos, Y., Battisti, B. and Grimm, K., 2008. 'Achieving Transformative Sustainability Learning: Engaging Head, Hands and Heart', *International Journal of Sustainability in Higher Education*, 9(1), 68–86.

Stroobants, V., 2005. 'Stories about Learning in Narrative Biographical Research', *International Journal of Qualitative Studies in Education*, 18(1), 47–61.

Vare, P. and Scott, W., 2007. 'Learning for a Change: Exploring the Relationship Between Education and Sustainable Development', *Journal of Education for Sustainable Development*, 1(2), 191–8.

Wals, A.E., 2010. 'Mirroring, Gestaltswitching and Transformative Social Learning: Stepping Stones for Developing Sustainability Competence', *International Journal of Sustainability in Higher Education*, 11(4), 380–90.

Wals, A.E., Kieft, G., Tröften, P.-E. and Westin, M., 2010. *Education for Sustainable Development: Research Overview*, Sida review/Swedisch International Development Cooperatioen Agency, 2010(13), Stockholm: SIDA.

Weidinger, C., Fischler, F. and Schmidpeter, R., 2014. 'Preface', in Weidinger, C., Fischler, F. and Schmidpeter, R. (eds), *Sustainable Entrepreneurship: Business Success through Sustainability, CSR, Sustainability, Ethics & Governance*. Heidelberg, New York, Dordrecht, London: Springer, xvii–xix.

27

ACADEMICS' OPINIONS AND PRACTICES OF EDUCATION FOR SUSTAINABLE DEVELOPMENT

Reflections on a nation-wide, mixed-methods, multidisciplinary study

Belinda Christie and Kelly Miller

Introduction

To ensure that Education for Sustainable Development (ESD) is present in the classroom of every university student, research is required to understand how those responsible for teaching value, understand and practice ESD (Reid and Petocz 2006). Given the relative academic freedom university teachers enjoy, the decision of what and how to teach lies largely with the individual academic (Åkerlind and Kayrooz 2003; Shephard and Furnari 2013). An academic's own perception of sustainability will influence if and how they teach it, and in turn influence the quality of their own students' understanding and potential practice of the concept (Cotton *et al.* 2007; Prosser and Trigwell 1997; Reid and Petocz 2006). Indeed, previous studies have noted that academics' perceptions of sustainability have been a major inhibitor to ESD curricula inclusion, with many believing that ESD is not relevant to their discipline (Cotton and Winter 2010; Dawe *et al.* 2005; Velazquez *et al.* 2005).

Furthermore, the subjective, controversial, ill-defined and contextual nature of the concept of ESD adds complication to gaining teaching academics' support for ESD (Scott and Gough 2004; Stevenson *et al.* 2013; Thomas and Nicita 2002; Wals and Blewitt 2010). ESD aligns with *postpositivist epistemology*, where knowledge is understood as fluid and as formed and shaped by interactions with a constantly evolving world (Littledyke and Manolas 2010). As such, there are many commentaries on the need for *constructivist* (where knowledge is understood as created from experience), learner-centred, approaches to teach sustainability (Christie *et al.* 2013; Littledyke 2008; Sipos *et al.* 2008). Such methods include the use of active, participatory, interdisciplinary, holistic and experiential learning approaches, where the teacher acts as a facilitator of learning, rather than a director or 'sage on the stage' transmitting information to their students (Cotton and Winter 2010; Dawe *et al.* 2005; Littledyke and Manolas 2010; Sipos *et al.* 2008; Thomas 2009; Tilbury and Cooke 2005).

Teaching methods like critical and holistic thinking, place-based education, role plays, stimulus activities, critical reading and writing, reflective accounts, group discussions and debates, field work, problem-based learning and case studies are therefore often advocated for teaching

ESD as they align with the epistemologies, ideologies and pedagogies that support postpositivist approaches to education (for a more detailed description of these teaching methods and their associated philosophies, see Christie *et al.* 2013).

Of particular importance to ESD, is the use of critical thinking within the classroom. While the definitions of critical thinking are varied (see for example Dewey 1933; Facione 1990; Lipman 1988; King and Kitchener 1994), the process is often described as when an individual reorientates their thinking; to knowledge being objective and observable, to the new understanding that knowledge is ever changing, uncertain and contextual (King and Kitchener 1994). As such, critical thinking is often widely promoted as essential to the understanding, evaluation and practice of sustainable development – as well as being a skill commonly iterated in university graduate attributes (Cotton and Winter 2010; Commonwealth of Australia 2007; Jickling 1992; McKeown and Hopkins 2003; Oulton *et al.* 2004; Rieckmann 2012; Seatter 2011; Thomas 2009; Wals and Jickling 2002; Wright and Horst 2013).

Conversely, teaching methods such as lectures, tutorials and rote learning are not often promoted for ESD, as they are viewed as passive forms of education which align with *positivist epistemology* – thereby emphasising the acquisition and clarification of what is seen as objective and factual information (Exley and Dennick 2009; Littledyke and Manolas 2010). This is not to say that lectures, tutorials, rote learning and the like cannot be used to engage students in postpositivist learning, rather that the literature and history of use of these teaching methods suggests that they are not often associated with constructivist learner-centred approaches (Christie *et al.* 2013).

Although there is some evidence that constructivist approaches to teaching and learning are gaining popularity in university classrooms (Biggs and Tang 2007; Kerka 1997), there is little research exploring to what extent these methods are already used, or valued, by teaching academics across disciplines, and if and how this is associated with ESD. Additionally, there is a common perception among academics and the general public, that ESD is the domain of the life sciences, geography and biology (Cotton *et al.* 2007). This perception has influenced the uptake of sustainability in different disciplines (Reid and Petocz 2006; Sherren 2006; Thomas and Nicita 2002). However, research regarding teaching academics' self-reported opinions and practice of ESD has failed to detect these differences (e.g. Cotton *et al.* 2007; Shephard and Furnari 2013; Stables and Scott 2002). General agreement on the ideal of ESD and small sample sizes may have masked differences in teaching academics' understanding and application of ESD across the disciplines (Christie *et al.* 2015). Although one should not seek to generalise disciplinary experience of any individual teacher (Littledyke 2008), identifying large scale differences between the disciplines can help ESD advocates tailor their approaches and programmes.

Despite the importance of research involving teaching academics from across disciplines, very few studies have explored these stakeholders' conceptions, beliefs, experiences and practices of ESD in higher education, or how their current teaching practices might align with ESD pedagogy (Christie *et al.* 2013, 2015; Cotton *et al.* 2007; Reid and Petocz 2006). Studies that have involved teaching academics are often based on qualitative research methods, employing case study, singular university or singular discipline approaches, and involving academics with a stated interest in ESD, rather than conducting research from a multidisciplinary, or sector-wide, perspective (Aznar Minguet *et al.* 2011; Carew and Mitchell 2006; Cotton *et al.* 2007; Dyball and Carpenter 2006; Joseph *et al.* 2013; McKeown-Ice 2000; Reid and Petocz 2006; Shephard and Furnari 2013; Brinkhurst *et al.* 2011; Barth and Rieckmann 2013; Wemmenhove and de Groot 2001). It is important to acknowledge that although each institution is unique (Corcoran *et al.* 2004), universities are not 'free standing' and that developments, trends and innovation in the higher education sector are indeed influenced by what is happening across the sector (Scott and Gough 2004: 243).

As seen across the university sector globally, many Australian universities have policies committing them to addressing sustainability[1] yet ESD curricular inclusion has been minimal (Bekessy *et al.* 2003; Christie *et al.* 2013; Lang *et al.* 2006; Leihy and Salazar 2011; Noonan and Thomas 2004; Tilbury *et al.* 2005). Much of the sector wide research investigating ESD in higher education has largely been based on information gathered from policy documents, university websites, or administrators, rather than seeking the empirical opinions and experiences of current teaching academics (e.g. Bekessy *et al.* 2003; Holdsworth *et al.* 2008; Lang *et al.* 2006; Leihy and Salazar 2011; Sherren 2006; Thomas and Nicita 2002; Tilbury *et al.* 2005). As such, lessons learnt within the Australian university sector can serve universities globally.

Nation-wide research was therefore conducted to investigate teaching academics' opinions and practice of ESD and ESD pedagogy across disciplines. The aims of the study were to:

1. Determine teaching academics' current conceptions of and attitudes towards ESD in higher education.
2. Determine current teaching practice of ESD: if ESD is taught, teaching methods used, challenges and solutions for including ESD in classrooms and identifying ESD pedagogy compatible with current teaching practices.
3. Identify the differences between the disciplines in regards to the first two aims.

Research design

Methodology

Given that ESD aligns with post-positivist epistemology (Littledyke and Manolas 2010), research in ESD is often 'real world', or applied research, in that it intends to initiate a change, inform policy or programmes, or has an action agenda as part of the research itself (Fien 2002; Robson 2011). As such, its focus is different from other academic research where the primary intent is to develop an academic discipline (Robson 2011). Suitably, much of the higher education research in ESD to date has been 'small in scale and modest in scope', as it seeks to identify and propose contextual solutions to real local problems (Barth and Rieckmann 2013; Corcoran *et al.* 2004; Huberman and Miles 2002; Robson 2011: 3; Wemmenhove and de Groot 2001). This necessarily post-positivist and real-world approach to ESD typically employs qualitative research methods where concepts, opinions and experiences are described verbally, or in non-numeric form, within their given context (Robson 2011).

However, to convince teaching academics from across disciplines, and increasingly market-driven, evidence-focused decision-makers in higher education (Ernst & Young Australia 2012; Marginson and Considine 2000), to accept, endorse or fund, new approaches to teaching and learning, such as ESD, large-scale *positivist* research may also be beneficial; where knowledge is seen as fixed, certain and measurable (Littledyke and Manolas 2010). Positivist approaches, in this context, seek to measure and quantify the meaning and use of ESD, so that its importance, demand and implementation can be weighed and assessed by the numerical measures that so much of the current business-model operated university sector requires to aid decision-making. Such positivist research methods often involve the use of quantitative and statistical approaches to provide significant representation of the sample population, thereby aiding the transferability of the findings (Corcoran *et al.* 2004; Onwuegbuzie *et al.* 2009; Robson 2011).

ESD research in higher education, therefore, may at times, hold two distinct requirements:

post-positivist research where the nature of the concept of sustainability and people's interactions with it can be explored, and positivist research where interactions with sustainability can be quantified to serve university decision-making.

Figure 27.1 has been designed to demonstrate how these competing, yet interrelated, requirements of ESD higher education research both serve to inform the practice of ESD in university classrooms. Higher ESD Research (the central circle in the figure) not only includes real-world, or applied, research with the intent of informing policy and practice, but it also necessarily includes 'action research' to evaluate programs, and purely academic research aimed at advancing the field itself (Robson 2011). This research, in turn, informs real-world research practices. While the relationship between Higher ESD Research, university decision-makers (left circle in the figure), on-ground action (right circle in the figure) and classroom ESD (square in the figure) is vastly more complex, non-linear (Stevenson 2004), and involves more players, than represented, the figure expresses where the different ESD research paradigms may hold some influence.

Although qualitative and quantitative research have traditionally been considered as different research paradigms (Kuhn 1962), either type of research can be, and is, carried out from a range of philosophical positions and with any of the (non-exhaustive) list of research methods provided in the figure (Corcoran *et al.* 2004; Maxwell and Mittapalli 2010; Robson 2001; Stevenson 2004). While the qualitative/quantitative paradigms present an over simplification of the choices in research approaches, and indeed most research is undertaken somewhere on a continuum (where not even quantitative research is completely value-free), there none-the-less remains a tendency for research, and the role of the researcher, to align closer to one or the other approach (Khagram *et al.* 2010; Robson 2011; Stevenson 2004). Researchers often forge philosophical considerations in their choice of research strategies, such as ontology and epistemology, due to the engrained research 'norms' within their field, thus perpetuating the typical research methods adopted (Corcoran *et al.* 2004; Fien 2002; Khagram *et al.* 2010; Robson 2011). While there are many other philosophical traditions to contemplate when conducting research (e.g. interpretivism, constructivism, emancipatory, etc.) and research styles (e.g. experimental, statistical, comparative, ethnographic, triangulation, etc.) these are too numerous to mention in this review (Fien 2002; Khagram *et al.* 2010; Robson 2011; Stevenson 2004). Suffice to say that researchers should engage in these questions before commencing their work and ensure that the type of knowledge they seek to generate aligns, as best it can, with their intended research outcome (be it, generating heightened understanding, providing universal generalisations, or deconstructing a discourse, etc.) (Corcoran 2004; Stevenson 2004).

Given the spectrum of research methodology described in Figure 27.1, the present study adopted a 'mixed-methods' approach, using both traditional post-positivist qualitative, and positivist quantitative, research methods. The present chapter will provide a reflection on the adopted research approach – what worked well, what did not work so well, and what the authors would do differently in similar circumstances. Prior to this discussion however, a review of the methods and results of the research, summarised from previously published research (Christie *et al.* 2013, 2015; Christie and Miller, under review), are provided below.

Methods and analysis

The research design employed a multi-strategy and mixed-methods approach. Three phases were used to explore the research aims and to triangulate the results (using more than one data collection method and qualitative/quantitative approaches) (Khagram *et al.* 2010; Robson 2011).

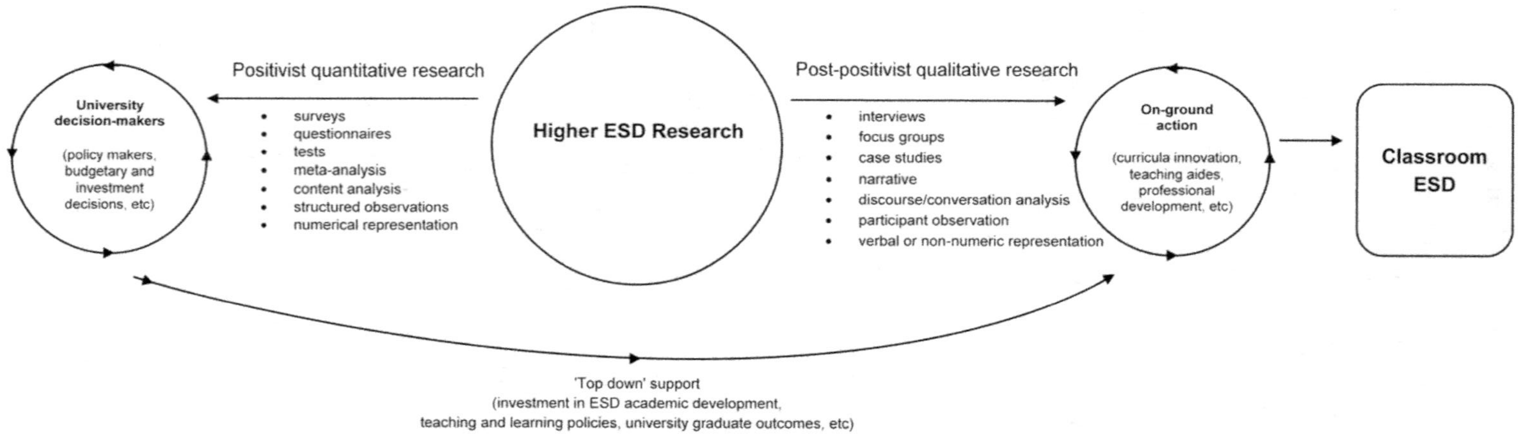

Figure 27.1 Conceptual diagram representing the relationship between positivist and post-positivist ESD research in higher education, decision-making processes, on-ground action, and implementation of ESD in the classroom

Phase one was a nation-wide, multidisciplinary study which intended to collect mostly quantitative data for inferential statistical analysis, and some qualitative data to further explore and triangulate evident quantitative themes. An online, 26-question questionnaire was sent to approximately one quarter of the teaching academics in every discipline of every Australian university (except one) on 24 January 2011 (n = 7,066).

Contact details for the academics were obtained by searching each Australian university's publically accessible web pages for the name and email address of every fourth academic listed (except one university where academics' contact details were not publically accessible). To intentionally exclude the use of any words that might bias the sample to those interested in sustainability or environment issues, the subject line of the email was labelled 'teaching methods'.

Academics were sent a personally addressed initial invitation to participate, a reminder five weeks later, and those who had not completed the questionnaire or had not indicated they did not wish to participate, were sent a shorter questionnaire at seven weeks. The shorter questionnaire consisted of three questions that were identical in words and format to the original questionnaire, allowing responses to the original and shorter questionnaires to be compared to check for any systematic bias. If the two samples of academics held similar views, then the original questionnaire was less likely to represent a bias towards those interested in the research topic (Krestser *et al.* 2009).[2]

Questions were designed by drawing on ESD and environmental education literature and best practice questionnaire design principles (e.g. see Dillman *et al.* 2009; Robson 2011). Both qualitative and quantitative approaches were used within the questionnaire, such as 'closed' questions (Likert scale; tick box; yes/no) and open-ended questions (providing space for the respondent's own descriptions) (McKernan 1996). Questions surrounded four main themes: Teaching practices (teaching methods used and why), critical thinking (definitions and use as a teaching method), Education for Sustainability (definitions, attitudes, use, teaching methods and experiences of constraints), and demographic questions. The same questionnaire was distributed to all so that disciplines could be compared. Spaces for qualitative responses provided alongside the quantitative questions allowed respondents to express their own views within their disciplinary framework.

Given that the questionnaire was designed to be completed by respondents of all academic disciplines, it was recognised that respondents would hold varying degrees of familiarity with the term Education for Sustainability.[3] As such, a definition of Education for Sustainability was developed to guide those whose first contact with the term was the questionnaire itself, while still allowing those familiar with the concept to articulate their own understanding through a qualitative response. A question was therefore created:

> For the purposes of this study, 'education for sustainability' is defined as: 'Building knowledge and skills to create environmentally sustainable citizens.' Often referred to as 'environmental education'. If you disagree with the above definition please give your own definition or explanation below (in 50 words or less).

The definition was created by referencing Australian university and government policy documents. The term Education for Sustainability was chosen, rather than any other variation such as ESD, as this was the most commonly used term within Australian university and government policy documents, and therefore more likely to be used within the respondents' university. During the pilot study it was evident that respondents felt the historically used term 'environmental education' was more self-explanatory, and so this term was also added to aid understanding.

Although there are numerous commentaries on how Education for Sustainability differs from environmental education (Monroe 2012; Kopnina 2012; McKeown and Hopkins 2003; Stevenson *et al.* 2013), it was felt that explanation of this debate would be too cumbersome in a questionnaire where using as little text as possible was essential to ensuring the high response rate required to enable statistical comparisons between disciplines (Dillman *et al.* 2009).

Questionnaire data were analysed using SPSS (v.17.0) with descriptive and inferential statistics for categorical data. Inferential statistical procedures conducted included: chi-square tests of independence, one-way between-groups analysis of variance (ANOVA), principal component analysis, factor analysis, and Cronbach's α reliability analysis (Cronbach 1990; Pallant 2011). For ease of reader interpretation, the 13 disciplines reported by academics were grouped into five categories or 'aggregate disciplines': environment, science, creative, humanities and interdisciplinary academics.[4]

The second phase of the study was conducted in 2012 through semi-structured in-depth interviews, to further explore the quantitative themes evident in the first phase of the study. Of the questionnaire respondents who indicated they would like to participate further in the research, 30 academics were randomly selected for an in-depth interview (phase two), and access to their students for classroom observation and student questionnaires (phase three, as discussed below). The process of seeking 'organisational approval' to contact staff and students from each university largely dictated the number, and timing, of the interviews conducted.

Academics were contacted via email and invited to participate in the research a second time through a face-to-face or telephone interview. Interview questions were designed in reference to ESD and environmental education literature and the evolving findings from the quantitative phase of the study (i.e. Christie *et al.* 2013, 2015). A semi-structured design was chosen to allow interview participants to say as much or as little as they liked, and to allow subjective conceptualisations of the subject matter, with the understanding that all interpretations would be equally valid.

Three broad questions were asked: 'What does the term Education for Sustainability mean to you', 'Tell me about the teaching methods you use in your classes', and 'Tell me about critical thinking in your teaching'. Simple demographic questions were also included. Prompts, to further explore the participants' conceptualisations of ESD, ESD pedagogy and their relationship with their own discipline, were used sparingly in the belief that if a concept or experience was important enough to a participant, then it would be mentioned unsolicited.

Interviews lasted between 13 and 42 minutes, with the majority nearing 30 minutes in length. Interviews were digitally voice recorded, transcribed verbatim and pseudonyms were assigned. Three pilot interviews were conducted at the researcher's own university, and were included in the final data set, as interview methods and questions did not change notably after the pilot study. The inclusion of the pilot interviews was carefully considered due to the risk of biasing the data towards one particular institutions' culture, practices or policy. However as the academics interviewed for the pilot study held diverse views and experiences, and given this stage of the study was designed to provide in-depth qualitative understanding, rather than establish a representative sample of academics across institutions, the pilot interviews were included in the final data set.

Five-phased thematic coding analysis was used, involving data familiarisation, code generation, theme identification, thematic network construction and processes of integration and interpretation (as in Robson 2011). The qualitative data analysis software QSR NVivo v10 was used to verify emerging themes. A 13-step process was then undertaken to scrutinise the data analysis (e.g. triangulating the data, replicating findings and finding rival explanations, etc.) (Robson 2011; Miles and Huberman 1994).

Phase three involved the use of student questionnaires and classroom observation conducted concurrently with the academic interviews. This phase was undertaken specifically to triangulate results of the academics interviews (e.g. reported vs actual teaching practices). For various reasons, to be discussed below, the student questionnaire data were found unsuitable to triangulate the academics' practices of ESD. As such, the student questionnaires were disregarded for this particular study. Classroom observation was abandoned for all but one university due to the time and financial constraints of travel, and the difficulties associated with gaining ethics approval from universities to access their students (discussed below).

Results

The results of the study are summarised briefly below from previously published work (Christie *et al.* 2013, 2015; Christie and Miller, under review). The study resulted in multidisciplinary, nation-wide representation of 1,819 teaching academics, equating to a 26 per cent response rate and providing a statistically fair representation of ~6 per cent of the entire academic teaching workforce of Australia. An additional 802 academics responded to the shorter questionnaire (used only to check for bias), equating to a total of 2,621 questionnaires returned, or 37 per cent of the sample. Results from the shorter questionnaire suggested that participation in the original questionnaire had not been biased by the opinions of academics keenly interested in the subject matter. Teaching academics represented the ratio of genders, and range of academic disciplines, employment status and years teaching within the sector.

Findings suggested that teaching academics supported the inclusion of ESD for all university students. Understanding of the term ESD was varied with most academics not providing further qualification to the broad definition given in the questionnaire, suggesting ambivalence or unfamiliarity with the concept, a finding reported previously (Cotton *et al.* 2007; Reid and Petocz 2006). Respondents preferred and employed lectures, tutorials, critical thinking and discussions in their teaching. Although ESD was largely not practiced within classrooms, when ESD was taught, teaching methods remained the same as when it was not taught, unlike in previous studies (Cotton *et al.* 2007) – this suggested that ESD was not pursued through the use of progressive pedagogies. Although the adoption of ESD pedagogies was low, there was evidence that academics actively sought to make their lessons more interactive within their lecture and tutorial format, often using critical thinking and discussions within their lessons.

Support, perceived relevance, reported difficulties with ESD, and adoption of ESD pedagogies were discipline specific. The environment disciplines (and to some extent the creative disciplines) were unsurprisingly most supportive of ESD, the creative disciplines were most engaged with ESD pedagogies, while the science disciplines were the least supportive of ESD and least engaged with ESD pedagogies. These previously unknown differences between the disciplines may have been due to the different epistemological traditions of each discipline.

These findings lead to two distinct considerations when developing the academic interview questions: exploring the use of critical thinking for sustainability and further explaining the differences between the disciplines in their understanding and practice of ESD.

From the eight institutions who granted approval in the six month time frame, 11 interviews were conducted. Despite the small number of interviews, participants represented a range of disciplines, genders and teaching experience within the university sector. While there were numerous similarities in results from the questionnaire and the interviews, the discrepancies between the results produced by the two methods, and the additional avenues of inquiry suggested by the questionnaire, yielded important findings.

Although teaching academics were largely unfamiliar with the term ESD, they assumed that it referred to education *about* sustainability, emphasising societal and economic issues, similar to previous studies (Christie *et al.* 2015; Christie and Miller, under review; Wright and Horst 2013). Sustainability or environment issues however were infrequently taught, although reported use appeared inflated compared to the academic questionnaire results.

Interview participants' conceptualisations and practice of critical thinking in their teaching aligned with ESD epistemology, and suggested that this teaching 'method' could be further promoted to teach, or engage with, sustainability. Counter to the findings in the academic questionnaire, interview participants did reflect on slightly shifting their approaches to teaching when discussing environment and sustainability issues with their students to include more constructivist learning principles (i.e. sustainability was, unlike other topics, up for discussion).

Although less pronounced as in the questionnaire, differences between the disciplines were evident in the academic interviews. In particular, science academics appeared less familiar with the term ESD than academics from the other disciplines, and many participants expressed disciplinary association with their chosen teaching methods. There were individual exceptions however, making the differences between the disciplines less clear. Had the present study solely relied on the small scale qualitative interviews to investigate the differences between the disciplines, few differences would have been visible.

The combined results of the two phases of the study suggested two specific research implications. Firstly, that the most realistic teaching methods to promote for ESD are discussions and critical thinking (those in the nexus of the pedagogies appropriate for teaching sustainability and methods that are already valued and used by teaching academics). Results suggested that academics' understanding and use of critical thinking in their classrooms appeared compatible with ESD epistemology. Further research regarding the understanding and use of critical thinking for sustainability would be of benefit.

Secondly, given the evident differences between the disciplines (especially in their support of ESD, perceived relevance to their discipline and use of ESD pedagogies), academics would respond positively to ESD framed within their disciplinary worldviews – such as using familiar language, cultures, pedagogy and experiences when exploring ESD. Further multidisciplinary research is required to explore these differences.

Reflecting on the research

The experience of conducting this nation-wide, mixed-methods and multidisciplinary study in ESD in higher education although in itself unique, offers insights into research approaches that may benefit researchers wishing to design similar studies. As such, the following offers some reflections on what worked well, what did not work so well, and what the researchers would do differently next time we tackle a nation-wide, mixed-methods or multidisciplinary study.

What worked well

Reflecting on the research process, there are a number of factors that contributed to the successful exploration of academics' opinions and practices of ESD across disciplines.

Comparing data between research methods enabled the findings from each phase of the research to be triangulated and further refined by the findings from the other phase (Khagram *et al.* 2010; Robson 2011). This 'mixed-methods' approach increased the rigour of the research and resulted in more meaningful and accurate representations of the research population (Khagram *et al.* 2010; Robson 2011). This would not have been achieved if only one research method was employed. Furthermore, given the large sample size, the quantitative results from the academic questionnaire may help communicate academic support, and desire, for ESD to university decision-makers, while the qualitative data from the academic questionnaire and interviews may help communicate the 'why' and 'how' of ESD to facilitate on-ground practice (Corcoran *et al.* 2004; Kyburz-Graber 2004;Yin 2009) (as seen in Figure 27.1).

The study successfully attracted a large sample size, allowing in-depth inferential analysis not often possible in other studies of ESD in higher education, due to their small scale approach (Barth and Rieckmann 2013; Fien 2002; Sherren 2006). The large sample size in the study can be attributed to a number of factors: the large initial sample (n=7,066), timing of the data collection, careful choice of words in the email heading, personally addressing each email, the online questionnaire format, avoiding ESD and discipline specific jargon, keeping the questionnaire as short as possible, and sending follow-up reminders (Dillman *et al.* 2009; Robson 2011). Foremost however, public open access to the academics' contact details was a vital factor in the success of the academic questionnaire, removing the lengthy (and sometimes unsuccessful) process of seeking 'organisational approval' from each university individually.

The chosen interview method of asking three broad semi-structured questions also provided valuable data that may not have appeared had the interview been rigid and overly structured (Robson 2011). Academics were easily drawn into discussion regarding their teaching methods and critical thinking, which lead to new unsolicited revelations regarding these themes (Christie and Miller, under review).

Crucial to the success of the mixed-methods research was also constructing a multidisciplinary research team. While much ESD research appears to be housed within, and undertaken by researchers with backgrounds in, education and humanities faculties, this research was conducted from within a science faculty. Although this, at times, meant less ESD research support (education research funding opportunities, collaboration with ESD specialists, etc.) it also meant that new approaches, ideas and perspectives on existing ESD research were cultivated. Without this 'outsider' cultivation, the present 'mixed-methods' research may not have materialised.[5]

What did not work so well

As with any study, there were of course aspects of the research that did not work as well as planned, or which added complexity to an already multifaceted project.

The large sample size for instance brought its own difficulties, as much of the data returned statistically significant results despite there being, at times, no real-world difference in the responses of the participants.[6] Although this was addressed through the use of percentages and effect size statistics (Pallant 2011), it indeed added further complexity to an already complex set of data analyses. Similarly, the volume of data collected in the questionnaire meant that the data had to be condensed to aid readability. Although this is helpful for creating 'bite size' pieces of information to pass on to decision-makers and ESD practitioners, much of the detail of academic opinions and practice of ESD became hidden within the resulting publications.[7] The academic interviews therefore held the added importance of helping to communicate this detail.

Another challenge was the task of defining Education for Sustainability within the questionnaire. Despite piloting the definition and terminology, and the term Education for Sustainability being the preferred language within most of the Australian university (and government) policy documents, respondents' qualitative responses suggest that they may have been more familiar with the term ESD (Christie *et al.* 2015). Whether or not the addition of the term 'environmental education', confused or clarified the term in respondents' minds is hard to determine. Open-ended questions soliciting respondents' own understandings of the term, both in the academic questionnaire and the interviews, were not the most ideal question formats to explore a concept which many respondents seemed unfamiliar with. Unavoidably, the given definition may have also slightly biased the opinions of respondents whose first encounter with the concept of ESD was the questionnaire itself.

One of the biggest difficulties experienced during the research project was gaining 'organisational approval' from each individual university for the academic interviews, student questionnaires and classroom observation. As autonomous institutions, each university necessarily has its own procedures, language, requirements and timeframe for approving research to be conducted on its campuses. This resulted in 'wasted' time and some asymmetry in the number of respondents that could be recruited for each phase of the research, further complicating comparisons between research methods and results.

Although the pooled data from the different classes of students in phase three of the research revealed interesting insights into student opinions of ESD, the data were not suitable to triangulate the academic interview findings. The students' ability to answer the questions was varied, and the enthusiasm of academics to administer the questionnaire in the face of competing demands on their class time was inconsistent. Without the classroom observation and student questionnaires to further triangulate the academic interview data, it is possible that the research may have over- or under-reported teaching and ESD practices (Robson 2011).

What we would do differently next time

Through the successes and challenges of the research, there are a number of research methods which would be approached differently in future research. These approaches may also serve others wishing to undertake similar cross institution, mixed-methods or multidisciplinary studies in higher education.

To explore an unfamiliar concept, such as ESD, with respondents, developing a conceptual framework alongside a more complete explanation of ESD, and its various iterations, would help engage respondents in the concept and solicit more in-depth responses. This section of the study would need to be carefully designed to ensure that the majority of respondents engage with the provided explanation (such as asking closed, or Likert scale, questions which solicit engagement with the ESD explanation, as opposed to an open-ended question) (Dillman *et al.* 2009).

Some of the difficulties experienced while conducting phase three of the research, the student questionnaires and classroom observations, also could have been rectified through a number of means: further piloting of the questionnaire, highly emphasising the importance to academics of following the questionnaire distribution instructions and timing, involving more on-ground researchers, and the researcher being present when the questionnaires were distributed (primarily, as with the abandoned classroom observations, a financial consideration) (Dillman *et al.* 2009; Robson 2011).

Foremost however, researchers should avoid approaching universities 'blind', without prior knowledge of their ethics approvals processes, culture and expectations. This contributed to the lengthy 'organisational approvals' process, as well as the small number of universities who granted access to their staff and students within the timeframe. Given ESD researchers are widespread among universities globally, connecting with one another through ESD research communities would help expedite the approvals process and advance cross-institution research. Especially important in multidisciplinary research such as ESD, these networks can also provide opportunities for funding higher education research and collaborating with specialists, which may be lacking in one's own faculty (whatever that faculty may be).

Concluding remarks

While the challenges of conducting nation-wide, mixed-methods and multidisciplinary research should not be underestimated, the present research demonstrates that perseverance with such multifaceted projects can lead one to new understandings. Above and beyond the practical impediments, and disciplinary traditions, that may direct our chosen methods (Khagram *et al.* 2010; Robson 2011), as researchers we should continue to reach outside of our disciplinary silos, consciously deliberate on, and select, research methods that best serve our research subject, and intended research outcomes (Corcoran *et al.* 2004; Khagram *et al.* 2010). We should equally remember to disseminate not just our research results, but to share learnings on the process of the research itself. In part, the successful inclusion of ESD in the classroom of every university student depends on our ability to do so.

Notes

1 For one example, 23 of the 39 Australian universities are signatories to the Talloires Declaration, committing them to addressing sustainability in their teaching, research and campus operations (ULSF 2014).

2 If the most common responses from both original and short questionnaire respondents were the same, then it is likely that the original questionnaire respondents did not participate solely because they were interested in ESD. For more detail regarding this procedure see Christie *et al.* (2013).

3 The most commonly used term in Australian university policy documents is Education for Sustainability, and so this term, rather than other variations, was used throughout the study (Christie *et al.* 2013, 2014; Christie and Miller, under review). The term Education for Sustainable Development (ESD) has been employed throughout the present chapter in keeping with the terminology of this Handbook.

4 Interdisciplinary respondents were respondents who fell into two or more of the aforementioned aggregate disciplines.

5 Although those within the field of sustainability education (often education academics) do indeed employ mixed-methods designs, these approaches are less common in this field of research (Barth and Rieckmann 2013) due, in part, to the disciplinary traditions of research (for example, the present research which was undertaken in a science faculty, had a strong quantitative focus) (Khagram *et al.* 2010; Robson 2011).

6 Particularly when sample sizes are large, statistical differences can sometimes occur, despite their being little real-world difference. For example, the environment disciplines might be 0.001 per cent more likely to agree to a statement than the humanities disciplines, but a difference of 0.001 is most likely not going to change how we approach that issue in ESD or higher education.

7 It should also be recognised that one of the limitations to such 'real-world' research is simply that decision-makers and academics outside of the field of ESD are unlikely to engage in ESD literature (Fien 2002). The shifting language of ESD also makes the literature less accessible to those outside ESD academia (Fien 2002; Sherren 2006). As such we need to find ways of crossing the boundaries of peer-reviewed literature, such as creating accessible executive reports (e.g. Tilbury *et al.* 2005), write for practitioner publications (such as newsletters or non-academic journals) and actively contribute our research findings to developing academic development programmes.

References

Åkerlind, G.S. and Kayrooz, C., 2003. 'Understanding Academic Freedom: The Views of Social Scientists', *Higher Education Research & Development*, 22(3), 327–44.

Aznar Minguet, P., Martinez-Agut, M.P., Palacios, B., Piñero, A. and Ull, M.A., 2011. 'Introducing Sustainability into University Curricula: An Indicator and Baseline Survey of the Views of University

Teachers at the University of Valencia', *Environmental Education Research*, 17(2), 145–66.

Barth, M. and Rieckmann, M., 2013. 'A Review on Research in Higher Education for Sustainable Development: Current Trends and Approaches (1992–2012)'. 7th World Environmental Education Congress 2013, 9–14 June 2013, Marrakech, Morocco.

Bekessy, S., Burgman, M., Wright, T., Leal Filho, W. and Smith, M., 2003. *Universities and Sustainability.* Carlton, VIC: Tela Series, Australian Conservation Foundation.

Biggs, J. and Tang, C., 2007. *Teaching for Quality Learning at University: What the Student Does.* Berkshire: Open University Press.

Brinkhurst, M., Rose, P., Maurice, G. and Ackerman, J.D., 2011. 'Achieving Campus Sustainability: Top-down, Bottom-up, or Neither?', *International Journal of Sustainability in Higher Education*, 12(4), 338–54.

Carew, A.L. and Mitchell, C.A., 2006. 'Metaphors used by some Engineering Academics in Australia for Understanding and Explaining Sustainability', *Environmental Education Research*, 12(2), 217–31.

Christie, B.A. and Miller, K.K., under review. '"Crikey! Education for sustainability?" A Qualitative Exploration of Academics' Understanding and Practice of Sustainability and Critical Thinking'.

Christie, B.A., Miller, K.K., Cooke, R. and White, J.G., 2013. 'Environmental Sustainability in Higher Education: How do Academics Teach?', *Environmental Education Research*, 19(3), 385–414.

Christie, B.A., Miller, K.K., Cooke, R. and White, J.G., 2015. 'Environmental Sustainability in Higher Education: What do Academics Think?' *Environmental Education Research*, 21(5), 655–86.

Commonwealth of Australia., 2007. *Caring for our Future: The Australian Government Strategy for the United Nations Decade for Education for Sustainable Development, 2005–2014.* Canberra: Australian Government Department of the Environment and Heritage.

Corcoran, P.B., Walker, K.E. and Wals, A.E.J., 2004. 'Case Studies, Make-your-case Studies, and Case Stories: A Critique of Case-study Methodology in Sustainability in Higher Education', *Environmental Education Research*, 10(1), 7–21.

Cotton, D. and Winter, J., 2010. '"It's not just bits of paper and light bulbs": A Review of Sustainability Pedagogies and their Potential for use in Higher Education', in Jones, P., Selby, D. and Sterling, S. (eds), *Sustainability Education: Perspectives and Practice across Higher Education.* London: Earthscan, 39–54.

Cotton, D., Warren, M., Maiboroda, O. and Bailey, I., 2007. 'Sustainable Development, Higher Education and Pedagogy: A Study of Lecturers' Beliefs and Attitudes', *Environmental Education Research*, 13(5), 579–97.

Cronbach, L.J., 1990. *Essentials of Psychological Testing.* New York: Harper Collins Publishers.

Dawe, G., Jucker, R. and Martin, S., 2005. *Sustainable Development in Higher Education: Current Practice and Future Developments.* York: A report for the Higher Education Academy.

Dewey, J., 1933. *How We Think: A Statement of the Relation of Reflective Thinking to the Educative Process.* Lexington, MA: D.C. Heath and Company.

Dillman, D.A., Smyth, J.D. and Christian, L.M., 2009. *Internet, Mail and Mixed-mode Surveys: The Tailored Design Method.* New Jersey: John Wiley and Sons.

Dyball, R. and Carpenter, D., 2006. 'Human Ecology and Education for Sustainability', in Leal Filho, W. and Carpenter, D. (eds), *Sustainability in the Australasian University Context.* Frankfurt: Peter Lang, 45–65.

Ernst & Young Australia., 2012. 'University of the Future: A Thousand Year Old Industry on the Cusp of Profound Change'. www.ey.com/Publication/vwLUAssets/University_of_the_future/$FILE/University_of_the_future_2012.pdf [accessed 24 February 2014].

Exley, K. and Dennick, R., 2009. *Giving a Lecture: From Presenting to Teaching*, 2nd edn. New York: Routledge.

Facione, P.A., 1990. 'Critical Thinking: A Statement of Expert Consensus for Purposes of Educational Assessment and Instruction'. Washington, DC: US Department of Education. (Eric Document No: ED315423). www.eric.ed.gov/ERICWebPortal/search/detailmini.jsp?_nfpb=true&_&ERICExtSearch_SearchValue_0=ED315423&ERICExtSearch_SearchType_0=no&accno=ED315423 [accessed 17 August 2014].

Fien, J., 2002. 'Advancing Sustainability in Higher Education: Issues and Opportunities for Research', *Higher Education Policy*, 15(2), 143–52.

Holdsworth, S., Wyborn, C., Bekessy, S. and Thomas, I., 2008. 'Professional Development for Education for Sustainability', *International Journal of Sustainability in Higher Education*, 9(2), 131–46.

Huberman, A.M. and Miles, M.B., 2002. *The Qualitative Researcher's Companion.* London: Sage Publications.

Jickling, B. 1992. 'Why I don't Want my Children to be Educated for Sustainable Development', *Journal of Environmental Education*, 23(3), 5–8.

Joseph, C., Nichol, E.O., Janggu, T. and Madi, N., 2013. 'Environmental Literacy and Attitudes among

Malaysian Business Educators', *International Journal of Sustainability in Higher Education*, 14(2), 196–208.
Kerka, S., 1997. *Constructivism, Workplace Learning, and Vocational Education*. Columbus, OH: ERIC Digest.
Khagram, S., Nicholas, K.A., Bever, D.M., Warren, J., Richards, E.H., Oleson, K., Kitzes, J., Katz, R., Hwang, R., Goldman, R., Funk, J. and Brauman, K.A., 2010. 'Thinking about Knowing: Conceptual Foundations for Interdisciplinary Environmental Research', *Environmental Conservation*, 37(4), 388–97.
King, P.M., and Kitchener, K.S., 1994. *Developing Reflective Judgement: Understanding and Promoting Intellectual Growth and Critical Thinking in Adolescents and Adults*. San Francisco, CA: Jossey-Bass.
Kopnina, H., 2012. 'Education for Sustainable Development (ESD): The Turn Away from "Environment" in Environmental Education?', *Environmental Education Research*, 18(5), 699–717.
Krestser, H.E., Curtis, P.D., Francis, J.D., Pendall, R.J. and Knuth, B.A., 2009. 'Factors Affecting Perceptions of Human-Wildlife Interactions in Residential Areas of Northern New York and Implications for Conservation', *Human Dimensions of Wildlife*, 14(2), 102–18.
Kuhn, T., 1962. The structure of scientific revolutions, Chicago: University of Chicago Press.
Kyburz-Graber, R., 2004. 'Does Case-study Methodology Lack Rigour? The Need for Quality Criteria for Sound Case-study Research, as Illustrated by a Recent Case in Secondary and Higher Education', *Environmental Education Research*, 10(1), 53–65.
Lang, J., Thomas, I. and Wilson, A., 2006. 'Education for Sustainability in Australian Universities: Where is the Action?', *Australian Journal of Environmental Education*, 22(2), 45–58.
Leihy, P. and Salazar, J., 2011. 'Education for Sustainability in University Curricula: Policies and Practice in Victoria, Melbourne, Centre for the Study of Higher Education, University of Melbourne'. Prepared for Sustainability Victoria. www.cshe.unimelb.edu.au/research/policy_dev/docs/EfS_CSHE.pdf [accessed 24 February 2014].
Lipman, M., 1988. 'Critical Thinking: What Can It Be?', *Educational Leadership*, 46(1), 38–43.
Littledyke, M., 2008. 'Science Education for Environmental Awareness: Approaches to Integrating Cognitive and Affective Domains', *Environmental Education Research*, 14(1), 1–17.
Littledyke, M. and Manolas, E., 2010. 'Ideology, Epistemology and Pedagogy: Barriers and Drivers to Education for Sustainability in Science Education', *Journal of Baltic Science Education*, 9(4), 285–301.
Marginson, S. and Considine, M., 2000. *The Enterprise University: Power, Governance and Reinvention in Australia*. Cambridge: Cambridge University Press.
Maxwell, J.A. and Mittapalli, K., 2010. 'Realism as a Stance for Mixed Methods Research', in Tashakkori, A. and Teddlie, C.B. (eds), *Handbook of Mixed Methods in Social and Behavioural Research*, 2nd edn. Thousand Oaks, CA: Sage, 145–67.
McKeown-Ice, R., 2000. 'Environmental Education in the United States: A Survey of Preservice Teacher Education Programs', *The Journal of Environmental Education*, 32(1), 4–11.
McKeown, R. and Hopkins, C., 2003. 'EE ≠ ESD: Defusing the Worry', *Environmental Education Research*, 9(1), 117–28.
McKernan, J., 1996. *Curriculum Action Research: A Handbook of Methods and Resources for the Reflective Practitioner*. London: Kogan Page.
Miles, M.B. and Huberman, A.M., 1994. *Qualitative Data Analysis: An Expanded Sourcebook*. Thousand Oaks, CA: Sage.
Monroe, M.C., 2012. 'The Co-evolution of ESD and EE', *Journal of Education for Sustainable Development*, 6(1), 43–47.
Noonan, D. and Thomas, I., 2004. 'Greening Universities in Australia: Process and Possibilities', *Australian Journal of Environmental Education*, 20(2), 67–79.
Onwuegbuzie, A.J., Johnson, R.B. and Collins, K.M.T., 2009. 'Call for Mixed Analysis: A Philosophical Framework for Combining Qualitative and Quantitative Approaches', *International Journal of Multiple Research Approaches*, 3(2), 114–39.
Oulton, C., Dillon, J. and Grace, M.M., 2004. 'Reconceptualizing the Teaching of Controversial Issues', *International Journal of Science Education*, 26(4), 411–23.
Pallant, J., 2011. *SPSS Survival Manual*. Crows Nest, NSW: Allen & Unwin.
Prosser, M. and Trigwell, K., 1997. 'Relations between Perceptions of the Teaching Environment and Approaches to Teaching', *British Journal of Educational Psychology*, 67(1), 25–35.
Reid, A. and Petocz, P., 2006. 'University Lecturers' Understanding of Sustainability', Higher Education, 51(1), 105–23.
Rieckmann, M., 2012. 'Future-oriented Higher Education: Which Key Competencies should be Fostered through University Teaching and Learning?', *Futures*, 44(2), 127–35.
Robson, C., 2011. *Real World Research*. West Sussex: John Wiley & Sons.

Scott, W. and Gough, S., 2004. 'Education and Sustainable Development in United Kingdom Universities: A Critical Exploration', in Corcoran, P.B. and Wals, A.E.J. (eds), *Higher Education and the Challenge of Sustainability: Problems, Promise, and Practice*. Dordrecht, The Netherlands: Kluwer Academic Publishers, 235–47.

Seatter, C., 2011. 'A Critical Stand of My Own: Complementarity of Responsible Environmental Sustainability Education and Quality Thinking', *The Journal of Educational Thought*, 45(1), 21–58.

Shephard, K. and Furnari, M., 2013. 'Exploring what University Teachers think about Education for Sustainability', *Studies in Higher Education*, 38(10), 1577–90.

Sherren, K., 2006. 'Core Issues: Reflections on Sustainability in Australian University Coursework Programs', *International Journal of Sustainability in Higher Education*, 7(4), 400–13.

Sipos, Y., Battisti, B. and Grimm, K., 2008. 'Achieving Transformative Sustainability Learning: Engaging Head, Hands and Heart', *International Journal of Sustainability in Higher Education*, 9(1), 68–86.

Stables, A. and Scott, W., 2002. 'The Quest for Holism in Education for Sustainable Development', *Environmental Education Research*, 8(1), 53–60.

Stevenson, R., 2004. 'Constructing Knowledge of Educational Practices from Case Studies', *Environmental Education Research*, 10(1), 39–51.

Stevenson, R., Wals, A.E.J., Dillon, J. and Brody, M., 2013. 'Introduction: An Orientation to Environmental Education and the Handbook', in Stevenson, R., Brody, M., Dillon, J. and Wals, A.E.J. (eds), *International Handbook of Research on Environmental Education*. New York: Routledge, 1–6.

Thomas, I., 2009. 'Critical Thinking, Transformative Learning, Sustainable Education, and Problem-based Learning in Universities', *Journal of Transformative Education*, 7(3), 245–64.

Thomas, I. and Nicita, J., 2002. 'Sustainability Education and Australian Universities', *Environmental Education Research*, 8(4), 475–92.

Tilbury, D. and Cooke, K., 2005. *A National Review of Environmental Education and its Contribution to Sustainability in Australia: Frameworks for Sustainability*. Canberra: Australian Government Department of the Environment and Heritage and Australian Research Institute in Education for Sustainability.

Tilbury, D., Keogh, A., Leighton, A. and Kent, J., 2005. *A National Review of Environmental Education and its Contribution to Sustainability in Australia: Further and Higher Education*. Canberra: Australian Government Department of the Environment and Heritage and Australian Research Institute in Education for Sustainability (ARIES).

ULSF, 2014. 'Talloires Declaration Institution Signatories List'. www.ulsf.org/programs_talloires_signatories.html [accessed 4 August 2014].

Velazquez, L., Munguia, N. and Sanchez, M., 2005. 'Deterring Sustainability in Higher Education Institutions: An Appraisal of the Factors which Influence Sustainability in Higher Education Institutions', *International Journal of Sustainability in Higher Education*, 6(4), 383–91.

Wals, A.E.J. and Blewitt, J., 2010. 'Third-wave Sustainability in Higher Education: Some (Inter)national Trends and Developments', in Jones, P., Selby, D. and Sterling, S. (eds), *Sustainability Education – Perspectives and Practice across Higher Education*. London: Earthscan, 55–74.

Wals, A.E.J. and Jickling, B., 2002. '"Sustainability" in Higher Education: From Doublethink and Newspeak to Critical Thinking and Meaningful Learning', *International Journal of Sustainability in Higher Education*, 3(3), 221–32.

Wemmenhove, R. and de Groot, W.T., 2001. 'Principles for University Curriculum Greening: An Empirical Case Study from Tanzania', *International Journal of Sustainability in Higher Education*, 2(3), 267–83.

Wright, T. and Horst, N., 2013. 'Exploring the Ambiguity: What Faculty Leaders really think of Sustainability in Higher Education', *International Journal of Sustainability in Higher Education*, 14(2), 209–27.

Yin, R.K., 2009. *Case Study Research: Design and Methods*, 4th edn. Thousand Oaks, CA: Sage Publications.

28

STUDENTS' COMPETENCY DEVELOPMENT IN THE CONTEXT OF SELF-ORGANISED AND PROJECT-ORIENTED SUSTAINABILITY SEMINARS

Research at the interface between self-description and real-life action

Mandy Singer-Brodowski

Introduction

Against a background of accelerating worldwide problems of sustainability and 'planetary boundaries' (Rockström *et al.* 2009), it is becoming increasingly important to identify the competencies that university graduates will need if they are to solve the 'wicked sustainability problems' (see Fadeeva and Mochizuki 2010). Recent years have seen the development of various ways of modelling sustainability competencies (e.g. de Haan 2006; Barth *et al.* 2007, de Kraker *et al.* 2009, Segales *et al.* 2009, UNECE 2012). Wiek *et al.* synthesised the various competency models in a reference framework focussed primarily on applying the required competencies operationally in real-life problem-solving processes in the context of sustainable development (Wiek *et al.* 2011).

However, the debate on higher education for sustainable development (HESD) should not foreground competency systematisation alone but also address the issue of how these sustainability competencies are to be developed in university study courses. While some existing case studies (e.g. Barth *et al.* 2007) describe sustainability students' learning, there is still a lack of systematic analyses concerned with the conditions for and processes of competency development in sustainability courses and environmental learning in general (Rickinson 2001; Rickinson 2006; Lundholm *et al.* 2013). The present chapter addresses this desideratum and introduces a qualitative approach to capturing competency at the interface between self-description and action.

Self-organised and problem-based learning

Development of student competency in sustainability is defined here by reference to two didactic contexts currently under discussion in the literature that together form a basic constant of student learning: problem-based learning and self-organised learning.

Problem-based learning involves learning situations that focus on either a societal issue (project) or a research problem (study) (on the distinction, see Brundiers and Wiek 2013). Problem-based learning motivates learners to integrate theory and practice and to find an appropriate solution for a pre-defined problem (Savery 2006). Key determinants for the quality of the learning process are selection of a complex, relatively unstructured problem, the inherent seriousness of the problem, and accompaniment of the process by a tutor (see ibid.). In recent years the problem-based learning is becoming increasingly important in higher education for sustainable development (Dobson and Tomkinson 2012; Brundiers and Wiek 2011; Schweizer-Ries *et al.* 2013, Bessant *et al.* 2013).

Problem-based learning is also closely associated with self-organised learning and self-regulated learning (Knowles 1975; Candy 1991; Boekarts 1999), which by definition include autonomous determination by the learner of all dimensions of his/her internal learning activity, of the learning topic and of the learning environment. Self-determination with regard to learning content significantly increases the intrinsic motivation of learners (Deci and Ryan 1985), and learners will develop a sense of ownership for projects and for their learning processes (Wheeler *et al.* 2010) if they are involved in decisions about the general conditions of their learning (places, composition of teams, reflections and evaluations of learning processes). Although the integration of self-organised courses demands additional resources from the institution, it tends to lead to better learning outcomes in comparison with 'conventional' courses (Murad and Varkey 2008). Last of all, self-organised aspects are a key prerequisite for competency development in general.

Requirements for capturing competent action

For purposes of reconstructing competency development processes in students participating in self-organised sustainability seminars, the first points to be determined are which working definition of competency is to be adopted, and how the associated competency development can be empirically captured. Many descriptions of competencies (e.g. Weinert 2001) treat competency as a dispositional characteristic that becomes visible only when the disposition in question is externalised in the context of action in a special domain (for the field of higher education, reference is made to Blömeke and Zlatkin-Troitschanskaia 2013). For the empirical capturing of previously defined competencies and for the reconstruction of general competency development this poses special methodological challenges: for example, the subjective judgement of the researchers as to which competency was successfully 'applied' in which situation.

Two possible approaches to an empirical reconstruction of students' competency development in sustainability courses are: 1) students' self-description (Schaeper 2013), i.e., their subjective theories with regard to their own competency development; 2) reconstruction of learners' competent action in the relevant real-life situation.

Overview of the chapter

In the research project described here, a combination of these two approaches was attempted, making the competent actions the basis for qualitative ESD competency research. For this purpose, two individual cases were selected from a bigger study, evaluated in depth, and reviewed from a methodological perspective. The over-arching study aimed to 'look inside' the learning processes and establish how the students come to terms cognitively with the concept of sustainable development. The central focus of the investigation was on the students' subjective theories with regard to sustainable development, and on the role of project-oriented and self-organised learning. The present chapter will not report the overall study's findings, instead discussing which methodologies may be used for reconstruction of competency development in students, with reference to two individual cases. In view of the methodological challenges posed by qualitative competency research, the approach used for the purpose was that of action validation. This may prove to be a rewarding approach for purposes of ESD competency research, and one which could be adopted elsewhere.

Research methodology: an overview

Constructivist grounded theory as a research methodology

Based on the epistemological theories of social constructivism, the study aimed at a consistent posture of observation and analytical review and reflection (Breuer *et al.* 2002) vis-à-vis the planning, execution and analysis of scholarly enquiry processes.

The reflective element was combined with the methodological paradigm of Grounded Theory (Glaser and Strauss 1967), used principally for generation of new knowledge through the exploration of a social phenomenon in a new research field. While numerous recent publications have dealt with the conceptualisation of necessary sustainability competencies, systematic description of competency *development* in the context of sustainability competencies is theoretical less explored terrain. The defining characteristics of student learning (problem-based and self-organised learning) on which the present study focuses have likewise not to date been subjected to systematic investigation. The Grounded Theory methodology enables the emergence of theoretical perspectives on a given subject that are grounded in the data (see e.g. Bryant and Charmaz 2007). It reshapes the entire research process of data collection and analysis, yoking analysis and collection of data together and introducing permanent feedback linkage between them. The ascertained data were coded at an early stage in the research process, making them accessible for ongoing analysis and the selection of new cases. This theoretical sampling (Glaser and Strauss 1967) was used in the study as a whole. Furthermore, in vivo codes were used (verbal expressions of the interviewees, which were incorporated into the theory in their original form; see Charmaz 2011), and theoretical memos contributed to the development of theory by focusing the attention of the researcher on undiscovered and abductive phenomena and processes.

The case study: samples and results

The objective of the overall study was an attempt to handle the complexity of capturing competent action and to develop a procedure for qualitative competency development – particularly with regard to competent action viewed as a combination of cognitive, motivational, volitional and emotional factors.

The study's setting was a self-organised interdisciplinary seminar at the University of Erfurt, Germany, in which students collaborated on real projects with partners from outside the university (NGOs, educational institutions, city administration). The course started with a lecture series about central issues and concepts of sustainability. Afterwards the students worked with the partners over an eight-week period, planning, executing and evaluating their special project, for example the creation of a vegan city map or a one-day workshop about renewables in a local school. They also had the option of devising their own projects without the demands of an external partner. The students were responsible for the whole project phase, for their meetings, and for the preparation and evaluation activities relating to the project. Over and above the actual projects there was an organising team of students responsible for handling practical arrangements for the seminar (lecture series, joint project selection session with outside partners, contacts with academic mentors, etc.).

For the process of gathering data, a combination of different survey approaches was used (three group discussions, 18 interviews and two observations using video recordings of about 18 hours of different planning sessions). In the context of the study as a whole, work on the construction of a typology of differing learning strategies, dependent on the students' previous affinity with sustainability, began during successive analysis of the first interviews. While the first cases has been chosen according to different categories (project team vs. organisation team, degree of scope to make independent decisions about content and strategies during the project), the last cases were selected according to this theoretical category of affinity with sustainability (theoretical sampling).

The two cases described here came from an organising team that set up a seminar for 60 other students in the summer semester of 2012. They were chosen because they had been interviewed twice, and because there were some video recordings of their project meetings. This made it possible to assess the competency development of the students at the interface between their subjective theories and their actions.

The two female students were interviewed at two different times about their own learning processes during the course, based on the dialogue approach of the problem-centred interview (Witzel 2000). In the second interview, the students were confronted with their statements from the first interview (communicative validation of subjective theories), which enabled the researcher to explore the students' concepts and theories in greater depth. A further step was to show the students selected clips from their own planning meetings, inviting them to express their reactions after viewing these.

The survey procedure involving the sequence 'video-recording, first interview, second interview' could not be consistently applied in more than two cases. This was because competent action in the selected situations was not always focused on aspects of sustainability, but might more generally demonstrate competent action by the students in uncertain and complex situations. Because the focus of the overall study was on the students' handling of the learning topic 'sustainable development', it was decided to include additional cases rather than confine the survey to detailed analysis of a very small number of cases.

Analysis involved coding the survey data in line with the principles of Grounded Theory and then subjecting them to analytical study. The coding interrupted the continuity of the texts being analysed (e.g. an interview transcript), while at the same time ensuring continued closeness to the material. In the course of the different phases of coding, the material became increasingly condensed, conceptual and theoretically abstract. The coding phases could be categorised in very general terms as initial coding, focused coding and conceptual coding (Charmaz 2011), with free movement between phases.

Methodological review with reference to three examples

In the second interview, video recordings from the planning meetings were shown to two subjects, who were asked to express their own opinion on key sequences in these recordings.

This provided the researcher with a communicative and an action validation of her reading of students' subjective theories (see Groeben and Scheele 1977) about their own learning.

At this point three practical case examples are briefly outlined for the inferences they suggest as to methodology in capturing qualitative competency. The students were asked about their own learning processes, about conditions that had been useful or detrimental to their own learning, and key situations during this learning.

One subject, in her first interview, outlined her subjective understanding of sustainable development as discourse. The researcher asked her to watch a video scene in which the project group had discussed aspects of sustainable activity in various fields (e.g. consumption, energy-saving, etc.), and then say to what extent that conformed to her idea of a discourse.

> Interviewee 1: Yeah, well. I do reckon it definitely could be, was a discourse, because we'd described all the aspects, ... Everyone suggested an aspect they thought was sustainability. And then we all discussed that. How far we'd go along with that. Or we came up with something else, quite a lot. Like, we were all more or less agreed. It wasn't like we were contradicting each other, or that. I reckon that's ... in a public discourse, usually, that's the way it is. ... Like, when you put these things up for public discussion, the way it is here in Germany at the moment, sort of. Then o' course you always get objectors, people just saying: 'No, that's not sustainability to me!' Or: 'Why should I bother doing that?' And er we all agreed, yes, it's important, sustainable, sustainable development, we should keep it going.

Validation of the understanding of sustainability as a discourse (in vivo code) took place in the second interview, which thus achieved an *exploration in greater depth of the subjective theory* held by the interviewee. The closer study afforded by revisiting her subjective theory in this way brought to light the similarities and differences most apparent in it between political and student discourse on the topic of sustainable development. At the same time, the interviewee emphasised elsewhere that she was surprised how similar the project group had proved to be at this point of the discussion – in the context of her work in the team following the meeting, the differences in a lived understanding of sustainability seemed to be far greater.

In the second scene played back to this subject, the project group were discussing the usefulness of having an attendance list for the seminar's framework meetings. This discussion takes place regularly in the seminar's organising teams and represents a change of role for students, who are responsible for running a formal class and yet at the same time enjoy no formal right of decision on issues of examination design, attendance monitoring and absences on the part of their fellow-students. They find this 'situation in limbo', occupying a role somewhere between student and course tutor, to be exceptionally challenging. In the playback scene, the student quoted above responds to a question by delivering a spirited plea for the abolition of attendance lists, on the grounds that a student-organised seminar on sustainability is an eminently suitable occasion for students' sense of responsibility to take centre stage. Yet in the first interview she has described herself as reticent, not good at asserting herself in group situations. The video clip shows the group deciding, as a result of her contribution, against the use of an attendance list.

> Interviewer: How was it for you in that scene?
>
> Interviewee: We – ell, a bit out on my own, really, I suppose, I think. Yes... And also a bit under pressure, because I was absolutely the only one – to start with – who was AGAINST having a list. ... because that actually mattered to me, I think. ...

> Seeing as I was absolutely the only one, at the time, I just felt like I had to stick to my guns and argue.
>
> Interviewer: You said at one point in our interview that you have begun … to learn how to assert yourself. … Now that was a scene where you were in quite a fraught situation, and you hit your way out of it, very positively, after being – as you say – perhaps the outsider to start with. … I'd be interested in how you reckon you managed to do that? …
>
> Interviewee: I think that was actually easy enough, because it mattered to me what happened. I think I was just fired up to do it. Yes. And if something matters to me, then I'm going to say so, make it clear. And then, and this is the bit, if it's something that affects other people too, then it's important to me to speak up for other people. … And I think another thing is, this whole attendance list business at university just turns me off, it really does. What they need to do is make the seminars more attractive. Rather than putting on this leverage, it's just external constraint. I don't like that on principle. … Exactly and then of course if I'm actually given the chance to help organise a seminar, well, I'm not going to want that kind of thing, am I? (laughing).

The action validation in this second case has resulted in the *uncovering of contradictions* between the interviewee's self-description and her actual competent action in a performance situation. In retrospective analysis of this self-contradiction, the salient point to emerge was that the subject's intrinsic motivation to create a congenial learning environment for her fellow students proved in practice to be a force enabling her to 'rise above herself'. She aimed to ensure that the self-organised teaching session – a format particularly well suited to these circumstances – was as well presented as possible, contrasting favourably with other university seminars.

The third example is provided by a subject from the same team of student organisers and derives from a video scene in which these students discuss how to structure their future business meetings. In this real action situation, the interview subject in question expresses great trepidation at the idea of chairing a meeting.

> Interview subject 2: Yes, I can remember that very very clearly, … I still can't explain even now what it was that made me, that I said 'no' and then 'ok chair it' and 'oh no, I don't want to, I don't want to, somehow'. … It was kind of like/ like being frightened … where I actually s- thought 'no, you don't want to, you can't do that' and at the end of the day of course it was all a fuss about nothing … So then I really was/I chaired the first meeting/ … but in fact it was no big deal at all, they didn't even notice I was chairing it. I just really I just got the agenda points agreed and … then I'd say: 'Right, fine, that's sorted, now let's … get on to the next point'. But/ but that it was anything like/ chairing it the way I'd imagined it/ panic and that, no it wasn't like that at all.

Later in the interview this subject says that in this situation she sees a resemblance to other 'uncertain', unpredictable situations in her life – for instance reporting that she would feel very apprehensive before oral exams. The effect of the action validation in this case was to prompt the subject to *reflect on and analyse an emotional challenge that had biographical roots*.

All three cases produced a deeper level of reflection on student learning processes, an outcome attributable primarily to the re-run of the actual action situation in the interviews. These reflections did not always include the students' confrontation with the concept of sustainable development – one reason why the procedure was not applied in all 13 cases covered by the overall study.

However, the study's findings point in particular to the significance of students' own subjective theories regarding the concept of sustainable development. From this it follows that student learning processes during a sustainability seminar can be categorised in terms of their pre-existing subjective theories on sustainability. Self-organised courses were particularly conducive to reconstructing the different learning processes, and more generally the competency development and motivation of the students. It thus seems likely that a survey capturing students' subjective theories and concepts together with relevant conceptual change occurring during a sustainability seminar would be an interesting starting-point for further studies.

A further point to emerge is that the didactic setting of a problem-oriented, self-organised seminar benefits the development of student competency by obliging participants to confront complex and 'wicked' sustainability problems (Tomkinson 2011), which do not have clear definitions and which include converging and sometimes conflicting perspectives of different actors. Furthermore, the students interact with fellow team members in arguing out a solution to an authentic problem. In the light of the overall study it can be regarded as a sound working hypothesis that self-organisation provides a didactic context especially conducive to deep learning processes that are emotionally challenging.

Conclusion

This chapter has described a study of student competency development in the context of self-organised and project-oriented sustainability seminars. This competency development study being understood as a permanent process of reconstruction of the competent action and thus interacting closely with the domain-specific application context, successful application of competencies was the central focus of the part-analysis of a wider study. Competency development in the context of the overall study was captured by means of a set of interlinked survey methods (group discussion, interviews, video recordings), and two cases were selected and subjected to methodical retrospective reflection and analysis for this study. In both cases the strategy used was a) video recording, b) 1st interview, and c) 2nd interview. The action validation made possible by this procedure could constitute methodological added value in the context of qualitative ESD-competency research.

For the specified research desideratum of studying competency development in students participating in self-organised and problem-oriented seminars on sustainability, the study's use of the *methodology of Grounded Theory* was an appropriate choice. The emergence during the overall study of a typology of differing learning strategies (depending on respective pre-existing theories regarding Sustainable Development) seems to afford fresh insight into the content of students' ESD learning (for a typology of different ESD-concepts of teachers see Shepard and Fumari 2013). However, these emerging differences posed challenging problems for in-depth analysis of the individual case – problems manifested in practice mainly in a shortfall in researcher hours. The increasing volume of cases included on the basis of theoretical sampling conflicted with the imperative of detailed and carefully considered analysis of each individual case.

The three examples described here have the special merit of demonstrating that in the context of sustainability topics it appears beneficial to work from a relatively broad concept of competency, viz. as cognition, emotion, motivation and volition operating in consort.

Video-based observation of the project's student groups during the study yielded a rich harvest of data; however, there was no systematic analysis of the video-recordings as an ethnographic record of the life and perceptions of the students. This was due in part to the fact that the recordings tended to provide evidence primarily of the cross-disciplinary key-competency development achieved by the students: a development independent of the sustainability topic in that it would have occurred to more or less the same degree in self-organised and project-oriented sessions dealing with other, unrelated topics. A second reason was that this video-based observation was confined to two teams at the beginning of the two-year research process, when the researcher had a close relationship to the students. As the research process went on, the researcher tried to detach herself increasingly from the students for the sake of a more distanced analytical perspective. This less close relationship (which was a major prerequisite for the students' personal reflections) made the suggested methodology for capturing the students' competency development more ethically and methodologically challenging. This fruitful tension between intimacy and distance, which as a feature of educational research studies in particular is in part dictated by relatively well-defined roles and hierarchies, deserves to be sensitively integrated into the design of future learning research. It could be advantageous in this context to deploy specially trained younger interviewers for their closeness to current student perspectives and dispositions.

The research approach that has constituted the central topic of this article, *action validation at the transition point where the students' real-world planning activity is followed up by individuals' reflective analysis*, in interviews, *of their own learning processes* proved extremely fruitful, and might well serve as an inspiration for future qualitative ESD competency studies. The reconstructive procedure of action validation in the context of capturing competent action can be said on the basis of the study described here to fulfil three related purposes:

1. *exploration in depth of subjective theories* (i.e. sustainability as a discourse):
   This exploration of the subjective theories was central to the results of the study as a whole, because it pointed to the different strategies students deploy when grappling with the concept of sustainability (dependent on their prior affinity towards sustainability).
2. *uncovering of contradictions between students' self-descriptions and their actions*:
   The analysis of these contradictions showed the high relevance of ownership and motivation during a self-organised learning process, which in one case led to active engagement in one aspect of a project (eliminating attendance lists), although the student's self-described characteristics seemed likely to prevent her from confidently presenting arguments in a group. Thus the competency development of students can be fostered by giving them more scope for deciding about their own learning (environment) – a finding also confirmed by the study as a whole.
3. *reflection on and analysis of emotional challenges, partly or wholly rooted in biography, experienced during a competency development process*:
   Reflection on and analysis of these emotional challenges showed the important but underestimated role of emotions in learning processes in general and also in environmental/sustainability learning (Rickinson *et al.* 2009; Shepard 2008), which could also be found in the study as a whole.

To sum up, it can be stated that action validation can afford a special empirical insight into student learning processes, because it makes it possible for the real-action determinants (brought into play during application of the competencies) to be viewed in relation to the students' subjective theories and self-assessments. In the long run the procedure ensures a richer and more nuanced perspective on student learning processes than could be achieved by interviews alone.

References

Barth, M., Godeman, J., Rieckmann, M. and Stoltenberg, U., 2007.' Developing Key Competencies for Sustainable Development in Higher Education', *International Journal of Sustainability in Higher Education*, 8(4), 416–30.

Bessant, S., Bailey, P., Robinson, Z., Tomkinson, B.C., Tomkinson, R., Ormerod, M.R. and Boast, R., 2013. 'Problem-Based Learning: A Case Study of Sustainability Education'. www.heacademy.ac.uk/assets/documents/ntfs/Problem_Based_Learning_Toolkit.pdf [accessed 9. February 2015].

Blömeke, S. and Zlatkin-Troitschanskaia, O., eds, 2013. 'The German Funding Initiative "Modeling and Measuring Competencies in Higher Education": 23 Research Projects on Engineering, Economics and Social Sciences, Education and Generic Skills of Higher Education Student. www.kompetenzen-im-hochschulsektor.de/Dateien/KoKoHs_WP3_Bloemeke_Zlatkin-Troitschanskaia_2013_neu.pdf. [accessed 27 February 2014].

Boekarts, M., 1999. 'Self-regulated Learning: Where we are Today', *International Journal of Educational Research*, 31(6), 445–57.

Breuer, F., Mruck, K. and Roth, W.M., 2002. 'Subjectivity and Reflexivity: An Introduction', *Forum: Qualitative Social Research*. www.qualitative-research.net/index.php/fqs/article/view/822/1785 [27 February 2014].

Brundiers, K. and Wiek, A., 2011. 'Educating Students in Real-world Sustainability Research: Vision and Implementation', *Innovative Higher Education*, 36(2), 107–24.

Brundiers, K. and Wiek, A., 2013. 'Do we Teach what we Preach? An International Comparative Appraisal of Problem- and Project-based Learning Courses in Sustainability', *Sustainability*, 5(4), 1725–46.

Bryant, A. and Charmaz, K., 2007. 'Introduction. Grounded Theory Research: Methods and Practice', in Bryant, A. and Charmaz, K. (eds), *The SAGE Handbook of Grounded Theory.* Los Angeles, CA: Sage, 1–28.

Candy, P.C., 1991. *Self-Direction for Lifelong Learning. A Comprehensive Guide to Theory and Practice.* San Francisco, CA: Jossey-Bass.

Charmaz, K., 2011. *Constructing Grounded Theory: A Practical Guide through Qualitative Analysis.* Los Angeles, CA: SAGE.

de Haan, G., 2006. 'The BLK '21 Programme in Germany: A Gestaltungskompetenz-based Model for Education for Sustainable Development', *Environmental Education Research*, 12(1), 19–32.

de Kraker, J., Lansu, A. and van dam Mieras, R., 2009. 'Competences and competence-based learning for sustainable development', in de Kraker, J., Lansu, A. and van dam Mieras, R. (eds), *Crossing Boundaries. Innovative Learning for Sustainable Development.* Frankfurt a.M.: VAS, 103–14.

Deci, E.L. and Ryan, R.M., 1985. *Intrinsic Motivation and Self-determination in Human Behavior.* New York: Plenum.

Dobson, H.E. and Tomkinson, C.B., 2012. 'Creating Sustainable Development Change Agents through Problem-based Learning. Designing Appropriate Student PBL Projects', *International Journal of Sustainability in Higher Education*, 13(3), 263–78.

Fadeeva, Z. and Mochizuki, Y., 2010. 'Higher Education for Today and Tomorrow: University Appraisal for Diversity, Innovation and Change towards Sustainable Development', *Sustanibility Science*, 5(2), 249–56.

Glaser, B.G. and Strauss, A., 1967. *The Discovery of Grounded Theory.* New York: de Gruyter.

Groeben, N. and Scheele, B., 1977. 'Dialogue-Hermeneutic Method and the "Research Program Subjective Theories"', *Forum: Qualitative Social Research*, 1(2), art. 22. www.qualitative-research.net/index.php/fqs/article/view/1079/2354 [accessed 9 February 2015].

Knowles, M., 1975. *Self-directed Learning. A Guide for Learners and Teachers.* New York: Englewood Cliffs.

Lundholm, C., Hopwood, N. and Rickinson, M., 2013. 'Environmental Learning. Insights from Research into the Students Experiences', in Stevenson, R.B, Brody, M., Dillon, J. and A.E.J. Wals (eds), *International Handbook of Research on Environmental Education.* New York/London: Routledge, 243–52.

Murad, H.M. and Varkey, P., 2008. 'Self-directed Learning in Health Professions Education', *Annals Academy of Medicine*, 37(7), 580–90.

Rickinson, M., 2001. 'Learners and Learning in Environmental Education: A Critical Review of the Evidence', *Environment Education Research*, 7(3), 207–320.

Rickinson, M., 2006. 'Researching and Understanding Environmental Learning', *Environmental Education Research*, 12(3–4), 445–57.

Rickinson, M., Lundholm, C. and Hopwood, N., 2009. *Environmental Learning: Insights from Research into the Student Experience.* Amsterdam: Springer.

Rockström, J., Steffen W., Noone, K., Persson, Å., Chapin, F.S. III, Lambin, E., Lenton, T.M., Scheffer, M., Folke, C., Schellnhuber, H., Nykvist, B., de Wit, C.A., Hughes, T., van der Leeuw, S., Rodhe, H., Sörlin, S., Snyder, P.K., Costanza, R., Svedin, U., Falkenmark, M., Karlberg, L., Corell, R.W., Fabry, V.J., Hansen, J., Walker, B., Liverman, D., Richardson, K., Crutzen, P. and Foley, J., 2009. 'Planetary Boundaries: Exploring the Safe Operating Space for Humanity', *Ecology and Society*, 14(2), www.ecologyandsociety.org/vol14/iss2/art32/ [accessed 9 February 2015].

Savery, J.R., 2006. 'Overview of Problem-based Learning: Definitions and Distinctions', *Interdisciplinary Journal of Problem-based Learning*, 1(1), 9–20.

Schaeper, H., 2013. 'The German National Educational Panel Study (NEPS): Assessing Competencies over the Life Course and in Higher Education', in Blömeke, S, Zlatkin-Troitschanskaia, O., Kuhn, C. and Fege, J. (eds), *Modeling and Measuring Competencies in Higher Education.* Rotterdam: Sense Publishers B.V., 147–58.

Schweizer-Ries, P., Pautzke, F., Metzner-Szigeth, A., Feldermann, J. and Biesenbach, R., 2013. *Bochum University of Applied Science on the Way to Establish Sustainability Education. Proceedings of the 9th International Symposium on Mechatronics and its Applications (ISMA13),* Amman. http://ieeexplore.ieee.org/xpl/articleDetails.jsp?arnumber=6547383 [27 February 2014].

Segalas, J., Ferrer-Balas, D., Svanstrom, M., Lundqvist, U. and Mulder, K.F., 2009. 'What has to be Learnt for Sustainability? A Comparison of Bachelor Engineering Education Competencies at Three European Universities', *Sustainability Science*, 4(1), 17–27.

Shepard, K., 2008. 'Higher Education for Sustainability: Seeking Affective Learning Outcomes', *International Journal of Sustainability in Higher Education*, 9(1), 87–98.

Shepard, K. and Fumari, M., 2013. 'Exploring what University Educators think about Education for Sustainable Development', *Studies in Higher Education*, 38(10), 1577–90.

Tomkinson, B., 2011. 'Education to Face the Wicked Challenges of Sustainability', *Journal of Social Sciences*, 7(1), 1–5.

UNECE, 2012. 'Learning for the future. Competencies for EDS'. www.unece.org/fileadmin/DAM/env/esd/ESD_Publications/Competences_Publication.pdf [29 July 2014].

Weinert, F.E., 2001. 'Concept of Competence: A Conceptual Clarification', in Rychen, D.S. and Salganik, L.H. (eds), *Defining and Selecting Key Competencies.* Seattle, WA: Hogrefe and Huber, 45–66.

Wheeler, G., Bergsman, K., Thumlert, C. and Kelly, B., 2010. 'Sustainable Design Project Teacher Manual'. Olympia, WA: Office of Superintendent of Public Instruction. www.k12.wa.us/environmentsustainability/pubdocs/sdpmanual2010.doc [accessed 9 February 2015].

Wiek, AD., Withycombe, L. and Redman, C.L., 2011. 'Key Competencies in Sustainability – A Reference Framework for Academic Program Development', *Sustainability Science*, 6(2), 203–18.

Witzel, A., 2000. 'The Problem-Centered Interview', *Forum: Qualitative Social Research*, 1(1), art. 22. www.qualitative-research.net/index.php/fqs/article/view/1132/2521 [accessed 9 February 2015].

29

TOWARDS CRITIQUE

Exploring the politics and praxis of sustainable higher education change from a discursive-praxeological perspective

Susanne Müller-Lindeque

A contested field: international policies and politics of sustainable higher education (SHE)

The context: SHE discourse at an international level

Although concerns regarding the nature and role of science in relation to ecological problems and societal transformation have a much longer history,[1] this debate has intensified in recent years as contested notions of environment and sustainability/sustainable development have increasingly been adopted from within the academic community and become a prominent issue for international policy making. Against this background, SHE has recently emerged as an academic field of inquiry and engagement, which is concerned with both the scholarly-professional and practical-administrative implications of socio-ecological crisis. Overall, it seeks to create an academe that is more relevant to, if not responsible for, a more democratic and ecologically sensitised social order.

In spite of its relative infancy SHE is a complex field with blurred boundaries (e.g. with respect to its 'siblings' environmental education [EE] and education for sustainable development [ESD]) and varying interpretations of its (academic) nature and role vis-à-vis the socio-ecological. Thus, whilst it may be relatively incontrovertible to suggest that the current 'sustainability imperative' implies 'a need to rethink the meaning of research and the relationship of research and teaching' (Wals and Blewitt 2010: 69), it should be noted that 'the sustainability in higher education research spectrum is vast, with scientific inquiry taking many different forms and pathways – with respect to research paradigms, designs, methodology and empirical work, theoretical conceptual foundations and theory building, and its practical goals and aspirations' (Beringer and Adomßent 2008: 607). Primarily this has to do with the complex character of sustainability/sustainable development individually and in relation to each other as well as in relation to 'academe' (cf. Beringer and Adomßent 2008; Gough and Scott 2007; Corcoran and Wals 2004). SHE has thus emerged as a contested field, in which ongoing discursive and social (re-)significations processes continue to contribute to development and difference. The following section very briefly introduces some of the major institutional influences that seem to have shaped the emergence of the field.

Since the 1990s, a range of international policy initiatives and documents in particular have contributed to the development and differentiation of SHE understandings and practice (e.g. Talloires Declaration, ULSF 1990; Lüneburg Declaration, UNESCO 2001). More recently, it has been the influence of a range of UN-driven policy initiatives and activities at the international and national level, featuring the current United Nations Decade of Education for Sustainable Development (UN DESD 2005–2014), which contributed to this diversification as well as increasingly also the institutionalisation of SHE. In particular, this was promoted through the range of SHE declarations uttered at an international level, that mobilised different themes and topics for debate (for a detailed discussion of three moments of SHE, see Müller 2013; see also Wright 2004; Wals and Blewitt 2010).

Following the initialising Talloires Declaration (ULSF 1990) SHE could be primarily understood as a strategy for addressing the environmental and sustainability crises identified at the Rio Earth Summit (UN 1992). In a certain sense, it could be said that in this document practical-administrative concerns outdo academic ones, especially if these are to be more narrowly defined as the academic core business of knowledge production and transfer. Contrastingly, the second majorly influential document, the Lüneburg Declaration (2001), characterises SHE as a matter of academic concern. In what finally might be regarded as a third 'moment' of SHE (i.e. roughly speaking the period beginning with the UN DESD), even if not bound to a single major document, SHE seemed to emerge as a (self-)regulative ideal for the professionalisation/responsibilitisation of academic selves (see Müller 2013 for a detailed analysis). Because of the inherent diversity and political nature of discursive developments in the field, it is of crucial importance to draw attention to the ways through which reality has come to be created in one way and not another (see Hart 2008).

Concerns about international policy influences

As a contested field, SHE continues to surface and actualise the aforementioned core issue of the status and role of science in society in highly different ways. Especially the later (UN-led) implementation of SHE during the UN DESD have stimulated critique and pointed to the need for further/ongoing critical reflection of the various influences that shape what the field can be now and in(to) the future. Critical commentators, such as Martens *et al.* (2010) for instance, have argued that, rather than breaking from the status quo, the initial phase of UN-led discourse on ESD implementation during the UN DESD was brought (back) onto UN 'pet' policy themes and areas for intervention. In this respect, the authors name buzzwords like 'quality', 'accountability', 'professionalisation' and 'lifelong learning' as particularly prominent areas of policy intervention.

The SHE policy analysis of my PhD study (Müller 2013), suggests that certain (UN) policies during the UN DESD introduce a 'new' regulative of individual academic self-activation. As a consequence, it may now be suggested that becoming active in SHE is a responsibility that every academic must consider in his/her professional life and daily practices. Yet, as a wave of sustainable professional regulation(s) articulated from within international policy-led, but also academic discourses, is (re-)structuring the field, the status and nature of their (sustainable) innovativeness is difficult to tell. For some, concerns remain to the extent 'that sustainability has become a diminishing prospect' (Corcoran 2010: xiii). Here Paul Hart's commentary on recent developments in EE seems instructive, when he asserts that 'in spite of increasing public awareness and professional status, environmental education continues to be marginalized by the practices of formal academic discourse as well as the conventions and assumptions of traditional education practice' (Hart 2008: 27). Considering existing sobering reviews of SHE progress during the UN DESD (Sterling and Scott 2008; Adomßent and Michelsen 2006), Hart's questioning of '(w)hether environmental educators should continue to seek embeddedness within dominant discourses particularly as the vehicle shifts toward sustainability education' (2008: 27), seems to also be of some relevance for SHE. To concretise these arguably somewhat 'abstract' concerns and critiques and to provide some anecdotal evidence of their contemporary relevance, I will now turn to a discussion of an example from my 'fieldwork' notes on SHE.

During my interviews I often asked my interviewees what it means to them to research 'sustainably'. Most interviewees more or less overtly stumbled when this question was brought up. Their responses tended to immediately jump to talk about their research topics as in one way or another relevant to the concepts of 'sustainability/sustainable development'. Without a doubt the selection of research topics plays an important role in relation to understanding researching as practice; nonetheless I would contend that a potentially richer exploration constructively aims to reach beyond this. Indeed, it was striking to see how my own attempts to take these conversations beyond the question of the choice of (relevant) research themes and, relatedly, conceptual and definitional debates over the right thematic content of 'sustainable development/sustainability', were found wanting. Overall, my attempts seemed to reverberate very little with most of my interviewee partners. Having said that, other interviewees enthusiastically highlighted the need for continuing or furthering a normatively motivated engagement in 'interdisciplinary' and/or 'transdisciplinary' method(ology) in the context of sustainable higher education research. There was only one person who referred explicitly to issues of research quality and validity. However, all this was framed in terms of revising the generally established quality criteria in sustainable higher education research towards this end. What is more, the apparent discursive 'irrelevance' of my question as to what it might mean to 'research sustainably' could also be regarded as manifesting terms of how my interviewees' would approach the negotiable, graded 'ethical consent form' I offered to them. More often than not this interaction would be resolved brusquely with, 'Where do I have to sign?'. This left little space for any dialogue on ethical terms we both could agree on. In fact, the impression may be seen as even more surprising considering how these observational 'snapshots' stand in stark contrast to a certain obviousness, natural ease and attention the very same question would receive with regard to 'teaching'.

This episode speaks of a repeated frustration I experienced during my 'fieldwork', i.e. the many conversations I had with variously engaged academics (see Table 29.1 in the Appendix). In these conversations, I saw academics performing traditional academic subjectivities (somewhat simplified here to be understood in the sense of particular social roles) through traditional academic practices, with these performances however being meant as reflections of those traditions (Hart 2008). In my experience sustainable higher education praxis as a form of change was characterised by somewhat frustrating ambivalences or perhaps even 'failure to innovate' (Hart 2008: 26).[2]

It is however crucial to understand, that this alleged lack of innovation in/through SHE praxis, for me, is less a matter of a lack of human consciousness or will, but rather has to do with the complex and contradictory nature of a relational ensemble of discursive and social practices themselves. If SHE is primarily understood as an ensemble of relational practices, a reflexive turn upon the field's making requires the (empirical) reconstruction of these relationalities. In the following section, I situate the particular research study underpinning this chapter in the context of ongoing SHE research.

Toward a critique of SHE: the research study

The present chapter against the background of SHE research

As I have already indicated above, this controversy also reflects on the field's (overall) research agenda and approaches, which are characterised by a broad range of different paradigms, methodologies and methods (e.g. Beringer and Adomßent 2008). The breadth of intellectual engagements within SHE is also reflected thematically in recent (research) topics, ranging from concerns with environmental management and university 'greening', to philosophical, pedagogical, political and participatory interests, and preoccupations with curriculum change (Wals 2014). However, it can also be noted that even if SHE publications seem to have significantly grown in number over recent years, it is the more eco-managerial, practical-administrative and implementatory-institutional interests that would seem to have been the most represented/popular, now perhaps also increasingly accompanied by a range of participatory concerns (e.g. Polk and Knuttson 2008). More recently issues of implementatory quality (auditing, assessment, quality assurance) have also gained in thematic and institutional impetus (Wals 2014). Moreover, the notion and practice of social learning has become a prominent reference point for most of the recent debates (e.g. Wals 2007). Finally, as noted by Wals (2014), whilst themes like 'research', 'professional development' and 'competencies' have played a subordinated role for a long time, most recently they seem to have shifted to the centre of attention. He points out that,

> Such engagement is also leading to alternative views of science itself and of the role of the university in society (Peters and Wals 2013). It is argued that empirical analytical and reductionist ways of understanding the world need to be complemented with more integrative and holistic ways of understanding the world and methodologies and methods that are better suited to cope with complexity, uncertainty and contested knowledge.
>
> *(Wals 2014: 10)*

The research study presented in this chapter engages thematically, conceptually and methodologically with these most recent topics, i.e. the current professionalisation/responsibilitisation of academics, as well as its relation to diverse understandings of sustainable researching. It draws on and uniquely combines a set of different theoretical and methodological perspectives that as yet have not received much attention in the field of SHE.[3] Working from within these post-structural and 'praxeological' perspectives, this SHE research begins to trace some of those elements of socially (re-)constitutive processes of sustainable academic practice that would seem to bring about, but also sometimes resist, innovation and transformation at all levels. In other words, it seeks to investigate the various relations between that particular ensemble of practices that currently make SHE. For me this implied researching the 'programmatics' of sustainable higher education from a governmentally-inspired perspective and to analytically focus on those practices at the micro level through which academic agents 'made' SHE in their everyday academic lives in more or less reflexive manners, through more or less reflexive choices respectively. This analytical focus on the relationalities of sustainable higher education practices thus seeks to provide a (more) nuanced picture of the current possibilities and limits/limitations of sustainable higher education change. The prospect of such work lies in its involvement of an 'ethics of everyday activity as coupled with those social perspectives that work to reinstate agency beyond narrow anthropomorphism through more reflexive actions in education' (Hart

2005: 397). To attempt to create such reflexive interaction between different (analytical) levels of practice I asked:

- How can I explore the social and discursive practices through which SHE is currently (re-)constituted?
- How can the concept of 'subjectivity' be heuristically mobilised to provide for a more nuanced and integrated sensitising instrument in the relationally-oriented study of the diverse ways of knowing and being that currently make the field of SHE and its academic subjects?
- How may this broadened understanding of diverse socially constitutive processes by which SHE and its academic subjects currently come about contribute to the facilitation of more situated, practical and relational engagements of reflexivity in the field?
- How can I become more (self-)reflexive of my own constitutive/constituted enmeshment in these inquiries?

Departing from a broadly 'discursive-praxeological' perspective on the constitution of social reality, SHE is conceptualised here as a historically and culturally contingent product, a highly particular social construction, whose contingent nature results from the indeterminacy and overdetermination of social praxis itself. My particular concern with the making of SHE commands attention to a particular understanding of such constitutive processes and practices, namely those that highlight SHE as always being an 'interactive matter of doing'. SHE as a field is therefore seen as being brought about in hybrid and interactive processes of a 'practical', 'relational' and 'powerful' quality that are also likely to occur and resonate within and across multiple contexts and sites.

This understanding requires forms of methodological combination that take into account the particularities and ambivalences of a relational understanding of praxis through more reflexive research frameworks. The next section accounts for the engagement of reflexivity in my own research practice. This is done through re-telling what happened in the 'field' *before* the perspective sketched above was 'found', as a way of contextualising this 'searching' process.

The (developing) research design

In order to understand how the analytical interests of this project developed in the course of the ongoing research process, it seems important to look back to its initial research design. The initial design was a (comparative) case study-design (e.g. Stake 2005), which reflected a broader interest in a cross-case comparison of individual academics' subjective perspectives on SHE (implementation) and innovative teaching (practices). It also sought to consider individual academic's thinking and understandings in relation to their respective national and institutional contexts, namely England, Germany and Austria. The study thus initially proceeded with conventional qualitative strategies and methods of purposive sampling, semi-structured interviewing and thematic analysis/content analysis (see Flick 2009). The actual data collection entailed episodic interviews of a cross-section of academics and to some degree also other 'stakeholders', which had in one way or another been engaged with SHE at the time of the interview. The interviews were both one-to-one, and where possible, group conversations. It stretched over the period of one year (April 2009 – April 2010), involving multiple day trips across England throughout that span, a compact two-week block of meetings in Austria in September 2009 as well as two short(er) interviewing trips to northern and southern Germany in February and March/April 2010.[4] All interviews were audio-recorded and most were additionally video-taped.

Interviewees were initially selected to develop a range of theoretically informed and sensitised insights and conversations about SHE (focusing on research and scholarship). When I pinned down the 'spatial scale' of this study I began the delineation task with theoretical selection strategies as regards relevant national-political contexts, as the excerpt taken from a proposal written at that stage of the developing research process succinctly illustrates:[5]

Case sampling I: scale of the study

As a starting point for limiting the scope of the study and to allow for some initial anchoring of inter-case comparability a sampling choice was made before the start of the actual data collection with regard to the political and cultural national contexts in which the cases are located, namely Germany, Austria and England.[6] This selection thus proceeded on the assumption of 'given' differences in terms of (sustainable) higher education policies and (higher) education cultures (e.g. different models of state governance, academic traditions, etc.), which seemed particularly relevant considering the originally stronger focus on ESD implementation policies and practices during the UN DESD.

The limitations of this design soon emerged as individual interviewee accounts seemed to 'spill over' (Saukko 2003) different sites and contexts as well as spheres of life, thereby disrupting the neatness of my carefully designed, but preliminary, selection process and units of analysis. That is, my first encounters with the field taught me that the ways in which these individuals have come to understand themselves as academics, in relation to particular contexts, is far more layered or multi-levelled, dynamic and complicated than an exploration of subjective perspectives alone allows, even under consideration of 'institutional' and 'national' contexts.

Thus, what increasingly mattered in the process was how the academics I approached responded to my request and where they positioned themselves: How did they see themselves as academics in relation to SHE? Did they consider themselves as SHE academics? Or, how (else) did they associate themselves with 'the field'? How did they want to be seen (by me, by others)? And, how/where did they situate themselves in relation to 'conventional' academe? This initial recognition of the fundamentally contingent nature of the multiple makings of SHE in/through academic practice, increasingly led me away from the qualitative-interpretative design sketched above.

In order to cope with these emerging methodological complexities I experimented with different styles of interviewing and gradually worked toward developing a combined framework, which is close to Flick's (2009) 'episodic interviewing' as a distinct method. The point of this strategy is to blend 'narrative' and 'semi-structured' methodical elements in such a way as to facilitate both reflection of 'episodic-situational forms of experiential knowledge' and of more 'conceptual knowledge' (Flick 2009: 186), as well as facilitating the exploration of the linkages between both approaches. Our (mutual) understandings concerning 'sustainability' and 'higher education' unfolded in a highly complex interactive process between my research participants, me, the storied knowledges we produced and the places in (relation to) which these conversations unfolded (see Somerville *et al.* 2011). In this way, these beginning dialogues encouraged me to continue with my 'person research' as the primary empirical concern of the study, now engaged through the lens of subjectivity, whilst at the same time complicating my reflexive understanding thereof in several ways.

Findings

In the following section an overview on the study's main heuristical and empirical findings is provided. These include:

- a *multidimensional heuristic tool* for investigating the multiple relational ways through which SHE is currently (re-)constituted. More precisely, this tool includes a particular selection and combination of discursive-praxeological approaches to (subject) analysis (see also above).
- a *selection of vignettes* providing impressionistic accounts of individual academics' meaning-making of the heterogeneous and arguably sometimes even conflicted concepts of sustainable development/sustainability, higher education and the relationship(s) between both. These stories of a variety of academic experiences in relation to the 'sustainability challenge' demonstrate a diverse range of ongoing struggles to make sense of the present situation, such as re-visiting once taken-for-granted or dearly held beliefs and re-formulating the blurring boundaries of professional/private grounds for action.
- *a literary documentation of the daily academic practices of three different academic subject positions* currently emerging in relation to SHE. This less conventional representation of an ordinary working day in the office life of three different SHE subject types (the 'dilettantish-cosmopolitan' subject, the 'unfinished-cosmopolitan' subject and the 'epistemic-entrepreneurial' subject) reflects the mundane practices and micropolitics of everyday academic life through which we 'accomplish' ourselves as (more) 'sustainable academics' here and now.
- *two case summaries of the complex material-semiotic entanglements* in the making of sustainable higher education, draw attention to instances of practical and relational 'movement' in which the previously discussed structural changes may be subject to change yet again. The positioning of the academics I met had a sense of its own and it was important to ask: 'Who assumes which positions and how? Who resists and who breaks out or mixes particular opportunities of becoming … How do normativities and ideas about appropriateness slide into new modes? How are they sedimented?' (Højgaard and Søndergaard 2011: 342).

It is important to note that the theoretical and methodological frameworks sketched in this chapter provide an alternate way of thinking about the social world and thus of thinking about SHE. In particular, this different way of thinking has consequences for how one can think about academic knowledge and research. It therefore also influences the findings and conclusions that can be drawn from such work (Müller 2013). Taking this into account, in the following I briefly comment on what seems (im-)possible in this respect.

The work discussed in this chapter proceeds on the assumption that due to its particular theoretical and methodological framing and unlike other forms of qualitative research, discursive-praxeological research cannot directly lead to better actions or should (but could?) serve as the grounds for deliberative learning processes towards this end. The relevance of this critique lies with the proposition that, even if we may not be able to emancipate from the workings of power through forms of critical consciousness, we still may be able to reflexively enable transformative social praxis (e.g. Somerville *et al.* 2011), even if this may remain an ambivalent endeavour (Davies *et al.* 2004).

One way of elaborating on this proposition is the specific (Foucauldian) understanding of critique as 'transgression'. In this view, '[c]ritique doesn't have to be on the premise of a deduction which concludes: this then is what needs to be done' (Foucault 1991a: 84 in Biesta 2008:

200). The reflexive potential of this kind of SHE research can be fleshed out further by pointing out how 'transgression' may be seen as an alternate, arguably more 'pragmatic' form of emancipation, that according Biesta (2008) unfolds its transformative effects 'on the ground':

'But what it can bring about is a situation in which people, "no longer know what to do", so that the acts, gestures, discourses which up until then has seemed to go without saying become problematic, difficult, dangerous' – and this effect is entirely *intentional* (Foucault 1991a: 84 in Biesta 2008: 200). '(t)he only important problem is what happens on the ground' (Foucault 1991a: 83 in Biesta 2008: 200). What this entails is a '*practical* critique that takes the form of a possible transgression' (Foucault 1984: 45; emphasis added in Biesta 2008: 200). Yet this tiny step is crucial, since it opens up the possibility 'of no longer being, doing, or thinking what we are, do or think' – and in precisely this sense 'it is seeking to give a new impetus ... to the undefined work of freedom' (Foucault 1984: 46 in Biesta 2008: 201).

Whilst it seems inappropriate to formulate direct recommendations for policy and practice from my study, it can contribute to the enablement of social transformation through seeing things differently. A mundane example may help to illustrate this: A typical comment from academic readers of the 'office stories' and the subject positions 'behind' them, was that they now wanted to become this SHE academic through adopting the respective positioning/practices. This is suggestive of how the reflexivities engaged through my work can inform the SHE judgements 'on the ground', which we need to make every day as we continue to engage our academic lives and worlds. This, then, is what lies at the heart of documenting sustainable academic 'becoming', since:

> All we are doing, as reflexive researchers, is to write in ways that reveal the limits of our knowledge, our political orientation and other dimensions of self, in ways that reveal the discourses that shape our work and open possibilities for thinking about our work as we get on with it.
>
> *(Hart 2005: 399)*

Methodological discussion and outlook

I argued that in spite of a considerable institutional shift towards embedding sustainable development into higher education before and during the UN DESD, there remains an important need for a 'reflexive turn' focusing on the makings of this field. I have further illustrated how a discursive-praxeological understanding of those makings may help with providing an enabling research framework in this respect. Yet, this particular theoretical and methodological framework may be considered to reside at 'the margins' of what currently counts as legitimate and/or valuable research in SHE. So, in closing this documentation of the 'becoming' of this SHE research(er), I want to draw your attention to certain aspects of this doing research 'at the margins' against the background of SHE research conceived more broadly.

As a field, SHE has as yet remained opened to multiple approaches of research, even if, more recently, one can note, in part, a politically induced trend towards promoting a variety of 'transdisciplinary' and/or 'participatory' approaches. According to Wals (2014), this can be seen as an indication of an increased concern with some very profound questions regarding the nature and role of science in ecologically challenged societies. Yet, especially against the background of a general climate of the neoliberalisation of higher education (e.g. Olsson and Peters 2005), the debate over different kinds of more applied forms of sustainable/social science(s), also runs 'the risk of assimilation and the reduction of qualitative [sic? research] to an instrumentalism that meets the demands of [environmental?, sustainable?] audit culture' (Lather 2013: 636, additions mine). In fact, considering some of my earlier confusions and frustrations, the research reflected in this chapter can be seen as an increasingly conscious attempt to engage epistemological and ontological reflexivity through producing academic knowledge about the field in an alternate manner. Even if I am still excited about the promises that these new 'post-post' forms of research hold (e.g. Lather 2013), to me it now seems crucial to engage more carefully with the questions that those perhaps less intrigued by 'this new' typically pose. In her thoughtful review of a recent Special Issue on 'post-qualitative' inquiry in the *International Journal of Qualitative Studies in Education*, Greene (2013) provides a helpful set of questions, which reflects where major concerns commonly tend to lie:

- Can this still be considered research?
- Where is this going?
- What is being lost in the new inquiry?

I briefly reflect on how some of these questions might be engaged with (more) productively in the afterward (Lather 2013):

Can this still be considered (accessive) research?

In more conventional terms, (qualitative) social science research is typically thought of as, 'the systematic process of recording and analyzing information about targeted phenomena … toward better understanding of these phenomena' (Greene 2013: 752). To this sketch, Greene adds the expectation that research – in one way or another – is supposed to make a contribution to the public good (2013: 752).

One of the typical concerns when engaging in more, say, experimental approaches to researching is a supposed lack of systematic method. Clearly, this concern taps into an age-old methodological debate, which I do not want to go into here. Having said that, it is equally clear that within the circle of 'post-qualitative' researchers, reflexivity in various spellings is the most common strategic 'response' to this concern. Hart (2005: 399) importantly states that 'in reauthorizing ourselves through practice rather than confession, researchers can demonstrate understanding of means of production, that is, be aware of the possibilities for appropriation and know the constraints of methodological techniques as well as the power relations of location and position'. In my experience this first issue directly plays onto another common concern with 'post-qualitative' inquiries, i.e. their tendency towards abstraction and exclusionary terminology (Greene 2013). Both issues are critiques that have been repeatedly uttered with respect to this research too and almost certainly impacted on some of the researcher-participant relationships during my fieldwork (see Müller 2013). With hindsight, a more intensive use of visual methodologies (e.g. Rose 2012) might have been an exciting methodological, but as yet underexplored option in this respect. In my more recent work, reconstructive collaboration on the basis of video clips of classroom teaching, has shown the potential to 'practically' work on the issues mentioned before in an unexpectedly productive manner (Müller-Lindeque and Wrana 2013).

What is being lost in the new inquiry? What role(s) in society does post-qualitative research fulfil?

Another typical concern is the arguable lack of (direct) contribution to 'policy and practice' in the name of a more democratic and ecologically sensitised social order. Alongside others, my aim was to contribute to 'creating openings toward as yet unimaginable futures' (Somerville *et al.* 2011: 3). This may sound less humble than it actually is intended to be (see above), but I do fully recognise its currently underdeveloped nature. Some pioneering work regarding a pedagogy of ethical uncertainty has been carried out by Somerville *et al.*'s (2011): ' pedagogy of ethical uncertainty, where ethical refers to our mutual responsibilities to other and to the more-than-human world, and uncertainty to the unpredictability inherent in our relationship with this world' (Somerville *et al.* 2011: 3). Apart from the ongoing need to engage and experiment with new methodologies, such as 'collective biography' (Davies *et al.* 2013), lastly to me this brings to the fore the much undervalued and underexplored 'political category of the everyday maker'. A '"form of lay citizenship shaped by everyday experience", in which we refuse to take on "professional, fulltime nor strategic identity" but instead do things where we are, in our own ways, when we have time or feel like it' (Bang 2005: 5, in McKenzie 2009: 220).

Acknowledgements

I wish to thank my supervisors Alan Reid, William Scott and Jill Porter for their sustained support in the realisation of the doctoral study referred to in this chapter. I also wish to thank the research participants for their important contribution to this study. The research project was made possible by funding from the ESRC and the University of Bath's Department of Education.

Notes

1 Rachel Carson's (1962) *Silent Spring* is often discussed as being a forerunner in this debate.
2 Of course, the intricacies of various failures to innovate make for a big topic in environmental education research and educational research more broadly, now even forming an (educational) area of research on its own (e.g. Rürup and Bormann 2012). This is not the place to discuss this topic/area in an adequate manner, but it should be noted that my approach is characterised by a discursive-praxeological take on these and related issues.
3 These are discourse theories and theories of social praxis as currently discussed and received in the more culturally inclined quarters of (German) education (e.g. Thompson *et al.* 2014). On the other hand, methodological discussions around 'post-critical' forms of inquiry as currently led in parts of the (Anglo-American) EE (e.g. Hart 2005; McKenzie 2005) but also the general education community (e.g. Lather 2013; Lather and St Pierre 2013) have been pivotal for this work.
4 In addition to this, two interviews with Swiss participants were conducted during the same time; but given the course of the study thereafter this material is not used in the present study.
5 As I went out into 'the field', often I was provided with further contacts of academics with whom I might be interested to speak. Thus, this initial selection process developed into a snowballing approach in combination with the more practical strategic moves and considerations of convenience and accessibility.
6 Following Flick (2009), for example, one might consider this approach an 'a priori determination of the sample structure', i.e. taking criteria for the drawing of samples, which 'are abstract, because they have been developed independently of the concrete material analysed and before its collection and analysis' (Flick 2009: 115).

References

Adomßent, M. and Michelsen, G., 2006. 'German Academia Heading for Sustainability? Reflections on Policy and Practice in Teaching, Research and Institutional Innovations', *Environmental Education Research*, 12(1), 85–99.

Beringer, A. and Adomßent, M., 2008. 'Sustainable University Research and Development: Inspecting Sustainability in Higher Education Research', *Environmental Education Research*, 14(6), 607–23.

Biesta, G.J.J., 2008. 'Encountering Foucault in Lifelong Learning', in Fejes, A. and Nicholl, K. (eds),

Foucault and Lifelong Learning. Governing the Subject. Abingdon: Routledge, 193–205.

Carson, R., 1962. *Silent Spring.* Harmondsworth: Penguin.

Corcoran, P.B., 2010. 'Foreword by Peter Blaze Corcoran', in Jones, P., Selby, D. and Sterling, S. (eds), *Sustainabiliy Education. Perspectives and Practice across Higher Education.* London and Washington, DC: Earthscan, xiii.

Corcoran, P.B. and Wals, A.E.J., eds., 2004. *Higher Education and the Challenge of Sustainability. Problematics, Promise and Practice.* Dordrecht: Springer.

Davies, B., Browne, J., Gannon, S., Honan, E., Laws, C., Mueller-Rockstroh, B. and Petersen, E.B., 2004. 'The Ambivalent Practices of Reflexivity', *Qualitative Inquiry*, 10(3), 360–89.

Davies, B., de Schauwer, E., Claes, L., De Munck., K., Van de Putte, I. and Verstichele, M., 2013. 'Recognition and Difference: A Collective Biography', *International Journal of Qualitative Studies in Education*, 26(6), 680–91.

Flick, U., 2009. *An Introduction to Qualitative Research*, 4th edn. London: Sage.

Gough, S. and Scott, W.A.H., 2007. 'Universities and Sustainable Development: The Necessity for Barriers to Change', *Perspectives: Policy and Practice in Higher Education*, 11(4), 109–18.

Greene, J.C., 2013. 'On Rhizomes, Lines of Flight, Mangles and Other Assemblages', *International Journal of Qualitative Studies in Education*, 26(6), 749–58.

Hart, P., 2005. 'Transitions in Thought and Practice: Links, Divergences and Contradictions in Post-critical Inquiry', *Environmental Education Research*, 11(4), 391–400.

Hart, P., 2008. 'Ontological/Epistemological Pluralism within Complex Contested EE/ESD Landscapes: Beyond Politics and Mirrors', in Gonzáles-Gaudiano, E. and Peters., M.A. (eds), *Environmental Education. Identity, Politics and Citizenship.* Rotterdam and Taipei: Sense Publishers, 25–38.

Højgaard, L. and Søndergaard, D.M., 2011. 'Theorizing the Complexities of Discursive and Material Subjectivity: Agential Realism and Poststructural Analyses', *Theory and Psychology*, 21(3), 338–54.

Lather, P., 2013. 'Methodology-21: What Do We Do in the Afterward?', *International Journal of Qualitative Studies in Education*, 26(6), 634–54.

Lather, P. and St Pierre, E.A., 2013. 'Post-qualitative Research', *International Journal of Qualitative Studies in Education*, 26(6), 629–33.

McKenzie, M., 2005. 'The "Post-post Period" and Environmental Education Research', *Environmental Education Research*, 11(4), 401–12.

McKenzie, M., 2009. 'Pedagogical Transgression: Toward Intersubjective Agency and Action', in McKenzie, M., Hart, P., Bai, H. and Jickling, B. (eds), *Fields of Green. Restorying Culture, Environment, and Education.* Cresskill, NJ: Hampton Press, 211–24.

Martens, P., Roorda, N. and Cörvers, R., 2010. 'Sustainability, Science and Higher Education. The Need for New Paradigms', *Sustainability*, 3(5), 294–303.

Müller, S., 2013. 'Making Sustainable Higher Education: A Critique of Scholarly Responsibilities, Professionalisation and Praxis'. Unpublished doctoral thesis, University of Bath.

Müller-Lindeque, S. and Wrana, D., 2013. '"Teacher diagnostics" as Affective Practices – A Heuristic Escapade'. Paper Presentation at MultiPluriTrans: Emerging Field in Educational Ethnography, Luxembourg, 21–23 November 2013.

Olsson, M. and Peters, M.A., 2005. 'Neoliberalism, Higher Education and the Knowledge Economy: From the Free Market to Knowledge Capitalism', *Journal of Education Policy*, 20(3), 313–45.

Polk, M. and Knuttson, P., 2008. 'Participation, Value Rationality and Mutual Learning in Transdisciplinary Knowledge Production for Sustainable Development', *Environmental Education Research*, 14(6), 643–53.

Rose, G., 2012. *Visual Methodologies. An Introduction to Researching with Visual Materials*, 3rd edn. Los Angelesc, CA: Sage.

Rürup, M. and Bormann, I., eds, 2012. *Innovationen im Bildungswesen. Analytische Zugänge und empirische Befunde.* Wiesbaden: Springer.

Saukko, P., 2003. *Doing Research in Cultural Studies. An Introduction to Classical and New Methodological Approaches.* London: Sage.

Somerville, M., Davies, B., Power, K., Gannon, S. and de Carteret, P., 2011. *PlacePedagogyChange.* Rotterdam: Sense Publishers.

Stake, R.E., 2005. *Multiple Case Study Analysis.* New York: Guilford Press.

Sterling, S. and Scott, W., 2008. 'Higher Education and ESD in England: A Critical Commentary on Recent Initiatives', *Environmental Education Research*, 14(4), 386–96.

Thompson, C., Jergus, K. and Breidenstein, G., eds, 2014. *Interferenzen. Perspektiven kulturwissenschaftlicher Bildungsforschung.* Weilerswist: Velbrück.

ULSF, 1990. 'The Talloires Declaration. Report and Declaration of the Presidents Conference'. www.ulsf.org/programs_talloires_report.html [accessed 9 February 2015].

UN, 1992. 'Earth Summit. Agenda 21. The United Nations Programme of Action from Rio'. www.un.org/esa/dsd/agenda21/res_agenda21_00.shtml [accessed 9 February 2015].

UNESCO (in co-operation with EUA, GHESP, IAU, ULSF), 2001. 'The Lüneburg Declaration on Higher Education for Sustainable Development'. Lüneburg: Authors. http://portal.unesco.org/education/en/files/37585/11038209883LuneburgDeclaration.pdf/LuneburgDeclaration.pdf [accessed 9 February 2015].

Wals, A.E.J., ed., 2007. *Social Learning Towards a Sustainable World: Principles, Perspectives and Praxis.* Wageningen: Wageningen Academic Publishers.

Wals, A.E.J., 2014. 'Sustainability in Higher Education in the Context of the UN DESD: A Review of leArning and Institutionalization Processes', *Journal of Cleaner Production*, 62(1), 8–15.

Wals, A.E.J. and Blewitt, J., 2010. 'Third-wave Sustainability in Higher Education: Some (Inter)national Trends and Developments', in Jones, P., Selby, D. and Sterling, S. (eds), *Sustainabiliy Education. Perspectives and Practice across Higher Education.* London: Earthscan, 55–74.

Wright, T., 2004. 'The Evolution of Sustainability Declarations in Higher Education', in Corcoran, P.B. and Wals, A.E.J. (eds), *Higher Education and the Challenge of Sustainability. Problematics, Promise, and Practice.* Dordrecht: Kluwer Academic Publishers, 7–20.

Appendix

Table 29.1 Overview of research participants and resources

Method	*England*	*Austria*	*Germany*
Interviews by positions			
Episodic interviews with 'junior' academics	1 (senior) teaching fellow 1 lecturer (programme director) 2 senior lecturers	1 habilitation candidate 2 lecturers 1 post-doc 1 doctoral student	1 habilitation candidate (focus group) 1 lecturer 1 post-doc 1 (doctoral) student
Episodic interviews with professors/research centre directors	3 professors 3 research centre directors	2 professors 1 professor emeritus	1 junior professor 2 professors 1 research centre director (focus group)
Short interviews and conversations with non academic (staff)	2 environmental/ sustainability managers 1 administrative staff HE policy making 1 freelance academic 1 masters student	1 NGO worker (1 administrative staff educational policy making) 1 short conversation with student representative	1 custodian 1 professor
Interviews by disciplines			
Episodic interviews with 'junior' academics	2 English Literature 1 Interdisciplinary 1 Education	2 Interdisciplinary 1 Economics 1 Anthropology 1 Geography	2 Interdisciplinary 1 Biology 1 Education
Episodic interviews with professors/research centre directors	1 Environmental Sciences 2 Interdisciplinary 1 Education	1 Interdisciplinary 2 Education	1 Biology 1 Management 1 (2) Education 1 Interdisciplinary

Table 29.1 continued

Method	*England*	*Austria*	*Germany*
Videos			
Episodic interview tapings	12 episodic interview video tapings	10 episodic interview video tapings	9 episodic interview video tapings
Documents (institutions)			
Academic publications		1 academic article on the RCE Graz-Styria 1 academic article on teaching (University of Graz)	5 academic articles on the Leuphana University Lüneburg sustainability project
Teaching materials	1 piece of course material (London South Bank University)	1 internet representation masters course 'joint degree sustainability' (University of Graz)	1 internet representation seminar description (Leuphana University Lüneburg)
Institutional sustainability policy documents	internet representation 1 sustainability portal (University of Gloucestershire) 1 sustainability portal (University of Plymouth)	2 internet representations (RCE Graz-Styria)	5 internet representations (Sustainability guidelines and portal of Leuphana University Lüneburg University of Osnabrück, University of Bremen, University of Göttingen and Free University
Berlin	1 environmental management (University of Bath)		
Sustainability reports (organisational management)	sustainability reports (University of Plymouth, University of Gloucestershire)	1 (2) sustainability reports (University of Graz) 1 sustainability report (University of Klagenfurt)	1 sustainability report (Leuphana) 1 climate protection report (University of Göttingen) 3 environmental reports (University of Osnabrück, University of Bremen, Free University Berlin)

30

COMPETENCIES FOR SUSTAINABILITY IN THE CURRICULA OF ALL NEW DEGREES FROM THE UNIVERSITY OF VALENCIA (SPAIN)

Pilar Aznar, M. Angeles Ull, Albert Piñero and M. Pilar Martínez-Agut

Introduction

This study aims at strengthening the inclusion of sustainability in all degree studies of the University of Valencia (UV).[1] University training of future professionals is a decisive factor to achieve a culture of sustainability; all university students should obtain a central understanding of the vision of sustainability in such a way that, in the future, they could consider this perspective in their professional activities (Aznar Minguet *et al.* 2011).

The specification of key competencies for sustainability, incorporated in the whole of general competencies, is a requirement determined by the regulations of our country for the development of the University new curricula within the European harmonisation process for Higher Education, the guidelines of which contain the principles for the implementation of guiding criteria for university studies towards sustainability. In this context, the objective of our research has been the review of the General and Specific Competencies of the Degrees, in order to know the level of inclusion of competencies dealing with sustainability in the curricula of the new degree titles of the UV.

Key competencies for sustainability on higher education are nowadays under research (Sterling 2005; Sherren 2006; Lozano 2006; Aznar Minguet 2006; Barth *et al.* 2007; Corney and Reid 2007; Martínez-Agut *et al.* 2007; Junyent and de Ciurana 2008; Sibbel 2009; Aznar Minguet and Ull 2009; de la Harpe and Thomas 2009; Thomas 2009; Ull *et al.* 2010; Barrón *et al.* 2010). Wiek *et al.* (2011) developed a comprehensive review about the various inputs, although focusing on the key competencies needed for specific studies of sustainability.

As indicated by Barth and Rieckmann (2012), the inclusion of competencies for sustainability in university curricula is a new challenge for the academic system. Many universities have introduced activities for their implementation over the last years, and a high number of study cases on these processes have been documented. Many of these cases identified the key competencies which are relevant for sustainable development and so must be developed in higher education institutions focused towards the future. Several approaches to the selection of key competencies have been made, and there is some kind of international agreement on the most important key competencies. For example, Rieckmann (2012) develops an analysis of the individual key competencies crucial for understanding the main changes that worldwide society must face. In order to move towards a more sustainable future this analysis, in which many European and Latin-American experts have been involved, proposes that such competencies are, among others: systemic thinking, anticipatory thinking, critical thinking, for cooperation in heterogeneous groups, for participation, for interdisciplinary work, for communication and use of media, for planning and realising innovative projects. However, while being important key competencies for sustainability, they are not unique to sustainability, and in our study we have been able to show that many of them are included among the general competencies of the majority of degree programmes, without involving the introduction of any reference to sustainability in them.

Thus, a different point of view to analyse the presence of sustainability was considered, searching for consistent competencies with the main issues raised in the Framework for the UN DESD International Implementation Scheme (UNESCO 2006). The legal framework has also been considered: Spain's Law 4/2007 of Universities, which regulates the arrangement of official university teaching (developed by the Royal Decree 1393/2007). In its preamble, it is stated that 'training on any professional activity should take account of the need to contribute to the knowledge and development of all human rights, democratic principles, principles of gender equality, solidarity, environmental protection, universal accessibility and design for all citizens, and the promotion of a culture of peace' (R.D. 1393/2007: 3).

Additionally, the 'Guidelines for the introduction of Sustainability in the curricula', adopted by the Working Group for Environmental Quality and Sustainable Development, of the Spanish University Rectors' Conference (CADEP-CRUE 2012), might also be mentioned. Although some universities' programmes reflected these guidelines, most of them have not provided precise instructions for the inclusion of these competencies, as was the case of the UV. The absence of prior definition implies that the decision about including general and specific competencies in the degrees is at the sole discretion of the different Commissions responsible for the development of the curricula of each degree. All this has led to the need for the present study to examine the current situation.

Methodology

The methodology that was followed is descriptive, empirical and ex-post, using both qualitative and quantitative techniques.

In order to carry out the review of the inclusion of sustainability competencies in the Educational Guides for the subjects of the different UV degree titles, all the existing guides in this university for the 2013–14 academic year have been analysed. They were distributed according to the five major areas of knowledge: Sciences, Engineering, Health Sciences, Social and Legal Sciences, and Arts and Humanities. The Thesaurus used for the review of curricula competencies, named 'Sustainability Thesaurus' (Aznar Minguet *et al.* 2014a), has also been applied for data collection. This document drew on the main issues identified throughout the UN Decade of Education for Sustainable Development (UNESCO 2006), and was supplemented by the Spanish legal frame and other considerations (Aznar Minguet *et al.* 2014b). This development has led to the identification of four analysis categories: sustainability, environmental, economic, and socio-cultural (SOSTENB, AMBIN, ECONM and SOCIOCULT, respectively, names which recall their Spanish acronyms). Each one of these categories has its corresponding sub-categories (eight in the socio-cultural category, nine environmental sub-categories, six economic subcategories, and only one for sustainability).

SOSTENB: assigned when the word 'Sustainability' or its derivatives (sustainable, unsustainable, etc.) referred to its global meaning, is found in the text of the analysed competency. Also, competencies that include the three variables of sustainability (environmental, economic and social) are considered SOSTENB, although the word 'Sustainability' or equivalent is not mentioned. This category does not have sub-categories of analysis.

SOCIOCLT: refers to the socio-cultural variable, and includes the following sub-categories: human rights (democratic, civil and political; economic, social and cultural; and solidarity); cultural diversity (peace and human security; universal accessibility and design for all citizens); gender equality (non-discrimination on the grounds of gender, defence of women's rights); health promotion; governance (social democratisation, civic participation); demography (changes, situation); equal access to ICTs (digital divide); ethical responsibility (ethical principles, values).

AMBIN: concerning the environmental perspective, and containing sub-categories dealing with: protection and sustainable use of natural resources; loss of biodiversity; conservation of the natural environment; climate change associated with global warming; rural transformation; sustainable urban design; environmental problems at global, regional or local level and disaster prevention and mitigation; human influence and interference on the environment (including chemical, biological or biotechnological risk; references to pollution and environmental policies); use of renewable energies and energy efficiency.

ECONM: concerning the economic perspective, and containing sub-categories dealing with: poverty reduction (training level implementation); responsible production and consumption (social and environmental consequences of consumption patterns); harmonisation of market requirements and environmental protection and the objective of social equity; corporate social responsibility; environmental and social impact assessment of economic activities; environmental management (socio-economic consequences of environmental management).

For the teachers' guides analysis Filemaker Pro, versión 11, has been used. The methodology has been based on the development of a relational database which incorporates the general and specific competencies contained in the guides.

Population and sample under study

Fifty-three degree titles from all major knowledge areas are offered in the UV, what means a total number of 2,835 educational guides (1,730 compulsory subject guides and 1,105 elective subject guides). All of them have been analysed and the number of degrees per area and the number of subject guides both compulsory (CS) and elective (ES), can be seen in Table 30.1.

Data collection procedure

A data sheet of competencies for sustainability has been developed for each one of the teachers' guides analysed. On the basis of the competencies specified in those areas, the corresponding categories of analysis from the Sustainability Thesaurus (SOSTENB, AMBIN, ECONM and SOCIOCULT), have been assigned considering the same criteria as used in previous studies (Aznar Minguet *et al.* 2013; Aznar Minguet *et al.* 2014a; Ull *et al.* 2013).

The implementation of the Thesaurus has resulted in the detection of competencies which make explicit reference to the sustainability category or to the three categories at the same time

Table 30.1 Number of guides of compulsory and elective subjects analysed, by major areas of knowledge

Major Areas of Knowledge	*Number UV Degrees/Area*	*Total Number of Teachers' Guides*	*Number of Compulsory Subjects Guides*	*Number of Elective Subjects Guides*
Sciences	7	298	215	83
Engineering	6	269	208	61
Health Sciences	11	508	394	114
Social Sciences	20	1005	642	363
Art and Humanities	9	755	271	484
Total	53	2835	1730	1105

(SOSTENB), and also competencies which only refer to one category (AMBIN, ECONM or SOCIOCULT). Additionally, a distinction between compulsory subjects (CS) and elective subjects (ES) from each degree, has been established.

Analysis and interpretation of the results

The results obtained from the analysis of the teachers' guides are presented below. The most relevant information is presented in summary tables with respect to major areas of knowledge.

Sciences area

In the UV, the Sciences area has seven degrees, assigned to four Faculties: four degrees for the Faculty of Biological Sciences (Biology, Biochemistry and Biomedical Sciences, Biotechnology, and Environmental Sciences), and one degree for the Faculties of Chemistry, Mathematics and Physics. The area is rather homogenous regarding the number of compulsory (varying between 27 and 36) and elective (varying between 9 and 15) subjects. A total number of 298 teachers' guides have been analysed.

If the four analysed categories are considered, competencies can be found in five of the seven degree guides (Table 30.2). No competencies have been found either in Maths or Physics, areas in which it seems difficult, but not impossible, to introduce sustainability; since Maths has a prominent instrumental role in Sustainability and Physics is involved in major problems such as the use of energy and climate change.

The number of guides with any of the four categories ranges from 10 in Biochemistry and Biomedical Sciences to 32 in Chemistry; yet, if we only focus on competencies which contain sustainability the number is significantly lower, as can be seen in the last two columns.

It is to be noted that in the Degree of Chemistry more than 50 per cent of the guides include two competencies: a general competency, '*Awareness on environmental issues and sustainability*', and a specific one, '*Ability to develop sustainable methodologies*'.

In the 'Totals' row of Table 30.2 and other similar ones, sums have only been made when considering number of guides, since information of each one of the degrees is what really matters.

Table 30.2 Results of the analysis of competencies of the Teachers' Guides from the Sciences area

Area of Knowledge	*Degrees*	*Total Number of Guides (CS+ES)*	*Number of Guides with Competencies in 4 Categories Totals (CS+ES)*	*Number of Guides with Competencies in SOSTENB Totals (CS+ES)*	*% of Compulsary Guides with Competencies in SOSTENB*
Sciences	Biology	38 (27+11)	14 (11+3)	7 (6+ 1)	22.2
	Biochemistry and Biomedical Sciences	41 (32+9)	10 (6+4)	2 (2+0)	6.2
	Biotechnology	44 (33+11)	18 (15+3)	0 (0 +0)	0.0
	Environmental Sciences	44 (31+13)	30 (21+9)	5 (2+3)	6.4
	Chemistry	44 (29+15)	32 (23+9)	24 (16+8)	55.2
	Physics	50 (36+14)	0 (0+0)	0 (0 +0)	0.0
	Maths	37 (27+10)	0 (0+0)	0 (0 +0)	0.0
Totals	7	298 (215+ 83)			

Engineering area

In the UV, the Engineering area has six degrees assigned to the School of Engineering (Table 30.3). A total number of 269 guides have been analysed. When considering the four categories, competencies can be found in the guides of all degrees. The number of guides with any of the four categories ranges between six and 23 across the six degrees, and the percentage of guides with any sustainability competency is high.

A general competency found in each degree is '*Ability to analyse and assess the social and environmental impact of technical solutions*'. Another example of a competency found is '*Consider the social and economic context in engineering solutions, being aware of diversity and multiculturality, and guaranteeing sustainability and the respect for human rights and for gender equality*'.

Health Sciences area

The Health Sciences area has 11 degrees, assigned to six different faculties (Table 30.4). A larger number of guides have been analysed (508) due to the large number of degrees and also because some of these degrees do not have 240 credits but 300 or 360, as in the case of Medicine. If the four analysed categories are considered, competencies are found in guides of all degrees. The number of guides with any of the four categories ranges between four and 29. Nevertheless, when only considering the competencies which contain sustainability, five of the 11 degrees do not have any guide.

As examples of general competencies, in Pharmacy we can also find: '*Knowing how to apply knowledge to the various possible modalities of professional practice, on the basis of respect for human rights, democratic principles, gender equality, solidarity, environmental protection, and promotion of a culture of peace, with a gender perspective*'. And within the Degree in Speech Therapy: '*Promote a culture of peace, democratic values and sustainability*'.

Table 30.3 Results of the analysis of competencies of the Teachers' Guides from the Engineering area

Area of Knowledge	*Degrees*	*Total Number of Guides (CS+ES)*	*Number of Guides with Competencies in 4 Categories Totals (CS+ES)*	*Number of Guides with Competencies in SOSTENB Totals (CS+ES)*	*% of Compulsary Guides with Competencies in SOSTENB*
Engineering	Chemistry Engineering	44 (36+8)	15 (10+5)	10 (10+0)	27.8
	Industrial Electronics Engineering	43 (35+8)	11 (9+2)	9 (9+0)	25.7
	Electronics and Telecommunication Engineering	41 (36+5)	8 (8+0)	6 (6 +0)	16.7
	Computer Engineering	45 (34+11)	6 (6+0)	6 (6 +0)	17.6
	Telematic Engineering	42 (34+8)	7 (7+0)	6 (6+0)	14.7
	Multimedia Engineering	54 (33+21)	23 (19+4)	12 (11+1)	33.3
Totals	6	269 (208+61)			

Table 30.4 Results of the analysis of competencies of the Teachers' Guides from the Health Sciences area

Area of Knowledge	*Degrees*	*Total Number of Guides (CS+ES)*	*Number of Guides with Competencies in 4 Categories Totals (CS+ES)*	*Number of Guides with Competencies in SOSTENB Totals (CS+ES)*	*% of Compulsary Guides with Competencies in SOSTENB*
Health Sciences	Pharmacy	55 (39+16)	13 (13+0)	10 (10+0)	25.6
	Science and Food Technology	40 (33+7)	20 (16+4)	17 (13+4)	39.4
	Human Nutrition and Dietetics	44 (34+10)	19 (16+3)	4 (3+1)	8.8
	Medicine	77 (53+24)	7 (7+0)	0 (0+0)	0.0
	Dentistry	43 (37+6)	17 (15+2)	0 (0+0)	0.0
	Physiotherapy	39 (33+6)	29 (26+3)	0 (0+0)	0.0
	Nursing	36 (31+5)	26 (24+2)	10 (10+0)	32.4
	Podiatry	41 (39+2)	5 (3+2)	0 (0+0)	0.0
	Optics and Optometry	38 (31+7)	19 (12+7)	17 (10+7)	44.7
	Psychology	57 (33+24)	4 (3+1)	0 0+0)	0.0
	Speech Therapy	38 (31+7)	18 (15+3)	4 (3+1)	9.7
Totals	11	508 (394+114)			

Arts and Humanities areas

The same type of information has been obtained from the nine degrees of the Arts and Humanities area, detecting Competencies for Sustainability in five of the nine degrees (Table 30.5).

As an example of the identified competencies, in Catalan Philology we can find: '*Development of the ethical commitment, focusing on gender equality, equal opportunities, culture of peace and democratic values, and environmental problems, as well as knowledge and appreciation of linguistic diversity and multiculturality*'.

Social Sciences

The Social Sciences area comprises 20 degrees, assigned to six faculties. From these degrees we have reviewed 1,005 educational guides of those 20 degrees, and have found guides, covering all degrees, that contain references to any of the four categories. Noticeably, all contain a competence related to the socio-cultural category, due to the characteristics of the area. Searching for competencies that make reference to the sustainability category, 16 of the 20 titles were found and even some, like the Degree in Labour Relations and Human Resource, presented some competencies in 97 per cent of their subjects; similarly for the Degree in Primary School Education (94 per cent). On the other hand, there are four degrees (Social Work, Finance and Accounting, Physical Activity and Sport Sciences, and Journalism) that do

Table 30.5 Results of the analysis of competencies of the Teachers' Guides from the Arts and Humanities area

Area of Knowledge	*Degrees*	*Total Number of Guides (CS+ES)*	*Number of Guides with Competencies in 4 Categories Totals (CS+ES)*	*Number of Guides with Competencies in SOSTENB Totals (CS+ES)*	*% of Compulsary Guides with Competencies in SOSTENB*
Arts and Humanities	Hispanic Studies	105 (32+73)	2 (0+2)	0 (0+0)	0.0
	Catalan Philology	102 (32+70)	16 (13+3)	16 (13+3)	40.6
	Classical Philology	99 (32+67)	0 (0+0)	0 (0+0)	0.0
	Modern Languages and their Literature	136 (10+126)	24 (7+17)	23 (6+17)	60.0
	English Studies	101 (31+70)	14 (8+6)	13 (8+5)	25.8
	Translation and Interlinguistic Mediation	62 (28+34)	38 (23+15)	37 (23+14)	82.1
	History	49 (36+13)	45 (35+10)	0 (0+0)	0.0
	Art History	52 (34+18)	17 (8+9)	3 (3+0)	8.8
	Philosophy	49 (36+13)	45 (35+10)	0 (0+0)	0.0
Totals	9	755 (271+484)			

not have any competence for sustainability in its educational guides. These big differences are due to each curriculum committee worked independently, and the inclusion or not of competencies has been dependent on the sensitivity of the members of each committee and their involvement in the sustainability issue. A table to summarise the results has not been included due to its length.

As examples of general competencies on this area, with respect to Sociology, there is the competence: '*Acquire and master the disciplinary knowledge needed to analyse contemporary society, its structure and dynamics, including population, resources and environment relationships, and social conditions of sustainability*'.

Further, regarding Teacher Training in Early Childhood Education, an example of a competency is: '*Analyse and incorporate in a critical manner the most relevant issues of the current society affecting family and school education: social and educative impact of audiovisual languages and screens; changes in gender and intergender relationships; multiculturality and interculturality; discrimination and social inclusion, and sustainable development; and, also, promote educative actions focused on the preparation of an active and democratic citizenship, committed to the equality, specially between men and women*'.

Looking at our results for all five areas of knowledge we have found important differences between degrees regarding the presence of Competencies for Sustainability (CfS) in curricula and educational guides that develop them. Only in the area of Engineering do we see the CfS present in all degrees, even if only in some subjects of the degree. In the other four areas there are some degrees in which there is no reference to CfS, while there are some degrees with a high percentage of subject guides containing CfS. We can speculate that this wide variability on the inclusion of CfS may not have occurred if there had been a statement from the Rector's office about inclusion of general Competencies for Sustainability in all subjects.

Conclusions

We have used the thesaurus for sustainability, extending the search to partial aspects of the concept (environmental, economic and socio-cultural topics) to reveal that, even if teachers have not been specific about the meaning of sustainability, aspects of sustainability have been included in the competencies listed in their teaching guide. In these cases, provided that partial aspects of sustainability are addressed when discussing, for example, gender perspective, human rights or environmental protection, we can identify that there is the intention to reflect on the concept of sustainability.

The research carried out has allowed us to have a complete overview concerning the introduction of competencies for sustainability in the subjects of all degrees at UV.

The information collected has been published in the website of the university, as a contribution to the strategic plan 'Sustainable Campus UV/2015', which in its Research and Education Programme sets as actions two of the objectives of the present study:

- Reporting about the inclusion of competencies for sustainability in all new curricula, and
- Review of Teachers' Guides of the compulsory subjects in the new curricula with respect to the inclusion of competencies for sustainability and its development through programming consistent activities.

Furthermore, the assessment made regarding the degrees assigned to each centre of the university has been forwarded to the Deans of the Faculties by the Vice-President of Sustainability, in order to be used in the revision of curricula following the recommendations of the *Campus Sostenible UV/2015* plan.

To count on the support of the University President it is important to spread the culture of sustainability. Development of this culture has been a long process beginning in 1997, when a small internal guide ('Greening the curriculum') was published and addressed to students in the UV. Importantly, having a research group that analyses its own institution, is able to make recommendations, and establish synergies with the institution's management staff, is good for the inclusion in the culture of sustainability.

The analysis conducted has highlighted, on the one hand, the existence of an important percentage of Teachers' Guides having general and/or specific competencies for sustainability, as well as the existence of several subjects which include sustainability in their conceptual corpus. On the other hand, it has been confirmed that a large diversity exists when specifying competencies related to sustainability in the degrees, and that their explanation is not, in some cases, appropriate for a general competency. In such cases we recommended that the Deans revise the key competencies and the introduction of the four key competencies recommended for CADEP-CRUE (2012).

The evaluation of the inclusion of sustainability into the curriculum in higher education required a tool powerful enough to cover the many facets that make up the variables that define it. For this reason the constructed thesaurus presents an ordered list of words that are grouped by their relationship with the meaning of sustainability, awarded by UNESCO, and represents a list of keys to search for topics that contain the multiple meanings of the term; as a documentary language and terminology control instrument, the thesaurus unifies the concepts expressed in the documents in order to allow analysis and review. However, its application to the analysis of the data contained in the curriculum has presented difficulties due to the subjectivity that, to a greater or lesser extent, affects all interpretations of the titles and education guides. For example, not all competencies that include references to health, the environment, equality of rights and citizen participation, can be regarded as a competence for sustainability, because such inclusion may be considered as inherent in the title, but sustainability was not necessarily evident in the substance of the subject. This would be an instance of an indication of awareness of sustainability, but not of a general competence for sustainability. To control for this difficulty and focus the search for sustainability competencies, the four members of the team independently evaluated each set of information, based on the competencies related to the four categories, which had been defined previously after discussion by the researchers. This issue delayed the research because we started reviewing the subject titles and guides by dividing the work among the researchers. However, given the difficulty of interpreting the material, we decided to begin the review again with each researcher examining all the material, after which we discussed our independent findings and came to a consensus about the assessment for each subject.

The inclusion of competencies for sustainability in the curricula of the subjects demands subject content activities that develop these competencies in the teaching-learning processes, as well as its evaluation through implementation benchmarks. The great challenge of developing competencies in such a way that curricula are really transformed into 'builders' of sustainability, still remains to be done. A teaching-learning process which is able to introduce transformational changes depends on the teachers and their skills and willingness to provide support (Barth and Rieckmann 2012). Teachers are thus the key component of the process. As a result it would be important to encourage synergies between the teachers already convinced about the need for changes in the curricula, since involving teachers' teams in the design and implementation of actions related to the introduction of competencies for sustainability in the curricula, is a key strategic factor (Aznar Minguet and Ull 2009). It should be made possible to provide well-trained coordinators committed to the process of implementation of such actions and, also, the commitment of all the teachers (Cotton *et al.* 2007); however, there will still be the challenge to overcome the hesitation of some teachers and other barriers to Education for Sustainable Development, already outlined by several authors (Holmberg and Samuelson 2006; Lozano 2006, Vilches and Gil Pérez 2009; Granados-Sánchez *et al.* 2012; Ull *et al.*, 2013).

In any innovation intended to be introduced in university, teachers are the centrepiece of the process, the motor of change. This requires facilitating their task by providing time and space availability to develop resources and tools which would contribute to the promotion of sustainability in their specific subjects. It would also encourage the exchange of experiences, particularly given that in this area greater emphasis is usually given to updating information and knowledge, rather than to ongoing training for teaching. The implementation of these requirements in order to move towards a sustainable future still remains to be done.

Note

1 This study is part of the Project 'Curriculum Sustainability in Grade training plans: review of basic competencies for sustainability in Educational Guides. Development and assessment' (EDU2010-21485). Ministry of Economy and Competitiveness.

References

Aznar Minguet, P., 2006. 'El reto educativo de la sostenibilidad en el marco europeo de la educación superior', in Escolano Benito, A., *Educación superior y desarrollo sostenible: Discursos y prácticas*. Madrid: Biblioteca Nueva, 167–88.

Aznar Minguet, P. and Ull, M.A., 2009. 'Education in Basic Competences for Sustainable Development. The Role of University', *Revista de Educación*, special issue, 219–237.

Aznar Minguet, P., Martínez-Agut, M., Palacios, B., Piñero, A. and Ull, M. A., 2011. 'Introducing Sustainability into University Curricula: An Indicator and Baseline Survey of the Views of University Teachers at the University of Valencia', *Environmental Education Research*, 17(2), 145–66.

Aznar Minguet, P., Ull, M.A., Piñero, A. and Martínez-Agut, M.P., 2013. 'Informe de investigación "Evaluación de la introducción de Competencias Generales para la Sostenibilidad en los Estudios de Grado de la Universitat de València"'. www.uv.es/campus-sostenible/ca/educacio-investigacio/-p2-sostenibilitzacio-academica-1285849973575.html [accessed 1 February 2015].

Aznar Minguet, P., Ull, M.A., Piñero, A. and Martínez-Agut, M.P., 2014a. 'El Tesauro de Sostenibilidad. Universidad de Valencia'. www.uv.es/acuveg (Sostenibilidad y Educación Superior) [accessed 10 February 2015].

Aznar Minguet, P., Ull, M.A., Piñero, A. and Martínez-Agut, M.P., 2014b. 'Sustainability in Higher Education: Challenges and Opportunities', *Educación XX1*, 17(1), 131–58.

Barrón, A., Navarrete, A. and Ferrer-Balasch, D., 2010. 'Sostenibilización curricular en las universidades españolas. ¿Ha llegado la hora de actuar?', *Rev. Eureka. Enseñanza y Divulgación de las Ciencias*, 7, N° Extra: La sostenibilidad en la universidad, 388–99.

Barth, M. and Rieckmann, M., 2012. 'Academic Staff Development as a Catalyst for Curriculum Change towards Education for Sustainable Development: An Output Perspective', *Journal of Cleaner Production*, 26(May), 28–36.

Barth, M., Godemann, J., Rieckmann, M. and Stoltenberg, U., 2007. 'Developing Key Competencies for Sustainable Development in Higher Education', *International Journal of Sustainability in Higher Education*, 8(4), 416–30.

CADEP-CRUE (Commission for Environmental Quality, Sustainable Development and the Prevention of Risks, CRUE), 2012. 'Guidelines for the Introduction of Sustainability into the Curriculum'. Document approved at the General Assembly held in Salamanca, 2012. www.crue.org/Sostenibilidad/CADEP/Documents/Documentos/1.pdf [accessed 9 February 2015].

Corney, G. and A. Reid., 2007. 'Student Teachers' Learning about Subject Matter and Pedagogy in Education for Sustainable Development', *Environmental Education Research*, 13(1), 33–54.

Cotton, D.R.E., Warren, M.F., Maiboroda, O. and Bailey, I., 2007. 'Sustainable Development, Higher Education and Pedagogy: A Study of Lecturers' Beliefs and Attitudes', *Environmental Education Research*,

13(5), 579–97.
de la Harpe B. and Thomas, I., 2009. 'Curriculum Change in Universities: Why Education for Sustainable Development is so Tough', *Journal of Education for Sustainable Development*, 3(1), 75–85.
Granados-Sánchez, J., Wals, A.E.J., Ferrer Balas, D., Waas, T., Imaz, M., Nortier, S., Svanström, M., van't Land, H. and Arriaga, G., 2012. 'Sustainability in Higher Education: moving from understanding to action, breaking barriers for transformation', in *Higher Education in the World 4. GUNI Series on the Social Commitment of Universities 4.* New York: Palgrave Macmillan, 193–207.
Holmberg, J. and Samuelson, B., eds., 2006. 'Drivers and Barriers for Implementing Sustainable Development in Higher Education', 7–11. Paris: UNESCO. http://unesdoc.unesco.org/images/0014/001484/148466E.pdf [accessed 9 February 2015].
Junyent, M. and de Ciurana, A.M.G., 2008. 'Education for Sustainability in University Studies: A Model for Reorienting the Curriculum', *British Educational Research Journal*, 34(6), 762–83.
Lozano, R., 2006. 'Incorporation and Institutionalization of Sustainable Development into Universities: Breaking through Barriers to Change', *Journal of Cleaner Production*, 14(9 & 11), 787–96.
Martínez-Agut, M.P., Aznar, P., Ull, A. and Piñero, A., 2007. 'Promoción de la sostenibilidad en los *currícula* de la enseñanza superior desde el punto de vista del profesorado: un modelo de formación por competencias', *Educatio Siglo XXI*, 25, 187–208.
Rieckmann, M., 2012. 'Future-oriented Higher Education: Which Key Competencies should be Fostered through University Teaching and Learning?', *Futures*, 44(1), 27–135.
Royal Decree 1393/2007, of 29 October (Ordenación de las enseñanzas universitarias oficiales) (Management of Official University) (BOE 30-10-2007). www.boe.es/boe/dias/2007/10/30/pdfs/A44037-44048.pdf [accessed 18 June 2015].
Sherren, K., 2006. 'Core Issues: Reflections on Sustainability in Australian University Coursework Programs', *International Journal of Sustainability in Higher Education*, 7(4), 400–41.
Sibbel, A., 2009. 'Pathways Towards Sustainability through Higher Education', *International Journal of Sustainability in Higher Education*, 10(1), 68–82.
Sterling, S., 2005. 'Higher Education, Sustainability, and the Role of Systemic Learning', in Blaze Corcoran, P.B. and Wals, A.E.J. (eds), *Higher Education and the Challenge of Sustainability: Problematics, Promise and Practice.* Dordretch: Kluwer Academic Press, 49–70.
Thomas, I., 2009. 'Critical thinking, Transformative Learning, Sustainable Education and Problem-Based Learning in Universities', *Journal of Transformative Education*, 7(3), 245–64.
Ull, M.A., Martínez-Agut, M.P., Piñero, A. and Aznar Minguet, P., 2010. 'Análisis de la introducción de la sostenibilidad en la enseñanza superior en Europa: compromisos institucionales y propuestas curriculares', *Revista Eureka sobre Enseñanza y Divulgación de las Ciencias*, special issue, 413–32.
Ull, M.A., Aznar Minguet, P., Martínez-Agut, M.P. and Piñero, A., 2013. 'Competencias para la sostenibilidad en los Planes de Estudio de los Grados de Ciencias de la Universidad de Valencia', *Revista Enseñanza de las Ciencias*, N° Extra. ISSN: 0212-4521. Actas IX Congreso Internacional sobre Investigación en Didáctica de las Ciencias.
UNESCO, 2006. *Framework for the UN DESD International Implementation Scheme.* Paris: UNESCO Education Sector.
Vilches, A. and Gil Pérez, D., 2009. 'Una situación de emergencia planetaria, a la que debemos y "podemos" hacer frente', *Revista de Educación*, special issue, 101–22.
Wiek, A., Withycombe, L. and Redman, Ch.L., 2011. 'Key Competencies in Sustainability: A Reference Framework for Academic Program Development', *Sustainability Science*, 6(2), 203–18.

31

IMPLEMENTING EDUCATION FOR SUSTAINABILITY IN HIGHER EDUCATION THROUGH STUDENT-CENTRED PEDAGOGIES

Neus (Snowy) Evans

Introduction

Scholars argue that effective education for sustainability (EfS – the preferred name in Australia) requires a re-imagination of pedagogy from traditional transmissive approaches to active and participatory student-centred teaching methods (Cotton and Winter 2010; Sterling 2004, 2012; Tilbury and Cooke 2005). Referred to as sustainability pedagogies (Cotton and Winter 2010; Sterling 2012), examples include role-plays and simulations, group discussions, stimulus activities, debates, critical incidents, case studies, reflexive accounts, critical reading and writing, problem-based learning, and futures visioning. Within higher education, however, such teaching and learning methods are found to be more aspirational than actual, with research identifying limited relevance, tensions between different approaches and conflict with conventional pedagogies as reasons for resistance (Christie *et al.* 2012; Cotton *et al.* 2009; Cotton *et al.* 2007). If sustainability pedagogies are being applied the processes and realities of application are poorly understood due to a lack of published empirical studies providing comparative and evaluative overviews of practice, or describing and reflecting on the processes, methods, outcomes and challenges (Tilbury 2011).

This chapter begins to address this gap by tracing my experiences, as a first year lecturer with a research background in EfS, during a first attempt to operationalise the concept of sustainability pedagogies within a core first year undergraduate sustainability education subject offered to pre-service teachers at a regional Australian university. The chapter begins by drawing on evidence from student-centred active teaching research and the development of sustainability pedagogies more broadly, then outlines the particular frameworks, theories, methods and processes underpinning my practice, and concludes with a personal reflection outlining the major challenges faced and how these may inform future research and practice of sustainability pedagogies.

Background

To date, most research-based work related to sustainability in teaching and learning has focused around curriculum change and course development (Corcoran and Wals 2004; Thomas 2004, 2009). Resulting resources for lecturers wishing to engage with EfS are available in the form of guidelines, toolkits and websites (see, for example, Shields and Hoggard 2013; Sterling 2012; Te Kete Ipurangi [TKI] n.d.; University of Gloucestershire 2009; University of Plymouth n.d.). Albeit useful for helping to frame practice, the reorientation of teaching and learning towards sustainability is a complex process requiring more than mere acquisition of a set of practices or methods such as those provided by the resources. The profoundly more difficult task, requiring practice and reflection, is understanding how to apply the methods (Ramsden 2003) in ways that produce sought-for outcomes.

Sustainability pedagogies originate from the broader concept of student-centred teaching, based on the premise that active forms of pedagogy improve student cognitive and affective outcomes (Biggs and Tang 2011; Howard 2002; Kogan and Laursen 2014). The reason for this, it is argued, is a shift in educational paradigm from one that focuses on teaching and the content to be taught, to one that focuses on learning and what the learner is doing (Barr and Tagg 1995; Biggs and Tang 2011). Proponents argue that the shift acts as a catalyst for active pedagogies that facilitate student interpretation and construction of knowledge that leads to deeper, more engaging, enduring and readily transferable learning, compared to traditional approaches where students passively receive information (Biggs and Tang 2011; Collins and O'Brien 2003; Deslauriers *et al.* 2011; Haak *et al.* 2011; Michael and Modell 2003; Walczyk and Ramsey 2003). Arguments for active learning have been criticised on the grounds that the evidence is ambiguous and lacks empirical support (Giles *et al.* 2006; Prince 2004). However, many of the sceptical studies are dated. For example, Prince (2004) sites research findings dating back to 1972 and 1991. More recent research provides compelling empirical evidence in support of active learning, including comparisons of real classrooms and randomised, controlled studies conducted under experimental laboratory conditions in which students are taught the same material in different ways (US President's Council of Advisors on Science and Technology [PCAST] 2012), quasi-experimental studies in a variety of science disciplines (Andrews *et al.* 2011) and reviews of research on active learning such as Prince (2004) and Freeman *et al.* (2014). For instance, Freeman *et al.*'s (2014) meta-analysis of 225 studies on the effects of active learning found that students achieve higher overall grades and less fail grades when lecturers use active learning methods. But what are the specific forms of student-centred active learning strategies or activities and how does one decide which ones to apply?

Resources on active-learning are replete. A Google search with the term 'active learning in higher education' returned 22,600,000 results, including books and other scholarly publications, websites and a journal (*Active Learning in Higher Education*) dedicated to the field. A variety of sources (Biggs and Tang 2011; Florida State University 2011; Michael and Modell 2003; Rosebrough and Leverett 2011; University of South Florida 2014) provide generic strategies; others speak to specific disciplines and much of the research originates from the science and engineering disciplines, based on an identified need for more Science, Technology, Engineering and Mathematics (STEM) professionals (PCAST 2012). Some student-centred pedagogies such as discussion and critical thinking are reported to be included within many disciplines (Ryan and Cotton 2013), while other strategies appear to be more specific to particular disciplines, for example, the use of case studies in medical, law and business education. More emergent active learning innovations are electronic student response systems and mobile applications.

Framing the research

My teaching and the research behind this chapter is underpinned by the premise that effective teaching and learning is transformational. Transformational teaching and learning is one of the important aspects of EfS and is evident when learners are enabled to reach beyond acquisition of disciplinary knowledge and concepts to a level of holism and depth capable of changing ways they understand, experience or conceptualise their world, a problem or phenomena (Mezirow 2000, 2009; Ramsden 2003; Rosebrough and Leverett 2011; Slavich 2005; Slavich and Zimbardo 2012). Simply put, transformational teaching and learning provokes change (Taylor 2009). This is particularly relevant to EfS which aims to change traditional ways of thinking, living and learning to build people's capacity for transformational change towards sustainability (Australian Research Institute in Education for Sustainability [ARIES] 2009; Sterling 2010–11).

Best practice to effect transformational learning is unclear (Taylor 2009). However, Mezirow (2009) provides a framework involving four processes of learning which I found helpful for framing the learning features of the sustainability pedagogies I applied. The first process, *elaborating existing meaning schemes*, involves learning that expands existing knowledge without affecting the learner's frame of mind. For example, at the end of a course the learner knows more than at the beginning, but their thinking and way of doing things remains unchanged. Second, *learning new meaning schemes*, is learning which leads to the development of a new point of view. Here the learner may develop a different perspective on a particular issue, but is not affected. So, instead of just having one perspective on an issue, the learner may now have two, but again core beliefs and actions remain unchanged. Third, *transforming meaning schemes*, is when learning provokes the revision and reframing of meaning-making schemes. In this case the learner changes their point of view or the way they conceive a particular issue. Last, *transforming meaning perspectives*, is learning which completely changes (transforms) the learner's perspective, worldview and way of doing things.

Similar to most academics, the drive underpinning my work as a lecturer is to help students learn. How best to go about that can be contentious because the way we teach is deeply rooted in epistemological, philosophical and ideological beliefs. Teaching for transformation, and by default sustainability, embodies a constructivist epistemology (Armstrong 2011) and so, unsurprisingly, calls for a purposeful redirection of pedagogy from teacher-centred transmission to student-centred active and collaborative approaches which engage students in, for example, critical thinking, experience and reflection (Littledyke and Manolas 2010; Moore 2005). This is germane to my own construct of effective teaching, which is underpinned by constructivist understandings and informed by EfS understandings and Ramsden (2003) and Biggs and Tang's (2011) approaches to teaching and learning in higher education. For me then, knowledge is not fixed, but constructed and reconstructed and a teaching and learning episode is one of many possible representations of a body of knowledge. Thereby, it makes sense that I am most comfortable with adopting student-centred, active pedagogies which encourage students to develop and refine their own representations. However, it is also the case that I do not solely subscribe to a one dimensional understanding of instruction and, hence, resist any binary. After Ramsden (2003), good teaching is not about prescribing any one particular model of instruction. Rather, it is about being open to change and 'constantly trying to find out what the effects of instruction are on learning, and modifying that instruction in the light of the evidence collected' (Ramsden 2003: 98).

Equally important is that, aside from epistemological, philosophical and ideological considerations, the way we teach (and learn) is also embedded in years of formal and informal (or hidden) training. The effects of conditioning and tradition are compelling. After years of traditional schooling, teachers and students become conditioned to rely on the transfer of information and skills as the dominant and, according to some, most reliable way of teaching and learning (Shor 1993). There is a certain comfort in familiarity. After all, as academics and students attending university, we can assume that traditional methods of teaching and learning have worked for us. For all my commitment to student-centred practice, I am not immune to such forces. However, I am cognisant that students are not *tabula rasa* and attend higher education with *personal foundations of experience*, comprised of their history in learning situations, as well as their assumptions, values, conceptual frameworks (Boud 2011). Therefore, it makes sense that traditional approaches do not suit all learners and, with the expansion of the higher education sector and as a pre-service teacher educator committed to inclusive practice, I feel obligated to apply a diversity of pedagogical approaches as well as to model what I teach students. Following Ramsden (2003), I also believe that student success is strongly aligned with teacher effectiveness; hence, I always feel a sense of responsibility for helping my students achieve their potential. This tension is illuminated through works I have sought to inform my practice, the looming predominant traditional teaching and learning frameworks that underpin university courses, and my negotiation of the subject which forms the focus of this research. I explore these tensions in the following section of the chapter.

Operationalising sustainability pedagogies

The research which is the focus of this chapter sits within a compulsory first year offering for students enrolled in the Bachelor of Education (primary and early childhood) across the Townsville and Cairns campuses of James Cook University (JCU). The student population comprises of a combination of school leavers, non-school leavers and mature aged students from a variety of backgrounds, educational and life experiences. The subject, called Foundations of Sustainability in Education (ED1411), was designed from an environmental science perspective by science educators with the aim to provide an introduction to the principles and practices of science and sustainability education. Hence, the subject has the dual focus of sustainability education and the science underpinning a range of sustainability issues, with the overarching intention to prepare students to implement EfS in future classroom practice. ED1411 takes a knowledge-centred approach to organise a series of six modules which draw upon the natural and social sciences to explore contemporary sustainability issues related to human population growth and urbanisation, water resource management, renewable and non-renewable energy, biodiversity, food security and agriculture, and climate change. ED1411 has been coordinated by the same academic across the two campuses since its inception in 2010 who, in line with JCU policy that requires students receive an equivalent experience regardless of where or how they are enrolled, is responsible for ensuring delivery is uniform. While some flexibility is afforded to suit different contexts, the content, assessment and face-to-face teaching experience in Townsville and Cairns has remained the same over the years.

Upon reviewing the materials in preparation for the semester's teaching, it immediately became apparent that the subject is very well conceptualised and developed with a strong rationale, with lectures designed to deliver large volumes of information through the traditional transmissive mode of content delivery and tutorials to guide students through a series of teacher-led inquiries and experiments. From a constructivist perspective, however, I am not convinced that spending two hours of lecture time teaching EfS through a transmissive style alone is the most effective way to develop student capacity for EfS – this requires students to do more than just listen to a lecturer talk. I do not dismiss the role of the lecture – it is useful for helping students master course content (Slavich and Zimbardo 2012). However, mastering course content is only part of what EfS aims to accomplish. The broader and more difficult task of transformational learning is more likely to be achieved through a diversity of student-centred and active pedagogies (Slavich and Zimbardo 2012). It was within the lecture component, then, where I identified the possibility of operationalising the concept of sustainability pedagogies.

As an early-career education academic with a research background in sustainability education, I have a developed understanding of education and teaching generally, as well as the theoretical and practical premises that guide EfS. However, I am also cognisant that the processes of teaching and learning are highly complex and that, being a first year lecturer, I bring fresh eyes to the field. As such, I set out to take an informed approach to teaching and learning by studying the works of Biggs and Tang (2013) and Ramsden (2003) in combination with relevant readings from the EfS field, which would directly inform my research (e.g., Cotton and Winter 2010). I began to prepare for teaching ED1411 in 2013 by reviewing 2012 materials. This included an online platform containing six modules, overviews of assignment tasks and support, weekly readings, recorded lectures and accompanying PowerPoint presentations, tutorial activities, student discussions and blogs. The process enabled me to consolidate my prior understandings with recent readings and the subject materials and frameworks. It became clear at this stage that I could not develop a pre-determined set of EfS pedagogies to implement each week, but that the process would necessitate an organic approach based on student development through the semester. My next move, then, was to search diverse sources for resources relevant to the realities within which I was working. Being mindful of Mezirow's (2009) framework of transformational learning, I sought provocative course-relevant resources with the aim of challenging learners' perspectives by, for example, selecting current newsworthy material in the form of images, video clips, websites and newspaper articles, as per Table 31.1, that I could use in the activities. These were then stored for recall, as needed each week.

Preparation of the lecture each week involved studying the material to be covered in the lecture, assessing which aspects would most lend themselves to teaching and learning through sustainability pedagogies, then designing suitable activities. I took care to ensure that activities met the intended subject learning outcomes while incorporating broader EfS outcomes related to connections, relationships and transformational learning as per Mezirow (2009). In this way, I sought to build the activities around current contentious issues and emphasised, questioned and, in conjunction with students, explored connections between the issues and the ecological, social, political and economic implications, together with subtexts related to power, interests and action and the week's materials. My intent for operationalising sustainability pedagogies within work already developed in the subject was not to replace, but to build and extend student learning. I wanted to move students from learning EfS as the teaching of isolated blocks of knowledge and issues to a more holistic and deep approach that emphasises complexity and connections, encouraging transformational learning. One instance of how I undertook to do this is provided in the group discussion example in Table 31.1. Here I intended to extend student understanding of links between the ecological and political sustainability pillars by combining traditional course material on biodiversity with a sustainability pedagogy (discussion) and relevant 'real world' political propaganda based on a topical and contested issue.

It was clear that lecturing would be required to explain concepts. However, considering that student attention in lectures is typically only maintained for about 15 minutes (Biggs and Tang 2013), I planned to combine periods of lecturing with student activities based on sustainability pedagogies. The stimulus activities in Table 31.1 provide good illustrations of how I balanced lecturer talk with student activity within one section of a two hour lecture. In both cases, I could

Table 31.1 Sustainability pedagogies applied

Process	*Rationale*
Stimulus activity	
In groups of three or four students discuss a stimulus diagram of the Earth system displaying the four subsystems (geosphere, hydrosphere, atmosphere and biosphere) and the sun. I use questions on the visualiser to prompt thinking and discussion: What do you see in this image? What do you understand is going on? How can you explain what's going on? I circulate the room, listening, commenting and speaking with students. Once I observe that each group has developed some consensual understanding and explanation, I play a short video clip on the earth system. The video clip focuses on the interconnections between the four subsystems. The aim of the video is to synthesise or extend student understanding, and to provide a backdrop for a concluding whole-class discussion which enables me to learn about student understanding and expand on connections and relationships. I finish by providing a summary. In a different session, students responded to a series of images on a web-based student response system called gosoapbox.com. The lecture focus was on energy and energy sources. In groups of three students were directed to log into app.soapbox.com, where I had set up the activity. I ran through a series of stimulus images of energy sources (e.g., kinetic, potential, light, sound, chemical energy) on a PowerPoint show and provided students with one or two minutes per image to respond to the image. Students were directed to brainstorm their collective understanding of the energy source displayed on each image and input a response in gosoap.box.com. I lead a discussion based on student responses to each image before progressing to the next – this enabled me to expand and/or clarify student understanding.	Through stimulus activities I aim to stimulate student thinking and understanding about a particular topic or issue as well as gather some formative feedback about student knowledge and understanding to guide the learning session. Two different examples are provided here. In the first case, I used the stimulus activity for teaching and learning about the Earth system. On another week, the stimulus activity was applied to initiate discussion and guide the lecture content by assessing existing student knowledge. This enables me to better meet student learning needs. In both cases, I found the stimulus activity broadened discussion, beyond what I might have expected, as a result of exposure to different perspectives.

Table 31.1 continued

Process	*Rationale*
Futures visioning The activity begins with a whole-group revision and discussion of *Campbell's (2007) article* on population, wherein the Nile in Egypt is presented as a case study. Once the group has built a whole picture of the article, including the different scenarios presented, students watch a video clip about Egypt (we watched www.youtube.com/watch?v=m1a0z469y38, however, there are many other available options). Following, as a whole-group, we bring the Nile case study to life by putting it into context. This involves discussing a range of images of the Nile. For example, I show students images of the 10 countries of the Nile Basin and we discuss the geography, populations' characteristics, economies, etc., that live within the catchment areas, as per Campbell (2007). Next, in groups of four, students are asked to envision what Egypt might look like in 2060 under each scenario presented in Campbell's (2007) article and to discuss concerns they have for the ecological, social, economic and/or political sustainability impact of each scenario. The session ends with a general discussion of the visioning and possible solutions to address concerns. The second futures visioning activity required students to (a) envision what a sustainable energy future might look like in Australia and (b) map-out how we could achieve such a vision. Students undertake this activity in groups of four or five. They have access to the Internet to undertake research and are required to record (a) and (b) on paper or electronic format, for collection and sharing with the class. The session finishes with a whole-group discussion with reference to some, if not all (time allowing) visions.	Futures visioning is an effective method for helping students understand how present decisions and actions may impact future wellbeing and sustainability. I applied the futures visioning pedagogy on two separate occasions. The first futures visioning example is directly related to the week's reading (Campbell, 2007) which provided a case study to exemplify the link between population and sustainability by outlining two possibilities for the future availability of the Nile water for Egypt by 2060. I applied this strategy to help students make links between population growth, urbanisation and sustainability. The second was undertaken as part of the weekly focus on energy and a lecture on renewable and non-renewable energy sources, including Australia's major sources of energy. The aim of the activity was to have students establish their own critical vision for how Australia may achieve a sustainable energy future.

Table 31.1 continued

Process	*Rationale*
Case study	
The first example I provide here was embedded in a lecture on local water resources and management of the Great Barrier Reef. The case study is the expansion of the Abbot Point coal terminal (Australia), a contemporary pertinent issue in 2013. I provided context for the activity by explaining the issue (including context and stakeholders) with the aid of images. Then, I posed the question: Should the application for the expansion be granted? Why? I provided students with six different sources of evidence, including from the Great Barrier Reef Marine Park Authority, *Mackay Daily Mercury*, ABC News, ABC Rural, World Wildlife Fund, and *The Australian* newspaper. In groups of three or four, students were required to consider all the evidence provided and argue for their case with reference to the evidence.	Case studies are useful for drawing student attention to and developing understanding and perspective of contemporary issues related to the topic under study. I found case studies useful for extending understanding of concepts which can be easily related to real-life situations, particularly if the concept is somewhat abstract. The case study can facilitate transfer from abstract to concrete understanding.
The second case study was undertaken during a lecture on climate change. To explore impacts of climate change, in groups of four, students developed and presented a case study around one of five possible impacts (rising sea levels, weather, biodiversity, food production and security, human health). I asked students to investigate their group's issue generally, then relate that to a local context. For example, what is rising sea level/what's the problem? Why does it take place? And what impact is it predicted to have on our local area.	I employed two different styles of case studies; one where I provide students with all the information and resources and the other where I provide the topic only. I applied the first type for a controversial issue to ensure students received a variety of perspectives.

Table 31.1 continued

Process	*Rationale*
Critical reading In groups of three or four, students were directed to three different local school web pages and asked to consider the different types of discourses reflected on the webpages – particularly the dominant one, the motivation behind the discourse, any counter discourses between the different school webpages, and how they relate to EfS. The schools chosen have a reputation for engaging with EfS, have won awards and feature in local newspapers for their sustainability work. As a backdrop to this activity, I led a whole-class discussion to ascertain what students already knew about each school and extended students' knowledge by providing an overview of the work undertaken by each school, including showcasing photographs and awards. In this way, students were able to compare and contrast the school's reputation and EfS achievements with the public webpage. Following the introduction, students moved into groups to undertake the critical reading exercise and I circulated the room, listening to and noting student conversations. We concluded the activity with a whole class discussion of student interpretations of the web pages and how these reflect or contrast with the sustainability work the schools are known for.	Critical reading is an important literacy practice which can enable development of higher order skills. Critical reading provides students with opportunities to develop critical literacy by deconstructing destructive, alternative or counter-discourses (Stibbe 2008). The module, readings and lecture leading up to this activity were based on EfS. The aim of the activity was to enable students to critically analyse current local school practices related to EfS by deconstructing published school web pages.
Group discussions Against a backdrop of the week's focus on biodiversity, students viewed and critically investigated propaganda from the Liberal National Party's (LNP) published vision for Northern Australia. In groups of three or four, students were asked to take a critical position on whether a northern food bowl should be developed. I provided some guiding questions: Is a northern food bowl a threat to Australia's biodiversity? What are the positives? What are the negatives? Can we develop Northern Australia sustainably? I circulated the room, listening and contributing, as necessary. Once I was satisfied that substantive group discussions had been undertaken and positions had been reached, I engaged students in a whole-group discussion and summary.	Group discussion is a more common pedagogy applied by lecturers and are useful for broadening perspectives (Cotton and Winter 2010). The example of a group discussion provided here took place during a lecture on biodiversity with a focus on the Australian context, major threats and contemporary approaches to sustaining biodiversity. The wider context was an Australian federal election and the Liberal National Party's (LNP) published vision for Northern Australia. The purpose of the activity was to enable students to link course content to contemporary policy and practice within a critical framework.

have simply delivered the content. Instead I interspersed lecturer talk with student activity by requiring students to activate and consider their own understandings of subject matter. Planning for implementing the specific pedagogies usually took one day per week, in addition to the usual planning, and required thinking about the week's learning outcome, relating it to an activity which would usefully and meaningfully extend the particular concept I wanted students to understand, designing the activities, then interspersing them within a pre-designed lecture PowerPoint presentation. Each lecture started with a revision exercise of the previous week's key learnings, followed by a short introduction to the current week's key concepts and lecture content. This was trailed by the first lecture segment, then to an activity focused around sustainability pedagogy. Table 31.1 provides examples of how I applied the sustainability pedagogies in practice along with rationales for implementation. Examples include stimulus activities, futures visioning, case studies, critical reading and group discussions. It is important to note that the intent is not to be prescriptive. The pedagogies I adopted build on examples provided by Cotton and Winter (2010), hence, I expect other scholars to critique and extend my work with the overall intent to develop teaching and learning for sustainability.

This chapter draws on data collected during the semester-long trial of the implementation of sustainability pedagogies within the lecture component of the subject on the Cairns campus. Data sources include a weekly planning and reflection journal, student feedback via a questionnaire at the end of the course and the university's student feedback process (a university online questionnaire administered to all students at the end of the semester to obtain feedback on student experiences of learning, teaching and curriculum within each subject), and a group interview with six students from a total cohort of 71 students. The six students were purposefully selected based on continued lecture and tutorial attendance, class participation, and observed engagement with subject materials and activities. Together, the participants represented a spread of backgrounds with two school leavers, one non-school leaver with general workforce experience and three mature-aged students from a range of vocational backgrounds. Selective sampling can bias study findings. In this case, focus group participants cannot be considered representative of the whole cohort undertaking the subject and, hence, findings cannot be generalised. Nevertheless, given that the purpose of this study is to enhance understanding about emergent EfS pedagogy, selecting the most productive sample is more likely to provide information-rich data capable of generating insights and in-depth understandings (Patton 2002).

Data were analysed via an inductive approach following Thomas (2006). Inductive analysis involves careful identification of frequent, dominant or significant themes, patterns and categories from the data (Patton 2002; Thomas 2006). After sorting the data into a workable format, I (a) read the texts four times, the first time to familiarise myself with the data and subsequent times to identify, mark and take notes about text segments (with different colour highlighter pens within the text and pencil in the margins) that captured central messages germane to the objectives of the study; (b) in an Excel worksheet, I developed category headings for the segments of text, then copied and pasted suitable segments of text under each heading; (c) I reduced overlap and redundancy among categories by comparing, combining and refining categories and data until I felt confident that my worksheet reflected the most important aspects of the themes identified in the data.

Reflections

In a recent interview (McKew 2014), Linda Darling-Hammond (a renowned world-leading authority on education and teacher training) commented that ideas enable us to think about what we can or might do, but if we do not know how or lack the resources to do it, then we will fail to get very far. The statement rings true for sustainability pedagogies. Available resources to date provide ideas about what we should and could do, but not much to guide us on how to do it or the effects of doing it. In the spirit of contributing to this gap, I have outlined how I conceived, planned and implemented sustainability pedagogies. Below I reflect on three key learnings emergent from my study which, together, capture my experience.

Conflicts and challenges

Barrett (2007) suggests that the power of dominant discourses and contradictory subjectivities may seriously constrain ways in which teachers teach EfS. I experienced this tension in relation to the traditional role of the lecture and lecturer, the dominant traditional framing of ED1411 and my own philosophical approach to teaching and learning which is tightly linked to the EfS pedagogical approach I adopted for the lecture component of ED1411. I felt secure that I had developed a robust plan to appeal to students cognitively through well-researched relevant content (Lange 2009) and pedagogically through student-centred (sustainability) pedagogies aimed at transforming students' meaning perspectives (Mezirow 2009). I also felt comfortable with the philosophy that underpins sustainability pedagogy and that such pedagogies transfer the locus of control from the teacher to the student and, hence, require the teacher to relinquish control. However, what I found in reality is that the adoption of such practices disturbed long-standing (subconscious) conventions about teaching and learning. The practice of implementing sustainability pedagogies, similar to other student-centred approaches, is actually unpredictable, messy and complex because it is non-linear. However comfortable I thought I felt with this state of affairs, I still found myself caught up with what critics call the traditional dominant practice in schools which, among other things, highlights the priority for teachers to dispense factual knowledge and maintain order and control (Stevenson 2007). Hence, I found myself lecturing for far longer time periods each lecture than I had intended. I questioned whether by giving up control (i.e. by not standing at the podium lecturing) I was somehow compromising student learning. I asked myself how I could be sure students were grasping what was intended because I was not lecturing, but facilitating. The reality, of course, is that we can never be sure that anything is understood the way it is meant, regardless of the strategies applied. Cognisant of this, my response was carefully structured reflection. I found it useful to triangulate subject and weekly learning outcomes with my commitment to transformational teaching and learning and EfS pedagogies with research on student-centred pedagogy and my own reflection notes taken after each lecture. The process of holistically mapping out the different components enabled me to negotiate the tensions I felt.

Researching own practice challenges conventional scientific standards (Stensland 2003). For me the epistemological and philosophical grounding of action research was not problematic and the process worked well. I am perfectly comfortable with an emergent research approach and the dual participant and observer role required in action research. Researching my own practice was worthwhile because it provided valuable insights into the personal and existential aspects of my teaching. The challenge, instead, lay in undertaking research by myself, as I set about this research without organising a mentor to consult. A more productive approach might have been to set up a formal peer review process, based on the intention to improve teaching and student success. Being an early career academic, this would have provided me the benefit of formal mentorship and feedback on the processes of the research through the semester long study and may have enriched my study and learning. The second related point is that if I were to undertake this research now, I would apply a more emergent and student-centred approach to the sustainability pedagogies I applied. As outlined in the methods section, each week I chose what I deemed to be the most suitable activity from Cotton and Winter's (2010) list of sustainability pedagogies to apply in the lecture segment of ED1411. What I realise in hindsight is that I was enforcing a framework in a literal sense which served to restrict, rather than expand my practice. Although Cotton and Winter's (2010) sustainability pedagogies are student-centred per se, a true student-centred approach can only be realised if the teacher has the students at the centre of all pedagogical decisions. My pedagogical decisions were not fully based on how I could best facilitate student learning, but on which of a certain set of pedagogies were most suitable. There are other active student-centred pedagogies which have enormous potential for developing EfS that are not captured by current sustainability pedagogy frameworks. For example, I applied the futures visioning activity, as outlined in Table 31.3, to help students develop understanding of the complex issues of population dynamics. While the activity might be considered innovative and engaging, it was very time consuming and required a lot of pedagogical skill. An equally rich and pedagogically easier learning experience to lead might be provided through student produced mind-maps of population dynamics. My point here is that in meeting the outcomes we set ourselves as sustainability educators we should not constrain ourselves to a single set of sustainability pedagogies, but rather take an organic and fluid approach. This point is expanded further below.

Student responses to and learning through sustainability pedagogies

I observed and received a variety of responses to the sustainability pedagogies. Student feedback indicates students enjoyed the subject overall, with some students emphasising they enjoyed the lectures, the teaching style and the content. The most personally challenging response, however, was from students who displayed passive resistance to the activities. These students resisted participation, opting instead to work on their own or ignore the activities. Research by Tormey and Henchy (2008), and Giles *et al.* (2006) points to student predisposition to passive learning through transmissive pedagogies. By the time students undertake university study they have already developed learning strategies based on dominant top-down knowledge-centred transmissive school education practices. This assumption is supported by one student's comment:

> I'm from a generation of explicit teaching and so I'm very much a convergent thinker. Tell me what the answer is, I'll memorise the answer and then I'll try to assimilate that. But this subject was open. You gave us a start 'let's talk about it', but I wanted a summary, like a finished summary that I could go 'yep, I know exactly what I need to study', and I never felt like I had that, right up to the end … I would learn better if you broke us up into groups then you teach each group the topic then say 'I want you to tell us about this aspect that I've taught you', then we can correlate the information you're giving us.

It seems that 'the influence of prior learning is more pervasive than we might imagine' (Boud 2011: 31). As Cotton *et al.* (2007) found, students themselves can act as a conservative force 'exhibiting a transactional view of education whereby lecturers are expected to provide all the answers' (594). However, I suggest the problem is much more complex. Brookfield's (2006) characteristics of student resistance to learning provide a link to the complex nature of learning. Beyond predisposition to passive learning, student resistance to active learning can be attributed to a range of reasons, including, but not limited to, poor self-image as learners, fear of the unknown, disjunction between learning and teaching styles, and apparent irrelevance of the learning activity (Brookfield 2006). It makes sense that students are less likely to engage in sustainability pedagogies if they do not think they can learn; are hesitant of the unknown; have a learning style that is at odds with that being presented, or do not understand what or how an activity contributes to learning. Although beyond the scope of this study, such notions can inform further development of sustainability pedagogies.

Positive responses to the sustainability pedagogies were also generated. Some students reported the lecture activities helped them understand and personally make sense of the content. In some instances, learning can even be linked with outcomes beyond knowledge acquisition only:

> The lectures were presented in such a way that made issues relevant to students. There was plenty of opportunity to seek clarification and explore concepts and ideas.
>
> [the lecturer] stimulated me to do my own research into previous, as well as current sustainability issues. This encouraged me to dig deeper into the course material, conduct my own research, and create my own conclusions.
>
> [the lecturer] made me want to be more involved with community issues.
>
> Before doing this subject I didn't care at all about politics, never paid any attention. Now I realise how important politics are, how integral, so I realise that I must start paying attention and being involved.

So, how do student responses to sustainability pedagogies relate to the broader concept of transformational learning? In considering learning through Mezirow's (2009) four processes of learning, student feedback data as a whole (distributed questionnaire, the university's student feedback process and the focus group interview) indicates that only a minority of students can be considered to have reached beyond the first two processes. Most students expanded their level of knowledge and/or developed new perspectives on issues. This is in keeping with an external (unpublished) review of ED1411 carried out in 2012 that found circumstantial evidence of transformative learning, as well as Mezirow's own finding that transformative learning is uncommon.

Clearly, the implication for transformational change with regards to EfS is that the level of change possible does to some extent depend on the learner's motivation or disposition to learning (Biggs and Tang 2011; Ramsden 2003) as well as the learner's personal foundation of experience (Boud 2011). If we consider that transformative learning requires different processes of learning and forms of appropriate educational intervention (Mezirow 1997), then there is a need to more intentionally develop ways to help students unblock constraints to learning. One way to do this is by focusing on broadening the face-to-face learning interactions we share with students (Boud 2011) as well as the particularities that underlie sources of student resistance to learning (Brookfield 2006).

Sustainability pedagogies – a panacea?

Without doubt, developing potential for EfS in higher education through multiple pathways is an important research focus and the concept of sustainability pedagogies serves to further focus attention. However, if we suppose that teaching for transformation and sustainability is complex; that pedagogy is more than a set of strategies to facilitate learning – that to be effective, pedagogy has to account for complex interactions between content, learners, teacher and context (Wink 2010); and that most academics are constrained, to a greater or lesser degree, by their own dominant discourses and the traditional system in which they work, then it is possible to conceive that privileging a set of pre-determined pedagogical methods for the teaching of sustainability is, in reality, a naïve conceptualisation of the teaching and learning process and has the potential to narrow learning, hinder creativity and maintain EfS on the margins. I expand on this below.

Teaching can be classified as a *wicked problem*. Hence, I am not convinced that prescribing a particular set of pedagogies will enable more effective EfS. There are multiple complex, context-based, uncontrollable variables that will naturally affect learning outcomes and no teaching method alone can guarantee learning (Michael 2006; Prince 2004; Westwood 2008). For example, student-centred pedagogies, and by default sustainability pedagogies, require more pedagogical skill and time for the planning and teaching cycle than teacher-centred methods (Cotton and Winter 2010; Dawe *et al.* 2005; Michael 2006), careful alignment to desired learning outcomes, and a certain level of student knowledge and skill as learners (Prince 2004). The complex nature of teaching and learning coupled with research on effective teaching (e.g. Hattie 2008; Westwood 2008) and reasons for low take-up by academics of pedagogies geared towards sustainability (Cotton *et al.* 2009; Cotton *et al.* 2007) points to avoiding any pre-determined pedagogies that confine us to particular normative ways of teaching EfS. Even though sustainability pedagogies are good pedagogies, intrinsically they are unlikely to lead to learning geared towards sustainability.

An alternative approach is to work organically within established norms to promote complimentary student-centred pedagogies. If underpinned by an overall aim to enrich and expand student learning outcomes, then by default an emergent approach will more likely promote the types of skills that sustainability scholars support. Taking the voluminous literature on student-centred pedagogies, founded on the same epistemology and ideology as sustainability pedagogies, it is possible to find inclusive pedagogies that serve to expand understanding. For example, strategies such as mind-mapping, concept mapping, schematic diagrams and one-minute papers are student-centred pedagogies that can be strategically applied to encourage extended thinking and reflection. Drawing from my own practice, one of the topics I explore with students in ED1411 is stratospheric ozone depletion – a topic that holds many student misconceptions. To facilitate and extend learning, I engage students through a number of different strategies including direct instruction where I very carefully explain the process with visual aids (lecture), facilitated student role-play and simulation of the process, student created drawings and explanations of the process, then thinking and discussion methods, such as think-pair-share, to focus on the consequences. While role-plays, simulations and discussions are considered in the list of sustainability pedagogies, lecture, drawing and explanations are not. Yet, a multi-method approach such as this can open opportunities for the type of deep reflexive and transformative learning that sustainability scholars advocate, and at the same time be more inclusive of lecturer backgrounds and needs.

Conclusion

Specific and context-based examples that narrate how lecturers have conceptualised, developed and applied particular pedagogies can provide powerful tools for those wishing to innovate. The intention of this chapter was to explore my experiences as a first year lecturer innovating pedagogy to begin to understand the *how* of implementing sustainability pedagogies with the intent of moving students towards transformative learning. The point was not to criticise or support any one approach, but apply a process of critical self-reflexivity (Lange 2009) and commitment to improvement to examine my experiences. What has become clear is that the current construct of sustainability pedagogies is not a panacea for enhancing lecturer practice towards sustainability. This does not mean that sustainability pedagogies per se will not be effective, just that enhancing pedagogy is a complex and challenging task.

References

Andrews, T.M., Leonard, M.J., Colgrove, C.A. and Kalinowski, S.T., 2011. 'Active Learning not Associated with Student Learning in a Random Sample of College Biology Courses', *CBE-Life Sciences Education*, 10(4), 394–405.

Armstrong, C., 2011. 'Implementing Education for Sustainable Development: The Potential Use of Time-honored Pedagogical Practice from the Progressive Era of Education', *Journal of Sustainability Education*, 2(March).

Australian Research Institute in Education for Sustainability [ARIES], 2009. *Education for Sustainability: The Role of Education in Engaging and Equipping People for Change.* Sydney: Macquarie University.

Barr, R. and Tagg, J., 1995. 'From Teaching to Learning – A New Paradigm for Undergraduate Education', *Change*, 27(6), 12–26.

Barrett, M.J., 2007. 'Homework and Fieldwork: Investigations into the Rhetoric-reality Gap in Environmental Education Resarch and Pedagogy', *Environmental Education Research*, 13(2), 209–23.

Biggs, J. and Tang, C., 2011. *Teaching for Quality Learning at University*, 4th edn. Berkshire: Open University Press.

Boud, D., 2011. 'Experience as the Base for Learning', in Kandlbinder, P. and Peseta, T. (eds), *Higher Education Research and Development Anthology*. Milperra, NSW: HERDSA, 25–36.

Brookfield, S.D., 2006. *The Skillful Teacher: On Technique, Trust, and Responsiveness in the Classroom*, 2nd edn. San Francisco, CA: Jossey-Bass.

Campbell, M., 2007. 'Why the Silence on Population?', *Population and Environment*, 28(4), 237–46.

Christie, B.A., Miller, K.K., Cooke, R. and White, J.G., 2012. 'Environmental Sustainability in Higher Education: How do Academics Teach?', *Environmental Education Research*, 19(3), 385–414.

Collins, J.W. and O'Brien, N.P., 2003. *The Greenwood Dictionary of Education.* Westport, CT: Greenwood.

Corcoran, P.B. and Wals, A.E.J., eds., 2004. *Higher Education and the Challenge of Sustainability: Problematics, Promise, and Practice.* Hingham, MA: Kluwer Academic Publishers.

Cotton, D. and Winter, J., 2010. '"It's Not Just Bits of Paper and Light Bulbs": A Review of Sustainability Pedagogies and their Potential for Use in Higher Education', in Jones, P., Selby, D. and Sterling, S. (eds), *Sustainability Education: Perspectives and Practice across Higher Education.* London: Earthscan, 39–54.

Cotton, D., Warren, M.F., Maiboroda, O. and Bailey, I., 2007. 'Sustainable Development, Higher Education and Pedagogy: A Study of Lecturers' Beliefs and Attitudes', *Environmental Education Research*, 13(5), 579–97.

Cotton, D., Bailey, I., Warren, M. and Bissell, S., 2009. 'Revolutions and Second-best Solutions: Education for Sustainable Development in Higher Education', *Studies in Higher Education*, 34(7), 719–33.

Dawe, G., Jucker, R. and Martin, S., 2005. *Sustainable Development in Higher Education: Current Practice and Future Developments – A Report for the Higher Education Academy.* York: Higher Education Academy.

Deslauriers, L., Schelew, E. and Wieman, C., 2011. 'Improved Learning in a Large-enrollment Physics Class', *Science*, 332(6031), 862–4.

Florida State University, 2011. 'Instruction at FSU: A Guide to Teaching and Learning Practices'. http://distance.fsu.edu/instructors/instruction-fsu-guide-teaching-learning-practices [accessed 9 February 2015].

Freeman, S., Eddy, S.L., McDonough, M., Smith, M.K., Nnadozie, O., Jordt, H. and Wenderoth, M.P., 2014. 'Active Learning Increases Student Performance in Science, Engineering, and Mathematics'. *Proceedings of the National Academy of Sciences of the United States of America (PNAS)*, 111(23), 8410–15.

Giles, J., Ryan, D.A.J., Belliveau, G., de Freitas, E. and Casey, R., 2006. 'Teaching Style and Learning in a Quantitative Classroom', *Active Learning in Higher Education*, 7(3), 213–25.

Haak, D.C., Hille Ris Lambers, J., Pitre, E. and Freeman, S., 2011. 'Increased Structure and Active Learning Reduce the Achievement Gap in Introductory Biology', *Science*, 332(6034), 1213–16.

Hattie, J., 2008. *Visible Learning: A Synthesis of over 800 Meta-analysis Relating to Achievement*. Abingdon: Routledge.

Howard, J.R., 2002. 'Do College Students Participate More in Discussion in Traditional Delivery Courses or in Interactive Telecourses? A Preliminary Comparison', *The Journal of Higher Education*, 73(6), 764–80.

Kogan, M. and Laursen, S.L., 2014. 'Assessing Long-term Effects of Inquiry-based Learning: A Case Study from College Mathematics', *Innovative Higher Education*, 39(3), 183–99.

Lange, E.A., 2009. 'Fostering a Learning Sanctuary for Transformation in Sustainability Education', in Mezirow, J. and Taylor, E.W. (eds), *Transformative Learning in Practice: Insights from Community, Workplace, and Higher Education*. San Francisco, CA: Jossey-Bass, 193–204.

Littledyke, M. and Manolas, E., 2010. 'Ideology, Epistemology and Pedagogy: Barriers and Drivers to Education for Sustainability in Science Education', *Journal of Baltic Science Education*, 9(4), 285–301.

McKew, M., 2014. 'In Conversation: Maxine McKew and Linda Darling-Hammond'. http://theconversation.com/in-conversation-maxine-mckew-and-linda-darling-hammond-22489 [accessed 9 February 2015].

Mezirow, J. and Associates, 2000. *Learning as Transformation*. San Francisco, CA: Jossey-Bass.

Mezirow, J., 2009. 'Transformative Learning Theory', in Mezirow, J., Taylor, E.W. and Associates (eds), *Transformative Learning in Practice: Insights from Community, Workplace, and Higher Education*. San Francisco, CA: John Wiley & Sons Inc, 18–31.

Michael, J., 2006. 'Where's the Evidence that Active Learning Works?', *Advances in Physiology Education*, 30(4), 159–67.

Michael, J.A. and Modell, H.I., 2003. *Active Learning in Secondary and College Science Classrooms: A Working Model of Helping the Learning to Learn*. Mahwah, NJ: Erlbaum.

Moore, J., 2005. 'Seven Recommendations for Creating Sustainability Education at the University Level', *International Journal of Sustainability in Higher Education*, 6(4), 326–39.

Patton, M.Q., 2002. *Qualitative Research and Evaluation Methods*, 3rd edn. Thousand Oaks, CA: Sage Publications.

Prince, M., 2004. 'Does Active Learning Work? A Review of the Research', *Journal of Engineering Education*, 93(3), 223–31.

Ramsden, P., 2003. *Learning to Teach in Higher Education*, 2nd edn. Oxon: Routledge Falmer.

Rosebrough, T.R. and Leverett, R.G., 2011. *Transformational Teaching in the Information Age: Making Why and How we Teach Relevant to Students*. Virginia: ASCD.

Ryan, A. and Cotton, D., 2013. 'Times of Change: Shifting Pedagogy and Curricula for Future Sustainability', in Sterling, S., Maxey, L. and Luna, H. (eds), *The Sustainable University: Progess and Prospects*. Oxon: Routledge, 151–67.

Shields, K. and Hoggard, L., 2013. *Sustainability for Educators: A Toolkit of Learning Activities and Resources*. Mullumbimby, NSW: Byron Community College.

Shor, I., 1993. 'Education is Politics: Paulo Freire's Critical Pedagogy', in McLaren, P. and Leonard, P. (eds), *Paulo Freire, A Critical Encounter*. New York: Routledge, 25–35.

Slavich, G.M., 2005. 'Transformational Teaching: E-xcellence in Teaching', *PsychTeacher Electronic Discussion List*, 5(October).

Slavich, G.M. and Zimbardo, P.G., 2012. 'Transformational Teaching: Theoretical Underpinnings, Basic Principles, and Core Methods', in Zinn, T., Saville, B.K. and Williams, J.E. (eds), *E-xcellence in Teaching*. Society for the Teaching of Psychology, Vol. 5, 55–9. http://teachpsych.org/ebooks/eit2005/index.php.

Stensland, P., 2003. 'Action Research on Own Practice: Methodological Challenges', *Scandinavian Journal of Primary Health Care*, 21(2), 77–82.

Sterling, S., 2004. 'Higher Education, Sustainability, and the Role of Systematic Learning', in Corcoran, P.B. and Wals, A.E.J. (eds), *Higher Education and the Challenge of Sustainability. Problems, Promise and Practice*. Dordrecht: Kluwer Academic Publishers, 49–70.

Sterling, S., 2010–11. 'Transformative Learning and Sustainability: Sketching the Conceptual Ground', *Learning and Teaching in Higher Education*, 5, 17–33.

Sterling, S., 2012. *The Future Fit Framework: An Introductory Guide to Teaching and Learning for Sustainability in HE*. York: The Higher Education Academy.

Stevenson, R.B., 2007. 'Schooling and Environmental Education: Contradictions in Purpose and Practice', *Environmental Education Research*, 13(2), 139–53.

Stibbe, A., 2008. 'Words and Worlds: New Directions for Sustainability Literacy', *Language and Ecology*, 2(3), 1–10.

Taylor, E.W., 2009. 'Fostering Transformative Learning', in Mezirow, J. and Taylor, E.W. (eds), *Transformative Learning in Practice: Insights from Community, Workplace, and Higher Education*. San Francisco, CA: Jossey-Bass, 3–17.

Te Kete Ipurangi [TKI], n.d. 'Effective Pedagogy in Education for Sustainability'. http://efs.tki.org.nz/EfS-in-the-curriculum/Effective-pedagogy [accessed 9 February 2015].

Thomas, D.R., 2006. 'A General Inductive Approach for Analyzing Qualitative Evaluation Data', *American Journal of Evaluation*, 27(2), 237–46.

Thomas, I., 2004. 'Sustainability in Tertiary Curricula: What is Stopping it Happening?', *International Journal of Sustainability in Higher Education*, 5(1), 33–47.

Thomas, I., 2009. 'Critical Thinking, Transformative Learning, Sustainable Education, and Problem-Based Learning in Universities', *Journal of Transformative Education*, 7(3), 245–64.

Tilbury, D., 2011. *Education for Sustainable Development: An Expert Review of Processes and Learning*. Paris: UNESCO.

Tilbury, D. and Cooke, K., 2005. *A National Review of Environmental Education and its Contribution to Sustainability: Frameworks for Sustainability*. Canberra: Australian Government Department of the Environment and Water Resources and the Australian Research Institute in Education for Sustainability (ARIES).

Tormey, R. and Henchy, D., 2008. 'Re-imagining the Traditional Lecture: An Action Research Approach to Teaching Student Teachers to 'Do' Philosophy', *Teaching in Higher Education*, 13(3), 303–14.

University of Gloucestershire, 2009. 'Education for Sustainability: A Guide for Educators on Teaching and Learning Approaches'. http://insight.glos.ac.uk/sustainability/Education/Documents/EfS%20 Educators%20Guide%20FINAL%207July11.pdfn [accessed 9 February 2015].

University of Plymouth, n.d. '7 Steps to Embedding Sustainability in your Teaching'. http://efsandquality.glos.ac.uk/toolkit/Plymouth_7_Steps_to_ESD_2012.pdf [accessed 9 February 2015].

University of South Florida, 2014. 'Interactive Techniques'. www.usf.edu/atle/teaching/interactive-techniques.aspx [accessed 9 February 2015].

US President's Council of Advisors on Science and Technology [PCAST], (2012). *Report to the President – Engage to Excel: Producing One Million Additional College Graduates with Degrees in Science, Technology, Engineering, and Mathematics*. Washington: Executive Office of the President of the United States.

Walczyk, J.J. and Ramsey, L.L., 2003. 'Use of Learner-centered Instruction in College Science and Mathematics Classrooms', *Journal of Research in Science Teaching*, 40(6), 566–84.

Westwood, P., 2008. *What Teachers Need to Know about Teaching Methods*. Camberwell, VIC: ACER Press.

Wink, J., 2010. *Critical Pedagogy: Notes from the Real World*, 4th edn. New York: Addison-Wesley Longman Inc.

INDEX

For Product Safety Concerns and Information please contact our EU representative GPSR@taylorandfrancis.com
Taylor & Francis Verlag GmbH, Kaufingerstraße 24, 80331 München, Germany

www.ingramcontent.com/pod-product-compliance
Lightning Source LLC
LaVergne TN
LVHW080117011026
849160LV00013B/1120
* 9 7 8 1 1 3 8 5 9 7 5 4 9 *